Classics
of
Eastern Thought

Lynn H. Nelson
University of Kansas

Patrick Peebles
*University of Missouri,
Kansas City*

WADSWORTH

™

THOMSON LEARNING

Wadsworth/Thomson Learning
10 Davis Drive
Belmont, CA 94002-3098
USA

For information about our products, contact us:
Thomson Learning Academic Resource Center
1-800-423-0563
http://www.wadsworth.com

International Headquarters
Thomson Learning
International Division
290 Harbor Drive, 2ⁿᵈ Floor
Stamford, CT 06902-7477
USA

UK/Europe/Middle East/South Africa
Thomson Learning
Berkshire House
168-173 High Holborn
London WCIV 7AA

Asia
Thomson Learning
60 Albert Street, #15-01
Albert Complex
Singapore 189969

Canada
Nelson Thomson Learning
1120 Birchmount Road
Toronto, Ontario M1K 5G4
Canada
United Kingdom

ISBN 0-15-507655-8

The Adaptable Courseware Program consists of products and additions to existing Wadsworth Group products that are produced from camera-ready copy. Peer review, class testing, and accuracy are primarily the responsibility of the author(s).

PREFACE

Humanities professors throughout the country are displaying an increasing awareness of the modern status and traditional cultures of Asian nations by recommending that the study of Asian civilizations be included in the student's general program. In response to such curricular development and in appreciation of the value and interest of the subject, both the number of Asian civilization courses and their enrollments have been increasing in recent years. We have designed *Classics of Eastern Thought* both as a resource for teaching such courses, whether their emphasis be historical, literary, philosophical, or broadly cultural, and as a means of integrating Eastern civilizations into broader world history coverage.

The source readings that make up this volume have been drawn from a wide variety of genres in order to illustrate both the richness and the diversity of the Asian heritage. They represent a fair selection of Asia's ancient and modern classics of thought and expression. They constitute a unique combination of poetry, novels, drama, autobiography, speeches, political and philosophical treatises, and even a screenplay. It is our hope that this diversity will allow the instructor sufficient flexibility in adapting these readings to his or her course.

In order to provide a degree of unity to what otherwise might be a simple assortment of excerpts from well-known works, a measure of selectivity and a means of discrimination are necessary. In making these choices, we have kept in mind certain themes: individualism and social obligation, tradition and change, and the relationship between thought and action. These particular themes recommend themselves as being common concerns of humanity that are also central to Asian thought and values. For this reason, we hope these readings will not only afford the student a better appreciation of Asian traditions but will provide an opportunity to relate these traditions to familiar and significant issues in Western life.

The work has been structured and sufficient background and explanatory material included to provide maximum adaptability—in Asian civilization and world history courses, in humanities, Eastern literature, and comparative literature courses, or in offerings on the history of China, India, or Japan.

We feel that this book contains the most extensive apparatus currently available in any offering of its type. The forty-nine selections are grouped into four chronological periods. Although not every selection is a complete work, we

v

have attempted to ensure that the material presented is both substantial and representative. Each of the four parts is preceded by an extensive overview of the era, providing a survey of the historical development of the region and furnishing the student with a context for the better appreciation of the individual selections. These historical surveys are not intended to supplant a core textbook on the history of the region; but they are sufficiently substantial so as to provide students with an adequate introduction to that history.

Each selection is prefaced by a detailed essay that discusses its specific historical context, the author, and the work. Since many of the readings are illustrative of historically significant events and movements, these essays supplement the historical overviews of the part introductions. A set of reading questions at the beginning of each selection directs the student's attention to major issues within the reading, and the selection is followed by an extensive annotated bibliography of relevant, related works. Finally, each of the four parts concludes with a series of at least ten discussion questions framed to encourage the reader to consider the scope and relevance of the issues presented, the interrelationships of the readings, and significant comparisons and contrasts in thought and approach.

This apparatus and structure enable both instructor and student to utilize the work at a number of levels and for a variety of functions. Readings might be assigned simply as supplemental to and illustrative of the material presented by a core textbook, or course activities could be structured around the readings themselves. One or more readings, together with their bibliographies, might serve as the starting point for a term paper. The part introductions and the background essays for each selection provide sufficient detail to furnish students with an introductory knowledge of Asian history and some of the critical moments in the development of the Asian nations; they might serve as the basis for the study of specific topics. Finally, the discussion questions raise issues suitable for student papers or discussions, or even as themes around which the instructor might wish to center classroom presentations.

We wish to acknowledge the valuable assistance and counsel we have received from Steven Drummond of the University of Kansas in the conception and preparation of this volume.

We would like to express our appreciation to the following individuals for their advice and suggestions in both the selection of materials and in the preparation of the accompanying apparatus: Professors Daniel Bays, John Dardess, and Wallace Johnson of the University of Kansas, and Mary Schuler of the South Asia Center of Cornell University. We owe particular thanks to Professors Edward Graham of Michigan State University and Conrad Schirokauer of City College of the City University of New York for their painstaking appraisals of the plan of this work and their many suggestions for its improvement.

We have enjoyed the full support of the editorial staff of Harcourt Brace Jovanovich, and wish to extend our particular thanks to Elizabeth Banks, Drake Bush, Eleanor Garner, Joan Harlan, Karen Hay, Lynn Knipe, and Diane Southworth for their assistance, encouragement, and forbearance.

Finally, we would like to make special note of the personal encouragement offered over the years by W. N. Drummond, Jr., David A. Drummond, Carolyn A. S. Nelson, and Mary H. Peebles.

LYNN H. NELSON
PATRICK PEEBLES

CONTENTS

Preface   v

PART I ✦ FOUNDATIONS ✦ 1
THE CLASSICAL WORLD: 4000 B.C. TO A.D. 300

VEDIC HYMNS 7
THE BOOK OF SONGS 15
SERMON AT THE DEER PARK   Siddhartha Gautama Buddha 30
THE BHAGAVAD GITA 39
THE ANALECTS   K'ung Fu-tzu 50
TAO TE CHING   Lao Tzu 58
THE ART OF WAR   Sun Tzu 67
ARTHASASTRA   Kautilya 81
THE CLASSIC OF FILIAL PIETY   (HSIAO CHING) 91
LESSONS FOR WOMEN   Pan Chao 101
Discussion Questions 112

PART II ✦ EXPANDING HORIZONS ✦ 116
CHALLENGES TO THE CLASSICAL HERITAGE:
A.D. 300 TO 1350

PEACH BLOSSOM SPRING   T'ao Ch'ien 123
THE PERFECT BRIDE   Dandin 126
THE TRAVELS OF SANUDASA THE MERCHANT 131
THE PURE LAND 144

COLD MOUNTAIN POEMS Han Shan 149

THE POETRY OF LI PO AND TU FU 160

MAN'YOSHU: A COLLECTION OF TEN THOUSAND
LEAVES 174

APPRAISAL OF WOMEN ON A RAINY NIGHT
Lady Murasaki Shikibu 189

REFLECTIONS OF THINGS AT HAND Chu Hsi 207

THE POETRY OF YI KYU BO Yi Kyu Bo 218

GITAGOVINDA Jayadeva 224

THE ROMANCE OF THE WESTERN CHAMBER
Wang Shih-fu 232

CONFESSIONS OF LADY NIJO 256

Discussion Questions 270

PART III ✦ IN THE LONG TRADITION ✦ 274

THE CRISIS OF THE CLASSICAL CULTURES:
A.D. 1350 TO 1750

KANEHIRA Zeami 280

SONGS OF KABIR Kabir 293

INQUIRY ON THE GREAT LEARNING Wang Yang-ming 299

SACRED WRITINGS OF THE SIKHS 309

AKBAR NAMA Abu-l Fazl 317

JOURNEY TO THE WEST Wu Ch'eng-en 324

HAGAKURE Tsunetomo Yamamoto 330

THE DREAM OF THE RED CHAMBER Tsao Hsueh-ch'in 341

TREASURY OF LOYAL RETAINERS Takeda Izumo, Namiki
Senryu, and Miyoshi Shoraku 358

THE SCHOLARS Wu Ching-tzu 376

Discussion Questions 397

PART IV ✦ MODERNIZATION AND TRADITION ✦ 400

HARMONY IN A NEW ERA: A.D. 1750 TO THE PRESENT

THE SORROWS OF MISFORTUNE *Shen Fu* 408

ON THE BURNING OF WIDOWS *Ram Mohan Roy* 415

THE TALE OF KIEU *Nguyen Du* 425

LETTER OF MORAL ADMONITION TO QUEEN
VICTORIA *Lin Tse-hsu* 442

CONFUCIUS AS A SOCIAL REFORMER AND THE AGE OF
GREAT UNITY *K'ang Yu-wei* 449

HIND SWARAJ *Mohandas K. Gandhi* 458

KOKORO *Natsume Soseki* 468

A MADMAN'S DIARY *Lu Hsun* 483

AN OUTLINE FOR THE RECONSTRUCTION OF JAPAN
Kita Ikki 496

FAMILY *Pa Chin* 505

THE VIETNAMESE DECLARATION OF INDEPENDENCE
Ho Chi Minh 525

ON THE PEOPLE'S DEMOCRATIC DICTATORSHIP
Mao Tse-tung 530

IKIRU *Akira Kurosawa* 544

BIRD OF PASSAGE *O Yongsu* 587

WHAT IS INDIA? *Jawaharlal Nehru* 602

WAITING FOR THE MAHATMA *R. K. Narayan* 609

Discussion Questions 618

To Professor James A. Seaver

——————— ✦ ———————

mentor, colleague, friend

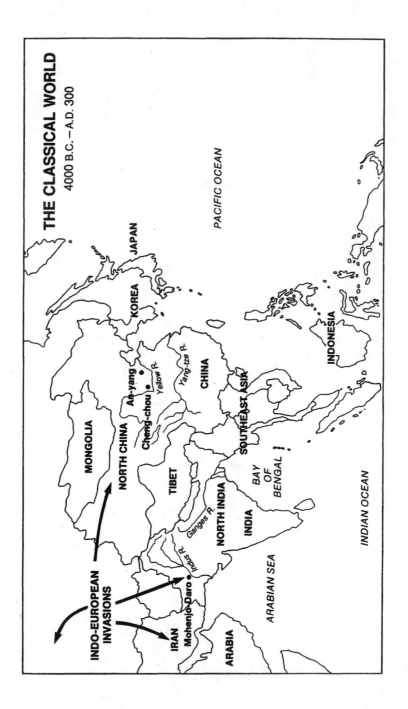

THE CLASSICAL WORLD
4000 B.C. – A.D. 300

PACIFIC OCEAN

JAPAN

KOREA

MONGOLIA

NORTH CHINA

Ah-yang

Cheng-chou

Yellow R.

Yang-tze R.

CHINA

SOUTHEAST ASIA

TIBET

INDONESIA

NORTH INDIA

Ganges R.

Indus R.

Mohenjo-Daro

IRAN

INDIA

BAY
OF
BENGAL

INDO-EUROPEAN
INVASIONS

ARABIA

ARABIAN SEA

INDIAN OCEAN

PART I

Foundations

The Classical World: 4000 B.C. to A.D. 300

Human history may be characterized in part by the tension and conflict that occurs when movements of people, concepts, or technologies bring new ideas and institutions to a given community, and that community tries to adapt these new influences to local conditions and indigenous traditions. Human diversity must have arisen with the spread of human beings from their original home, perhaps in Africa, throughout the world. Moving as hunters and gatherers, adapting to great variations of climate, terrain, and available food supplies, humans took hundreds of thousands of years to complete the process of populating the globe.

In the course of this process, the original human stock began to differentiate in matters such as stature, skin color, and various physical attributes. Other differences arose as the result of variations in local resources. Some fisher folk, exploiting an abundant and reliable food supply, were able to establish permanent settlements and develop a relatively high level of material culture; other peoples, following migratory herds, were able to carry with them only a limited amount of material wealth; yet others, ranging widely in search of scarce and scattered sources of food, were able to develop little material culture at all. Thus highly differentiated human communities, with varied modes of life, different levels of material wealth, and, presumably, diverse attitudes and values arose as the natural result of the expansion of the human race.

These differences were accentuated with the Neolithic Revolution that occurred in the Middle East sometime before 8000 B.C. The domestication of animals and the development of agriculture by some groups of people made it possible for them to concentrate and control their food supplies. This innovation had numerous significant effects on their ways of life. Permanent settlements were now possible, as were a rational division of labor and a substantial increase in material wealth. Communities became larger; whereas the hunting-gathering groups could not have numbered more than a hundred, except under special circumstances, the Neolithic village communities could have populations of over a thousand. This created certain problems within these villages. The small hunting-gathering bands had been little more than extended families, with their mutual obligations and responsibilities defined by ties of blood kinship and the relatively simple division of labor required by their economy.

1

The situation was far different in the more populous and more complex Neolithic villages, and elaborate systems of ritual, religion, legend, and social conventions were developed to create a sense of communal identity within which the obligations incumbent upon the individual could be defined and justified. Thus the Neolithic Revolution gave rise to still greater differences within the human race as numerous Neolithic communities each developed its own distinctive culture, ideology, and sense of identity.

Like the spread of human population, the diffusion of farming and animal husbandry was a relatively slow process. Indeed, it is not yet complete. It would be safe to say, however, that the major river valleys of the Asian continent, districts providing the ample and assured source of water necessary for farming, were all the sites of Neolithic villages by about 2400 B.C., this being the date assigned to the earliest Neolithic archaeological sites found in the Yellow River valley of North China. It was in the valley of the Tigris and Euphrates rivers of Mesopotamia that the next great influence for change arose: the Urban Revolution and the emergence of civilization. The growing populations of the villages in this region led to increasingly complex religious, political, and economic systems. A greater degree of social control was required, necessitating the growth of a managerial class, at first priestly, later secular. In order to regulate and dominate the mass of the population, these rulers developed a number of devices, including more reliable calendars, advanced systems of arithmetic and geometry, and increasingly complex religious systems based on the concept of powerful ruling deities who had to be propitiated through ritual and sacrifice to assure the safety and prosperity of the community. Most important from the viewpoint of the historian, in about 4500 B.C. these Mesopotamian priest-managers developed a system of recording information through the use of a written script. Literature soon followed, and the Mesopotamians produced such impressive works as *The Epic of Gilgamesh*. With the development of writing, the study of history, as opposed to that of archaeology, begins to play a role in deciphering the human record.

Civilization also spread slowly. By about 3100 B.C. the Old Kingdom had been established in the Nile Valley of Egypt, and sometime about 2500 B.C. the two great Indian cities of Harappa and Mohenjo-Daro had arisen along the banks of the Indus River. Although each of these centers was in contact with the others through trade, each adapted the techniques of civilization to the local traditions that had become established during the long period of Neolithic development. All faced the problems created by the growing sizes of their dependent territory and population and the increased secularization of their societies. In the course of their expansion and consolidation, these civilizations had conquered many villages in the name of their local god, and, as a sign of their dominance, demanded that the conquered peoples recognize the supremacy of that deity. By so doing, they crushed their new subjects' sense of communal identity. Although the empires absorbed many of their subjects' gods as lesser members of a state-recognized pantheon, the conquered subjects of these new empires could no longer identify with the community as a whole on purely religious grounds, and their rulers began to substitute secular laws and civil constraints for the religious sanctions that were no longer an effective method of controlling their increasingly heterogeneous subjects.

Sometime about 1700 B.C., while these processes were still underway, new developments occurred in the great expanse of grasslands stretching from the Yellow Sea to Europe that would threaten these rich, but relatively fragile, river-valley civilizations. Somewhere in this region to the north, perhaps around the Caspian Sea, a tribe of people managed to combine advanced techniques of bronze metallurgy with a knowledge of horse-handling to create war chariots, a fearsome weapon that would dominate the field of battle for the next thousand years. This group of people, known to historians as the Aryans or Indo-Europeans, swept out in all directions from their northern homeland, conquering as they went. Although the Aryans appear in history under various names—Hittites, Hyksos, Kassites, Mitanni—and appear to have left little distinctive material culture for archaeologists to recognize, they had a common culture and social organization that greatly influenced the peoples of the regions into which they entered.

Their social organization was male-dominated, reflected in their characteristic pantheon of male sky and nature gods. They shared a linguistic tradition, demonstrated by the close relationships between such languages as Latin, Greek, the major western European tongues, Persian, Sanskrit, and Hindi, all of which are derived from the language of the Indo-European conquerors. The fundamental and defining characteristic of the Indo-Europeans, however, was their fighting chariots and war horses. An incomparable weapon for the times, it was also very expensive. This meant that only a few of the Indo-Europeans could be chariot warriors, and this meant, in turn, that their society was of necessity aristocratic. As is the case with all warlike aristocratic societies, their songs were epic and their gods the embodiments of virile power and prowess. They were organized for war, and the labors of the mass of the people were devoted to the support of the warriors who protected them, fought in the forefront of their battles, and led them in their expansion.

About 1500 B.C., the Indo-Europeans reached both the advanced Indian civilization of the Indus Valley and the Neolithic villages of the Yellow River of China, but in different manners. Mohenjo-Daro and Harappa were both destroyed, and the Indus civilization was brought to an end. The Indo-Europeans entered the Punjab and northern India as proud conquerors, singing the praises of their leaders and gods. Some of these songs survived and later were collected into the *Rig-Veda*, selections from which are presented here in *Vedic Hymns*. Settling in the region, the Indo-Europeans formed a number of petty aristocratic kingdoms, often at war with each other. Although its final form dates from much later, the *Bhagavad Gita*, a song within the great epic, *Mahabharata*, typifies the attitudes and ideals of these Bronze Age warriors and their descendants. As time passed, life within these petty Indian kingdoms grew more elaborate. A written language was developed, and an hereditary priestly class rose to share status and prestige with the warriors. The importance of trade and commerce to the welfare of the community was recognized, and another hereditary status, that of merchant and artisan, became a regular feature of Indian societies. In this fashion, the caste system that characterized Indian society until the modern era evolved from the tribal structure of the Indo-European conquerors of North India. Indian culture, now an amalgam of a native heritage and Indo-European cultural and social influences, developed the power to resist further incursions from the north, although it was not until the fourth century B.C., and then under Persian and Greek influences, that the various kingdoms of the land acquired any real capacity for political unity.

It is uncertain whether the Indo-European invaders were able to conquer the inhabitants of the Yellow River, but it is clear that they exerted considerable influence on them. The first Chinese dynasty for which archaeological evidence has been found is the Shang (1523–c. 1027 B.C.). Shang cities excavated at Cheng-chou and An-yang were heavily fortified, and the graves of these sites attest to an aristocratic society based on a chariot-driving warrior class. Religion appears to have been characterized by a pantheon of nature and sky gods similar to the Indo-European model, and a nascent priestly class had developed a pictographic script that shows some slight relationships to Sumerian. Shang rule was severe, and the testimony of historical records and archaeological excavations indicate a widespread practice of human sacrifice. In about 1050, Shang culture was conquered by their western neighbors, who established the Chou dynasty (1027–256 B.C.). The Chou rulers justified their conquest of a 500-year-old civilization by the political concept of the "Mandate of Heaven" and their development of an elaborate system of state ritual. They centralized the state and brought about a more humane administration. Under the rule of the Chou, indigenous traditions were finally harmonized with the influences of the chariot peoples and the needs of a centralized state, and Chinese culture began to flourish. *The Book of Songs* of Chou China, contrasted with the Indian *Vedic Hymns*, illustrates the degree to which Chinese and Indian civilizations had each evolved their own distinctive characteristics, even if the basic elements of a Neolithic economy and an aristocratic warrior-dominated society had originally been relatively similar.

About 1000 B.C., the techniques of iron metallurgy began to be perfected, perhaps in Asia Minor, and slowly began to spread eastward. The long-term effect of this development was to weaken the social and political structures of the Bronze Age empires. Since iron was cheaper than bronze, many more men could be armed, and formations of spearmen could effectively challenge the dominance of the chariot warriors. The power of the Bronze Age empires and their capacity to maintain central control of their dominions had consisted of their ability to secure and control supplies of bronze and thus keep a warlike aristocracy dependent on the central government. With the advent of iron, the aristocracy no longer controlled the field of battle and could not justify their status by their superior military power. As a consequence, they sought political power. By arming their peasants with cheap iron weapons, it became possible for the aristocracy to challenge the authority of the central government and establish their own independent states. The result of this new possibility in China was the breakup of the Chou empire. Although the emperor retained nominal power until 256 B.C., by 770 B.C. he was in fact virtually powerless, and North China was composed of a number of petty kingdoms. Much the same process occurred in India, with the exception that no tradition of centralized imperial control existed, and, therefore, relatively little change occurred in the political institutions and attitudes of the inhabitants of the land.

The disintegration of the Bronze Age empires was a tumultuous period in which centuries-old traditions were overthrown. It must have appeared to the populace of the time that stability and certainty had vanished from their world, and that ancestral values no longer provided a satisfactory guide to living. Individuals found themselves called upon to make personal decisions in a world in which social control had broken down, and sought to discover the bases on which such decisions should be made. The result was a rise throughout Eurasia of a series of ethical religions. From Hesiod and Amos in the West to K'ung Futzu and Lao-tzu in the East, during the seventh and sixth centuries B.C., individuals began to formulate religious and philosophical systems based on the notion that the moral and ethical conduct of the individual was the necessary foundation of justice and order.

Naturally, each of these thinkers built on the local traditions and the perceived problems of his age. In China, the scholar K'ung Fu-tzu (551–478 B.C.) developed the concepts of "humane conduct" and "proper proportion" discussed in selections from the *Analects*. At about the same time, the legendary sage Lao-tzu supposedly discussed the essential, but undefinable, relationship between the individual and the universe of nature. Selections from this discussion, the *Tao te ching*, illustrate the power of Chinese mysticism. In India, the prince Siddartha Gautama Buddha (c. 566–489 B.C.) produced a personal and mystical alternative to the relatively mechanistic concept of personal "salvation" provided by traditional Hinduism, illustrated in the *Bhagavad Gita*, and explained his doctrine in the famous *Sermon at the Deer Park*, traditionally dated about 530 B.C.

Meanwhile, of course, the social and political turbulence continued, and other scholars attempted to adapt to it both politically and militarily. Advisors attended the petty kings of the period, providing the ruler with guidance, and sometimes admonition, in technical matters. The sage Sun-tzu (c. 500 B.C.?) was such an advisor and excerpts from his classical manual on *The Art of War* provide some idea of the moral rootlessness of the times. Near the close of the period under discussion, the earliest portions of the Indian manual of government known as the *Arthasastra*, later completed by Kautilya (c. 300 B.C.), was formulated by similar advisors, and display a similar concern for practical results.

As time passed, the dangers inherent in the new iron technology were overcome, and stable and dynamic societies arose once again. In China, this was the special role of the Ch'in (221–206 B.C.) and Han (221 B.C.–A.D. 220) dynasties. During this period, the rulers made strenuous efforts to establish a stable state through the centralization of authority, a pattern that occurred across the Eurasian continent with the exception of India. Here, the disintegration of the Mauyran Empire (321–184 B.C.) had been succeeded by a great growth of Indian trade and commerce that developed its own pattern of institutions and traditions. The personal and individualistic religions and philosophies of the earlier era of turmoil were standardized and adapted to the needs of an expanding society. Various scattered Buddhist teachings were organized into a canon of scripture to serve the needs of a mystical philosophy that had become a missionary church.

The Han Empire was particularly demanding in its desire that philosophy should serve the needs of the state and society. New Confucian texts that often bore little relationship to the original teachings of K'ung Fu-tzu received official endorsement and gained great currency. *The Classic of Filial Piety* extolled the virtues of respect for family, a fundamental institution in Han society, while *Lessons for Women* by Pan Chao (A.D. 45–114?) specified the attitudes and actions for the proper woman to cultivate and practice in order to be a good wife. The selections from each of these demonstrate the essentially conservative nature of scholarly thought under the Han emperors.

The period under discussion ends with the forces of standardization and institutionalization dominant, deepening and strengthening traditional culture. At the same time, both Chinese and Indian civilizations were dynamic and expanding, China militarily and politically, and India commercially and culturally. Both were again subject to new influences and faced new challenges. Not the least of the latter was the growth of another power to the north. Not dependent on cumbersome and expensive chariots, the new invaders were horsemen, ranging widely and striking at will. The Huns would soon disturb the happy state of affairs that had been achieved within the classic civilizations of the Old World.

VEDIC HYMNS

The Aryans, one of the Indo-European tribes of chariot-driving conquerors, were a pastoral and nomadic people who brought the Sanskrit language, a pantheon of deities, and a ritualistic cult (based on sacrificial fire and an intoxicating drink called soma) into India some time after 2000 B.C. As nomads seizing new grazing lands, the Aryans valued cattle as their primary source of wealth, and the importance of these animals to the conquerors was perhaps the origin of the later Hindu reverence for the cow. The Aryans did not come to India peacefully, but destroyed the Indus River civilization of India and subjugated the previous inhabitants of the land, whom they called *dasa*, a word that later came to mean "slave."

The Aryans were organized into patriarchal tribes that were in turn composed of hereditary classes, or castes. The Aryans themselves formed the noble class, divided into the warriors (*Rajanya* or *Kshatriya*) and the priests (*Brahman*). Commoners (*Vaisya*) filled all the other respectable occupations. The conquered inhabitants of India, who formed the bulk of the population, were either serfs (*Sudra*) or slaves. These four classes survived long after purely Aryan society disappeared. A fifth category was reserved for those people so low in status that they did not belong to any caste. Such people were called in English "untouchables," since the other castes felt that they were defiled by even touching them.

Early Aryan religion was designed to placate the natural and supernatural forces that influenced human life; it was simple and straightforward, attributing unexplainable events as well as natural phenomena—thunder, lightning, rain, and the fertility of the soil—to the actions of their gods. These gods favored the Aryans when the priests performed sacrifices regularly and correctly. The magical power of the sacrifice to persuade the gods to do what humans wanted them to do was called *brahman*, from which the name of the priestly class derived. The Brahmans were not only the priests of the Aryans, but also their wise men, preserving traditions, laws, and—most of all—knowledge of the gods and their ways for future generations. The Brahmans transmitted this knowledge orally for hundreds of years almost perfectly unchanged, until they were able to write it down. One of the earliest collections of Aryan lore is that known as the Vedas, composed of hymns, prayers, and songs that are now considered sacred by Hindus. The hymns of the *Rig Veda* are the earliest Vedic texts, composed between 1500 and 1200 B.C.

The Vedas preserve songs of homage to the deities, myths, formulas for rituals and sacrifices, and philosophical speculation. Some of the deities to

From *Hinduism*, ed. Louis Renou (New York: George Braziller, 1961), pp. 61–66, 67–69, 71.

whom these hymns are addressed have their counterparts in the pantheons of other Indo-European peoples, especially those of Iran, Greece, and Rome, which suggests a common origin in prehistoric times for all of these religions. Varuna, the greatest of the early Aryan deities, for instance, appears to be related to the god Uranus, famed in Greek mythology.

Many of the hymns of the *Rig Veda* glorify the martial character of the conquerors. Indra, originally a rain-god associated with thunder, was later worshipped as a heroic champion of the Aryans in their destruction of the citadels, dams, and irrigation works of Mohenjo-Daro and Harappa. As the Aryans settled in the land of the five rivers, or Punjab, and extended their conquests into the Ganges plain, Indra began to assume a central role among their other gods. The Aryan pantheon continued to evolve, and the belief system grew more complex. Vishnu, who is a minor deity mentioned in the *Rig Veda* only in the hymn given here, later became perhaps the greatest of the Hindu gods. The idea of transmigration, or the cycle of rebirth, is not mentioned in the earliest sacred texts that have survived; like other Indo-European peoples, the Aryans appear to have believed in a kind of paradise in which the gods dwelled and in a hell ruled by the god Yama, who tortured wicked souls after death. Only later did they develop the belief that souls did not go to an afterlife, but instead returned to another life in a continuous cycle of rebirth and death.

Questions

1. How do the hymns "To Night" and "To Dawn" view nature?
2. In the hymns, what evidence is given of the Aryan transition from pastoral nomadism to settled agriculture?
3. The hymns to creation and the Hymn of Man are dated to a later period on the basis of linguistic evidence. Do they show evidence of the evolution of Indian religious thought?

VEDIC HYMNS

TO VARUNA

Sing forth a hymn sublime and solemn, grateful to glorious
    Varuna, imperial ruler,
Who hath struck out, like one who slays the victim, earth
    as a skin to spread in front of the sun.

In the tree-tops the air he hath extended, put milk in kine[1]
    and vigorous speed in horses,
Set intellect in hearts, fire in the waters, the sun in heaven
    and Soma on the mountain.

Varuna lets the big cask, opening downward, flow through
    the heaven and earth and air's mid-region.
Therewith the universe's sovran waters earth as the shower
    of rain bedews the barley.

When Varuna is fain for milk, he moistens the sky, the
    land, and earth to her foundation.
Then straight the mountains clothe them in the rain-cloud:
    the heroes, putting forth their vigour, loose them.

I will declare this mighty deed of magic, of glorious Varuna,
    the lord immortal,
Who, standing in the firmament, hath meted the earth out
    with the sun as with a measure.

None, verily, hath ever let or hindered this the most wise
    god's mighty deed of magic,
Whereby with all their flood, the lucid rivers fill not one sea
    wherein they pour their waters.

If we have sinned against the man who loves us, have ever
    wronged a brother, friend, or comrade,
The neighbour ever with us, or a stranger, O Varuna,
    remove from us the trespass.

If we, as gamesters cheat at play, have cheated, done wrong
    unwittingly or sinned of purpose,
Cast all these sins away like loosened fetters, and, Varuna,
    let us be thine own beloved.

[1]Cows.

TO VISNU

I will declare the mighty deeds of Visnu, of him who
    measured out the earthly regions,
Who propped the highest place of congregation, thrice
    setting down his footstep, widely striding.

For this his mighty deed is Visnu lauded, like some wild
    beast, dread, prowling, mountain roaming;
He within whose three wide-extended paces all living
    creatures have their habitation.

Let the hymn lift itself as strength to Visnu, the Bull, far-
    striding, dwelling on the mountains,
Him who alone with triple step hath measured this
    common dwelling-place, long, far extended,

Him whose three places that are filled with sweetness,
    imperishable, joy as it may list them,
Who verily alone upholds the threefold, the earth, the
    heaven, and all living creatures.

May I attain to that his well-loved mansion where men
    devoted to the gods are happy.
For there springs, close akin to the wide-strider, the well of
    meath in Visnu's highest footstep.

Fain would we go unto your dwelling-places where there are
    many horned and nimble oxen,
For mightily, there, shineth down upon us the widely-
    striding Bull's sublimest mansion.

TO DAWN

She hath shone brightly like a youthful woman, stirring to
    motion every living creature.
Agni hath come to feed on mortals' fuel. She hath made
    light and chased away the darkness.

Turned to this all, far-spreading, she hath risen and shone
    in brightness with white robes about her.

She hath beamed forth lovely with golden colours, mother
of kine, guide of the days she bringeth.

Bearing the gods' own eye, auspicious lady, leading her
courser white and fair to look on,
Distinguished by her beams, Dawn shines apparent, come
forth to all the world with wondrous treasure.

Dawn nigh will wealth and dawn away the foeman: prepare
for us wide pasture free from danger.
Drive away those who hate us, bring us riches: pour bounty,
opulent lady, on the singer.

Send thy most excellent beams to shine and light us, giving
us lengthened days, O Dawn, O goddess,
Granting us food, thou who hast all things precious, and
bounty rich in chariots, kine, and horses.

O Dawn, nobly-born, daughter of heaven, whom the
Vasisthas[2] with their hymns make mighty,
Bestow thou on us vast and glorious riches. Preserve us
evermore, ye gods, with blessings.

TO NIGHT

With all her eyes the goddess Night looks forth approaching
many a spot:
She hath put all her glories on.

Immortal, she hath filled the waste, the goddess hath filled
height and depth:
She conquers darkness with her light.

The goddess as she comes hath set the Dawn her sister in
her place:
And then the darkness vanishes.

So favour us this night, O thou whose pathways we have
visited
As birds their nest upon the tree.

[2] Poet seers.

The villagers have sought their homes, and all that walks
    and all that flies,
  Even the falcons fain for prey.

Keep off the she-wolf and the wolf; O Night, keep the thief
    away:
  Easy be thou for us to pass.

Clearly hath she come nigh to me who decks the dark with
    richest hues:
  O morning, cancel it like debts.

These have I brought to thee like kine. O Night, thou child
    of heaven, accept
  This laud as for a conqueror.

THE HYMN OF MAN

A thousand heads hath Purusa, a thousand eyes, a thousand
    feet.
On every side pervading earth he fills a space ten fingers
    wide.

This Purusa is all that yet hath been and all that is to be,
The lord of immortality which waxes greater still by food.

So mighty is his greatness; yea, greater than this is Purusa.
All creatures are one-fourth of him, three-fourths eternal
    life in heaven.

With three-fourths Purusa went up; one-fourth of him again
    was here.
Thence he strode out to every side over what eats not and
    what eats.

From him Viraj was born; again Purusa from Viraj was born.
As soon as he was born he spread eastward and westward
    o'er the earth.

When gods prepared the Sacrifice with Purusa as their
    offering,
Its oil was spring; the holy gift was autumn; summer was the
    wood.

They balmed as victim on the grass Purusa born in earliest
time.
With him the deities and all Sadhyas[3] and Rsis[4] sacrificed.

From that great general Sacrifice the dripping fat was
gathered up.
He formed the creatures of the air, and animals both wild
and tame.

From that great general Sacrifice Rcs[5] and Sama-hymns[6]
were born;
Therefrom were spells and charms produced; the Yajus[7] had
their birth from it.

From it were horses born, from it all cattle with two rows of
teeth:
From it were gathered kine, from it the goats and sheep
were born.

When they divided Purusa, how many portions did they
make?
What do they call his mouth, his arms? What do they call
his thighs and feet?

The Brahman was his mouth, of both his arms was the
Rajanya made.
His thighs became the Vaisya, from his feet the Sudra was
produced.

The moon was gendered from his mind, and from his eye
the sun had birth;
Indra and Agni from his mouth were born, and Vayu from
his breath.

Forth from his navel came mid-air; the sky was fashioned
from his head;
Earth from his feet, and from his ear the regions. Thus they
formed the worlds.

[3]Celestial beings.
[4]Ancient seers.
[5]Verses.
[6]Hymns of the *Sama-Veda*; meant to be chanted.
[7]Hymns of the *Vaju-Veda*; sung at sacrifices.

Seven fencing-sticks had he, thrice seven layers of fuel were
    prepared,
When the gods, offering sacrifice, bound, as their victim,
    Purusa.

Gods, sacrificing, sacrificed the victim: these were the
    earliest holy ordinance.
The mighty ones attained the height of heaven, there
    where the Sadhyas, gods of old, are dwelling.

THE SONG OF CREATION

Then was not non-existent nor existent: there was no realm
    of air, no sky beyond it.
What covered in, and where? and what gave shelter? Was
    water there, unfathomed depth of water?

Death was not then, nor was there aught immortal: no sign
    was there, the day's and night's divider.
That one thing, breathless, breathed by its own nature:
    apart from it was nothing whatsoever.

Darkness there was: at first concealed in darkness, this All
    was indiscriminated chaos.
All that existed then was void and formless: by the great
    power of warmth was born that unit.

Thereafter rose desire in the beginning, Desire, the primal
    seed and germ of spirit.
Sages who searched with their heart's thought discovered
    the existent's kinship in the non-existent.

Transversely was their severing line extended: what was
    above it then, and what below it?
There were begetters, there were mighty forces, free action
    here and energy up yonder.

Who verily knows and who can here declare it, whence it
    was born and whence came this creation?
The gods are later than this world's production. Who
    knows, then, whence it first came into being?

He, the first origin of this creation, whether he formed it all
　　or did not form it,
Whose eye controls this world in highest heaven, he verily
　　knows it, or perhaps he knows not.

FURTHER READINGS

Several translations of Vedic hymns are available; two of the standard editions are Ralph T. H. Griffith, trans., *The Hymns of the Rgveda*, 5th ed., 2 vols (Varanasi: Chowkhamba Sanskrit Series Office, 1971) and A. A. Macdonnell, trans., *Hymns from the Rgveda* (London: Oxford University Press, 1923). Raymond and Bridget Allchin, *The Rise of Civilization in India and Pakistan* (Cambridge, UK: Cambridge University Press, 1982) is the authoritative account of prehistoric South Asia. The Classic introduction to Indian civilization is Arthur L. Basham, *The Wonder That Was India: A Survey of the Culture of the Indian Subcontinent Before the Coming of the Muslims* (New York: Grove Press, 1959), supplemented by the essays in Arthur L. Basham, ed., *A Cultural History of India* (Oxford, UK: Oxford University Press, 1976). For an anthropological analysis of Hinduism see Wendy O'Flaherty, *Hindu Myths* (Baltimore: Penguin, 1975).

THE BOOK OF SONGS

Chinese literature begins with the *Shih Ching*, or *Book of Songs*, one of the world's great collections of poetry. This ancient treasury of traditional songs dates from a period between the twelfth and seventh centuries B.C., during the Chou dynasty. Like the earliest classics of other ancient civilization—such as the *Vedic Hymns* of India, the *Epic of Gilgamesh* of Mesopotamia, and the *Iliad* of Greece—the songs of the *Shih Ching* represent an oral tradition written down, sometime around the seventh century B.C., only after centuries of modification and sophistication of both form and language. The collection was originally accompanied by music and was known to the Chinese as the *Shih*, or "songwords." Later it became known as the *Shih Ching*, or "classic of song-words."

The source of Chinese poetry and the inspiration for much of Eastern philosophy, the *Book of Songs* occupies a primary place in Chinese literary history. No other single work in the Chinese language has been more powerful and significant in shaping what is essentially a lyrical tradition. In it are found most

From *The Book of Songs*, trans. Arthur Waley (New York: Grove Press, 1960), pp. 25, 35, 60, 67–68, 71, 113, 153, 161–162, 177, 193, 204–205, 209–211, 227, 233, 324.

of the themes that recur throughout the long and distinguished Chinese poetic heritage.

Tradition credits Confucius with the compilation of the 305 songs that comprise the *Book of Songs*. In the *Analects*, the Sage expresses the deepest respect for the *Book of Songs* and ascribes the deepest moral and ethical significance to its contents. His followers frequently employed the songs as texts for moral instruction and as examples of the highest wisdom. With the passage of time, the anthology became numbered among the Five Confucian Classics[1] and became one of the basic texts of Chinese education. An educated person was expected to have memorized the *Book of Songs* and to be able to recognize an allusion drawn from any poem in the collection.

Poetry has always occupied an important place in Chinese life and society. Poems are composed to express friendship, as entertainment at banquets or parties, as intellectual exercises, or simply for the fun of it. Anything can inspire a poem: a flower or mountain, a desire to praise one's ancestors, the joys of love and courtship, the sorrow of parting, the sight of snow, or dissatisfaction with government policy. Poetry expresses the personal and intimate side of Chinese life and thought as does no other genre, and the results are interwoven into the history of the Chinese people.

The *Book of Songs* already displays the human and individual character of Chinese poetry as well as the vast variety of topics it treats. The *Songs* vividly portray much of daily life and, as a result, afford invaluable glimpses into village life and human activities during ancient times. Besides songs about working the fields and gathering the harvests, there are songs about hunting, feasting, performing sacrifices, honoring the emperors, and making love and war. All are charming in their freshness and surprising in their frankness. The sixteen selections that follow present some of the common topics in the *Book of Songs* and exhibit the qualities of China's most ancient and revered literary treasure.

Questions

1. Western literature often glorifies war in the form of the epic poem. What is the attitude towards war in the *Book of Songs*?

2. The *Book of Songs* is a valuable aid in the reconstruction of daily life in ancient China. After reading these poems, discuss the various social and economic activities typical of the period.

3. The ideal Chinese female was often characterized in literature by a humble, yielding, and respectful attitude towards males. Do the love poems of the *Book of Songs* also reflect this view?

[1] The others are *The Book of Changes (I Ching)*, *The Classic of History*, *The Spring and Autumn Annals*, and *The Book of Rites*. A now-lost *Classic of Music* was sometimes added to form the Six Classics.

COURTSHIP

Elms of the Eastern Gate,
Oaks of the Hollow Mound—
The sons of the Tzu-chung
Trip and sway beneath them.

It is a lucky morning, hurrah!
The Yuan girls from the southern side
Instead of twisting their hemp
In the market trip and sway.

It is a fine morning at last!
"Let us go off to join the throng."
"You are lovely as the mallow."
"Then give me a handful of pepper-seed!"

Mao #137

SECRET COURTSHIP

I beg of you, Chung Tzu,
Do not climb into our homestead,
Do not break the willows we have planted.
Not that I mind about the willows,
But I am afraid of my father and mother.
Chung Tzu I dearly love;
But of what my father and mother say
Indeed I am afraid.

I beg of you, Chung Tzu,
Do not climb over our wall,
Do not break the mulberry-trees we have planted.
Not that I mind about the mulberry-trees,
But I am afraid of my brothers.

Chung Tzu I dearly love;
But of what my brothers say
Indeed I am afraid.

I beg of you, Chung Tzu,
Do not climb into our garden,
Do not break the hard-wood we have planted.
Not that I mind about the hard-wood,
But I am afraid of what people will say.
Chung Tzu I dearly love;
But of all that people will say
Indeed I am afraid.

Mao #76

The rural lover in China frequently visited his lady at night. He was expected to display his courage and resourcefulness by cleverly and quietly overcoming all obstacles in reaching her side. Although sometimes difficult, he was obligated to leave her home by daylight.

COURTSHIP AND SEDUCTION

In the wilds there is a dead doe;
With white rushes we cover her.
There was a lady longing for the spring;
A fair knight seduced her.

In the wood there is a clump of oaks,
And in the wilds a dead deer
With white rushes well bound;
There was a lady fair as jade.

"Heigh, not so hasty, not so rough;
Heigh, do not touch my handkerchief. [1]
Take care, or the dog will bark."

Mao #23

[1] Which was worn at the girdle.

If people find a dead deer in the woods, they cover it piously with rushes. But there are men who "kill" a girl, in the sense that they seduce her and then fail to "cover up" the damage by marrying her. Such is the burden in the preceding poem, its last three lines calling up "elliptically" the scene of the seduction.

MARRIAGE

Over the southern hill so deep
The male fox drags along,
But the way to Lu is easy and broad
For this Ch'i lady on her wedding-way.
Yet once she has made the journey,
Never again must her fancy room.

Fibre shoes, five pairs;
Cap ribbons, a couple.[2]
The way to Lu is easy and broad
For this lady of Ch'i to use.
But once she has used it,
No way else must she ever go.

When we plant hemp, how do we do it?
Across and along we put the rows.
When one takes a wife, how is it done?
The man must talk with her father and mother.
And once he has talked with them,
No one else must he court.

When we cut firewood, how do we do it?
Without an axe it would not be possible.
When one takes a wife, how is it done?
Without a match-maker he cannot get her.
But once he has got her,
No one else must he ever approach.[3]

Mao #101

---

[2] Marriage gifts.
[3] With a view to marriage. It does not, of course, mean that he may not have concubines.

MARRIAGE

Tossed is that cypress boat,
Wave-tossed it floats.
My heart is in turmoil, I cannot sleep.
But secret is my grief.
Wine I have, all things needful
For play, for sport.

My heart is not a mirror,
To reflect what others will.
Brothers too I have;
I cannot be snatched away.
But lo, when I told them of my plight
I found that they were angry with me.

My heart is not a stone;
It cannot be rolled.
My heart is not a mat;
It cannot be folded away.
I have borne myself correctly
In rites more than can be numbered.

My sad heart is consumed, I am harassed
By a host of small men.
I have borne vexations very many,
Received insults not few.
In the still of night I brood upon it;
In the waking hours I rend my breast.

Oh sun, ah, moon,
Why are you changed and dim?
Sorrow clings to me
Like an unwashed dress.
In the still of night I brood upon it,
Long to take wing and fly away.

Mao #26

This is the song of a lady whose friends tried to marry her against her
inclinations.

BLESSINGS

The fish caught in the trap
Were yellow-jaws and sand-eels.
Our lords have wine
Good and plentiful.

The fish caught in the trap
Were bream and tench.
Our lords have wine
Plentiful and good.

The fish caught in the trap
Were mud-fish and carp.
Our lords have wine
Good and to spare.

Things they have in plenty,
Only because their ways are blessed.
Things they have that are good,
Only because they are at peace with one another.
Things they have enough and to spare,
Only because their ways are lovely.

Mao #170

WELCOME

The red bow is unstrung,
When one is given it, one puts it away.
I have a lucky guest;
To the depths of my heart I honour him.
The bells and drums are all set;
The whole morning I feast him.

The red bow is unstrung,
When one is given it, one stores it.
I have a lucky guest;
To the depths of my heart I delight in him.

The bells and drums are all set;
The whole morning I ply him.

The red bow is unstrung,
When one is given it, one puts it in its press.
I have a lucky guest;
To the depths of my heart I love him.
The bells and drums are all set;
The whole morning I drink pledges with him.

Mao #175

THE CLAN FEAST

Ting, ting goes the woodman's axe;
Ying, ying cry the birds,
Leave the dark valley,
Mount to the high tree.
"Ying" they cry,
Each searching its mate's voice.

Seeing then that even a bird
Searches for its mate's voice,
How much the more must man
Needs search out friends and kin.
For the spirits are listening
Whether we are all friendly and at peace.

"Heave ho," cry the woodcutters.
I have strained my wine so clear,
I have got a fatted lamb
To which I invite all my fathers.[4]
Even if they choose not to come
They cannot say I have neglected them.

Spick and span I have sprinkled and swept,
I have set out the meats, the eight dishes of grain.
I have got a fatted ox,
To which I invite all my uncles,

[4] Paternal uncles.

And even if they choose not to come
They cannot hold me to blame.

They are cutting wood on the bank.
Of strained wine I have good store;
The dishes and trays are all in rows.
Elder brothers and younger brothers, do not stay afar!
If people lose the virtue that is in them,
It is a dry throat that has led them astray.

When we have got wine we strain it, we!
When we have none, we buy it, we!
Bang, bang we drum, do we!
Nimbly step the dance, do we!
And take this opportunity
Of drinking clear wine.

Mao #165

AGRICULTURE

Abundant is the year, with much millet, much rice;
But we have tall granaries,
To hold myriads, many myriads and millions of grain.
We make wine, make sweet liquor,
We offer it to ancestor, to ancestress,
We use it to fulfil all the rites,
To bring down blessings upon each and all.

Mao #279

AGRICULTURE

They clear away the grass, the trees;
Their ploughs open up the ground.
In a thousand pairs they tug at weeds and roots,
Along the low grounds, along the ridges.
There is the master and his eldest son,
There the headman and overseer.

They mark out, they plough.
Deep the food-baskets that are brought;
Dainty are the wives,
The men press close to them.
And now with shares so sharp
They set to work upon the southern acre.
They sow the many sorts of grain,
The seeds that hold moist life.
How the blade shoots up,
How sleek, the grown plant;
Very sleek, the young grain!
Band on band, the weeders ply their task.
Now they reap, all in due order;
Close-packed are their stooks[5]—
Myriads, many myriads and millions,
To make wine, make sweet liquor,
As offering to ancestor and ancestress,
For fulfilment of all the rites.
"When sweet the fragrance of offering,
Glory shall come to the fatherland.
When pungent the scent,
The blessed elders are at rest."[6]
Not only here is it like this,
Not only now is it so.
From long ago it has been thus.

Mao #290

DYNASTIC SONG

The charge that Heaven gave
Was solemn, was for ever.
And ah, most glorious
King Wen in plentitude of power!
With blessings he has whelmed us;
We need but gather them in.

---

[5]Bundles of grain.
[6]Or, "are reassured."

High favours has King Wen[7] vouchsafed to us;
May his descendants hold them fast.

Mao #267

Kings rule by virtue of a charge (*ming*), an appointment assigned to them by Heaven.

DYNASTIC SONG

Pity me, your child,
Inheritor of a House unfinished,
Lonely and in trouble.
O august elders,
All my days I will be pious,
Bearing in mind those august forefathers
That ascend and descend in the courtyard.
Yes, I your child,
Early and late will be reverent.
O august kings,
The succession shall not stop!

Mao #286

A song from the legend of King Ch'eng. It is said that when he came to the throne he was a mere child and had to be helped in his rule by his uncle, the Duke of Chou. He also had wicked uncles, who rebelled against him, making common cause with the son of the last Shang king. The story in its main features is probably historical. But the part played by the Duke of Chou has perhaps been exaggerated by the Confucians, who made the duke into a sort of patron saint of their school.

---

[7]Father of King Wu, who conquered the Yin. The standard chronology puts his accession in 1134 B.C. The twenty-six kings from 770 to 249 B.C. had an average reign-length of twenty years. If we apply this average to the twelve kings who preceded them, the date 1134 works out as a hundred years too early.

WARRIOR SONG

How few of us are left, how few!
<u>Why do we not go back</u>?
Were it not for our prince and his concerns,
What should we be doing here in the dew?

How few of us are left, how few!
Why do we not go back?
Were it not for our prince's own concerns,
What should we be doing here in the mud?

Mao #36

WARRIOR SONG

How can you plead that you have no wraps?
I will share my rug with you.
The king is raising an army;
I have made ready both axe and spear;
You shall share them with me as my comrade.

How can you plead that you have no wraps?
I will share my under-robe with you.
The king is raising an army,
I have made ready both spear and halberd;
You shall share them with me when we start.

How can you plead that you have no wraps?
I will share my skirt[8] with you.
The king is raising an army,
I have made ready both armour and arms;
You shall share them with me on the march.

Mao #133

[8]As a rug at night.

LAMENTATION

Oh, the flowers of the bignonia,
Gorgeous is their yellow!
The sorrows of my heart,
How they stab!

Oh, the flowers of the bignonia,
And its leaves so thick!
Had I known it would be like this,
Better that I should never have been born!

As often as a ewe has a ram's head,
As often as Orion is in the Pleiads,
Do people to-day, if they find food at all,
Get a chance to eat their fill.

Mao #233

SACRIFICE

Thick grows the star-thistle;
We must clear away its prickly clumps.
From of old, what have we been doing?
We grow wine-millet and cooking-millet,
Our wine-millet, a heavy crop;
Our cooking-millet doing well.
Our granaries are all full,
For our stacks were in their millions,
To make wine and food,
To make offering, to make prayer-offering,
That we may have peace, that we may have ease,
That every blessing may be vouchsafed.

In due order, treading cautiously,
We purify your oxen and sheep.
We carry out the rice-offering, the harvest offering,
Now baking, now boiling,

Now setting out and arranging,
Praying and sacrificing at the gate.
Very hallowed was this service of offering;
Very mighty the forefathers.
The Spirits and Protectors[9] have accepted;
The pious descendant shall have happiness,
They will reward him with great blessings,
With span of years unending.

We mind the furnaces, treading softly;
Attend to the food-stands so tall,
For roast meat, for broiled meat.
Our lord's lady hard at work
Sees to the dishes, so many,
Needed for guests, for strangers.
Healths and pledges go the round,
Every custom and rite is observed,
Every smile, every word is in place.
The Spirits and Protectors will surely come
And requite us with great blessings,
Countless years of life as our reward.

Very hard have we striven
That the rites might be without mistake.
The skilful recitant conveys the message,
Goes and gives it to the pious son:
"Fragrant were your pious offerings,
The Spirits enjoyed their drink and food.
They assign to you a hundred blessings.
According to their hopes, to their rules,
All was orderly and swift,
All was straight and sure.
For ever they will bestow upon you good store;
Myriads and tens of myriads."

The rites have all been accomplished,
The bells and drums are ready.
The pious son goes to his seat
And the skilful recitant conveys the message:
"The Spirits are all drunk."

[9] An ancestor.

The august Dead One then rises
And is seen off with drums and bells;
The Spirits and protectors have gone home.
Then the stewards and our lord's lady
Clear away the dishes with all speed,
While the uncles and brothers
All go off to the lay feast.

The musicians go in and play,
That after-blessings may be secured.
Your viands are passed round;
No one is discontented, all are happy;
They are drunk, they are sated.
Small and great all bow their heads:
"The Spirits," they say, "enjoyed their drink and food
And will give our lord a long life.
He will be very favoured and blessed,
And because nothing was left undone,
By son's sons and grandson's grandsons
Shall his line for ever be continued."

Mao #209

At Chinese sacrifices a young man, usually the grandson of the sacrificer, impersonated the ancestor to whom the sacrifice was being made. For the time being the spirit of the ancestor entered into him. It was, however, no frenzied "possession"; . . . on the contrary, the demeanor of the Dead One was extremely quiet and restrained.

FURTHER READINGS

The multivolume Dennis Twitchett and John K. Fairbanks, eds., *Cambridge History of China* (Cambridge, UK: Cambridge University Press, 1978–), is the standard reference work on Chinese history. Edward H. Shaefer, *Ancient China* (New York: Time, 1967), is a finely illustrated overview of early Chinese history. Joseph R. Levenson and Franz Schurmann, *China: An Interpretive History* (Berkeley: University of California Press, 1969), covers Chinese history from the earliest times to the end of the Han dynasty. Henri Maspero, *China in Antiquity*, trans. Frank A. Kierman, Jr. (Amherst: University of Massachusetts Press, 1978), offers a sound presentation of the development of Chinese literature and philosophy from primitive times to the founding of the Ch'in dynasty. Notable among numerous general works on ancient China are William Watson,

China before the Han Dynasty (New York: Frederick Praeger, 1961), David N. Keightley, The Origins of Chinese Civilization (Berkeley: University of California Press, 1983), Leonard Cottrell, The Tiger of Ch'in: The Dramatic Emergence of China as a Nation (New York: Holt, Rinehart and Winston, 1962), Kwang-chih Chang, Shang Civilization (New Haven, CT: Yale University Press, 1980), and Jacques Gernet, Ancient China from the Beginnings to the Empire, trans. Raymond Rudorff (London: Faber and Faber, 1968).

William Naughton, The Book of Songs (New York: Twayne, 1971), provides an excellent critical analysis of both the subjects and style of the Songs. C. H. Wang, The Bell and the Drum: Shih Ching as Formulaic Poetry in an Oral Tradition (Berkeley: University of California Press, 1974), and W. A. Dobson, The Language of the Book of Songs (Toronto: University of Toronto Press, 1968), are two helpful linguistic studies. Burton Watson, Early Chinese Literature (New York: Columbia University Press, 1961), provides a critical study of early Chinese literature in general.

Cyril Birch, ed., Anthology of Chinese Literature from Early Times to the Fourteenth Century (New York: Grove Press, 1965), affords an excellent sampling of a vast field. Wu-chi Liu and Irving Yucheng Lo, eds., Sunflower Splendor: Three Thousand Years of Chinese Poetry (Bloomington, IN: Indiana University Press, 1975), is a comprehensive anthology of Chinese poetry from ancient times to the present. The text provides helpful background material and bibliographies for poets and poems. A third useful anthology is Burton Watson, ed. and trans., The Columbia Book of Chinese Poetry (New York: Columbia University Press, 1984), a work that begins with the Book of Songs.

SERMON AT THE DEER PARK
Siddhartha Gautama Buddha

Religious reformers appeared in India in the middle of the first millennium B.C., contemporary with Confucius, the Hebrew prophets, the earliest Greek philosophers, and possibly Zoroaster in Persia. Among their contributions to Hinduism are a series of commentaries on, and explanations of, the Hindu faith. The most important of these are called Upanishads, some of which were written about 550 B.C. Most of the Upanishads speculate on the mechanics of

From The Gospel of Buddha, According to Old Records, told by Paul Carus, 4th rev. ed. (Chicago: Open Court Publishing Company, 1896), pp. 30–33, 37–43.

transmigration, concluding that one's actions (*karma*) determine how one is reborn. If one's deeds are good, the soul (*atman*) is reborn into a higher status; if they are evil, one will live one's next lifetime in a lower status. Transmigration (*samsara*) is not mentioned in the early Vedas, but the Upanishads combined their concept of the brahman mentioned in the Vedic sacrifices with the atman or soul that transmigrates. The brahman was the "universal soul," and salvation was the reunification of the atman with brahman.

Karma and transmigration are the nearest things to religious dogma in Hinduism. By the sixth century B.C., the concept of karma increasingly came to mean ritually prescribed behavior; that is, karma was not so much a matter of good deeds as it was of fulfilling religious obligations. This enhanced the role of the Brahmans, since they were the only caste allowed to perform sacrifice, and other castes had to turn to them for assistance in fulfilling their religious debts. It was believed that only the Brahmans' sacrifices had the magical power to compel the gods to respond to human prayers. At the same time, individual duty (*dharma*) ceased being interpreted in broad human terms, and increasingly came to be defined in terms of caste occupation. In this way, the individual was removed from the center of religious activity in favor of the Brahmans, and individual morality tended to become merely a means of reinforcing a stratified and unequal social system.

The sages who wrote the Upanishads built on the foundations of the Vedas, accepting and elaborating their principles, but others rejected the authority of the Vedas with their emphasis on sacrifice and the inequality between classes and their neglect of personal moral responsibilities. Much of this heterodox thought appears to have come from tribal kingdoms on the fringes of the Ganges plain that had only recently and incompletely absorbed Aryan social institutions. One such kingdom, that of the Sakyas, lying in the foothills of the Himalayas, gave birth to the greatest challenger of Hindu orthodoxy, the founder of Buddhism, Gautama Siddhartha (*c.* 566–486 B.C.), the son of a Sakya chieftain.

The goal of religious effort in the Buddha's teachings was enlightenment (*nirvana*)—a release from the constant cycle of birth and rebirth and a cessation of any consciousness of self. On the surface, this would appear quite similar to the Upanishads' view that salvation consists of the merging of individual and universal souls, but was really quite different. The Buddha explicitly denied the existence of the soul and explained transmigration as merely the movement of a life-force, like a flame passing from candle to candle. On a more institutional level, he also denied that the Brahmans had any special status or peculiar power in the cosmic order. In this sense, he founded a democratic and personal religion, in which each individual was to seek personal enlightenment.

The biography of the "historical Buddha" is an important part of Buddhist beliefs, particularly for Theravada Buddhists, for whom he is a model of the path of renunciation and moderation that leads to enlightenment. There is no full version of his life in early texts, and the following is summarized from later works. Prince Siddartha Gautama left his protected and pampered life in his father's court at the age of twenty-nine to become an ascetic. He practiced various systems of self-mortification and remained with the five ascetics mentioned in this selection for six years, practicing asceticism in an effort to understand the meaning of things and the path to enlightenment. He increased his psychic powers considerably in this fashion, but decided that this alone had not brought him any closer to enlightenment; that it had, in fact, prevented him from maintaining the inner calm necessary for successful meditation. The ascetics left him in disgust when he abandoned his extreme practices. He then meditated alone under the Tree of Wisdom at Gaya and repulsed the temptation from the demon Mora.

The following selection describes his enlightenment and first actions as conceived by the sect of saffron-robed mendicants (*bhikkhu*) who followed his teachings in later centuries. He discovered the "Four Noble Truths" and became a buddha, or "enlightened one," and returned to Benares, where he found the five ascetics who had been his disciples. In the Deer Park outside the city, he preached his first sermon, in which he set out the basic principles of his teachings. The Buddha chose not to pass into the state of nirvana, but remained on earth for forty more years, teaching and collecting disciples.

Questions

1. Why does the Buddha say that ignorance is the root of all evil?
2. How did the five ascetics greet the Buddha? Why?
3. What does the Buddha mean by "the instability of the ego"?

SERMON AT THE DEER PARK

Bodhisattva having put to flight Mara, gave himself up to meditation. All the miseries of the world, the evils produced by evil deeds and the sufferings arising therefrom passed before his mental eye, and he thought:

"Surely if living creatures saw the results of all their evil deeds, they would turn away from them in disgust. But selfhood blinds them, and they cling to their obnoxious desires.

"They crave for pleasure and they cause pain; when death destroys their individuality, they find no peace; their thirst for existence abides and their self-hood reappears in new births.

"Thus they continue to move in the coil and can find no escape from the hell of their own making. And how empty are their pleasures, how vain are their endeavors! Hollow like the plantain-tree and without contents like the bubble.

"The world is full of sin and sorrow, because it is full of error. Men go astray because they think that delusion is better than truth. Rather than truth they follow error, which is pleasant to look at in the beginning but causes anxiety, tribulation, and misery."

And Bodhisattva began to expound the dharma. The dharma is the truth. The dharma is the sacred law. The dharma is religion. The dharma alone can deliver us from error, sin, and sorrow.

Pondering on the origin of birth and death, the Enlightened One recognised that ignorance was the root of all evil; and these are the links in the development of life, called the twelve nidanas:

"In the beginning there is existence blind and without knowledge; and in this sea of ignorance there are appetences formative and organising. From appetences, formative and organising, rises awareness or feelings. Feelings beget organisms that live as individual beings. These organisms develop the six fields, that is, the five senses and the mind. The six fields come in contact with things. Contact begets sensation. Sensation creates the thirst of individualised being. The thirst of being creates a cleaving to things. The cleaving produces the growth and continuation of selfhood. Selfhood continues in renewed births. The renewed births of selfhood are the cause of suffering, old age, sickness, and death. They produce lamentation, anxiety, and despair.

"The cause of all sorrow lies at the very beginning; it is hidden in the ignorance from which life grows. Remove ignorance and you will destroy the wrong appetences that rise from ignorance; destroy these appetences and you will wipe out the wrong perception that rises from them. Destroy wrong perception and there is an end of errors in individualised beings. Destroy errors in individualised beings and the illusions of the six fields will disappear. Destroy illusions and the contact with things will cease to beget misconception. Destroy misconception and you do away with thirst. Destroy thirst and you will be free of all morbid cleaving. Remove the cleaving and you destroy the selfishness of selfhood. If the selfishness of selfhood is destroyed you will be above birth, old age, disease, and death, and you escape all suffering."

The Enlightened One saw the four noble truths which point out the path that leads to Nirvana or the extinction of self:

"The first noble truth is the existence of sorrow. Birth is sorrowful, growth is sorrowful, illness is sorrowful, and death is sorrowful. Sad it is to be joined with that which we do not like. Sadder still is the separation from that which we love, and painful is the craving for that which cannot be obtained.

"The second noble truth is the cause of suffering. The cause of suffering is lust. The surrounding world affects sensation and begets a craving thirst, which clamors for immediate satisfaction. The illusion of self originates and manifests itself in a cleaving to things. The desire to live for the enjoyment of self entangles us in the net of sorrow. Pleasures are the bait and the result is pain.

"The third noble truth is the cessation of sorrow. He who conquers self will be free from lust. He no longer craves, and the flame of desire finds no material to feed upon. Thus it will be extinguished.

"The fourth noble truth is the eightfold path that leads to the cessation of sorrow. There is salvation for him whose self disappears before Truth, whose will is bent upon what he ought to do, whose sole desire is the performance of his duty. He who is wise will enter this path and make an end of sorrow.

"The eightfold path is (1) right comprehension; (2) right resolutions; (3) right speech; (4) right acts; (5) right way of earning a livelihood; (6) right efforts; (7) right thoughts; and (8) the right state of a peaceful mind."

This is the dharma. This is the truth.

Now the Blessed One thought: "To whom shall I preach the doctrine first? My old teachers are dead. They would have received the good news with joy. But my five disciples are still alive. I shall go to them, and to them shall I first proclaim the gospel of deliverance."

At that time the five bhikshus dwelt in the Deer Park at Benares, and the Blessed One not thinking of their unkindness in having left him at a time when he was most in need of their sympathy and help, but mindful only of the services which they had ministered unto him, and pitying them for the austerities which they practised in vain, rose and journeyed to their abode.

The five bhikshus saw their old teacher approach and agreed among themselves not to salute him, nor to address him as a master, but by his name only. "For," so they said, "he has broken his vow and has abandoned holiness. He is no bhikshu but Gautama, and Gautama has become a man who lives in abundance and indulges in the pleasures of worldliness."

But when the Blessed One approached in a dignified manner, they involuntarily rose from their seats and greeted him in spite of their resolution. Still they called him by his name and addressed him as "friend."

When they had thus received the Blessed One, he said: "Do not call the Tathagata by his name nor address him 'friend,' for he is Buddha, the Holy One. Buddha looks equally with a kind heart on all living beings and they therefore call him 'Father.' To disrespect a father is wrong; to despise him, is sin.

"The Tathagata," Buddha continued, "does not seek salvation in austerities, but for that reason you must not think that he indulges in worldly pleasures, nor does he live in abundance. The Tathagata has found the middle path.

"Neither abstinence from fish or flesh, nor going naked, nor shaving the head, nor wearing matted hair, nor dressing in a rough garment, nor covering oneself with dirt, nor sacrificing to Agni, will cleanse a man who is not free from delusions.

"Reading the Vedas, making offerings to priests, or sacrifices to the gods, self-mortification by heat or cold, and many such penances performed for the sake of immortality, these do not cleanse the man who is not free from delusions.

"Anger, drunkenness, obstinacy, bigotry, deception, envy, self-praise, disparaging others, superciliousness, and evil intentions constitute uncleanness; not verily the eating of flesh.

"Let me teach you, O bhikshus, the middle path, which keeps aloof from both extremes. By suffering, the emaciated devotee produces confusion and sickly thoughts in his mind. Mortification is not conducive even to worldly knowledge; how much less to a triumph over the senses!

"He who fills his lamp with water will not dispel the darkness, and he who tries to light a fire with rotten wood will fail.

"Mortifications are painful, vain, and profitless. And how can any one be free from self by leading a wretched life if he does not succeed in quenching the fires of lust.

"All mortification is vain so long as self remains, so long as self continues to lust after either worldly or heavenly pleasures. But he in whom self has become extinct is free from lust; he will desire neither worldly nor heavenly pleasures, and the satisfaction of his natural wants will not defile him. Let him eat and drink according to the needs of the body.

"Water surrounds the lotus-flower, but does not wet its petals.

"On the other hand, sensuality of all kind is enervating. The sensual man is a slave of his passions, and pleasure-seeking is degrading and vulgar.

"But to satisfy the necessities of life is not evil. To keep the body in good health is a duty, for otherwise we shall not be able to trim the lamp of wisdom, and keep our mind strong and clear.

"This is the middle path, O bhikshus, that keeps aloof from both extremes."

And the Blessed One spoke kindly to his disciples, pitying them for their errors, and pointing out the uselessness of their endeavors, and the ice of ill-will that chilled their hearts melted away under the gentle warmth of the Master's persuasion.

Now the Blessed One set the wheel of the most excellent law a-rolling, and he began to preach to the five bhikshus, opening to them the gate of immortality, and showing them the bliss of Nirvana.

And when the Blessed One began his sermon, a rapture thrilled through all the universes.

The devas left their heavenly abodes to listen to the sweetness of the truth; the saints that had parted from life crowded around the great teacher to receive the glad tidings; even the animals of the earth felt the bliss that rested upon the words of the Tathagata: and all the creatures of the host of sentient beings, gods, men, and beasts, hearing the message of deliverance, received and understood it in their own language.

Buddha said:

"The spokes of the wheel are the rules of pure conduct; justice is the uniformity of their length; wisdom is the tire; modesty and thoughtfulness are the hub in which the immovable axle of truth is fixed.

"He who recognises the existence of suffering, its cause, its remedy, and its cessation has fathomed the four noble truths. He will walk in the right path.

"Right views will be the torch to light his way. Right aims will be his guide. Right words will be his dwelling-place on the road. His gait will be straight, for it is right behavior. His refreshments will be the right way of earning his livelihood. Right efforts will be his steps: right thoughts his breath; and peace will follow in his footprints."

And the Blessed One explained the instability of the ego.

"Whatsoever is originated will be dissolved again. All worry about the self is vain; the ego is like a mirage, and all the tribulations that touch it will pass away. They will vanish like a nightmare when the sleeper awakes.

"He who has awakened is freed from fear; he has become Buddha; he knows the vanity of all his cares, his ambitions, and also of his pains.

"It easily happens that a man, when taking a bath, steps upon a wet rope and imagines that is is a snake. Horror will overcome him, and he will shake from fear, anticipating in his mind all the agonies caused by the serpent's venomous bite. What a relief does this man experience when he sees that the rope is no snake. The cause of his fright lies in his error, his ignorance, his illusion. If the true nature of the rope is recognised, his tranquillity of mind will come back to him; he will feel relieved; he will be joyful and happy.

"This is the state of mind of one who has recognised that there is no self, that the cause of all his troubles, cares, and vanities is a mirage, a shadow, a dream.

"Happy is he who has overcome all selfishness; happy is he who has attained peace; happy is he who has found the truth.

"The truth is noble and sweet; the truth can deliver you from evil. There is no saviour in the world except the truth.

"Have confidence in the truth, although you may not be able to comprehend it, although you may suppose its sweetness to be bitter, although you may shrink from it at first. Trust in the truth.

"The truth is best as it is. No one can alter it; neither can any one improve it. Have faith in the truth and live it.

"Errors lead astray; illusions beget miseries. They intoxicate like strong drinks; but they fade away soon and leave you sick and disgusted.

"Self is a fever; self is a transient vision, a dream; but truth is wholesome, truth is sublime, truth is everlasting. There is no immortality except in truth. For truth alone abideth forever."

And when the doctrine was propounded, the venerable Kaundinya, the oldest one among the five bhikshus, discerned the truth with his mental eye, and he said: "Truly, O Buddha, our Lord, thou hast found the truth."

And the devas and saints and all the good spirits of the departed generations that had listened to the sermon of the Tathagata, joyfully received the doctrine and shouted: "Truly, the Blessed One has founded the kingdom of righteousness. The Blessed One has moved the earth; he has set the wheel of Truth rolling, which by no one in the universe, be he god or man, can ever be turned back. The kingdom of Truth will be preached upon earth; it will spread; and righteousness, good-will, and peace will reign among mankind."

FURTHER READINGS

Henry Clark Warren, *Buddhism in Translations* (New Delhi: Motilal Banarasidas, 1987) is a reprint of the 1896 edition of one of the pioneering works of Buddhist studies in the United States; there are well-edited selections of readings in Richard A. Gard, ed., *Buddhism* (New York: George Braziller, 1962) and Edward Conze, ed., *Buddhist Texts through the Ages* (Oxford: Cassirer, 1954). Richard F. Gombrich, *Theravada Buddhism: A Social History from Ancient Benares to Modern Colombo* (London: Routledge and Kegan Paul, 1988) briefly surveys the school of Buddhism that traces its origins to the earliest teachings of the Buddha. Jeannine Auboyer, *Buddha: A Pictorial History of His Life and Legacy* (New York: Crossroad, 1983), offers a superbly illustrated account of the life of Buddha. Edward Conze, *A Short History of Buddhism* (London: Allen & Unwin, 1980), provides an excellent and readable coverage of an extensive subject in a brief work. Arthur R. Wright, *Buddhism in Chinese History* (Stanford, CA: Stanford University Press, 1970) considers the introduction of Buddhism to China and the important role it occupies in the Chinese legacy.

THE BHAGAVAD GITA

The culture and civilization that developed in ancient India is nowhere more clearly reflected than in its two great epic poems, the *Ramayana* and the *Mahabharata*. Transmitted orally for centuries, the two epics were reworked so frequently that today it is impossible to know which elements are the most ancient. The two poems were quite likely secular in origin, but by the time they were placed in their final written form (c. A.D. 200), they had become scripture. These epics have had a profound influence on Indian society, both ancient and modern. They have provided the common ideas and ideals that have been instrumental in maintaining the unity and stability of Hindu life.

The *Mahabharata*, which in its present form consists of some one hundred thousand couplets, holds the distinction of being the world's longest poem. It is part heroic tale, part religious lesson and tells the story of a great battle fought on the plains near modern Delhi between the sons of a blind king on the one hand, and their cousins, the rightful heirs to the throne, on the other. Contained within this vast epic is a literary masterpiece of about fourteen hundred lines that stands out as an independent work. It is known as the *Bhagavad Gita*, or "Lord's Song," and it is universally regarded as the most important and influential of all Hindu scripture. The *Gita* is not an integral part of the *Mahabharata* and was simply inserted into the epic at an appropriate place.

The *Bhagavad Gita* consists of a battlefield dialogue between Arjuna and the god Krishna, who appears in human form and serves as Arjuna's charioteer. Krishna consoles and instructs Arjuna as the prince prepares to go into battle against family and friends to defend his older brother's claim to the throne. Arjuna, a man renowned for his bravery and skill in war, recoils from the thought of killing relatives and friends and cries out to Krishna for help. Krishna, in his answer, touches on almost all the main themes of the *Gita*. Arjuna is told not to worry over the slaying of friends and relatives, for the soul is eternal and only the body dies. In fact, the souls of those killed in battle will only move on to the next life sooner than those who live to old age. Krishna further counsels the prince by pointing out that it is Arjuna's duty (*dharma*) as a member of the warrior class to fight, and that he cannot obtain salvation unless he does his duty. Eventually Arjuna is made to understand that, although he must do his duty, he must act selflessly in doing so. Arjuna must fight not for his own sake, but for the welfare of all. He should perform his duty for its own sake rather than for any personal benefits.

From *The Bhagavad Gita*, trans. Eknath Easwaran (Petaluma, CA: Nilgiri Press, 1985), pp. 52–56, 61–69, 75–79.

The *Bhagavad Gita* occupies a unique position in the ethical tradition of India. It stands out as a timeless, practical manual for daily life. The *Gita* places human destiny solely in human hands. One's actions determine one's destiny. Individuals must fulfill their obligations, but must do so without selfish attachment to personal satisfactions. It is the universality of these themes that has made the *Bhagavad Gita* one of India's most important contributions to world literature.

Questions

1. According to the *Bhagavad Gita*, how should we conduct ourselves in our daily lives? How can we obtain the highest good?
2. What questions does Arjuna ask Krishna regarding life and death? How does Krishna answer these questions? What impact does such knowledge have on everyday actions?
3. What is the *Bhagavad Gita*'s attitude towards war?
4. Describe the relationship between man and god as expressed in this selection.
5. The *Bhagavad Gita* is said to have a universality that crosses time and place. What relevance does its message possess for you?

THE BHAGAVAD GITA

THE WAR WITHIN

DHRITARASHTRA

O Sanjaya, tell me what happened at Kurukshetra, the field of dharma,[1] where my family and the Pandavas gathered to fight.

SANJAYA

Having surveyed the forces of the Pandavas arrayed for battle, prince Duryodhana approached his teacher, Drona, and spoke, "O my teacher, look at this mighty army of the Pandavas, assembled by your own gifted disciple, Yudhishthira. There are heroic warriors and great archers who are the equals of

[1]The obligations of an individual; duty, responsibility.

Bhima and Arjuna: Yuyudhana, Virata, the mighty Drupada, Dhrishtaketu, Chekitana, the valiant king of Kashi, Purujit, Kuntibhoja, the great leader Shaibya, the powerful Yudhamanyu, the valiant Uttamaujas, and the son of Subhadra, in addition to the sons of Draupadi. All these command mighty chariots.

"O best of brahmins, listen to the names of those who are distinguished among our own forces: Bhishma, Karna, and the victorious Kripa; Ashvatthama, Vikarna, and the son of Somadatta. There are many others, too, heroes giving up their lives for my sake, all proficient in war and armed with a variety of weapons. Our army is unlimited and commanded by Bhishma; theirs is small and commanded by Bhima. Let everyone take his proper place and stand firm supporting Bhishma!"

Then the powerful Bhisma, the grandsire, oldest of all the Kurus, in order to cheer Duryodhana, roared like a lion and blew his conch horn. And after Bhishma, a tremendous noise arose of conchs and cowhorns and pounding on drums.

Then Sri Krishna and Arjuna, who were standing in a mighty chariot yoked with white horses, blew their divine conchs. Sri Krishna blew the conch named Panchajanya, and Arjuna blew that called Devadatta. The mighty Bhima blew the huge conch Paundra. Yudhishthira, the king, the son of Kunti, blew the conch Anatavijaya; Nakula and Sahadeva blew their conchs as well. Then the king of Kashi, the leading bowman, the great warrior Shikhandi, Dhrishtadyumna, Virata, the invincible Satyaki, Drupada, all the sons of Draupadi, and the strong-armed son of Subhadra joined in, and the noise tore through the heart of Duryodhana's army. Indeed, the sound was tumultuous, echoing throughout heaven and earth.

Then, O Dhritarashtra, lord of the earth, having seen your son's forces set in their places and the fighting about to begin, Arjuna spoke these words to Sri Krishna:

ARJUNA

O Krishna, drive my chariot between the two armies. I want to see those who desire to fight with me. With whom will this battle be fought? I want to see those assembled to fight for Duryodhana, those who seek to please the evil-minded son of Dhritarashtra by engaging in war.

SANJAYA

Thus Arjuna spoke, and Sri Krishna, driving his splendid chariot between the two armies, facing Bhishma and Drona and all the kings of the earth, said: "Arjuna, behold all the Kurus gathered together."

And Arjuna, standing between the two armies, saw fathers and grandfathers, teachers, uncles, and brothers, sons and grandsons, in-laws and friends. Seeing his kinsmen established in opposition, Arjuna was overcome by sorrow. Despairing, he spoke these words:

ARJUNA

O Krishna, I see my own relations here anxious to fight, and my limbs grow weak; my mouth is dry, my body shakes, and my hair is standing on end. My skin burns, and the bow Gandiva has slipped from my hand. I am unable to stand; my mind seems to be whirling. These signs bode evil for us. I do not see that any good can come from killing our relations in battle. O Krishna, I have no desire for victory, or for a kingdom or pleasures. Of what use is a kingdom or pleasure or even life, if those for whose sake we desire these things—teachers, fathers, sons, grandfathers, uncles, in-laws, grandsons, and others with family ties—are engaging in this battle, renouncing their wealth and their lives? Even if they were to kill me, I would not want to kill them, not even to become ruler of the three worlds. How much less for the earth alone?

O Krishna, what satisfaction could we find in killing Dhritarashtra's sons? We would become sinners by slaying these men, even though they are evil. The sons of Dhritarashtra are related to us; therefore, we should not kill them. How can we gain happiness by killing members of our own family?

Though they are overpowered by greed and see no evil in destroying families or injuring friends, *we* see these evils. Why shouldn't we turn away from this sin? When a family declines, ancient traditions are destroyed. With them are lost the spiritual foundations for life, and the family loses its sense of unity. Where there is no sense of unity, the women of the family become corrupt; and with the corruption of its women, society is plunged into chaos. Social chaos is hell for the family and for those who have destroyed the family as well. It disrupts the process of spiritual evolution begun by our ancestors. The timeless spiritual foundations of family and society would be destroyed by these terrible deeds, which violate the unity of life.

It is said that those whose family dharma has been destroyed dwell in hell. This is a great sin! We are prepared to kill our own relations out of greed for the pleasures of a kingdom. Better for me if the sons of Dhritarashtra, weapons in hand, were to attack me in battle and kill me unarmed and unresisting.

SANJAYA

Overwhelmed by sorrow, Arjuna spoke these words. And casting away his bow and his arrows, he sat down in his chariot in the middle of the battlefield.

THE ILLUMINED MAN

SANJAYA

These are the words that Sri Krishna spoke to the despairing Arjuna, whose eyes were burning with tears of pity and confusion.

SRI KRISHNA

This despair and weakness in a time of crisis are mean and unworthy of you, Arjuna. How have you fallen into a state so far from the path to liberation? It does not become you to yield to this weakness. Arise with a brave heart and destroy the enemy.

ARJUNA

How can I ever bring myself to fight against Bhishma and Drona, who are worthy of reverence? How can I, Krishna? Surely it would be better to spend my life begging than to kill these great and worthy souls! If I killed them, every pleasure I found would be tainted. I don't even know which would be better, for us to conquer them or for them to conquer us. The sons of Dhritarashtra have confronted us; but why would we care to live if we killed them? My will is paralyzed, and I am utterly confused. Tell me which is the better path for me. Let me be your disciple. I have fallen at your feet; give me instruction. What can overcome a sorrow that saps all my vitality? Even power over men and gods or the wealth of an empire seems empty.

SANJAYA

This is how Arjuna, the great warrior, spoke to Sri Krishna. With the words, "O Krishna, I will not fight," he fell silent.

As they stood between the two armies, Sri Krishna smiled and replied to Arjuna, who had sunk into despair.

SRI KRISHNA

You speak sincerely, but your sorrow has no cause. The wise grieve neither for the living nor for the dead. There has never been a time when you and I and the kings gathered here have not existed, nor will there be a time when we will cease to exist. As the same person inhabits the body through childhood, youth, and old age, so too at the time of death he attains another body. The wise are not deluded by these changes.

When the senses contact sense objects, a person experiences cold or heat, pleasure or pain. These experiences are fleeting; they come and go. Bear them patiently, Arjuna. Those who are not affected by these changes, who are the same in pleasure and pain, are truly wise and fit for immortality. Assert your strength and realize this!

The impermanent has no reality; reality lies in the eternal. Those who have seen the boundary between these two have attained the end of all knowledge. Realize that which pervades the universe and is indestructible; no power can affect this unchanging, imperishable reality. The body is mortal, but he who dwells in the body is immortal and immeasurable. Therefore, Arjuna, fight in this battle.

One man believes he is the slayer, another believes he is the slain. Both are ignorant; there is neither slayer nor slain. You were never born; you will never die. You have never changed; you can never change. Unborn, eternal, immutable, immemorial, you do not die when the body dies. Realizing that which is indestructible, eternal, unborn, and unchanging, how can you slay or cause another to slay?

As a man abandons worn-out clothes and acquires new ones, so when the body is worn out a new one is acquired by the Self, who lives within.

The Self cannot be pierced by weapons or burned by fire; water cannot wet it, nor can the wind dry it. The Self cannot be pierced or burned, made wet or dry. It is everlasting and infinite, standing on the motionless foundations of eternity. The Self is unmanifested, beyond all thought, beyond all change. Knowing this, you should not grieve.

O mighty Arjuna, even if you believe the Self to be subject to birth and death, you should not grieve. Death is inevitable for the living; birth is inevitable for the dead. Since these are unavoidable, you should not sorrow. Every creature is unmanifested at first and then attains manifestation. When its end has come, it once again becomes unmanifested. What is there to lament in this?

The glory of the Self is beheld by a few, and a few describe it; a few listen, but many without understanding. The Self of all beings, living within the body, is eternal and cannot be harmed. Therefore, do not grieve.

Considering your dharma, you should not vacillate. For a warrior, nothing is higher than a war against evil. The warrior confronted with such a war should be pleased, Arjuna, for it comes as an open gate to heaven. But if you do not participate in this battle against evil, you will incur sin, violating your dharma and your honor.

The story of your dishonor will be repeated endlessly: and for a man of honor, dishonor is worse than death. These brave warriors will think you have withdrawn from battle out of fear, and those who formerly esteemed you will treat you with disrespect. Your enemies will ridicule your strength and say things that should not be said. What could be more painful than this?

Death means the attainment of heaven; victory means the enjoyment of the earth. Therefore rise up, Arjuna, resolved to fight! Having made yourself alike in pain and pleasure, profit and loss, victory and defeat, engage in this great battle and you will be freed from sin.

You have heard the intellectual explanation of Sankhya, Arjuna; now listen to the principles of yoga.[2] By practicing these you can break through the bonds of karma.[3] On this path effort never goes to waste, and there is no failure. Even a little effort toward spiritual awareness will protect you from the greatest fear.

---

[2]Mental and physical discipline through which the individual attempts to reach the state of "pure soul," in which the soul is freed of both dharma and karma.
[3]The accumulated weight of past deeds and misdeeds on the individual soul.

Those who follow this path, resolving deep within themselves to seek Me alone, attain singleness of purpose. For those who lack resolution, the decisions of life are many-branched and endless. There are ignorant people who speak flowery words and take delight in the letter of the law, saying that there is nothing else. Their hearts are full of selfish desires, Arjuna. Their idea of heaven is their own enjoyment, and the aim of all their activities is pleasure and power. The fruit of their actions is continual rebirth. Those whose minds are swept away by the pursuit of pleasure and power are incapable of following the supreme goal and will not attain samadhi.[4]

The scriptures describe the three gunas.[5] But you should be free from the action of the gunas, established in eternal truth, self-controlled, without any sense of duality or the desire to acquire and hoard.

Just as a reservoir is of little use when the whole countryside is flooded, scriptures are of little use to the illumined man or woman, who sees the Lord everywhere.

You have the right to work, but never to the fruit of work. You should never engage in action for the sake of reward, nor should you long for inaction. Perform work in this world, Arjuna, as a man established within himself—without selfish attachments, and alike in success and defeat. For yoga is perfect evenness of mind.

Seek refuge in the attitude of detachment and you will amass the wealth of spiritual awareness. Those who are motivated only by desire for the fruits of action are miserable, for they are constantly anxious about the results of what they do. When consciousness is unified, however, all vain anxiety is left behind. There is no cause for worry, whether things go well or ill. Therefore, devote yourself to the disciplines of yoga, for yoga is skill in action.

The wise unify their consciousness and abandon attachment to the fruits of action, which binds a person to continual rebirth. Thus they attain a state beyond all evil.

When your mind has overcome the confusion of duality, you will attain the state of holy indifference to things you hear and things you have heard. When you are

---

[4]The state of "pure soul"; also called nirvana.
[5]The three elements or attributes of which all things and actions are composed: *sattva*, the luminous, noble element; *rajas*, the colored, passionate element; and *tamas*, the dark, indifferent element.

unmoved by the confusion of ideas and your mind is completely united in deep samadhi,[6] you will attain the state of perfect yoga.

ARJUNA

Tell me of those who live established in wisdom, ever aware of the Self, O Krishna. How do they talk? How sit? How move about?

SRI KRISHNA

They live in wisdom who see themselves in all and all in them, who have re-nounced every selfish desire and sense craving tormenting the heart.

Neither agitated by grief nor hankering after pleasure, they live free from lust and fear and anger. Established in meditation, they are truly wise. Fettered no more by selfish attchments, they are neither elated by good fortune nor de-pressed by bad. Such are the seers. Even as a tortoise draws in its limbs, the wise can draw in their senses at will. Aspirants abstain from sense pleasures, but they still crave for them. These cravings all disappear when they see the highest goal. Even of those who tread the path, the stormy senses can sweep off the mind. They live in wisdom who subdue their senses and keep their minds ever ab-sorbed in me.

When you keep thinking about sense objects, attachment comes. Attachment breeds desire, the lust of possession that burns to anger. Anger clouds the judg-ment; you can no longer learn from past mistakes. Lost is the power to choose between what is wise and what is unwise, and your life is utter waste. But when you move amidst the world of sense, free from attachment and aversion alike, there comes the peace in which all sorrows end, and you live in the wisdom of the Self. The disunited mind is far from wise; how can it meditate? How be at peace? When you know no peace, how can you know joy? When you let your mind follow the call of the senses, they carry away your better judgment as storms drive a boat off its charted course on the sea.

Use all your power to free the senses from attachment and aversion alike, and live in the full wisdom of the Self. Such a sage awakes to light in the night of all creatures. That which the world calls day is the night of ignorance to the wise.

As rivers flow into the ocean but cannot make the vast ocean overflow, so flow the streams of the sense-world into the sea of peace that is the sage. But this is not so with the desirer of desires.

[6]Concentrated mental discipline; a form of meditation.

They are forever free who renounce all selfish desires and break away from the ego-cage of "I," "me," and "mine" to be united with the Lord. This is the supreme state. Attain to this, and pass from death to immortality.

SELFLESS SERVICE

ARJUNA

O Krishna, you have said that knowledge is greater than action; why then do you ask me to wage this terrible war? Your advice seems inconsistent. Give me one path to follow to the supreme good.

SRI KRISHNA

At the beginning of time I declared two paths for the pure heart: *jnana yoga,* the contemplative path of spiritual wisdom, and *karma yoga,* the active path of selfless service. He who shirks action does not attain freedom; no one can gain perfection by abstaining from work. Indeed, there is no one who rests for even an instant; every creature is driven to action by his own nature.

Those who abstain from action while allowing the mind to dwell on sensual pleasure cannot be called sincere spiritual aspirants. But they excel who control their senses through the mind, using them for selfless service.

Fulfill all your duties; action is better than inaction. Even to maintain your body, Arjuna, you are obliged to act. Selfish action imprisons the world. Act selflessly, without any thought of personal profit.

At the beginning, mankind and the obligation of selfless service were created together. "Through selfless service, you will always be fruitful and find the fulfillment of your desires": this is the promise of the Creator.

Honor and cherish the devas[7] as they honor and cherish you; through this honor and love you will attain the supreme good. All human desires are fulfilled by the devas, who are pleased by selfless service. But anyone who enjoys the things given by the devas without offering selfless acts in return is a thief.

The spiritually minded, who eat in the spirit of service, are freed from all their sins; but the selfish, who prepare food for their own satisfaction, eat sin. Living

[7]The gods, demigods, and spirits of Hindu belief.

creatures are nourished by food, and food is nourished by rain; rain itself is the water of life, which comes from selfless worship and service.

Every selfless act, Arjuna, is born from Brahman, the eternal, infinite Godhead. He is present in every act of service. All life turns on this law, O Arjuna. Whoever violates it, indulging his senses for his own pleasure and ignoring the needs of others, has wasted his life. But those who realize the Self are always satisfied. Having found the source of joy and fulfillment, they no longer seek happiness from the external world. They have nothing to gain or lose by any action; neither people nor things can affect their security.

Strive constantly to serve the welfare of the world; by devotion to selfless work one attains the supreme goal of life. Do your work with the welfare of others always in mind. It was by such work that Janaka[8] attained perfection; others, too, have followed this path.

What the outstanding person does, others will try to do. The standards such people create will be followed by the whole world. There is nothing in the three worlds for me to gain, Arjuna, nor is there anything I do not have; I continue to act, but I am not driven by any need of my own. If I ever refrained from continuous work, everyone would immediately follow my example. If I stopped working I would be the cause of cosmic chaos, and finally of the destruction of this world and these people.

The ignorant work for their own profit, Arjuna; the wise work for the welfare of the world, without thought for themselves. By abstaining from work you will confuse the ignorant, who are engrossed in their actions. Perform all work carefully, guided by compassion.

All actions are performed by the gunas of prakriti.[9] Deluded by his identification with the ego, a person thinks, "I am the doer." But the illumined man or woman understands the domain of the gunas and is not attached. Such people know that the gunas interact with each other; they do not claim to be the doer.

Those who are deluded by the operation of the gunas become attached to the results of their action. Those who understand these truths should not unsettle

[8]King of Mithila who sacrificed to the gods personally, rather than through a Brahman priest, and thus became a Brahman through his own efforts. Janaka was also the father-in-law of Rama, hero of the epic *Ramayana*.
[9]The material basis of the universe, as opposed to *purusha*, the spiritual basis.

the ignorant. Performing all actions for my sake, completely absorbed in the Self, and without expectations, fight!—but stay free from the fever of the ego.

Those who live in accordance with these divine laws without complaining, firmly established in faith, are released from karma. Those who violate these laws, criticizing and complaining, are utterly deluded, and are the cause of their own suffering.

Even a wise man acts within the limitations of his own nature. Every creature is subject to prakriti; what is the use of repression? The senses have been conditioned by attraction to the pleasant and aversion to the unpleasant. Do not be ruled by them; they are obstacles in your path.

It is better to strive in one's own dharma than to succeed in the dharma of another. Nothing is ever lost in following one's own dharma, but competition in another's dharma breeds fear and insecurity.

ARJUNA

What is the force that binds us to selfish deeds, O Krishna? What power moves us, even against our will, as if forcing us?

SRI KRISHNA

It is selfish desire and anger, arising from the guna of rajas; these are the appetites and evils which threaten a person in this life.

Just as a fire is covered by smoke and a mirror is obscured by dust, just as the embryo rests deep within the womb, knowledge is hidden by selfish desire—hidden, Arjuna, by this unquenchable fire for self-satisfaction, the inveterate enemy of the wise.

Selfish desire is found in the senses, mind, and intellect, misleading them and burying the understanding in delusion. Fight with all your strength, Arjuna! Controlling your senses, conquer your enemy, the destroyer of knowledge and realization.

The senses are higher than the body, the mind higher than the senses; above the mind is the intellect, and above the intellect is the Atman. Thus, knowing that which is supreme, let the Atman rule the ego. Use your mighty arms to slay the fierce enemy that is selfish desire.

FURTHER READINGS

Notable among the many commentaries on the *Bhagavad Gita* is Singh Balbir, *Essence of the Bhagavad Gita* (Atlantic Highlands, NJ: Humanities Press, 1981). A recent study of the comparative and intercultural aspects of the *Gita*, in particular, dealing with Western interpretations, is provided in Eric Sharpe, *The Universal Gita* (London: Duckworth, 1985). Prem Nath Bazaz, *The Role of the Bhagavad Gita in Indian History* (New Delhi: Sterling, 1975) is a critical examination of the *Gita* and its role in the historical development of India. Among the numerous works providing a general background for ancient India are Arthur L. Basham, *Aspects of Ancient Indian Culture* (Bombay: Asia Publishing House, 1966); Bridget Allchin, *The Rise of Civilization in India and Pakistan* (Cambridge, UK: Cambridge University Press, 1982); and Jeannine Auboyer, *Daily Life in Ancient India* (New York: Macmillan, 1966).

THE ANALECTS

K'ung Fu-tzu

K'ung Fu-tzu (551–478 B.C.), commonly known in the West as Confucius, was the greatest of the Chinese sages and is generally regarded as having done more than any other single individual to shape Chinese character and culture over the centuries. He was born into an age in which society appeared to be disintegrating. For four centuries, the Chou dynasty (1122–770 B.C.) had maintained order and stability in North China, but had lost all real power some two centuries earlier. During Kung's lifetime, attempts to maintain a measure of peace and political unity through a "concert of princes" was failing. The intricate social and political relations and the highly developed religious ritual and sophisticated culture that had evolved over the preceding thousand years were decaying. Ancient values and attitudes provided the people with little sense of purpose and direction as China continued its decline toward that period that would become known as the "Era of the Warring States" (453–221 B.C.).

K'ung entered the civil service of the prince of Lu, a small state in what is now the province of Shantung. During this period, tradition credits him with having rescued from neglect a group of books that he considered as embodying the best traditions of the golden age of Chou. These works, *The Book of Songs*, *The Book of History*, *The Book of Changes*, *The Spring and Autumn Annals*, and *The Book of Rites*, became known as the Five Classics, and the Confucian system of education was based on their study. K'ung soon began teaching, and quickly

From *The Analects of Confucius*, trans. Arthur Waley (London: Allen & Unwin, 1938), pp. 83–93.

gathered numerous disciples about him. He taught that the welfare of the people and the good of the state depend on individuals conducting themselves properly in their relations with others, and virtuous individuals teach others by example. Virtue is its own reward, and proper conduct ennobles the individual more certainly than high birth. One of history's great moralists, K'ung displayed little interest in metaphysics or cosmological speculation. Humanity lay at the center of his philosophical world, and a sense of proportion (*li*) and a humane spirit (*jen*) were the fundamental qualities necessary to restore order to a disorderly world. Although K'ung wrote little, his disciples copied down his discourses and spread his reputation far and wide. *The Analects*, from which this reading is taken, is the main surviving work of this sort.

K'ung longed to become an advisor of one of the ruling princes in order to gain enough influence to help restore a sense of order to the world. He and his students wandered throughout China, spreading his teachings far and wide, and seeking a ruler willing to accept his direction. Despite his increasing fame, and although the princes admired and honored him, none was willing to accept him as counsellor and trust his fortunes to such fragile values as moderation and humane conduct. K'ung died frustrated and a failure in his own eyes.

In the ensuing years, his followers were persecuted and scattered, but Confucian teachings survived and were adopted as doctrine by the great Han emperors who once again brought unity to China (206 B.C.–A.D. 200). The *Analects* itself assumed the stature of a classic, and the Han emperors expected their administrators to be thoroughly familiar with its teachings. The Confucians characteristically paid little attention to metaphysics and theology; if virtue is its own reward, there is little reason to speculate about the gods and the afterlife. In the *Analects*, which takes the form of brief quotations of the Master (K'ung) and various of his early disciples, or short exchanges between them, there are no hidden doctrines or complex theorizing. Social and political obligations, the Chinese tradition of the veneration of ancestors, the qualities necessary to the good man, the principles of effective government, and other similar topics are the subjects of concern, often presented in a seemingly random fashion. These short discourses are unified, however, by their constant concern with the principles of proportion and humane conduct, the twin pillars of Confucian thought and the enduring ideals of traditional Chinese culture.

Questions

1. Why does filial respect play such a large role in Confucian thought?
2. What are the qualities of a "gentleman"?
3. Why do K'ung and his disciples place so much emphasis on tradition and ritual?
4. What does K'ung consider to be the bases of good government?

THE ANALECTS

BOOK I

1. The Master said, To learn and at due times to repeat what one has learnt, is that not after all a pleasure? That friends should come to one from afar, is this not after all delightful? To remain unsoured even though one's merits are unrecognized by others, is that not after all what is expected of a gentleman?

2. Master Yu[1] said, Those who in private life behave well towards their parents and elder brothers, in public life seldom show a disposition to resist the authority of their superiors. And as for such men starting a revolution, no instance of it has ever occurred. It is upon the trunk that a gentleman works.[2] When that is firmly set up, the Way grows. And surely proper behaviour towards parents and elder brothers is the trunk of Goodness?

3. The Master said, "Clever talk and a pretentious manner" are seldom found in the Good.

4. Master Tseng said, Every day I examine myself on these three points: in acting on behalf of others, have I always been loyal to their interests? In intercourse with my friends, have I always been true to my word? Have I failed to repeat the precepts that have been handed down to me?

5. The Master said, A country of a thousand war-chariots cannot be administered unless the ruler attends strictly to business, punctually observes his promises, is economical in expenditure, shows affection towards his subjects in general, and uses the labour of the peasantry only at the proper times of year.[3]

6. The Master said, A young man's duty is to behave well to his parents at home and to his elders abroad, to be cautious in giving promises and punctual in keeping them, to have kindly feelings towards everyone, but seek the intimacy of the Good. If, when all that is done, he has any energy to spare, then let him study the polite arts.[4]

7. Tzu-hsia said, A man who

> Treats his betters as betters,
> Wears an air of respect,
> Who into serving father and mother
> Knows how to put his whole strength,

[1] Master Yu, Master Tseng, Tzu-hsia, disciples of Confucius.
[2] The gentleman concentrates on basic issues, causes rather than effects.
[3] Leaving them free to plant and harvest at the necessary times.
[4] Such as archery, music, and essay writing.

- respect authority
- keep word integrity

Who in the service of his prince will lay down his life,
Who in intercourse with friends is true to his word——

others may say of him that he still lacks education,[5] but I for my part should certainly call him an educated man.

8. The Master said, If a gentleman is frivolous, he will lose the respect of his inferiors and lack firm ground upon which to build up his education. First and foremost he must learn to be faithful to his superiors, to keep promises, to refuse the friendship of all who are not like him. And if he finds he has made a mistake, then he must not be afraid of admitting the fact and amending his ways.

9. Master Tseng said, When proper respect towards the dead is shown at the End and continued after they are far away the moral force of a people has reached its highest point.

10. Tzu-Ch'in[6] said to Tzu-kung, When our Master arrives in a fresh country he always manages to find out about its policy. Does he do this by asking questions, or do people tell him of their own accord? Tzu-kung said, "Our Master gets things by being cordial, frank, courteous, temperate, deferential. That is our Master's way of enquiring—a very different matter, certainly, from the way in which enquiries are generally made.

11. The Master said, While a man's father is alive, you can only see his intentions; it is when his father dies that you discover whether or not he is capable of carrying them out. If for the whole three years of mourning he manages to carry on the household exactly as in his father's day, then he is a good son indeed.

12. Master Yu said, In the usages of ritual it is harmony that is prized; the Way of the Former Kings from this got its beauty. Both small matters and great depend upon it. If things go amiss, he who knows the harmony will be able to attune them. But if harmony itself is not modulated by ritual, things will still go amiss.

13. Master Yu said,

In your promises cleave to what is right,
And you will be able to fulfil your word.
In your obeisances cleave to ritual,
And you will keep dishonour at bay.
Marry one who has not betrayed her own kin,
And you may safely present her to your Ancestors.[7]

[5]Formal learning and social graces.
[6]Tzu-Ch'in, Tzu-kung: other disciples of Confucius.
[7]The presentation of a bride to the bridegroom's ancestors was an important part of the marriage ritual.

-responsibility

14. The Master said, A gentleman who never goes on eating till he is sated, who does not demand comfort in his home, who is diligent in business and cautious in speech, who associates with those that possess the Way and thereby corrects his own faults—such a one may indeed be said to have a taste for learning.

15. Tzu-kung said, "Poor without cadging, rich without swagger." What of that? The Master said, Not bad. But better still, "Poor, yet delighting in the Way; rich, yet a student of ritual." Tzu-kung said, The saying of the *Songs,*

> As thing cut, as thing filed,
> As thing chiselled, as thing polished

refers, I suppose, to what you have just said? The Master said, Ssu,[8] now I can really begin to talk to you about the *Songs,* for when I allude to sayings of the past, you see what bearing they have on what was to come after.

16. The Master said, (the good man) does not grieve that other people do not recognize his merits. His only anxiety is lest he should fail to recognize theirs. *import of learning*

1. The Master said, He who rules by moral force is like the pole-star, which remains in its place while all the lesser stars do homage to it.

2. The Master said, If out of the three hundred *Songs* I had to take one phrase to cover all my teaching, I would say "Let there be no evil in your thoughts."

3. The Master said, Govern the people by regulations, keep order among them by chastisements, and they will flee from you, and lose all self-respect. Govern them by moral force, keep order among them by ritual, and they will keep their self-respect and come to you of their own accord.

4. The Master said, At fifteen I set my heart upon learning. At thirty, I had planted my feet firm upon the ground. At forty, I no longer suffered from perplexities. At fifty, I knew what were the biddings of Heaven. At sixty, I heard them with docile ear. At seventy, I could follow the dictates of my own heart; for what I desired no longer overstepped the boundaries of right.

5. Meng I Tzu[9] asked about the treatment of parents. The Master said, Never disobey! When Fan Ch'ih was driving his carriage for him, the Master said, Meng asked me about the treatment of parents and I said, Never disobey! Fan Ch'ih said, In what sense did you mean it? The Master said, While they

[8]Perhaps Tzu-kung's personal name; but also an exclamation, like "Ah!"

[9]Meng I Tzu (d. 481 B.C.), Fan Ch'ih, disciples of Confucius; Meng Wu Po, a disciple and son of Meng I Tzu.

virtuous teach by being virtuous

are alive, serve them according to ritual. When they die, bury them according to ritual and sacrifice to them according to ritual.

6. Meng Wu Po asked about the treatment of parents. The Master said, Behave in such a way that your father and mother have no anxiety about you, except concerning your health.

7. Tzu-yu asked about the treatment of parents. The Master said, "Filial sons" nowadays are people who see to it that their parents get enough to eat. But even dogs and horses are cared for to that extent. If there is no feeling of respect, wherein lies the difference?

8. Tzu-hsia asked about the treatment of parents. The Master said, It is the demeanour that is difficult. Filial piety does not consist merely in young people undertaking the hard work, when anything has to be done, or serving their elders first with wine and food. It is something much more than that.

9. The Master said, I can talk to Yen Hui[10] a whole day without his ever differing from me. One would think he was stupid. But if I enquire into his private conduct when he is not with me I find that it fully demonstrates what I have taught him. No, Hui is by no means stupid.

10. The Master said, Look closely into his aims, observe the means by which he pursues them, discover what brings him content—and can the man's real worth remain hidden from you, can it remain hidden from you?

11. The Master said, He who by reanimating the Old can gain knowledge of the New is fit to be a teacher.

12. The Master said, A gentleman is not an implement.[11]

13. Tzu-kung asked about the true gentleman. The Master said, He does not preach what he practises till he has practised what he preaches.

14. The Master said, A gentleman can see a question from all sides without bias. The small man is biased and can see a question only from one side.

15. The Master said, "He who learns but does not think, is lost." He who thinks but does not learn is in great danger.

16. The Master said, He who sets to work upon a different strand destroys the whole fabric.

17. The Master said, Yu, shall I teach you what knowledge is? When you know a thing, to recognize that you know it, and when you do not know a thing, to recognize that you do not know it. That is knowledge.

[10]Yen Hui, a favorite disciple of Confucius.
[11]That is, fit only for a single purpose. The gentleman is liberally educated.

18. Tzu-chang was studying the Song Han-lu.[12] The Master said, Hear much, but maintain silence as regards doubtful points and be cautious in speaking of the rest; then you will seldom get into trouble. See much, but ignore what it is dangerous to have seen, and be cautious in acting upon the rest; then you will seldom want to undo your acts. He who seldom gets into trouble about what he has said and seldom does anything that he afterwards wishes he had not done, will be sure incidentally to get his reward.

19. Duke Ai[13] asked, What can I do in order to get the support of the common people? Master K'ung[14] replied, If you "raise up the straight and set them on top of the crooked," the commoners will support you. But if you raise the crooked and set them on top of the straight, the commoners will not support you.

20. Chi K'ang-tzu asked whether there were any form of encouragement by which he could induce the common people to be respectful and loyal. The Master said, Approach them with dignity, and they will respect you. Show piety towards your parents and kindness towards your children, and they will be loyal to you. Promote those who are worthy, train those who are incompetent; that is the best form of encouragement.

21. Someone, when talking to Master K'ung, said, How is it that you are not in the public service? The Master said, The Book[15] says: "Be filial, only be filial and friendly towards your brothers, and you will be contributing to government." There are other sorts of service quite different from what you mean by "service."

22. The Master said, I do not see what use a man can be put to, whose word cannot be trusted. How can a waggon be made to go if it has no yoke-bar or a carriage, if it has no collar-bar?

23. Tzu-chang asked whether the state of things ten generations hence could be foretold. The Master said, We know in what ways the Yin modified ritual when they followed upon the Hsia.[16] We know in what ways the Chou modified ritual when they followed upon the Yin. And hence we can foretell what the successors of Chou will be like, even supposing they do not appear till a hundred generations from now.

24. The Master said, Just as to sacrifice to ancestors other than one's own is presumption, so to see what is right and not do it is cowardice.

[12]Tzu-chang, disciple of Confucius. The song "Han-lu" is from the Book of Songs, knowledge of which was an essential part of a gentleman's education.
[13]Ruler of the state of Lu, 494–468 B.C.
[14]Master K'ung: Confucius.
[15]The Book of History, one of the Five Classics.
[16]Yin, Hsia, Chou, imperial dynasties.

FURTHER READINGS

For the history of China, the multivolume Denis Twitchett and John K. Fairbanks, eds., *Cambridge History of China* (Cambridge, UK: Cambridge University Press, 1978–), is an excellent scholarly reference. The Chou dynasty is discussed by Cho-yun Hsu, *Western Chou Civilization*, Chinese Civilization Series (New Haven, CT: Yale University Press, 1988), and Hsueh-ch'in Li, *Eastern Zhou and Qin Civilizations*, trans. K. C. Chang, Chinese Civilization Series (New Haven, CT: Yale University Press, 1985). Richly illustrated presentations of early Chinese history are provided by C. P. Fitzgerald, *The Horizon History of China* (New York: American Heritage, 1969), Yong Yap Cotterell and Arthur Cotterell, *The Early Civilization of China* (New York: Putnam's Sons, 1975), and Bambier Gascoigne, *The Dynasties and Treasures of China* (New York: Viking Press, 1973). Michael Lowe, *Chinese Ideas of Life and Death: Faith, Myth, and Reason in the Han Period* (London: Allen & Unwin, 1982) examines some intellectual and religious beliefs of the Ch'in and Han periods. Herrlee Creel, *The Birth of China, a Study of the Formative Period of Chinese Civilization* (New York: Reynal and Hitchcock, 1937), discusses aspects of early Chinese life. Benjamin I. Schwartz, *The World of Thought in Ancient China* (Cambridge, MA: Harvard University Press, 1985) provides information on the relationship between moral qualities and the family.

Although the life of K'ung Fu-tzu has been heavily influenced by legend, it has been treated by a number of authors, including Maurice Collis, *The First Holy One* (New York: Knopf, 1948); Raymond S. Dawson, *Confucius* (New York: Hill & Wang, 1982); Carl Crow, *Master K'ung: The Story of Confucius* (New York: Harper & Brothers, 1938); and Chang Ch'i-yun, *A Life of Confucius*, trans. Shih Chao-yin (Taipei: China News Press, 1957). The standard English translation of the basic work of Confucian thought is still Arthur Waley, trans., *The Analects of Confucius* (New York: Allen & Unwin, 1938), but those of Willam E. Soothill (London: Oxford University Press, 1951) and D. C. Lau (Hong Kong: Chinese University Press, 1983) are also worthwhile. Representative later texts of Confucian philosophy are provided in Ch'u Chai and Winberg Ch'ai, eds. and trans., *The Sacred Books of Confucius and Other Confucian Classics* (New York: Bantam, 1965), and Jordan D. Paper, ed. and trans., *The Fu-tsu: A Post-Han Confucian Text* (Leiden, Netherlands: Brill, 1987).

Perhaps the most comprehensive introduction to Chinese philosophy is that of Fung Yu-lan, *A History of Chinese Philosophy*, 2nd ed., 2 vols (Princeton, NJ: Princeton University Press, 1959–1960), available in a shorter edition designed for the general reader, *A Short History of Chinese Philosophy*, ed. Derk Bodde (New York: Macmillan, 1948). Arthur F. Wright discusses Confucian philosophy generally in *The Confucian Persuasion* (Palo Alto, CA: Stanford University Press, 1960), while Arthur F. Waley, *Confucianism and Chinese*

Civilization (Stanford: Stanford University Press, 1975), presents Confucianism within its wider cultural context. For the reader interested in pursuing Confucian philosophy further, David L. Hall, *Thinking through Confucius* (Albany: State University of New York Press, 1987), and William McNaughton, *The Confucian Vision* (Ann Arbor: University of Michigan Press, 1974), provide useful introductions.

TAO TE CHING
Lao Tzu

Few books are as enigmatic, or as intriguing, as the Chinese classic, *Tao te ching*, sometimes translated as "The Classic of the Way and the Power." Scholars argue about the date of its writing, although they generally are willing to admit that it was composed sometime between 600 and 200 B.C. They dispute whether it is the product of a single mind or simply a collection of adages drawn from various ancient sources. Students of the work have viewed it variously as a metaphysical, mystical, or ethical treatise, a manual of administrative methods, or even a book of hidden meanings that, if properly understood, can give the reader power over the forces of nature and enable him to gain immortality. And yet, even without any general agreement on its nature or purpose, this little book has exerted a compelling influence over the centuries. Chinese scholars have written literally hundreds of commentaries on it, attempting to fathom its mysteries. A body of popular belief and ritual has grown up around it that continues to be practiced as one of the major religions in China today. Its attraction is not confined to the East, however, but extends to Westerners. It is said to be the most translated book, after the Bible, in history.

According to tradition, Lao Tzu was born in the province of Honan and was court archivist in the kingdom of Chou. K'ung Fu-tzu supposedly visited him, an encounter that has become famous in Chinese legend and art. The interview was brief; Lao Tzu suggested that K'ung should attempt to rid himself or arrogant airs and selfish desires, and bade him goodbye. Lao Tzu finally became disgusted with the kings of Chou, and decided to leave for the West. Reaching a pass on the border of the kingdom, he was stopped by the frontier guard, who begged him to write a book of instruction before he departed forever. Lao Tzu sat down by the roadside, wrote the five thousand characters that

From *The Way and the Power*, trans. Arthur Waley (London: Allen & Unwin, 1934), pp. 141, 143, 145–147, 149–152, 154, 159, 166, 180.

comprise the *Tao te ching*, and, handing them over to the guard, disappeared to the west.

It is difficult to discuss Taoist philosophy; the opening line of the *Tao te ching* can be translated as, "The Way that can be talked about is not the real Way." Basically, however, it would appear that the early Taoists regarded rational knowledge or, indeed, any knowledge at all, of physical nature as unattainable. Because all physical aspects of things are purely relative, they are indistinguishable and indescribable: "Water is life for a fish, death for a man." Moreover, the relativity is such that all things exist only in reference to their opposites: "It is only because everyone thinks that beauty exists that they think that ugliness exists." Even existence is a reflection of nonexistence: a house is a house only because of the holes that comprise the doors and windows; a wheel is a wheel only because of the empty space where the axle is fitted; a jug is useful only because it contains an emptiness, and that emptiness is significant only because it can be filled. All things that exist eventually pass into nothingness, and out of this nothingness, new things emerge. Thus all of nature, being and nothingness, is all mixed up together. The Universe is essentially a single whole and is in reality indivisible. This being so, it is humanly incomprehensible. Since knowledge of the universe is unattainable by reason, reason is of no use to anyone. Human knowledge is only an illusion. Wisdom is the realization of realizing this illusion, accepting that one cannot control nature, and learning to become a part of it. By refusing to struggle against the natural course of things, one gains power. By flowing along with nature, rather than swimming against the current, one's ends can be achieved without effort or action.

Though knowledge of the external world cannot be acquired, this is not necessarily true of the inner world of the mind. It must be remembered, however, that inner knowledge cannot be achieved through reason or analysis, and bears no relationship to any external reality. How it is to be gained is therefore impossible to describe in words. A later Taoist poet suggested that one forget everything one ever knew and "work on it." What "it" is, is, unfortunately, also impossible to describe.

Taoism flourished in early China in part because it provided a complement to Confucianism, which was essentially a social and moral philosophy, lacking any transcendent vision of the universe and making little provision for the satisfaction of human emotional needs. Confucianism was directed almost entirely towards the external world and stressed proper action as the means to achieve success. Obviously, however, not everyone in the world can, or even wants to, succeed. Taoism provided an alternative to those who were unable, or who refused to try, to prosper within the existing social and economic system.

As a consequence, Taoism proved attractive to the peasant masses. Seizing on the idea that one could achieve power through harmony with nature, they evolved a popular form of Taoism that mixed superstition, the shamanistic practices of China's northern neighbors, and ancient fertility rituals. Popular Taoism found it easy to borrow some of the practices of Indian Yoga, and to seek herbs that would not only exalt the spirit but gain one immortality. Even some educated Taoists came to believe that self-knowledge could gain one immortality and the power to control natural phenomena. Taoism thus eventually gave rise to the practice of magic, alchemy, and foretelling the future. At the popular level, at least, the teachings of the *Tao te ching* were perverted from what appears to have been their original intent.

And yet, Taoism continued to hold a fascination for the Chinese and, in recent times, for Westerners. The secret of its durability and attraction lies in the *Tao te ching* itself. Its five thousand characters are a mass of dense and ambiguous meanings, and the reader feels compelled to discover its message. Each brings his or her own individual needs and desires to the task, and each finds a message that seems personally right and true. Tao is described as an uncarved block, in which all things are potentially present. The same could be said of the *Tao te ching*; this may account for its enduring appeal.

Questions

1. How does Taoism describe the relativity of the physical universe?
2. What are the various characteristics of the Way?
3. How does the Sage exert power?
4. What is the Taoist view of how to govern?

TAO TE CHING

1

The Way that can be told of is not an Unvarying Way;
The names that can be named are not unvarying names.
It was from the Nameless that Heaven and Earth sprang;
The named is but the mother that rears the ten thousand
      creatures,[1] each after its kind.
Truly, "Only he that rids himself forever of desire can see
      the Secret Essences";

---

[1] The physical world in general, humankind in particular.

He that has never rid himself of desire can see only the
      Outcomes.
These two things issued from the same mould, but
      nevertheless are different in name.
This "same mould" we can but call the Mystery,
Or rather the "Darker than any Mystery,"
The Doorway whence issued all Secret Essences.

2

It is because every one under Heaven recognizes beauty as
      beauty, that the idea of ugliness exists.
And equally if every one recognized virtue as virtue, this
      would merely create fresh conceptions of wickedness.
For truly "Being and Not-being grow out of one another;
Difficult and easy complete one another.
Long and short test one another;
High and low determine one another.
Pitch and mode give harmony to one another.
Front and back give sequence to one another."
Therefore the Sage relies on actionless activity,   *— exertion of power*
Carries on wordless teaching,
But the myriad creatures are worked upon by him; he does
      not disown them.
He rears them, but does not lay claim to them,
Controls them, but does not lean upon them,
Achieves his aim, but does not call attention to what he
      does;
And for the very reason that he does not call attention to
      what he does
He is not ejected from fruition of what he has done.

3

If we stop looking for "persons of superior morality" (*hsien*) to put in power,
there will be no more jealousies among the people. If we cease to set store by
products that are hard to get, there will be no more thieves. If the people never
see such things as excite desire, their hearts will remain placid and undisturbed.
Therefore the Sage rules

    By emptying their hearts
    And filling their bellies,

[handwritten: sage's exertion of power]

Weakening their intelligence
And toughening their sinews
Ever striving to make the people knowledgeless and
    desireless.

Indeed he sees to it that if there be any who have knowledge, they dare not interfere. Yet through his actionless activity all things are duly regulated.

4

The Way is like an empty vessel
That yet may be drawn from
Without ever needing to be filled.
It is bottomless; the very progenitor of all things in the
    world.
[handwritten: dull] In it all sharpness is blunted,
All tangles untied,
All glare tempered,
All dust smoothed.
It is like a deep pool that never dries.
Was it too the child of something else? We cannot tell.
But as a substanceless image it existed before the Ancestor.[2]

5

Heaven and Earth are ruthless;
To them the Ten Thousand Things are but as straw dogs.[3]
The Sage too is ruthless;
To him the people are but as straw dogs.
Yet Heaven and Earth and all that lies between
Is like a bellows
[handwritten: universe] In that it is empty, but gives a supply that never fails.
Work it, and more comes out.
Whereas the force of words is soon spent.
Far better is it to keep what is in the heart.

6

The Valley Spirit never dies.
It is named the Mysterious Female.

[2] The "Ancestor" separated the heavens from the earth and thus created the world as we know it.
[3] Dolls made of straw to be used in celebrations and then disgarded; things without souls or worth.

And the Doorway of the Mysterious Female
Is the base from which Heaven and Earth sprang.
It is there within us all the while;
Draw upon it as you will, it never runs dry.

7

Heaven is eternal, the Earth everlasting.
How come they to be so? It is because they do not foster
        their own lives;
That is why they live so long.
Therefore the Sage
Puts himself in the background; but is always to the fore.
Remains outside; but is always there.
Is it not just because he does not strive for any personal end
That all his personal ends are fulfilled?

8

The highest good is like that of water. The goodness of water is that it benefits
the ten thousand creatures; yet itself does not scramble, but is content with the
places that all men disdain.[4] It is this that makes water so near to the Way.

And if men think the ground the best place for building a
        house upon,
If among thoughts they value those that are profound,
If in friendship they value gentleness,
In words, truth; in government, good order; — *valued in gov't*
In deeds, effectiveness; in actions, timeliness—
In each case it is because they prefer what does not lead to
        strife,
And therefore does not go amiss.

9

Stretch a bow[5] to the very full,
And you will wish you had stopped in time;
Temper a sword-edge to its very sharpest,
And you will find it soon grows dull.

[4] Water naturally seeks the lowest places, while people generally strive for the heights.
[5] A fully stretched bow may snap.

When bronze and jade fill your hall
It can no longer be guarded.
Wealth and place breed insolence
That brings ruin in its train.
When your work is done, then withdraw!
Such is Heaven's Way.

10

Can you keep the unquiet physical-soul from straying, hold
      fast to the Unity, and never quit it?
Can you, when concentrating your breath, make it soft like
      that of a little child?
Can you wipe and cleanse your vision of the Mystery till all
      is without blur?
Can you love the people and rule the land, yet remain
      unknown?
Can you in opening and shutting the heavenly gates play
      always the female part?[6]
Can your mind penetrate every corner of the land, but you
      yourself never interfere?
Rear them, then, feed them,
Rear them, but do not lay claim to them.
Control them, but never lean upon them;
Be chief among them, but do not manage them.
This is called the Mysterious Power. *of a sage?*

11

We put thirty spokes together and call it a wheel;
But it is on the space where there is nothing that the
      usefulness of the wheel depends.[7]
We turn clay to make a vessel;
But it is on the space where there is nothing that the
      usefulness of the vessel depends.
We pierce doors and windows to make a house;
And it is on these spaces where there is nothing that the
      usefulness of the house depends.

[6]Passivity.
[7]The hub, where the axle is placed.

Therefore just as we take advantage of what is, we should
recognize the usefulness of what is not.

14

Because the eye gazes but can catch no glimpse of it,
It is called elusive.
Because the ear listens but cannot hear it,
It is called the rarefied.
Because the hand feels for it but cannot find it,
It is called the infinitesimal.
These three, because they cannot be further scrutinized,
Blend into one.
Its rising brings no light;
Its sinking, no darkness.
Endless the series of things without name
On the way back to where there is nothing.
They are called shapeless shapes;
Forms without form;
Are called vague semblances.
Go towards them, and you can see no front;
Go after them, and you see no rear.
Yet by seizing on the Way that was
You can ride[8] the things that are now.
For to know what once there was, in the Beginning,
This is called the essence of the Way.

The Way =

19

Banish wisdom, discard knowledge,
And the people will be benefited a hundredfold.
Banish human kindness, discard morality,
And the people will be dutiful and compassionate.
Banish skill, discard profit,
And thieves and robbers will disappear.
If when these three things are done they find life too plain
and unadorned,
Then let them have accessories;

[8]Control, dominate.

Give them Simplicity to look at, the Uncarved Block
    to hold,
Give them selflessness and fewness of desires.

30

He who by Tao purposes to help a ruler of men
Will oppose all conquest by force of arms;
For such things are wont to rebound.
Where armies are, thorns and brambles grow.
The raising of a great host
Is followed by a year of dearth.
Therefore a good general effects his purpose and then stops;
    he does not take further advantage of his victory.
Fulfils his purpose and does not glory in what he has done;
Fulfils his purpose and does not boast of what he has done;
Fulfils his purpose, but takes no pride in what he has done;
Fulfils his purpose, but only as a step that could not be
    avoided.
Fulfils his purpose, but without violence;
For what has a time of vigour also has a time of decay.
This is against Tao,[9]
And what is against Tao will soon perish.

FURTHER READINGS

Numerous introductions to the history of Taoist philosophy and religion are available, but three of the best are Holmes Welch, *Taoism: The Parting of the Way* (Boston: Beacon Press, 1957); Max Kaltenmark, *Lao Tzu and Taoism*, trans. Roger Greaves (Stanford: Stanford University Press, 1969); and Liu Da, *The Tao and Chinese Civilization* (New York: Schocken Books, 1979). As has been noted, there are a large number of English translations of the *Tao te ching* (sometimes entitled *Lao Tzu*). That of one of the leaders of the rise of Victorian interest in Taoism has been reprinted as James Legge, *The Tao te ching: The Writings of Chuang-tzu; the Thai-Shan Tractate of Actions and Their Retributions* (Taipei: World Book, 1963). Arthur Waley, *The Way and the Power* (London: Allen & Unwin, 1934), did much to encourage modern interest. Dim C. Lau, *Tao te ching* (Baltimore: Penguin, 1963), is perhaps the most easily available, while Gia-fu Feng and Jane English, *Tao te ching* (New York: Vintage Books, 1972), is one of the more luxurious. Art photographs and calligraphic presentations of

[9]Violence is against the Way, as is all action, negative or positive.

each section appear on facing pages. Wang Pi, *Commentary on the "Lao Tzu,"* trans. Ariane Rump (Honolulu: University Press of Hawaii, 1979), presents the text of the *Tao te ching*, together with the commentary of Wang Pi (A.D. 226–249), author of the oldest surviving commentary on Lao Tzu, of which several hundred have been written. This is not a book for a beginner, nor is Paul J. Lin, *A Translation of Lao Tzu's "Tao te ching" and Wang Pi's "Commentary"* (Ann Arbor: Center for Chinese Studies, University of Michigan, 1977). Lin provides a scholarly translation of the *Tao te ching*, with Wang Pi's commentary as footnotes, together with Ssu-ma Ch'ien's biography of Lao Tzu and Ho Shao's biography of Wang Pi. Ch'en Ku-ying, *Lao Tzu: Text Notes, and Comments,* trans. and adapted by Rhett Y. W. Young and Roger T. Ames (San Francisco: Chinese Materials Center, 1977), is probably the fullest available presentation of the *Tao te ching*, being a translation of the Chinese edition of 1970. It offers an extensive introduction, an excellent English translation, the full Chinese text, and notes taken from the major commentators on the *Tao te ching*. An appendix lists and discusses these major commentators. An early Taoist classic is provided in Huai nan-tzu, *The Huai nan-tzu, Book Eleven: Behavior, Culture, and the Cosmos,* trans. Benjamin E. Wallacker (New Haven, CT: American Oriental Society, 1962). Chuang Tzu, a major contributor to Taoist scripture, who probably wrote in the early third century B.C., is the subject of Michael R. Saso, *The Teachings of Taoist Master Chuang* (New Haven, CT: Yale University Press, 1978), and Wu Kuang-ming, *Chuang tzu: World Philosopher at Play* (New York: Crossroad, 1982). The literature of Taoism is very large, and this list of important works could be extended considerably. The bewildered reader is advised to turn to Benjamin Hoff, *The Tao of Pooh* (New York: Dutton, 1982), for a welcome diversion.

THE ART OF WAR

Sun Tzu

Warfare in China during the height of the Chou dynasty (c. 1000–771 B.C.) was typical of a Bronze Age society. The crucial element in battle was an armored, chariot-driving nobility, and combat was governed by a strict, almost chivalrous, code of conduct. As the emperors lost political power, a number of independent states emerged, each with its own prince, and each contending with the other. Nevertheless, the princes endeavored to lessen the effects of

From Sun Tzu, *The Art of War*, trans. Samuel B. Griffith (New York: Oxford University Press, 1963), pp. 57–59, 63–71, 77–84.

increasing warfare by preserving at least a modicum of political order. These attempts were doomed, however. Confucius, living near the end of this period, attempted and failed to persuade various of the princes to adopt his rules of good conduct and end the process of steady disintegration. In 453 B.C., a quarter century after Confucius's death, the state of Chin was dismembered in a brutal fashion, and the "era of the warring states" (453–221 B.C.) had begun.

This era was characterized by almost incessant warfare as the larger states steadily absorbed the smaller. Concepts of moderation, honor, and humanity were subordinated to the desire for military success. Although China made substantial economic, demographic, and even organizational advances during the period, these changes were in spite of, and not because of, the dominant social and political structure of the country. It was during this period that The Art of War (Sun Tzu) was written.

The great Chinese biographer Ssu-ma Ch'ien ascribed the work to Sun Wu, and suggested that the work was completed in about 500 B.C., which would have placed it in the "classical period" of Chinese literature. Tradition has accepted Ssu-ma's biographical material, and this selection begins with a biographical sketch based on these traditions. The material is fictive, however; little is really known about the author of The Art of War, and he is still generally known as Sun Tzu. The era of the warring states was a period that saw professional counsellors, advisors in military and political affairs, attain great influence. It is likely that the author of The Art of War was such a man. In this strife-filled era, these advisors depended on the success of their counsel not only to secure their political positions but to safeguard their very lives. An unsuccessful advisor was as often killed as dismissed, and such men were not likely to theorize overmuch. The Art of War is empirical and eminently practical.

The entire work consists of thirteen chapters, of which the first and third, dealing with "Estimates" and "Offensive Strategy," are included in this selection. These are sufficient to gain the flavor of the whole. Considerations such as loyalty and bravery, which were important in an earlier period, are largely ignored; warfare has become a science.

Questions

1. Are the principles of The Art of War still valid, or have mechanized warfare and the rise of airpower rendered them out of date?

2. How applicable are the principles of The Art of War to forms of competition other than warfare?

3. How do the comments added by later scholars help to clarify the principles of The Art of War?

4. In "Offensive Strategy," The Art of War appears to recommend a humane approach to war. Why?

THE ART OF WAR

BIOGRAPHY OF SUN TZU

Sun Tzu was a native of Ch'i who by means of his book on the art of war secured an audience with Ho-lü, King of Wu.

Ho-lü said, "I have read your thirteen chapters, Sir, in their entirety. Can you conduct a minor experiment in control of the movement of troops?"

Sun Tzu replied, "I can."

Ho-lü asked, "Can you conduct this test using women?"

Sun Tzu said, "Yes."

The King thereupon agreed and sent from the palace one hundred and eighty beautiful women.

Sun Tzu divided them into two companies and put the King's two favourite concubines in command. He instructed them all how to hold halberds. He then said, "Do you know where the heart is, and where the right and left hands and the back are?"

The women said, "We know."

Sun Tzu said, "When I give the order 'Front,' face in the direction of the heart; when I say 'Left,' face toward the left hand; when I say 'Right' toward the right; when I say 'Rear,' face in the direction of your backs."

The women said, "We understand."

When these regulations had been announced the executioner's weapons were arranged.

Sun Tzu then gave the orders three times and explained them five times, after which he beat on the drum the signal "Face Right." The women all roared with laughter.

Sun Tzu said, "If regulations are not clear and orders not thoroughly explained, it is the commander's fault." He then repeated the orders three times and explained them five times, and gave the drum signal to face to the left. The woman again burst into laughter.

Sun Tzu said, "If instructions are not clear and commands not explicit, it is the commander's fault. But when they have been made clear, and are not carried out in accordance with military law, it is a crime on the part of the officers." Then he ordered that the commanders of the right and left ranks be beheaded.

The King of Wu, who was reviewing the proceedings from his terrace, saw that his two beloved concubines were about to be executed. He was terrified, and hurriedly sent an aide with this message: "I already know that the General is able to employ troops. Without these two concubines my food will not taste sweet. It is my desire that they be not executed."

Sun Tzu replied: "Your servant has already received your appointment as Commander and when the commander is at the head of the army he need not accept all the sovereign's orders."

Consequently he ordered that the two women who had commanded the ranks be executed as an example. He then used the next seniors as company commanders.

Thereupon he repeated the signals on the drum, and the women faced left, right, to the front, to the rear, knelt and rose all in strict accordance with the prescribed drill. They did not dare to make the slightest noise.

Sun Tzu then sent a messenger to the King and informed him: "The troops are now in good order. The King may descend to review and inspect them. They may be employed as the King desires, even to the extent of going through fire and water."

The King of Wu said, "The General may go to his hostel and rest. I do not wish to come to inspect them."

Sun Tzu said, "The King likes only empty words. He is not capable of putting them into practice."

Ho-lü then realized Sun Tzu's capacity as a commander, and eventually made him a general. Sun Tzu defeated the strong State of Ch'u to the west and entered Ying; to the north he intimidated Ch'i and Chin. That the name of Wu was illustrious among the feudal lords was partly due to his achievements. (The Yüeh *Chüeh Shu* says: "Outside the Wu Gate of Wu Hsieh, at a distance of ten *li*,[1] there was a large tomb which is that of Sun Tzu.")

ESTIMATES

SUN TZU SAID:

1. War is a matter of vital importance to the State; the province of life or death; the road to survival or ruin. It is mandatory that it be thoroughly studied.

   Li Ch'üan[2]: "Weapons are tools of ill omen." War is a grave matter; one is apprehensive lest men embark upon it without due reflection.

2. Therefore, appraise it in terms of the five fundamental factors and make comparisons of the seven elements later named. So you may assess its essentials.

---

[1] A *li* is about one-third of a mile.
[2] Li Ch'üan, Chang Yü, and the others whose names appear in italics here are later commentators on *The Art of War* whose explanations and examples have come to be included within the text of the work.

3. The first of these factors is moral influence; the second, weather; the third, terrain; the fourth, command; and the fifth, doctrine.

   Chang Yü: The systematic order above is perfectly clear. When troops are raised to chastise transgressors, the temple council first considers the adequacy of the rulers' benevolence and the confidence of their peoples; next, the appropriateness of nature's seasons, and finally the difficulties of the topography. After thorough deliberation of these three matters a general is appointed to launch the attack. After troops have crossed the borders, responsibility for laws and orders devolves upon the general.

4. By moral influence I mean that which causes the people to be in harmony with their leaders, so that they will accompany them in life and unto death without fear of mortal peril.

   Chang Yü: When one treats people with benevolence, justice, and righteousness, and reposes confidence in them, the army will be united in mind and all will be happy to serve their leaders. The Book of Changes says: "In happiness at overcoming difficulties, people forget the danger of death."

5. By weather I mean the interaction of natural forces; the effects of winter's cold and summer's heat and the conduct of military operations in accordance with the seasons.

6. By terrain I mean distances, whether the ground is traversed with ease or difficulty, whether it is open or constricted, and the chances of life or death.

   Mei Yao-ch'en: . . . When employing troops it is essential to know beforehand the conditions of the terrain. Knowing the distances, one can make use of an indirect or a direct plan. If he knows the degree of ease or difficulty of traversing the ground he can estimate the advantages of using infantry or cavalry. If he knows where the ground is constricted and where open he can calculate the size of force appropriate. If he knows where he will give battle he knows when to concentrate or divide his forces.

7. By command, I mean the general's qualities of wisdom, sincerity, humanity, courage, and strictness.

   Li Ch'üan: These five are the virtues of the general. Hence the army refers to him as "The Respected One."
   Tu Mu: . . . If wise, a commander is able to recognize changing circumstances and to act expediently. If sincere, his men will have no doubt of the

certainty of rewards and punishments. If humane, he loves mankind, sympathizes with others, and appreciates their industry and toil. If courageous, he gains victory by seizing opportunity without hesitation. If strict, his troops are disciplined because they are in awe of him and are afraid of punishment.

Shen Pao-hsu . . . said: "If a general is not courageous he will be unable to conquer doubts or to create great plans."

8. By doctrine I mean organization, control, assignment of appropriate ranks to officers, regulation of supply routes, and the provision of principal items used by the army.

9. There is no general who has not heard of these five matters. Those who master them win; those who do not are defeated.

10. Therefore in laying plans compare the following elements, appraising them with the utmost care.

11. If you say which ruler possesses moral influence, which commander is the more able, which army obtains the advantages of nature and the terrain, in which regulations and instructions are better carried out, which troops are the stronger;

Chang Yü: Chariots strong, horses fast, troops valiant, weapons sharp—so that when they hear the drums beat the attack they are happy, and when they hear the gongs sound the retirement they are enraged. He who is like this is strong.

12. Which has the better trained officers and men;

Tu Yu: . . . Therefore Master Wang said: "If officers are unaccustomed to rigorous drilling they will be worried and hesitant in battle; if generals are not thoroughly trained they will inwardly quail when they face the enemy."

13. And which administers rewards and punishments in a more enlightened manner;

Tu Mu: Neither should be excessive.

14. I will be able to forecast which side will be victorious and which defeated.

15. If a general who heeds my strategy is employed he is certain to win. Retain him! When one who refuses to listen to my strategy is employed, he is certain to be defeated. Dismiss him!

16. Having paid heed to the advantages of my plans, the general must create situations which will contribute to their accomplishment. By "situations" I

mean that he should act expediently in accordance with what is advantageous and so control the balance.

17. All warfare is based on deception.

18. Therefore, when capable, feign incapacity; when active, inactivity.

19. When near, make it appear that you are far away; when far away, that you are near.

20. Offer the enemy a bait to lure him; feign disorder and strike him.

   Tu Mu: The Chao general Li Mu released herds of cattle with their shepherds; when the Hsiung Nu had advanced a short distance he feigned a retirement, leaving behind several thousand men as if abandoning them. When the Khan heard this news he was delighted, and at the head of a strong force marched to the place. Li Mu put most of his troops into formations on the right and left wings, made a horning attack, crushed the Huns and slaughtered over one hundred thousand of their horsemen.

21. When he concentrates, prepare against him; where he is strong, avoid him.

22. Anger his general and confuse him.

   Li Ch'üan: If the general is choleric his authority can easily be upset. His character is not firm.
   Chang Yü: If the enemy general is obstinate and prone to anger, insult and enrage him, so that he will be irritated and confused, and without a plan will recklessly advance against you.

23. Pretend inferiority and encourage his arrogance.

   Tu Mu: Toward the end of the Ch'in dynasty, Mo Tun of the Hsiung Nu first established his power. The Eastern Hu were strong and sent ambassadors to parley. They said: "We wish to obtain T'ou Ma's thousand-*li* horse."[3] Mo Tun consulted his advisers, who all exclaimed: "The thousand-*li* horse! The most precious thing in this country! Do not give them that!" Mo Tun replied: "Why begrudge a horse to a neighbour?" So he sent the horse.
      Shortly after, the Eastern Hu sent envoys who said: "We wish one of the Khan's princesses." Mo Tun asked advice of his ministers who all angrily said: "The Eastern Hu are unrighteous! Now they even ask for a princess! We implore you to attack them!" Mo Tun said: "How can one begrudge his neighbour a young woman?" So he gave the woman.
      A short time later, the Eastern Hu returned and said: "You have a thousand *li* of unused land which we want." Mo Tun consulted his advisers.

[3] A horse able to travel a thousand *li* (over three hundred miles) without stopping to eat or drink.

Some said it would be reasonable to cede the land, others that it would not. Mo Tun was enraged and said: "Land is the foundation of the State. How could one give it away?" All those who had advised doing so were beheaded.

Mo Tun then sprang on his horse, ordered that all who remained behind were to be beheaded, and made a surprise attack on the Eastern Hu. The Eastern Hu were contemptuous of him and had made no preparations. When he attacked he annihilated them. Mo Tun then turned westward and attacked the Yueh Ti. To the south he annexed Lou Fan . . . and invaded Yen. He completely recovered the ancestral lands of the Hsiung Nu previously conquered by the Ch'in general Meng T'ien.

Ch'en Hao: Give the enemy young boys and women to infatuate him, and jades and silks to excite his ambitions.

24. Keep him under a strain and wear him down.

Li Ch'üan: When the enemy is at ease, tire him.

Tu Mu: . . . Toward the end of the Later Han, after Ts'ao Ts'ao had defeated Liu Pei, Pei fled to Yuan Shao, who then led out his troops intending to engage Ts'ao Ts'ao. T'ien Fang, one of Yuan Shao's staff officers, said: "Ts'ao Ts'ao is expert at employing troops; one cannot go against him heedlessly. Nothing is better than to protract things and keep him at a distance. You, General, should fortify along the mountains and rivers and hold the four prefectures. Externally, make alliances with powerful leaders; internally, [establish colonies of soldier-farmers along your borders.] Later, select crack troops and form them into extraordinary units. Taking advantage of spots where he is unprepared, make repeated sorties and disturb the country south of the river. When he comes to aid the right, attack his left; when he goes to succour the left, attack the right; exhaust him by causing him continually to run about. . . . Now if you reject this victorious strategy and decide instead to risk all on one battle, it will be too late for regrets." Yuan Shao did not follow this advice and therefore was defeated.

25. When he is united, divide him.

Chang Yü: Sometimes drive a wedge between a sovereign and his ministers; on other occasions separate his allies from him. Make them mutually suspicious so that they drift apart. Then you can plot against them.

26. Attack where he is unprepared; sally out when he does not expect you.

Ho Yen-hsi: . . . Li Ching of the T'ang proposed ten plans to be used against Hsiao Hsieh, and the entire responsibility of commanding the armies was entrusted to him. In the eighth month he collected his forces at K'uei Chou.

As it was the season of the autumn floods the waters of the Yangtze were overflowing and the roads by the three gorges were perilous, Hsiao Hsieh thought it certain that Li Ching would not advance against him. Consequently he made no preparations.

In the ninth month Li Ching took command of the troops and addressed them as follows: "What is of the greatest importance in war is extraordinary speed; one cannot afford to neglect opportunity. Now we are concentrated and Hsiao Hsieh does not yet know of it. Taking advantage of the fact that the river is in flood, we will appear unexpectedly under the walls of his capital. As is said: 'When the thunder-clap comes, there is no time to cover the ears.' Even if he should discover us, he cannot on the spur of the moment devise a plan to counter us, and surely we can capture him."

He advanced to I Ling and Hsiao Hsieh began to be afraid and summoned reinforcements from south of the river, but these were unable to arrive in time. Li Ching laid siege to the city and Hsieh surrendered.

"To sally forth where he does not expect you" means as when, toward its close, the Wei dynasty sent Generals Chung Hui and Teng Ai to attack Shu. . . . In winter, in the tenth month, Ai left Yin P'ing and marched through uninhabited country for over seven hundred *li*, chiselling roads through the mountains and building suspension bridges. The mountains were high, the valleys deep, and this task was extremely difficult and dangerous. Also, the army, about to run out of provisions, was on the verge of perishing. Teng Ai wrapped himself in felt carpets and rolled down the steep mountain slopes; generals and officers clambered up by grasping limbs of trees. Scaling the precipices like strings of fish, the army advanced.

Teng Ai appeared first at Chiang Yu in Shu, and Ma Mou, the general charged with its defence, surrendered. Teng Ai beheaded Chu-ko Chan, who resisted at Mein-chu, and marched on Ch'eng Tu. The King of Shu, Liu Shan, surrendered.

27. These are the strategist's keys to victory. It is not possible to discuss them beforehand.

   Mei Yao-ch'en: When confronted by the enemy respond to changing circumstances and devise expedients. How can these be discussed beforehand?

28. Now if the estimates made in the temple before hostilities indicate victory it is because calculations show one's strength to be superior to that of his enemy; if they indicate defeat, it is because calculations show that one is inferior. With many calculations, one can win; with few one cannot. How much less chance of victory has one who makes none at all! By this means I examine the situation and the outcome will be clearly apparent.

OFFENSIVE STRATEGY

SUN TZU SAID:

1. Generally in war the best policy is to take a state intact; to ruin it is inferior to this.

   Li Ch'üan: Do not put a premium on killing.

2. To capture the enemy's army is better than to destroy it; to take intact a battalion, a company or a five-man squad is better than to destroy them.

3. For to win one hundred victories in one hundred battles is not the acme of skill. To subdue the enemy without fighting is the acme of skill.

4. Thus, what is of supreme importance in war is to attack the enemy's strategy;

   Tu Mu: . . . The Grand Duke said: "He who excels at resolving difficulties does so before they arise. He who excels in conquering his enemies triumphs before threats materialize."
   Li Ch'üan: Attack plans at their inception. In the Later Han, K'ou Hsün surrounded Kao Chun. Chun sent his Planning Officer, Huang-fu Wen, to parley. Huang-fu Wen was stubborn and rude and K'ou Hsün beheaded him, and informed Kao Chun: "Your staff officer was without propriety. I have beheaded him. If you wish to submit, do so immediately. Otherwise defend yourself." On the same day, Chun threw open his fortifications and surrendered.
       All K'ou Hsün's generals said: "May we ask, you killed his envoy, but yet forced him to surrender his city. How is this?"
       K'ou Hsün said: "Huang-fu Wen was Kao Chun's heart and guts, his intimate counsellor. If I had spared Huang-fu Wen's life, he would have accomplished his schemes, but when I killed him, Kao Chun lost his guts. It is said: 'The supreme excellence in war is to attack the enemy's plans'."
       All the generals said: "This is beyond our comprehension."

5. Next best is to disrupt his alliances:

   Tu Yu: Do not allow your enemies to get together.
   Wang Hsi: . . . Look into the matter of his alliances and cause them to be severed and dissolved. If an enemy has alliances, the problem is grave and the enemy's position strong; if he has no alliances the problem is minor and the enemy's position weak.

6. The next best is to attack his army.

   Chia Lin: . . . The Grand Duke said: "He who struggles for victory with naked blades is not a good general."
   Wang Hsi: Battles are dangerous affairs.
   Chang Yü: If you cannot nip his plans in the bud, or disrupt his alliances when they are about to be consummated, sharpen your weapons to gain the victory.

7. The worst policy is to attack cities. Attack cities only when there is no alternative.

8. To prepare the shielded wagons and make ready the necessary arms and equipment requires at least three months; to pile up earthen ramps against the walls an additional three months will be needed.

9. If the general is unable to control his impatience and orders his troops to swarm up the wall like ants, one-third of them will be killed without taking the city. Such is the calamity of these attacks.

   Tu Mu: . . . In the later Wei, the Emperor T'ai Wu led one hundred thousand troops to attack the Sung general Tsang Chih at Yu T'ai. The Emperor first asked Tsang Chih for some wine.[4] Tsang Chih sealed up a pot full of urine and sent it to him. T'ai Wu was transported with rage and immediately attacked the city, ordering his troops to scale the walls and engage in close combat. Corpses piled up to the top of the walls and after thirty days of this the dead exceeded half his force.

10. Thus, those skilled in war subdue the enemy's army without battle. They capture his cities without assaulting them and overthrow his state without protracted operations.

    Li Ch'üan: They conquer by strategy. In the Later Han the Marquis of Tsan, Tsang Kung, surrounded the "Yao" rebels at Yüan Wu, but during a succession of months was unable to take the city. His officers and men were ill and covered with ulcers. The King of Tung Hai spoke to Tsang Kung, saying: "Now you have massed troops and encircled the enemy, who is determined to fight to the death. This is no strategy! You should lift the siege. Let them know that an escape route is open and they will flee and disperse. Then any village constable will be able to capture them!" Tsang Kung followed this advice and took Yüan Wu.

---

[4]Exchange of gifts and compliments was a normal preliminary to battle.

11. Your aim must be to take All-under-Heaven intact. Thus your troops are not worn out and your gains will be complete. This is the art of offensive strategy.

12. Consequently, the art of using troops is this: When ten to the enemy's one, surround him;

13. When five times his strength, attack him;

    Chang Yü: If my force is five times that of the enemy I alarm him to the front, surprise him to the rear, create an uproar in the east and strike in the west.

14. If double his strength, divide him.

    Tu Yu: . . . If a two-to-one superiority is insufficient to manipulate the situation, we use a distracting force to divide his army. Therefore the Grand Duke said: "If one is unable to influence the enemy to divide his forces, he cannot discuss unusual tactics."

15. If equally matched you may engage him.

    Ho Yen-hsi: . . . In these circumstances only the able general can win.

16. If weaker numerically, be capable of withdrawing;

    Tu Mu: If your troops do not equal his, temporarily avoid his initial onrush. Probably later you can take advantage of a soft spot. Then rouse yourself and seek victory with determined spirit.
    Chang Yü: If the enemy is strong and I am weak, I temporarily withdraw and do not engage. This is the case when the abilities and courage of the generals and the efficiency of troops are equal.
    If I am in good order and the enemy in disarray, if I am energetic and he careless, then, even if he be numerically stronger, I can give battle.

17. And if in all respects unequal, be capable of eluding him, for a small force is but booty for one more powerful.

    Chang Yü: . . . Mencius said: "The small certainly cannot equal the large, nor can the weak match the strong, nor the few the many."

18. Now the general is the protector of the state. If this protection is all-embracing, the state will surely be strong; if defective, the state will certainly be weak.

    Chang Yü: . . . The Grand Duke said: "A sovereign who obtains the right person prospers. One who fails to do so will be ruined."

19. Now there are three ways in which a ruler can bring misfortune upon his army:

20. When ignorant that the army should not advance, to order an advance or ignorant that it should not retire, to order a retirement. This is described as "hobbling the army."

    Chia Lin: The advance and retirement of the army can be controlled by the general in accordance with prevailing circumstances. No evil is greater than commands of the sovereign from the court.

21. When ignorant of military affairs, to participate in their administration. This causes the officers to be perplexed.

    Ts'ao Ts'ao: . . . An army cannot be run according to rules of etiquette.
    Tu Mu: As far as propriety, laws, and decrees are concerned, the army has its own code, which it ordinarily follows. If these are made identical with those used in governing a state the officers will be bewildered.
    Chang Yü: Benevolence and righteousness may be used to govern a state but cannot be used to administer an army. Expediency and flexibility are used in administering an army, but cannot be used in governing a state.

22. When ignorant of command problems to share in the exercise of responsibilities. This engenders doubts in the minds of the officers.

    Wang Hsi: . . . If one ignorant of military matters is sent to participate in the administration of the army, then in every movement there will be disagreement and mutual frustration and the entire army will be hamstrung. That is why Pei Tu memorialized the throne to withdraw the Army Supervisor; only then was he able to pacify Ts'ao Chou.
    Chang Yü: In recent times court officials have been used as Supervisors of the Army and this is precisely what is wrong.

23. If the army is confused and suspicious, neighbouring rulers will cause trouble. This is what is meant by the saying: "A confused army leads to another's victory."

    Meng: . . . The Grand Duke said: "One who is confused in purpose cannot respond to his enemy."
    Li Ch'üan: . . . The wrong person cannot be appointed to command. . . .
    Lin Hsiang-ju, the Prime Minister of Chao, said: "Chao Kua is merely able to read his father's books, and is as yet ignorant of correlating changing circumstances. Now Your Majesty, on account of his name, makes him the commander-in-chief. This is like glueing the pegs of a lute and then trying to tune it."

24. Now there are five circumstances in which victory may be predicted:

25. He who knows when he can fight and when he cannot will be victorious.

26. He who understands how to use both large and small forces will be victorious.

    Tu Yu: There are circumstances in war when many cannot attack few, and others when the weak can master the strong. One able to manipulate such circumstances will be victorious.

27. He whose ranks are united in purpose will be victorious.

    Tu Yu: Therefore Mencius said: "The appropriate season is not as important as the advantages of the ground; these are not as important as harmonious human relations."

28. He who is prudent and lies in wait for an enemy who is not, will be victorious.

    Ch'en Hao: Create an invincible army and await the enemy's moment of vulnerability.
    Ho Yen-hsi: . . . A gentleman said: "To rely on rustics and not prepare is the greatest of crimes; to be prepared beforehand for any contingency is the greatest of virtues."

29. He whose generals are able and not interfered with by the sovereign will be victorious.

    Tu Yu: . . . Therefore Master Wang said: "To make appointments is the province of the sovereign; to decide on battle, that of the general."
    Wang Hsi: . . . A sovereign of high character and intelligence must be able to know the right man, should place the responsibility on him, and expect results.
    Ho Yen-hsi: . . . Now in war there may be one hundred changes in each step. When one sees he can, he advances; when he sees that things are difficult, he retires. To say that a general must await commands of the sovereign in such circumstances is like informing a superior that you wish to put out a fire. Before the order to do so arrives the ashes are cold. And it is said one must consult the Army Supervisor in these matters! This is as if in building a house beside the road one took advice from those who pass by. Of course the work would never be completed!
    To put a rein on an able general while at the same time asking him to suppress a cunning enemy is like tying up the Black Hound of Han and then ordering him to catch elusive hares. What is the difference?

30. It is in these five matters that the way to victory is known.

31. Therefore I say: "<u>Know the enemy and know yourself</u>; in a hundred battles you will never be in peril.

32. When you are ignorant of the enemy but know yourself, your chances of winning or losing are equal.

33. If ignorant both of your enemy and of yourself, you are certain in every battle to be in peril."

Li Ch'üan: Such people are called "mad bandits." What can they expect if not defeat?

FURTHER READINGS

Edward H. Schafer, *Ancient China* (New York: Time, 1967), provides a finely illustrated general overview of early Chinese history. An informative analysis of the character of early Chinese military forces is provided in Herrlee Creel, *The Origins of Statecraft in China* (Chicago: University of Chicago Press, 1970). Hans Bielenstein, *The Bureaucracy of Han Times* (New York: Cambridge University Press, 1980), offers a brief look at military organization during the Han period. Cho-yun Hsu, *Ancient China in Transition: An Analysis of Social Mobility, 722–222 B.C.* (Stanford: Stanford University Press, 1965), examines the effect of warfare on the social structure of ancient China. Original materials from ancient China that convey a more human perspective on warfare than *The Art of War* are the warriors and battles sections from Arthur Waley, trans., *The Book of Songs* (New York: Grove Press, 1960). Readers particularly interested in military theory may care to compare *The Art of War* with European theorists such as Saxe, Clausewitz, and Moltke.

ARTHASASTRA
Kautilya

Throughout most of its history, India has been composed of numerous weak, fragmented, and decentralized states that displayed little stability or permanence. Although some states persisted for generations as the territorial base of power of a single family, more commonly boundaries and ruling families were constantly changing. Petty courts throughout India replicated those of the richer and more powerful states, but on a smaller scale. Their rulers patronized

From *The Kautilya Arthasastra, Part II, An English Translation with Critical and Explanatory Notes*, R. P. Kangle, 2nd ed. (Bombay: University of Bombay, 1972), pp. 45–48, 314, 315, 317–324.

the Brahmans, or priestly caste, employing them to perform state rituals and allowing them great authority as administrators and advisors. The religious recognition accorded by the Brahmans gave the kings greater legitimacy, but the influence of the Brahmans also limited the ability of the kings to act independently. When they did act, they did so in accordance with the rules set forth in Brahman textbooks on statecraft, of which the *Arthasastra* is the most famous.

There were exceptional periods of unity when great empires arose, such as when Chandragupta Maurya (r. 324–301 B.C.) united all but the southernmost tip of India and established the Mauryan Empire. This empire did not last, however, and fragmented a generation after the death of Asoka in 232 B.C. The later Gupta Empire (c. A.D. 320–500) achieved cultural grandeur, but its political power was essentially restricted to North India. The emperor Harsha (A.D. 606–648) never succeeded in reuniting that limited territory.

In the *Arthasastra*, Kautilya describes a political system in which there are many small states, each either the ally or the enemy of the others. Warfare was endemic, but had curiously little effect on the basic cultural and economic life of the region. The goal of battle was "righteous victory" (*dharmavijaya*), in which the conqueror released his enemy unharmed, without looting or destroying his capital, and the conquered admitted his subservience, at least for a time. This propriety was far removed from the goal of warfare in other civilizations, where the destruction of the enemy was usually the aim of battle. In India, however, the mutability of fortune appeared to be widely accepted among rulers—in another generation, for all one knew, the conquered lineage might reestablish its power and come to collect tribute from the formerly dominant state, which might have grown weak in the interim. This being the case, ruthless behavior was in no one's interest.

Over the years, these many weak kingdoms prevented one strong kingdom from arising. Although each of the petty kings surrounded himself with an aura of divinity, this emphasis on appearances brought no real stability to the system. Political alignments were in a constant state of flux, boundaries changed constantly, and kings fell, only to be replaced by others. Ruling dynasties disappear from historical records, only to reappear centuries later. This fluid and fragmented political system nevertheless coexisted within a stable and confident civilization, tolerant of cultural diversity but resistant to change.

The warfare of the kings had little lasting effect at the local level, where society was regulated by caste and custom, and ruled by prominent families of the district, who were often Brahmans. Indian life was concentrated in its thousands of agricultural villages, where the pace of life was dictated by the seasons and it seemed as if very little ever changed. The peasant would still pay taxes, often to the same tax collector, regardless of which king ended up with the money. Without the homogenizing effect of a strong central ruler, local customs persisted and village life remained relatively unaltered by time. This stability at the local level promoted extraordinary conservatism, particularly among the peasant masses. Indian civilization maintained a continuity throughout this era, but it was the continuity of a religious and cultural tradition based on popular participation, rather than of political institutions imposed from above.

The *Arthasastra*, like many other classical Indian texts, reached its final written form in the era between the Mauryan and Gupta empires. This was a period of great intellectual creativity, when the many small courts encouraged scholarship and art as important obligations. The *Arthasastra*, like numerous texts of the time, has as one of its main concerns the deference due the Brahmans, who were, after all, often the authors of the works in question.

Questions

1. What is the role of Brahmans in the political system?
2. How does a ruler determine whether another ruler is a friend or a foe?
3. What are the conditions necessary for peace?

ARTHASASTRA

SECTION 16   RULES FOR THE KING

1   When the king is active, the servants become active following his example. 2   If he is remiss, they too become remiss along with him. 3   And they consume his works. 4   Moreover, he is over-reached by enemies. 5   Therefore, he should himself be (energetically) active.

6   He should divide the day into eight parts as also the night by means of *nalikas*, or by the measure of the shadow (of the gnomon).

7   (A shadow) measuring three *paurusas*, one *paurusa*, (and) four *angulas*, and the midday when the shadow disappears, these are the four earlier eighth parts of the day. 8   By them are explained the later (four). 9   Out of them, during the first eighth part of the day, he should listen to measures taken for defence and (accounts of) income and expenditure. 10   During the second, he should look into the affairs of the citizens and the country people. 11   During the third, he should take his bath and meals and devote himself to study. 12   During the fourth, he should receive revenue in cash and assign tasks to heads of departments. 13   During the fifth, he should consult the council of ministers by sending letters, and acquaint himself with secret information brought in by spies. 14   During the sixth, he should engage in recreation at his pleasure or hold consultations. 15   During the seventh, he should review elephants, horses, chariots, and troops. 16   During the eighth, he should

deliberate on military plans with the commander-in-chief. 17   When the day is ended, he should worship the evening twilight.

18   During the first (eighth) part of the night, he should interview secret agents. 19   During the second, he should take a bath and meals and engage in study. 20   During the third, he should go to bed to the strains of musical instruments and sleep during the fourth and the fifth (parts). 21   During the sixth, he should awaken to the sound of musical instruments and ponder over the teaching of the science (of politics) as well as over the work to be done. 22   During the seventh, he should sit in consultation (with councillors) and despatch secret agents. 23   During the eighth, he should receive blessings from priests, preceptors and chaplain, and see his physician, chief cook and astrologer. 24   And after going round a cow with her calf and a bull, he should proceed to the assembly hall.

25   Or, he should divide the day and night into (different) parts in conformity with his capacity and carry out his tasks.

26   Arriving in the assembly hall, he should allow unrestricted entrance to those wishing to see him in connection with their affairs. 27   For, a king difficult of access is made to do the reverse of what ought to be done and what ought not to be done, by those near him. 28   In consequence of that, he may have to face an insurrection of the subjects or subjugation by the enemy. 29   Therefore, he should look into the affairs of temple deities, hermitages, heretics, Brahmins learned in the Vedas, cattle and holy places, of minors, the aged, the sick, the distressed and the helpless and of women, in (this) order, or, in accordance with the importance of the matter or its urgency.

30   He should hear (at once) every urgent matter, (and) not put it off. An (affair) postponed becomes difficult to settle or even impossible to settle.

31   He should look into the affairs of persons learned in the Vedas and of ascetics after going to the fire sanctuary (and) in the company of his chaplain and preceptor, after getting up from his seat and saluting (those suitors).

32   But he should decide the affairs of ascetics and of persons versed in the practice of magic, (in consultation) with persons learned in the three Vedas, not by himself (alone), for the reason that they might be roused to anger.

33   For the king, the (sacrificial) vow is activity, sacrifice the administration of affairs; the sacrificial fee, however, is impartiality of behaviour, (and) sacrificial initiation for him is the coronation.

34   In the happiness of the subjects lies the happiness of the king and in what is beneficial to the subjects his own benefit. What is dear to himself is not beneficial to the king, but what is dear to the subjects is beneficial (to him).

35   Therefore, being ever active, the king should carry out the management of material well-being. The root of material well-being is activity, of material disaster its reverse.

36 In the absence of activity, there is certain destruction of what is obtained and of what is not yet received. By activity reward is obtained, and one also secures abundance of riches.

SECTION 96 EXCELLENCES OF THE CONSTITUENT ELEMENTS

1 The king, the minister, the country, the fortified city, the treasury, the army and the ally are the constituent elements (of the state).

2 Among them, the excellences of the king are:

3 Born in a high family, endowed with good fortune, intelligence and spirit, given to seeing elders, pious, truthful in speech, not breaking his promise, grateful, liberal, of great energy, not dilatory, with weak neighbouring princes, resolute, not having a mean council (of ministers), desirous of training,—these are the qualities of one easily approachable.

4 Desire to learn, listening, learning, retention, thorough understanding, reflecting, rejecting (false views) and intentness on truth,—these are the qualities of intellect.

5 Bravery, resentment, quickness, and dexterity,—these are the qualities of energy.

6 Eloquent, bold, endowed with memory, intellect, and strength, exalted, easy to manage, trained in arts, free from vices, able to lead the army, able to requite obligations and injury in the prescribed manner, possessed of a sense of shame, able to take suitable action in calamities and in normal conditions, seeing long and far, attaching prominence to undertakings at the proper place and time and with appropriate human endeavour, able to discriminate between peace and fighting, giving and withholding, and (observance of) conditions and (striking at) the enemy's weak points, well-guarded, not laughing in an undignified manner, with a glance which is straight and without a frown, devoid of passion, anger, greed, stiffness, fickleness, troublesomeness, and slanderousness, sweet in speech, speaking with a smile and with dignity, with conduct conforming to the advice of elders,—these are personal excellences.

SECTION 97 CONCERNING PEACE AND ACTIVITY

1 Peace and activity constitute the source of acquisition and security. 2 Activity is that which brings about the accomplishment of works undertaken. 3 Peace is that which brings about security of enjoyment of the fruits of works.

4   The source of peace and activity is the six-fold policy. 5   Decline, stability, and advancement are the consequences of that (policy).

6   (Acts) of human agency are good policy and bad policy; of divine agency good fortune and misfortune. 7   For, it is acts of human and divine agency that make the world go. 8   That caused by an unseen agency is the divine (act). 9   In that, the attainment of the desired fruit is good fortune; of undesired (fruit), misfortune. 10   That caused by a seen agency is the human (act). 11   In that, the coming into being of well-being is good policy; (its) ruin, bad policy. 12   That can be thought about; the divine is incalculable.

13   The king, endowed with personal excellences and those of his material constituents, the seat of good policy, is the would-be conqueror. 14   Encircling him on all sides, with territory immediately next to his is the constituent called the enemy. 15   In the same manner, one with territory separated by one (other territory) is the constituent called the ally.

16   A neighbouring prince possessed of the excellences of an enemy is the foe; one in calamity is vulnerable; one without support or with a weak support is fit to be exterminated; in the reverse case, fit to be harassed or weakened. 17   These are the different types of enemies.

18   Beyond him, the ally, the enemy's ally, the ally's ally, and the enemy's ally's ally are situated in front in accordance with the proximity of the territories; behind, the enemy in the rear, the ally in the rear, the rear enemy's ally and the rear ally's ally (one behind the other).

19   One with immediately proximate territory is the natural enemy; one of equal birth is the enemy by birth; one opposed or in opposition is the enemy made (for the time being).

20   One with territory separated by one other is the natural ally; one related through the mother or father is the ally by birth; one who has sought shelter for wealth or life is the ally made (for the time being).

21   One with territory immediately proximate to those of the enemy and the conqueror, capable of helping them when they are united or disunited and of suppressing them when they are disunited, is the middle king.

22   One outside (the sphere of) the enemy, the conqueror and the middle king, stronger than (their) constituents, capable of helping the enemy, the conqueror and the middle king when they are united or disunited and of suppressing them when they are disunited, is the neutral king.

23   These are the constituents (of the circle of kings).

24   Or, the conqueror, the ally and the ally's ally are the three constituents of this (circle of kings). 25   They, each individually united with its five constituent elements, the minister, the country, the fort, the treasury, and the army, constitute the eighteen-fold circle. 26   By that is explained a separate

circle (for each of) the enemy, the middle, and the neutral kings. 27   Thus there is a collection of four circles.

28   There are twelve constituents who are kings, sixty material constituents, a total of seventy-two in all. 29   Each of these has its own peculiar excellences.

30   Power and success (are to be explained). 31   Power is (possession of) strength. 32   Success is (obtaining) happiness.

33   Power is three-fold: the power of knowledge is the power of counsel, the power of the treasury and the army is the power of might, the power of valour is the power of energy.

34   In the same way, success is also three-fold: that attainable by the power of counsel is success by counsel, that attainable by the power of might is success by might, that attainable by the power of energy is success by energy.

35   Thriving with these, the (king) becomes superior; reduced (in these), inferior; with equal powers, equal. 36   Therefore, he should endeavour to endow himself with power and success, or, if similar, (to endow with power and success) the material constituents in accordance with their immediate proximity or integrity. 37   Or, he should endeavour to detract (these) from treasonable persons and enemies.

38   Or, if he were to see, "My enemy, possessed of power, will injure his subjects with verbal or physical injury or appropriation of their property, or, when endowed with success, will become negligent because of (addiction to) hunting, gambling, wine or women, thus with subjects disaffected or (himself) become weakened or remiss, he will be easy to overpower for me; or, being attacked in war, he will remain in one place or not in his fort, with all his troops collected together, thus with his army brought together, (and himself) separated from his ally and fort, he will be easy to over-power for me; or, he will render help to me when I am attacked by a strong king, (thinking) 'the strong king is desirous of exterminating my enemy elsewhere; after exterminating him, he might exterminate me,' or (help me) when my undertakings have failed;" and when seeking to seize the middle king (the enemy's help is needed);—for these and other reasons, he may wish power and success even to the enemy.

39   Making the kings separated by one (intervening territory) the felly and those immediately proximate the spokes, the leader should stretch himself out as the hub in the circle of constituents.

40   For, the enemy situated between the two, the leader and the ally, becomes easy to exterminate or to harass, even if strong.

Herewith ends the Sixth Book of the Arthasastra of Kautilya
"The Circle (of Kings) as the Basis"

SECTION 98 ENUMERATION OF THE SIX MEASURES OF FOREIGN POLICY

SECTION 99 DETERMINATION OF (MEASURES IN) DECLINE, STABLE CONDITION, AND ADVANCEMENT

1   The circle of constituent elements is the basis of the six measures of foreign policy.

2   "Peace, war, staying quiet, marching, seeking shelter, and dual policy constitute the six measures," say the teachers.

3   "There are (only) two measures," says Vatavyadhi. 4   "For, out of peace and war the six measures come into being."

5   "These are really six measures, because of differences in the situations," says Kautilya.

6   Among them, entering into a treaty is peace. 7   Doing injury is war. 8   Remaining indifferent is staying quiet. 9   Augmentation of (powers) is marching. 10   Submitting to another is seeking shelter. 11   Resorting to peace (with one) and war (with another) is dual policy. 12   These are the six measures of foreign policy.

13   When in decline as compared to the enemy, he should make peace. 14   When prospering, he should make war. 15   (When he thinks) "The enemy is not able to do harm to me, nor I to him," he should stay quiet. 16   When possessed of a preponderance of excellent qualities, he should march. 17   Depleted in power, he should seek shelter. 18   In a work that can be achieved with the help of an associate, he should resort to a dual policy. 19   Thus are the measures established.

20   Of them, he should follow that policy by resorting to which he may be able to see, "By resorting to this, I shall be able to promote my own undertakings concerning forts, water-works, trade-routes, settling on waste land, mines, material forests and elephant forests, and to injure these undertakings of the enemy." 21   That is advancement. 22   Perceiving "My advancement will be quicker or greater or leading to a greater advancement in the future, the reverse (will be) that of the enemy," he should remain indifferent to the enemy's advancement. 23   In case the advancement takes the same time or bears an equal fruit (for both), he should make peace.

24   He should not follow that policy by resorting to which he were to see the ruin of his own undertakings, not of (those of) the other (party). 25   This is decline. 26   Perceiving "I shall decline after a longer time or to a lesser extent or in such a way that I shall make a greater advancement, the enemy (will

decline) in the reverse manner," he should remain indifferent to his decline. 27 In case the decline lasts for the same period or leads to equal results (for both), he should make peace.

28 The policy, following which he were to see neither the advancement nor the decline of his own undertakings, constitutes stable condition. 29 Perceiving "I shall remain stable for a shorter period or in such a way that I shall make a greater advancement, the enemy (will do so) in the opposite way," he should remain indifferent to his stable condition. 30 "In case the stable condition lasts for the same period or leads to equal consequences (for both), he should make peace," say the teachers. 31 This is not disputed, says Kautilya.

32 Or, if he were to see, "Remaining at peace, I shall ruin the enemy's undertakings by my own undertakings bearing abundant fruits; or, I shall enjoy my own undertakings bearing abundant fruits or the undertakings of the enemy; or, by creating confidence by means of the peace, I shall ruin the enemy's undertakings by the employment of secret remedies and occult practices; or, I shall easily entice away the persons capable of carrying out the enemy's undertakings by (offering) a greater remuneration from my own undertakings, with facilities of favours and exemptions; or, the enemy, in alliance with an extremely strong king, will suffer the ruin of his own undertakings; or, I shall keep prolonged his war with the king, being at war with whom he is making peace with me; or, he will harass the country of the king, who is in alliance with me (but is) hostile to me; or, his country, laid waste by his enemy, will come to me, so that I shall achieve advancement in my undertakings; or, the enemy, with his undertakings ruined (and himself) placed in a difficult situation, would not attack my undertakings; or, with my undertakings started elsewhere, I shall achieve advancement in my undertakings, being in alliance with both; or, by making peace with the enemy I shall divide from him the circle of (kings) which is attached to the enemy, (and) when divided, I shall secure it (for myself); or, by giving support to the enemy by favouring him with troops when he seeks to seize the circle, I shall create hostility towards him, (and) when he faces hostility I shall get him destroyed by that same (circle)," he should secure advancement through peace.

33 Or, if he were to see, "My country, consisting mostly of martial people or fighting bands, or secure in the protection of a single entrance through a mountain-fort, a forest-fort or a river-fort, will be able to repulse the enemy's attack; or, taking shelter in an impregnable fort on the border of my territory, I shall be able to ruin the enemy's undertakings; or, the enemy, with his energy sapped by the troubles caused by a calamity, has reached a time when his undertakings face ruin; or, when he is fighting elsewhere, I shall be able to carry off his country," he should secure advancement by resorting to war.

34 Or, if he were to think, "The enemy is not able to ruin my undertakings nor am I able to ruin his undertakings; or, (when) he is in a calamity, or

(engaged) as in a conflict between a hound and a boar, I shall advance (myself), being intent on carrying out my own undertakings," he should secure advancement by staying quiet.

35   Or, if he were to think, "The ruin of the enemy's undertakings can be brought about by marching, and I have taken steps to secure the protection of my own undertakings," he should secure advancement by marching.

36   Or, if he were to think, "I am not able to ruin the enemy's undertakings nor to avert the ruin of my own undertakings," he should seek shelter with a strong king and by carrying out his own undertakings, should seek to progress from decline to stable condition and from stable condition to advancement.

37   Or, if he were to think, "I shall promote my own undertakings by peace on one side and ruin the enemy's undertakings by war on the other side," he should secure advancement through a dual policy.

38   Situated in the circle of constituent elements, he should, in this manner, with these six measures of policy, seek to progress from decline to stable condition and from stable condition to advancement in his own undertakings.

FURTHER READINGS

The standard political history of India is Vincent A. Smith, *The Oxford History of India*, Mortimer Wheeler, et al., eds., 3rd ed. (Oxford: Clarendon, 1958), while the classic account of life in the times of the *Arthasastra* may be found in Jeannine Auboyer, *Daily Life in Ancient India from 200 B.C. to A.D. 700*, trans. by Simon W. Taylor (New York: Macmillan, 1965).

For an analysis of statecraft at the time of the Arthasastra see John Spellman, *The Political Theory of Ancient India: A Study of Kingship from the Earliest Times to A.D. 300* (Oxford: Clarendon, 1964). The standard history of Asoka's empire is Romila Thapar, *Asoka and the Decline of the Mauryas* (London: Oxford University Press, 1961). The final version of the Arthasastra has been dated at A.D. 250 by computer analysis in Thomas R. Trautmann, *Kautilya and the Arthasastra: A Statistical Investigation of the Authorship and Evolution of the Text* (Leiden, Netherlands: Brill, 1971).

THE CLASSIC OF FILIAL PIETY

Hsiao Ching

K'ung Fu-tzu, commonly known in the West as Confucius, was the greatest of the Chinese sages and is generally regarded as having done more than any other single individual to shape Chinese character and culture over the centuries. His life spanned the years 551 to 478 B.C., years of turmoil and unrest in China. The Chou dynasty had lost all real power some two centuries earlier, and attempts to maintain a measure of peace and political unity through a "concert of princes" was failing. The intricate social and political relations, the highly developed religious ritual, and the sophisticated culture that had evolved over the preceding thousand years were disintegrating. Ancient values and attitudes provided the people with little sense of purpose and direction as China continued towards the period known as the "era of the warring states" (453–221 B.C.).

K'ung entered the civil service of the prince of Lu, a state in what is now the province of Shantung. He soon began teaching, and quickly gathered numerous disciples. He taught that the welfare of the people and the good of the state depend on individuals conducting themselves properly in their relations with others, and that the virtuous individual teaches others by example. Virtue is its own reward, and proper conduct ennobles the individual more certainly than high birth. Although K'ung wrote little, his disciples copied down his discourses and spread his reputation far and wide. Nevertheless, as would later be the case with Plato, although the princes admired and honored him, none was willing to accept him as counsellor.

Though his followers were persecuted and scattered, Confucian teachings survived and were adopted as doctrine by the great Han emperors as they once again brought unity to China (206 B.C.–A.D. 220). *The Classic of Filial Piety* (*Hsiao Ching*), although ascribed to Confucius's disciple Tseng Tzu, was probably written much later than Confucius's time and is a good example of how Confucian teachings reached Han China. Although K'ung Fu-tzu himself does not seem to have emphasized filial piety to such a degree, in this work it becomes the fundamental social virtue upon which all other relationships rest. The *Hsiao Ching* was not only the manual of conduct for every educated individual of Han China, but a required elementary textbook in all schools.

From *The Humanist Way in Ancient China*, ed. and trans. Ch'u Chai and Winberg Chai (New York: Bantam, 1965), pp. 326–334.

It is characteristic of the Confucians that they paid little attention to metaphysics and theology. If virtue is its own reward, there is little reason to speculate about the gods and the afterlife. In this little piece, which takes the form of a dialogue between Tseng Tzu and K'ung, there are no hidden doctrines or complex theorizing. Social and political obligations on the one hand, and the Chinese tradition of the veneration of ancestors on the other, are brought together in a single and practical doctrine.

Questions

1. How is filial piety defined in this work?
2. How does filial piety lead the individual to a concern for his own welfare?
3. What is the *Tao* that is frequently mentioned?
4. What is the purpose of the frequent quotations from the *Shih King*, a collection of ancient poems compiled by K'ung Fu-tzu?

THE CLASSIC OF FILIAL PIETY

THE GENERAL THEME

Chung'ni[1] was at leisure, and Tseng Tzu attended him. The Master said: "The early kings possessed the supreme virtue and the basic *Tao* for the regulation of the world. On account of this, the people lived in peace and harmony; neither superiors nor inferiors had any complaints. Do you know this?"

Tseng Tzu rose from his seat and said: "How can Sheng,[2] dull of intelligence, know this?"

The Master said: "Filial piety is the basis of virtue and the source of culture. Sit down again, and I will explain it to you. The body and the limbs, the hair and the skin, are given to one by one's parents, and to them no injury should come; this is where filial piety begins. To establish oneself and practice the *Tao* is to immortalize one's name and thereby to glorify one's parents; this is where filial piety ends. Thus, filial piety commences with service to parents; it proceeds with service to the sovereign; it is completed by the establishment of one's own personality.

[1] Confucius.
[2] Tseng Tzu's name: this was a courteous way of addressing seniors.

"In the *Shih* it is said:

> May you think of your ancestors,
> And so cultivate their virtues!"

THE SON OF HEAVEN

The Master said: "One who loves one's parents does not dare to hate others. One who reveres one's parents does not dare to spurn others. When love and reverence are thus cherished in the service of one's parents, one's moral influence transforms the people, and one becomes a pattern to all within the four seas. This is the filial piety of the Son of Heaven.

"In the *Fu Code*, it is said:

> When the One Man has blessings,
> The millions of people rely on him."

THE FEUDAL PRINCES

When the prince is not proud and arrogant, he will be secure in his position, however high it may be. When the prince is frugal and prudent, he will keep his wealth, however abundant it may be. When he secures himself in his high position, he will remain unimpaired in his dignity; when he keeps his abundant wealth, he will remain rich. And thus, preserving his wealth and dignity, he will be able to protect his country and pacify his people. This is the filial piety of feudal princes.

In the *Shih* it is said:

> In fear and trembling,
> With caution and care,
> As if standing by a deep abyss,
> As if treading on thin ice.

THE HIGH OFFICERS

They do not presume to be in costume not prescribed by the early kings; they do not presume to use words not sanctioned by the early kings; they do not presume to act contrary to the virtuous conduct of the early kings. Thus, none of their words [is] contrary to sanctions, and none of their actions [is] not in accordance with the *Tao*. Their words are not improper; nor are their actions indecent. Their words spread over the world, and yet no fault is found in them. Their actions spread over the world, and yet no complaint is caused by them. When these three things are properly observed, they will be able to preserve their ancestral temples. This is the filial piety of high officers.

In the *Shih* it is said:

> Day and night, never slacken
> In the service of the One Man.

THE SCHOLARS

One serves one's mother in the same manner in which one serves one's father, and the love toward them is the same. One serves one's prince in the same manner in which one serves one's father, and the reverence toward them is the same. Thus, to the mother one shows love and to the prince one shows reverence, but to the father one shows both love and reverence. Therefore, to serve the prince with filial piety is to show loyalty; to serve the senior with reverence is to show obedience. Not failing in loyalty and obedience in the service of one's superiors, one will be able to preserve one's emolument and position and to carry on one's family sacrifices. This is the filial piety of scholars.

In the *Shih* it is said:

> Rise early and go to sleep late;
> Never disgrace those who bore you.

THE COMMON PEOPLE

In order to support their parents, they follow the *Tao* of Heaven; they utilize the earth in accordance with the quality of its soil, and they are prudent and frugal in their expenditure. This is the filial piety of the common people.

Therefore, from the Son of Heaven down to the common people, there has never been one on whom, if filial piety was not pursued from the beginning to end, disasters did not befall.

THE TRINITY—HEAVEN, EARTH, AND MAN

Tseng Tzu said: "How great is filial piety!" The Master said: "Filial piety is the basic principle of Heaven, the ultimate standard of earth, and the norm of conduct for the people. Men ought to abide by the guiding principle of Heaven and earth as the pattern of their lives, so that by the brightness of Heaven and the benefits of earth they would be able to keep all in the world in harmony and in unison. On this account, their teachings, though not stringent, are followed, and their government, though not rigorous, is well ordered. The early kings, knowing that their teachings could transform the people, made themselves an example of practicing all-embracing love; thereby the people did not neglect their parents. They expounded the virtuous and righteous conduct, and the people enthusiastically complied. They made of themselves an example of respectful and prudent behavior, and the people were not contentious. They guided themselves with *li*[3] and music, and the people lived in concord. They verified the distinction between good and evil, and the people knew restraint.

"In the *Shih* it is said:

> Oh, majestic Master Yin,
> The people all look up to thee!"

GOVERNMENT BY FILIAL PIETY

The Master said: "Formerly the enlightened kings governed the world by filial piety. They did not dare to neglect the ministers of small states—to say nothing of the dukes, marquises, earls, viscounts, and barons! They thereby gained the good will of all the states to serve their early kings.

"Those who governed the states did not dare to ignore the widows and widowers—to say nothing of scholars and the people! They thereby gained the good will of all the subjects to serve their former princes.

"Those who regulated their families did not dare to mistreat their servants and concubines—to say nothing of their wives and children! They thereby gained the good will of others who served their parents.

"Accordingly, while living, the parents enjoyed comfort; after their death, sacrifices were offered to their spirits. In this way the world was kept in peace; disasters did not arise, nor did riots occur. Such was the way in which the early enlightened governed the world by filial piety.

"In the *Shih* it is said:

> Glorious was his virtuous conduct,
> And all states submitted themselves."

GOVERNMENT BY THE SAGE

Tseng Tzu said: "I venture to ask whether in the virtue of the sage there is anything that surpasses filial piety."

The Master said: "It is the nature of Heaven and earth that man is the most honorable of all beings. Of all human conduct none is greater than filial piety. In filial piety nothing is greater than to revere one's father. In revering

---

[3]Order, propriety; the rules of proper conduct.

one's father, nothing is greater than making him a peer of Heaven. The Duke of Chou did this. Formerly the Duke of Chou sacrificed to Hou Chi in the suburbs as the peer of Heaven. He sacrificed to King Wen [his father] at the Ming T'ang [Bright Temple] as the peer of Shang Ti [Supreme Being]. Therefore, all the feudal princes within the four seas came, each with his tribute, to join in the sacrifices. How can there be anything in the virtue of the sage that surpasses filial piety?

"Affection is fostered by parents during childhood, and from there springs the child's reverence, which grows daily, while sustaining his parents. The sage was to follow this innate development by teaching reverence and to follow this piety. In filial piety nothing is greater than to revere one's father. In revering innate feeling of affection by teaching love. Thus, the teachings of the sage, though not stringent, were followed, and his government, though not rigorous, was well ordered. All this was brought about because of this innate disposition.

"The *Tao* of father and son is rooted in the Heaven-endowed nature, and develops into the equity between sovereign and ministers. Parents give one life; no bond is stronger. They bring up and care for their child; no kindness is greater. Therefore, one who does not love one's parents, but others, acts to the detriment of virtue. One who does not revere one's parents, but others, acts to the detriment of *li*. Should the rules of conduct be modeled on such perversity, the people would have no true norm by which to abide. Therein is found no goodness but only evil. Although such a person may gain a high position, the *chün-tzu* will not esteem him.

The *chün-tzu* is not like this. His speech is consistent with the *Tao*, his action with what is good. His virtuous equity is respected; his administration is commendable; his demeanor is pleasing; his movements are proper. In this way he governs the people, and therefore they look upon him with awe and love— make him their model and follow him. Thus he is able to realize his virtuous teachings and to carry out his edicts and orders.

"In the *Shih* it is said:

> The *chun-tzu*[4] our princely lord—
> His fine demeanor is without fault."

THE PRACTICE OF FILIAL PIETY

The Master said: "In serving his parents, a filial son reveres them in daily life; he makes them happy while he nourishes them; he takes anxious care of them in sickness; he shows great sorrow over their death and he sacrifices to them with

[4]"Masterly scion": an enlightened member of the ruling class.

solemnity. When he has performed these five duties, he has truly served his parents.

"He who really serves his parents will not be proud in a high position; he will not be rebellious in an inferior position; among the multitude he will not be contentious. To be proud in a high position is to be ruined; to be rebellious in an inferior position is to incur punishment; to be contentious among the multitude is to bring about violence. As long as these three evils are not discarded, a son cannot be called filial, even though he treats his parents daily with the three kinds of meat."[5]

THE FIVE PUNISHMENTS

The Master said: "There are five punishments for three thousand offenses, and of these offenses there is no greater crime than lack of filial piety. To intimidate the sovereign is to defy a superior; to denounce the sage is to disregard the law; to decry filial piety is to not acknowledge parents. This is the way of great chaos."

ILLUSTRATION OF THE BASIC TAO

The Master said: "There is nothing better than filial piety to teach the people love for one another. There is nothing better than brotherly deference to teach the people propriety and prudence. There is nothing better than music to transform their manners and to change customs. There is nothing better than *li* to safeguard the sovereign and to govern the people.

"*Li* is but reverence. When the parents are revered, the son is pleased; when the elder brother is revered, the younger brother is pleased; when the sovereign is revered, the ministers are pleased; when the One Man is revered, the millions of men are pleased. Thus, those who are revered are few, but those who are pleased are many. This is said to be the 'basic *Tao.*'"

ILLUSTRATION OF THE SUPREME VIRTUE

The Master said: "The *chun-tzu* in teaching filial piety need not go daily to visit the families. He need only teach filial piety and he will show reverence due to all the fathers of the world. He need only teach brotherly deference and thereby show reverence due to all the elder brothers of the world. He need only teach

[5]Beef, lamb, and pork.

the duties of ministers and thereby show reverence due to all the sovereigns of the world.

"In the *Shih* it is said:

> The princely man, cheerful and pleasant,
> Is the father and mother of the people!

"Without possessing the supreme virtue how can he keep the people in such harmony?"

ILLUSTRATION OF PERPETUATING THE NAME

The Master said: "The *chun-tzu* serves his parents with filial piety: thus his loyalty can be transferred to his sovereign. He serves his elder brother with brotherly deference; thus his respect can be transferred to his superiors. He orders his family well; thus his good order can be transferred to his public administration.

"Therefore, when one cultivates one's conduct within oneself, one's name will be perpetuated for future generations."

THE DUTY OF ADMONITION

Tseng Tzu said: "I have heard about parental love, loving respect, cherishing care for parents, and making their name known. I venture to ask whether a son, by obeying every command of his father, can be called filial?"

The Master said, "What are you talking about? What are you talking about? In the old days, the Son of Heaven,[6] who had seven ministers to admonish him, would not have lost his world, even if he were devoid of virtue. A state prince, who had five officers to admonish him, would not have lost his state, even if he were devoid of virtue. A minister, who had three assistants to admonish him, would not have lost his family, even if he were devoid of virtue.

"Thus, if a scholar has a friend to admonish him, he will not deviate from his good name. If a father has a son to admonish him, he will not commit gross wrong. In case of gross wrong, the son should never fail to admonish his father against it; nor should the minister fail to admonish his sovereign. Hence when there is gross wrong, there should be admonition. How can a son, by obeying the command of his father, be called filial?"

---

[6]The emperor in the era of the Chou dynasty.

filial piety ≠ just obedience,
(≠ just provision)

INFLUENCE AND EFFECT

The Master said: "Formerly the enlightened kings were filial in the service of their fathers and thereby became enlightened in the service of Heaven. They were filial in the service of their mothers and thereby became discreet in the service of earth. When the young deferred to the elders, superiors governed inferiors well. When they were enlightened and discreet in the service of Heaven and earth, the blessings of spirits were manifest.

"Hence, even the Son of Heaven has someone to honor—his father. He has someone to respect—his elder brothers. He sacrifices at the ancestral temple, lest he forget his parents. He cultivates his person and acts with prudence, lest he disgrace his elders. He pays reverence, at the ancestral temples, to the spirits and ghosts, so as to enjoy their blessings. When his filial piety and brotherly deference reach perfection, he is endowed with divine enlightenment. His virtuous influence illuminates the four seas and penetrates far and wide.

"In the *Shih* it is said:

> From the west to the east,
> From the south to the north,
> None thought of not submitting."

SERVING THE SOVEREIGN

The Master said: "In serving his sovereign, the *chun-tzu* endeavors to be utterly loyal when he is in office; he contemplates, in retirement, to remedy his shortcomings. Then he tries to conform to what is good in the sovereign, and to rectify what is wrong in him. In this way a mutual affection will be fostered between superiors and inferiors.

"In the *Shih* it is said:

> In my heart I love him,
> Why should I not tell it?
> I keep him in my heart,
> When shall I forget him?"

MOURNING FOR PARENTS

The master said: "In mourning for his parents, a filial son weeps without wailing, he observes funeral rites without heeding his personal appearance, he speaks without regard for eloquence, he finds no comfort in fine clothing, he feels no joy on hearing music, he has no appetite for good food; all this is the innate expression of grief and sorrow. After three days, he breaks his fast, so as to teach the people that the dead should not hurt the living and that disfigurement should not destroy life; this is the rule of the sages. Mourning only extends to the period of three years, so as to show the people that sorrow comes to an end.

"The body, dressed in fine robes, is placed in the encased coffin. The sacrificial vessels are set out with grief and sorrow. Beating the breasts and stamping the feet, weeping and wailing, the mourners escort the coffin to the resting-place selected by divination. A shrine is built, and there offerings are made to the spirits. Spring and autumn sacrificial rites are performed, for the purpose of thinking about them at the proper season.

"When parents are alive, they are served with love and reverence; when they are dead, they are mourned with grief and sorrow. This is the performance of man's supreme duty, fulfillment of the mutual affection between the living and the dead, and the accomplishment of the filial son's service to his parents."

FURTHER READINGS

For the history of China, the multivolume Denis Twitchett and John K. Fairbanks, eds., *Cambridge History of China* (Cambridge: Cambridge University Press, 1978–), is an excellent scholarly reference. Arthur F. Wright discusses Confucian philosophy generally in *The Confucian Persuasion* (Palo Alto: Stanford University Press, 1960). The standard English translation of the basic work of Confucian thought is still Arthur Waley, trans. *The Analects of Confucius*, (New York: George Allen and Unwin, 1938).

Michael Lowe, *Chinese Ideas of Life and Death: Faith, Myth and Reason in the Han Period* (London: Allen & Unwin, 1982) examines some intellectual and religious beliefs of the Ch'in and Han periods. Hugh Baker, *Chinese Family and Kinship* (New York: Macmillan, 1979) and Paul Chao, *Chinese Kinship* (London: Kegan Paul, 1983) each offer informative material on the importance of filial piety in Chinese society. Benjamin I. Schwartz, *The World of Thought in Ancient China* (Cambridge, MA: Harvard University Press, 1985) provides information on the relationship between moral quality and the family. A brief examination of the Confucian emphasis on filial piety is included in Yu-lan Feng, *A Short History of Chinese Philosophy*, ed. Derk Bodde (New York: Macmillan, 1948) and Herrlee Creel, *Confucius and the Chinese Way* (New York: Harper, 1960). A brief but informative section on family life in China is included in Herrlee Creel, *The Birth of China, a Study of the Formative Period of Chinese Civilization* (New York: Reynal & Hitchcock, 1937).

LESSONS FOR WOMEN
Pan Chao

Throughout the long history of Chinese literature, the contribution of women has been relatively small in comparison with that of men. This is largely the result of a strong social and cultural tradition, existing since antiquity, that emphasized women's responsibilities within the household and required their subservience to the needs of men. This tradition, strengthened by legal restrictions, combined to bar women from full participation in political, social, economic, and cultural life. Moreover, women were inculcated with principles that justified and perpetuated this situation. Chinese women were taught, almost from birth, that the ideal female was humble, yielding, and respectful towards males. The accepted mode of female conduct was characterized by self-effacement and deference.

In spite of these obstacles, individual women of exceptional talent and courage have occasionally attained positions of political and scholarly distinction. One woman who unquestionably deserves to be counted among the first rank of Chinese scholars is Pan Chao (A.D. 45–114?), a renowned educator, moralist, writer, and the only female to attain the position of Historian to the Imperial Court.

Pan Chao lived during the Eastern, or Later, Han period (A.D. 25–220), an era remarkable for both its political and cultural achievements. The Han emperors required their ministers and public officials to be learned in the Confucian classics and to be able to discourse on the moral and ethical doctrines embodied in those writings. Thus government officers were united by a common literary and cultural background, as well as by a common adherence to the principles of proper conduct central to Confucius's teachings. The Han were thus able to staff an elaborate bureaucracy with loyal and able scholar-administrators dedicated to the ideal of selfless service. Two works contained in this anthology, *The Classic of Filial Piety* and *Lessons for Women*, are products of the Later Han period and reflect the emphasis placed by Han administrators on the principles of obedience and service.

Pan Chao belonged to a scholarly family and received an exceptional education from her parents. Her father, a noted historian, and her mother provided her with both a literary education as well as training in acceptable manners. Since her father and elder brothers were recognized scholars, her home often received learned guests, and Pan Chao profited from the discussions that

From Nancy Lee Swann, *Pan Chao: Foremost Woman Scholar of China* (New York: Russell & Russell, 1968, 1932), pp. 82–90.

took place. She was married at the age of fourteen and, following the early death
of her husband, followed the accepted, although often ignored, custom of permanent widowhood. Well-trained in mathematics and astronomy, she was appointed by the emperor to complete her brother Pan Ku's (d. A.D. 92) famous
historical record of the previous dynasty, *The History of the Former Han*. Her
other literary works were both numerous and varied, including narrative poems,
commemorations, eulogies, commentaries, and essays. Although much of her
work has been lost, her most famous and influential treatise, *Lessons for Women*,
survives in its entirety.

Lessons for Women was the first manual devoted to the practical lives of
women in the home. It contains a complete statement of feminine ethics, a
system of moral principles, and advice on the practical application of these
principles. *Lessons* is addressed to "unmarried girls" and concentrates on instructing its audience in personal deportment and the proper appreciation of
family relationships. Pan Chao depicts the model woman as one who has succeeded in adjusting to married life through an attitude of respect and obedience.
Her formula for proper female conduct is simple and unquestioning: once a
young woman has accepted the principles that men are superior to women, and
the old are superior to the young, she will easily know how to comport herself
with the various members of her new family.

Where Pan Chao departs from previous tradition is in the area of education. Perhaps drawing on her own experience, she argues that, if education is
the path to learning the principles of proper conduct, then it is equally important for men and women, since proper conduct is just as important within the
home as outside of it. She held that the lack of a proper education for girls
hindered the establishment of successful relations between men and women.
This appeal was unique in the history of Chinese thought, and *Lessons for
Women* continued to exert a great influence for many generations. As a historical document, it demonstrates how the training of Han scholars could on occasion lift them above the burden of tradition to new visions of justice and equity.

Questions

1. What is the primary virtue of the ideal young woman?
2. Pan Chao regards strength as the chief glory of men. What does she consider
   the chief ornament of a woman's character?
3. How does Pan Chao present her case for equal education for young girls?
4. Pan Chao stresses the importance of a young woman's relationship with her
   husband, her parents-in-law, and her brothers- and sisters-in-law. Of these
   three, which is most important and why?

LESSONS FOR WOMEN[1]

INSTRUCTIONS IN SEVEN CHAPTERS FOR A WOMAN'S ORDINARY WAY OF LIFE IN THE FIRST CENTURY A.D.

INTRODUCTION

I, the unworthy writer, am unsophisticated, unenlightened, and by nature unintelligent, but I am fortunate both to have received not a little favor from my scholarly father,[2] and to have had a (cultured) mother and instructresses upon whom to rely for a literary education as well as for training in good manners. More than forty years have passed since at the age of fourteen I took up the dustpan and the broom[3] in the Ts'ao family. During this time with trembling heart I feared constantly that I might disgrace my parents, and that I might multiply difficulties for both the women and the men (of my husband's family). Day and night I was distressed in heart, (but) I labored without confessing weariness. Now and hereafter, however, I know how to escape (from such fears).

Being careless, and by nature stupid, I taught and trained (my children) without system. Consequently I fear that my son Ku may bring disgrace upon the Imperial Dynasty by whose Holy Grace he has unprecedentedly received the extraordinary privilege of wearing the Gold and the Purple, a privilege for the attainment of which (by my son, I) a humble subject never even hoped. Nevertheless, now that he is a man and able to plan his own life, I need not again have concern for him. But I do grieve that you, my daughters,[4] just now at the age for marriage, have not at this time had gradual training and advice; that you still have not learned the proper customs for married women. I fear that by failure in good manners in other families you will humiliate both your ancestors and your clan. I am now seriously ill, life is uncertain. As I have thought of you all in so untrained a state, I have been uneasy many a time for you. At hours of leisure I have composed in seven chapters these instructions under the title, "Lessons for Women." In order that you may have something wherewith to

[1] Pan Chao's successors in the field of moral writings have been so much more widely quoted than herself that modern China as well as the West has failed to appreciate the ethical value of this treatise.

[2] Pan Chao was the daughter of Pan Piao. Her elder brother, the historian Pan Ku, wrote the *Han Shu* or *History of the Former Han*.

[3] An expression for the marriage of the young woman.

[4] Not necessarily only her own daughters, but girls of her family.

Fear of bringing disgrace to family and country.

benefit your persons, I wish every one of you, my daughters, each to write out a copy for yourself.

From this time on every one of you strive to practise these (lessons).

CHAPTER I

HUMILITY

On the third day after the birth of a girl the ancients[5] observed three customs: (first) to place the baby below[6] the bed; (second) to give her a potsherd with which to play;[7] and (third) to announce her birth to her ancestors by an offering. Now to lay the baby below the bed plainly indicated that she is lowly and weak, and should regard it as her primary duty to humble herself before others. To give her potsherds with which to play indubitably signified that she should practise labor and consider it her primary duty to be industrious. To announce her birth before her ancestors clearly meant that she ought to esteem as her primary duty the continuation of the observance of worship[8] in the home.

These three ancient customs epitomize a woman's ordinary way of life and the teachings of the traditional ceremonial rites and regulations. Let a woman modestly yield to others; let her respect others; let her put others first, herself last. Should she do something good, let her not mention it; should she do something bad, let her not deny it. Let her bear disgrace; let her even endure[9] when others speak or do evil to her. Always let her seem to tremble and fear. (When a woman follows such maxims as these,) then she may be said to humble herself before others.

Let a woman retire late to bed, but rise early to duties; let her not dread tasks by day or by night. Let her not refuse to perform domestic duties whether easy or difficult. That which must be done, let her finish completely, tidily, and systematically. (When a woman follows such rules as these,) then she may be said to be industrious.

Let a woman be correct in manner and upright in character in order to serve her husband. Let her live in purity and quietness (of spirit), and attend to

---

[5]Pan Chao does not indicate that any such custom existed in her time, it was the custom of ancients—people who were "ancient" more than eighteen hundred years ago.

[6]That is, on the floor, or the ground.

[7]An honorable symbol of domesticity, being used in ancient times as a weight for the spindle.

[8]The worship and obedience due to parents and ancestors.

[9]Literally "Let her hold filth in her mouth, let her swallow insult."

her own affairs. Let her love not gossip and silly laughter. Let her cleanse and purify and arrange in order the wine and the food for the offerings to the ancestors. [10] (When a woman observes such principles as these,) then she may be said to continue ancestral worship.

No woman who observes these three (fundamentals of life) has ever had a bad reputation or has fallen into disgrace. If a woman fails to observe them, how can her name be honored; how can she but bring disgrace upon herself?

CHAPTER II

HUSBAND AND WIFE

The Way of husband and wife is intimately connected with *Yin* and *Yang*, [11] and relates the individual to gods and ancestors. Truly it is the great principle of Heaven and Earth, and the great basis of human relationships. [12] Therefore the "Rites" honor union of man and woman; and in the "Book of Poetry" the "First Ode" manifests the principle of marriage. For these reasons the relationship cannot but be an important one.

If a husband be unworthy then he possesses nothing by which to control his wife. If a wife be unworthy, then she possesses nothing with which to serve her husband. If a husband does not control his wife, then the rules of conduct manifesting his authority are abandoned and broken. If a wife does not serve her husband, then the proper relationship (between men and women) and the natural order of things are neglected and destroyed. As a matter of fact the purpose of these two (the controlling of women by men, and the serving of men by women) is the same.

Now examine the gentlemen of the present age. They only know that wives must be controlled, and that the husband's rules of conduct manifesting his authority must be established. They therefore teach their boys to read books and (study) histories. But they do not in the least understand that husbands and masters must (also) be served, and that the proper relationship and the rites should be maintained.

---

[10]The wife had special duties to perform in the periodical sacrifices. It was her duty to prepare the sacrificial cakes, the rice, the millet, and the fruits, and to see to it that they were served in the proper vessels.

[11]The fundamental basis of the Chinese conception of nature lies in the revolution of the seasons, in the alternation of heat and cold, of darkness and light. The two antithetic principles were later named *Yin—Yang*.

[12]The Chinese have always considered marriage as the most solemn and important act of life.

Yet only to teach men and not to teach women—is that not ignoring the essential relation between them? According to the "Rites," it is the rule to begin to teach children to read at the age of eight years, and by the age of fifteen years they ought then to be ready for cultural training. Only why should it not be (that girls' education as well as boys' be) according to this principle?

CHAPTER III   #1 : respect

RESPECT AND CAUTION

As *Yin* and *Yang* are not of the same nature, so man and woman have different characteristics. The distinctive quality of the *Yang* is rigidity; the function of the *Yin* is yielding. Man is honored for strength; a woman is beautiful on account of her gentleness. Hence there arose a common saying: "A man though born like a wolf may, it is feared, become a weak monstrosity; a woman though born like a mouse may, it is feared, become a tiger."

Now for self-culture[13] nothing equals respect for others. To counteract firmness nothing equals compliance. Consequently it can be said that the Way of respect and acquiescence is woman's most important principle of conduct. So respect may be defined as nothing other than holding on to that which is permanent; and acquiescence nothing other than being liberal and generous. Those who are steadfast in devotion know that they should stay in their proper places; those who are liberal and generous esteem others, and honor and serve (them).

If husband and wife have the habit of staying together, never leaving one another, and following each other around within the limited space of their own rooms, then they will lust after and take liberties with one another. From such action improper language will arise between the two. This kind of discussion may lead to licentiousness. Out of licentiousness will be born a heart of disrespect to the husband. Such a result comes from not knowing that one should stay in one's proper place.

Furthermore, affairs may be either crooked or straight; words may be either right or wrong. Straightforwardness cannot but lead to quarreling; crookedness cannot but lead to accusation. If there are really accusations and quarrels, then undoubtedly there will be angry affairs. Such a result comes from not esteeming others, and not honoring and serving (them).

(If wives) suppress not contempt for husbands, then it follows (that such wives) rebuke and scold (their husbands). (If husbands) stop not short of anger,

---

[13]The cultivation of the person was of the utmost importance.

then they are certain to beat (their wives). The correct relationship between husband and wife is based upon harmony and intimacy, and (conjugal) love is grounded in proper union. Should actual blows be dealt, how could matrimonial relationship be preserved? Should sharp words be spoken, how could (conjugal) love exist? If love and proper relationship both be destroyed, then husband and wife are divided.

CHAPTER IV

WOMANLY QUALIFICATIONS

A woman (ought to) have four qualifications: (1) womanly virtue; (2) womanly words; (3) womanly bearing; and (4) womanly work. Now what is called womanly virtue need not be brilliant ability, exceptionally different from others. Womanly words need be neither clever in debate nor keen in conversation. Womanly appearance requires neither a pretty nor a perfect face and form. Womanly work need not be work done more skillfully than that of others.

To guard carefully her chastity; to control circumspectly her behavior; in every motion to exhibit modesty; and to model each act on the best usage, this is womanly virtue.

To choose her words with care; to avoid vulgar language; to speak at appropriate times; and not to weary others (with much conversation), may be called the characteristics of womanly words.

To wash and scrub filth away; to keep clothes and ornaments fresh and clean; to wash the head and bathe the body regularly, and to keep the person free from disgraceful filth, may be called the characteristics of womanly bearing.

With whole-hearted devotion to sew and to weave; to love not gossip and silly laughter; in cleanliness and order (to prepare) the wine and food for serving guests, may be called the characteristics of womanly work.

These four qualifications characterize the greatest virtue of a woman. No woman can afford to be without them. In fact they are very easy to possess if a woman only treasure them in her heart. The ancients had a saying: "Is Love afar off? If I desire love, then love is at hand!" So can it be said of these qualifications.

CHAPTER V

WHOLE-HEARTED DEVOTION

Now in the "Rites" is written the principle that a husband may marry again, but there is no Canon that authorizes a woman to be married the second time.

Therefore it is said of husbands as of Heaven, that as certainly as people cannot run away from Heaven, so surely a wife cannot leave[14] (a husband's home).

If people in action or character disobey the spirits of Heaven and of Earth,[15] then Heaven punishes them. Likewise if a woman errs in the rites and in the proper mode of conduct, then her husband esteems her lightly. The ancient book, "A Pattern for Women," (*Nu Hsien*)[16] says: "To obtain the love of one man is the crown of a woman's life; to lose the love of one man is to miss the aim in woman's life."[17] For these reasons a woman cannot but seek to win her husband's heart. Nevertheless, the beseeching wife need not use flattery, coaxing words, and cheap methods to gain intimacy.

Decidedly nothing is better (to gain the heart of a husband) than wholehearted devotion and correct manners. In accordance with the rites and the proper mode of conduct, (let a woman) live a pure life. Let her have ears that hear not licentiousness; and eyes that see not depravity. When she goes outside her own home, let her not be conspicuous in dress and manners. When at home let her not neglect her dress. Women should not assemble in groups, nor gather together (for gossip and silly laughter). They should not stand watching in the gateways. (If a woman follows) these rules, she may be said to have wholehearted devotion and correct manners.

If, in all her actions, she is frivolous, she sees and hears (only) that which pleases herself. At home her hair is dishevelled, and her dress is slovenly. Outside the home she emphasizes her femininity to attract attention; she says what ought not to be said; and she looks at what ought not to be seen. (If a woman does such as) these, (she may be) said to be without whole-hearted devotion and correct manners.

CHAPTER VI

IMPLICIT OBEDIENCE

Now "to win the love of one man is the crown of a woman's life; to lose the love of one man is her eternal disgrace." This saying advises a fixed will and a whole-

---

[14]Even following a husband's death, the worthy wife does not leave her husband's home.

[15]Deeply implanted in Chinese faith was the belief in the personal intervention of their gods in human affairs.

[16]Thought to be the title of a long lost book.

[17]The full translation is: "To become of like mind with one man may be said to be the final end; to fail to become of like mind with one man may be said to be the eternal end."

hearted devotion for a woman. Ought she then to lose the hearts of her father-and mother-in-law?[18]

There are times when love may lead to differences of opinion (between individuals); there are times when duty may lead to disagreement. Even should the husband say that he loves something, when the parents-in-law say "no," this is called a case of duty leading to disagreement. This being so, then what about the hearts of the parents-in-law? Nothing is better than an obedience which sacrifices personal opinion.

Whenever the mother-in-law says, "Do not do that," and if what she says is right, unquestionably the daughter-in-law obeys. Whenever the mother-in-law says, "Do that," even if what she says is wrong, still the daughter-in-law submits unfailingly to the command.

Let a woman not act contrary to the wishes and the opinions of parents-in-law about right and wrong; let her not dispute with them what is straight[19] and what is crooked. Such (docility) may be called obedience which sacrifices personal opinion. Therefore the ancient book, "A Pattern for Women," says: "If a daughter-in-law (who follows the wishes of her parents-in-law) is like an echo and a shadow, how could she not be praised?"

CHAPTER VII

HARMONY WITH YOUNGER BROTHERS- AND SISTERS-IN-LAW

In order for a wife to gain the love of her husband, she must win for herself the love of her parents-in-law. To win for herself the love of her parents-in-law, she must secure for herself the good will of younger brothers- and sisters-in-law. For these reasons the right and the wrong, the praise and the blame of a woman alike depend upon younger brothers- and sisters-in-law. Consequently it will not do for a woman to lose their affection.

They are stupid both who know not that they must not lose (the hearts of) younger brothers- and sisters-in-law, and who cannot be in harmony with them in order to be intimate with them. Excepting only the Holy Men, few are able to

---

[18] In the Chinese family system, children, even mature sons and their wives, were morally bound to dwell under the same parental roof. This often resulted in conflicts between the mother-in-law and the daughter-in-law, as well as between a wife and the wives of her husband's brothers, a wife and the unmarried daughters of the family, or the widows of deceased sons, or the young children of the family. There were many opportunities for friction.

[19] Proper.

be faultless. Now Yen Tzu's[20] greatest virtue was that he was able to reform. Confucius praised him (for not committing a misdeed) the second time. (In comparison with him) a woman is the more likely (to make mistakes).

Although a woman possesses a worthy woman's qualifications, and is wise and discerning by nature, is she able to be perfect? Yet if a woman lives in harmony with her immediate family, unfavorable criticism will be silenced (within the home. But) if a man and woman disagree, then this evil will be noised abroad. Such consequences are inevitable. The "Book of Changes" says:

> "Should two hearts harmonize,
> The united strength can cut gold.
> Words from hearts which agree,
> Give forth fragrance like the orchid."[21]

This saying may be applied to (harmony in the home).

Though a daughter-in-law and her younger sisters-in-law are equal in rank, nevertheless (they should) respect (each other); though love (between them may be) sparse, their proper relationship should be intimate. Only the virtuous, the beautiful, the modest, and the respectful (young women) can accordingly rely upon the sense of duty to make their affection sincere, and magnify love to bind their relationships firmly.

Then the excellence and the beauty of such a daughter-in-law becomes generally known. Moreover, any flaws and mistakes are hidden and unrevealed. Parents-in-law boast of her good deeds; her husband is satisfied with her.[22] Praise of her radiates, making her illustrious in district and in neighborhood; and her brightness reaches to her own father and mother.

But a stupid and foolish person as an elder sister-in-law uses her rank[23] to exalt herself; as a younger sister-in-law, because of parents' favor, she becomes filled with arrogance. If arrogant, how can a woman live in harmony with others? If love and proper relationships be perverted, how can praise be secured? In such instances the wife's good is hidden, and her faults are declared. The mother-in-law will be angry, and the husband will be indignant. Blame will reverberate and spread in and outside the home. Disgrace will gather upon the daughter-in-law's person, on the one hand to add humiliation to her own father and mother, and on the other to increase the difficulties of her husband.

---

[20] A favorite disciple of K'ung Fu-tzu.
[21] In loving unity there is strength and beauty as the two (or the group) meet life's responsibilities.
[22] Literally "praises the beauty of her character."
[23] The eldest daughter-in-law had control over other sons' wives.

harmony in relationships

Such then is the basis for both honor and disgrace; the foundation for reputation or for ill-repute. Can a woman be too cautious? Consequently to seek the hearts of young brothers- and sisters-in-law decidedly nothing can be esteemed better than modesty and acquiescence.

Modesty is virtue's handle; acquiescence is the wife's (most refined) characteristic. All who possess these two have sufficient [virtues] for harmony with others. In the "Book of Poetry" it is written that "here is no evil; there is no dart." So it may be said of (these two, modesty and acquiescence).

FURTHER READINGS

Edmund Capen and William MacQuitty, *Princes of Jade* (New York: Dutton, 1973), provides a basic introduction to the Han period. Hans Bielstein, *The Bureaucracy of Han Times* (Cambridge, UK: Cambridge University Press, 1980), and T'ung-tsu Ch'u, *Law and Tradition in Traditional China* (Paris: Mouton, 1961), are helpful in understanding the social structure of Han China. Michael Loewe, *Crisis and Conflict in Han China* (London: Allen & Unwin, 1974), discusses the political situation from 104 B.C. to A.D. 9. Two useful examinations of law in Ch'in and Han times are provided in Derk Bodde and Clarence Morris, *Law in Imperial China* (Cambridge, MA: Harvard University Press, 1967), and A. F. P. Hulsewe, *Remnants of Han Law*, Vol. I (Leiden, Netherlands: Brill, 1955).

Arthur F. Wright discusses Confucian philosophy in *The Confucian Persuasion* (Stanford: Stanford University Press, 1960). The standard English translation of the basic work of Confucian thought is still Arthur Waley, trans. *The Analects of Confucius*, (New York: Allen & Unwin, 1938). Pan Ku's work is available in *The History of the Former Han*, trans. Homer H. Dubs, 3 vols., (Baltimore: Waverly Press, 1938–1955).

T'ung-tsu Ch'u, "The Position of Women in Han China," in *Han Social Structure*, ed. Jack L. Dull (Seattle: University of Washington Press, 1972), pp. 33–62, provides an excellent analysis of the subject. Further useful material on the status of women in ancient China is provided by Albert O'Hara, *The Position of Women in Early China* (Westport, CT: Hyperion, 1980), and Florence Ayscough, *Chinese Women: Yesterday and Today* (New York: Da Capo, 1975). Nancy Lee Swann, *Pan Chao: Foremost Woman Scholar of China* (New York: Russell and Russell, 1968), provides an informative study of Pan Chao's life and works. Female sexuality is discussed in Robert van Gulik, *Sexual Life in Ancient China* (Atlantic Highlands, NJ: Humanities Press International, 1974). An interesting view of women's life at court is offered by C. P. Fitzgerald, *The Empress Wu* (London: Cresset, 1968).

PART I

1. Respect for the individual would seem to be a necessary characteristic of the just society. What role does individual integrity play in the societies described in the *Bhagavad Gita* and the *Arthasastra*, *The Analects* and *The Classic of Filial Piety*? How would you explain the differences of attitude that appear among these selections?

2. A society can be defined as a group of people bound together by mutual obligations. These obligations form an important part of the society's traditions. Where do these mutual obligations come from? Why should one respect one's parents or refrain from actions that might bring harm to others? What do K'ung Fu-tzu, Krishna, and Pan Chao suggest? What is your own view?

3. The things that we can sense are our inner self and the outer world. Do we gain more knowledge by studying the outside world or by learning more about ourselves? Which knowledge is more important? What are the views of Buddha in *The Sermon at the Deer Park*? How do these compare with the philosophy of K'ung Fu-tzu in *The Analects*? What would Lao Tzu, in the *Tao te ching*, say about this question? Of what value is knowledge gained from within? How can it be put to use, or is such a question unanswerable?

4. Two of the basic questions that every culture tries to answer are where the physical world came from and of what it really consists. What answers do the *Vedic Hymns* give, and how do they compare with Krishna's statements in the *Bhagavad Gita*? What is Lao Tzu's view, as expressed in the *Tao te ching*? How does *The Book of Songs* view these questions? What are the modern Western views? Are they consistent and understandable?

5. A question that constantly intrigues authors, both male and female, is what qualities are desirable in a woman. One can get a picture from *The Book of Songs* and *Lessons for Women* of how the Chinese thought about this over a period of time. During this period, what characterized an admirable woman, and did these qualities change between the Chou and Han dynasties? If so, why do you think such changes occurred? Are women regarded as individuals, or as creatures who should adapt themselves to the customs of a male-dominated society? What qualities are admirable in a woman today?

Does the modern attitude show any greater respect for the woman as an individual?

6. Most cultures hold that beyond the realities of the inner self and the physical world lies the reality of the gods, and elaborate explanations have been developed of the proper relationship to be maintained between the gods and the individual. What is the view, expressed in the *Vedic Hymns* and the *Bhagavad Gita*, of the nature of the gods and the proper relationship between gods and humans? How do K'ung Fu-tzu and Buddha approach the same questions? What are their differences, and why do you think changes occurred in Indian and Chinese thought? Which view most appeals to you, and which belief do you think would lead to the better society? Why?

7. Both the *Arthasastra* and Sun Tzu's *The Art of War* are regarded as practical manuals. What role do considerations of morality and humane conduct play in each? Are morality and humane conduct primarily means to an end, or are they desirable in and of themselves? Why does K'ung Fu-tzu, in *The Analects*, hold that these qualities are of value? What justification does Buddha offer for them in *The Sermon at the Deer Park*? Are *The Classic of Filial Piety* and *Lessons for Women* concerned with real morality or simply socially approved behavior? How can one tell the difference?

8. If humane conduct is the ideal, then war would seem to be the greatest of evils. And yet societies seem to go to war with great ease and considerable enthusiasm. What justifications for war are offered in the *Bhagavad Gita*, *Arthasastra*, and *The Art of War*? Are these legitimate reasons, or are they only rationalizations? To what extent do you think societies develop values and beliefs that justify and legitimize their going to war against others and among themselves? What reasons has the United States advanced for entering its recent conflicts? Do these appear valid to you in retrospect?

9. One of the early concepts the Chinese had about the nature of the universe concerns the balance of *yang*, the principle of action, and *yin*, the principle of passivity. Simply put, a falling rock possesses yang, the ground that it strikes possesses yin. After the two have met, there is a harmonious balance. How is this concept reflected in *The Book of Songs* and the *Tao te ching*? After looking at the *Vedic Hymns*, the *Bhagavad Gita*, and *The Sermon at the Deer Park*, what sort of view do you feel the early Indians had of nature and natural laws? Which view do you think is more valid? How well do yang and yin compare with the modern Western views of energy and matter?

10. *The Analects* implies that yang is the dominant element in human beings, while the *Tao te ching* would claim that, for the enlightened person, yin should dominate. What position do you think Buddha would take on this issue? What are the basic positions of *The Classic of Filial Piety* and *Lessons for Women*? Should humans really be active, making all their own decisions, or should they be predominately passive, fulfilling the obligations placed upon them by tradition and social custom? How many individualists can a society take before it ceases to unite people? What sort of a balance should be struck, and how?

11. Are human beings basically good or basically depraved? This is a question many philosophers have asked. What position does *The Analects* take, and how does it compare with that of the *Arthasastra*? Do the *Bhagavad Gita* and *The Sermon at the Deer Park* agree or differ on this issue? What is the view of *The Book of Songs*? What position would the Han emperors have taken, and why? How is this question related to the kind of traditions and government a society develops? What do you believe, and how do you think this belief affects your attitudes towards other social and economic problems of the day?

12. It may be noted that early Confucianism, particularly the tradition established during the Han dynasty, lacked any real curiosity about the physical world. Compare *The Analects*, *The Classic of Filial Piety*, and *Lessons for Women* in this regard. Does this lack of curiosity spring from the basic approach of K'ung Fu-tzu or from the preoccupations of the scholars of the Han period? What might there have been about the Han period that discouraged philosophical speculation on the nature of the physical world? What is it about modern society that encourages such speculation?

13. The early Indians seem to have had little interest in the writing of history. Review the *Bhagavad Gita* and suggest why this should be. The Chinese, on the other hand, compiled histories from an early date. Review the *Analects* and discuss why this should be true. Would the writing of history have flourished under societies accepting the doctrines of either *The Sermon at the Deer Park* or the *Tao te ching*? Why, or why not? The popularity of history seems to vary from society to society and from time to time. How popular is history in American society today, and what does this tell you about our society and its philosophical values?

14. It has been suggested that one of the attractive aspects of Hinduism is its "majestic" view of the universe and man. To what degree would you con-

sider the teachings of Krishna in the *Bhagavad Gita* to be majestic? What qualities do you find in Krishna's teachings, besides Krishna's "divinity," that are lacking in the teachings of K'ung Fu-tzu in *The Analects*? Does the majesty of a philosophical view diminish the importance of the individual? Which teaching is most appealing to you personally? Why?

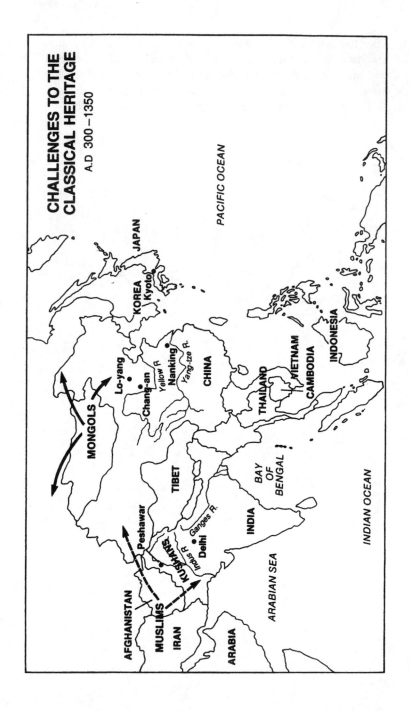

CHALLENGES TO THE CLASSICAL HERITAGE

A.D 300—1350

PACIFIC OCEAN

KOREA
JAPAN
Kyoto

MONGOLS

Lo-yang
Chang-an
Yellow R
Nanking
Yang-tze R.
CHINA

THAILAND
VIETNAM
CAMBODIA
INDONESIA

AFGHANISTAN
Peshawar
MUSLIMS
IRAN
KUSHANS
TIBET
Indus R
Ganges R.
Delhi
INDIA
BAY OF BENGAL

ARABIA
ARABIAN SEA

INDIAN OCEAN

PART II
Expanding Horizons
Challenges to the Classical Heritage: A.D. 300 to 1350

The Han Empire, much like the Roman Empire to the west, succeeded in defining the basic values and patterns of Chinese tradition and in extending that tradition to new territories. The regions south of the Yang-tze River were brought within the Chinese orbit, and Han outposts were established in northern Vietnam and Korea. Han commerce exported textiles to the West along the "silk road" and imported musical and artistic motifs, as well as new crops that increased the food supply. All of these influences were so well harmonized within Han China that Han traditions would constitute the enduring core of Chinese culture, providing the Chinese of later centuries with inspiration, stability, and a sense of national identity. And yet, much like the Later Roman Empire in the West, the Later Han dynasty was in decay, and the central government was incapable of maintaining unity. China split into three kingdoms, and the way was open for invaders.

In 316,[1] a band of Hsiung-nu, as the Huns were called by the Chinese, sacked Loyang, the capital of the kingdom of Wei. North China fell into anarchy, and many Chinese fled to the South, where a successor dynasty had set up its imperial capital at Nanking. China remained divided in this fashion for almost four centuries (316–589), while the southern dynasties wasted their substance in ineffectual attempts to reconquer the North. Thrown into disorder, the Chinese were particularly vulnerable to foreign influences, and the period was distinguished by the defense of traditional culture as well as the adaptation of foreign ideas to Chinese needs. The first tendency is illustrated by the fable *Peach Blossom Spring*, by T'ao Ch'ien (365–427), which is both a glorification of the tenacity of traditional Chinese life and a lament over the present unstable state of affairs. The second tendency is exemplified in the Buddhist text *The Pure Land Sutra*. The most important single foreign influence in China during the period lay in the spread of various forms of Indian Buddhism. One such sect, the Pure Land movement, which promised salvation through a personal savior, held particular appeal for the peasant classes of China, and became the most

---

[1] All dates not designated by the epoch time designation B.C. refer to the period A.D. Unless required for clarification, A.D. will no longer be used throughout the text.

popular form of Buddhism in the land. It is interesting to note that Buddhism was accepted into the Chinese tradition at approximately the same time that it was supplanted in India by the spread of reformed Hinduism.

The power of the traditional cultural forms established in Han times eventually prevailed. Indian Buddhism became a Chinese institution, just as the "barbarian" invaders from the North adopted Chinese speech, Chinese ways, and were absorbed into the Chinese population. Although this did not bring immediate political unity, a new cultural unity and an era of relative peace led to the emergence of a dynamic and confident society. Foreign importations, such as tea, and the refinement of such native inventions as paper, porcelain, and the like were readily accepted as welcome improvements of Chinese material culture and soon became important elements of the Chinese heritage.

The influence exercised by the invaders of India was also beneficial in the long run, but only indirectly. The Kushans entered India from the north about 185 B.C., shortly after the collapse of the Mauryan Empire (322–185 B.C.). They soon controlled Afghanistan and the northern Punjab, and dominated the trade routes uniting China and the West. From their capital at Peshawar, they held the petty states of North India in vassalage. With the collapse of their empire in the early fourth century A.D., the Kushans left behind a political vacuum that the descendants of the Mauryan emperors were quick to fill. The Guptan emperors (320–c. 535) restored unity to North India after a lapse of five centuries and established an opulent court, encouraging surprisingly sophisticated examples of sculpture, architecture, and literature. The Hindu Indian heritage was defined during the Guptan age in much the same way that Chinese tradition had crystallized during the Han era. As has been noted, reformed Hinduism supplanted Buddhism. Sanskrit was revived and refined as a literary language, and blossomed in such works as the plays of Kalidasa, and a great body of romances, fables, and adventures. The selections from *The Perfect Bride* and *The Travels of Sanudasa the Merchant* have been taken from this popular literature, which offers an unusually intimate picture of India during its Classic era.

During the period that followed the disintegration of the Guptan Empire, India again lost political cohesion, but still possessed a cultural and economic vitality that helped spread Indian influence widely. Indianized states soon arose in Burma, Thailand, Cambodia, Malaysia, and throughout western Indonesia. Thus by the sixth century, China and India, although subject to many of the same forces and continually influencing each other, had each developed a distinctive culture and a high degree of civilization. East Asia now had two major cultural centers, and the various peoples of the region began slowly to coalesce into two great blocs, the Indian and Chinese cultural worlds.

The belt of civilizations that lay across the Eurasian continent had been able to beat back the assault of Central Asian horsemen at least partly because of the Iranian development of a new and larger breed of horse. Such horses were capable of carrying heavily armored men who were more than a match for the lightly armed nomadic cavalry. They were expensive, however, and consumed a great deal of grain, and only a few professional warriors could be so equipped. The pendulum began to swing once again toward an aristocratization of society, a tendency that reached its height in the feudal age of Western Europe. In China, such horses had made possible the consolidation of North China under the Wei dynasty (386–535), and later enabled their successors, the Sui (581–618), finally to conquer the South and reunite China after almost four hundred years of division. The great accomplishments made possible by this reunification, however, were reserved for the emperors of the T'ang dynasty (618–907).

The T'ang dynasty addressed itself to the task of centralizing the state and ending the concentration of land and power in the hands of the aristocracy. One of their greatest instruments in the accomplishment of these policies was the creation of an able and loyal class of local administrators who supplanted the authority of the rich land owners and war-chieftains. In order to achieve this end, the emperors revived and greatly elaborated the Han system of examining potential administrators on the basis of their command of the Chinese classics. In this fashion, they secured an effective civil service who efficiently managed the greatly increased wealth of the land and were, by education, committed to the preservation of the traditions of Chinese society. The wealth gathered by imperial tax collectors made military expansion possible, and T'ang armies conquered Tibet, portions of Sinkiang, and Korea, while other, more distant peoples were subjected to Chinese vassalage. Literature and the arts, particularly poetry, flourished, and the selections from the works of Li Po and Tu Fu suggest the high levels of sophistication and personal expression that the artists of the time could achieve. T'ang society was characterized by a sense of tolerance, and the period saw the harmonization of disparate elements within Chinese culture, a process illustrated by the mixture of religious elements in the selection from the Han Shan poems. The T'ang were also receptive to foreign contacts and more than willing to share their culture with others, a trait that led to the birth of Japanese civilization.

Although Chinese influences, including Buddhism, had been slowly penetrating Japan through Korea for many years, under the guidance of Japanese Prince Shotoku (574–622) the process became conscious and rapid. In 587, Shotoku determined to reorganize Japan on the Chinese model, and succeeded to a surprising degree in doing so. He established a new capital, modeled on the T'ang capital of Chang-an, at Nara, and made it a center for the cultivation of Chinese literature, learning, and governmental institutions. The great poetry collection of the *Man'yoshu*, inspired by the *Book of Songs* of Chou China, was compiled there in 759. For various reasons, the capital was eventually moved to

Heian (modern Kyoto), and the ensuing period of Japanese history is known as the Heian period (794–1185). Chinese models were prized and cultivated, but not imitated slavishly, and these foreign influences were slowly modified by the native Japanese heritage. The aristocracy of Heian developed a sophisticated and refined society, well portrayed by the selection entitled *Appraisal of Women on a Rainy Night* (taken from the great novel *The Tale of Genji*, written 1008–1020), but it was a society that was uniquely Japanese. The rarefied culture of the Heian aristocracy owed much to Chinese models, but had clearly maintained a distinctively Japanese pattern of values.

The Heian rulers ignored significant developments outside their capital and court circle. Great estates throughout Japan were consolidated by local rulers and clan leaders, and the taxes gathered from these estates were used to maintain large bands of professional and dedicated warriors known as *samurai*. After numerous challenges to imperial rule, a full-scale civil war broke out, and, in a climactic battle in 1185, imperial power was broken. The victorious leader of the opposition, Yoritomo (1147–1199), declared himself *shogun*, or military ruler of Japan, and established a system of military dictatorship that was to endure, with a few interruptions, until the nineteenth century. The emperor continued to enjoy respect, as is amply illustrated by the selections from *The Confessions of Lady Nijo* (written about 1307), but exercised little real power. Real authority rested with the shogun and was enforced by his vassals and their bands of samurai. Japan had entered a feudal age, which was, nevertheless, perhaps the most peaceful and productive age the country had yet experienced.

On the continent, yet a new force had emerged. Carried from Arabia in the years after 632, the new and evangelistic religion of Islam conquered and converted as it spread. By the eighth century, Muslim sailors had wrested control of the Arabian Sea and Indian Ocean from Indian merchants and isolated India from its cultural and commercial hinterland to the east, thus allowing Southeast Asia and Indonesia to develop their own traditions apart from a permanent Indian presence. Muslim forces seized Sind, on the Indian border with Persia, and, by occupying the Tamir basin in Central Asia, severed the overland route by which China and India had maintained contact over the ages. The arrival of the Gurjara nomads from Central Asia, and their establishment of a dynasty that controlled much of North India (740–1036), provided a power that defended India for a time against further Muslim advances, but also increased Hindu India's virtual isolation. Under such conditions, Indians naturally came to regard the outside world as foreign and hostile, and tended toward greater conservatism. Indian tradition drew in upon itself, influenced more by the enduring values of virtually unchanging village life, and less by the artificial culture of sophisticated and opulent courts. This tendency was reflected to a degree in the growth of popular Hinduism, in which Krishna, portrayed as the awesome warrior companion in the *Bhagavad Gita* is transformed into the playmate of dairymaids in the *Gitagovinda*. Slowly adapting itself to peasant values, Indian culture turned increasingly from the science, tolerance, and innovation of Guptan times to the conservativism and relative passivity of later ages. This tendency, coupled with the lack of any durable tradition of centralized government, rendered India even more vulnerable to further conquest.

The Muslim expansion also had its impact on China. When Muslim forces defeated the T'ang army west of the Pamir Mountains in 751 and took control of extensive areas of western Asia, they dealt the T'ang economy a severe blow. Already financially overextended by conquest, great public works, and courtly extravagance, the T'ang dynasty could not survive the loss of the trade of its western vassal states. Its collapse was internal; provincial commanders seized local control, and the owners of large estates freed themselves from government obligations. Although the process was fitful, by 907 China had again been divided, and the South was in a state of virtual anarchy. The disintegration of T'ang China no doubt contributed to the contemporary divergence of the Japanese from purely Chinese models. Thus the expansion of the Muslims had the dual effect of weakening both India and China, while also allowing the societies surrounding them a greater freedom to develop their own institutions. Forces of division and differentiation were dominant in East Asia by the middle of the tenth century.

It would appear, however, that the tradition of centralized rule and common heritage had become so strong in China that disunity could not persist for long. In any event, after only fifty years, the country was once again unified under the Sung Dynasty (960–1126). In 1069 to 1076, the great reformer Wang An-shih reorganized the government so effectively that a period of unprecedented peace and prosperity followed. Commercial and technological innovations made China the richest, most populous, and most advanced state in the world. Ports were opened to Muslim and Korean merchants, and the loss of the overland silk routes was more than compensated for by a tremendous growth of overseas trade. Art, literature, and scholarship flourished. Han Confucianism, which had always lacked a scientific interest or curiosity about the physical world, was reshaped by a series of Sung philosophers, culminating in Chu Hsi (1130–1200). The selections from his *Reflections of Things at Hand* show the influence of Buddhist and Taoist thought in developing a coherent view of a rational physical universe. Chu Hsi's world view and ethical formulations, the foundations of Neo-Confucianism, were to govern Chinese philosophical and scientific thought until 1912.

With the collapse of the Gujara dynasty, North India was again politically divided and vulnerable, while China was invitingly wealthy. The combination was irresistible, and yet another group of invading peoples appeared out of the

North. Under the leadership of Chinggis Khan (*c.* 1155–1227), Mongol horse-men, wielding deadly bows, swept out of the steppes of Mongolia, swiftly gather-ing defeated tribesmen into their ranks. Pressure from similar attacks had al-ready divided China, but even so, the Mongol conquest took a long time (1222–1279). When it was completed, China had become part of a Mongol empire that stretched from Korea to the plains of Hungary. China nevertheless contin-ued in its customary ways, since its Mongol conquerors soon found that the country was too large and populous, and native traditions too ingrained, to be altered by a small ruling class. Adopting the dynastic name of Yüan (1279–1368), the Mongols gained the hatred of the Chinese for various distasteful innovations, particularly that of importing large numbers of foreigners to assist in the rule of their new possessions. Nevertheless, they remained only a minor force within the wider context of traditional Chinese culture, the progress of which continued almost unimpeded. This is illustrated by selections from *The Dream of the Western Chamber*—a clearly Chinese play, although written under alien rule.

It was not the Mongols, but the Muslims who posed the great challenge for traditional Indian culture. In 1192, a Hindu confederacy was decisively de-feated by the Muslims, leading to the establishment of the Muslim kingdom of Delhi. Muslim conquests continued from this center until virtually all India was under their control. Religiously opposed to polytheists and idol-worshipers, the Muslims were not kind to Hindu Indian culture. Many of the great monuments of the past were destroyed, and Indian culture was constantly subjected to the religious and cultural imperialism of their rulers. India ended this period disor-ganized and exhausted by the grandiose schemes of world conquest pursued by their half-mad ruler Muhammad Tughluk (1325–1351).

The period 300 to 1350 ended with both of the great cultural centers of Asia under the rule of aliens essentially hostile to the native traditions. Only the peripheral states were still free to pursue their own paths of development unim-peded by foreign domination. China, with a unified cultural heritage, was most successful in dealing with the situation. The Chinese cultural tradition contin-ued to develop, enriched by new influences, but relatively unaffected by a numerically inferior ruling class with little sophisticated culture of its own. Nev-ertheless, the growing Chinese hatred for their alien rulers became institu-tionalized in a general contempt for foreigners that was eventually to prove very disadvantageous for China. The experience of alien rule was different in India. Here the ruling class was numerous and unified by Persian culture and the Isla-mic religion. Indian culture survived by retreating to its roots in village life, but, by so doing, lost contact with most of its native political institutions and the heritage of Mauryan and Guptan political unity.

PEACH BLOSSOM SPRING
T'ao Ch'ien

In 316, the Hsiung-nu invaded China and pillaged the Han capital of Loyang. This catastrophe, as shocking to the Chinese as the sack of Rome in 410 was to the Romans, was only the beginning. North China became the scene of incessant warfare between various barbarian bands, and thousands of Chinese fled the devastation to the relative safety of the mountains of Szechuan and the lands south of the Yang-tze River. Here a member of the Chin royal family set himself up as emperor in the city of Nanking ("Southern Capital"). This Eastern Chin dynasty ruled in great luxury, but its corrupt government, arrogant generals, and ineffectual attempts to reconquer the North drained the country of wealth and led to general disorder.

T'ao Ch'ien (365–427) was a scholar administrator in the service of the Eastern Chin emperors, but abandoned his career at the age of thirty-three and devoted himself to poetry praising the joys of the simple rustic life. His little fable, Peach Blossom Spring, is perhaps his most famous work, and has become a standard allusion in Chinese and Japanese literature to an earthly paradise.

There is an ironic undertone to Peach Blossom Spring that requires some historical background to appreciate fully. The inhabitants of Peach Blossom Spring village tell a fisherman, who has stumbled on their long-hidden valley, that they had fled to this secluded spot to escape "the troubles of the age of Ch'in." The Ch'in dynasty (246–206 B.C.) was the creation of a single man, Ch'in Shih-huang, who took the title "First Emperor." He ruled the land with an iron hand, assembled great armies to extend his realms to the north and east, and drafted tens of thousands of peasants to construct what has become known as the "Great Wall of China," as well as to build numerous roads, canals, irrigation ditches, and ornate palaces. Many peasants fled the land to escape these forced labors, and the rest lost any sense of loyalty to the dynasty. Four years after the death of the First Emperor in 410 B.C., the dynasty simply disintegrated, and the First Emperor entered Chinese tradition as the very embodiment of tyranny.

For over seven hundred years, the peasants in Tao Ch'ien's fable had led a secluded and peaceful life in Peach Blossom Spring village. After hearing of the outside world, more particularly of the world of the Chin, the villagers pleaded with the fisherman not to disclose their hiding place, and seem to have taken

From *Anthology of Chinese Literature from Earliest Times to the Fourteenth Century*, ed. Cyril Birch (New York: Grove Press, 1965), pp. 167–68.

great care to ensure that the path to their village would not be discovered again. The parallel between the tyranny of Ch'in and the disorders of the Chin is gentle, but clear. Moreover, the villagers in the fable are the descendants of those who had repudiated the government of the First Emperor, joined the disgruntled aristocracy in rebellion against his successor, and condemned his "ten thousand generation dynasty" to oblivion. T'ao Ch'ien implies that the abused subjects of the Chin emperor could very well do the same. As an added piece of ambiguous irony, one should note that the bearer of the tale of Peach Blossom Spring village is a fisherman. In Chinese tradition, "hidden sages" were men who, distressed by the corruption and decadence of the world in which they lived, would retire to live in anonymity among the rural population. They would often become fishermen, and sometimes offer wisdom or warnings that were obscured by their apparently humble station in life. T'ao Ch'ien leaves it up to the reader to decide whether the fisherman had found his way to a hidden village paradise or was a hidden sage, offering some advice to the local government.

The lasting attraction of *Peach Blossom Spring* lies not so much in its subtle ironic undertone, however, as in its appeal to the yearning that many have felt through the ages for a fulfilling, quiet, and peaceful life. Brigadoon and Shangri-la are popular Western expressions of that same yearning; the hermit Liu Tzu-chi who died searching for Peach Blossom Spring village was only following a dream that many men and women harbor within themselves even today.

Questions

1. How would you characterize the life led by the inhabitants of Peach Blossom Spring village?
2. What sort of people are they?
3. Why do you think the fisherman told the prefect about the village after having been asked not to?

PEACH BLOSSOM SPRING

During the reign-period T'ai yuan [326–397] of the Chin dynasty there lived in Wu-ling a certain fisherman. One day, as he followed the course of a stream, he became unconscious of the distance he had travelled. All at once he came upon a grove of blossoming peach trees which lined either bank for hundreds of paces. No tree of any other kind stood amongst them, but there were fragrant flowers, delicate and lovely to the eye, and the air was filled with drifting peachbloom.

The fisherman, marvelling, passed on to discover where the grove would end. It ended at a spring; and then there came a hill. In the side of the hill was a small opening which seemed to promise a gleam of light. The fisherman left his boat and entered the opening. It was almost too cramped at first to afford him passage; but when he had taken a few dozen steps he emerged into the open light of day. He faced a spread of level land. Imposing buildings stood among rich fields and pleasant ponds all set with mulberry and willow. Linking paths led everywhere, and the fowls and dogs of one farm could be heard from the next. People were coming and going and working in the fields. Both the men and the women dressed in exactly the same manner as people outside; white-haired elders and tufted children alike were cheerful and contented.

Some, noticing the fisherman, started in great surprise and asked him where he had come from. He told them his story. They then invited him to their home, where they set out wine and killed chickens for a feast. When news of his coming spread through the village everyone came in to question him. For their part they told how their forefathers, fleeing from the troubles of the age of Ch'in, had come with their wives and neighbours to this isolated place, never to leave it. From that time on they had been cut off from the outside world. They asked what age was this: they had never even heard of the Han, let alone its successors the Wei and the Chin. The fisherman answered each of their questions in full, and they sighed and wondered at what he had to tell. The rest all invited him to their homes in turn, and in each house food and wine were set before him. It was only after a stay of several days that he took his leave.

"Do not speak of us to the people outside," they said. But when he had regained his boat and was retracing his original route, he marked it at point after point; and on reaching the prefecture he sought audience of the prefect and told him of all these things. The prefect immediately despatched officers to go back with the fisherman. He hunted for the marks he had made, but grew confused and never found the way again.

The learned and virtuous hermit Liu Tzu-chi heard the story and went off elated to find the place. But he had no success, and died at length of a sickness. Since that time there have been no further "seekers of the ford."

FURTHER READINGS

Albert R. Davis provides an excellent biography of T'ao Ch'ien and a compilation of his poetry in *Tao Yuan-ming, His Works and Their Meaning* (New York: Cambridge University Press, 1984). The discovery of the tomb of Chin Shih-huang and its great army of life-size terra-cotta figures is one of the most dramatic Chinese archaeological discoveries of modern times and has been justly celebrated by Arthur Cotterell, *The First Emperor of China: The Greatest*

Archaeological Find of Our Time (New York: Holt, Rinehart and Winston, 1981), and Gary Geddes, *The Terra-Cotta Army* (Toronto: Oberon, 1984). Arthur Cotterell concentrates on the lasting accomplishments of Chin Shih-huang in *The Tiger of Ch'in: The Dramatic Emergence of China as a Nation* (New York: Holt, Rinehart and Winston, 1962), while Li Hsueh-chin provides an overview of life under the short-lived dynasty in *Eastern Zhou and Qin Civilizations*, Early Chinese Civilizations Series (New Haven, CT: Yale University Press, 1985). The legal and administrative system instituted by the dynasty is considered by Anthony F. P. Hulsewe, *Remnants of Ch'in Law: An Annotated Translation of the Ch'in Legal and Administrative Documents of the Third Century* B.C. *Discovered in the Yun-meng Prefecture, Hu-pei Province in 1975* (Leiden, Netherlands: Brill, 1985). A small selection of the poetry of T'ao Ch'ien may be found in Cyril Birch, ed., *Anthology of Chinese Literature from Early Times to the Fourteenth Century*, (New York: Grove Press, 1965).

THE PERFECT BRIDE

Dandin

The Perfect Bride is one of an impressive collection of Sanskrit romances dating from approximately the fifth to the seventh centuries A.D. The action of these tales is set in the time of the great Guptan Empire of India (c. 320–550), an era in which Indian civilization reached great political and cultural heights. It was an age of great prosperity, in which Indian merchants dominated the seas and carried Indian commerce and culture into Southeast Asia, Indonesia, and elsewhere along the littoral of the Indian Ocean. At the same time, Buddhist missionaries carried Indian religion, philosophy, and art overland to the north and east. Culture flourished, and Indian literature and art reached heights that set the standard for centuries to come.

During this period, a great revival occurred in the sacred Sanskrit language. It again became a living and literary language, one in which secular works of great sophistication were composed. Guptan literature was vibrant and dynamic, excelling in such varied forms as the fable, lyric poetry, drama, and romance. In all, however, the emphasis was less on the warrior or king than on the merchant and traveler. The three most popular themes were the pursuit of profit, virtue, and love.

From *Tales of Ancient India*, trans. J. A. B. van Buitenen (Chicago: University of Chicago Press, 1959), pp. 157–60.

The three great writers of narrative prose during the period are generally considered to be Subandhu, Dandin, and Bana, roughly contemporary during the late sixth and early seventh centuries. *The Perfect Bride* is taken from Dandin's *Tales of Ten Princes*, a fascinating collection of sometimes humorous, and often scandalous, stories. These tales are particularly interesting for the relatively realistic view they present of the life of the times. During their adventures, the ten princes encounter a virtual cross-section of Guptan society, including thieves, princesses, prostitutes, and peasants.

The leading characters of *The Perfect Bride* are Saktikumara, the son of a merchant prince, and a young girl who becomes the object of his romantic interest. The story revolves around Saktikumara's desire for a bride who is not only physically attractive, but possesses "all the wifely virtues." He puts the young woman to a difficult test, which she ingeniously passes. Content that he has found a woman possessing all the qualities he desires, he marries her and then, of course, begins to take her for granted. The story ends with Saktikumara, finally won over by his wife's qualities, abandoning his shameful ways and adopting a more virtuous way of life.

Questions

1. What are the virtues Saktikumara seeks in a wife? Do you consider these valid?
2. What do the "markings" that he looks for signify?
3. What qualities does Saktikumara's test seek to discover, and how?
4. On the basis of *The Perfect Bride*, discuss the role of women in medieval Indian society.

THE PERFECT BRIDE

In Tamil Land in a city called Kanci lived the millionaire son of a merchant prince. His name was Saktikumara, and when he was about eighteen years old, he began to worry.

"There is no happiness without a wife," he reflected, "nor with a wife if she is disagreeable. But how to find a wife who has all the wifely virtues?"

Distrusting the purely accidental aspect of marriage with a wife taken at the recommendation of others, he became an astrologer and palmist and, tucking two pounds of unthreshed rice in the hem of his garment, wandered through the land. Everyone who had daughters displayed them before him, saying "Here

is a fortune teller!" But however well marked and suitable the girl was, Saktikumara would ask, "Are you able, my dear, to prepare a complete meal for us
with these two pounds of rice?" Thus, he roamed from house to house, entering
only to be laughed at and thrown out.

One day, in a hamlet on the southern bank of the Kaveri in Sibi country,
an ayah[1] showed him a young girl with but a few jewels, who, together with her
parents, had gone through a large fortune of which only a decrepit house was
left. He stared at her.

"Here is a girl," he thought, "with a perfectly proportioned figure—not
too heavy, not too thin, neither too short nor too tall—with regular features
and a fair complexion. Her toes are pink inside; the soles are marked with
auspicious lines, of barley grain, fish, lotus, and pitcher; her ankles are symmetrical and the feet well rounded and not muscular. The calves are perfectly
curved, and the knees are hardly noticeable, as though they were swallowed by
the sturdy thighs. The loin dimples are precisely parallel and square and shed
lustre upon buttocks round as chariot wheels. Her abdomen is adorned by three
folds and is slender around the deep navel, even a little caved. The broad-based
breasts with proud nipples fill the full region of her chest. Her copper-red fingers, straight and well rounded, with long, smooth, polished nails like glistening
gems, adorn hands which show the happy signs of abundance of grain, wealth,
and sons. Her arms, which start from sloping shoulders and taper to the wrists,
are very delicate. Her slender neck is curved and bent like a seashell. Her lotus-
like face shows unblemished red lips that are rounded in the middle, a lovely and
unabbreviated chin, firm but fully rounded cheeks, dark brows that arch a little
but do not meet, and a nose like a haughty Sesamum blossom. The wide eyes, jet
black, dazzling white, and reddish brown, are radiant and tender and profound
and languidly roving. Her forehead is shapely like the crescent moon, her locks
darkly alluring like a mine of sapphires. The long ears are twice adorned, by
a fading lotus and a playful stalk. Her long, abundant, and fragrant locks
are glossy black, every single hair of them, and do not fade to brown even at
the ends.

"When her figure is so beautiful, her character cannot be different. My
heart goes out to her. However, I shall not marry her before I have tried her: for
those who act without circumspection inevitably reap repentance in abundance."

So he asked with a kindly look, "Would you be able, my dear, to make me
a complete meal with this rice?"

The girl gave her old servant a meaningful glance; whereupon the woman
took the two pounds of rice from him and placed it on the terrace before the
door after sprinkling and scrubbing it thoroughly. Then she washed the girl's

[1]Household servant.

feet. The girl then dried the sweet-smelling rice measure by measure, repeatedly turning it over in the sun, and when it was thoroughly dry, she spread it on a hard, smooth part of the floor, threshed it very, very gently with the edge of a reed-stalk, and finally took all the rice grains out of the husks without breaking them.

Then she said to her ayah: "Mother, jewelers want these husks; they use them to polish jewelry. Sell it to them and, with the pennies they give you, you must buy good hard firewood sticks, neither too dry nor too damp, a small-sized pan, and two shallow bowls."

When the servant had done that, the girl placed the rice grains in a shallow mortar of kakubha wood with a flat, wide bottom and began pounding them with a long, heavy, iron-tipped, smooth-bodied pestle of khadira wood that was slightly recessed in the middle to form a grip. She tired her arms in a charming play of raising and dropping, picking up and picking out single grains, which she then cleaned of chaff and awn in a winnowing basket, washed repeatedly in water, and, after a small offering to the fireplace, dropped in boiling water, five parts water to one part rice.

As the grains softened and started to jump and swelled to the size of a bud, she lowered the fire and, holding the lid on the pot, poured out the scum. Then she plunged her spoon in the rice, turned the grains with the spoon, and, having satisfied herself that they were evenly boiled, turned the pot upside down on its lid to let the rice steam. She poured water over those firesticks which had not burned up entirely, and when the fire had died and the heat was gone, she sent this charcoal to the dealers: "Buy with the coin you receive as much of vegetables, ghee, curds, oil, myrobalan, and tamarinds as you can get."

When this had been done, she added two or three kinds of spices, and once the rice broth was transferred to a new bowl placed on wet sand, she cooled it with gentle strokes of a palmleaf fan, added salt, and scented it with fragrant smoke. Then she ground the myrobalan to a fine lotus-sweet powder, and finally relayed through her servant the invitation to a bath. The old nurse, clean from a bath herself, gave Saktikumara myrobalan and oil, whereupon he bathed. After his bath he sat down on a plank placed on sprinkled and swept stones. He touched the two bowls that were placed on a light, green banana-tree leaf from her own garden—a quarter of one leaf was used—and she set the rice broth before him. He drank it and, feeling happy and content after his journey, let a sweet lassitude pervade his body. Then she served him two spoonsful of rice porridge and added a serving of butter, soup, and condiment. Finally, she served him the remaining boiled rice with curds mixed with mace, cardamon, and cinnamon, and fragrant cool buttermilk and fermented rice gruel. He finished all the rice and side dishes. Then he asked for water. From a new pitcher with water that was scented with the incense of aloe wood, permeated with the fragrance of fresh Bignonia blossoms and perfumed with lotus buds, she poured out an even thin stream. He held his mouth close to the vessel; and while the snow-cold spattering drops bristled and reddened his eyelashes, his ears rejoiced in the tinkling sound of the stream, his cheeks tickled and thrilled at the pleasurable touch, his nostrils opened to the fragrance of the lotus buds, and his sense of taste delighted in the delicious flavor, he drank the water to his heart's content. With a nod of his head he indicated that she stop pouring, and she gave him, from another vessel, fresh water to rinse his mouth. When the old woman had removed the scraps of the meal and had cleaned the stone floor with yellow cowdung, he spread his ragged upper cloth on the ground and took a short nap.

Highly satisfied, he married the girl with proper rites and took her with him. Once he had brought her home, he ignored her and wooed a courtesan; the bride treated even that woman as her dear friend. She waited on her husband as if he were a god, untiringly. She did the household chores without fail and, wonder of tact, won the affection of the servants. Conquered by her virtues, her husband put the entire household in her charge and, depending body and soul on her alone, applied himself to the pursuit of Virtue, Wealth, and Love. Thus, I say, a wife's virtue is a man's happiness.

FURTHER READINGS

A translation of Dandin's major work is available in *The Ten Princes (Dandin's Dasakumaracarita)*, Arthur W. Ryder, trans. (University of Chicago Press, 1927). A. Keith, *A History of Sanskrit Literature* (London: Oxford University Press, 1928) provides a general survey of Sanskrit literature.

Arthur L. Basham, *The Wonder That Was India* (London: Sidgwick & Jackson, 1961) is an excellent introduction to Indian culture before the Muslim invasions. S. K. Maitz, *Gupta Civilization* (Calcutta: Pustak Bhandar, 1974) offers a brief account of various facets of life in the Guptan period. Jeannine Auboyer, *Daily Life in Ancient India from 200* B.C. *to* A.D. *700*, S. W. Taylor, trans. (New York: Macmillan, 1965); Padmini Sendgupta, *Everyday Life in Ancient India* (New York: Oxford University Press, 1950); and Yagyendra Bakadur Singh, *Social Life in Ancient India* (New Delhi: Light and Life, 1981) all deal with various aspects of daily life, including courtship and marriage, in ancient and medieval India.

THE TRAVELS OF SANUDASA THE MERCHANT

The tale of *Sanudasa the Merchant* is drawn from a great collection of Sanskrit romances written down in about the eighth century A.D. Its action, however, dates from a yet earlier age, that of the great Guptan Empire (320–c. 535), a truly golden age of Indian culture and society.

Some time in the third century, for reasons still unknown, the Kushan Empire collapsed. The Kushans, with their capital at Peshawar, had controlled Afghanistan and great stretches of northern India, and had dominated the overland trade routes between China, India, and the Mediterranean. The disappearance of the Kushans left a power vacuum in northern India that was slowly occupied by the rulers of the small state of Lichchhavi, located on the Ganges. Claiming descent from the Guptan rulers of the Mauryan Empire (322–185 B.C.), the founder of this new dynasty took the name Chandragupta I (r. 320–330). Gaining powerful allies by means of an advantageous marriage, Chandragupta began to expand his power to the north and west. By the reign of Chandragupta II (r. c. 380–413), the empire extended across northern India from the mouth of the Ganges to the Arabian Sea.

It is clear that Chandragupta II brought to India a period of unparalleled peace and plenty, but virtually nothing is known of the means by which he accomplished this feat—the Indians of the age showed little interest in writing political or administrative histories. A Chinese Buddhist monk, Fa-hsien, traveled through India during the years 401 to 410 and noted the wealth of its people, the mildness of the administration, and the general air of toleration throughout the realm, but offered little in the way of details. The best evidence of the effectiveness of Guptan rule, however, is its remarkable scientific, literary, and artistic legacy. Indian astronomers, such as Aryabhata (b. 476) and Varahamihira (b. 505), advanced their science to new heights; and Indian mathematicians developed the so-called arabic numerals, decimal notation, and the use of the zero. In literature, such famous and influential works as the animal fables of the Panchitantra, the plays of Kalidasa, and Vatsyayana's *Kama Sutra* date from this period. Although the Muslims, who later occupied much of northern India, destroyed much of Guptan art and architecture, some of the

From "The Travels of Sanudasa the Merchant," from *Tales of Ancient India*, trans. J. A. B. van Buitenen (Chicago: University of Chicago Press, 1959), pp. 227–29, 243–53.

pieces that have survived must be judged as the finest examples of Hindu sculpture and art. All of these accomplishments, both in their magnitude and content, reflect a confident, vibrant, and opulent society.

Much of this opulence was made possible by the energy and adventurous spirit of Guptan merchants and traders. The variety of products within India itself, as well as the overland caravan routes to China and Central Asia, assured Indian merchants of ample opportunities for profit, but the traders of the Guptan era also took to the sea and, often in company with Hindu or Buddhist missionaries, traveled throughout the Indian Ocean. Evidence of the spread of Indian civilization during the Guptan age is found in the Indian-style kingdoms that emerged in Thailand, Cambodia and Vietnam, as well as on the islands of Java, Sumatra, and Borneo in and about the fifth century. Even at the height of this cultural and religious expansion, however, a movement of peoples known as the Huns was pressing on the borders of the Guptan Empire, as well as on the Chinese, Persian, and Roman states. By 647, after a period of poorly documented struggles in which Guptan territories were slowly diminished and Guptan power steadily reduced, the unity of northern India had been broken and the Guptan Empire came to an end. During its golden age, however, it had succeeded in laying the foundations of Classic Indian culture. Much as Westerners look to the Roman Empire, Indians of later ages would look to the Guptan era as the source from which their traditions were derived. Moreover, they would remember it as an age of wealth, romance, and adventure.

The Travels of Sanudasa the Merchant is an example of this tradition. Sanudasa was not a historical figure, but an ideal model. In Western literature, the hero of a quest adventure is usually a warrior or a thief, such as Jason, Ulysses, or Aeneas. In India, he is more often a merchant, such as Sindbad the Sailor or Sanudasa. Within this story, Sanudasa fulfills his destiny by striving for profit, but, as will be seen, the Indian concept of profit encompasses more than simple considerations of economic gain.

Sanudasa was the rich and pampered only son of a famous merchant of the city of Campa. By the time he had reached manhood, and his father had died, his fastidiousness and self-righteousness had made him a burden to his friends and family. His friends conspired to get him drunk and introduce him to the charms of a prostitute of the city. Sanudasa was so captivated by these unfamiliar pleasures that he stayed with the prostitute and quickly squandered his fortune on her. She then threw him out of her house. Returning to his own home, he was informed that it had been sold and that his destitute mother, wife, and child had been forced to move to the pauper's quarter on the outskirts of the city. The story, as told by Sanudasa himself, begins at this point.

Questions

1. What sort of a person is Sanudasa at heart?
2. What does Sanudasa learn in the course of his gold-seeking expedition?
3. What are the special qualities of the hermit?
4. What treasure did Sanudasa gain in his travels?

THE TRAVELS OF SANUDASA THE MERCHANT

Slowly I trod along the road to the village of the poor, and I looked at the dispossessed, wasted by consumption, more dead than alive. Then, under a common nim tree, I saw my little son Dattaka. He was surrounded by a band of children. He was the king and the others his ministers and subjects, and he was sharing with them the little balls of half-ripe barley which he had brought. One of the boys who played the chamberlain snatched the ball that was reserved for the king and swallowed it hungrily. Dattaka, robbed of his single piece, began to scream for his mother. He ran to a little cabin, the front yard of which was littered with rubbish. A fence of straw mats ran around the place, but it was rotten and loose, and the roof let sun and moon in through an infinite number of holes.

I followed Dattaka to the front yard. A servant girl recognized me and went in to tell Mitravati. My mother came out in great confusion and embraced me, even in the state I was in. She held me tight and did not move or even breathe, as though at last she had found rest in a deep sleep. The poor woman who had lost her husband and only today had found her son washed me with her tears which were neither hot nor cold. Then I saw my wife. She was hiding in a corner of the hut and—— But why enlarge on the misery of it all? She was the image of poverty itself.

By rubbing my skin carefully with kodrava grains still in the husk, my mother removed the stuff which that malicious wench at the brothel had smeared on me. A water pitcher had to be borrowed next door to give me a hot bath; it was full of holes patched with lac, the brim was chipped, the neck cracked. The servant who was giving me my bath broke this miserable pitcher in a moment of carelessness, and the woman who owned it beat her breast and screamed wildly. "Ayi, my little pitcher, my princess of a pitcher, now you are gone and the world is empty and my mother dead. Mother got you as a present from her family when she married, and I cry over you as my second mother. . . ."

My heart grew weak with compassion for the woman who was weeping so pitifully; and I cut my cloak in two and gave her one half. Like elephants who drink the water in which they have bathed I ate a soup of kodrava seasoned with rice gruel; but it took effort. Enough! You have heard too much already about life of the poor, and hearing more can only upset a man of your sensibilities.

Somehow I got through a night that lasted a hundred thousand years. An inescapable gloom came over me, and when morning broke, I said to my mother: "I shall return to your house with four times more than I have wasted— or I shall never return. You, mother, you must pass your days as if you had never had a son or as if your son had died, with whatever distraction your misery and your labor can provide."

"Don't go, my child," she begged. "I shall do the meanest kind of work to keep you alive and happy with your wife and son."

"Praised be the life of the talented man who lives on the wretched labor of his old mother! Stop worrying about me, mother. Are you not the wife of a man whose mind was as lofty as the Meru?"

My insistence won out, and I bowed to my mother and departed from that terrible colony of the poor as from the inferno itself. My mother followed me a long way, giving me all kinds of good advice. "Go to Tamralipti, son. My brother Gangadatta lives there, and when a man is in need, his mother's people are his only refuge. An intelligent man leaves his father's relations alone, for they are his born enemies!"

She gave me a bowl full of rice cakes, and with a last word of advice she turned back. I went on and took the road that goes east. On the road I saw a company of travelers from foreign parts. Their umbrellas and sandals were worn, and they carried old leather haversacks and cooking pots slung over the shoulder. They looked exactly as I did; but when they saw me, they said to one another in pitying voices, "Aho, look at the cruel workings of fate! Who would have thought to see the upright Sanudasa in this state? But why should we pity him? He has not lost his fortune yet: for so long as a man of character has not lost his talents, he has lost nothing!"

Sanudasa then underwent a series of adventures—shipwreck, robberies, persecution—always seeking to make his fortune and always failing. Despite offers of help and pleas to return home, he continued his quest. Profit had become more than simply a means of freeing his family from the horrors of poverty; it had become the only means by which Sanudasa felt he could justify his own existence.

One day I met a merchant by the name of Acera who was going to the Gold Countries with a large company of traders. I embarked with him on his ship, and when we had completed part of our journey on sea, we landed, beached our ship, and continued on land down the coast.

When the sun reddened at dusk, we halted in wooded country at the foot of a majestic mountain whose peak pierced the clouds. That night, after we had finished eating and were sitting on our beds of leaves, the caravan leader gave us instructions.

"Merchants, when we are climbing the mountain, tie your rucksacks with provisions tightly to your backs with three windings of rope and hang your leather oil-flasks around your necks. While climbing, use a flexible and sturdy cane stick, not too dry or brittle, and hold it firmly with both your hands. Any fool who uses any other kind of stick is bound to get killed on the mountain. They call this the Cane Trail. It is like the great Lord of Obstacles, and it seeks to frustrate all the efforts of those who are driven by the prospects of gold."

He sounded discouraging; but, devoured by our cupidity, we did as he told us. When one of our party had already climbed a good part of the way, the end of his cane broke; and, like a warrior whose bowstring is cut by a blade, he tumbled and fell to the valley. All the others in our party made it to the summit. We mourned our companion's death and made him a water oblation. We passed the night on the peak.

The next morning we traveled a long way until we found a river full of large rocks that were shaped like cows, horses, goats, and sheep. Acera, at the head of our column, stopped us from going any farther.

"Don't touch the water, don't! Hey, there, stop at once, stop! Any fool who touches this water is changed into stone. Can't you see for yourselves, friends? Now look at the bamboo trees across the river. There is a sharp wind blowing this way which bends the trees all the way across to this bank. Get a firm grip on one of these bamboos with both your hands, but it should not be too brittle, soft, rotten, or dry. When the wind dies down, the bamboos will straighten themselves and swing you, if you are careful enough, to the other bank. But if anybody holds onto the wrong kind of bamboo, he'll fall in the river and be turned into stone. This is the Bamboo Trail, and it is terrifying like the Last Trail itself. But with some agility and luck any one with courage can jump it."

Like the fool who entered the demon's cave at the sorcerer's bidding, we did what he wanted. One of us had got hold of a thin bamboo; it broke and he fell; and, abandoning his petrified body, he went to God's heaven. We climbed down our bamboos and left the river far behind. We made an oblation of water for his soul at another river where we camped.

The next morning when we had covered about five leagues, I saw in front of me an extremely narrow ledge which snaked along the side of a horrifying abyss. The bottom receded from sight in an intense darkness which even the sun was afraid to penetrate. Acera instructed the travelers.

"We must make a smoking fire with damp wood, leaves, and straw. The highlanders will come out when they see the smoke, to sell us their mountain goats which are covered with tiger skins. You have got to buy them, giving saffron, indigo, or sakala-dyed clothes or even sugar, rice, vermilion, salt, or oils in exchange. Mount the goats and carry bamboo poles with you, then ride on to the circuitous ledge, death's crooked eyebrow. . . .

"Now it is possible that on the ledge there will be another party of travelers returning with gold from the gold mines, and we may come face to face with each other halfway. And that means we die in the ravine with our gold or our hopes. The ledge is too narrow for a goat train to pass or to turn. Therefore we need a powerful man who is used to handling a spear and has a butcher's experience to ride at the head of our train. One man like that can kill off an entire row of enemies as long as he is not himself slain by the enemies. This terrible road is known as the Goat Trail. Those who don't mind the fall are sure to meet Bhrgu!"

Acera was interrupted by the arrival of a band of tribesmen, armed with tall bows, who drove a troop of goats ahead of them. When the buying and selling was done, they departed. The travelers bathed and prayed in loud voices to Siva and K'rsna. Thereupon the long train of goats carrying the travelers started along, moving fast enough, yet precisely balanced like a becalmed ship on the high seas. I was the seventh from the rear, and Acera, immediately behind me, the sixth. As we were riding on, we heard in the distance ahead of us the loud clatter of bamboos striking against one another—zing zing!—and the cries of men and beasts—meh meh! and aah aah!—as they fell into the abyss of darkness and mud, terrifying even to a brave man's heart.

A moment later the ranks of the enemy were annihilated save for one man, and in our own ranks the seventh from the rear had suddenly become the first. Our leader prodded me: "Come on, what are you waiting for? There is only one enemy left. Send him to heaven!"

The man opposite me threw his bamboo stick away, folded his hands at his forehead, and, now that his entire caravan had been destroyed and he was left unprotected, sought my protection. "My family is perishing," he cried, "and I am the only one left to continue it. Don't destroy it completely by cutting down the last branch! My parents are blind, and I, their only son, their only love, am the stick to guide them. Brother, don't kill me!"

I thought, "Damn the life that is smeared with the filth of sin, thrice damn the gold that must be won by killing the living. Let the wretch kill me. He clings to life, and his life means sight to the dead eyes of his parents."

Red with rage and pale with despair Acera sneered at me between clenched teeth in a harsh and hissing voice. "Ayi! stupid ass, have you no sense of time? This is not the time to use pity, but to use a sword. Bah, you and your theories: we know all about your pity in practice! Are you going to sacrifice sixteen for the sake of one scoundrel? Kill him and his goat, and at least fourteen lives are saved. If you don't, he and you and the goats and all of us will perish. A man's life is sacred and should not be sacrificed to save one scoundrel! 'One must always protect one's self, with one's wife as well as one's wealth,'" and so on and so forth. He read me a sermon as long as the Bhagavadgita, prompting me to an act of cruelty as Visnu prompted Arjuna. Deeply ashamed, blaming myself for the cruelty of my deed, I struck my enemy's goat very lightly on the legs. And as the animal sank like a ship in the ocean of darkness, the traveler who sailed it drowned with his cupidity. We came away from the perilous road like the survivors from the Bharata wars:[1] our thin ranks annihilated, seven saved their souls but lost their hearts.

We continued our journey through the country until we reached a Ganges. There we offered a handful of water, mixed with our tears, to our dead. Soon our grief, bitter though it was, gave way to our appetite; for man knows no pain like the pain of hunger. We prepared our meal and lay down on a bed of leaves.

When the leader woke us up, our eyes were still heavy from too little sleep. "These goats," he said, "have to be killed. We shall eat the meat; the skins we turn inside out and sew up to form sacks. Then we wrap ourselves in these sacks—no room for squeamishness here, it will only delay us!—in such a way that the bloody inside is turned outside. There are birds here as large as the winged mountains of legend, with beaks wide as caverns. They come here from the Gold Country. They will mistake us for lumps of meat and carry us in their beaks through the sky all the way to the Gold Country. That is what we must do."

I said, "It is true what people say, 'Throw this gold away that cuts your ears!' How could I be so cruel as to kill my goat, this good spirit that has saved me from peril as virtue saves a man from hell? I am done with money and done with living if I have to kill my best friend to save the life he gave me."

Acera said to the travelers, "Everyone kill his own goat. And take Sanudasa's goat out of the way." One of the traders took my goat somewhere and came back with a goatskin hanging from his stick.

"I swapped Sanudasa's goat for another," he said. "Look, I have its skin here." But I recognized it; it was the skin of my own goat. "You did not take it out of the way," I cried, "you *put* it out of the way!"

---

[1] The conflict described in the *Mahabharata*, of which the *Bhagavad Gita* is a part.

Thereupon, taking our leader's word for it, we prepared ourselves for a voyage through the sky, which is more terrible than a voyage by sea because there is no way of escape. Soon all the heavens were filled with huge gray birds thundering ominously like autumn clouds. Under the wind of their wings the heavy tree trunks on the mountains were crushed to the ground as though they were the mountain's wings being cut by the blades of Indra's arrows. Seven birds swooped down and carried the seven of us, each with his heart in his throat, to the sky. One bird was left without its share, and, cheated out of its expectations, it started to tear me violently away from the bird that had got me. This started a gruesome fight between the two vultures, each greedy for its own share, which, like the battle of Jatayus and Ravana, terrified all the inhabitants of heaven. I was torn between the two birds, passing from beak to beak and sometimes rolling over the ground. I prayed to Siva. Their pointed beaks and claws, hard as diamond points, ripped the skin until it was worn like a sieve. I was dragged from the torn skin bag and tumbled into a pond of astonishing beauty.

I rubbed my bloodsmeared body with lotuses and bathed. Next I made a thanksgiving offering to the gods and the fathers, and only then tasted the nectar of the pond. I sank down on the shore and lay until I was rested. My eyes wandered over the woods that had been the scene of prodigious adventures and forgot the anxieties of the battle between the giant birds, forgot them like a man who has escaped from the Hell of the Swordblades to stroll in Paradise. There was not a tree with a withered or faded leaf; not one was burned by lightning and brushfire or empty of bloom and fruit. The blossoms of cadamba, malati and kunda jasmine, and spring creepers were thickly dotted by armies of bees. The ground was covered with a carpet of grass four fingers high, blue-green like Siva's throat, and as soft as rabbit fur. Lions, tigers, peacocks, snakes, and all kinds of game lived peaceably like hermits on nothing but leaves, flowers, water, and wind. My eyes did not tire of looking as I roamed in the woods.

Then I discovered a faint track, a path made by some man's footsteps. Slowly I followed the track, which led me far into the woods to a river with low banks and shallow bed; both bottom and banks were covered with precious stones and gold-dust. I crossed the stream, bathed, and paid homage to the gods and my elders.

Near the riverbank I saw a hermitage surrounded by banana trees where monkeys were crouching quietly. And within the hermitage I saw a great hermit with a matted tuft of hair, golden like a flash of lightning, who was sitting on a sheaf of dwarf kusa grass like the image of the sacrificial fire resting in the womb of a pit, its base and kindling sprinkled with butter oblations.

When I approached to greet him, he was like a rising moon of graciousness, like a winter sun without summer glare. His cheeks were moist with tears of joy as he spoke to me: "A blessing to merchant Sanudasa!"

I thought, "Then it is true that hermits have second sight, for he sees what is hidden to the eyes of the flesh. My name, which could have been anything, and the vocation that governs my action—he has named them before he was told."

While I was thinking, he directed me to a grass cushion, and I sat down slowly for I was embarrassed. But the recluse smiled and said, "It is as you think, my boy. But the mere mention of a name is none too miraculous a feat of austerity. I know everything about you: how Dhruvaka and his friends inveigled you into drinking spirits, how you met the harlot Ganga in the park, and from there on until your escape from the battle of the birds, the very mouth of death, and your arrival here.

"Yes, you have seen ships wrecked and you have explored inaccessible mountains, forests, and rivers. Why have you toiled so tirelessly? Ah, your mother Mitravati will tell you that. You expended all that effort just to find gold. It is within your reach now; don't despair any longer, for where can the gold go? It is easy to find for people with energy and intelligence, for a man of character like you who listens to the counsel of one like me. Stay in my hermitage for a few days; you will sleep in a hut of leaves and eat the fruits of trees."

So I ate forest fare, nutritious, invigorating, and purifying; and it tasted so good that I lost all taste for grown vegetables. And as I slept on the bed of leaves I had made in a hut of foliage, I learned to hate Gangadatta's house with its high-legged couches. Yet, although these simple joys which are outside a common man's experience made me oblivious of my sorrows, I never forgot that my mother was living in a slum. The misfortunes I had suffered so far till my abortive journey through the sky I now regarded as blessings; for misfortune that leads to the discovery of gold is fortune indeed!

One day I saw a celestial chariot arrive from heaven, splendid like Mount Meru; it had come for the sage, the incarnation of his merit. Heavenly maidens alighted, illuminating the forest with their radiance, as flashes of lightning alight from a beloved rainbow-hued cloud. They bowed before the prince of hermits, made a circumambulation to honor him, and returned to heaven like the rays of the moon.

One girl had remained behind. The hermit raised her to his breast, and with his eyes streaming and his voice stammering for joy, he said, "Gandharvadatta my daughter, you must forget me and devote yourself to your father Sanudasa!"

I thought that her meticulous attentiveness was merely mockery, and I felt like a humble attendant of Siva's whom the great White Goddess is amused to greet respectfully. One day I asked her, "Who is he? And who are you?"

"Listen," she said and told their history. "The sage, who is the sitting stone of all hermits, is of the clan of Bharadvaja. He is Bharadvaja of the Aerial

Spirits whose science he has sought to acquire. So powerful were his mortifications that Indra himself was perturbed and worried lest he be thrown off his
mountain throne. Even as he lay in the arms of his wife, Indra could not help
thinking that there was a hermit somewhere. When Narada, the messenger of
the gods, reported that this hermit was Bharadvaja, Visnu summoned Suprabha, the daughter of the king of Gandharvas, the celestial musicians.

"'It is common knowledge in all the worlds,' Visnu said, 'that you surpass
even Urvasi, however vain she may be of her youth, her beauty, and her charms.
Therefore, my lovely girl, go to Bharadvaja and attend to him so that your
beauty and charm be suitably rewarded.'

"Suprabha tried her best to seduce the saint with all the stratagems of
love, with words, glances, and meaningful gestures, but the saint's mind remained fixed on truth. When she failed, even though she spent years, she was so
discouraged that she became his handmaiden. She did all the chores so well,
plucking flowers, fetching water, sweeping the cell, that the sage was pleased
and asked her to choose a boon.

"'Sir,' she said, 'your imperturbability has made a mockery of charms for
which the wives of all thirty-three gods envy me. Beauty, ornaments, garlands,
and ointments are valueless to women unless their value can be measured by
their power to arouse the passions of their men. Therefore I pray you, if you
are pleased to grant me a boon, then may you, the greatest man in the world, be
a man to me! If a young girl's heart is smitten with love, what greater boon is
there than a husband who charms her eyes and heart? Please, although you
hate passion, submit to your mercy and love me so that you may restore my
charm to me!"

"He was agreeable and gave her one daughter; for even a contrary man will
be won in the end by devotion. Suprabha took the girl to the house of her father
Visvavasu, and she reared her there and educated her in the arts and sciences.
Then the king of the Gandharvas took his granddaughter to Bharadvaja and
asked him to give her a name. The name the sage gave her was full of meaning.
'Let her be Gandharvadatta,' he said, 'the Gift of the Gandharva, for you have
given her to me.'

"So a girl was born to Bharadvaja and Suprabha and given the name
Gandharvadatta. And I am this girl," she concluded.

One dark night I happened to notice that the trees on a rocky hillock were
aglow with a golden light. I thought, "This hill must be pure gold ore. That is a
piece of luck to find gold here! It will bring me luck." What sense I had was
caught in the noose of greed, and I completely filled one large hut with rocks.
When Gandharvadatta the next morning saw the rocks, she asked me what they
were, and I told her. She told her father, and he called me.

"This is not gold ore, my boy," he said, "just rock. That golden glow you saw in the darkness comes from the herbs. Sunlight obscures it, but at night it spreads freely. You see nothing but gold, even in rocks: thus a man with a jaundiced eye sees the whole world yellow. At the right time I myself shall arrange for your gold and your return to Campa. It will be soon now. Now free yourself of your confusions!"

It took me a whole day of increasing misery to throw out the rocks which had taken an hour of increasing contentment to bring in.

Then one day the hermit handed me a lute made of tortoise shell and said, "Hear what I am going to say and do as I tell you. The story which Gandharvadatta has told you about me is true; she is indeed my daughter. She is the future bride of the future emperor of Aerial Spirits: the goddess that rose from the ocean could never be any but Visnu's bride. You must take Gandharvadatta to Campa and give her to the emperor. I shall tell you how you can recognize him, and you must plant the signs firmly in your memory. Every six months you will assemble all the Gandharvas, and when they are assembled, Gandharvadatta will chant for them the 'Hymn to Narayana.' If one of the Gandharvas is able to accompany her song on the lute and to chant it himself, you must give him my daughter.

(*"Sire, he predicted exactly what you yourself would do at the meeting of the Gandharvas, everything, including your chanting the hymn and accompanying her on your lute!"*)

The sage continued. "Children, you have been bored for a long time now. To relieve your boredom, start for Campa."

I threw myself at his feet; and my happiness made me so nervous that the whole long night had passed before I fell asleep.

When I woke up, I heard the divine music of two wooden vinas and a flute, enchanting to ear and heart, and, interrupted by the crowing of cocks, the loud benedictions and greetings of heralds which at once dispelled my sleep. Wide awake now, I found myself in a palanquin framed in gold and aglitter with precious stones. It stood on a shining clean stone floor in the center of a pavilion that was thatched with colorful silks which were supported by polished golden tentpoles. Gandharvadatta was sitting in the lap of a blue crystal bench under an awning to bar the sun, and she was playing her vina with great concentration. My pavilion was surrounded by a host of smaller tents in flamboyant colors, and their beautifully dressed proprietors happily moved between the sacks of gold that filled their tents. Merchants were busily buying and selling such costly wares as gold and jewelry, and all around the encampment crowded herds of camels and bullocks. But how could a dumb man describe the spectacle? Impossible! No man has ever seen such wealth in all his dreams.

I asked Gandharvadatta, "What is this miracle? Is it fantasy, is it magic, is it a dream?"

"These are the fruits of Bharadvaja's austerities," she said, "which have become a very Tree of Wishes. For if rightly observed the mortifications of the just have a power that is beyond the imagination. You can spend as you wish, for your wealth has no limit. Spend it on anybody, worthy or worthless, but don't bury it in the ground. Don't worry how to gain; worry how to spend! You can draw forever on Bharadvaja's mountain of gold. And don't worry any more about when you will see your mother. Campa is only ten miles from this caravan camp." She was like wisdom whose soul is Certainty, and as she spoke, all my doubts about magic or dream dissolved instantly.

Then I saw Dhruvaka, the scoundrel. He did not dare to look me in the face, and he hung his head; and so did his friends around him. Getting up from my bed, I hugged him affectionately and gave him my own chair; his embarrassment vanished at once. Grandly he favored his friends with a gracious word or two, an embrace, and a seat, strictly according to seniority.

Soon after, all Campa's people came out dancing behind their dancers and surrounded the caravan. They were uproariously happy, so happy indeed that several of them lost their breath—one found it back in the end, but another died. I showered presents on the crowd: delicacies of food and drink, jewels, robes, garlands, perfumes, and liberal quantities of gold. And especially did I rescue from the hell of poverty those who had had to clean their streets with cowdung when I passed by on my way back from the brothel.

At last I said to Dhruvaka, "Friend, get my mother out of that ghastly slum and bring her to her own house. Give the owner a hundred times as much as he paid when he bought it from my mother. Perish the life of a man who can see his wealthy mother in a poor man's quarters and live!"

Dhruvaka smiled. "Madame poor? Who has seen the Ganges run dry? The house is her own and her wealth as solid as ever. But now that you have returned, she will bloom like a lotus pond in the moonlight."

Day and night passed like an instant, and early the next morning I rode into Campa, as Kubera into Alaka.[2] Preceded by a parade of all the different guilds, I went along the highways and avenues to call upon our glorious king. I prostrated myself before him at a respectful distance, but the king addressed me joyfully and embraced me without dissimulation. When he had honored me with costly gems and robes without end, he said, "Son, now go and see your mother." I filled the insatiable hellhole of royal cupidity with a mass of gold and precious stones that was worth Mount Meru and, surrounded by the king's boon companions and chanting brahmins, returned to my old house. It is a wonder I

[2]The residence of the god of wealth.

was not trampled by the townspeople who with the energy that only rapture can arouse danced wildly in the streets to the soft beat of drums. But when they saw my mother from a distance, carrying in her hand the little bowl with the water of hospitality, the crowd shrank away in confusion. For the masses of commoners are unnerved by the sight of a lady and disperse as darkness disperses before the full moon.

His mother then revealed to Sanudasa that he had been tricked. She had not been destitute and his family had not been forced to live in a slum. It had all been a deception concocted by her, the king of Campa, and all his friends and relations. They had sought to force him to become a man and to seek his fulfillment as a merchant in search of profit. This he had done, and his fame would live forever.

FURTHER READINGS

Long a classic survey, Vincent A. Smith, *The Oxford History of India*, 3rd ed., ed. Mortimer Wheeler, et al. (Oxford, UK: Clarendon, 1958), presents a detailed account, concentrating on political history. Romila Thapar, *A History of India*, Vol. 1 (New York: Penguin, 1966), provides an easily available history of India from the Aryan invasions to the coming of the Mughals in 1576. Hugh Tinker, *South Asia. A Short History* (New York: Praeger, 1966), provides a brief survey that includes not only India, but also Pakistan, Sri Lanka, Burma, and Nepal. Francis Watson, *A Concise History of India* (New York: Scribner's, 1975), is briefer still, but contains some excellent illustrations. A. L. Bashan, *The Wonder That Was India*, 3rd ed. (New York: Taplinger, 1968), is a general account of Indian civilization to the coming of the Mughals. Organized topically, its chapters include State, Society, Everyday Life, Art, Religion, and Language and Literature, as well as a series of appendices on distinct aspects of the Indian heritage such as the calendar, mathematics, and astronomy. Perhaps the classic account of early Indian society, however, is that of Jeannine Auboyer, *Daily Life in Ancient India from 200 B.C. to A.D. 700*, trans. Simon W. Taylor (New York: Macmillan, 1965). Topically organized, it covers a wide range of ancient Indian life. The best available economic history is that of Rajaram N. Saletore, *Early Indian Economic History* (Bombay: Tripathi, 1973). Lucille Schulberg, *Historic India* (New York: Time-Life Books, 1968), provides a richly illustrated work with a readable historical text.

The revival of Sanskrit during the Guptan age forms part of the general survey of A. B. Keith's standard work, *A History of Sanskrit Literature* (Oxford, UK: Oxford University Press, 1928). Guptan literature available in translation includes Kalidasa, *The Cloud Messenger*, trans. Franklin and Eleanor Edgerton (Ann Arbor: University of Michigan Press, 1964); Richard F. Burton, trans.,

The Kama Sutra of Vasyayana (New York: Dutton, 1964), and Arthur W. Ryder, trans., *Panchitantra*, (Chicago: University of Chicago Press, 1956). Fa-hsien's account of his travels in Guptan India may be read in K. A. Giles, trans., *The Travels of Fa-hsien*, (Cambridge, UK: Cambridge University Press, 1923).

THE PURE LAND

The Buddhist attitude towards death is fundamentally conditioned by a belief in reincarnation. In common with the Hindus, the Buddhists believe that, after death, the soul is reborn in another body. The kind of body and station in life into which the individual is reborn depends on the kind of life he or she has led. Those who have led virtuous lives and have attained merit are reborn into such conditions as will allow them to practice even greater virtue and merit them a yet more advanced incarnation. The obverse also holds true; those who lead depraved lives can suffer a series of rebirths, each lower and more wretched than the last. This process is not endless, however. The soul seeks the upward path and, after innumerable incarnations, can reach the position where, through meditation and contemplation, it becomes aware of the universal meaning of things. This state is often called enlightenment, and the individual who achieves it is called Buddha. The Buddha is released from the cycle of death and rebirth, transcends the forms and changes of the material universe, and dwells forever in a timeless, formless, and unchanging state known as *nirvana*.

The doctrine of Buddhism was established by the Indian prince Siddhartha Gautama (563–483 B.C.?), who taught that the path to nirvana was two-fold—personal morality and ascetic meditation. Although Buddhism never displaced Hinduism in India, missionaries took its doctrines to China, Korea, and Japan, where it became a leading pattern of belief. Its teachings became increasingly more complex for various reasons, not the least of which was that as individuals gained enlightenment, they became Buddhas and their teachings and examples were absorbed into the body of belief.

One of the great attractions of Buddhism lay in its promised release, achievable through personal effort, from the sufferings of the human condition. One of the great difficulties of Buddhism, however, lay in the belief that the release it promised could take many lifetimes, and most people were in no position to practice the asceticism, seclusion, and meditation that made enlighten-

From *Buddhist Texts through the Ages*, ed. and trans. Edward Conze, et. al. (New York: Philosophical Library, 1954), pp. 202–206.

ment possible. The mass of the people, leading lives of hardship and often misery, had no hope of imminent release; faith, however strong, brought one no closer to nirvana.

Over a thousand years ago, a branch of Buddhism arose that sought to overcome these difficulties. According to the belief of the Pure Land school of Buddhism, an Indian ascetic named Dharmakara, seeking enlightenment, made forty-eight vows that helped him gain Buddhahood as Amitabha. The eighteenth vow promised that if anyone at the point of death and wishing enlightenment should call on him by name, he would come and lead that person to rebirth in Sukhavati, Amitabha's own Buddha-world, in which the believer would assuredly gain enlightenment and release from the human condition. This belief proved immensely popular, particularly among the common folk of China, and millions called on his name to lead them from the miseries of this world into his Western Paradise, the Pure Land of Sukhavati.

This selection is taken from *The Pure Land Sutra* (*Sukhavativyuha*), the fundamental text of the Pure Land school. It attempts to describe, in sensual terms, the delights of that promised land that is but one sure step towards nirvana.

Questions

1. How are the senses delighted in Sukhavati?
2. Is Sukhavati a purely sensual paradise?
3. How does Sukhavati lead the resident to supreme enlightenment?
4. What does the dweller in Sukhavati need in order to achieve nirvana?

THE PURE LAND

This world Sukhavati, Ananda,[1] which is the world system of the Lord Amitabha, is rich and prosperous, comfortable, fertile, delightful and crowded with many Gods and men. And in this world system, Ananda, there are no hells, no animals, no ghosts, no Asuras[2] and none of the inauspicious places of rebirth. And in this our world no jewels make their appearance like those which exist in the world system Sukhavati.

[1] Favorite disciple of Buddha.
[2] Evil spirits.

And that world system Sukhavati, Ananda, emits many fragrant odours, it is rich in a great variety of flowers and fruits, adorned with jewel trees, which are frequented by flocks of various birds with sweet voices, which the Tathagata's[3] miraculous power has conjured up. And these jewel trees, Ananda, have various colours, many colours, many hundreds of thousands of colours. They are variously composed of the seven precious things, in varying combinations, i.e. of gold, silver, beryl, crystal, coral, red pearls or emerald. Such jewel trees, and clusters of banana trees and rows of palm trees, all made of precious things, grow everywhere in this Buddha-field. On all sides it is surrounded with golden nets, and all round covered with lotus flowers made of all the precious things. Some of the lotus flowers are half a mile in circumference, others up to ten miles. And from each jewel lotus issue thirty-six hundred thousand kotis of rays. And at the end of each ray there issue thirty-six hundred thousand kotis of Buddhas, with golden-coloured bodies, who bear the thirty-two marks of the superman, and who, in all the ten directions, go into countless world systems, and there demonstrate Dharma.[4]

And further, Ananda, in this Buddha-field there are nowhere any mountains—black mountains, jewel mountains, Sumerus, kings of mountains, circular mountains, and great circular mountains. But the Buddha-field is everywhere even, delightful like the palm of the hand, and in all its parts the ground contains a great variety of jewels and gems. . . .

And many kinds of rivers flow along in this world system Sukhavati. There are great rivers there, one mile broad, and up to fifty miles broad and twelve miles deep. And all these rivers flow along calmly, their water is fragrant with manifold agreeable odours, in them there are bunches of flowers to which various jewels adhere, and they resound with various sweet sounds. And the sound which issues from these great rivers is as pleasant as that of a musical instrument, which consists of hundreds of thousands of kotis of parts, and which, skilfully played, emits a heavenly music. It is deep, commanding, distinct, clear, pleasant to the ear, touching the heart, delightful, sweet, pleasant, and one never tires of hearing it, it always agrees with one and one likes to hear it, like the words "Impermanent, peaceful, calm, and not-self." Such is the sound that reaches the ears of those beings.

And, Ananda, both the banks of those great rivers are lined with variously scented jewel trees, and from them bunches of flowers, leaves and branches of all kinds hang down. And if those beings wish to indulge in sports full of heavenly delights on those river-banks, then, after they have stepped into the water, the water in each case rises as high as they wish it to,—up to the

[3] Buddha.
[4] Proper action.

ankles, or the knees, or the hips, or their sides, or their ears. And heavenly
delights arise. Again, if beings wish the water to be cold, for them it becomes
cold; if they wish it to be hot, for them it becomes hot; if they wish it to be hot
and cold, for them it becomes hot and cold, to suit their pleasure. And those
rivers flow along, full of water scented with the finest odours, and covered with
beautiful flowers, resounding with the sounds of many birds, easy to ford, free
from mud, and with golden sand at the bottom. And all the wishes those beings
may think of, they all will be fulfilled, as long as they are rightful.

And as to the pleasant sound which issues from the water (of these rivers),
that reaches all the parts of this Buddha-field. And everyone hears the pleasant
sound he wishes to hear, i.e., he hears of the Buddha, the Dharma,[5] the Sam-
gha,[6] of the (six) perfections, the (ten) stages, the powers, the grounds of self-
confidence, of the special dharmas[7] of a Buddha, of the analytical knowledges,
of emptiness, the signless, and the wishless, of the uneffected, the unborn, of
non-production, non-existence, non-cessation, of calm, quietude and peace, of
the great friendliness, the great compassion, the great sympathetic joy, the great
evenmindedness, of the patient acceptance of things which fail to be produced,
and of the acquisition of the stage where one is consecrated (as a Tathagata).
And, hearing this, one gains the exalted zest and joyfulness, which is associated
with detachment, dispassion, calm, cessation, Dharma, and brings about the
state of mind which leads to the accomplishment of enlightenment. And nowhere in this world-system Sukhavati does one hear of anything unwholesome,
nowhere of the hindrances, nowhere of the states of punishment, the states of
woe and the bad destinies, nowhere of suffering. Even of feelings which are
neither pleasant nor unpleasant one does not hear here, how much less of suffering! And that, Ananda, is the reason why this world-system is called the
"Happy Land" (Sukhavati). But all this describes it only in brief, not in detail.
One aeon might well reach its end while one proclaims the reasons for happiness
in the world-system Sukhavati, and still one could not come to the end of (the
enumeration of) the reasons for happiness.

Moreover, Ananda, all the beings who have been reborn in this world-
system Sukhavati, who are reborn in it, or who will be reborn in it, they will be
exactly like the Paranirmitavasavartin Gods: of the same colour, strength, vigour, height and breadth, dominion, store of merit, and keenness of super-
knowledges; they enjoy the same dresses, ornaments, parks, palaces and pointed
towers, the same kind of forms, sounds, smells, tastes, and touchables, just the
same kinds of enjoyments. And the beings in the world-system Sukhavati do not

[5]Teachings of Buddha.
[6]Community of believers.
[7]Duties.

eat gross food, like soup or raw sugar; but whatever food they may wish for, that they perceive as eaten, and they become gratified in body and mind, without there being any further need to throw the food into the body. And if, after their bodies are gratified, they wish for certain perfumes, then the whole of that Buddha-field becomes scented with just that kind of heavenly perfumes. But if someone does not wish to smell that perfume, then the perception of it does not reach him. In the same way, whatever they may wish for, comes to them, be it musical instruments, banners, flags, etc.; or cloaks of different colours, or ornaments of various kinds. If they wish for a palace of a certain colour, distinguishing marks, construction, height, and width, made of various precious things, adorned with hundreds of thousands of pinnacles, while inside it various heavenly woven materials are spread out, and it is full of couches strewn with beautiful cushions,—then just such a palace appears before them. In those delightful palaces, surrounded and honoured by seven times seven thousand Apsaras,[8] they dwell, play, enjoy, and disport themselves.

. . . And the beings who are touched by the winds, which are pervaded with various perfumes, are filled with a happiness as great as that of a monk who has achieved the cessation of suffering.

And in this Buddha-field one has no conception at all of fire, sun, moon, planets, constellations, stars or blinding darkness, and no conception even of day and night, except (where they are mentioned) in the sayings of the Tathagata. There is nowhere a notion of monks possessing private parks for retreats.

And all the beings who have been born, who are born, who will be born in this Buddha-field, they all are fixed on the right method of salvation, until they have won Nirvana. And why? Because there is here no place for and no conception of the two other groups, i.e., of those who are not fixed at all, and those who are fixed on wrong ways. For this reason also that world-system is called the "Happy Land." . . .

And further again, Ananda, in the ten directions, in each single direction, in Buddha-fields countless like the sands of the river Ganges, Buddhas and Lords countless like the sands of the river Ganges, glorify the name of the Lord Amitabha, the Tathagata, praise him, proclaim his fame, extol his virtue. And why? Because all beings are irreversible from the supreme enlightenment if they hear the name of the Lord Amitabha, and, on hearing it, with one single thought only raise their hearts to him with a resolve connected with serene faith.

And if any beings, Ananda, again and again reverently attend to this Tathagata, if they will plant a large and immeasurable root of good, having raised their hearts to enlightenment, and if they vow to be reborn in that world

[8]Female supernatural beings.

system, then, when the hour of their death approaches, that Tathagata Amitabha, the Arhat,[9] the fully Enlightened One, will stand before them, surrounded by hosts of monks. Then, having seen that Lord, and having died with hearts serene, they will be reborn in just that world-system Sukhavati. And if there are sons or daughters of good family, who may desire to see that Tathagata Amitabha in this very life, they should raise their hearts to the supreme enlightenment, they should direct their thought with extreme resoluteness and perseverance unto this Buddha-field and they should dedicate their store of merit to being reborn therein.

FURTHER READINGS

An excellent account of the life of Buddha, accompanied by superb illustrations, is provided by Jeannine Auboyer, *Buddha. A Pictorial History of His Life and Legacy* (New York: Crossroad, 1983). Edward Conze, *A Short History of Buddhism* (London: Allen & Unwin, 1980), offers a readable account with excellent coverage of the subject in a limited space. The introduction of Buddhism to China is discussed in a scholarly manner by Erik Zurcher, *The Buddhist Conquest of China: The Spread and Adaptation of Buddhism in Early Medieval China*, 2 vols. (Leiden, Netherlands: Brill, 1959). Two excellent surveys of the history of Buddhism in China are Kenneth Ch'en, *Buddhism in China* (Princeton, NJ: Princeton University Press, 1964) and Arthur R. Wright, *Buddhism in Chinese History* (Stanford: Stanford University Press, 1970).

COLD MOUNTAIN POEMS
Han Shan

As the Han Empire declined, Buddhism gained in popularity and slowly spread throughout its realm. The Chinese were not simply passive recipients of Indian practices but adapted many Buddhist beliefs to traditional patterns of Chinese thought. This adaptation was particularly easy because many basic Buddhist concepts were quite similar to those of Taoism, a well-established and popular Chinese religion.

[9]One who has achieved nirvana.

From "Cold Mountain Poems," trans. Gary Snyder, in *Anthology of Chinese Literature*, ed. Cyril Birch (New York: Grove Press, 1965), pp. 194–202.

The origins of Taoism are obscure since its practitioners were hardly interested in writing historical accounts. According to legend, Lao Tzu, a contemporary of K'ung Fu-tzu in the fifth century B.C., was a philosopher who served at
the court of the Chou emperors. Becoming disgusted with the inability of his
countrymen to understand his teachings, he decided to leave. He was stopped
by a border-guard at the western frontier of the empire and was told that he
would have to write down his philosophy before he would be allowed to depart.
Sitting by the roadside, he wrote the five thousand characters that comprise the
Tao te ching (Classic of the Way and of Virtue), one of the two fundamental
scriptures of Taoism. The basic tenet of Taoism is that Nature is the only force in
the universe. Nature is impersonal and unchangeable; the best, and perhaps
only, course of action for the individual is to recognize this and accept it. However, many practices were absorbed into Taoism that, on the surface, may appear
to contradict this teaching. Taoists practiced meditation and controlled breathing as did Buddhist monks, and, like the Buddhists, they believed in enlightenment and a form of Nirvana. Some also practiced alchemy and nature magic,
and were popularly believed to be able to cure disease, control the elements, and
even achieve eternal life.

The poems of Han Shan together with a preface by Liu-ch'iu Yin are
illustrative of that period during the T'ang dynasty (618–907) in which Buddhism and Taoism were still closely connected. Han Shan and his friend Shih-te
are described to Governor Yin as being members of specialized Buddhist sects
(*Manjusri* and *Samantabhadra*). Moreover, their words suggest that Feng-kan,
who had cured Governor Lü-ch'iu, may have belonged to the Pure Land sect.
Through their actions and powers, however, Lü-ch'iu sees them as "men of Tao."
Historically, an important event was occurring. Taoism and Buddhism were
acting on each other to create yet another pattern of belief and practice, Ch'an
Buddhism, which was further refined in Japan as Zen Buddhism, perhaps the
most familiar form of Buddhist practice in the West.

Something of the human concern behind the *Cold Mountain Poems* is
revealed within this context. Han Shan was a Manjusri and also a Taoist hermit,
and the two traditions conflicted in certain areas. The Manjusri sect believed
that the enlightened ones should help others to achieve enlightenment. Taoism, on the other hand, suggests that real truths cannot be revealed with
words—"The Way that can be spoken is not the Way." Han Shan had found a
"way" as a Taoist and wished, as a Manjusri, to teach it. Since he could not
teach his doctrine in words, he was ridiculed as a madman or clown when he
attempted to explain himself. He ended by scattering his poems about the countryside for anyone to read and for those with insight to understand. It was a
device that a modern Zen master might view with approval.

Questions

1. How many different meanings does "Han Shan" have in the selection? What are they?
2. In what ways is Han Shan's residence on Cold Mountain the "good life?"
3. What is there about life on Cold Mountain that leads one to enlightenment?
4. In some poems, Han Shan describes Cold Mountain as pleasant, in others as unpleasant. Why are there these apparent contradictions?

COLD MOUNTAIN POEMS

PREFACE TO THE POEMS OF HAN-SHAN BY LÜ-CH'IU YIN, GOVERNOR OF T'AI PREFECTURE

No one knows just what sort of man Han-shan was. There are old people who knew him: they say he was a poor man, a crazy character. He lived alone seventy li[1] west of the T'ang-hsing district of T'ien-t'ai at a place called Cold Mountain (Han-shan). He often went down to the Kuo-ch'ing Temple. At the temple lived Shih-te, who ran the dining hall. He sometimes saved leftovers for Han-shan, hiding them in a bamboo tube. Han-shan would come and carry it away, walking the long veranda, calling and shouting happily, talking and laughing to himself. Once the monks followed him, caught him, and made fun of him. He stopped, clapped his hands, and laughed greatly—Ha Ha!—for a spell, then left.

He looked like a tramp. His body and face were old and beat. Yet in every word he breathed was a meaning in line with the subtle principles of things, if only you thought of it deeply. Everything he said had a feeling of the Tao in it, profound and arcane secrets. His hat was made of birch bark, his clothes were ragged and worn out, and his shoes were wood. Thus men who have made it hide their tracks: unifying categories and interpenetrating things. On that long veranda calling and singing, in his words of reply—Ha Ha!—the three worlds revolve. Sometimes at the villages and farms he laughed and sang with the cowherds. Sometimes intractable, sometimes agreeable, his nature was happy of itself. But how could a person without wisdom recognize him?

---

[1] A *li* is about one-third of a mile.

I once received a position as a petty official at Tan-ch'iu. The day I was to depart, I had a bad headache. I called a doctor, but he couldn't cure me and it turned worse. Then I met a Buddhist Master named Feng-kan, who said he came from the Kuo-ch'ing Temple of T'ien-t'ai especially to visit me. I asked him to rescue me from my illness. He smiled and said, "The four realms are within the body; sickness comes from illusion. If you want to do away with it, you need pure water." Someone brought water to the Master, who spat it on me. In a moment the disease was rooted out. He then said, "There are miasmas in T'ai prefecture, when you get there take care of yourself." I asked him, "Are there any wise men in your area I could look on as Master?" He replied, "When you see him you don't recognize him, when you recognize him you don't see him. If you want to see him, you can't rely on appearances. Then you can see him. Han-shan is a Manjusri hiding at Kuo-ch'ing. Shih-te is a Samantabhadra. They look like poor fellows and act like madmen. Sometimes they go and sometimes they come. They work in the kitchen of the Kuo-ch'ing dining hall, tending the fire." When he was done talking, he left.

I proceeded on my journey to my job at Tan-ch'iu, not forgetting this affair. I arrived three days later, immediately went to a temple, and questioned an old monk. It seemed the Master had been truthful, so I gave orders to see if T'ang-hsing really contained a Han-shan and Shih-te. The District Magistrate reported to me: "In this district, seventy li west, is a mountain. People used to see a poor man heading from the cliffs to stay awhile at Kuo-ch'ing. At the temple dining hall is a similar man named Shih-te." I made a bow, and went to Kuo-ch'ing. I asked some people around the temple, "There used to be a Master named Feng-kan here. Where is his place? And where can Han-shan and Shih-te be seen?" A monk named Tao-ch'iao spoke up: "Feng-kan the Master lived in back of the library. Nowadays nobody lives there; a tiger often comes and roars. Han-shan and Shih-te are in the kitchen." The monk led me to Feng-kan's yard. Then he opened the gate: all we saw were tiger tracks. I asked the monks Tao-ch'iao and Pao-te, "When Feng-kan was here, what was his job?" The monks said, "He pounded and hulled rice. At night he sang songs to amuse himself." Then we went to the kitchen, before the stoves. Two men were facing the fire, laughing loudly. I made a bow. The two shouted HO! at me. They struck their hands together—Ha Ha!—great laughter. They shouted. Then they said, "Feng-kan—loose-tongued. You don't recognize Amitabha, why be courteous to us?" The monks gathered round, surprise going through them. "Why has a big official bowed to a pair of clowns?" The two men grabbed hands and ran out of the temple. I cried, "Catch them"—but they quickly ran away. Han-shan returned to Cold Mountain. I asked the monks, "Would those two men be willing to settle down at this temple?" I ordered them to find a house, and to ask Han-shan and Shih-te to return and live at the temple.

I returned to my district and had two sets of clean clothes made, got some incense and such, and sent it to the temple—but the two men didn't return. So I had it carried up to Cold Mountain. The packer saw Han-shan, who called in a loud voice, "Thief! Thief!" and retreated into a mountain cave. He shouted, "I tell you, man, strive hard!"—entered the cave and was gone. The cave closed of itself and they weren't able to follow. Shih-te's tracks disappeared completely.

I ordered Tao-ch'iao and the other monks to find out how they had lived, to hunt up the poems written on bamboo, wood, stones, and cliffs—and also to collect those written on the walls of people's houses. There were more than three hundred. On the wall of the Earth-shrine Shih-te had written some short poems, *gatha*. It was all brought together and made into a book.

I hold to the principle of the Buddha-mind. It is fortunate to meet with men of Tao, so I have made this eulogy.

1

The path to Han-shan's place is laughable,
A path, but no sign of cart or horse.
Converging gorges—hard to trace their twists
Jumbled cliffs—unbelievably rugged.
A thousand grasses bend with dew,
A hill of pines hums in the wind.
And now I've lost the shortcut home,
Body asking shadow, how do you keep up?

2

In a tangle of cliffs, I chose a place—
Bird-paths, but no trails for men.
What's beyond the yard?
White clouds clinging to vague rocks.
Now I've lived here—how many years—
Again and again, spring and winter pass.
Go tell families with silverware and cars
"What's the use of all that noise and money?"

3

In the mountains it's cold.
Always been cold, not just this year.

Jagged scarps forever snowed in
Woods in the dark ravines spitting mist.
Grass is still sprouting at the end of June,
Leaves began to fall in early August.
And here am I, high on mountains,
Peering and peering, but I can't even see the sky.

4

I spur my horse through the wrecked town,
The wrecked town sinks my spirit.
High, low, old parapet-walls.
Big, small, the aging tombs.
I waggle my shadow, all alone;
Not even the crack of a shrinking coffin is heard.
I pity all these ordinary bones,
In the books of the Immortals they are nameless.

5

I wanted a good place to settle:
Cold Mountain would be safe.
Light wind in a hidden pine—
Listen close—the sound gets better.
Under it a gray-haired man
Mumbles along reading Huang and Lao.
For ten years I haven't gone back home
I've even forgotten the way by which I came.

6

Men ask the way to Cold Mountain
Cold Mountain: there's no through trail.
In summer, ice doesn't melt
The rising sun blurs in swirling fog.
How did I make it?
My heart's not the same as yours.
If your heart was like mine
You'd get it and be right here.

7

I settled at Cold Mountain long ago,
Already it seems like years and years.
Freely drifting, I prowl the woods and streams
And linger watching things themselves.
Men don't get this far into the mountains,
White clouds gather and billow.
Thin grass does for a mattress,
The blue sky makes a good quilt.
Happy with a stone underhead
Let heaven and earth go about their changes.

8

Clambering up the Cold Mountain path,
The Cold Mountain trail goes on and on;
The long gorge choked with scree and boulders,
The wide creek, the mist-blurred grass.
The moss is slippery, though there's been no rain
The pine sings, but there's no wind.
Who can leap the world's ties
And sit with me among the white clouds?

9

Rough and dark—the Cold Mountain trail,
Sharp cobbles—the icy creek bank.
Yammering, chirping—always birds
Bleak, alone, not even a lone hiker.
Whip, whip—the wind slaps my face
Whirled and tumbled—snow piles on my back.
Morning after morning I don't see the sun
Year after year, not a sign of spring.

10

I have lived at Cold Mountain
These thirty long years.
Yesterday I called on friends and family:

More than half had gone to the Yellow Springs.
Slowly consumed, like fire down a candle;
Forever flowing, like a passing river.
Now, morning, I face my lone shadow:
Suddenly my eyes are bleared with tears.

11

Spring-water in the green creek is clear
Moonlight on Cold Mountain is white
Silent knowledge—the spirit is enlightened of itself
Contemplate the void: this world exceeds stillness.

12

In my first thirty years of life
I roamed hundreds and thousands of miles.
Walked by rivers through deep green grass
Entered cities of boiling red dust.
Tried drugs, but couldn't make Immortal;
Read books and wrote poems down on history.
Today I'm back at Cold Mountain:
I'll sleep by the creek and purify my ears.

13

I can't stand these bird-songs
Now I'll go rest in my straw shack.
The cherry flowers out scarlet
The willow shoots up feathery.
Morning sun drives over blue peaks
Bright clouds wash green ponds.
Who knows that I'm out of the dusty world
Climbing the southern slope of Cold Mountain?

14

Cold Mountain has many hidden wonders,
People who climb here are always getting scared.

When the moon shines, water sparkles clear
When wind blows, grass swishes and rattles.
On the bare plum, flowers of snow
On the dead stump, leaves of mist.
At the touch of rain it all turns fresh and live
At the wrong season you can't ford the creeks.

15

There's a naked bug at Cold Mountain
With a white body and a black head.
His hand holds two book-scrolls,
One the Way and one its Power.
His shack's got no pots or oven,
He goes for a walk with his shirt and pants askew.
But he always carries the sword of wisdom:
He means to cut down senseless craving.

16

Cold Mountain is a house
Without beams or walls.
The six doors left and right are open
The hall is blue sky.
The rooms all vacant and vague
The east wall beats on the west wall
At the center nothing.
Borrowers don't bother me
In the cold I build a little fire
When I'm hungry I boil up some greens.
I've got no use for the kulak[2]
With his big barn and pasture—
He just sets up a prison for himself.
Once in he can't get out.
Think it over—
You know it might happen to you.

[2]Rich peasant.

17

If I hide out at Cold Mountain
Living off mountain plants and berries—
All my lifetime, why worry?
One follows his karma through.
Days and months slip by like water,
Time is like sparks knocked off flint.
Go ahead and let the world change—
I'm happy to sit among these cliffs.

18

Most T'ien-t'ai men
Don't know Han-shan
Don't know his real thought
& call it silly talk.

19

Once at Cold Mountain, troubles cease—
No more tangled, hung-up mind.
I idly scribble poems on the rock-cliff,
Taking whatever comes, like a drifting boat.

20

Some critic tried to put me down—
"Your poems lack the Basic Truth of Tao"
and I recall the old-timers
Who were poor and didn't care.
I have to laugh at him,
He misses the point entirely,
Men like that
Ought to stick to making money.

21

I've lived at Cold Mountain—how many autumns.
Alone, I hum a song—utterly without regret.
Hungry, I eat one grain of Immortal-medicine
Mind solid and sharp; leaning on a stone.

22

On top of Cold Mountain the lone round moon
Lights the whole clear cloudless sky.
Honor this priceless natural treasure
Concealed in five shadows, sunk deep in the flesh.

23

My home was at Cold Mountain from the start,
Rambling among the hills, far from trouble.
Gone, and a million things leave no trace
Loosed, and it flows through the galaxies
A fountain of light, into the very mind—
Not a thing, and yet it appears before me:
Now I know the pearl of the Buddha-nature
Know its use: a boundless perfect sphere.

24

When men see Han-shan
They all say he's crazy
And not much to look at—
Dressed in rags and hides.
They don't get what I say
& I don't talk their language.
All I can say to those I meet:
"Try and make it to Cold Mountain."

FURTHER READINGS

Aspects of the intellectual milieu of Han China are discussed in Michael Lowe, *Chinese Ideas of Life and Death: Faith, Myth, and Reason in the Han Period* (London: Allen & Unwin, 1982). Charles O. Hucker, *China's Imperial Past: An Introduction to Chinese History and Culture* (Stanford: Stanford University Press, 1975) provides a general history of China, stressing cultural and intellectual factors, from the earliest times to 1850. Edward Conze, *A Short History of Buddhism* (London: Allen & Unwin, 1980) is a well-organized and readable general history, while Buddhism in China is discussed in six essays by Arthur F. Wright, *Buddhism in Chinese History* (New York: Atheneum, 1965). The introduction of Buddhism into China is the subject of Erik Zürcher, *The Buddhist Conquest of China: The Spread and Adaptation of Buddhism in Early Medieval China* (Leiden,

Netherlands: Brill, 1959), while its progress under the T'ang dynasty is discussed in Stanley Weinstein, *Buddhism under the T'ang* (Cambridge, UK: Cambridge University Press, 1987). The *Tao te ching*, sometimes called the *Lao Tzu*, is available in numerous translations, while general evaluations of Taoism are presented by Liu Da, *The Tao and Chinese Civilization* (New York: Schocken Books, 1979) and Holmes Welch, *Taoism: The Parting of the Way* (Boston: Beacon Press, 1966). Taoism as practiced in Modern Taiwan is the subject of Michael R. Saso, *Taoism and the Rite of Cosmic Renewal* (Pullman, WA: Washington State University Press, 1972). Heinrich Dumoulin, *The History of Zen Buddhism*, trans. Paul Peachy (New York: Pantheon, 1963) is a standard history of the sect. The origins of Ch'an Buddhism are studied in John R. McRae, *The Northern School and the Foundation of Ch'an Buddhism* (Honolulu: University of Hawaii Press, 1987), and three eighth-century Zen texts are provided by J. C. Cleary, trans., *Zen Dawn: Early Zen Texts from Tung Huang*, (New York: Random House, 1986).

THE POETRY OF LI PO AND TU FU

Rising from the struggles accompanying the disintegration of the Sui Empire (A.D. 581–617), the T'ang dynasty (618–907) established the greatest empire of its day and ushered in one of the most brilliant periods of Chinese history. T'ang power extended from Siberia to Southeast Asia and from the Caspian Sea to Korea. Politically and culturally, T'ang China became the model for all of eastern Asia. Turks, Persians, Koreans, Japanese, and others traveled to China to profit from the example of T'ang civilization. Painting, music, and dance prospered under the influence of peace and imperial patronage. Religious and philosophical thought flourished in a general atmosphere of tolerance. The state employed Confucian learning, many of the emperors were Taoists, and Buddhism spread widely among the people. Each made its own contribution to the cultural and social achievements of the period.

It was also a golden age for Chinese poetry in terms of both quality and quantity. No less than forty-eight thousand poems by some twenty-two hundred authors have been preserved from the period. Most of these poets came from the

From *Sunflower Splendor: Three Thousand Years of Chinese Poetry*, ed. Wu-Chi Liu and Irving Yuching Lo (Garden City, NY: Anchor, 1975), pp. 104–106, 109–10, 112, 118–21, 127, 129–30, 134–36.

scholar class, and many served as government officials. In fact, the Literary Examination, the most prestigious of the civil service examinations, required the composition of a poem in a set verse form. Thus, literary training was essential to political advancement, and men often obtained high posts on the strength of their poetic ability.

This flowering of poetry reached its height in the reign of Hsuan-tsun (712–770) with the works of Li Po (701–763) and Tu Fu (712–770), generally regarded as the greatest and most beloved of Chinese poets. The two had much in common. They both were court officials, knew and respected each other, and both had suffered hardship during the An Lushan rebellion of 755–763. Although for different reasons, neither was ever much of a political success.

Li Po was a romantic figure around whom a rich body of legends arose. He possessed a boundless vitality, a sensitivity to beauty, and a reckless nature that often led him to personal disasters and humiliations. A swordsman, heavy drinker, and patron of prostitutes, he displayed an arrogant disregard for rules. Once, when summoned to court, he sent a message to the emperor that he was with the god of wine and could not be bothered to leave his tavern. He was a noted wanderer, and many of his journeys were the result of his exile from court for one reason or another. On one occasion, he forced the chief imperial eunuch, an influential and corrupt official, to remove his dirty shoes for him, and suffered ten years' exile as a consequence.

Educated in both the Confucian and Taoist classics, he possessed a fondness for nature and the mountains, often retreating into the wilderness to compose poems that reflected his Taoist background. There is almost no subject on which Li Po did not write. He is believed to have composed some twenty thousand poems, of which some eighteen hundred have survived. Most celebrate the fairyland wonder of nature and of life. A legend relates that, when traveling by boat in 762, he drank himself into a stupor. Rousing, he saw the reflection of the moon in the water and attempted to embrace it, drowning himself as a result. The tale is unlikely, but it is part of Li Po's enduring image.

Tu Fu also composed poems in praise of friendship and wine, but is most admired for his social conscience and compassion. He was a frequent traveler, and some of his most impassioned poems describe the troubles of the times and the sufferings of the common people. He presents his experiences and observations with emotion and candor. It is his humaneness and concern for others that most endear him to the Chinese people.

Born into a distinguished literary family, Tu Fu received an education in the Confucian classics that lent him a sense of duty and responsibility often reflected in his poetry. He never abandoned his desire to serve in political capacities, although his attempts at the administrative life were generally unsuccessful. He had difficulty passing the civil service examination and, having passed, refused the police position he was offered. He spent time as a captive of the An Lushan rebels, but escaped to join the new emperor's government-in-exile. Here he took an unpopular position in defending a military official and was exiled for his display of honesty. He served briefly in a provincial government post, but spent most of his later years in retirement. It was during this period that he composed more than half of the fourteen hundred fifty poems that have survived.

The poems that follow are but a few examples of the works of China's two greatest poets: Li Po, the free spirit with a monumental love of life, and Tu Fu, who infused his work with personal insight and emotion unequaled in Chinese literature.

Questions

1. Chinese poetry is usually didactic or a means of self-expression. How do the poems of Li Po and Tu Fu conform to this observation? Is either more concerned with didacticism than the other? What about self-expression?
2. Tu Fu not only valued Li Po's friendship but greatly admired his work. After reading both, what was there in Li Po's work that Tu Fu esteemed so highly?
3. Taoism and Buddhism provided much inspiration for T'ang poetry. Is their influence apparent in the works of Li Po and Tu Fu? If so, in what manner?

THE POETRY OF LI PO (701–763)

THOUGHTS WHILE STUDYING AT HANLIN ACADEMY SENT TO MY COLLEAGUES AT THE CHI-HSIEN ACADEMY

At dawn I hasten toward the Purple Hall,
At dusk I await edicts from the Golden Gate.
I read book after book, scattering rare manuscripts all around.
I study antiquity to search for the ultimate essence,
Whenever I feel I understand a word,
I close my book and suddenly smile.
Black flies too easily defile the pure,
A lofty tune like "White Snow" finds few echoes.

By nature carefree and unrestrained,
I've often been rebuked for eccentricity.
When the cloudy sky becomes clear and bright,
I long for visits to woods and hills.
Sometimes when the cool breezes rise,
I'll lean on the railings and whistle aloud.
Yen Kuang[1] angled in his T'ung-lu Creek,
And Hsieh K'e[2] climbed his Ling-hai Peak.
When I finish my task in this world,
I shall follow them and try my fishhook.

(*Trans. Joseph J. Lee*)

THE ROAD TO SHU IS HARD

Alas! behold! how steep! how high!
The road to Shu is hard, harder than climbing to the heavens.
The two kings Ts'an-ts'ung and Yu-fu[3]
Opened up this land in the dim past;
Forty-eight thousand years since that time,
Sealed off from the frontier region of Ch'in!
The Great White Peak blocks the west approach, a bird track,
Just wide enough to be laid across the top of Mount Omei.
Earth tottered, mountain crumbled, brave men perished,[4]
And then came stone hanging-bridges, sky-ascending ladder
    interlocked.
Above, on the highest point, the Six-Dragon Peak curls around
    the sun;

---

[1](37 B.C.–A.D. 43), friend and adviser to Liu Hsiu, who later became Emperor Kuang-wu of Eastern Han (r. A.D. 25–58).

[2]The Poet Hsieh Ling-yun (A.D. 385–433).

[3]Shu, the ancient name for Szechwan, was said to be ruled at one time by five brothers, the eldest being Ts'an-ts'ung and the third being Yu-fu. Having no language, the people lived in peace and had no contact with Ch'in until 311 B.C.

[4]According to legend, a king of Ch'in promised five young women in marriage to the ruler of Shu, who sent five brave men to meet and escort the young women. On the way, they encountered a huge snake; and while they were fighting off the snake, mountains crumbled and all the party met death. The five women were transformed into five mountain peaks.

Below, the gushing, churning torrents turn rivers around.
White geese[5] cannot fly across,
And gibbons in despair give up climbing.
How the Mud Mountain twists and turns!
Nine bends within a hundred steps, zigzagging up the cliffside
To where one can touch the stars, breathless!
Beating my breast, I heave a long sigh and sit down.

May I ask if you expect to return, traveling so far west?
Terrifying road, inaccessible mountain peaks lie ahead,
Where one sees only dismal birds howling in ancient woods
Where the female and the male fly around and around.
One also hears cuckoos crying beneath the moon at night,
Grief overfills the empty mountain.
The road to Shu is hard, harder than climbing to the heavens;
Just hearing these words turns one's cheeks pale.

Peak upon peak less than a foot from the sky,
Where withered pines hang inverted from sheer cliffs,
Where cataracts and roaring torrents make noisy clamor,
Dashing upon rocks, a thunderclap from ten thousand glens.
An impregnable place like this—
I sigh and ask why should anyone come here from far away?

There the Dagger Peak stands erect and sharp:
With one man guarding the pass,
Ten thousand people can't advance.
Should those on guard prove untrustworthy,
They could have turned into leopards and wolves.
Mornings, one runs away from fierce tigers;
Evenings, one runs away from long snakes—
They gnash their fangs, suck human blood,
And maul people down like hemp.
The Brocade City might be a place for pleasure,
But it's far better to hurry home.
The road to Shu is hard, harder than climbing to the heavens.
Sideways I look westward and heave a long sigh.

(Trans. Irving Y. Lo)

[5]Reading ku (snow-white goose) for ho (crane).

DRINKING ALONE BENEATH THE MOON, TWO SELECTIONS

1

A pot of wine among the flowers:
I drink alone, no kith or kin near.
I raise my cup to invite the moon to join me;
It and my shadow make a party of three.
Alas, the moon is unconcerned about drinking,
And my shadow merely follows me around.
Briefly I cavort with the moon and my shadow:
Pleasure must be sought while it is spring.
I sing and the moon goes back and forth,
I dance and my shadow falls at random.
While sober we seek pleasure in fellowship;
When drunk we go each our own way.
Then let us pledge a friendship without human ties
And meet again at the far end of the Milky Way.

2

If Heaven weren't fond of wine
Wine Star would not be found in Heaven.[6]
If Earth weren't fond of wine
There could be no Wine Spring[7] on earth.
Since Heaven and Earth are fond of wine,
In Heaven being fond of wine can't be judged wrong.
Clear wine, I've heard, is compared to sages,
Also the unstrained wine spoken of as worthies.[8]
Since I've drunk both sages and worthies
Why must I seek out the immortals?
Three cups penetrate the Great Truth;

---

[6] According to the chapter on astronomy in *Tsin Shu* (*History of Tsin Dynasty*), written by the T'ang mathematician Li Shun-feng (seventh century), the "Wine Pennant Star" (*chiu-ch'i hsing*) was the name of three stars situated south and at the right corner of Hsuan-yuan, or Leo; it was also the pennant of wine officials.

[7] Name of a town in Kansu since Han times, known for its underground spring with the taste of wine.

[8] "Sages" and "worthies" were slang expressions referring respectively to strained and unstrained wine used in a time of prohibition in T'ang times.

One gallon accords with Nature's laws.
Simply find pleasure in wine:
Speak not of it to the sober ones.

                              (Trans. Irving Y. Lo)

WRITTEN IN BEHALF OF MY WIFE

To cleave a running stream with a sword,
The water will never be severed.
My thoughts that follow you in your wanderings
Are as interminable as the stream.
Since we parted, the grass before our gate
In the autumn lane has turned green in spring.
I sweep it away but it grows back,
Densely it covers your footprints.
The singing phoenixes were happy together;
Startled, the male and the female each flies away.
On which mountaintop have the drifting clouds stayed?
Once gone, they never are seen to return.
From a merchant traveling to Ta-lou,
I learn you are there at Autumn Cove.
In the Liang Garden[9] I sleep in an empty embroidered bed;
On the Yang Terrace you dream of the drifting rain. [10]
Three times my family has produced a prime minister;
Then moved to west Ch'in since our decline.
We still have our old flutes and songs,
Their sad notes heard everywhere by neighbors.
When the music rises to the purple clouds,
I cry for the absence of my beloved.
I am like a peach tree at the bottom of a well,
For whom will the blossoms smile?
You are like the moon high in the sky,
Unwilling to cast your light on me.
I cannot recognize myself when I look in the mirror,

[9] A region in southeastern Honan.
[10] Yang Terrace refers to the general area on the Yangtze. The line alludes not only to Li Po's whereabouts, but also to Sung Yu's "Shen-nu Fu."

I must have grown thin since you left home.
If only I could own the fabled parrot
To tell you of the feelings in my heart!

(Trans. Joseph J. Lee)

THE POETRY OF TU FU (712–770)

FRONTIER SONGS, FIRST SERIES, THREE SELECTIONS

1

Sad, sad they leave their old village,
Far, far they go to the Chiao River.
Officials have an appointed time of arrival,
To flee from orders is to run afoul of capture.
The ruler is already rich in lands,
Expanding the frontier brings no gain!
Abandoned forever is the love of father, mother,
Sobbing, they march away with spears on their backs.

(Trans. Ronald C. Miao)

2

Sharpen the sword in the Sobbing Waters,[11]
The water reddens, the blade wounds my hand.
How much I want to hush the sound of anguish;
Too long entangled are the strands of my heart!
When a man of courage promises life to his country,
Then what is there to regret and lament?
Deeds of fame live on in the Unicorn Pavilion,
Bones of soldiers will quickly decay.

(Trans. Irving Y. Lo)

---

[11] Wu-yen Shui is also the name of a river in Sui-te, Shensi, where, according to legend, the eldest son of the First Emperor of Ch'in, Fu-su, was sent and murdered under instructions of Chao Kao, who forged the emperor's edict; hence the sobbing sounds of the river keep on lamenting the heir apparent's fate.

3

If you draw a bow, draw the strongest,
If you use an arrow, use the longest:
To shoot a man, first shoot his horse,
To capture rebels, first capture their chief.
In killing men, also, there are limits,
And each state has its own borders.
So long as invasion can be curbed,
What's the use of much killing?

(*Trans. Ronald C. Miao*)

CH'IANG VILLAGE, TWO SELECTIONS

1

From the jagged edges of purple clouds to the west,
The sun sets its foot on level plain.
Above wicket gate sparrows start chattering,
As I return home from a thousand-*li* journey.
My wife and children, amazed at my being alive,
Wipe their tears when they get over their surprise.
In these troubled times I have drifted thither and yond;
Returning home alive is but an accident.
Neighbors are all over the garden wall;
They sigh and sob uncontrollably.
As night draws on, I call for candles;
Then we look at each other as if in a dream.

2

Flocks of chicken clucking from every corner,
They fight each other as visitors arrive.
After I have chased the chickens up the tree,
I could hear the knocks at the wicket gate.
Elders of the village, four or five,
Come to ask me about my long journey.
Each carrying something in his hand,
They pour out jugs of good and poor wine.

"Hope you won't mind if the wine tastes too weak:
No one has been able to attend to farming.
And since we're still in the midst of battles,
All our children have gone to the eastern front."
Then I ask to sing for the elders a song;
In these hard times, I'm deeply moved by their affection.
Singing done, I look up to the heavens and sigh,
And tears stream down the cheeks of all who sit around.

(*Trans. Irving Y. Lo*)

MEANDERING RIVER,[12] TWO POEMS

1

A single petal swirling diminishes the spring.
Ten thousand dots adrift in the wind, they sadden me.
Shouldn't I then gaze at flowers about to fall before my eyes?
Never disdain the hurtful wine that passes through my lips.
In a small pavilion by the river nest the kingfisher birds;
Close by a high tomb in the royal park lie stone unicorns.
This, a single law of nature: seek pleasure while there's time.
Who needs drifting fame to entangle this body?

2

Returning from court day after day, I pawn my spring clothes;
Every time I come home drunk from the riverbank.
Wine debts are common affairs wherever I go;
Life at seventy is rare since time began.
Deep among the flowers, butterflies press their way;
The slow-winged dragonflies dot the water.
I'd whisper to the wind and light: "Together let's tarry;
We shall enjoy the moment, and never contrary be."

(*Trans. Irving Y. Lo*)

---

[12]This is the Ch'u-chiang, "meandering river," located in the southeast corner of Ch'ang-an. Tu Fu wrote the poem while serving briefly in the new government.

FAREWELL OF AN OLD MAN

"No peace or quiet in the countryside,
Even in old age I find no rest.
My sons and grandsons lost in war,
What's the use of staying home to save my skin?"
He throws away his cane and strides out the gate;
Tears come to his old comrades-in-arms.

"I'm lucky. I still have my own teeth
Though I regret the marrow dried in my bones.
Now that I'm a soldier properly clad in armor,
I'll make a long bow to bid farewell to the magistrate.

"My dear old woman lies crying by the road,
It's late winter; her clothes are thin.
Who can be sure this won't be our final farewell—
I cannot stop worrying over her suffering in the fierce cold.
I do not expect to return from this march,
Yet her gentle urging to eat well stays with me.

"The walls at T'u-men have been fortified;
The ferry at Hsing-yuan will thwart the foe.
Conditions are different from our defeat at Yeh;
Even if I must die, there is still some time left.
Life has its partings and reunions,
Why fuss about your age; everyone must die.
But when I think back on the days of my youth
I can't help pausing—and sighing.

"The whole empire is a military camp;
Beacon fires have spread to each ridge and peak.
Corpses in piles foul fields and woods,
Blood reddens streams and plains.
If I knew where Heaven was
I wouldn't linger on this earth longer.
To leave for good this humble cottage and home
Will crush a man."

(Trans. Michael E. Workman)

RANDOM PLEASURES: NINE QUATRAINS

1

See a traveler in sorrow; deeper is his grief
As wanton spring steals into the river pavilion—
True, the flowers will rush to open,
Yet how the orioles will keep up their songs.

2

Those peach and plum trees planted by hand are not without
   a master:
The rude wall is low; still it's my home.
But 'tis just like the spring wind, that master bully:
Last night it blew so many blossomed branches down.

3

How well they know my study's low and small—
The swallows from the riverside find reason to visit me often:
Carrying mud to spot and spoil my lute and books,
And trailing a flight of gnats that strike my face.

4

March is gone, and April's come:
Old fellow, how many more chances to welcome the spring?
Don't think of the endless affairs beyond the hereafter;
Just drain your lifetime's few allotted cups.

5

Heartbroken—there springtime river trickles to its end:
Cane in hand, I slowly pace and stand on fragrant bank.
How impertinent the willow catkins to run off with the wind;
So fickle, the peach blossoms to drift with the stream!

6

I've grown so indolent I never leave the village;
At dusk I shout to the boy to shut the rustic gate.
Green moss, raw wine, calm in the grove;
Blue water, spring breeze, dusk on the land.

7

Path-strewn catkins spread out a white carpet;
Stream-dotting lotus leaves mound up green coins.
By the bamboo roots, a young pheasant unseen;
On the sandbank, ducklings by their mother, asleep.

8

West of my house, young mulberry leaves are ready for picking;
Along the river, new wheat, so tender and soft.
How much more is left of life when spring has turned to summer?
Don't pass up good wine, sweeter than honey.

9

The willows by the gate are slender and graceful
Like the waist of a girl at fifteen.
Morning came, and who could fail to see
Mad wind had snapped the longest branch.

(Trans. Irving Y. Lo)

FURTHER READINGS

Charles O. Hucker, *China's Imperial Past: An Introduction to Chinese History and Culture* (Stanford: Stanford University Press, 1975), provides a general history of China from the earliest times to 1850, stressing cultural and intellectual developments. Charles P. Fitzgerald, *The Empress Wu*, 2nd ed. (London: Cresset, 1968), is a biographical study of one of the most famous figures of the T'ang period. Edward H. Schafer, *The Vermillion Bird: T'ang Images of the South* (Berkeley: University of California Press, 1967), offers an interesting study of the influence of T'ang culture. Howard Wechsler, *Offerings of Jade and Silk: Ritual and Symbol in the Legitimation of the T'ang Dynasty* (New Haven, CT: Yale

University Press, 1985), offers another perceptive examination of the T'ang period.

The expansion of Buddhism during the T'ang period is the subject of Stanley Weinsten, *Buddhism Under the T'ang* (Cambridge, UK: Cambridge University Press, 1987). Kenneth Ch'en, *Buddhism in China* (Princeton, NJ: Princeton University Press, 1964), and Arthur R. Wright, *Buddhism in Chinese History* (Stanford: Stanford University Press, 1970), provide helpful surveys of the history of Buddhism in China.

Stephen Owen, *The Great Age of Chinese Poetry: The High T'ang* (New Haven, CT: Yale University Press, 1980), includes an excellent treatment of the works of both Li Po and Tu Fu, as does Francois Cheng, *Chinese Poetic Writing*, trans. Donald A. Riggs and Jerome P. Seaton (Bloomington, IN: Indiana University Press, 1983). Sidney S. K. Fung and S. T. Lai, *25 T'ang Poets: Index to English Translations* (Seattle: University of Washington Press, 1984), provides valuable bibliographic information. Wu-Chi Liu and Irving Yuching Lo, eds., *Sunflower Splendor: Three Thousand Years of Chinese Poetry* (Garden City, NY: Anchor Press, 1975), contains a large sampling of works by Li Po and Tu Fu. Soame Jenyns, trans., *Selections from the Three Hundred Poems of the T'ang Dynasty*, (London: John Murray, 1952), is a translation from a famous and widely read collection of T'ang poetry.

Works are available dealing specifically with Li Po and Tu Fu. A. R. Davis, *Tu Fu* (New York: Twayne, 1971), offers an invaluable biographical sketch followed by a critical discussion of his poetry. William Hung, *Tu Fu: China's Greatest Poet* (New York: Russell & Russell, 1969), provides an excellent picture of the subject. David Hawkes, *A Little Primer of Tu Fu* (Oxford: Clarendon, 1967), examines some of the poems by Tu Fu contained in the Chinese anthology, *Three Hundred T'ang Poems*. Fewer studies are concerned with Li Po. Arthur Waley, *The Poetry and Career of Li Po* (London: Allen & Unwin, 1950), is a short and rather unsympathetic biography. Obata Shigiyoski, *The Works of Li Po the Poet* (New York: Dutton, 1922), is old but useful. A perceptive analysis of Li Po's poetry may be found in Eiling O. Eide, "On Li Po," in *Perspectives on the T'ang*, ed. Arthur F. Wright and Denis Twitchett (New Haven, CT: Yale University Press, 1973).

MAN'YOSHU

A COLLECTION OF TEN THOUSAND LEAVES

Japan experienced one of its most vigorous eras of cultural development during the century from 686 to 784. It was at this time that the Japanese established their first permanent capital at Nara and began solidifying their government with an elaborate bureaucracy and formal administrative structures. Along with these institutional developments came remarkable achievements in art, religion, architecture, and literature.

Much of this political and cultural flowering sprang from the interplay between native Japanese traditions and imported elements. Chinese concepts of government, architecture, law, taxation, writing, and calendars, as well as Chinese moral and religious ideas embodied in Buddhism and Confucianism, were welcomed in Japan. Although the influence of the mainland was important in the development of Nara Japan, it did not eclipse native traditions. Many of the accomplishments of the period display a growing pride in things uniquely Japanese. In part due to its geographical separation from the mainland, Japan was able to maintain a distinctive character, including its own language, its traditional Shinto religion, and a characteristically Japanese society and state.

Nara Japan witnessed the first great flowering of Japanese literature. Japan's oldest literary works, the traditional histories *Kojiki* and *Nihon Shoki*, both written in Chinese script, date from this period. Even more notable, however, are the two great collections of poetry, the *Man'yoshu* (*Collection of Ten Thousand Leaves*, compiled in 759) and the *Kaifuso* (compiled in 751). The first was written in Chinese characters that transliterated spoken Japanese, while the second was essentially Chinese poetry written by Japanese. It is not surprising that the poems composed by the Japanese in their own language possess a superior literary merit and have enjoyed a greater lasting popularity.

Just as the Chinese literary tradition began to blossom a millennium earlier with the *Book of Songs*, so Japanese poetry flowered with the great collection of songs, ballads, and verse contained in the *Man'yoshu*. Consisting of some forty-five hundred works dating from about the mid-seventh to the mid-eighth

From *An Introduction to Japanese Court Poetry*, ed. Earl Miner (Stanford: Stanford University Press, 1968), pp. 40–44, 46–49, 51–52, 73–77.

century, the *Man'yoshu* includes poems by people of various classes, including peasants and artisans, as well as emperors and aristocrats. The subjects of these poems are as varied as their authors and provide a mirror of early Japanese life and thought; descriptions as far-ranging as aristocratic life at court and military life in lonely outposts are included. Numerous poems about the landscape, the seasons, moonlight, hills, birds, and clouds display the appreciation of nature that has remained an enduring element in Japanese literature, art, and life. Folk songs, songs in praise of rice wine, longer poems with legendary themes, and poems of life and love all contribute to the rich variety of the *Man'yoshu.*

Japanese poetry is not based on rhyme, meter, or stress, as is Western poetry, but on the number of syllables that comprise the poem and the pattern in which these syllables are arranged. Although some long poems (called *choka*) possess a considerable sustained power, the most common type of poem in the *Man'yoshu* is the *tanka.* This is a poem of thirty-one syllables arranged in five lines with a pattern of 5–7–5–7–7 syllables. The tanka remained the dominant verse form in Japan for the next five centuries.

The following selections are by two of the greatest of the poets represented in the *Man'yoshu*, Kakinamoto Hitomaro (flourished *c.* 680–700) and Otomo Yakamochi (716–785). Much about Hitomaro's life is obscure. He was an aristocrat of middle rank who was frequently dispatched to the provinces on court business. He wrote about himself and those close to him, as well as about those at court and in the provinces. Although most of his surviving work consists of tanka, he is best known for his masterful longer poems such as "On Seeing the Body of a Man Lying among the Stones on the Island of Samine in Sanuki Province," which describes the result of a storm on Japan's Inland Sea, and "On the Lying-in-state of Prince Takechi," written in 696. His works demonstrate his considerable love of the land and its people, both great and humble. Otomo Yakamochi was probably one of the compilers of the *Man'yoshu.* He was a wellbred individual who possessed broad experience in life and literature. The Otomo clan had occupied a prominent position at court for centuries, but, by the eighth century, its influence had declined. Yakamochi, through the brilliance of his poetry, restored prestige to the family name. The *Man'yoshu* contains some five hundred of his poems, which deal mainly with love. His ability to reflect inwardly in his works is a characteristic that makes his poetry particularly appealing to the modern reader.

By the time of Hitomaro and Yakamochi, Japanese poets had demonstrated that they were quite capable of producing a poetic tradition based on their own unique culture. The *Man'yoshu* ushered in the first great age of Japanese poetry and laid the foundations for much of what was to follow.

Questions

1. The theme of separation is common among the works of the *Man'yoshu*. How does this theme appear in the works of Hitomaro and Yakamochi? Does this emphasis on separation suggest anything about social and cultural conditions in early Japan?

2. What topics do you find in these poems that reflect an appreciation of nature? What in the Japanese cultural heritage might account for this high regard for nature?

3. Loyalty and responsibility are recurring themes in Japanese poetry. How does "On the Lying-in-state of Prince Takechi" deal with these themes? What are Hitomaro's views on loyalty? On responsibility?

MAN'YOSHU

ON THE LYING-IN-STATE OF PRINCE TAKECHI

To think of it
Fills my soul with a holy fear,
    And to speak of it
Makes my voice quiver with dread:
    Our sovereign Lord
Who ruled over all the land in peace,
    Who with royal wisdom
In a manner befitting his godliness,
    Appointed in the past
The site for his august palace,
    Lofty as the heavens,
Upon the divine plain of Makami
    In the land of Asuka,
Vanishing within its rock-bound walls—
    Yes, that very sovereign
Once crossed the pine-clad crest of Fuwa
    Far off to the north
In the vast domain beneath his sway,
    Vouchsafing to descend
Upon the hill-ringed plain of Wazami—
    Ringed like a Korean sword.

For a time he set his palace in the fields,
    Where, with divine intent
To bring stability to the world
    And order to his realm,
He summoned to his imperial side
    Bold warriors from the East,
Where the speech of men sounds as strange
    As the crowing of cocks,
And saying, "Let the belligerence
      of the people
    Now be pacified,
And let the rebelliousness of the provinces
    Swiftly be put down,"
He bestowed command over all his men
    Upon our noble Prince,
To carry out the royal will.

    So it was our Prince
Quickly buckled to his waist
    His great long sword,
Seized his war bow in his hand,
    And with fierce battle cry
Urged on the valiant fighting men.
    Through his serried ranks
The booming of the war drums echoed
    Like crashing thunder;
To the enemies' affrighted ears
    The awful music
Of battle horns blown with fierce resolve
    Seemed like the roaring
Of tigers as they spring upon their prey;
    Their stoutest men
Trembled in terror at the alarm.
    Fluttering in the wind,
The banners that our Prince had raised
    Looked like the hungry flames
Of the fires they kindle on all the fields
    In the early spring
To burn away the grasses withered
    By the winter's cold.
His warriors aimed their great war bows:

A myriad bowstrings
All released as one upon the air
    Was frightful to the ears;
The sound was like a violent whirlwind
    Rushing through the trees
Of some forest in the grip of winter,
    Whose savage blizzards
Fill all the air with blinding snow—
    Yes, like a great blizzard
Came the swirling cloud of arrows
    That burst upon them,
Driven like snow before the wind.
    The armies clashed,
For even the enemies of our Prince,
    Rebels that they were,
Knowing they must perish like dew or frost
    Fading beneath the sun,
Took courage in their desperation,
    Each striving to be first
Like birds that vie upon the wing—
    When, lo, from Itsuki,
From the Great Shrine in holy Watarai,
    A divine wind sprang up,
Blowing confusion upon the enemy,
    Bearing heavenly clouds
To blacken the sacred sun's bright form,
    Covering the earth
With an impenetrable darkness:
    Thus did our great Prince
Bring peace to this rice-abounding land,
    And while a very goddess
Reigned in splendor from her throne,
    He graciously undertook
To govern the earth on her behalf.

So the land prospered,
Like flowers of the mulberry tree,
    And all men thought
It would flourish for a thousand ages,
    When suddenly
The palace of our noble Prince
    Became a shrine

Entombing his divine remains.
   Now the courtiers
Who waited on our Lord in life
   Were robed in hempen white,
Yes, clothed in the white hemp of
     mourning,
   And day by day
Beneath the madder-colored sun
   They crept about,
Falling to the ground like stricken deer
   Upon the fields
Before his palace gate at Haniyasu,
   And when the night
Grew to darkness like a head of jet,
   They crawled away,
Bowing in grief to the ground like quails
   And glancing back
Toward the great palace of their Lord.
   Though they would serve him,
He was no longer theirs to serve;
   They could only raise
Weak-throated cries like birds in spring.
   And before their grief
Had even begun to pass away,
   Before their longing
Had lost its first shocked anguish,
   He was borne away
In holy procession across the fields
   Of Kudara, whose very name
Sounds remote as the speech of
     far Cathay;
   He was laid to rest
Forever in the sacred shrine
   Of lofty Kinoe,
Pure as cloth of the whitest hemp,
   A veritable god
Enshrined forever in those sacred halls.
   But though our Prince,
Our royal master, is taken from us,
   There still remains
On the Holy Hill of Kagu his
     great palace

That he erected,
Intending that it should endure
    Ten thousand ages—
Yes, though ten thousand ages pass away
    It will endure,
And we shall gaze up at its eminence
    As to the heavens,
In longing for our royal master
Though holy dread may fill our hearts.

Envoys

Although our Lord
Now reigns in splendor from his shrine
    As a god on high,
Our yearning for him knows no changing
With the passing of the days and months.

Just as the waters
Pent up by walls in Haniyasu Pool
    Do not know where to flow,
So now the courtiers of the Prince
Are trapped with no direction to their lives.

                            Hitomaro, II: 199–201

ON PASSING THE RUINED CAPITAL OF ŌMI

It was Mount Unebi,
Fair as a maiden gird with lovely scarf,
    Where from the first age
Of our sun-sovereigns there rose up
    Kashihara Palace;
And there each of our divinities
    Ruled in a line unbroken
Like a column of many evergreens,
    Beginning their sway
Of this nation under the heavens
    In Yamato province,
Which adds its brightness to the sky.
What purpose was there

To leave it, to cross the hills of Nara,
  Rich in colored earth,
To establish a new capital in a land
  Beyond the horizon,
To choose a palace site off in the country?
  But it was in Ōmi province,
Where the water rushes over rocks,
  In Sasanami
At this lofty Ōtsu palace,
  Where our ruler
Began his rule over all our nation;
  Here beneath the heavens
Yes, here it was our sovereign lord
  Made his imperial court.

Though men relate how at this site
  There rose a palace,
Though they insist high halls
    stood here,
  Now wild grasses grow
In a springtime of profusion
  And haze-streamers float
Across the mild spring sun, misting over
  The ruins of a palace
Built on foundations multi-walled,
And just to look upon it makes me sad.

  Envoys

  The Cape of Kara
At Shiga in Sasanami still remains
  As it ever was,
But though it waits throughout the ages,
The courtiers' pleasure boats will
    not return.

  Although the waters
Off the Shiga coast in Sasanami
  Stand still and wait,
Never again can they hope to greet
The men now vanished in the past.

                    Hitomaro, I: 29–31

ON SEEING THE BODY OF A MAN LYING AMONG THE STONES
ON THE ISLAND OF SAMINE IN SANUKI PROVINCE

O the precious land of Sanuki,
Resting where the seaweed glows
    like gems!
  Perhaps for its precious nature
I never tire in my gazing on it,
  Perhaps for its holy name
It is the most divine of sights.
  It will flourish and endure
Together with the heavens and earth,
  With the shining sun and moon,
For through successive ages it has
    come down
  That the landface is the face of a god.

Having rushed our ship upon the breakers
  From the port of Naka,
We came rowing steadily until the wind
  That rises with the tides
Stormed down from the dwelling of
    the clouds—
  Looking back upon the open sea
I saw waves gather in their mounting
    surges,
  And looking off beyond the prow
I saw the white waves dashing on
    the surf.

  In awe of the terrible sea,
Where whales are hunted down as prey,
  We clutched the steering oar,
Straining the plunging ship upon its
    course;
  And though here and there
We saw the scattered island coasts
  To dash upon for safety,
We sought haven on rugged Samine,
  The isle so beautiful in name.
Erecting a little shelter, we looked about,
  And then we saw you:

Pillowed upon your shaking beach,
  Using those wave-beaten rocks
As if the coasts were spread out for
    your bedding;
  On such a rugged place
You have laid yourself to rest.
  If I but knew your home,
I would go tell them where you sleep;
  If your wife but knew this place,
She would come here searching for you,
  But knowing nothing of the way—
The way straight as a jeweled spear—
  How must she be waiting,
How anxiously now longing for you,
She so dear who was your wife.

  Envoys

  If your wife were here,
She would be out gathering your food,
  She would pick the greens
From the hill slopes of Samine—
But is there season not now past?

  So you rest your head,
Pillowed on the rocky spread-out bedding
  Of this rugged shore,
While the furious, wind-driven surf
Pounds ever in from off the sea.

Hitomaro, II: 220–22

ON PARTING FROM HIS WIFE AS HE SETS OUT FROM IWAMI FOR THE CAPITAL

  It was by the sea of Iwami
When the clinging ivy creeps across
    the rocks,
  By the waters off Cape Kara,
A land remote as the speech of far
    Cathay—

Yes, there where the seaweed grows,
Clinging to rocks fathoms beneath the
    waves,
And where on the stony strand
The seaweed glows like polished gems.
    My young wife dwells there,
Who like seaweed bent to the
    current of love,
The girl who slept beside me
Soft and lithesome as the gem-like
    water plants.
Now those nights seem few
When we held each other close in sleep.

We parted unwillingly,
Clinging to each other like ivy creepers;
    My heart ached and swelled
Against the ribs that would hold it,
And when my yearning drew me
To pause, look back, and see her
    once again
Waving her sleeves in farewell,
They were already taken from my sight,
    Hidden by the leaves
Falling like a curtain in their yellow whirl
    At the crest of Mount Watari,
A crest like a wave's that bears a
    ship away.

Although I longed for her—
As for the voyaging moon when it glides
    Into a rift of clouds
That swallow it up on Mount
    Yakami, where,
    They say, men retire with their wives—
I took my lonely way, watching the sun
    Coursing through the sky
Till it sank behind the mountains.

Though I always thought
Myself a man with a warrior's heart,

I found that my sleeves—
Wide as they were, like our bedclothes—
Were all soaked through with tears.

Envoys
My gray-white horse
Has carried me at so swift a pace
  That I have left behind
The place where my beloved dwells
Beneath the cloudland of the distant sky.

O you yellow leaves
That whirl upon the autumn slopes—
  If only for a moment
Do not whirl down in such confusion,
That I may see where my beloved dwells.

                Hitomaro, II: 135–37

LAMENT

  Since that ancient time
When the heavens and earth began,
  It has been decreed
That of the eighty noble clans
  Each living man
Shall follow obediently the commands
  Of our great Sovereign.
So I, an official of the court,
  Heard with veneration
The sacred words of our great
    Sovereign;
  And now I live,
Governing this distant province
  Here in the wilds,
Cut off from home by hills and streams.
  Since my coming here
You and I have had but winds and clouds
  To bear our messages;

And as days have piled on days and still
   We have not met again,
I have longed to see you more and more,
   And sighed with yearning.

Straight as a jeweled spear
   Was the road he came on,
The traveler who has brought these
      tidings:
   He reports that you,
My amiable and noble friend,
   Are struck in grief
And lately spend your days in mourning.
   <u>Truly the span of life</u>
<u>Is filled with sorrow and suffering</u>:
   The very flowers open
Only to wither and fall with time,
   <u>And we living men</u>
<u>Are creatures of a like impermanence.</u>
   Surely it must be
That even your most noble mother,
   At whose breasts you fed,
Must like others have a fatal hour.
   And now this news:
That in the full bloom of her
      womanhood,
   When one might still gaze
Upon her beauty with such rare delight
   As on a polished mirror,
Cherishing her like a string of jewels,
   Even she has faded away,
Vanished like the rising mists,
   Like dew upon the grass;
That she lay listless as the gem-like
      seaweed
   Bending to the tide;
That like a running stream she ebbed
      away
   And could not be held back.
Can this be some fantastic tale I hear?

Is not the message false,
Merely a rumor of a passing traveler?
   Though from afar—
Like the warning of bowstrings twanged
   By palace guards at night—
I hear this news, my grief is fresh,
   And I cannot keep
The tears from flowing down my cheeks
Like rivulets from a sudden shower.

Envoys

This news I hear,
That you, my friend, are plunged in grief,
   Comes from afar,
But still I must raise my voice in weeping:
Your distant sorrow weighs upon my heart.

You know as I
The nature of this illusory world,
   How nothing stays—
Endeavor to be brave and stalwart,
Do not wear out that heart in grief.

        Yakamochi, XIX: 4214–16

THREE SPRING POEMS

   Across spring fields
The haze drifts along in banners
   Pleasing to the heart,
And in the dusk a warbler
Sings out amid the crimson light.

   From my garden
Where bamboo stands in little clusters,
   Faintly comes the sound
Of the leaves that rustle darkly
In the breeze of this spring dusk.

> The lark flies up
> Into a sky glowing with the light
>   Of a fair spring day,
> And I alone stand here to feel it
> Bring such gladness to the heart.

Yakamochi, XIX: 4290–92

FURTHER READINGS

The Kodansha Encyclopedia of Japan (Tokyo: Kodansha, 1983) is a major resource. John W. Hall, *Japan from Prehistory to Modern Times* (New York: Delacorte, 1970), presents a general history focusing particularly on institutional development. Two useful introductions to Japan are W. Scott Morton, *Japan: Its History and Culture* (New York: Crowell, 1970), and Ian Nish, *A Short History of Japan* (New York: Praeger, 1968). H. Paul Varley, *Japanese Culture* (New York: Praeger, 1973), provides a particularly helpful survey of the subject and includes religion, theater, literature, and the visual arts. George Sansom, *A History of Japan to 1334* (London: Cresset, 1958), examines social and political aspects of Japanese history from the earliest times and contains a brief but useful introduction to the *Man'yoshu*. Two surveys of the archaeology of early Japan are J. Edward Kidder, *Japan Before Buddhism* (New York: Praeger, 1966), and his *Early Buddhist Japan* (New York: Praeger, 1972).

Harold Wright, trans., *Ten Thousand Leaves: Love Poems from the Man'yoshu* (Woodstock, NY: Overlook, 1986) provides an attractively illustrated collection of love poems from the *Man'yoshu*. Robert H. Brower and Earl Miner, *Japanese Court Poetry* (Stanford: Stanford University Press, 1961), is an exhaustive examination of Japanese court poetry, and includes translations of over three hundred poems. Donald Keene, ed., *Anthology of Japanese Literature* (London: Allen & Unwin, 1955), offers translations of a number of selections from the *Man'yoshu*. Miyamori Asataro, trans., *Masterpieces of Japanese Poetry, Ancient and Modern*, 2 Vols. (Westport, CT: Greenwood, 1970), contains translations of a number of poems from the *Man'yoshu* in Volume 1 along with helpful background material on a number of the poets. Daisaku Ikeda, *On the Japanese Classics*, Burton Watson, trans. (New York: Weatherhill, 1974), is an examination of four early Japanese literary classics, including the *Man'yoshu*.

APPRAISAL OF WOMEN ON A RAINY NIGHT

The Tale of Genji

Lady Murasaki Shikibu

Medieval Japan reached its cultural zenith with the flowering of Heian society between 794 and 1185. During this period, Murasaki Shikibu, a lady-in-waiting to the empress, wrote the classic love story *The Tale of Genji*. Her work received immediate acclaim and today ranks as the unquestioned masterpiece of Japanese literature. The world's first novel, as well as one of its longest, *The Tale of Genji* was unique in both its style and content. Earlier Japanese authors had confined their efforts to tales of no great length featuring fairies and other fantastic elements. Lady Murasaki, by contrast, drew upon her personal experiences at the imperial court in the capital city of Kyoto to paint a vivid portrait of contemporary court life.

The literature describing the elegant and refined society of the Heian court was produced almost exclusively by women. Writing in Japanese, rather than the Chinese cultivated by the men, women of this circle produced an enormous collection of letters, diaries, poems, and, following the example of Lady Murasaki, novels. These described in intimate detail the values, tastes, and pastimes of a tiny portion of the Japanese population, living virtually in a world of their own. Isolated in great degree from the rest of society, the inhabitants of this world cultivated rarified standards of cultural appreciation and social grace.

Fascinated by beauty, color, and ceremony, and untroubled by mundane concerns, they devoted themselves to the leisurely pursuit of elegant pleasures and romance. Thus it is not surprising to find the genteel love affair to be the dominant theme of Heian literature in general, and of *The Tale of Genji* in particular. Although the tale encompasses four generations of Genji's relations, its focus is on his many romances. Prince Genji was the handsome young son of an emperor and was the paragon of Heian gentility; he possessed all the virtues most valued in a lover: beauty and grace, talent and sensitivity. His social position afforded Genji the choice of any of the young ladies attending his father's court, but they served merely as the backdrop for his continual pursuit of an elusive ideal woman.

The following selection, the famous *Appraisal of Women on a Rainy Night*, has been regarded as the key to the organization of the entire novel. The

From Lady Murasaki, *The Tale of Genji*, trans. Arthur Waley (Boston: Houghton Mifflin, 1936), pp. 21–37.

action takes place on a stormy evening at the estate of Genji's wife. Here Genji and his brother-in-law, To no Chujo, are talking of their past romances and women in general. They are soon joined by two other young men, Hidari no Uma no Kami and To Shikibu no Jo, and the friends begin a lengthy discussion of the different types of women they have known and the merits of each. These types foreshadow the various women with whom Genji will become involved, sometimes with tragic consequences, as the novel progresses. Within itself, however, the passage could be an analogy of the court life of Heian Japan. Although the storm rages outside, within there is comfort, urbane conversation, mutual deference, and a general agreement as to the attributes of the perfect woman.

The refinement of the Heian age did not last, and the artificial world of the court soon vanished. Within a few years, the Heian gentlemen of Kyoto found themselves attacked by bands of armed Buddhist monks. Unable to defend themselves, they called in warrior clans to protect them. However, the warriors quickly supplanted the gentlemen, civil war broke out between the clans, and a turbulent and brutal period of Japanese history had begun.

Questions

1. What kind of woman would Genji consider ideal? Does his concept change during the course of the conversation?

2. What virtues do the four gentlemen consider to be the most admirable in a woman?

3. What methods of courtship are described? What is the primary purpose of courtship?

4. What function does poetry play in the text? How effectively does it fulfill that function?

APPRAISAL OF WOMEN ON A RAINY NIGHT

Genji the Shining One. . . . He knew that the bearer of such a name could not escape much scrutiny and jealous censure and that his lightest dallyings would be proclaimed to posterity. Fearing then lest he should appear to after ages as a mere good-for-nothing and trifler, and knowing that (so accursed is the blabbing of gossips' tongues) his most secret acts might come to light, he was obliged always to act with great prudence and to preserve at least the outward appearance of respectability. Thus nothing really romantic ever happened to him and Katano no Shosho[1] would have scoffed at his story.

While he was still a Captain of the Guard and was spending most of his time at the Palace, his infrequent visits to the Great Hall[2] were taken as a sign that some secret passion had made its imprint on his heart. But in reality the frivolous, commonplace, straight-ahead amours of his companions did not in the least interest him, and it was a curious trait in his character that when on rare occasions, despite all resistance, love did gain a hold upon him, it was always in the most improbable and hopeless entanglement that he became involved.

It was the season of the long rains. For many days there had not been a fine moment and the Court was keeping a strict fast. The people at the Great Hall were becoming very impatient of Genji's long residence at the Palace, but the young lords, who were Court pages, liked waiting upon Genji better than upon anyone else, always managing to put out his clothes and decorations in some marvelous new way. Among these brothers his greatest friend was the Equerry, To no Chujo, with whom above all other companions of his playtime he found himself familiar and at ease. This lord too found the house which his father-in-law, the Minister of the Right, had been at pains to build for him, somewhat oppressive, while at his father's house he, like Genji, found the splendour somewhat dazzling, so that he ended by becoming Genji's constant companion at Court. They shared both studies and play and were inseparable companions on every sort of occasion, so that soon all formalities were dispensed with between them and the inmost secrets of their hearts freely exchanged.

It was on a night when the rain never ceased its dismal downpour. There were not many people about in the palace and Genji's rooms seemed even quieter than usual. He was sitting by the lamp, looking at various books and papers. Suddenly he began pulling some letters out of the drawers of a desk which stood near by. This aroused To no Chujo's curiosity. 'Some of them I can show to you' said Genji 'but there are others which I had rather . . .' 'It is just those which I want to see. Ordinary, commonplace letters are very much alike and I do not suppose that yours differ much from mine. What I want to see are passionate letters written in moments of resentment, letters hinting consent, letters written at dusk . . .'

He begged so eagerly that Genji let him examine the drawers. It was not indeed likely that he had put any very important or secret documents in the ordinary desk; he would have hidden them away much further from sight. So he felt sure that the letters in these drawers would be nothing to worry about. After

[1] The hero of a lost popular romance.
[2] His father-in-law's house, where his wife Princess Aoi still continued to live.

turning over a few of them, 'What an astonishing variety!' To no Chujo exclaimed and began guessing at the writers' names, and made one or two good hits. More often he was wrong and Genji, amused by his puzzled air, said very little but generally managed to lead him astray. At last he took the letters back, saying 'But you too must have a large collection. Show me some of yours, and my desk will open to you with better will.' 'I have none that you would care to see,' said To no Chujo, and he continued: 'I have at last discovered that there exists no woman of whom one can say "Here is perfection. This is indeed she." There are many who have the superficial art of writing a good running hand, or if occasion requires of making a quick repartee. But there are few who will stand the ordeal of any further test. Usually their minds are entirely occupied by admiration for their own accomplishments, and their abuse of all rivals creates a most unpleasant impression. Some again are adored by over-fond parents. These have been since childhood guarded behind lattice windows and no knowledge of them is allowed to reach the outer-world, save that of their excellence in some accomplishment or art; and this may indeed sometimes arouse our interest. She is pretty and graceful and has not yet mixed at all with the world. Such a girl by closely copying some model and applying herself with great industry will often succeed in really mastering one of the minor and ephemeral arts. Her friends are careful to say nothing of her defects and to exaggerate her accomplishments, and while we cannot altogether trust their praise we cannot believe that their judgment is entirely astray. But when we take steps to test their statements we are invariably disappointed.'

He paused, seeming to be slightly ashamed of the cynical tone which he had adopted, and added 'I know my experience is not large, but that is the conclusion I have come to so far.' Then Genji, smiling: 'And are there any who lack even one accomplishment?' 'No doubt, but in such a case it is unlikely that anyone would be successfully decoyed. The number of those who have nothing to recommend them and of those in whom nothing but good can be found is probably equal. I divide women into three classes. Those of high rank and birth are made such a fuss of and their weak points are so completely concealed that we are certain to be told that they are paragons. About those of the middle class everyone is allowed to express his own opinion, and we shall have much conflicting evidence to sift. As for the lower classes, they do not concern us.'

The completeness with which To no Chujo disposed of the question amused Genji, who said 'It will not always be so easy to know into which of the three classes a woman ought to be put. For sometimes people of high rank sink to the most abject positions; while others of common birth rise to be high officers, wear self-important faces, redecorate the inside of their houses and think themselves as good as anyone. How are we to deal with such cases?'

At this moment they were joined by Hidari no Uma no Kami and To Shikibu no Jo, who said they had also come to the Palace to keep the fast. As both of them were great lovers and good talkers, To no Chujo handed over to them the decision of Genji's question, and in the discussion which followed many unflattering things were said. Uma no Kami spoke first. 'However high a lady may rise, if she does not come of an adequate stock, the world will think very differently of her from what it would of one born to such honours; but if through adverse fortune a lady of highest rank finds herself in friendless misery, the noble breeding of her mind is soon forgotten and she becomes an object of contempt. I think then that taking all things into account, we must put such ladies too into the "middle class." But when we come to classify the daughters of Zuryo,[3] who are sent to labour at the affairs of distant provinces—they have such ups and downs that we may reasonably put them too into the middle class.

'Then there are Ministers of the third and fourth classes without Cabinet rank. These are generally thought less of even than the humdrum, ordinary officials. They are usually of quite good birth, but have much less responsibility than Ministers of State and consequently much greater peace of mind. Girls born into such households are brought up in complete security from want or deprivation of any kind, and indeed often amid surroundings of the utmost luxury and splendour. Many of them grow up into women whom it would be folly to despise; some have been admitted to Court, where they have enjoyed a quite unexpected success. And of this I could cite many, many instances.'

'Their success has generally been due to their having a lot of money,' said Genji smiling. 'You should have known better than to say that,' said To no Chujo, reproving him, and Uma no Kami went on: 'There are some whose lineage and reputation are so high that it never occurs to one that their education could possibly be at fault; yet when we meet them, we find ourselves exclaiming in despair "How can they have contrived to grow up like this?"

'No doubt the perfect woman in whom none of those essentials is lacking must somewhere exist and it would not startle me to find her. But she would certainly be beyond the reach of a humble person like myself, and for that reason I should like to put her in a category of her own and not to count her in our present classification.

'But suppose that behind some gateway overgrown with vineweed, in a place where no one knows there is a house at all, there should be locked away some creature of unimagined beauty—with what excitement should we discover her! The complete surprise of it, the upsetting of all our wise theories and classifications, would be likely, I think, to lay a strange and sudden enchantment

[3] Provincial officials.

upon us. I imagine her father rather large and gruff; her brother, a surly, ill-looking fellow. Locked away in an utterly blank and uninteresting bedroom, she will be subject to odd flights of fancy, so that in her hands the arts that others learn as trivial accomplishments will seem strangely full of meaning and importance; or perhaps in some particular art she will thrill us by her delightful and unexpected mastery. Such a one may perhaps be beneath the attention of those of you who are of flawless lineage. But for my part I find it hard to banish her . . . ' and here he looked at Shikibu no Jo, who wondered whether the description had been meant to apply to his own sisters, but said nothing. 'If it is difficult to choose even out of the top class . . . ' thought Genji, and began to doze.

He was dressed in a suit of soft white silk, with a rough cloak carelessly slung over his shoulders, with belt and fastenings untied. In the light of the lamp against which he was leaning he looked so lovely that one might have wished he were a girl; and they thought that even Uma no Kami's 'perfect woman,' whom he had placed in a category of her own, would not be worthy of such a prince as Genji.

The conversation went on. Many persons and things were discussed. Uma no Kami contended that perfection is equally difficult to find in other spheres. The sovereign is hard put to it to choose his ministers. But he at least has an easier task than the husband, for he does not entrust the affairs of his kingdom to one, two or three persons alone, but sets up a whole system of superiors and subordinates.

But when the mistress of a house is to be selected, a single individual must be found who will combine in her person many diverse qualities. It will not do to be too exacting. Let us be sure that the lady of our choice possesses certain tangible qualities which we admire; and if in other ways she falls short of our ideal, we must be patient and call to mind those qualities which first induced us to begin our courting.

But even here we must beware; for there are some who in the selfishness of youth and flawless beauty are determined that not a dust-flick shall fall upon them. In their letters they choose the most harmless topics, but yet contrive to colour the very texture of the written signs with a tenderness that vaguely disquiets us. But such a one, when we have at last secured a meeting, will speak so low that she can scarcely be heard, and the few faint sentences that she murmurs beneath her breath serve only to make her more mysterious than before. All this may seem to be the pretty shrinking of girlish modesty; but we may later find that what held her back was the very violence of her passions.

Or again, where all seems plain sailing, the perfect companion will turn out to be too impressionable and will upon the most inappropriate occasions display her affections in so ludicrous a way that we begin to wish ourselves rid of her.

Then there is the zealous housewife, who regardless of her appearance twists her hair behind her ears and devotes herself entirely to the details of our domestic welfare. The husband, in his comings and goings about the world, is certain to see and hear many things which he cannot discuss with strangers, but would gladly talk over with an intimate who could listen with sympathy and understanding, someone who could laugh with him or weep if need be. It often happens too that some political event will greatly perturb or amuse him, and he sits apart longing to tell someone about it. He suddenly laughs at some secret recollection or sighs audibly. But the wife only says lightly 'What is the matter?' and shows no interest.

This is apt to be very trying.

Uma no Kami considered several other cases. But he reached no definite conclusion and sighing deeply he continued: 'We will then, as I have suggested, let birth and beauty go by the board. Let her be the simplest and most guileless of creatures so long as she is honest and of a peaceable disposition, that in the end we may not lack a place of trust. And if some other virtue chances to be hers we shall treasure it as a godsend. But if we discover in her some small defect, it shall not be too closely scrutinized. And we may be sure that if she is strong in the virtues of tolerance and amiability her outward appearance will not be beyond measure harsh.

There are those who carry forbearance too far, and affecting not to notice wrongs which cry out for redress seem to be paragons of misused fidelity. But suddenly a time comes when such a one can restrain herself no longer, and leaving behind her a poem couched in pitiful language and calculated to rouse the most painful sentiments of remorse, she flies to some remote village in the mountains or some desolate seashore, and for a long while all trace of her is lost.

'When I was a boy the ladies-in-waiting used to tell me sad tales of this kind. I never doubted that the sentiments expressed in them were real, and I wept profusely. But now I am beginning to suspect that such sorrows are for the most part affectation. She has left behind her (this lady whom we are imagining) a husband who is probably still fond of her; she is making herself very unhappy, and by disappearing in this way is causing him unspeakable anxiety, perhaps only for the ridiculous purpose of putting his affection to the test. Then comes along some admiring friend crying "What a heart! What depth of feeling!" She becomes more lugubrious than ever, and finally enters a nunnery. When she decided on this step she was perfectly sincere and had not the slightest intention of every returning to the world. Then some female friend hears of it and "Poor thing" she cries; "in what an agony of mind must she have been to do this!" and visits her in her cell. When the husband, who has never ceased to mourn for her, hears what she has become, he bursts into tears, and some servant or old nurse, seeing this, bustles off to the nunnery with tales of the husband's despair, and "Oh Madam, what a shame, what a shame!" Then the nun, forgetting where and what she is, raises her hand to her head to straighten her hair, and finds that it has been shorn away. In helpless misery she sinks to the floor, and do what she will, the tears begin to flow. Now all is lost; for since she cannot at every moment be praying for strength, there creeps into her mind the sinful thought that she did ill to become a nun and so often does she commit this sin that even Buddha must think her wickeder now than she was before she took her vows; and she feels certain that these terrible thoughts are leading her soul to the blackest Hell. But if the *karma* of their past lives should chance to be strongly weighted against a parting, she will be found and captured before she has taken her final vows. In such a case their life will be beyond endurance unless she be fully determined, come good or ill, this time to close her eyes to all that goes amiss.

'Again there are others who must needs be forever mounting guard over their own and their husband's affections. Such a one, if she sees in him not a fault indeed but even the slightest inclination to stray, makes a foolish scene, declaring with indignation that she will have no more to do with him.

'But even if a man's fancy should chance indeed to have gone somewhat astray, yet his earlier affection may still be strong and in the end will return to its old haunts. Now by her tantrums she has made a rift that cannot be joined. Whereas she who when some small wrong calls for silent rebuke, shows by a glance that she is not unaware; but when some large offence demands admonishment knows how to hint without severity, will end by standing in her master's affections better than ever she stood before. For often the sight of our own forbearance will give our neighbor strength to rule his mutinous affections.

'But she whose tolerance and forgiveness knows no bounds, though this may seem to proceed from the beauty and amiability of her disposition, is in fact displaying the shallowness of her feeling: "The unmoored boat must needs drift with the stream." Are you not of this mind?'

To no Chujo nodded. 'Some' he said 'have imagined that by arousing a baseless suspicion in the mind of the beloved we can revive a waning devotion. But this experiment is very dangerous. Those who recommend it are confident that so long as resentment is groundless one need only suffer it in silence and all will soon be well. I have observed however that this is by no means the case.

'But when all is said and done, there can be no greater virtue in woman than this: that she should with gentleness and forbearance meet every wrong whatsoever that falls to her share.' He thought as he said this of his own sister, Princess Aoi; but was disappointed and piqued to discover that Genji, whose comments he awaited, was fast asleep.

Uma no Kami was an expert in such discussions and now stood preening his feathers. To no Chujo was disposed to hear what more he had to say and was now at pains to humour and encourage him.

'It is with women' said Uma no Kami 'as it is with the works of craftsmen. The wood-carver can fashion whatever he will. Yet his products are but toys of the moment, to be glanced at in jest, not fashioned according to any precept or law. When times change, the carver too will change his style and make new trifles to hit the fancy of the passing day. But there is another kind of artist, who sets more soberly about his work, striving to give real beauty to the things which men actually use and to give to them the shapes which tradition has ordained. This maker of real things must not for a moment be confused with the carver of idle toys.

'In the Painters' Workshop too there are many excellent artists chosen for their proficiency in ink-drawing; and indeed they are all so clever it is hard to set one above the other. But all of them are at work on subjects intended to impress and surprise. One paints the Mountain of Horai; another a raging sea-monster riding a storm; another, ferocious animals from the Land beyond the sea, or faces of imaginary demons. Letting their fancy run wildly riot they have no thought of beauty, but only of how best they may astonish the beholder's eye. And though nothing in their pictures is real, all is probable. But ordinary hills and rivers, just as they are, houses such as you may see anywhere, with all their real beauty and harmony of form—quietly to draw such scenes as this, or to show what lies behind some intimate hedge that is folded away far from the world, and thick trees upon some unheroic hill, and all this with befitting care for composition, proportion, and the like—such works demand the highest master's utmost skill and must needs draw the common craftsman into a thousand blunders. So too in handwriting, we see some who aimlessly prolong their cursive strokes this way or that, and hope their flourishes will be mistaken for genius. But true penmanship preserves in every letter its balance and form, and though at first some letters may seem but half-formed, yet when we compare them with the copy-books we find that there is nothing at all amiss.

'So it is in these trifling matters. And how much the more in judging of the human heart should we distrust all fashionable airs and graces, all tricks and smartness, learnt only to please the outward gaze! This I first understood some while ago, and if you will have patience with me I will tell you the story.'

So saying, he came and sat a little closer to them, and Genji woke up. To no Chujo, in wrapt attention, was sitting with his cheek propped upon his hand. Uma no Kami's whole speech that night was indeed very much like a chaplain's sermon about the ways of the world, and was rather absurd. But upon such occasions as this we are easily led on into discussing our own ideas and most private secrets without the least reserve.

'It happened when I was young, and in an even more humble position than I am today' Uma no Kami continued. 'I was in love with a girl who (like the drudging, faithful wife of whom I spoke a little while ago) was not a full-sail beauty; and I in my youthful vanity thought she was all very well for the moment, but would never do for the wife of so fine a fellow as I. She made an excellent companion in times when I was at a loose end; but she was of a disposition so violently jealous, that I could have put up with a little less devotion if only she had been somewhat less fiercely ardent and exacting.

'Thus I kept thinking, vexed by her unrelenting suspicions. But then I would remember her ceaseless devotion to the interest of one who was after all a person of no account, and full of remorse I made sure that with a little patience on my part she would one day learn to school her jealousy.

'It was her habit to minister to my smallest wants even before I was myself aware of them; whatever she felt was lacking in her she strove to acquire, and where she knew that in some quality of mind she still fell behind my desires, she was at pains never to show her deficiency in such a way as might vex me. Thus in one way or another she was always busy in forwarding my affairs, and she hoped that if all down to the last dewdrop (as they say) were conducted as I should wish, this would be set down to her credit and help to balance the defects in her person which meek and obliging as she might be could not (she fondly imagined) fail to offend me; and at this time she even hid herself from strangers lest their poor opinion of her looks should put me out of countenance.

'I meanwhile, becoming used to her homely looks, was well content with her character, save for this one article of jealousy, and here she showed no amendment. Then I began to think to myself "Surely, since she seems so anxious to please, so timid, there must be some way of giving her a fright which will teach her a lesson, so that for a while at least we may have a respite from this accursed business." And though I knew it would cost me dear, I determined to make a pretence of giving her up, thinking that since she was so fond of me this would be the best way to teach her a lesson. Accordingly I behaved with the greatest coldness to her, and she as usual began her jealous fit and behaved with such folly that in the end I said to her, "If you want to be rid for ever of one who loves you dearly, you are going the right way about it by all these endless poutings over nothing at all. But if you want to go on with me, you must give up suspecting some deep intrigue each time you fancy that I am treating you unkindly. Do this, and you may be sure I shall continue to love you dearly. It may well be that as time goes on, I shall rise a little higher in the world and then . . . "

'I thought I had managed matters very cleverly, though perhaps in the heat of the moment I might have spoken somewhat too roughly. She smiled faintly and answered that if it were only a matter of bearing for a while with my failures and disappointments, that did not trouble her at all, and she would gladly wait till I became a person of consequence.

"But it is a hard task" she said "to go on year after year enduring your coldness and waiting the time when you will at last learn to behave to me with some decency; and therefore I agree with you that the time has come when we had better go each his own way." Then in a fit of wild and uncontrollable jealousy she began to pour upon me a torrent of bitter reproaches, and with a woman's savagery she suddenly seized my little finger and bit deep into it. The unexpected pain was difficult to bear, but composing myself I said tragically "Now you have put this mark upon me I shall get on worse than ever in public society; as for promotion, I shall be considered a disgrace to the meanest public office and unable to cut a genteel figure in any capacity, I shall be obliged to withdraw myself completely from the world. You and I at any rate shall certainly not meet again," and bending my injured finger as I turned to go, I recited the verse "As on bent hand I count the times that we have met, it is not one finger only that bears witness to my pain." And she, all of a sudden bursting into tears . . . "If still in your heart only you look for pains to count, then were our hands best employed in parting." After a few more words I left her, not for a moment thinking that all was over.

'Days went by, and no news. I began to be restless. One night when I had been at the Palace for the rehearsal of the Festival music, heavy sleet was falling; and I stood at the spot where those of us who came from the Palace had dispersed, unable to make up my mind which way to go. For in no direction had I anything which could properly be called a home. I might of course take a room in the Palace precincts; but I shivered to think of the cheerless grandeur that would surround me. Suddenly I began to wonder what she was thinking, how she was looking; and brushing the snow off my shoulders, I set out for her house. I own I felt uneasy; but I thought that after so long a time her anger must surely have somewhat abated. Inside the room a lamp showed dimly, turned to the wall. Some undergarments were hung out upon a large, warmly-quilted couch, the bed-hangings were drawn up, and I made sure that she was for some reason actually expecting me. I was priding myself on having made so lucky a hit, when suddenly, "Not at home!"; and on questioning the maid I learnt that she had but that very night gone to her parents' home, leaving only a few necessary servants behind. The fact that she had till now sent no poem or conciliatory message seemed to show some hardening of heart, and had already disquieted me. Now I began to fear that her accursed suspiciousness and jealousy had but been a stratagem to make me grow weary of her, and though I could recall no further proof of this I fell into great despair. And to show her that, though we no longer met, I still thought of her and planned for her, I got her some stuff for a dress, choosing a most delightful and unusual shade of colour, and a material that I knew she would be glad to have. "For after all" I thought "she cannot want to put me altogether out of her head." When I informed her of this purchase she did not rebuff me nor make any attempt to hide from me, but to all my questions she answered quietly and composedly, without any sign that she was ashamed of herself.

'At last she told me that if I went on as before, she could never forgive me; but if I would promise to live more quietly she would take me back again. Seeing that she still hankered after me I determined to school her a little further yet, and said that I could make no conditions and must be free to live as I chose. So the tug of war went on; but it seems that it hurt her far more than I knew, for in a little while she fell into a decline and died, leaving me aghast at the upshot of my wanton game. And now I felt that, whatever faults she might have had, her devotion alone would have made her a fit wife for me. I remembered how both in trivial talk and in consideration of important matters she had never once shown herself at a loss, how in the dyeing of brocades she rivalled the Goddess of Tatsuta who tints the autumn leaves, and how in needlework and the like she was not less skillful than Tanabata, the Weaving-lady of the sky.'

Here he stopped, greatly distressed at the recollection of the lady's many talents and virtues.

'The Weaving-lady and the Herd boy' said To no Chujo 'enjoy a love that is eternal. Had she but resembled the Divine Semptress in this, you would not, I think, have minded her being a little less skillful with her needle. I wonder that with this rare creature in mind you pronounce the world to be so blank a place.'

'Listen' replied Uma no Kami. 'About the same time there was another lady whom I used to visit. She was of higher birth than the first; her skill in poetry, cursive writing, and lute-playing, her readiness of hand and tongue were all marked enough to show that she was not a woman of trivial nature; and this indeed was allowed by those who knew her. To add to this she was not ill-looking and sometimes, when I needed a rest from my unhappy persecutress, I used to visit her secretly. In the end I found that I had fallen completely in love with her. After the death of the other I was in great distress. But it was no use brooding over the past and I began to visit my new lady more and more often. I soon came to the conclusion that she was frivolous and I had no confidence that I should have liked what went on when I was not there to see. I now visited her only at long intervals and at last decided that she had another lover.

'It was during the Godless Month, on a beautiful moonlight night. As I was leaving the Palace I met a certain young courtier, who, when I told him that I was driving out to spend the night at the Dainagon's, said that my way was his and joined me. The road passed my lady's house and here it was that he alighted, saying that he had an engagement which he should have been very sorry not to fulfill. The wall was half in ruins and through its gaps I saw the shadowy waters of the lake. It would not have been easy (for even the moonbeams seemed to loiter here!) to hasten past so lovely a place, and when he left his coach I too left mine.

'At once this man (whom I now knew to be that other lover whose existence I had guessed) went and sat unconcernedly on the bamboo skirting of the portico and began to gaze at the moon. The chrysanthemums were just in full bloom, the bright fallen leaves were tumbling and tussling in the wind. It was indeed a scene of wonderful beauty that met our eyes. Presently he took a flute out of the folds of his dress and began to play upon it. Then putting the flute aside, he began to murmur "Sweet is the shade" and other catches. Soon a pleasant-sounding native zithern began to tune up somewhere within the house and an ingenious accompaniment was fitted to his careless warblings. Her zithern was tuned to the autumn-mode, and she played with so much tenderness and feeling that though the music came from behind closed shutters it sounded quite modern and passionate, and well accorded with the soft beauty of the moonlight. The courtier was ravished, and as he stepped forward to place himself right under her window he turned to me and remarked in a self-satisfied way that among the fallen leaves no other footstep had left its mark. Then plucking a chrysanthemum, he sang:

> Strange that the music of your lute,
> These matchless flowers and all the beauty of the night,
> Have lured no other feet to linger at your door!

and then, beseeching her pardon for his halting verses, he begged her to play again while one was still near who longed so passionately to hear her. When he had paid her many other compliments, the lady answered in an affected voice with the verse:

> Would that I had some song that might detain
> The flute that blends its note
> With the low rustling of the autumn leaves.

and after these blandishments, still unsuspecting, she took up the thirteen-stringed lute, and tuning it to the *Banjiki* mode she clattered at the strings with all the frenzy that fashion now demands. It was a fine performance no doubt, but I cannot say that it made a very agreeable impression upon me.

'A man may amuse himself well enough by trifling from time to time with some lady at the Court; will get what pleasure he can out of it while he is with her and not trouble his head about what goes on when he is not there. This lady too I only saw from time to time, but such was her situation that I had once fondly imagined myself the only occupant of her thoughts. However that night's work dissolved the last shred of my confidence, and I never saw her again.

'These two experiences, falling to my lot while I was still so young, early deprived me of any hope from women. And since that time my view of them has but grown the blacker. No doubt to you at your age they seem very entrancing, these "dewdrops on the grass that fall if they are touched," these "glittering hailstones that melt if gathered in the hand." But when you are a little older you will think as I do. Take my advice in this at least; beware of caressing manners and soft, entangling ways. For if you are so rash as to let them lead you astray, you will soon find yourselves cutting a very silly figure in the world.'

To no Chujo as usual nodded his assent, and Genji's smile seemed such as to show that he too accepted Uma no Kami's advice. 'Your two stories were certainly very dismal' he said, laughing. And here To no Chujo interposed: 'I will tell you a story about myself. There was a lady whose acquaintance I was obliged to make with great secrecy. But her beauty well rewarded my pains, and though I had no thought of making her my wife, I grew so fond of her that I soon found I could not put her out of my head and she seemed to have complete confidence in me. Such confidence indeed that when from time to time I was obliged to behave in such a way as might well have aroused her resentment, she seemed not to notice that anything was amiss, and even when I neglected her for many weeks, she treated me as though I were still coming every day. In the end indeed I found this readiness to receive me whenever and however I came very painful, and determined for the future to merit her strange confidence.

'Her parents were dead and this was perhaps why, since I was all she had in the world, she treated me with such loving meekness, despite the many wrongs I did her. I must own that my resolution did not last long, and I was soon neglecting her worse than before. During this time (I did not hear of it till afterwards) someone who had discovered our friendship began to send her veiled messages which cruelly frightened and distressed her. Knowing nothing of the trouble she was in, although I often thought of her I neither came nor wrote to her for a long while. Just when she was in her worst despair a child was born, and at last in her distress she plucked a blossom of the flower that is called "Child of my Heart" and sent it to me.'

And here To no Chujo's eyes filled with tears.

'Well' said Genji 'and did she write a message to go with it?' 'Oh nothing very out-of-the-ordinary' said To no Chujo. 'She wrote: "Though tattered be the hillman's hedge, deign sometimes to look with kindness upon the Child-flower that grows so sweetly there." This brought me to her side. As usual she did not reproach me, but she looked sad enough, and when I considered the dreary desolation of this home where every object wore an aspect no less depressing than the wailing voices of the crickets in the grass, she seemed to me like some unhappy princess in an ancient story, and wishing her to feel that it was for the mother's sake and not for the child's that I had come, I answered with a poem in which I called the Child-flower by its other name "Bed-flower," and she replied with a poem that darkly hinted at the cruel tempest which had attended this Bed-flower's birth. She spoke lightly and did not seem to be downright angry with me; and when a few tears fell she was at great pains to hide them, and seemed more distressed at the thought that I might imagine her to be unhappy than actually resentful of my conduct towards her. So I went away with an easy mind and it was some while before I came again. When at last I returned she had utterly disappeared, and if she is alive she must be living a wretched vagrant life. If while I still loved her she had but shown some outward sign of her resentment, she would not have ended thus as an outcast and wanderer; for I should never have dared to leave her so long neglected, and might in the end have acknowledged her and made her mine for ever. The child too was a sweet creature, and I have spent much time in searching for them, but still without success.

'It is, I fear, as sorrowful a tale as that which Uma no Kami has told you. I, unfaithful, thought that I was not missed; and she, still loved, was in no better case than one whose love is not returned. I indeed am fast forgetting her; but she, it may be, cannot put me out of her mind and I fear there may be nights when thoughts that she would gladly banish burn fiercely in her breast; for now I fancy she must be living a comfortless and unprotected life.'

'When all is said and done' said Uma no Kami, 'my friend, though I pine for her now that she is gone, was a sad plague to me while I had her, and we must own that such a one will in the end be sure to make us wish ourselves well rid of her. The zithern-player had much talent to her credit, but was a great deal too light-headed. And your diffident lady, To no Chujo, seems to me to be a very suspicious case. The world appears to be so constructed that we shall in the end be always at a loss to make a reasoned choice; despite all our picking, sifting and comparing we shall never succeed in finding this in all ways and to all lengths adorable and impeccable female.'

'I can only suggest the Goddess Kichijo[4] said To no Chujo 'and I fear that intimacy with so holy and majestic a being might prove to be impracticable.'

At this they all laughed and To no Chujo continued: 'But now it is Shikibu's turn and he is sure to give us something entertaining. Come Shikibu, keep the ball rolling!' 'Nothing of interest ever happens to humble folk like myself' said Shikibu; but To no Chujo scolded him for keeping them waiting and after reflecting for a while which anecdote would best suit the company, he began: 'While I was still a student at the University, I came across a woman who was truly a prodigy of intelligence. One of Uma no Kami's demands she certainly fulfilled, for it was possible to discuss with her to advantage both public matters and the proper handling of one's private affairs. But not only was her mind capable of grappling with any problems of this kind; she was also so learned that ordinary scholars found themselves, to their humiliation, quite unable to hold their own against her.

'I was taking lessons from her father, who was a Professor. I had heard that he had several daughters, and some accidental circumstance made it necessary

[4]Goddess of Beauty.

for me to exchange a word or two with one of them who turned out to be the learned prodigy of whom I have spoken. The father, hearing that we had been seen together, came up to me with a wine-cup in his hand and made an allusion to the poem of The Two Wives.[5] Unfortunately I did not feel the least inclination towards the lady. However, I was very civil to her; upon which she began to take an affectionate interest in me and lost no opportunity of displaying her talents by giving me the most elaborate advice how best I might advance my position in the world. She sent me marvelous letters written in a very far-fetched epistolary style and entirely in Chinese characters; in return for which I felt bound to visit her, and by making her my teacher I managed to learn how to write Chinese poems. They were wretched, knock-kneed affairs, but I am still grateful to her for it. She was not however at all the sort of woman whom I should have cared to have as a wife, for though there may be certain disadvantages in marrying a complete dolt, it is even worse to marry a blue-stocking. Still less do princes like you and Genji require so huge a stock of intellect and erudition for your support! Let her but be one to whom the *karma* of our past lives draws us in natural sympathy, what matter if now and again her ignorance distresses us? Come to that, even men seem to me to get along very well without much learning.'

Here he stopped, but Genji and the rest, wishing to hear the end of the story, cried out that for their part they found her a most interesting woman. Shikibu protested that he did not wish to go on with the story, but at last after much coaxing, pulling a comical wry face he continued: 'I had not seen her for a long time. When at last some accident took me to the house, she did not receive me with her usual informality but spoke to me from behind a tiresome screen. Ha, Ha, thought I foolishly, she is sulking; now is the time to have a scene and break with her. I might have known that she was not so little of a philosopher as to sulk about trifles; she prided herself on knowing the ways of the world and my inconstancy did not in the least disturb her.

'She told me (speaking without the slightest tremor) that having had a bad cold for some weeks she had taken a strong garlic-cordial, which had made her breath smell rather unpleasant and that for this reason she could not come very close to me. But if I had any matter of special importance to discuss with her she was quite prepared to give me her attention. All this she had expressed with solemn literary perfection. I could think of no suitable reply, and with an "at your service" I rose to go. Then, feeling that the interview had not been quite a success, she added, raising her voice, "Please come again when my breath has lost its smell." I could not pretend I had not heard. I had however no intention of prolonging my visit, particularly as the odour was now becoming definitely unpleasant, and looking cross I recited the acrostic "On this night

---

[5] A poem pointing out the advantages of marrying a poor wife.

marked by the strange behaviour of the spider, how foolish to bid me come back tomorrow"[6] and calling over my shoulder "There is no excuse for you!" I ran out of the room. But she, following me, "If night by night and every night we met, in daytime too I should grow bold to meet you face to face." Here in the second sentence she had cleverly concealed the meaning, "If I had had any reason to expect you, I should not have eaten garlic."

'What a revolting story!' cried the young princes, and then, laughing, 'He must have invented it.' 'Such a woman is quite incredible, it must have been some sort of ogress. You have shocked us, Shikibu!' and they looked at him with disapproval. 'You must try to tell us a better story than that.' I do not see how any story could be better' said Shikibu, and left the room.

'There is a tendency among men as well as women' said Uma no Kami 'so soon as they have acquired a little knowledge of some kind, to want to display it to the best advantage. To have mastered all the difficulties in the Three Histories and Five Classics is no road to amiability. But even a woman cannot afford to lack all knowledge of public and private affairs. Her best way will be without regular study to pick up a little here and a little there, merely by keeping her eyes and ears open. Then, if she has her wits at all about her, she will soon find that she has amassed a surprising store of information. Let her be content with this and not insist upon cramming her letters with Chinese characters which do not at all accord with her feminine style of composition, and will make the recipient exclaim in despair "If only she could contrive to be a little less mannish!" And many of these characters, to which she intended the coloquial pronunciation to be given, are certain to be read as Chinese, and this will give the whole composition an even more pedantic sound than it deserves. Even among our ladies of rank and fashion there are many of this sort, and there are others who, wishing to master the art of verse-making, in the end allow it to master them, and, slaves to poetry, cannot resist the temptation, however urgent the business they are about or however inappropriate the time, to make use of some happy allusion which has occurred to them, but must needs fly to their desks and work it up into a poem. On festival days such a woman is very troublesome. For example on the morning of the Iris Festival, when everyone is busy making ready to go to the temple, she will worry them by stringing together all the old tags about the "matchless root"[7] or on the 9th day of the 9th month, when everyone is busy thinking out some difficult Chinese poem to fit the rhymes which have been prescribed, she begins making metaphors about the "dew on the chrysanthemums," thus diverting our attention from the far more important business which is in hand. At another time we might have found these compositions

---

[6]Omens were drawn from the behavior of spiders.

[7]The irises used for the Tango festival (fifth day of fifth month) had to have nine flowers growing on a root.

quite delightful; but by thrusting them upon our notice at inconvenient moments, when we cannot give them proper attention, she makes them seem worse than they really are. For in all matters we shall best commend ourselves if we study men's faces to read in them the "Why so?" or the "As you will" and do not, regardless of times and circumstances, demand an interest and sympathy that they have not leisure to give.

'Sometimes indeed a woman should even pretend to know less than she knows, or say only a part of what she would like to say . . . '

All this while Genji, though he had sometimes joined in the conversation, had in his heart of hearts been thinking of one person only, and the more he thought the less could he find a single trace of those shortcomings and excesses which, so his friends had declared, were common to all women. 'There is no one like her' he thought, and his heart was very full. The conversation indeed had not brought them to a definite conclusion, but it had led to many curious anecdotes and reflections. So they passed the night, and at last, for a wonder, the weather had improved. After this long residence at the Palace Genji knew he would be expected at the Great Hall and set out at once. There was in Princess Aoi's air and dress a dignified precision which had something in it even of stiffness; and in the very act of reflecting that she, above all women, was the type of that single-hearted and devoted wife whom (as his friends had said last night) no sensible man would lightly offend, he found himself oppressed by the very perfection of her beauty, which seemed only to make all intimacy with her the more impossible.

FURTHER READINGS

An enormous number of commentaries and scholarly studies have been written on *The Tale of Genji*. Notable among these is Ivan Morris, *The World of the Shining Prince* (New York: Knopf, 1964), which provides an informative and delightful look at the life of the Heian aristocracy. For Heian institutional history, see John W. Hall and Jeffrey P. Maas, eds., *Medieval Japan: Essays in Institutional History* (New Haven, CT: Yale University Press, 1974), about half of which deals with the Heian period. J. Puette, *Guide to the Tale of Genji* (Rutland, VT: Tuttle, 1983) is a helpful commentary that includes a brief analysis of each chapter of the *Tale*. Sir George Samson, *A History of Japan to 1334* (Stanford: Stanford University Press, 1958) provides the standard general history of the period. Earl Miner, *An Introduction to Japanese Court Poetry* (Stanford: Stanford University Press, 1968) is a classic study of poetry in medieval Japan.

Important translations of Heian literature include Ivan Morris, trans., *The Pillow Book of Sei Shonagon*, 2 vols. (New York: Columbia University Press, 1967); H. Jay Harris, trans., *The Tales of Ise* (Rutland, VT: Tuttle, 1972); Helen Craig McCullough, trans., *Okagami—The Great Mirror: Fujiwara Michinaga*

(966–1027) (Princeton, NJ: Princeton University Press, 1980). Annie Shepley Omori and Kochi Dei, trans., *Diaries of Court Ladies of Old Japan* (Boston: Houghton Mifflin, 1920) includes translations of the diaries of three women of the Heian period, including that of Murasaki Shikibu.

REFLECTIONS OF THINGS AT HAND
Chu Hsi

Under the Northern Sung dynasty (960–1126), China was the scene of extraordinary administrative, technological, and intellectual advances. The commanding figure of the era was the imperial minister Wang An-shih, who, in the seven years 1069–1076, brought about revolutionary changes. Costs of government were reduced by half; a new system of revenue collection was instituted based on bills of exchange, paper money, and rationalization of commodities distribution; agricultural methods and financing were improved; taxes and labor services were lowered. The result was an unprecedented period of peace and growth. By 1083, the population of the Chinese empire had risen to ninety million. Wang was equally influential in the field of education, where he introduced science and technology into the civil service examinations. This innovation provided the impetus that made China the most technologically advanced culture in the world at the time. A less celebrated, but even more influential, figure of the period was the Confucian scholar and minor official, Chou Tun-i (1017–1073).

Although the popularity of Buddhism had waned since the tenth century, the majesty of its conception of the nature and forces of the universe still served to emphasize the limitations of traditional Confucianism in coming to grips with the realities of nature. Chou Tun-i met this challenge by formulating a Confucian cosmology based on rational principles. In so doing, he set forth a vision of a universe functioning in accordance with a cosmic pattern of order (*li*)—a universe which needed no magic, gods, or legends to be explained, and which could be understood through observation, study, and thought. This conception was the beginning of the transformation of traditional Confucian thought into what is known as Neo-Confucianism, a philosophy that was to dominate Chinese intellectual life for the next 850 years.

From *Reflections of Things at Hand: The Neo-Confucian Anthology Compiled by Chu Hsi and Lü Tsu-ch'ien*, trans., with notes, Wing-tsit Chan (New York: Columbia University Press, 1967), pp. 1–2, 5–7, 174–81, 219–20.

Other scholars quickly built upon the foundations Chou Tun-i had laid. Shao Yung (1011–1077), Chang Tsai (1020–1077), and the Ch'eng brothers, Hao (1032–1085) and I (1035–1107) became known as the Five Masters, and their commentaries on *The Analects, The Book of Mencius, The Great Learning,* and *The Doctrine of the Mean* soon cast traditional Confucian thought in a fresh light. Old words gained new meanings, and new attitudes modified traditional values. It was an era of intellectual ferment and transformation.

The fall of the northern portions of the empire to the barbarian Chin horsemen in 1126, the retreat of the Sung dynasty to the south, and the transfer of the imperial capital to Hangchow did little to impede the cultural and technological advances begun in the Northern Sung. The Southern Sung emperors placed an even greater reliance on scholar administrators than had their predecessors, and both artists and scholars flourished in the southern port that soon became what Marco Polo would describe as a "city greater and nobler than any other in the world." It was an era in which many of the advances of the previous dynasty were consolidated. In Confucian philosophy, this was the peculiar contribution of Chu Hsi (1130–1200).

Chu Hsi was born in Fukien, the son of a scholar administrator, and studied the Confucian classics as a youth. His father also ensured that he became familiar with the new directions set out by the Five Masters. He passed his civil service examination in 1148, and embarked on a life of political turmoil, reluctant to serve a government he felt to be weak and corrupt. His scholarly life was intensely productive, however. He succeeded in absorbing the best of Taoist thought into a rationalist, even skeptical Confucian framework, in elaborating the metaphysical foundations which had been laid by the Five Masters, and in preserving the strong ethical orientation of traditional Confucian thought. The resulting synthesis was Neo-Confucianism.

Chu Hsi was the author of many works, but the *Chin-ssu lu,* or *Reflections of Things at Hand,* is unquestionably the most significant. Indeed, it has been called the most important philosophical work to appear in the Far East in the last thousand years. And yet it is not an original work, but an anthology of quotations from the Five Masters, compiled, as Chu Hsi states in his preface, so that a poor boy in a remote village without an adequate teacher might nevertheless achieve some understanding. Its importance lies perhaps in its organization and methodical approach. Chu Hsi explains the title, *Reflection of Things at Hand,* by saying that one should concentrate on the question at hand until one has gained some understanding of it before proceeding to the next issue. Learning is like a series of ladders: *Reflections of Things at Hand* is the ladder to the study and understanding of the works of the Five Masters. The Five Masters are the ladder to the study of the Four Books: *The Analects, The Book of Mencius, The Great Learning,* and *The Doctrine of the Mean.* These in turn are the ladder to the study of the Five Classics: *The Book of Songs, The Book of Changes, The Book of Rites, The Spring and Autumn Annals,* and *The Book of History.* The study of these books, finally, is the ladder to the understanding of things themselves. *Reflections of Things at Hand* is more than an anthology, then; it is the foundation of an integrated system of Neo-Confucian learning.

The following selections represent only a small part of the whole work, but reflect some of the major issues it addresses: the metaphysical underpinnings of the universe, the proper conduct of the individual, the proper arrangement of family life, and the proper governance of the state. Although Neo-Confucianism marked a new era of Confucian thought, bringing added depth and breadth of vision to traditional learning, it did not break with the past. The fundamental concerns of the scholar-administrator remained the same, and the means by which he sought to achieve his ends were basically unaltered.

Questions

1. How well does *Reflections of Things at Hand* serve its purpose? How good a teaching instrument is it?
2. What is the function of yin and yang in Chu Hsi's view of the universe?
3. How has Chu Hsi been influenced by Buddhism?
4. Why is Chu Hsi considered a rationalist?

REFLECTIONS OF THINGS AT HAND

PREFACE BY CHU HSI

In the summer of the second year of the Ch'un-hsi period [1175], Lu Po-kung of Tung-lai came from Tung-yang to my Han-ch'uan Study and stayed for [over] ten days. Together we read the works of Masters Chou Tun-i, Ch'eng Hao, Ch'eng I, and Chang Tsai, and lamented over the fact that their doctrines are as extensive and broad as a sea without shores. Fearing that a beginner may not know where to start, we have selected passages concerned with fundamentals and closely related to daily application to constitute this volume, making a total of 622 items divided into 14 chapters. I believe that the essentials of the student's search for the beginnings of things, exerting effort, conducting himself, and managing others, as well as the gist of understanding the heterodox schools and observing the sages and worthies can be seen in rough outline. Thus if a young man in an isolated village who has the will to learn, but no enlightened teacher or good friend to guide him, obtains this volume and explores and broods over its material in his own mind, he will be able to find the gate to enter. He can then read the complete works of the four gentlemen, deeply sift their meanings and repeatedly recite their words, and absorb them at leisure, so as to achieve an extensive learning and return to the simple truth. He can then acquire all the beauties of the ancestral temple and all the richness of the governmental offices. Someone may shrink from effort and be contented with the simple and convenient, thinking that all he needs is to be found here, but this is not the purpose of the present anthology.

> Respectfully,
> Chu Hsi of Hsin-an
> The fifth day of the fifth month[1]

ON THE SUBSTANCE OF THE WAY

CHOU TUN-I SAID: The Ultimate of Nonbeing and also the Great Ultimate

> "The operations of Heaven have neither sound nor smell." And yet this [Ultimate of Nonbeing] is really the axis of creation and the foundation of things of all kinds [ultimate being]. Therefore "the Ultimate of Nonbeing and also the Great Ultimate." It does not mean that outside of the Great Ultimate there is an Ultimate of Nonbeing. (Chu Hsi, Commentary on the T'ai-chi-t'u shuo.)

The Great Ultimate through movement generates yang. When its activity reaches its limit, it becomes tranquil. Through tranquillity the Great Ultimate generates yin. When tranquillity reaches its limit, activity begins again. So movement and tranquillity alternate and become the root of each other, giving rise to the distinction of yin and yang, and the two modes are thus established.

By the transformation of yang and its union with yin, the Five Agents of Water, Fire, Wood, Metal, and Earth arise. When these five material forces are distributed in harmonious order, the four seasons run their course.

The Five Agents constitute one system of yin and yang, and yin and yang constitute one Great Ultimate. The Great Ultimate is fundamentally the Ultimate of Nonbeing. The Five Agents arise, each with its specific nature.

> The Five Agents differ in substance, and the four seasons differ in material force, but none of them can be outside yin or yang. Yin and yang differ in position, and activity and tranquillity differ in time, but none of them can be outside the Great Ultimate. The Great

[1]26 May 1175.

Ultimate itself is originally without either sound or smell. It is so because the original substance of its nature makes it so. Is there anything in the universe without nature? As the Five Agents arise, each follows its own physical nature and is different in its endowment. Hence each has its specific nature (Ibid).

When the reality of the Ultimate of Nonbeing and the essence of yin, yang, and the Five Agents come into mysterious union, integration ensues. Heaven constitutes the male element, and Earth constitutes the female element. The interaction of these two material forces engenders and transforms the myriad things. The myriad things produce and reproduce, resulting in an unending transformation.

It is man alone who receives the material forces in their highest excellence, and therefore he is most intelligent. His physical form appears, and his spirit develops consciousness. The five moral principles of his nature are aroused by, and react to, the external world and engage in activity; good and evil are distinguished; and human affairs take place.

The sage settles these affairs by the principles of the Mean, correctness, humanity, and righteousness (for the way of the sage is none other than these four), regarding tranquillity as fundamental. (Having no desire, there will therefore be tranquillity.) Thus he establishes himself as the ultimate standard for man. Hence the character of the sage is "identical with that of Heaven and Earth; his brilliancy is identical with that of the sun and moon; his order is identical with that of the four seasons; and his good and evil fortunes are identical with those of spiritual beings." The superior man cultivates these moral qualities and enjoys good fortune, whereas the inferior man violates them and suffers evil fortune.

> This is to say that the sage completely possesses the characters of activity and tranquillity but always considers tranquillity as the basis. Man is born with the endowment of the excellent forces of yin, yang, and the Five Agents, and the sage is born with the most excellent. Therefore his action is in accord with the Mean, his handling of things is correct, whatever issues from him is characterized by humanity, and his decisions are guided by righteousness. Whether active or tranquil, he always preserves the way of the Great Ultimate completely. In this way, anyone who is overcome by passion because he has been aroused by selfish desires, or has in his mind a conflict between benefit and harm, can settle himself. But tranquillity means returning to sincerity and true nature. Unless one's mind is tranquil by being absolutely quiet and without desire, how can one handle changing events and become one with the activities of the world? Therefore the sage abides by the Mean, correctness, humanity, and righteousness. His activity and tranquillity are all-pervasive but in

his activity tranquillity is always fundamental. This is why he can occupy the central position, and neither Heaven, Earth, the sun and moon, the four seasons, nor the spiritual beings can oppose him. (*Ibid.*)

Therefore it is said that "yin and yang are established as the way of Heaven; the weak and the strong as the way of Earth; and humanity and righteousness as the way of man." It is also said that "if we investigate the cycle of things, we shall understand the concepts of life and death." Great is the *Book of Changes*! Herein lies its excellence!

THE ESSENTIALS OF LEARNING

1. MASTER LIEN-HSI [CHOU TUN-I] SAID: The sage aspires to become Heaven, the worthy aspires to become a sage, and the gentleman aspires to become a worthy. I-yin and Yen Yüan were great worthies. I-yin was ashamed that his ruler would not become a sage-emperor like Yao and Shun, and if a single person in the empire was not well adjusted, he felt that he himself was as disgraced as if he had been whipped in public. Yen Yüan "did not transfer his anger; he did not repeat a mistake," and "for three months there would be nothing in his mind contrary to humanity (jen)." If one desires what I-yin desired and learns what Yen Tzu learned, he will become a sage if he reaches the highest degree and a worthy if he reaches the proper degree. Even if he does not, he will not miss a good reputation.

2. The Way of the Sage is to be heard through the ear, to be preserved in the heart, to be deeply embraced there to become one's moral character, and to become one's activities and undertakings when it is put into practice. Those who are engaged purely in literary expression are vulgar people.

3. [CH'ENG I] Someone asked: "In the school of Confucius there were three thousand pupils. Yen Tzu alone was praised as loving to learn. It is not that the three thousand scholars had not studied and mastered the Six Arts such as the *Book of Odes*[2] and the *Book of History*. Then what was it that Yen Tzu alone loved to learn?"

   Master I-ch'uan [CH'ENG I] said: "It was to learn the way of becoming a sage."

   "Can one become a sage through learning?"

   "Yes."

   "What is the way to learn?"

   "From the essence of life accumulated in heaven and earth, that which receives the Five Agents in their highest excellence becomes man.

[2] *Book of Songs.*

Heaven and earth accumulate the essence of the two material forces and can therefore produce the myriad things. (Chu Hsi, *Chu Tzu yü-lei*, 30:14b).

"That which receives the Five Agents in their highest excellence becomes man." Only the Five Agents, and not yin and yang, are mentioned because man requires the Five Agents to be produced. Yin and yang are inherent in the Five Agents. (*Ibid.*, 15a)

"His original nature is pure and tranquil. Before it is aroused, the five moral principles of his nature, called humanity, righteousness, propriety, wisdom, and faithfulness, are complete. As his physical form appears, it comes into contact with external things and is aroused from within. As it is aroused from within, the seven feelings, called pleasure, anger, sorrow, joy, love, hate, and desire, ensue. As feelings become strong and increasingly reckless, his nature becomes damaged."

> Someone asked, "How can one's nature be called damaged?"
> Chu Hsi answered, "Of course nature cannot be damaged that way. But when man disobeys principle and foolishly acts as he pleases, he hurts his nature." (*Ibid.*, 15b)

"For this reason the enlightened person controls his feelings so that they will be in accord with the Mean. He rectifies his mind and nourishes his nature. The stupid person does not know how to control them. He lets them loose until they are depraved, fetter his nature, and destroy it. In the way of learning, the first thing is to be clear in one's mind and to know where to go and then to act vigorously in order that one may arrive at sagehood. This is what is meant by 'sincerity resulting from enlightenment.'

> "The enlightened . . . nourishes his nature" deals with general principles, while "In the way of learning . . . arrive at safehood" deals with details (*Ibid.*, 14b)
> To be clear in the mind and know where to go is a matter of investigation of principle, whereas to practice vigorously in order to arrive at sagehood is a matter of practice (*Ibid.*, 16a)

"The way to make the self sincere lies in having firm faith in the Way. As there is firm faith in the Way, one will put it into practice with determination. When one puts it into practice with determination, he will keep it securely. Then humanity, righteousness, loyalty, and faithfulness will never depart from his heart. 'In moments of haste, he acts according to them. In times of difficulty and confusion, he acts according to them.' And whether he is at home or outside, speaking or silent, he acts according to them. As he holds on to them for a long time without fail, he will then be at home with them and, in his movements and expressions, he will always be acting in a proper manner, and no depraved thought will arise in him. This is the reason why Yen Tzu, in his behavior, 'did not look at what was contrary to propriety, did not listen to what was contrary to propriety, did not speak what was contrary to propriety, and did not make any movement which was contrary to propriety.' Confucius praised him, saying, 'When he got hold of one thing that was good, he clasped it firmly, as if wearing it on his breast, and never lost it.' He also said, '[Yen Tzu] did not transfer his anger: he did not repeat a mistake.' Whenever he did anything wrong, he never failed to realize it. Having realized it, he never did it again.' This is the way he earnestly loved and learned.

"However, the sage 'apprehends without thinking and hits upon what is right without effort.' Yen Tzu had to think before apprehending, and had to make an effort before hitting upon what is right. The difference between him and the sage is as little as a moment of breathing. What was lacking in him was that he held onto [goodness] but was not yet completely transformed [into goodness itself]. Since he loved to learn, had he lived longer, he would have achieved transformation in a short time.

> Since the sage has no anger, what is there to transfer? And since he makes no mistakes, what is there to repeat? While Yen Hui did not transfer his anger or repeat his mistake, some idea still lingered in him, such as the idea he had when he said, "I should like not to boast of my excellence nor to show my meritorious deeds." It is like people today saying they wish not to be as they have been. This means they were this or that way all along and have only now become different. This is what is meant by holding on to something but not being transformed. (Ibid., 16a)
>
> When asked about holding on but not being transformed, Chu Hsi said, "A sage does not do that. Yen Hui still wavered between transferring or repeating and not transferring and repeating." (Ibid., 6a)

"Not understanding the true meaning of this, in later years people thought that sagehood was basically due to inborn knowledge [of the good] and could not be achieved through learning. Consequently the way to learn has been lost to us. Men do not seek within themselves but outside themselves and engage in extensive learning, effortful memorization, artful style, and elegant diction, making their words elaborate and beautiful. Thus few have arrived at the Way. This being the case, the learning of today and the learning that Yen Tzu loved are quite different."

> This treatise is very systematic. If in one's learning one follows it, he has enough to last all his life. (Ibid., 14a)

THE WAY TO REGULATE THE FAMILY

My late father was a chief officer of the first rank. His private name was Hsiang and his courtesy name Po-wen [1006-90]. Over the years he obtained five hereditary positions due an official's son and gave them to descendants of his brothers. When he gave orphaned girls in the community in marriage, he always did his best. He gave away his official remuneration to support poor relatives. His brother's wife, whose maiden name was Liu, became a widow, and he supported and took care of her wholeheartedly. When her son-in-law died, he welcomed my cousin, supported and provided her son with an education, and treated him like his own son and nephew. Later, when my cousin's own daughter also became a widow, fearing that my cousin was deeply grieved, he took the widowed daughter home and gave her in marriage. At that time his official position was minor and his remuneration slight. He denied himself in order to be charitable to others. People felt that he did what was difficult for others to do.

> Someone asked, "Taking the widowed grandniece home and giving
> her in marriage seems to contradict the teaching that a widow should
> not remarry. How about it?"
> Chu Hsi answered, "Generally speaking, that should be the
> case. But people cannot follow that absolutely." (Chu Hsi, *Chu Tzu
> yü-lei*, 96:13a)

Father was kindhearted and altruistic but at the same time firm and decisive. In his daily associations with the young and the lowly, he was always careful lest he hurt them. But if they violated any moral principle, he would not give in. Not a day passed when he did not inquire whether those who served him were adequately fed and clothed.

He married Miss Hou. My mother was known for filial piety and respectfulness in serving her parents-in-law. She and father treated each other with full respect as guests are treated. Grateful for her help at home, father treated her with even greater reverence. But mother conducted herself with humility and obedience. Even in small matters, she never made decisions alone but always asked father before she did anything. She was humane, altruistic, liberal, and earnest. She cared for and loved the children of my father's concubines just as she did her own. My father's cousin's son became an orphan when very young, and she regarded him as her own.

She was skillful in ruling the family. She was not stern, but correct. She did not like to beat servants but, instead, looked upon little servants as her own children. If we children should scold them, she would always admonish us, saying, "Although people differ in noble and humble stations, they are people just the same. When you grow up, can you do the same thing?" Whenever father got angry, she always gently explained the matter to him. But if we children were wrong, she would not cover up. She often said, "Children become un-worthy because a mother covers up their wrongdoings so the father is unaware of them."

Mother had six sons. Only two are still living. Her love and affection for us were of the highest degree. But in teaching us she would not give in a bit. When we were only several years old, sometimes we stumbled when we walked. People in the family would rush forward to hold us, for fear we might cry. Mother would always scold us with a loud voice and say, "If you had walked gently, would you have stumbled?" Food was always served us by her side. If we swallowed the sauces, as we often did, she would immediately shout and stop us, saying, "If you seek to satisfy your desires when you are young, what will you do when you grow up?" Even when we gave orders to others, we were not allowed to scold in harsh language. Consequently my brother and I are not particular in our food and clothing, and do not scold people in harsh language. It is not that we are this way by nature but that we were taught to be like this. When we quarreled with others, even though we were right, she would not take sides with us. She said, "The trouble is that one cannot bend and not that one cannot stretch out." When we were somewhat older, we were always told to keep company with good teachers and friends. Although we were poor, whenever someone wanted to invite a guest, she would gladly make preparations for it.

When mother was seven or eight, she read an ancient poem, which says,

> Women do not go out of doors at night.
> If they do, they carry a lighted candle.

From then on, she never went outside the gate of her living quarters after dark. As she grew up, she loved literature but did not engage in flowery compositions. She considered it vastly wrong for present-day women to pass around literary compositions, notes, and letters.

ON GOVERNING

[CH'ENG HAO] SAID TO THE EMPEROR: The foundation of government is to make public morals and customs correct and to get virtuous and talented men to serve. The first thing to do is politely to order the virtuous scholars among close attendants, and all officers, to search wholeheartedly for those whose moral characters and achievements are adequate as examples and teachers, and then for those who are eager to learn and have good ability and fine character. Invite them, appoint them, and have them courteously sent to the capital where they will gather. Let them discuss correct learning with each other from morning to evening. The moral principles to be taught must be based on human relations and must make clear the principles of things. The teaching, from the elementary training of sweeping the floor and answering questions on up, must consist in the cultivation of filial piety, brotherly respect, loyalty, and faithfulness, as well as proper behavior and the qualities derived from ceremonies and music. There must be a proper pace and order in inducing, leading, arousing, and gradually shaping the students and in bringing their character to completion. The essential training should be the way of choosing the good and cultivating the self until the whole world is transformed and brought to perfection so that all people from the ordinary person up can become sages. Those whose learning and conduct completely fulfill this standard are people of perfect virtue. Select students of ability and intelligence, who are capable of advancing toward the good, to study under them every day. Choose graduates of brilliant learning and high virtue to be professors at the national university and send the rest to teach in various parts of the country.

In selecting students, let county schools promote them to prefecture schools, and let prefecture schools present them, as though presenting guests, to the national university. Let them come together and be taught there. Each year the superior graduates will be recommended to the government for service.

All scholars are to be chosen to serve on the basis of their correct and pure character, their filial piety and brotherly respect demonstrated at home, their sense of integrity, shame, propriety, and humility, their intelligence and scholarship, and their understanding of the principles of government.

FURTHER READINGS

The general story of the emergence of Neo-Confucianism is recounted in J. Percy Bruce, *Chu Hsi and His Masters: An Introduction to Chu Hsi and the Sung School of Chinese Philosophy* (New York: AMS Press, 1973), and Carsun Chang, *The Development of Neo-Confucian Thought* (New Haven, CT: College and University Press, 1963). Wing-tsit Chan is clearly the outstanding modern authority on Chu Hsi and his works. His translations and commentaries include *Chu Hsi and Neo-Confucianism*, (Honolulu: University of Hawaii Press, 1986); *Chu Hsi, Life and Thought* (New York: St. Martin's Press, 1987); and his translation of *Reflections of Things at Hand* (Princeton, NJ: Princeton University Press, 1963). Another of Chu Hsi's contributions to Confucian thought is discussed in Daniel K. Gardner, *Chu Hsi and the Ta-hsueh: Neo-Confucian Reflection on the Confucian Canon*, Harvard East Asian Monographs, no. 118 (Cambridge, MA: Harvard University Press, 1986), and Chu Hsi himself is considered in Donald J. Munro, *Images of Human Nature: A Sung Portrait* (Princeton, NJ: Princeton University Press, 1988). Conrad M. Schirokauer, "Chu Hsi's Political Career: A Study in Ambivalence," in *Confucian Personalities*, ed. Arthur Wright and Denis Twitchett (Stanford: Stanford University Press, 1962), considers in detail Chu

Hsi's reluctance to serve an administration that he felt was failing to meet its responsibilities. Chu Hsi's emphasis on philosophical issues was challenged by many scholar-administrators who sought to maintain Confucianism as predominantly a tradition of statecraft. Not the least of these was Chen Liang (1141–1191), treated by Hoyt C. Tillman, *Utilitarian Confucianism: Chen Liang's Challenge to Chu Hsi*, Harvard East Asian Monographs, no. 101 (Cambridge, MA: Harvard University Press, 1982). "The Two Sungs" and "The Sung Achievement" in Yong Yap Cotterell and Arthur Cotterell, *The Early Civilization of China* (New York, NY: G. P. Putnam's Sons, 1985), present a well-illustrated account of the life and culture of the Northern and Southern Sung dynasties (960–1279), including a brief account of Chu Hsi's place in the intellectual achievements of the era, while Yoshinobu Shiba, *Commerce and Society in Sung China*, translated by Mark Elvin (Ann Arbor, MI: University of Michigan Center for Chinese Studies, 1970), and Richard Von Glahn, *The Country of Streams and Grottoes: Expansion, Settlement, and the Civilizing of the Sichuan Frontier in Song Times*, Harvard East Asian Monographs, no. 123 (Cambridge, MA: Harvard University Press, 1987), discuss more specific aspects of the government and economy of the period.

THE POETRY OF YI KYU BO

The political history of Korea began in A.D. 668 with the unification of most of the peninsula by the native state of Silla. For centuries prior to this development, the region had been a melting pot for wandering tribes from Manchuria, the Urals, Central Asia, and China. Alliances among these peoples gradually became more permanent unions until, by the fourth century A.D., three relatively stable states had emerged: Koguryo, Paekche, and Silla. With the success of Silla in establishing its predominance, Korea became an important force in the political and cultural development of East Asia.

T'ang China was the greatest state in the world at the time, and contacts between China and Korea were both numerous and influential. Korean princes, students, and monks flocked to the T'ang capital at Ch'ang-an and brought back knowledge and skills that resulted in a burst of cultural brilliance. The effect of T'ang models on Korean literature was clearly apparent in both themes and

From Joan Savell Grigsby, ed. and trans., *The Orchid Door* (New York: Paragon, 1970), pp. 49–54.

style. Chinese poets such as Tu Fu became immensely popular in Korea and stimulated Koreans to compose their literary works in Chinese. In fact, Silla poets composing in the Chinese tradition became widely admired.

Buddhism, another import from T'ang China, flourished under the rulers of Silla and became a dominant religious and cultural force in Korean society until its decline in the fourteenth century. Its views of man and the universe, its concepts of vast and limitless time, and its belief in a series of births and rebirths struck a responsive chord in a society still clinging to tribal shamanistic practices, and Buddhist teachings gained great popular acceptance. Confucianism, on the other hand, remained more an official ethical system. A Korean National Academy had already been established by 651, and Confucian studies in Chinese formed its curriculum of studies. Students began with the study of the *Classic of Filial Piety* and part of *The Book of Rites*, advanced to *The Analects*, and concluded their formal studies with the *Anthology of Literature* and the complete *Book of Rites*. Popular acceptance of Confucianism in Korea was relatively slow, but Confucian concern with interpersonal relationships and with the secular life complemented Buddhist other-worldliness, and the two philosophies coexisted harmoniously and fruitfully for some five hundred years.

In 957, the system of government examinations that had evolved in China was introduced in Korea. Success in these examinations, which became essential in acquiring government posts, was achieved by a mastery of the Confucian classics and skill in writing commentary, verse, and essays in an elegant and learned Chinese style. During the Koryu period (935–1392), scholar-officials trained in the Chinese classics came to form a nobility of civil ministers and maintained a high level of literary cultivation in Korea for some four centuries. Administrative ability and literary talent did not always coincide, of course. Some able ministers were uncreative writers, and some talented poets were incompetent administrators. Often enough, however, the system produced cultured and perceptive scholars with a fine grasp of the intricacies of government and management.

Yi Kyu Bo (1168–1241) was just such an individual. As a youth, he struggled with poverty and even flirted with starvation as he pursued his studies. Life was never for him an aesthetic abstraction. Naturally kind and perceptive, he developed an honesty and frankness that was attractive, but was something of an impediment for someone hoping to advance through court service. On the successful completion of his examination, he was awarded a position at court, but appears to have been soon sent into exile. As in many stories where virtue and talent eventually prevail, however, he was recalled to service a year later. His later rise in power and prestige was steady; he eventually became prime minister and was appointed to the highly honored post of chief of the official examiners.

Throughout his career, he continued to produce poetry that remains remarkable for its individuality and variety. In many ways, Yi Kyu Bo, with his passion, humor, individuality, and love of nature, typifies the best of Korean poetry in its classic age.

Questions

1. Although Yi Kyu Bo was a Confucian, do you see any Buddhist influences in his poetry? Please explain.
2. Korean poetry often expresses a deep love of nature. How does this observation fit the works of Yi Kyu Bo?

THE POETRY OF YI KYU BO

ON THE DEATH OF HIS LITTLE DAUGHTER

My little girl with face like shining snow—
How empty now the silent courtyards seem
Where once her gay skirt flashed among the flowers!

At two she talked like some wise parrot's tongue.
At three, retiring, sweet and very shy,
She hid herself behind the outer gate.

This year, being four, her tiny hand should hold
Her first small brush. I would have taught her well.
But she is gone. Only the brush remains.

My little pigeon of this troubled nest,
Why did you fly away so very soon?
A flash of light—you came. A flash—you fled.

I, who have learned to watch the passing days,
Can count them calmly still. But who shall dry
A mother's falling tears?
                              Across the fields
A raging storm draws near.

                              The ripening grain
Will fall before the howling wind tonight.
Of all we sow how little do we reap!

THE LOUSE AND THE DOG

Louse or dog, it's all the same,
  Each goes to meet his written end.
Yet why, if the dog dislikes to die,
  Does he kill the louse?

              Now go, my friend,
Consider this, and when you learn
  To rate the snail and wren as high
As the stately ox or horse, return
  And we'll talk religion, you and I.

MORNING THOUGHTS

Sunbeam with sunbeam chases mist away
From mountain tops at dawn.

Grey crags now gleam like gold above the sea,
Forgetful of the clouds that covered them,
Hiding, last night, the lustre of the moon.

Would that I so might chase away the dreams
Which held me all night long and still pursue
My spirit through the day!

DEPARTURE

The falling petals of the Flower Pavilion
Fashion his perfumed bed.

There, through the last watch of the moon he rests.

Into his sleep a purple wineflower drips
The fragrance of her dew.

Laughing he wakes. Drunken with blossom breath
He wanders through the garden, seeking love.

Whom will he take to share his ecstasy?
The peach? Her wanton gifts have wearied him.
The mountain apricot? Too harsh her tone.

But the silk skirts of the peony shimmer like tinted moths.
Her scarlet petals tremble. She falters forth his name.
Even in the Western Garden[1] he would find no fairer flower.

Swiftly the last watch of the moon goes down
And flames of morning leap from hill to hill.

Retreating steps—   At dawn an empty courtyard,
Departing echoes of his cavalcade.
Peony petals fall in the Flower Pavilion.
There is a sound of tears.

THE PINE TREE PICTURE SCREEN

He built this hermit house amid the pines
And here he lived his life, alone with trees.
Each breath he drew was fragrant with their breath.
He understood their speech. Their silences
Brought him the wisdom that the sages sought.
His ears were opened to the sound that dwells
Beyond the rim of silence.

                        Thus he heard
Music which has no voice for lesser men.
His eyes perceived forms beyond creature forms.

Day after day I sit and gaze until,
Drunken with beauty, wonder seizes me
That ink and brush could ever bring such life,
Repeating through ten thousand silences,
The hidden things this master learned from trees.

How dark these hills! How dim that lonely shore
Where serpents slowly move towards the tide
That, swinging back, has left them stripped and bare.

---

[1]The Western Garden is one of many poetic similes frequently applied to the "Land of Immortals" where perfection is realized.

Terrible monsters rest their bony forms
Against the crags, their heads against the sky.
Mysterious faces flicker through the trees
As daylight changes in this silent room
And night brings shadows to the pictured hills.
Among those awful rocks a dragon wails,
Will he come forth, with moonlight, from the trees?

HIS SHADOW IN THE WATER

Walking beside the river
I watch my shadow dance
From ripple to ripple in wild contortionings.
I think of So Tongpu by the Yungsoo Pool.
What did he see?
Only a windblown shadow?
Two hundred eyebrows and one hundred beards?

Or did he gaze until, beneath his shadow,
He found the wisdom I am always seeking?

LOOKING INTO THE WELL

Living alone, who cares to use a mirror?
I had forgotten how my face was fashioned.
Now, gazing in the well, I heave a sigh
For one half recognised—

               Can this be I?

FURTHER READINGS

A good general introduction to the history and culture of traditional Korea, prior to the reign of Kojong (1864–1907), is available in William E. Henthorn, *A History of Korea* (New York: Free Press, 1971). Ki-baik Lee, *A New History of Korea*, trans. Edward W. Wagner (Cambridge, MA: Harvard University Press, 1984) provides a useful survey of Korean history with an exceptional coverage of cultural developments. Two other introductions to Korean history, notable for their social and economic focus, are Bong-youn Choy, *Korea: A History* (Rutland, VT: C. E. Tuttle, 1971), and Takashi Hatada, *A History of Korea*, trans. Warren W. Smith, Jr. and Benjamin H. Hazard (Santa Barbara, CA: ABC-Clio, 1969).

Sin-yong Chon, *Buddhist Culture in Korea* (Seoul, Korea: International Cultural Foundation, 1974), and Frederick Starr, *Korean Buddhism* (Boston: Marshall Jones, 1918) provide an overview of Korean Buddhism. Confucianism in Korea is discussed in Gregory Henderson, "Chong Tasan: A Study in Korea's Intellectual History," *Journal of Asian Studies*, 3 (1957); Yang Key Baik and Gregory Henderson, "An Outline of Korean Confucianism," *Journal of Asian Studies*, 1 (1958) and 2 (1959); Wu-song Lee, *A Chapter on Korean Confucianism: Neo-Confucianism and the 'Practical Learning,'* in *Upper-Class Culture in Yi-Dynasty Korea* (Seoul, Korea: International Cultural Foundation, 1973), pp. 27–39.

Peter Lee, *Korean Literature: Topics and Themes* (Tucson: University of Arizona Press, 1965) provides a useful survey of Korean literature. Some good translations of Korean literature are easily available. Joan Savell Grigsby, ed. and trans., *The Orchid Door* (New York: Paragon, 1970), is an excellent collection of Korean poetry from ancient times to the seventeenth century and includes a brief but helpful introduction to the subject. Jesse Hoyt, trans., *Songs of the Dragons Flying to Heaven* (Seoul, Korea: Korean National Commission for UNESCO, 1971), is a fine translation of a Korean epic written around 1445–1447, celebrating the founding of the Yi dynasty. Peter Lee, *Songs of Flying Dragons* (Cambridge, MA: Harvard University Press, 1975), provides a useful critical analysis of this important work.

GITAGOVINDA
Jayadeva

Classical India was a land of great linguistic and political diversity, united by what anthropologists call the "great tradition." This consisted of the higher philosophical concepts, rituals, and mythology of Hinduism; the literary culture of the royal courts; the laws of the Brahmans; and the practices and customs of learned Brahmans themselves, which formed a model of behavior for the rest of society. The "little tradition" of village life, within which the great mass of the

From *Love Song of the Dark Lord: Jayadeva's Gitagovinda*, ed. and trans. Barbara Stoller Miller (New York: Columbia University Press, 1977), pp. 69, 72–74, 77, 122–25.

Indian population lived out their lives, encompassed the close interrelationships of family and friends, the familiarity with the fields and orchards, the cycle of seasons with their festivals of fertility and thanksgiving, and a general sense of harmony with the world of nature. These gave the individual peasant a sense of the rightness and stability of things. Local customs and traditions dominated Indian daily life, and Brahman families living within the village community linked the peasants with the more sophisticated traditions of Brahmanic legend and lore. It was the combination of these two traditions, and their mutual interaction, that gave Indian culture unity and continuity it would not otherwise have possessed. One of the important factors joining the great and little traditions was their common devotion to the great god Vishnu, in his earth-dwelling form of Krishna.

Vishnu appears in the *Rig Veda* only as the dwarf who measured the earth in three strides. In later centuries, this dwarf was considered to have been only one of Vishnu's ten *avatars* or incarnations, for Vishnu was a god who visited the earth. Some of these legendary incarnations, such as his appearance as a fish or as a boar, were probably myths originally unconnected with Vishnu. Other incarnations, such as Rama (of the epic poem *The Ramayana*) and Krishna, were probably heroic warrior-kings famed in legend long before they came to be identified as personifications of Vishnu.

By the seventh century, Vishnu began to gain greater importance in Indian religion, perhaps because he appeared as a god of love and kindness for humanity, and one who could be approached by the individual without the intermediation of a Brahman. Cults emphasizing personal devotion to Vishnu flourished in South India, and in succeeding centuries also gained followers in North India. Hindu devotionalism came to be expressed in terms of a reciprocal love between the worshipper and the god, and the acceptance of this concept by the Brahmans gave India a worship in which all could join as individuals and equals. Thus the effects of the caste system, the dominance of the Brahmans in religion and learning, and the great differences of wealth that characterized the Indian economic system were, in some measure, mitigated by a concept of a god who admitted all equally to his worship and his love. Moreover, Vishnu was not an abstract being, dwelling in a realm apart from his worshippers. To be with them, he took earthly form and lived among the men and women of India. Of all the forms he took, none was more beloved to the Indians than the fun-loving and ardent Krishna.

The life and deeds of Krishna are the theme of many myths and legends, from his birth and mischievous childhood to his role as the awesome charioteer in the *Bhagavad Gita*. In the tenth-century *Bhagavata Purana*, the most popular of the eighteen Sanskrit *puranas*, he appears in the form of a cowherd (*govinda*). In this tale, the young Krishna flirts and sports with a group of pretty cowherdesses (*gopi*), finally falling in love with Radha, one of their number. Krishna's choice of occupation and playmates in the *Gitagovinda* is in part a popular explanation for the sacredness of India's holy animal, the cow. In the *Vedic Hymns*, cattle signify wealth and the spoils of battle, and the Aryan nobles apparently protected this symbol of their wealth by forbidding anyone else to kill or harm one of them. This original secular restraint appears to have evolved into a religious tabu. Later, cows became sacrificial animals and were therefore dedicated to the gods. By the time of the *Gitagovinda*, they had come to symbolize maternal love and the spirit of devotion to Krishna. In the *Gitagovinda*, Jayadeva explains through myth why this came to be.

Jayadeva was a court poet in Bengal in the latter part of the twelfth century. The *Gitagovinda*, his greatest work, portrays personal devotion to God in terms of physical love. In the West, the poem has been criticized for its openly erotic character, but in India it remains one of the central works of devotion to Vishnu. It draws not only on earlier devotional literature, but also on Tantric ritual, the character of which is amply illustrated by the erotic themes in temple sculpture of the period. For the Indians of the time, it was only reasonable to describe abstract concepts in concrete terms through allegory. It seemed perfectly natural to them to describe their joyous love for their god in terms of the most ecstatic physical pleasure they knew.

The *Gitagovinda* has been translated into all modern Indian languages and is presented in theater, music, and dance throughout the country. The poem presents the story of the love of Radha and Krishna, and the only other character is another gopi who is Radha's confidante. The excerpts in this selection come from the beginning and from the end of the poem. The first excerpt is from Jayadeva's invocation, after which the narrative begins with Radha's description of how she observed Krishna's lovemaking with the other gopis. She hides in anger and jealousy; Krishna, realizing his love for Radha, searches unsuccessfully for her. He then waits for Radha to come to him. Radha wastes away from the anguish of separation and from the thought that Krishna no longer cares for her. Radha's friend passes back and forth between the two, describing the agony of the one to the other and urging each to overcome pride and to take the first step toward reconciliation. After a night and a day of separation, it is Krishna who comes to Radha and declares his love. He then returns to his home in the forest; Radha follows him to his hut, and the loveplay given here concludes the poem. Jayadeva stresses the cosmic significance of the relationship by referring to Krishna by various names that invoke Hindu mythology: Madhava (descendant of Madhu, or Spring), Hari (a demon), Narayana, and Yadu or Yadava (hero). Radha is called Sri, "radiance" or "beauty," which is another name of the goddess Laksmi, consort of Vishnu. To peasant worshippers, the allegory was clear; after a winter of short days, cold winds, and perhaps diminishing supplies of food, the god Vishnu arrives as Spring, a hero defeating death and Winter and, with joy and love, blesses humankind with the fruits of the season to come.

Questions

1. What does Jayadeva say are his motives for composing this work?
2. Some people claim that uninhibited eroticism, such as that demonstrated in the *Gitagovinda*, is a sign of decline in a civilization. What evidence for and against this argument can you find in this example?
3. The *Gitagovinda* is written in an ornate Sanskrit understood by few people, yet it was intended to be sung and danced publicly. How might ordinary Hindus have interpreted the story?

GITA GOVINDA

JOYFUL KRISHNA

"Clouds thicken the sky.
Tamala trees darken the forest.
The night frightens him.
Radha, you take him home!"
They leave at Nanda's order,
Passing trees in thickets on the way,
Until secret passions of Radha and Madhava
Triumph on the Jumna riverbank.

Jayadeva, wandering king of bards
Who sing at Padmavati's lotus feet,
Was obsessed in his heart
By rhythms of the goddess of speech,
And he made this lyrical poem
From tales of the passionate play
When Krishna loved Sri.

Umapatidhara is prodigal with speech,
Sarana is renowned for his subtle flowing sounds,
But only Jayadeva divines the pure design of words.

Dhoyi is famed as king of poets for his musical ear,
But no one rivals master Govardhana
For poems of erotic mood and sacred truth.

If remembering Hari enriches your heart,
If his arts of seduction arouse you,
Listen to Jayadeva's speech
In these sweet soft lyrical songs.

◆

Your beauty is fresh as rain clouds.
You hold the mountain to churn elixir from the sea.
Your eyes are night birds drinking from Sri's moon face.
    Triumph, God of Triumph, Hari!

Poet Jayadeva joyously sings
This song of invocation
In an auspicious prayer.
    Triumph, God of Triumph, Hari!

As he rests in Sri's embrace,
On the soft slope of her breast,
The saffroned chest of Madhu's killer
Is stained with red marks of passion
And sweat from fatigue of tumultuous loving.
May his broad chest bring you pleasure too!

When spring came, tender-limbed Radha wandered
Like a flowering creeper in the forest wilderness,
Seeking Krishna in his many haunts.
The god of love increased her ordeal,
Tormenting her with fevered thoughts,
And her friend sang to heighten the mood.

◆

When he quickens all things
To create bliss in the world,
His soft black sinuous lotus limbs
Begin the festival of love
And beautiful cowherd girls wildly
Wind him in their bodies.

Friend, in spring young Hari plays
Like erotic mood incarnate.

Winds from sandalwood mountains
Blow now toward Himalayan peaks,
Longing to plunge in the snows
After weeks of writhing
In the hot bellies of ground snakes.
Melodious voices of cuckoos
Raise their joyful sound
When they spy the buds
On tips of smooth mango branches.

"Joyful Krishna" is the first part in Gitagovinda

ECSTATIC KRISHNA

When her friends had gone,
Smiles spread on Radha's lips
While love's deep fantasies
Struggled with her modesty.
Seeing the mood in Radha's heart,
Hari spoke to his love;
Her eyes were fixed
On his bed of buds and tender shoots.

Leave lotus footprints on my bed of tender shoots, loving Radha!
Let my place be ravaged by your tender feet!
 Narayana is faithful now. Love me, Radhika!

I stroke your foot with my lotus hand—You have come far.
Set your golden anklet on my bed like the sun.
 Narayana is faithful now. Love me, Radhika!

Consent to my love; let elixir pour from your face!
To end our separation I bare my chest of the silk that bars your breast.
 Narayana is faithful now. Love me, Radhika!

Throbbing breasts aching for loving embrace are hard to touch.
Rest these vessels on my chest! Quench love's burning fire!
 Narayana is faithful now. Love me, Radhika!

Offer your lips' nectar to revive a dying slave, Radha!
His obsessed mind and listless body burn in love's desolation.
  Narayana is faithful now. Love me, Radhika!

Radha, make your jeweled girdle cords echo the tone of your voice!
Soothe the long torture my ears have suffered from cuckoo's shrill cries!
  Narayana is faithful now. Love me, Radhika!

Your eyes are ashamed now to see me tortured by baseless anger;
Glance at me and end my passion's despair!
  Narayana is faithful now. Love me, Radhika!

Each verse of Jayadeva's song echoes the delight of Madhu's foe.
Let emotion rise to a joyful mood of love in sensitive men!
  Narayana is faithful now. Love me, Radhika!

<blockquote>

Displaying her passion
In loveplay as the battle began,
She launched a bold offensive
Above him
And triumphed over her lover.
Her hips were still,
Her vine-like arm was slack,
Her chest was heaving,
Her eyes were closed.
Why does a mood of manly force
Succeed for women in love?

Then, as he idled after passionate love,
Radha, wanting him to ornament her,
Freely told her lover,
Secure in her power over him.

</blockquote>

Yadava hero, your hand is cooler than sandalbalm on my breast;
Paint a leaf design with deer musk here on Love's ritual vessel!
  She told the joyful Yadu hero, playing to delight her heart.

Lover, draw kohl glossier than a swarm of black bees on my eyes!
Your lips kissed away the lampblack bow that shoots arrows of Love.
  She told the joyful Yadu hero, playing to delight her heart.

My ears reflect the restless gleam of doe eyes, graceful Lord.
Hang earrings on their magic circles to form snares for love.
  She told the joyful Yadu hero, playing to delight her heart.

Pin back the teasing lock of hair on my smooth lotus face!
It fell before me to mime a gleaming line of black bees.
  She told the joyful Yadu hero, playing to delight her heart.

Make a mark with liquid deer musk on my moonlit brow!
Make a moon shadow, Krishna! The sweat drops are dried.
  She told the joyful Yadu hero, playing to delight her heart.

Fix flowers in shining hair loosened by loveplay, Krishna!
Make a flywhisk outshining peacock plumage to be the banner of Love.
  She told the joyful Yadu hero, playing to delight her heart.

My beautiful loins are a deep cavern to take the thrusts of love—
Cover them with jeweled girdles, cloths, and ornaments, Krishna!
  She told the joyful Yadu hero, playing to delight her heart.

Make your heart sympathetic to Jayadeva's splendid speech!
Recalling Hari's feet is elixir against fevers of this dark time.
  She told the joyful Yadu hero, playing to delight her heart.

> "Paint a leaf on my breasts!
> Put color on my cheeks!
> Lay a girdle on my hips!
> Twine my heavy braid with flowers!
> Fix rows of bangles on my hands
> And jeweled anklets on my feet!"
> Her yellow-robed lover
> Did what Radha said.

> His musical skills, his meditation on Vishnu,
> His vision of reality in the erotic mood,
> His graceful play in these poems,
> All show that master-poet Jayadeva's soul
> Is in perfect tune with Krishna—
> Let blissful men of wisdom purify the world
> By singing his *Gitagovinda*

> Bhojadeva's heir, Ramadevi's son, Jayadeva,
> Expresses the power of poetry
> In the *Gitagovinda*.
> Let his poem be in the voice
> Of devotees like sage Parasara.

"Ecstatic Krishna" is the twelfth part in Gitagovinda

FURTHER READINGS

There are many translations of the *Gitagovinda* in English, beginning with that of William Jones in 1792. The best known are the loose renderings of Edwin Arnold, *India's Song of Songs*, first published in 1875, and George Keyt, *Sri Jayadeva's Gita Govinda: The Loves of Krishna and Radha* (Bombay: Kutub-Popular, 1940). Hindu religious eroticism in general is discussed in Lee Siegel, *Sacred and Profane Dimensions of Love in Indian Traditions as Exemplified in the Gitagovinda of Jayadeva* (Delhi: Oxford University Press, 1978). Suniti Kumar Chatterji, *Jayadeva: Makers of Indian Literature* (New Delhi: Sahitya Akademi, 1973) is a biography of Jayadeva; worshippers of Vishnu regarded it as inspired. There is a splendid collection of scholarly essays on Krishna in Milton B. Singer, *Krishna: Myths, Rites, and Attitudes* (Honolulu: East-West Center, 1966). Two recent examples of American scholarship on Krishna in literature are Noel Sheth, *The Divinity of Krishna* (New Delhi: Munshiram Manorharlal, 1984), and John Stratton Hawley, *Krishna, the Butter Thief* (Princeton, NJ: Princeton University Press, 1983). Much Indian art centers on the figure of Krishna; this is beautifully illustrated in W. G. Archer, *The Loves of Krishna in Indian Painting and Poetry* (New York: Macmillan, 1957). Nigel Frith, *The Legend of Krishna* (New York: Schocken, 1976), provides popular narratives of many of the stories associated with Krishna.

THE ROMANCE OF THE WESTERN CHAMBER
Wang Shih-fu

Through the centuries, numerous love stories have delighted the Chinese both as literature and as popular entertainment. Prominent among these is the thirteenth-century play, *The Dream of the Western Chamber*. Written during the Yuan (or Mongol) dynasty (1260–1367), a period in which Chinese drama reached its zenith, it is generally regarded as the finest example extant of its genre. The work consists of five parts. The first four were written by Wang Shih-

From Wang Shih-fu, *The Romance of the Western Chamber*, trans. S. I. Hsiung (New York: Columbia University Press, 1968), pp. 165-203.

fu, of whom little is known, and the fifth part, a continuation, is traditionally ascribed to another great poet of the period, Kwang Han-ch'ing.

The plot, revolving around the romance between Chang Chun-jui, a young scholar, and the beautiful Ts'ui Ying-ying, was not an original one, but was based on an autobiographical short story written by the eighth-century poet Yuan Cheng. Wang's version of this love story begins with scholar Chang's encounter with Ying-ying at a temple where she is staying with her recently widowed mother and awaiting her father's burial. Accompanying the two women is their serving-maid Hung-niang. The young Chang falls deeply in love with Ying-ying, but her mother, having promising Ying-ying to another, blocks their relationship. When a robber threatens the two women and demands Ying-ying's hand, her mother offers the girl to whoever can save them. Scholar Chang secures the aid of a friend and saves them. Nevertheless, Ying-yang's mother fails to honor her promise to Chang, and refuses to allow their marriage. Chang's noble behavior and her mother's injustice towards him cause Ying-ying, already attracted to the young man, to give him her heart. At the same time, the serving-maid becomes a valuable ally of the young lovers.

In the following excerpt from *The Romance of the Western Chamber*, Chang has already been rejected by Ying-ying's mother and has fallen ill with lovesickness. Hung-niang comes to his aid and secretly brings the two young people together. As is common in Yuan drama, the emphasis here is on the physical fulfillment of their love. The mother learns what has taken place and, to save honor, agrees to their marriage on the conditions that Chang pass his state examinations and obtain official rank. In a very touching scene, the two lovers are parted as Chang leaves for the all-important examinations. This presentation of youthful love has seldom been matched in literature. Chang and Ying-ying vividly display their emotions, delight, impatience, ecstasy, sorrow, and passion so common to young lovers.

Questions

1. How does the courtship of Chang and Ying-ying differ from modern practice? What reasons can you give for this difference?

2. Why do you think Ying-ying is so receptive to this clandestine courtship? What does this say about the life and position of young women in Yuan China?

3. Chinese drama always possesses an underlying didactic purpose. What ethical lessons are taught in this play?

4. Discuss the conflict between natural impulse and conventional morality in this play.

THE ROMANCE OF THE WESTERN CHAMBER

ACT I

FULFILLMENT OF THE BILLET-DOUX

YING-YING *enters, and says:*   Hung Niang has gone with my missive, making an assignation with Mr. Chang to-night. I must await her return and decide how to act.

HUNG NIANG *enters, and says:*   My Young Mistress ordered me to take a missive to Mr. Chang, making an assignation with him to-night. But being afraid that she would change her mind and drive him to destruction, which would be no trifle, I must go and see my Young Mistress and hear what she has to say.

YING-YING *says:*   Hung Niang, get my bed ready. I am going to sleep.

HUNG NIANG *says:*   It is all right about your going to sleep, but what is to be done with the man?

YING-YING *says:*   What man?

HUNG NIANG *says:*   My Young Mistress! There you are again. If you drive him to destruction, it would be no trifle! If you go back on your promise, I will inform my Mistress that you told me to take the missive making an assignation with Mr. Chang.

YING-YING *says:*   You little cat, how artful you are!

HUNG NIANG *says:*   It is not I who am artful but it is you who must not play the same trick again.

YING-YING *says:*   But the very idea of this overwhelms me with bashfulness!

HUNG NIANG *says:*   But who will see you? There is no one else except myself.

HUNG NIANG, *urging her, says:*   Let us be off! Let us be off!

(YING-YING *maintains silence.*)

HUNG NIANG, *urging her, says:*   My Young Mistress, there is nothing for it but for us to be off at once.

(YING-YING *maintains silence and reveals her feelings in dumb show.*)

HUNG NIANG, *urging her, says:* My Young Mistress, let us be off! Let us be off!

(YING-YING *maintains silence; proceeds, and then stands still.*)

HUNG NIANG, *urging her, says:* My Young Mistress, why do you stand still? Let us be off! Let us be off!

(YING-YING *maintains silence and proceeds.*)

HUNG NIANG *says:* Although my Young Mistress is determined in her speech, her steps have already yielded.

She sings: 'As my Young Mistress is pure in spirit and as beautiful as
the flowers,
Her lover thinks of her incessantly from morn till eve!
To-night she has made a firm and sincere resolve
Which will cancel all the false promises I have made
Leaving her boudoir, she proceeds to the library,
While he, like the Prince of Ch'u, who left his country to meet the
Fairy of Love,
Is using the arts of old to become united with her whom he loves.
My Young Mistress is like the Fairy of Love, and Mr. Chang is like
the Prince of Ch'u.
The Prince of Ch'u is sure to be in readiness to meet his loved one at
the trysting-place.'   [*Exeunt.*

MR. CHANG *enters, and says:* The Young Lady ordered Hung Niang to bring a missive, making an assignation with me to-night. But the first watch of the night is already passed. Why has she not come?

'This beautiful night on Earth is wrapped in silence,
But will the Fair One from Heaven ever come?'

He sings: 'I stand on the silent steps.
The night is far advanced and a fragrant vapour is spread throughout
this golden space.
Solitary is the library,
And sad unto death is the student.

Where are the clouds with their varied colours which will bring me
good news?

The light of the moon, like a flood, covers the pavilion and the
terraces:
The priests repose in their cells.
The crows cry in the trees of the courtyard.
The sound of the wind in the bamboos
Makes me think that it is the jingling of her gold ornaments.
As the shadows of the flowers move in the moonlight,
I think it is the Fair Lady approaching.
My mind is in suspense, my gaze is fixed,
And my loving heart is full of agitation.
I can find no repose either for body or mind.
In this time of stress I lean on the door, waiting.
But not a word of news arrives either by the Blue Phoenix or the
Yellow Dog.

With confused love thoughts of her, I am so wearied that I can no
longer keep my eyes open.
On my lonely pillow, I dreamt that I had almost reached the trysting-
place.
Had I foreseen that I should be tormented night and day by thoughts
of her,
I think it would have been much better had I never met the beauty
who could overthrow cities.
When one has made a mistake, he should blame himself and be not
afraid to correct it.
Even if I were prepared to withdraw my mind from the love of beauty
and apply it as sincerely to the love of the virtuous, and to reform
my heart,
How could I prevent her from possessing it?

I still lean on the door, resting my cheek on my hand,
How can I possibly guess whether she will come or not?
It may be that she will certainly find it difficult to leave the side of her
mother.
My eyes seem to burst with looking for her,
My heart to quail with thoughts of her.
Probably she, who is making me her victim, is herself not at ease.'

He says: She has not yet come. Is she not proving false again?

He sings: 'If she is willing to come, she will have already left her noble home;
And should she arrive she will fill my humble library with happiness.
But if she does not come, my hopes will be gone like a stone sunk in
the vast ocean!
Counting my footsteps, I pace to and fro,
And then lean against the window-sill,
To send word to her so talented:
Although you have rebuffed me so cruelly,
I have never borne you malice in my heart,
So as to effect a change of mind and heart in you,
And to make you promise me to come at night and stay till morning,
We have exchanged love glances for half a year,
During which period my feelings have been beyond endurance.

I am ready to suffer wrong and prepared to be tricked.
I reflect that I, a stranger in a strange land, try to force myself just to
eat and drink enough to keep myself alive,
All for the sake of you, whom I love to distraction!
I have steeled my heart to patient endurance.
It is only by my resolution and sincerity that I have been able to
preserve my body from death.
Were an astrologer to be consulted about my six months of grief,
He would certainly say that it will require more than ten years for me
to recover.'

HUNG NIANG *enters, and says:*   My Young Mistress, I will go ahead while you
wait here.

(She knocks at the door.)

MR. CHANG *says:*   The Young Lady has arrived.

HUNG NIANG *says:*   My Young Mistress has arrived. You take her coverlet and
pillow.

MR. CHANG, *bowing, says:*   Miss Hung Niang, at this moment, words fail to
express my feelings. Only Heaven could reveal them.

HUNG NIANG *says:*   Not so loud or you will frighten her. You stay here and I
will bring her in.

HUNG NIANG, *pushing* YING-YING *forward, says:*   My Young Mistress, you go
in, and I will await you outside the window.   [Exit.

MR. CHANG, *when he sees* YING-YING, *kneels and embraces her, saying:*   How fortunate I am to have been able to trouble you to come here, my Young Lady!

He sings: 'The sudden appearance of her whom I love to distraction
Has already almost entirely cured my sickness!
Who could have hoped that you, who formerly rebuffed me, would
to-night treat me so cordially?
As you, my Young Lady, have shown such affection,
It is only right that your stupid admirer, Chang Kung, should salute
you on his knees.
I have neither the grace of Sung Yü,
Nor the good looks of P'an An,
Nor the talents of Tzu-chien.
Fair Lady! you must take pity on me, a stranger in a strange land.'

(YING-YING *maintains silence.*)
(MR. CHANG *rises and sits close to* YING-YING.)

He sings: 'Her embroidered shoes are only half a span long;
Her willowy waist, one hand could enfold.
Overwhelmed with bashfulness, she refuses to raise her head,
And rest it on the pillow embroidered with love-birds.
Her golden hair-pins seem to be falling from her locks.
The more disarranged her hair becomes, the more beautiful she
appears!
I will unbutton your robe and untie your silk girdle.
A fragrance like that of the lily and musk permeates the solitary
library.
You wicked one! Well do you know how to enslave me!
Oh! why do you not turn your face to me?'

(MR. CHANG *embraces* YING-YING.)
(YING-YING *remains silent.*)

He sings: 'I clasp to my breast her who is like jade, but softer, and who is
fragrant and warm.
Ah! At last, like Liu and Yüan, I am in paradise.
The spring is here and the flowers are in bloom.
Her waist is like a willow in its pliancy.
The heart of the flower has been gently plucked,
And the drops of dew make the peony open.

Overwhelmed with joy,
I am as happy as a fish delighting in water.
And, like a butterfly, which keeps gathering the sweet fragrance from
the delicate buds.
You half reject me and half welcome me,
While I am filled with surprise and love!
With my fragrant mouth I kiss your sweet cheeks.

The pure, white silk handkerchief
Is stained with spots of delicate red.
As I take a furtive glance at her under the light of the lamp,
I see her lovely, swelling breast.
And to my great surprise and wonder,
So exquisite and pure is her full figure,
That I do not know where her loveliness begins!
Poor student Chang, a lonely traveller from the West of Lo-yang!
Ever since he met her, he has never been able to forget her.
He was consumed in sorrow because of the separation,
And had no means to cure his love-sickness!
Now thanks to this charming girl, who has pardoned his rudeness, the
romance is fulfilled.

I love you with all my heart and soul.
I have defiled your virgin purity.
I had forgotten my meals and abandoned my sleep, and was prepared
for the worst.
If I had not borne all this with sincerity and patience,
How could I have been able to end the bitterness of love with
perfect bliss!

To-night I have completed my happiness.
My soul seems to have flown to the highest heavens.
I have at last met you, my Young Lady, so full of love.
Behold! how my figure has wasted and how my body has become as
thin as a stalk!
The happy union of to-night still seems to me unreal.
But the dew is falling on the fragrant earth,
The breeze is blowing gently over the lonely steps,
the moonlight is shining on the library,
And the clouds are enveloping the trysting-place.

> Observing clearly these surroundings,
> How can I say that our meeting is only a dream?'

MR. CHANG *rises, kneels, thanks her, and says:*   I, Chang Kung, having been able to wait upon you to-night, will be for ever grateful to you.

> (YING-YING *maintains silence.*)

HUNG NIANG *enters, and, prompting* YING-YING, *says:*   My Young Mistress, you had better return, in case the Mistress may discover our absence.

> (YING-YING *arises, starts to go, and maintains silence.*)
> (MR. CHANG, *holding* YING-YING'S *hand, keeps gazing at her.*)

He sings: 'Sadness seems inevitable!

> How full of charm, how perfect in beauty she is!
> At first sight she makes one love her;
> When not seen for a moment, she fills one with regret;
> And the sight of her, even for a short time, inspires affection!
> To-night we have met within the blue gauze curtains,
> But when shall I again untie the fragrant silk girdle?'

HUNG NIANG, *urging her, says:*   My Young Mistress, let us return quickly, in case the Mistress may discover our absence.

> (YING-YING, *remaining silent, descends the steps.*)
> (MR. CHANG, *holding both* YING-YING'S *hands, keeps gazing at her.*)

MR. CHANG *sings:*

> 'The feelings of love have permeated her snow-white bosom.
> The expression of love is revealed through her black eyebrows,
> Making the most precious things poor in comparison with her
> attractive beauty.
> Her face, like an apricot, and her cheeks, like peaches,
> In the bright moonlight
> Show more clearly the beautiful contrast of red and white.
> In descending the fragrant steps,
> She treads the green moss with hesitation,
> Not on account of her shoes, embroidered with the phoenix, being
> too small.

I regret that the poor scholar is unworthy of your love;
I thank you, who are full of charm, for the love you have mistakenly
bestowed on me,
And hope that you will try to find time to come again earlier than
to-night! [*Exeunt.*

ACT II

HUNG NIANG IN THE DOCK

MADAM *enters with her adopted son,* HUAN LANG, *and says:* During the last few days I have noticed that Ying-ying is confused in her speech, most unusually wrapped in thought; that her figure and her manner are not the same as formerly; and this makes me feel very uneasy.

HUAN LANG *says:* The other night, when you were asleep, I saw the Young Lady and Hung Niang go to the garden to burn incense. Though I waited half the night, they had not come back.

MADAM *says:* Go and tell Hung Niang to come here.

(HUAN LANG *calls* HUNG NIANG.)

HUNG NIANG *enters, and says:* My Young Master, what have you called me for?

HUAN LANG *says:* The Mistress has learned that you and the Young Mistress have been to the garden. Now she wants to question you.

HUNG NIANG, *alarmed, says:* Alas! My Young Mistress, you have compromised me! My Young Master, you go ahead and I will come directly.

'*The precious pond is full of water, on which the lovebirds sleep.*
The wind has blown open the embroidered curtain of the door and the
parrot has learned the secret.'

She sings: '*Had you but gone by night and returned at dawn*
Your joys could have lasted as long as Heaven and Earth endure.
It is only because you wished to meet in happy union,
You always made me as anxious as if my heart were in my mouth.
You ought to have gone at moonlight and returned with the morning
stars.
Who would ever have allowed you to sleep there all night long?

The Mistress is of a very ingenious mind and staid nature;
And furthermore, by plausible words and specious arguments, can
make something out of nothing.
She must have suspected that this poor wretch of a Scholar has made
himself her son-in-law.
That you, my Young Mistress, have become his sweet wife.
And that I, the maid Hung Niang, have pulled the strings.
Furthermore, not to speak of the beauty of your clearly marked
eyebrows, and the sparkling of your bright eyes,
If you only try your girdle and the buttons of your robe,
And compare it with the size of your former figure,
You will find that you have a vitality and grace quite different from
before!'

She says: I feel sure when I have to appear before my Mistress she will say:
'Oh, you little wretch!'

She sings: 'I ordered you to go with the sole object of watching her at every turn;
What on earth made you lead her astray into such bad ways?
Should she thus address me, what have I to say in my defence?'

She says: Then I will simply say to her: 'I, your maid Hung Niang, ever
since my childhood, have never dared to deceive you, my Mistress.'

She sings: 'And then I will make a clean breast of the whole affair!'

She says: What had I to gain from their liaison?

She sings: 'Their heads were as close together as two lilies on one stem,
Like two love-birds, they indulged their affection to the full,
While I, remaining outside the window alone, never dared to cough
even slightly,
And stood on the damp moss until my embroidered shoes were frozen
like ice.
Now my delicate skin is about to receive the impact of a thick rod.
What profit have I, the go-between of these two lovers, derived?'

She says: Well, my Young Mistress, I am off! If I can explain matters to her
satisfaction, don't you be too joyful; and if I fail, don't be too down-hearted!
You remain here and await the news.

HUNG NIANG *appears before* MADAM, *who says:*   You little wretch! Why don't you kneel down at once? Do you confess your guilt?

HUNG NIANG *says:*   Your maid, Hung Niang, has no guilt to confess!

MADAM *says:*   Do you still insist on denying it with your lips? If you tell the truth I will pardon you. If you do not I will beat you to death, you little wretch! You, with the Young Lady, went at midnight to the garden.

HUNG NIANG *says:*   Never! Who saw us?

MADAM *says:*   My son, Huan Lang, saw you, and you still deny it?

(She beats her.)

HUNG NIANG *says:*   My Mistress, withdraw your noble hand! I beseech you to calm your wrath while you listen to what your maid, Hung Niang, has to say.

She sings: *'When we were sitting at night, having finished our sewing and*
            embroidery,
            I chatted with my Young Mistress about nothing in particular.
            It was mentioned that elder brother (Mr. Chang) had been sick for
            long,
            So it was decided that we two, unknown to Madam, should go to the
            library to inquire after him.'

MADAM *says:*   To inquire? What did he say?

HUNG NIANG *sings:*
            'He said that recently the Mistress had returned evil for good,
            And had suddenly caused his joy to be turned to sadness.
            He said: "Hung Niang, you go back first!"
            He said further, "The Young Mistress will remain behind
            temporarily."'

MADAM *says:*   Ai! Yah! You wretch! She, an unmarried girl, to be left behind?

HUNG NIANG *sings:*
            'Of course! To enable him to be treated by the ever-healing needle
            and the moxa[1] cure.
            But who would have thought it could end in the case of the swallows
            mating and the orioles pairing!
            The young couple have continued to keep each other company for
            more than a month.

---

[1]Medicine made from wormwood leaves.

What necessity is there to go into minute detail?
They both know not grief nor sorrow,
Being devoted to each other in heart and soul!
My Mistress, do overlook the matter if you can!
Why should you probe into it too deeply?

MADAM *says:*   It is you, you little wretch, who are the cause of all this trouble.

HUNG NIANG *says:*   This trouble has nothing to do with Mr. Chang, my Young Mistress, or your maid, Hung Niang, but is entirely your fault, my Mistress!

MADAM *says:*   You little wretch, you are unjustly implicating me! How is it my fault?

HUNG NIANG *says:*   Good faith is the base of human dealings. Without such good faith one is not worthy of the name of man. When P'u Chiu Monastery was surrounded by the army of bandits you promised to give your daughter as wife to him who made the bandits retire. If Mr. Chang had not been the devoted admirer of the beauty of my Young Mistress, why should he, who had nothing to do with the matter, have contrived such a good plan? You, my Mistress, after the bandits retreated and you were left in peace, repented and went back on your former promise. Was not this a breach of good faith? Being unwilling to consent to the match, you ought to have rewarded him with money and made him go away far from here. It was very wrong of you to keep him in the library, immediately adjoining the Young Lady's abode, thereby enabling the pining maid and the lonely bachelor to peep at each other, which has thus resulted in this trouble. If you, my Mistress, do not cover up this scandal, in the first place, the family records of the Prime Minister will be overwhelmed with disgrace; in the second place, Mr. Chang, who has been our benefactor, will be unjustly insulted by us; and in the third place, if the matter is taken up officially, you, my Mistress, will be the first to suffer for the offence of not having looked after your family properly. According to Hung Niang's humble opinion, nothing is better than to forgive small offences as so to carry out to completion a great event. Such a course would certainly be of great advantage in the present case.

She sings: 'The proverb says: When a girl is grown up, it is no good to keep her
        at home.
        One is a leading literary luminary,
        And the other is the foremost lady scholar;
        One is thoroughly versed in the three religions and the nine schools,
        And the other is an expert in drawing and embroidering the phoenix.*

> *When there is such a romance as this, which is not unusual in this*
> *world, it is best to let it take its course and not to interfere with it.*
> *How can you make an enemy of a great benefactor,*
> *Who summoned his old friend, the General of the White Horse,*
> *Who came and beheaded the miserable bandit, the Flying Tiger?*
> *Putting aside the impossibility of keeping Mr. Chang, the Scholar,*
> *apart from his beloved, and merely regarding them as if they were two*
> *stars arising at different times,*
> *There is still to be considered what a disgrace and dishonour it would*
> *be to the family of the Prime Minister, Ts'ui, if the matter became*
> *known!*
> *And as this is, after all, a case which concerns one of your own flesh*
> *and blood,*
> *You, my Mistress, should not probe into it farther.'*

MADAM *says:* After all, what the little wretch has said is quite reasonable. It is my misfortune that I am the mother of such an unworthy girl. If the case is brought before the authorities it will certainly overwhelm our family with disgrace. Well! Well! My family has never had any male guilty of any offence against the law or any female who has married a second time. So I must give my daughter to this beast. Hung Niang, first go and tell that bad girl to come here.

HUNG NIANG *calls her* YOUNG MISTRESS, *and says:* My Young Mistress, the rod was brandished over the whole of my body without cessation. But, by speaking out straight, I was spared. Now my Mistress asks you to go to see her.

YING-YING *says:* How can I go to see my mother when I am overwhelmed with shame?

HUNG NIANG *says:* Ah, my Young Mistress, you are at it again! Why should you feel ashamed in the presence of your mother? If you feel ashamed you should not have acted as you did!

> *She sings:* *'When the bright moon had just risen over the top of the willows,*
> *You had already fulfilled your assignation with your lover in the dusk.*
> *This made me feel so ashamed that I turned my face away and bit*
> *into the sleeves of my robe with my teeth.*
> *How could I dare to fix my gaze on you?*
> *All that I saw was the delicate points of the soles of your shoes.*
> *One abandoned himself to love with ardour unceasing,*
> *While the other doted on him in silence.*
> *At that time you did not show the slightest sign of shame.'*

YING-YING *meets her* MOTHER, *who says:* My dear child!

> (MADAM *weeps.*)
> (YING-YING *weeps.*)
> (HUNG NIANG *weeps.*)

MADAM *says:* My dear child, you have been imposed upon and wronged. The act you have committed is entirely due to my sins in a former existence. How can I blame anybody else? Should I report the matter officially it would be an overwhelming disgrace to your father. Such an act is not one of which a Prime Minister's family like ours would be guilty.

> (YING-YING *weeps very bitterly.*)

MADAM *says:* Hung Niang, help your Young Mistress. Well! Well! The whole trouble is due to my daughter not having proved herself worthy. Go to the library and tell that beast to come.

> (HUNG-NIANG *calls* MR. CHANG.)

MR. CHANG *says:* Who is calling me?

HUNG NIANG *says:* Your affair has been discovered. My Mistress is calling for you.

MR. CHANG *says:* There seems to be no way out of the difficulty but for you to screen me a little. I wonder who told Madam this! I am trembling with fear. How can I go to see her?

HUNG NIANG *says:* Don't appear to be afraid but put on a bold air and go at once to see her.

> *She sings:* 'The truth having leaked out, the matter could not stop there,
> So I had to confess at once.
> She has now prepared tea and wine to entertain you,
> Reversing the usual custom of the man having to make the first
> approach,
> And you are full of anxiety instead of being pleased.
> What need is there of a betrothal arranged by a go-between,
> Though I have not discharged thoroughly my duty as chaperon?
> You are really as useless as a stalk of grain that bears no ears,
> And as a spear-head that looks like silver but is really wax!'

(MR. CHANG *meets* MADAM.)

MADAM *says:*   You are a fine scholar, indeed! Have you not heard that conduct unworthy of the ancient sages should never be indulged in? Should I hand you over to the authorities, that would only overwhelm my family with disgrace. There is therefore nothing left for me but to take my daughter, Yingying, and marry her to you as your wife. But for three generations past our family has never had a son-in-law who had no official rank. So you must proceed to the Capital to-morrow to attend the highest examination. In the meantime I will take care of your future wife. If you succeed in getting office you may come to see me; but if you fail do not come.

(MR. CHANG, *maintaining silence, kneels and makes his bows.*)

HUNG NIANG *says:*   Thank Heaven, thank Earth, and thanks to my Mistress!

She sings: '*Your love-affair having been entirely forgiven,*
You can forthwith raise your eyebrows which were formerly knitted;
And now will really commence the enjoyment of your devoted love in peace.
Who would hope for such bliss?
The beauty of such a delightful maiden can only be enjoyed by him who is worthy of it!'

MADAM *says:*   Hung Niang, you give orders for the luggage to be packed, and prepare the wine, viands, and sweetmeats, so that to-morrow, when we escort Mr. Chang to the Pavilion of Farewell, we may give him a farewell feast.

'*Send word to the willows that grow by the bank of the West river,*
To look kindly on the traveller who is about to depart.'

[*Exit* MADAM *with* YING-YING.

HUNG NIANG *says:*   Mr. Chang, do you feel happy or sad?

She sings: '*We must just wait till you come back again,*
When flutes and drums will sound at that joyful time throughout the painted hall,
And when you two love-birds are joined in matrimony,
Then, and only then, I will receive from you a reward for my acting as go-between,
And drink a cup of wine offered by you in appreciation of my services.'

[*Exeunt.*

ACT III

A FEAST WITH TEARS

MADAM *enters, and says:*   To-day we are going to see Mr. Chang start for the Capital, so, Hung Niang, go at once and tell your Young Mistress that she must come with us to the Pavilion of Farewell. I have already given orders for a feast to be prepared, and have also sent an invitation to Mr. Chang. I feel sure that he must have finished his packing by this time.

YING-YING, *with* HUNG NIANG, *enters, and says:*   To-day, we are going to see him off. To say good-bye at any time is very sad, but how much more painful is it when the time is late autumn!

MR. CHANG *enters, and says:*   Last night Madam said I must go to the Capital to attend the highest examination, and if I return, having obtained office, she will then give me her daughter in marriage. There is nothing for it but for me to go, as she directed. I now start first for the Pavilion of Farewell to wait there for the Young Lady so that I may bid her farewell.   [*Exit.*

YING-YING *says:*

> 'Whether there be joy at meeting or sorrow at parting, a glass of wine is drunk;
> To the four corners of the world, man, mounted on his horse, is always on the move.'

She sings: 'Grey are the clouds in the sky and faded are the leaves on the ground,
> Bitter is the west wind as the wild geese fly from the north to the south.
> How is it that in the morning the white-frosted trees are dyed as red as a wine-flushed face?
> It must have been caused by the tears of those who are about to be separated.
>
> My regret is that we met so late,
> And my sorrow is that we have to part so soon,
> Long though the willow branches may be, it is impossible to tie to them the white steed in order to delay his departure.
> I pray you, O autumn forest, to hinder the setting of the sun for my sake.
> May his steed go slowly,
> And may my carriage follow it without delay.

> *Just as we had declared our love openly for each other,*
> *The first thing to happen to us is that we are to be separated.*
> *When suddenly I heard a voice say "I am going",*
> *The shock made my golden bracelets too large for me!*
> *When I saw in the distance the Pavilion of Farewell,*
> *My body seemed to waste away.'*

HUNG NIANG *says:*   My Young Mistress, you have not made your toilet to-day!

YING-YING *says:*   Hung Niang, how can you know the feelings of my heart?

She sings: 'Who can understand this sorrow of mine?

> *When I have seen the carriage and horse ready to start,*
> *How can I fail to feel full of anguish and sorrow?*
> *And how can I have the heart to make myself look beautiful and*
> *charming?*
> *All I want is to prepare my coverlet and my pillow*
> *And have a sound sleep.*
> *Who cares that my robe and its sleeves are wet through with my*
> *never-ceasing tears?*
> *Oh! how sorrowful unto death am I!*
> *Yea unto death!*
> *Later on I will write to him and give him tidings,*
> *Sad and lonely though I may feel!'*

(MADAM, YING-YING, *and* HUNG NIANG *arrive at the Pavilion of Farewell.*)
(MR. CHANG *profoundly salutes* MADAM.)
(YING-YING *turns her face away.*)

MADAM *says:*   Mr Chang, come nearer. Now that you are my own flesh and blood, it is not necessary for you and my daughter to avoid each other. My child, you come here to meet him.

(MR. CHANG *and* YING-YING *meet each other.*)

MADAM *says:*   Mr. Chang, you sit down there. I will sit here, and my child there. Hung Niang, pour out the wine. Mr. Chang, you drink this cup and leave no heel-tap. Since I have promised to marry my daughter to you, you must go to the Capital and prove yourself worthy of my child. You must make every effort to come out first on the list at the highest examination.

MR. CHANG *says:*   I, Chang Kung, am a man of poor talents and shallow
learning, but depending entirely on the favour and deserved good fortune of
the late Prime Minister, and of you, Madam, whatever happens, I must come
back with my name first on the list, so that the Young Lady may in due course
be ennobled!

> *(They all sit down.)*
> *(YING-YING sighs.)*

YING-YING *sings:*

> 'The west wind blows and the faded leaves are scattered everywhere.
> Covered by the cold mist, the decayed grass presents a sorry sight.
> He sits uneasily at the feast,
> And I see him knitting his eyebrows in sorrow as if he is about to die.
> I dare not let the tears which fill my eyes fall,
> Lest others should know my sorrow.
> When I am suddenly seen by others, I lower my head,
> And, sighing deeply, I pretend to arrange my white silk robe.

> Although in future ours will be a happy union,
> How can I at this moment refrain from sorrow and weeping?
> I am so mad and intoxicated with love,
> That since last night
> My slight figure has become to-day still slighter.
> Before the joy of our happy union had been completed
> The sorrow of departure arrived.
> Formerly we loved each other in secret,
> Last night our love was clearly revealed,
> But to-day we have to separate!
> Though I have just realized the bitterness of those days when we
> suffered from love-sickness,
> Who would have thought that the sorrow of separation is ten times
> worse?'

MADAM *says:*   Hung Niang, help your Young Mistress to pour out the wine.

> *(YING-YING pours out the wine.)*
> *(MR. CHANG sighs.)*

YING-YING *whispers to him:*   You drink this cup of wine as I hold it in my hand.

She sings: 'You are abandoning me, treating lightly a long farewell
As if entirely oblivious of our happy union
When your cheeks rested on mine,
And when we held each other by the hand.
To be the son-in-law of the Prime Minister Ts'ui
Will ennoble you as being the husband of a wife of a distinguished
family.
Is not such a happy match, like two lotuses on one stem,
Better than the attainment of the highest literary honours?'

(YING-YING *sits down at the table again, and sighs.*)

She sings: 'The feast is passing too quickly.
This moment we are together
But in another moment we shall be separated.
Were it not for the presence of my mother at the feast, which
necessitates my acting with usual propriety,
I should like to show my respect for him by raising the dish for him to
the level of my eyebrows.
Although this joyous meeting is but for a moment,
We, as husband and wife, should have enjoyed it sitting at the same
table.
I have tried in vain to show my devotion to him with my eyes,
And as I kept thinking over the whole matter
I was almost petrified into stone like the wife who longed for the
return of her husband.'

MADAM *says:* Hung Niang, pour out the wine.
After having poured out a cup for MR. CHANG, HUNG NIANG *pours out a cup
for* YING-YING, *and says:*
My Young Mistress, you have not had breakfast this morning, so will you
please drink a little?

YING-YING *sings:*
'The wine and food you have offered to me
Taste like earth and mud,
But even if they were earth and mud,
They would have some of the aroma of earth and the flavour of mud.

This warmed wine of highest quality
Seems to me as tasteless and cold as water,
And the cup appears to be more than half full of tears of love.

The tea and rice before me remain untasted,
Because I am filled with regrets and sorrow.
It is only for empty fame, as unimportant as a snail's horn,
And for trifling profit, as large as a fly's head,
That the two love-birds are torn apart and made to stay in different
places,
One in one place, and one in another,
Heaving deep sighs for each other.

In a moment cups and dishes will be removed,
And the carriage will go east and the horse west;
Both lingering on their way
As the sun sets behind the green hills.
How can I know where he will dwell to-night?
Even in my dreams it will be impossible to find him.'

MADAM *says:*   Hung Niang, order them to get ready the carriage and request Mr. Chang to mount his pony. I am going to return with your Young Mistress.

(They all get ready to start.)
(MR. CHANG makes his bow to MADAM.)

MADAM *says:*   I have nothing else to say to you except that I hope you will keep in mind the desirability of securing high rank, and come back soon.

MR. CHANG, *thanking her, says:*   I will be careful to obey your strict instructions.

(MR. CHANG and YING-YING bow to each other.)

YING-YING *says:*   Now you are going, whether you secure official rank or not see that you come back again as quickly as possible.

MR. CHANG *says:*   My Young Lady, make yourself easy on that score. If the highest literary rank is not to be gained by your family, what other family can gain it? I must now bid you farewell.

YING-YING *says:*   Wait a moment. I have no other farewell gift to present to you except an impromptu short poem.

'Deserted and abandoned, what can I say now—
I, whom once you loved so fondly?
But may your devotions of old
Be bestowed on her whom you love next.'

MR. CHANG *says:* My Young Lady, you quite mistake me! How could I ever think of loving any one else but you? As to this poem, my heart at this moment is in a state of confusion. My Young Lady will not believe what I might say, so I must wait until I have returned, after having attained the highest literary honours, when I will respond to your poem with one of mine.

YING-YING *sings:*

> 'My red sleeves are soaked with my tears of love,
> But well I know that your blue gown is more soaked still.
> The oriole flies to the east and the swallow to the west.
> Even before he starts I ask the date of his return.
> Although he, who is now before my eyes, is about to go afar,
> I will, for the present, drink a cup of wine in his honour.
> Before I have even tasted it, my heart is intoxicated.
> My eyes shed tears of blood,
> My feelings of love are turned to ashes.
>
> When you arrive at the Capital,
> May the climate agree with you.
> As you pursue your route
> Be moderate in what you drink and eat,
> Take care of your all-precious health at every season.
> In the deserted villages, at the time of rain and dew, you should seek
> sleep early;
> In the country inn, when there is wind and frost, you should rise late.
> When riding in the chilly autumn wind,
> With no one to look after you,
> You yourself should pay every attention to your well-being.
> To whom can I tell my cares and sorrows?
> It is only I, myself, who know the pains of love.
> Even Heaven cares nothing for human sufferings.
> My tears would more than fill the winding waters of the Yellow River,
> And the load of my grief would weigh down the three peaks of the
> Hua Mountain.
> When night falls in the upper story of the Western Chamber,
> I will watch the evening sun falling on the old road,
> And the withered willows by the long embankment.
>
> Not long ago we came together from one place,
> And now we are departing each on a separate way.
> When I reach home, I shall dread to look inside the silken curtains of
> my couch.

> *Last night the embroidered coverlet was unusually warm where love
> still dwelt;*
> *To-day the green counterpane will be cold, and he will be present to
> me only in my dreams.*
> *I can devise no plans to detain him here.*
> *He has mounted his steed,*
> *While both of us have tears in our eyes and sorrow in our looks.*
>
> *I am not anxious as to whether your good fortune will be as perfect as
> your learning,*
> *But my sole anxiety is whether you will give up one wife for another!*
> *The fish of the river and the wild goose in the sky will be the bearers
> of many letters from you.*
> *While I here will frequently send you tidings by the Blue Phoenix.*
> *Swear not that you will never come back unless your name is on the
> list of honours at the examinations!*
> *But bear in mind that if elsewhere you see fair beauties,*
> *You must not linger there as you have done here.'*

MR. CHANG *says:*   My Young Lady, your words, as precious to me as gold and
jade, are imprinted on my heart. We will meet again soon, so you need not be
too sad. I am now going.

> *'I restrain my tears, and try to conceal them by hanging down my
> head;*
> *Though overwhelmed by my feelings, I assume a look of delight.'*

YING-YING *says:*

> *'My soul has already gone from me,*
> *How can I follow you even in my dreams?*

>> [*Exit* MR. CHANG.

(YING-YING *sighs.*)

She sings: *'The green mountain that separates us prevents me from seeing him
> off.*
> *The thin-planted wood seems to bear me a grudge by obscuring him
> from my sight.*
> *The slight mist and the night vapours screen him from view.*
> *The evening sun falls on the old road and no human voice is heard,*
> *But only the rustling of the crops in the autumn wind and the neigh
> of the horse.*

> *Reluctantly I mount my carriage.*
> *How very hurriedly I came,*
> *But how slowly I return!'*

MADAM *says:* Hung Niang, help your Young Mistress to mount her carriage. The time is already late; let us return at once.

> *'Though I have indirectly appeared to give way to my dear daughter,*
> *I may be considered, after all, to have acted as a correct and stern*
> *mother!'* [Exit.

HUNG NIANG *says:* The chariot with your mother is already a long way ahead, so, my Young Mistress, you must quickly return.

YING-YING *says:* Hung Niang, where do you think he has reached?

> *She sings:* *'He is now in the midst of the mountains,*
> *And his whip can be seen in the dying rays of the sun.*
> *All the sorrows of the world seem to be accumulated in my breast.*
> *How can a carriage of this size bear such a burden?'*
>   [Exeunt.

FURTHER READINGS

A treatment of classical Yuan drama is provided in James Irving Crump, *Chinese Theatre in the Days of Kublai Khan* (Tucson: University of Tucson Press, 1980). Included in this work are chapters on the social and historical background of the drama, as well as stages, theaters, actors, and complete texts of three Yuan plays. Chung-wen Shih, *The Golden Age of Chinese Drama* (Princeton, NJ: Princeton University Press, 1976) is an extensive survey of Yuan drama, containing an excellent bibliography. Lewis Charles Arlington, *The Chinese Drama from the Earliest Times until Today* (New York: Blom, 1966) and Colin Mackerras, ed., *Chinese Theater: From its Origins to the Present Day* (Honolulu: University of Hawaii Press, 1983) are helpful surveys of major aspects of Chinese theater. Three interesting examinations of specific topics in Yuan drama are James I. Crump, "The Conventions and Craft of Yuan Drama," *Journal of the American Oriental Society*, 91, no. 1 (Jan.–Mar. 1971), 14–29, and Richard Fus-sen Yang's two articles, "The Social Background of Yuan Drama," *Monumenta Serica*, 17 (1958), 331–52, and "The Function of Poetry in the Yuan Drama," *Monumenta Serica*, 29 (1970–71), 163–92.

THE CONFESSIONS OF LADY NIJO
Lady Nijo

The Confessions of Lady Nijo, written about 1307 but lost until the twentieth century, is a masterful autobiographical narrative chronicling thirty-six years (1271–1306) in the life of this remarkable woman. In relating her story, Lady Nijo discloses much about the age in which she lived. She wrote during Japan's early feudal age, the Kamakura period (1185–1333). This was a transitional era from the aristocratic tradition typical of the earlier Heian period (794–1184) to a culture dominated by the warrior or samurai class. Two important centers existed in Japan during the Kamakura period: the old imperial court in Kyoto and the military headquarters in Kamakura where the shogun actually administered the country's affairs. By the time of Lady Nijo's birth in 1258, both these cities housed large official bureaucracies.

Lady Nijo's story is especially valuable because it vividly portrays the many crosscurrents of life during the Kamakura period. Her youth was spent as a concubine at the imperial court at Kyoto, and the first half of her work reflects much of the world of the Heian court lady. At the age of thirty-two, following her exile from the imperial court, she began a new life of pilgrimage, traveling intermittently for seventeen years as a Buddhist nun. On her journeys, she encountered a variety of individuals, ranging from priests and warriors to commoners and prostitutes. She visited famous temples, shrines, and places of literary renown. Her experiences provide a fascinating and valuable insight into the social and religious life of medieval Japan.

Her account begins in 1271 when, at the age of fourteen, she became the concubine of the retired emperor GoFukakusa. He had taken Nijo into his palace when she was four and took her as his mistress when she was fourteen. Enjoying GoFukakusa's favor, she became a high-ranking lady of the imperial court, and she relates much about her personal life during this period, especially her love affairs, parties, and the ceremonies of court. Eventually, her amorous adventures, combined with the jealousy and hostility of GoFukakusa's wife, caused the emperor to exile Nijo from the court at the age of twenty-six. Lady Nijo's story resumes some six years later, by which time she had become a wandering nun, fulfilling vows to copy holy scriptures and to travel to holy sites. During this period, Nijo grew from a sophisticated and often vain court lady into

From Lady Nijo, *The Confessions of Lady Nijo*, trans. Karen Brazel (Garden City, NY: Anchor Books, 1973), pp. 206–25.

a thoughtful, mature, and patient woman. Nowhere is this transformation more apparent than in the following selection, covering the years 1291 and 1292. The account of her two meetings with her former imperial lover is a poignant example, in which Lady Nijo exhibits a compassion and sensitivity that she formerly lacked.

Lady Nijo continued her life of travels, and recorded various stories and traditions of the shrines and temples she visited. She crossed paths with a variety of people outside the confines of aristocratic life and discovered that she possessed a common bond of humanity with them. The individuals in her story are real, living people, and she has related her story and theirs with masterly skill. *The Confessions of Lady Nijo* is a personal document of one woman's experiences in thirteenth-century Japan and certainly ranks as one of the finest works in classical Japanese literature.

Questions

1. What was Lady Nijo's purpose in writing this account of her life?
2. Describe the personal characteristics of Lady Nijo. Would you consider them to be virtues? If so, why?
3. Discuss the social and religious aspects of Japanese society as portrayed in this work.
4. Describe the meeting between GoFukakusa and Lady Nijo. What emotions did they display? What conflicts took place?

THE CONFESSIONS OF LADY NIJO

1291

In the second month of the following year I visited the Iwashimizu Hachiman Shrine on my way back to the capital. It was a long journey from Nara to Iwashimizu, and the sun was setting when I arrived and began to climb the Inohana trail leading to the inner garden. Among the pilgrims on the road was a dwarf from Iwami province. Talk centered on his deformity; no one could imagine what kind of karma might have caused it. I noticed in passing that the residence facing the riding ground was open. That was where members of the imperial family stayed when visiting the shrine, but it was also open when the supervising priest was in residence. No one along the road had mentioned an imperial visit, and that was the farthest thing from my mind as we passed by. I was climbing up to the shrine itself when a man who seemed to be an imperial messenger approached and told me to go to the residence facing the riding ground. I asked him, "Who is staying there? Do you really know who I am? Certainly the message cannot be meant for me. Are you sure it is not for that dwarf?"

"No, I'm quite certain there's been no mistake. The summons is for you. Retired Emperor GoFukakusa has been here since yesterday."

I was dumbfounded. In all these months I had never forgotten him, but when I committed myself to a new way of life and took my leave from Lady Kyogoku's apartments, I thought I would never see him again in this world. Besides, I had no idea anyone could recognize me now, dressed in these humble clothes that had been through frost and snow and hail. Indeed, I wondered who had spotted me. It was unlikely to have been His Majesty, but perhaps one of the ladies thought she recognized me and was even now wondering if she had made a mistake. I stood there in bewilderment until a junior imperial guardsman came to hurry me along. There was no opportunity to flee as they led me to an entrance on the north side of the building.

"Come inside where you won't be so conspicuous. Come on." It was His Majesty's voice, unchanged, speaking directly from the past. I did not know what he wanted, and my heart was so agitated that I was unable to move at all. "Hurry up, hurry up!" he urged. Hesitantly, I entered.

"I recognized you easily," he said. "You must realize that even though many months have passed, I have never forgotten you." He began talking of events past and present and of his weariness with this constantly changing world. We stayed up the entire night, until all too soon the sky began to brighten. "I must complete the religious retreat I have begun," he said. "We can have a more leisurely meeting another time." Before leaving he took off the three smallsleeved gowns he was wearing next to his skin and presented them to me. "Don't let anyone know of these keepsakes, yet keep them with you always." At that I forgot completely the past, the future, and the darkness of worlds yet to come. My heart filled with an inexpressible agony as the dawn brightened inexorably. His Majesty murmured goodbye, and I gazed fondly after him as he retired to an inner room. His presence lingered in the fragrance of his scent still clinging to my black robes. The gowns he had given me were so conspicuous they would certainly attract attention. I would have to wear them under my own dark robes, awkward though that was.

> To wear your gowns—
> Love tokens from the distant past,
> Now tears stain dark sleeves.

It seemed a dream within a dream as I departed with his image futilely contained in the tears on my sleeves. We had at least met this once, but I doubted that the opportunity for another quiet tryst would ever come. My wretched appearance must have shocked His Majesty; perhaps he even regretted having called me. To remain here brazenly as though awaiting another summons would have been much too indelicate. And so I prepared to set out for the capital, suppressing my emotions by lecturing my heart.

Before actually leaving, however, I wanted to observe for one last time—now as an outsider—His Majesty make the rounds of the shrine. Fearing that I might attract his attention in my nun's habit, I decided to put on the gowns he had given me over my own robes. Then I mingled with a group of court ladies to watch. Garbed now in priestly robes, His Majesty looked utterly different from how he had appeared in the past, and the change affected me deeply. When he began to ascend the steps to the shrine, Middle Counselor Suketaka, who was at that time still only an imperial adviser and chamberlain, took His Majesty's arm and helped him up. Last night His Majesty had remarked that our similar attire made him feel nostalgic, and he had recalled events going back as far as my childhood. His words still echoed in my ears, and his image shimmered in my tears as I descended the holy mountain. Even after I had turned north toward the capital, I felt as though part of me had remained behind on the mountain.

Aware that I could not remain in the capital for long, I returned to the Atsuta Shrine and attempted to fulfill the vow I had made last year to copy some more of the Buddhist sutras there. I was working late one night when a fire broke out in one of the shrine buildings. You can imagine the consternation of the shrine officials. Unenlightened man seemed unable to contain this sacred fire, and within minutes the building had gone up in smoke. By daybreak nothing remained but ashes. Carpenters arrived, and the head priest and the master of ritual prayer came around to inspect the ruins. The building had been known as the Unopened Shrine and was said to have been constructed in the distant past by a god who then dwelt there. Now amid the still-smoldering remains of offerings on the foundation, there appeared a lacquered box about a foot wide and four feet long. Everyone gathered around to look at it in astonishment. The master of ritual prayer, a man said to be especially close to the gods, opened one side of the box a crack and peered inside. "I see a red brocade bag with something in it. It must be the sacred sword,"[1] he reported. The box was consecrated and deposited in the Yatsurugi part of the shrine complex.

---

[1] This sword, a mirror kept at Ise Shrine, and a jewel at the imperial palace are the three regalia of the Japanese emperor. Because it houses this sword, Atsuta Shrine is considered the second most sacred shrine in Japan; Ise, which is the major shrine to the sun goddess from whom the imperial family was believed to descend, ranks first.

Shrine documents that survived the fire related the miraculous history of this sword: "The god of this shrine, Prince Yamato-takeru, who had been born in the tenth year of the reign of his father, Emperor Keiko,[2] received an imperial command to go and subdue the eastern barbarians. On his way to battle he stopped to take leave of the gods at Ise Shrine, where he was given a sword and a brocade bag and told: 'In a former incarnation, when you were known as Susanoo no Mikoto,[3] you took this sword from the tail of an enormous dragon in Izumo and presented it to me. Here is a brocade bag also. When your life is endangered by the enemy, open it and look inside.'

"Later, in the plain of Mikarino in Suruga province, when the prince's life was threatened by a fire, the sword that he was wearing unsheathed itself and began cutting down the grass around him. The prince then used the flint he found in the brocade bag to start a fire, which immediately spread toward his enemies, blinding and then destroying them. Consequently the area was known as Yakitsuno, which means burning field, and the sword was named Kusanagi no Tsurugi, grass-mowing sword." This legend was particularly awe-inspiring because it confirmed a vision I had once had.

All this excitement, however, left me in no mood to concentrate on copying sutras, so I went to Tsushima and took a ferry to Ise. It was early in the fourth month, and the tips of the branches of the trees had all turned to delicate shades of green. I went first to the outer shrine at Yamada no Hara, where the grove of Japanese cedar was indeed the very place one would choose to await the first song of the cuckoo. There were several priests in attendance at the shrine office, and I was aware that since I was wearing a Buddhist habit, I would need to be circumspect in my actions at this Shinto shrine, so I inquired where and how I might carry out my pilgrimage. They told me I could go through the second gate as far as the garden.

The place was awe-inspiring. I lingered near the office until several men who appeared to be shrine officials came out and inquired where I was from. "I've come here from the capital on a pilgrimage," I replied.

"We are usually reluctant about allowing people in Buddhist orders to visit the shrine," one of them said, "but you look so tired I am sure the gods would understand." They invited me in and treated me hospitably, even to the extent of offering to show me around. "You're not permitted inside the shrine itself, but you can look in from the outside," they explained. Then one of them guided me to the edge of a pond overhung with the branches of an enormous

[2] Keiko was a prehistoric emperor believed to have reigned from A.D. 71 to 130.
[3] Susanoo was the brother of the sun goddess, Amaterasu, whose adventures and mischievous pranks are described in early legends and myths.

cedar, where a priest solemnly purified us and prepared some *nusa*[4] offerings. I wondered how that kind of purification could cleanse the taint buried deep within my heart.

I had arranged for lodging in a small house nearby, and as I prepared to return there I asked the names of the men who had been so kind to me. "I am Yukitada, and I'm the third assistant head priest," one replied. "I am in charge of the shrine office. The man who showed you around is Tsuneyoshi, the second son of the first assistant head priest." Their kindness would be hard to forget.

> The gods descend to earth for all mankind:
> What kindness you who serve the gods
> Have shown toward a moss-cloaked nun.

I wrote this on a scrap of prayer paper, attached it to a branch of sacred *sakaki*, and sent it to the priests, who replied:

> Know that we who dwell
> Deep in the shade of holy cedars
> Share the blessings of the gods with all.

I remained here for a week praying for greater understanding of the nature of life and death. The shrine officials helped time to pass pleasantly by sending me poems and inviting me to join them in composing linked verse. There was, of course, no reading of Buddhist sutras within the shrine precincts, but less than a half mile away was the Horakusha, where Buddhist services were continually performed. One evening at dusk, as I was walking over toward Horakusha, I stopped at the Kannon Hall, where some nuns were worshiping, and asked for lodging. "Impossible!" was the sharp reply. So cruelly turned away, I composed this poem:

> Weary of the world like you,
> I wear the same black robes.
> What means this hue if you reject me so?

I wrote this on a prayer slip, attached it to a branch from the nandin evergreen growing before the gate, and sent it inside. They didn't answer my poem, but they did let me stay, and we soon became acquainted.

---

[4]Folded strips of paper hung from a vertical stick and used in Shinto purification rites.

A week later, when I decided to go to the inner shrine, my former guide Tsuneyoshi sent me this poem:

> Now the wanderer rolls on like
> A wave on the Bay of Poetry
> Where our friendship arose;
> Regrettable our parting.

I replied:

> And were I not a wanderer
> How would it matter?
> Can one remain forever in this world?

There were some people of refinement at the inner shrine who had heard of my visit to the outer shrine and were anticipating my arrival. The knowledge of their expectations made me uneasy, but not to the point of preventing me from going. I stayed at a place in Okuda that was right next to the home of a lady of some importance. Soon after I arrived a young servant girl delivered a letter from the lady with this poem:

> To hear of the capital
> Fills me with yearning,
> Involuntary tears
> Glisten on my sleeves.

"I would very much like to meet you," she added, and I learned that she was the widow of Nobunari, the second assistant head priest of the inner shrine. I replied:

> Questioned about the past
> I cannot forget,
> Grief quells
> All words of response.

Early one night when the moon was to rise late, I set out to visit the shrine. Since the Buddhist garb I wore limited my freedom of movement, I worshiped from the upper bank of the Mimosuso River. The shrine was surrounded by dense rows of *sakaki* trees as well as by a series of sacred fences, so that I felt distant from it; yet when I remembered that the crossed beams on top of the roof were cut horizontally in order to insure the protection of the imperial line,[5] a heartfelt prayer for the emperor flowed effortlessly from my lips.

---

[5] A chief feature of shrine architecture is the crossed beams that stick up at each end of the roof. The tips of the beams are cut either horizontally to indicate that a goddess is enshrined within or vertically for a male god.

> Deeply dyed in love
> My heart's hue unchanging
> Like my prayer remains
> Long life for my lord.

A chilling breeze swept through the sacred precincts, and the waters of the Mimosuso River flowed quietly on. The light of the moon, rising now from Mount Kamiji, was so brilliant that I felt sure it shone far beyond our land.

Leaving the sacred precincts after a quiet period of worship, I passed before the building that served as the office and living quarters of the first assistant head priest, Hisayoshi. With its entrances all closed up, the building stood out conspicuously in the brilliant moonlight. It struck me that the outer shrine was known as the Moon Shrine,[6] and so I composed this poem:

> Your element is sunlight,
> But why shut out
> The bright rays of the moon?

I wrote this on a prayer slip, attached it to a *sakaki* branch, and placed it on the veranda of the office. The priest must have found it at dawn, for soon afterward this poem arrived, also attached to some *sakaki*:

> Why shut out the moon?
> My doors are kept unopened
> That an old man might sleep.

After spending a week in quiet retreat at the inner shrine, I inquired about the possibilities of a trip to Futami Beach, wanting to visit that place that had so attracted the goddess.[7] A priest named Munenobu offered to be my guide, and we set off together. We viewed the beach where pilgrims purify themselves, the strand of pine behind it, and a rock said to have been split in two by lightning, and then proceeded down the beach to the Sabi no Myojin Shrine, where we boarded a boat for a tour of the islands of Tateshi, Gozen, and Toru. Gozen Island got its name, which means "offering," from the great clusters of edible *miru* seaweed growing near the island. The priests from Ise Shrine gather this seaweed and offer it to the gods. *Toru* means "to pass through," for this island is a gigantic rock, a portion of which has been worn away by the sea, leaving an

---

[6]It was a common though mistaken belief of Lady Nijo's time that since the inner shrine was dedicated to the sun goddess, the outer shrine was dedicated to a moon god.

[7]The name Futami means "two looks." According to a Japanese myth, when the goddess Yamatohime was searching for a place to deposit the sacred mirror, this piece of shore so attracted her that she came back for a second look.

opening for boats to pass under what now looks like a huge roof beam. There were many other beautiful sights in the vast seascape.

A sacred mirror made by a god to reflect the image of the sun goddess was enshrined at Koasakuma. It is said that it was once stolen and dropped into deep water. When it was recovered and presented at the shrine, the goddess spoke through an oracle: "I have vowed to save all living things—even the fishes in the boundless sea." Then, by its own power, the mirror vanished from the shrine and reappeared on the top of a rock, beside which grew a lone cherry tree. At high tide the mirror lodged in the top of the tree; at low tide it remained on the rock. This illustration of the vow of universal salvation filled me with great hope and made me decide to remain quietly in this vicinity for several more days. I obtained a room in the Shioai district at the residence of the chief administrative official of Ise Shrine, where everyone's kindness made me feel very much at home.

Several days after arriving I went with some of the ladies one night to view the moon at Futami Beach, reputed to be a lovely sight. I was profoundly moved by the beauty of the scene. All through the night we engaged in pleasant pastimes at the beach, returning home as dawn broke.

> Could I ever forget?
> Clear moon shining
> On sparkling beach,
> Its image lingers in dawn's sky.

Somehow word of my visit to the shore reached GoFukakusa's palace, most likely through a serving girl named Terutsuki, who was related to someone at the shrine headquarters. When an unexpected letter came, I presumed it was from a lady I knew at the palace, yet I felt a strange sensation upon opening it. "Now that you are making friends with the moon at Futami, I suppose you've forgotten me completely. I'd like to talk with you again, as we did so unexpectedly that night." The letter transmitted His Majesty's sentiments at some length. Unable to trust my own feelings, I sent this poem in reply:

> Though I live elsewhere,
> Could I ever forget
> The clear moon shining down
> On that familiar palace?

There was no purpose in my staying longer, so I returned to the outer shrine for a brief visit before heading back to Atsuta to finish my sutra copying. Surely the disturbance caused by the fire had quieted down enough now to permit this. I realized, however, that I was not at all eager to leave Ise. I wrote this poem of parting and offered it at the shrine:

> O god of Ise, guide me
> Through the span of life
> Alotted to me still
> In this world of grief.

I was prepared to set out the next day at dawn when a letter arrived from Hisa-yoshi, the first assistant head priest of the inner shrine. "Your parting fills me with great regret," he wrote. "Be sure to return for the festival in the ninth month." How kind he was! I responded with this poem:

> Long life and prosperity
> To my Lord and you!
> In the ninth month I shall return.

About midnight I received an answer, which said: "Others might not understand your heartfelt blessing. What can I reply to a poem that blesses our Lord and me?" With this came two bolts of famous Ise silk and this poem:

> As long as pines are
> Evergreen at the sacred fence,
> Endless years I would wait
> For that joyous autumn day.

While it was still night I went to Ominato Harbor in order to catch the boat that left with the dawn tide. As I rested beside the salt kiln of some humble shore dweller, I recalled the words of an old song: "Among the rocks where cormorants live, or on a beach frequented only by whale, it matters not, if one has a lover." What was my own fate to be? Were I to wait forever, there would be no one to comfort me; were I to cross distant mountains, there would be no place of rendezvous.

We were to depart at daybreak. While it was still dark a letter came from Priest Tsuneyoshi of the outer shrine: "I had intended to send this to you at the inner shrine, but I forgot, so I am sending it now."

> You go with the tide I heard
> And wept, though a stranger.
> Those waves lap strange and distant shores
> Whose very names sound sad.

I replied:

> Our bond is that of strangers
> Yet now that I depart
> To return to distant shores
> Receding waves dampen my sleeves.

At Atsuta Shrine there was still the hubbub and confusion of reconstruction, but I was unwilling to postpone the completion of my pledge any longer, and I managed to arrange for a place to finish copying out the remaining thirty scrolls of the *Kegon Sutra*, which I then dedicated at the shrine. The ceremony of dedication was in the hands of an insignificant country priest who did not seem to understand what he was doing, but I made sure that various services were performed, including some music to please the guardian gods of the sutra. Then I returned to the capital.

1292 OR 1293

I knew I would remember until my death that unexpected meeting with His Majesty at the Iwashimizu Shrine. Afterward from time to time he would send one of his relatives to my old home with a message, but he refrained from importuning me to make decisions, and I was grateful for his continued sympathy as I passed the days and months in idleness until the ninth month of the following year. At that time His Majesty sent several letters urging me to visit him at the detached palace in Fushimi, where he was staying. "This is a quiet, relaxing place," he wrote, "and there is little chance of gossip spreading."

My love-filled, guilt-ridden heart acquiesced, and I went secretly to the lower palace at Fushimi. The oddness of the situation fully dawned on me when someone came to show me in. While waiting for His Majesty to appear, I went out on the veranda of the Kutai Hall and gazed at the Uji River and its lonely scene until the ever-flowing ripples of the river found their way to my cheeks, bringing to mind the old poem: "Where wind-rippled waves are all there is to see."

I lingered in reverie until His Majesty appeared late in the evening. The moon was bright, yet at the sight of him so changed from his past appearance, tears clouded my eyes. Once again we had a long talk ranging from that time in the distant past when I had played at his knees as a young child to the day I fled his palace certain that all was over. Yet these events, all from my own past, somehow failed to touch any deep feelings in me.

"Why have you let so much time pass without ever expressing your feelings about things?" he asked. "As long as we are living in this world of sorrow we are beset with grief." Indeed, what grievance did I have besides that of having to live as I did? Often I had thought of how it would feel to be able to disclose my sufferings and thoughts to someone and be comforted, but now I could find no words to express this wish. As His Majesty continued talking, I could hear the mournful cries of the deer on Mount Otowa and the sound of the dawn bell at Sokujoin warning us that day was breaking.

> The cries of deer
> Joined by the bell's sound
> Inquire about my tears
> As the sky brightens with dawn.

I kept this poem to myself.

Daybreak approached, and I prepared to leave, tears streaming down my face. His image lay deep within my heart. GoFukakusa said, "I hope that we can meet again on another moonlit night in this lifetime, but you persist in placing your hopes for our meeting only after the far distant dawn of salvation. What kind of vows are you cherishing? A man is more or less free to travel eastward or even to China, but there are so many hindrances for a traveling woman that I understand it to be impossible. Who have you pledged yourself to as a companion in your renunciation of this world? I still cannot believe it is possible for you to travel alone. What about Iinuma, from whom, as you wrote, you parted over a 'river of tears,' or the man at Kasuga and his hedge of chrysanthemums, or Tsunayoshi and that 'joyous autumn day'? These were surely more than frivolous exchanges. You must have made some deep and lasting pledges. And there must certainly have been others too with whom you have traveled." His Majesty kept at me with questions and remarks of this sort.

At last I replied, "Ever since I left the mist-shrouded palace to wander perplexed in frost-covered places, I have understood the scriptural passage: 'The restless world of unenlightened men is like a burning house,' for I have known no rest even for a single night. The sutras also say, 'Examine your present state to discover your past karma.' I am well aware of the wretchedness of my condition. Bonds that are once severed cannot be retied. I have certainly not met good fortune in this life, even though my Minamoto lineage puts me under the protection of the god Hachiman. When I traveled east for the first time, I went directly to the Tsurugaoka Shrine just to worship him. In this life I think constantly of salvation, petitioning the gods to dissolve my sins that I may be reborn in paradise.

"The vow of the gods to reward honesty has marvelous efficacy. I swear to you that though I traveled eastward as far as the Sumida River in Musashino, I did not so much as make a single night's pledge to any man. If I did, may I be excluded from the promise of Amida to save all mankind and may I sink to the deepest hell for all eternity. And if any bond of love attracted me when I visited the pure waters of the sacred river at Ise, may I incur the punishment of the great god Dainichi, who is said to rule both the diamond and the womb realms. My poem on the autumn chrysanthemums at Kasuga was simply a means of dispelling my nostalgia. If there is a man from the slopes of Nara southward to whom I have pledged my troth, may the four great gods whom I worshiped at the Kasuga Shrine withdraw their protection, leaving me to suffer the eight tortures of hell.

"I grieve over the fact that I have never known the face of my mother, who died when I was two, and I shed tears of longing when I recall the care my father gave me until he too passed away when I was only fifteen. I was yet a child when you kindly blessed me with your concern and generously bestowed on me your deep compassion. Under your tutelage, the sorrow of being orphaned gradually disappeared, and I grew up and received your favor. Why did I not value it fully? What an inept, stupid ass I was—although even an ass understands the four debts of gratitude.[8] How then, as a human being, could I have possibly forgotten your love? Your kindness shone on me when I was young like the light of the sun and moon combined, and as I grew, you lavished more affection on me than a pair of doting parents. Many years have drifted past since we parted so unexpectedly, yet I shed tears for the past whenever I meet you on one of your excursions, and I am never unaffected when official positions and ranks are conferred and I learn of another family's prosperity or of the rise of an old acquaintance. When I try to still the feeling prompted by these occasions I find I am unable to hold back my tears, so I journey far and wide in an attempt to overcome my emotions. Sometimes I stay at cloisters; other times I mix with common men. When I find a place where people are sympathetic and compose poetry, I stay for several days, and of course there is no dearth of people who enjoy starting rumors, whether in the capital or in the countryside. I have heard that sometimes, against her better judgment, a nun will get involved with an ascetic or mendicant she happens to meet, but I have never fallen into such a relationship. I spend my idle nights in solitude. If only I had such a relationship even in the capital. If only I had someone to share my bed, it might help ward off the mountain winds on cold and frosty nights. But there is no such person; no one awaits me, and I pass idle days under the blossoms. In the autumn, when leaves turn, the insect voices, weakening as the frost deepens, reflect my own unhappy fate as I spend night after night in travelers' lodgings."

His Majesty continued to press me: "On pilgrimages to holy places I'm sure you keep your vows in purity, but here in the capital, where you have no vows to keep, what is to prevent you from renewing an old friendship?"

---

[8]According to Confucian thought, one owed debts of gratitude to heaven, the sovereign, one's parents, and mankind.

"I have not even reached the age of forty yet, and I have no idea what the future holds—though I doubt that I shall have a very long life—but now, as of this very moment, I assure you I have no such relationships, either old or new. If I am lying, may all the works in which I've placed my hope for salvation—the two thousand days of reading the *Lotus Sutra*, the considerable time I have spent copying sutras in my own hand—may all these become but burdens in hell; may all my hopes come to naught; may I never live to see the dawn of Miroku's salvation, but instead remain forever damned to hell."

I could not tell the effect of what I had said, for he remained quiet for a time before replying. Then he said, "The feelings of a person in love are never logical. It is true that after you lost your mother and then your father, I willingly accepted the responsibility of raising you, but things did not go as I had intended, and I felt that our relationship was, after all, only a shallow one. All this time has passed without my realizing how much you cared for me. The Bodhisattva Hachiman first made this known to me when we met on his sacred mountain." As His Majesty spoke, the setting moon slipped behind the ridge of the mountains to the west, and the rays of the rising sun lit up the eastern sky.

I left quickly, feeling the need to be discreet in my nun's garb. As I returned to my lodgings, I wondered if His Majesty's parting words, "We must meet again soon," might not be a promise I would carry with me beyond death.

After His Majesty had returned to the capital I was somewhat surprised by the person he chose to bear a message of such genuine concern that I felt pleased and honored. I would have been content with even the slightest expression of affection, so the extent of the love revealed by his message left me overjoyed— even though I could share its words with no one. Since the end of our relationship long ago, his treatment of me had been beyond reproach, and I no longer had vivid memories of our love. Yet now that I knew more clearly some of the feelings His Majesty had hitherto concealed, those events of long ago would not recede from my memory.

Several years went by after this until I decided to go back to Futami Shore. If the gods themselves had visited there twice, I thought my return was in order, particularly since I wanted to pray for enlightenment. From Nara I took the Iga Road, visiting the Kasaoki Temple en route.

FURTHER READINGS

Although dealing with the earlier Heian period, aspects of court life typical of Lady Nijo's day are presented in Ivan Morris, *The World of the Shining Prince: Court Life in Ancient Japan* (New York: Knopf, 1964). John Whitney Hall, *Government and Local Power in Japan, 500 to 1700* (Princeton, NJ: Princeton

University Press, 1966) treats the origins of feudalism and the nature of provincial government during the Kamakura period. A more general account of feudal life in Japan is available in Peter Duus, *Feudalism in Japan* (New York: Knopf, 1969). Peter Varley, *The Samurai* (London: Weidenfeld and Nicolson, 1970) includes a brief discussion of the origin and rise of the samurai. Notable among the histories of the period is Sir George Samson, *A History of Japan to 1334* (Stanford, CA: Stanford University Press, 1958).

Helen Craig McCullough has provided translations of two important works from medieval Japan: *The Taiheiki: A Chronicle of Medieval Japan* (New York: Columbia University Press, 1959) and *Yoshitsune: A Fifteenth-Century Japanese Chronicle* (Stanford, CA: Stanford University Press, 1966). The tradition of Japanese court poetry is examined by Earl Miner, *An Introduction to Japanese Court Poetry* (Stanford, CA: Stanford University Press, 1968).

PART II

Discussion Questions

1. In *Cold Mountain Poems*, Han Shan has studied his inner self and has learned something very important that he wishes to teach us. He finds it difficult to express himself, however, and states, "All I can say to those I meet: 'Try and make it to Cold Mountain.'" On the other hand, Chu Hsi, in *Reflections of Things at Hand*, simply produces a manual that will lead one, even without the guidance of a qualified teacher, to the knowledge of things. What accounts for the difference in these two approaches to gaining knowledge? Why did Buddha find it so simple to express himself about inner knowledge in *The Sermon at the Deer Park*?

2. Saktikumara, in *The Perfect Bride*, and Genji, in *Appraisal of Women on a Rainy Night*, are looking for the perfect woman. What qualities do they value in a woman? Would either of them have been particularly satisfied with one who followed completely all of the *Lessons for Women* (Part I)? What qualities might they admire in Lady Nijo, in the *Confessions of Lady Nijo*? On the other hand, what might Lady Nijo have thought of Saktikumara and Genji?

3. Which is the more important aspect of individual virtue, doing good or abstaining from evil? What would Sanudasa's friends in *The Travels of San-*

udasa the Merchant say? What would the hermit in the same story say? Three figures from Part I might each contribute their own answers: Kung Fu-tzu, in *The Analects*; Krishna, in the *Bhagavad Gita*; and Buddha, in *The Sermon at the Deer Park*. How do you account for such disagreement regarding such a relatively straightforward question?

4. Is it possible that neither doing good nor abstaining from evil are really very important for salvation and fulfillment? What role does individual virtue play in *The Pure Land* and *Cold Mountain Poems*? *The Pure Land* was particularly popular in Japan; what connection do you think this might have had with the rapid spread of Christianity among the Japanese during the sixteenth century?

5. Human beings seem to yearn for two often conflicting qualities: personal liberty and social order. Which of the two is the more important in maintaining human happiness? How would the authors of *Arthasastra* (Part I), *Cold Mountain Poems*, and *Peach Blossom Spring* respond to the question, and how do you account for the differences in their answers?

6. One might argue that the conflict between personal liberty and social order can be reconciled if crucial values and attitudes are shared by everyone. How would the Heian nobles in *Appraisal of Women on a Rainy Night* respond to this argument? How would the women they are appraising react? The question of liberty versus order does not seem even to be considered in *The Pure Land*. Why is this? If one agrees with the basic position that liberty and order can be reconciled in this fashion, does this imply that such a conflict will always exist in a pluralistic society?

7. It is, perhaps, the dream of every individual to reach a permanently happy state, and many cultures concern themselves with the question of the means of obtaining this goal. It must be remembered, however, that the nature of that goal is culturally defined; much of the West considers it under the term "salvation." The following works address the issue more or less directly: *The Sermon at the Deer Park* (Part I), *The Pure Land*, and *Cold Mountain Poems*. How does each define ultimate happiness, and what suggestions are given for its attainment?

8. Perhaps the closest bond between two individuals is that of love between a man and a woman. Historians generally consider the concept of romantic love to be a Western European development, arising in the eleventh to twelfth centuries. Do you consider this to be the case? Can the relationship between Chang and Ying-ying in *The Romance of the Western Chamber* be considered romantic love? What was the quality of the love that Lady Nijo felt for GoFukakusa in *Confessions of Lady Nijo*, and how did it differ from

romantic love? Do the poems by Li Po, "Written in Behalf of my Wife," in *The Poetry of Li Po and Tu Fu*, and by Hitomaro, "On Parting from His Wife as He Sets Out from Iwami for the Capital" in *A Collection of Ten Thousand Leaves* strike you as being romantic love poems? What do you consider the definition of romantic love? Does it include mutual respect? Do you think romantic love was one of the factors considered by Genji in *Appraisal of Women on a Rainy Night*? How do you account for the absence of romantic love in *The Perfect Bride*?

9. The traditional Western concept of the origin of the physical universe is that it was created by God, and many Westerners find it difficult to approach philosophies based on a godless universe. How does Lao Tzu in the *Tao te ching* (Part I) explain the origin of the physical world and the orderly way in which it appears to operate? Compare this view with that of Chu Hsi, in *Reflections of Things at Hand*. What differences and what similarities do you find in their approaches? Do you find either view satisfactory? How do their views compare with the modern scientific "big bang" concept?

10. Subjects of a weak government often complain about lack of security, while others, under a strong government, complain about the weight of their obligations. What can you determine about the nature of the Tang government from *The Poetry of Li Po and Tu Fu*? What does the poetry of Hitomaro and Yakamochi, in *A Collection of Ten Thousand Leaves*, tell you about the Nara government? What complaints against life under a strong government are legitimate, and which are not? What does *Peach Blossom Spring* tell us about the government of the Eastern Chin dynasty?

11. Compare the Krishna of the *Bhagavad Gita* in Part I with the Krishna appearing in the *Gitagovinda*. In what ways has the nature of this god changed over the years? Do people alter their concepts of the character and nature of their deities to suit their needs? If so, is it possible to determine if an unalterable reality exists behind these inconstant traditions? How?

12. Village and family have been two of the basic and enduring institutions of Chinese society. While the literary views of the family often tend to be ambivalent, those of village life are normally loving. This is exemplified in *The Poetry of Li Po and Tu Fu* and *Peach Blossom Spring*. What elements of village life so capture the affection of the Chinese?

13. The differences between men and women are reflected in the traditions and institutions of most societies. Men and women play different roles and often have quite different values. It is well to keep this in mind when attempting to generalize about societies. In *Appraisal of Women on a Rainy Night*, do Genji and his friends reflect the views of Heian nobles in their discussion, or

do they reflect the manner in which Lady Murasaki Shikubu felt that Heian nobles should discuss the qualities of the perfect woman? Is their vision of the perfect woman that of Heian men or of Heian women? Lady Nijo knows the deference due an emperor, but is her description of the actions and attitudes of her old lover, the emperor GoFukakusa, all it seems to be on the surface? How has he treated her, and what does he want from her? What does she want, and what is her response when he finally leaves the scene? If inner knowledge is reality, and both men and women can obtain inner knowledge, then reality should be the same for both men and women. Try to imagine that the hermit Han Shan was a woman, and that it was she who had written all of these poems for you to try to understand. Would you feel differently about them? Why? Finally, in *The Perfect Bride*, which is the more admirable character, Saktikumara or his bride? The story seems to be merely funny, but it has a serious undertone. What is Dandin trying to tell us about women in the India of his time?

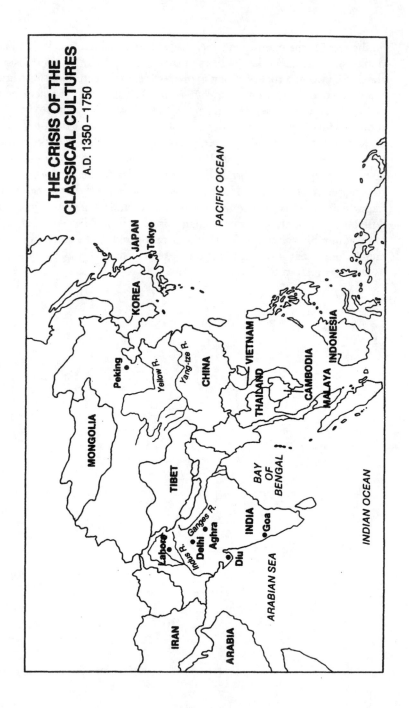

THE CRISIS OF THE
CLASSICAL CULTURES
A.D. 1350 – 1750

PACIFIC OCEAN

JAPAN
Tokyo

KOREA

MONGOLIA

Peking

Yellow R.

Yang-tze R.

CHINA

VIETNAM

THAILAND

CAMBODIA

MALAYA INDONESIA

TIBET

BAY
OF
BENGAL

INDIA

Ganges R.

Lahore

Indus R.

Delhi

Aghra

Goa

Diu

INDIAN OCEAN

IRAN

ARABIA

ARABIAN SEA

PART III

In the Long Tradition

The Crisis of the Classical Cultures: A.D. *1350 to 1750*

Mongol power in China was finally ended by a wave of rebellions against a weakened and hated alien government. The Mongol's successors, the Ming dynasty (1368–1644), restored Chinese institutions and secured for the inhabitants of China 276 years of relative peace and prosperity. Although the Ch'ing dynasty (1644–1912) that followed was composed of foreign Manchurians, they had already adopted many Chinese customs and by and large simply continued the institutions of Ming government and society insofar as conditions allowed them to do so. Thus for the next five centuries the pattern of Chinese history was set by the peculiar features of the Ming restoration of native Chinese rule.

Throughout this period, life and culture in the interior of China progressed at a peaceful pace. This was partly due to the return of imperial administration to Chinese hands, the restoration of the civil service examination system, and the conscious policy of Ming rulers to turn for inspiration to the traditions of the period preceding the arrival of the despised Mongols. An important aspect of this process was the need to restore to Confucian scholars a sense of the importance of moral conduct and enlightened action, a sense that had been weakened by their long exclusion from active participation in political and economic decision making. This task was performed by the philosopher Wang Yang-ming (1472–1529), who, in *Inquiry on the Great Learning*, declares that knowledge should not exist for its own sake but be expressed in action. An example of this doctrine is *Journey to the West*, written in 1570 by Wu Ch'en-en after he had traveled to India and returned to China. In *Journey* he effectively admonishes the declining Ming dynasty by comparing it unfavorably with Indian life and institutions and with the glorious days of the T'ang dynasty.

The Ming emperors restored the tributary and vassal state system established by the T'ang dynasty in the seventh century. Japan, Korea, Vietnam, and Tibet all sent tribute to the imperial court at Peking, although real submission was not as important a factor in these missions as was that of recognizing the restoration of the cultural center of the East Asian world. The Ming emperors had even more grandiose schemes for proclaiming their supremacy. Imperial fleets sent out from Chinese ports, sailed the coast of Southeast Asia, and ranged widely through the Indian Ocean and Arabian Sea (1405–1433) eighty

275

years before the Europeans entered those waters. Ming China had the opportunity to become the mistress of Asian seas and to develop overseas commerce on an unprecedented scale but never exploited this potential. Instead, the government ended these naval expeditions and turned its back on the possibilities of overseas trade. The reasons for this extraordinary attitude are complex, but the effect was to exclude China from the commercial revolution and from participation in the great acceleration of technological innovations that took place during the period. Once the technological leader of the world, China steadily fell further behind other societies, particularly those of Western Europe. Meanwhile, Chinese life continued along its traditional paths relatively unaffected, as is illustrated by excerpts that follow from two novels written near the end of the period, *The Dream of the Red Chamber* (1744) and *The Scholars* (1750).

Despite its nominal tributary status, Japan was hardly subordinated to China. Quite to the contrary, the rich coasts of China provided an irresistible attraction for Japanese adventures. Even as Ming China withdrew from overseas trade, Japanese vessels, both merchant and pirate, filled the vacuum. The result was the rapid growth in Japan of commercial cities and a dynamic middle class. This development was felt throughout Japanese society, but is nowhere better illustrated than in the two major forms of drama that evolved during the period. *No* dramas, derived from Heian times, are generally aristocratic and stylized. An example is *Kanehira*, which was written in 1440. *Kabuki* theater, on the other hand, is popular, adventurous, and comical. The most famous such play is the *Chushingura*, written in 1748. A typical episode of this play is offered here in *The Treasury of Loyal Retainers*.

The theme of both of these plays, separated in time by three centuries, is the samurai warrior, an emphasis that illustrates the prevalence of warfare throughout the era. The samurai became, during this period, a class of professional warriors admired by all levels of society and who exerted an influence on Japanese society disproportionate to their numbers. Their professional code of ethics, such as is expressed in the excerpts from *Hagakure*, became a form of popular philosophy, and samurai values and attitudes became deeply embedded in Japanese culture. The reason for this emphasis on military values and ideals lay in the essentially feudal character of Japanese governmental institutions. Japanese government under the shoguns was never much more than a confederation of great clan leaders and their bands of samurai, and politics consisted of the shifting patterns of alliances among those families. Stability depended on the personal character of the shogun and on the strength and support of his allies.

From 1336 to 1392, Japan was divided between two rival courts, and the Ashikaga shoguns (1392–1573), who reunited the country, could never fully control their followers. Their failure to do so led to a century of civil wars (1467–1568). Local military leaders, known as daimyos, took advantage of the lack of order to seize the great estates in their jurisdictions and to consolidate the lands under their control into independent feudal units. Three successive leaders of the sixteenth century, culminating in Hideyoshi (1537–1598) and Tokugawa Ieyasu (1543–1616) were able to gather a number of daimyos under their strong leadership and finally to create an effective central government, the Tokugawa shogunate (1600–1868). The daimyos were eventually converted into administrative officials, serving at the order of the shogun. The capital was moved to Edo (modern Tokyo), and the daimyos' loyalty and obedience was ensured by requiring their wives and children to reside in the capital, under the power of the shogun, while the daimyos had to live there every other year.

Europe had opened trade with Japan in 1545, and the Tokugawas were eager to expand this commerce as well as increase their own overseas trade throughout East Asia. European ships, guns and cannon, and navigational instruments particularly intrigued the Japanese, who clearly saw their superiority to native products. The Europeans brought more than trade goods and technological innovations with them, however, and large numbers of Japanese converted to Christianity. Distrusting such a weakening of Japanese cultural integrity, the shoguns began discouraging the tendency by persecuting and humiliating Christians, both Japanese and European. A Christian revolt in 1637–1638 turned this distrust into fanatic hatred, and hundreds of Christians were executed. In their determination to isolate Japan from further Christian, and therefore European, influence, the shoguns were willing to give up foreign trade. In 1635, Japanese were forbidden to leave Japan and return, thus throwing the rich commercial and manufacturing life of the islands into turmoil. In 1641, Westerners were barred from the islands except for a few Dutch merchants, who were kept isolated on a small island and allowed to conduct only a minimum of business. Japan had met the challenge of foreign influences, and responded by rejecting them completely. Although art and literature flourished under the Tokugawa shogunate, and commerce and manufacturing soon revived, Japan, like China, fell ever further behind the Westerners in technological and organizational development.

From a Hindu's point of view, at least, India met the challenges of the period much less successfully than China and Japan. From their capitals at Delhi and later Aghra, Muslim rulers extended their political power and Muslim culture over much of the subcontinent. Even the South, which generally had been spared the rigors of invasion and foreign rule, and in which native Hindu culture was now concentrated, was not free from Muslim attack. Persian replaced Sanskrit as the language of administration and refined literature. The leading philosophers were concerned with Islamic theology, and artists and architects worked with Muslim themes. Indian culture was now preeminently that of the Muslim North, and even the terrible and destructive raid of Timur-i-lang through that region in 1398 did little to alter that fact. This is not to say that native Indian culture had lost all vitality; indeed it provided a constant influence upon the Muslims. The eclectic philosophy of the poet Kabir, illustrated in the selections chosen from his work, displays this blending of Islamic and Hindu values and attitudes.

At the beginning of the sixteenth century, a new power emerged on the Indian scene. Following the first explorers, the Portuguese admiral Affonso Alburquerque established European control of the Arabian Sea and Indian Ocean (1509–1515). Portuguese commercial colonies were established at Goa and Diu, and the forces of Westernization and Christianity were introduced into the Indian world. Shortly after these events, Mughal forces under Babur (1483–1530) seized Lahore, Delhi, and Aghra. In 1527, a confederacy of Rajput warriors, once more hoping to restore Hindu dominance in North India, met Babur in battle and were decisively defeated. The great Mughal Empire had been established. By 1562, the emperor Akbar (1542–1605) began the process of uniting all of North India and much of eastern Persia under Mughal rule, a process that was substantially completed by his death. The greatest Indian ruler of the early modern period, Akbar was distinguished for his tolerance and eclecticism. He proclaimed the principle that the emperor should be sovereign over all, and the oppression of Hinduism ceased. Many Hindus served as his generals and administrators, and he called a council of representatives of the various faiths of India to develop the tenets of a syncretic religion called Divine Faith, which he then proposed to propagate throughout the world in the interests of peace. This visionary scheme failed, but illustrates the idealism of this ruler and the pattern of tolerance and cultural sharing that prospered under his rule. The eclectic religion of the Sikhs had begun much earlier, but they chose this era to close the canon of their scriptures. The Sacred Songs of the Sikhs, some early examples of which appear here, illustrate the amalgamation of traditions that had occurred under the beneficent rule of Akbar. He was himself a scholar, and under his patronage art and literature began to flourish once more. The great hero of the Mogul dynasty, his praises were sung in the Akbar Nama, selections from which follow.

The wars for empire in Western Europe during the seventeenth and eighteenth centuries had as one of their great prizes the commerce of India. Portuguese power declined, and other nations arrived to seek trading stations along the Indian coast. Soon Dutch, English, and French enclaves were beginning to tap the commerce and resources of the interior while squabbling among themselves for primacy in the Indian trade. It must be remembered that Western technological superiority over the Asians was still slight, and lay mainly in artillery and naval architecture. The Europeans had neither the numbers nor the means to penetrate the interior of the Asian nations. Instead, they sought favorable locations along the coast, which they could fortify and defend, and treaties that would allow them to establish business relations with native merchants of the interior. As a consequence, European influence in India during much of this period remained restricted and indirect.

The emperor Aurangzeb (1659–1707) reversed many of the policies of Akbar and, inspired by religious zeal, attempted to extend the Mughal Empire at the expense of the last few independent Hindu states. He thus alienated the Hindu supporters of the Mughal Empire and created more enemies for it. His exaggerated suspicion of his subordinates made orderly administration impossible, and the empire began to decline. Stung by persecution into armed opposition to the Mughals, the pacifistic and anti-caste Sikh religion transformed itself into an hereditary class of professional warriors. Despite all his ill-advised policies, by the time of his death Aurangzeb had succeeded in uniting almost all of India under his rule. After his reign, however, his accumulated errors of judgment began to tell, and his empire had disintegrated within twenty years after his death.

Throughout most of the period from 1350 to 1750, Western technological and military superiority over Asians was marginal at best. Europeans could control the sea lanes and defend favorably situated coastal sites, but posed no serious threat to the interiors of the Asian states. This was particularly true because, without steam power, their ships were virtually defenseless when attempting to sail upriver. For this reason, even weak Asian states could determine the terms on which they would allow a European presence and accept Western influences. If this was true in a disunited and anarchic India, it was even more so in strong and well-organized countries such as China and Japan. Since Westerners were willing to trade anything, including their technology, this presented a golden opportunity for Asia to learn from the West and to close the technological gap that existed between them. Neither China nor Japan were willing to accept this opportunity, however. From the heights of their two thousand years of tradition and from the perspective of their highly developed culture, the Chinese could see the Europeans, with their strange dress, talk, and interesting toys, only as another "barbarian" people, to be treated as potential tributaries but not to be allowed to disturb the even tenor of Chinese life. They thus restricted Western presence to a few trading ports, and refused even to consider what real advantages European learning and technology might have to offer. The Japanese, on the other hand, were quite well aware of the advantages to be gained and craved cannon, ships, and guns on the European model. They had encountered a problem, however, that would cause even greater difficulties in the future: how to acquire Western technology without having to accept other Western ways. They wanted Western trade goods and technology, but not at the cost of having to try to absorb Christian ideas into the fabric of traditional

Japanese life. Finding no immediate answer to this dilemma, they avoided it altogether by turning their backs on Western ideas and cultivating their own native heritage. Despite their internal problems, however, during the period 1350–1750, the Asian nations enjoyed a respite from devastating foreign invasions during which they might have avoided completely losing technological superiority to the Europeans. Instead, they turned inward, ignoring the facts that their technological inferiority was growing constantly more marked and the European powers would not always be willing to deal with Asian nations on the Asians' terms.

KANEHIRA
Zeami

Drama has attracted more attention from the Western world than any other form of Japanese literature. Of the four major forms of Japanese drama existing today, No is undoubtedly the most popular with Western readers. No is a uniquely native theater form that evolved from the singing and dancing performances popular in Heian times or even earlier. The development of this sophisticated theater into its present forms is attributed chiefly to the genius of two men, Kan'ami (1333–1384), a Shinto priest, and his son Zeami (1363–1443). They not only composed plays, but also acted in them, while Zeami in addition formulated the critical and aesthetic criteria of the art.

A performance of No is presented on a simple stage without any special scenery. The tone of the play is serious, and the presentation symbolic. The actors' movements are carefully choreographed, and extensive dancing highlights the performance. A chorus, seated at the side of the stage, expresses what is in the actor's mind and sings his lines while he dances. The actors and chorus are all men, and the principal characters wear beautifully fashioned masks, some of which are masterpieces of sculpture. Music of drums and flutes is combined with dancing, elegant costumes, poetic dialogue, and symbolic pantomime to produce one of the world's great art forms.

No plays draw heavily on Japanese literary tradition and recreate many of the most beloved and deeply moving scenes of such works as The Tale of Genji and The Tale of the Heike. No drama is of particular historical importance since it reflects vividly the emotions and customs of the Japanese during the four centu-

From Zeami, Kanehira, trans. Stanleigh H. Jones, Jr., in Twenty Plays of the No Theatre, ed. Donald Keene (New York: Columbia University Press, 1970), pp. 268–79.

ries of their medieval period. This stormy age, dominated by the samurai class with its rigid code of chivalry and loyalty, began amidst the violence of the civil wars that wracked Japan in the twelfth century.

No plays are classified by subject matter and fall into the categories of god plays, warrior plays, female-wig plays, mad woman plays, and concluding plays. It became customary to include one play of each type in a full program. The play presented here, *Kanehira* belongs to the class of warrior plays. It has traditionally been attributed to Zeami, but this has recently been questioned.

The theme of the play is drawn from the *Heike Monogatari*, a thirteenth-century work describing the civil wars between the Heike and Genji clans. The major characters, Kiso Yoshinaka (1154–1184) and Imai Kanehira (d. 1184), were historical figures who played significant roles in these conflicts. Yoshinaka was a Minamoto general in the war against the Taira, and a quarrel with his ally Yoshitsune led to fighting between the two. Kanehira, a long-time friend of Yoshinaka, served as his chief of staff in this conflict, and the deaths of these two tragic figures form the central theme of the play. *Kanehira* is notable for its travel description, the longest in No drama, which serves to heighten the suspense for the narration that follows, and for its powerful descriptions of battle in the second part of the play.

Questions

1. Discuss Kanehira's conduct. What does it tell us about the code of the samurai?
2. What is the samurai attitude toward death?
3. What aspects of religious life are presented in this work?

KANEHIRA

PERSONS   A priest from Kiso Province (*waki*)
An old boatman, later revealed to be Kanehira's
Ghost (*mae-jite*)
A ferryman at Yabase (*kyogen*)
The ghost of Imai Kanehira (*nochi-jite*)

PLACE   Part I: a boat traveling between Yabase and Awazu
in Omi Province
Part II: Awazu Plain in Omi

TIME   Early summer, the Fourth Month

PART 1

(The Priest enters to the naming-place and faces the rear of the stage.)

PRIEST   *I begin my journey from Shinano,*
            I begin my journey from Shinano—
            I shall seek the grave of Lord Kiso.

(He faces front.)

I am a priest from the mountain village of Kiso. I have heard that Lord Kiso met his death upon the Plain of Awazu in the province of Omi. I shall go there to pray for his soul's repose.

            And now I hasten on to Awazu Moor.
            Ah, the road through Shinano
            Famed for Kiso's hanging bridge
            Famed for Kiso's swinging bridge.
            I will pray before his grave!
            Night after night in wayside fields,

            (He takes two or three steps to his right, then returns.)

            Brief hours of sleep under shading grass,
            Day after day I journey,
            And now before I know it
            I am on the road of Omi,
            I have reached the strand at Yabase,
            Reached Yabase shore.

            (His return signifies his arrival at Yabase. He kneels at the waki-position. The stage attendant brings on a representation of the boat, and places it near the shite-pillar. The Boatman enters, wearing the asakurajo mask and carrying a bamboo pole.)

BOATMAN   *I bear the weight*
            Of years of fruitless labor,
            Piled high like the brushwood in my boat.
            But before these fagots kindle
            My heart will char with flames of longing.

            (The Priest rises and faces the Boatman.)

PRIEST　Ho there! Take me across in your boat.

BOATMAN　This is not the ferry between Yabase and Yamada. Look, the boat is loaded with brushwood. I cannot ferry you across.

PRIEST　I can see that you carry firewood in your boat, but there is no other boat at the crossing now. I am a priest—as a special favor, please ferry me across.

BOATMAN　True indeed, being a priest you are not the same as other men. Yes, it says in the *Sutra*, "like finding a ferry at a crossing."[1]

PRIEST　*To wait at dusk of a long day's journey.*
And find at last a ship . . .

BOATMAN　How strange that chance brings us together.

TOGETHER　*If this were the boat for Yabase*
On the Sea of Omi,[2]
It would be a traveler's ferry, nothing more.

CHORUS *(for the Boatman).*
But this craft carries fagots
Across an inconstant world—
Hauling firewood, for a wretched living.
My sleeve is never dry, seasoned to my tears
As my bamboo pole to the water.
You are a stranger, yet a man of the Law.
How can I begrudge you passage?

(He beckons to the Priest.)

Hurry come board,
Hurry hurry come abroad.

(The Priest kneels in the boat. The Boatman makes poling motions.)

PRIEST　Boatman, I've something to ask you. These shores and mountains I see, surely they are all famous places. Please tell me their names.

BOATMAN　Yes, all are well-known places. Ask and I will tell you about them.

(The Priest looks upward.)

[1]From a passage in the Lotus Sutra which describes the Buddha's merciful compassion as being "like a child who has a mother, like having a ferry at a crossing, like having a doctor in time of illness, like having a lamp in darkness."
[2]Lake Biwa, northeast of Kyoto. Because of its size (Japan's largest lake) it is often referred to in literature as the Sea of Omi.

PRIEST   First of all, the great mountain over there—is that Mount Hiei?

(The Boatman looks up too.)

BOATMAN   Yes, that indeed is Mount Hiei.

(He turns a little to his right.)

At the foot are the twenty-one shrines of Sanno. And on that peak so green with foliage is Hachioji Shrine. You can see all the houses in Tozu-Sakamoto.

(He turns to the Priest.)

PRIEST   Mount Hiei lies northeast of the Capital, does it not?

BOATMAN   You are right. Mount Hiei guards the demons' gateway into the Capital and wards off evil spirits. It is called the Pinnacle of the Highest Doctrine after the example of Vulture Peak[3]—you must have heard of it. It is known also as Mount Tendai because of its resemblance to the Cavern of the Four Lights in China.[4] The Great Teacher Dengyo, in common cause with the Emperor Kammu, founded his temple there in the Enryaku era. He wrote the lines, "Send down your divine grace upon these timbers that I raise." You can see all the way to the Main Central Hall at the crest.

PRIEST   Is the place they call the Covered Bridge of Omiya also in Sakamoto?

BOATMAN   Yes, that rather thickly wooded spot at the foot of the mountain is the Omiya Covered Bridge.

PRIEST   I am grateful when I hear the Buddha's words, "All living creatures equally possess the Buddha nature," that even we, so humble, can hope for grace.

BOATMAN   So, the Buddha and all living things being one, there is no gulf between us, even a priest like you, and me.

PRIEST   *From that peak of loftiest doctrine,*
Thick as branches on a tree,
His teachings can be seen everywhere.

BOATMAN   *And at its base, the sea of contemplation*
Overflows its banks,

---

[3]Mountain in central India sacred because Shakyamuni preached his doctrines there.
[4]Referring to Mount T'ien T'ai in China which was supposed to have a cave on its peak with openings in the four directions, thus being illuminated by the sun and moon.

PRIEST   *Revealing to us the triple teachings:*
           The holy rules, meditation, wisdom—

BOATMAN   The names we give the three pagodas.[5]

CHORUS *(for the Boatman).*
        In one thought three thousand worlds revealed;[6]
        So here are placed three thousand priests.
        This law of perfect harmony
        Is cloudless as the moon above Yokawa.

        (The Boatman turns to the right.)

        At the mountain's foot, the little waves

        (He looks toward the bridgeway.)

        Lap at the single pine of Kara Cape in Shiga,
        From where the sacred car will cross the water.[7]

        (He looks upward.)

        The ruffling waves, like ripples from the plying pole,
        Roll in bubbles onto the opposite shore;
        Distant Awazu forest now is near.
        The little waves lick at the now more distant shore behind them.
        And the mountain cherries, known from long ago,
        Are green with leaves; no blossoms now remain
        In mountains tressed with summer foliage.
        The brushwood boat has crossed the blue-hued waters;
        The priest, impatient for his destination,
        Urges the boat across the last low waves.
        Quickly they have reached Awazu beach,
        Quickly they have reached Awazu.

        (The Priest gets out of the boat and goes to kneel at the waki-position. *The Boatman gets out too, and exits. The stage assistant removes the boat. The Ferryman enters with a pole over his shoulder.)*

[5]The Eastern Tower, the Western Tower, and Yokawa Tower, three towers said to have been built as symbols of these three teachings.

[6]The Buddhist teaching of the Tendai sect that in one concentrated prayer one can comprehend the three thousand manifestations of the Buddhist Law.

[7]Reference to the festival of the Hiyoshi Shrine at the foot of Mount Hiei during which the God's palanquin is taken across Lake Biwa from Kara Cape.

INTERLUDE

FERRYMAN   I am the ferryman of Yabase Beach. I am on duty at the ferry today and I think I shall take the boat across. I am glad the weather is so fine.

(He sees the Priest.)

You there, sir, if you wish to cross over I will take you.

PRIEST   I have just come from the other side.

FERRYMAN   That cannot be. Our regulations say I cannot put my boat out on another's day of duty. He cannot interfere on days when I am on duty. Today is my turn, so no one could have ferried you across. Are you telling the truth?

PRIEST   I do not lie. But come here, I want to ask you more.

(The Ferryman puts down his pole at stage center, and kneels.)

FERRYMAN   Yes sir, What do you want to ask?

PRIEST   Something unusual. I would like you to tell me how Lord Kiso and Kanehira died.

FERRYMAN   Strange indeed! I do not know the details. I will try and tell you what I have heard.

PRIEST   Please do.

FERRYMAN   First, as to how Lord Yoshinaka[8] died and what then happened to Imai no Shiro Kanehira: Lord Kiso, victorious in the battle with the Taira in the north, took advantage of his triumph and marched to the capital at Kyoto. He was astonished to learn that more than sixty thousand troops were coming from Kamakura to attack him, all because of his arrogance and tyranny in the Capital. At once he set about to defend Uji and Seta, and since Seta was his main defense point he sent Kanehira there. To Uji he ordered Tate no Rokuro, Nunoi no Oyata, Nishina, Takanashi and Yamada no Jiro. Coming from the eastern provinces, Noriyori and Yoshitsune divided their troops into two forces. With Noriyori in command, over thirty thousand made for Seta and camped at Seta Bridge. Toward Uji twenty thousand troops led by Yoshitsune crossed through Iga and arrived at Uji Bridge. At both Uji and Seta the bridges had been torn down. It was past the twentieth of the first month, and the snow on the lofty peak of Mount Hiei had melted. The waters of the rivers were high and it seemed unlikely that the force at Uji would be able to cross. But Kajiwara Genta and Sasaki no Shiro took the lead

[8]Lord Kiso.

and the whole force plunged shouting into Uji River and crossed over. The approaches to Uji thus attacked and destroyed, Lord Kiso's soldiers fled to Mount Kobata, to Fushimi and Daigo. At Seta, Inage no Saburo also devised a means of crossing and the main defenses there were breached. Lord Kiso wished to see Kanehira again, and to his delight, while he was retreating toward Seta they came upon each other on the beach of Uchide at Otsu. Then Kanehira raised aloft his banner and some three hundred of their fleeing allies saw it and gathered round them. Deciding that with this force they could make one last valiant stand, furiously they fought. Then when only these two, lord and vassal, were left Kanehira said to Lord Kiso: "Make your way to that grove of pine over there and take your life." Kanehira remained behind and fought, but as soon as he heard the cry that Lord Kiso had been slain, he killed himself right then, they say. Lord Kiso, while heading for the pine grove, had been killed by Ishida no Jiro. That is the story as I have heard it. But what had you in mind when you asked me?

PRIEST Thank you for telling me these things. I am a priest from the mountain village of Kiso. I have come here to pray for the repose of the spirits of Lord Kiso and Kanehira. Before I met you an old man who looked like a ferryman came by. I asked him to carry me across, which he did, and on the way he told me about all the famous places we passed. The boat came to this place, but when I turned to look for him again he had vanished from sight.

FERRYMAN I think the ghost of Kanehira appeared to you and has brought you to this beach. Stay here awhile. I think you should pray for Kanehira's repose.

PRIEST Yes. I will stay here awhile, recite the blessed scriptures, and pray for his spirit's peace.

FERRYMAN If you need anything from me, please call on me again.

PRIEST I will.

FERRYMAN I am at your service.

(He exits.)

PART II

(The scene is now the Plain of Awazu.)

PRIEST *I lie upon a dew-laden mat of grass,*
I lie upon a dew-laden mat of grass.
Day darkens and night has come
And for that body, that dead soul,

> Departed from this bitter world
> Upon Awazu Moor,
> Now I offer up my litany,
> For Kanehira's remains
> I now shall pray.

(The ghost of Kanehira enters, wearing the heita mask and a long sword. He stands at the shite-position.)

KANEHIRA   Horror of naked blades
> Smashing on bone,
> Scenes of eyes gouged out,
> And shields floating on crimson waves
> Like scattered blossoms
> Breaking against a weir.

(He turns to the right.)

> In the morning wind of Awazu
> Fleeting as a cloud, as foam,

CHORUS *(for Kanehira).*
> A swelling chorus of war cries,

KANEHIRA   And in those shouting voices
> The din of Hell's own crossroads.

(He stamps in place. The Priest turns to him.)

PRIEST   What sort of man are you
> Who, girded in armor, comes beside
> My pillow of grass upon Awazu Field?

KANEHIRA   You talk like a fool!
> Was it not your wish to pray for my remains
> That brought you here?
> Kanehira stands before you!

PRIEST   No longer, then, of this world,
> Imai no Shiro Kanehira.
> Can this be a dream?

KANEHIRA   You think that what you see now is a dream? You have already
seen me in reality. Have you forgotten we met and talked in my boat?

PRIEST   *Then he whom I saw in that boat,*
              The boatman at Yabase beach . . .

KANEHIRA   I am that boatman—that was my true form.

PRIEST   *Yes, from the first word*
              I thought your manner strange.
              And that boatman yesterday . . .

KANEHIRA   No boatman he.

PRIEST   A fisherman then . . .

KANEHIRA   Certainly not!

CHORUS *(for Kanehira).*
              The warrior who appeared before you
              Looking like the boatman of Yabase strand,
              The boatman at the bay of Yabase—
              None other than myself!
              Oh, make of this boat
              A vessel of the Law
              And bear me to that far shore![9]

              (He takes two steps toward the Priest.)

CHORUS   *How quickly we come and go*
              Along the crossroads of life and death.
              It is not always true
              That old men die before the young:
              Dreams, fantasies, bubbles, shadows—
              Which one lasts the longest?

              (During the above lines Kanehira moves to stage center and sits on a stool.)

KANEHIRA   Brief is our glory
   As the one-day blossom of the rose of Sharon.

CHORUS *(for Kanehira).*
              With scarcely seven soldiers left
              Of all those born to warrior's blood,
              In the moon's thin trickle of light
              Away went Lord Kiso,
              Down this road through Omi.

---

[9]Paradise is here likened to a distant shore.

KANEHIRA   *And I, Kanehira, found him*
As I was coming from Seta.

CHORUS (for Kanehira).
We became more than three hundred strong.

KANEHIRA   *Then the fighting began.*
We battled, we struggled,
Till at last, all but two,
Lord and vassal, had perished.

CHORUS   *Now there is no chance.*
"Make for the pine grove and take your life there,"
Kanehira says; with sad hearts they ride hard,
Fleeing, lord and liege,
To the stand of pine on Awazu Moor.
Then shouts Kanehira:
"The enemy is coming with many men.
I will hold them off with my arrows."
But as he grasps the reins and wheels his mount about,
Lord Kiso stops him; "I fled the enemy
Only because I hoped to be with you."
He too turns his steed.
Kanehira speaks proudly.
"It breaks my heart to hear you say these words;
What disgrace to ages yet unborn
Should Lord Kiso die at another's hands!
I beg you, by your hand take your life.
I will presently be with you."
Shamed thus by Kanehira,
Again Kiso veers his horse and rides away.
Dejected and alone, he rides
Across Awazu Heath to the copse of pine.

(He looks toward the bridgeway.)

KANEHIRA   *It is now the end of the first month.*

CHORUS   *Spring is in the air.*

(He sweeps his gaze across the front of the stage.)

Still, though, the wind bites in the misty chill.
The sky grows dark, and aimless clouds
Are blown by mountain winds of Hiei.

Lord Kiso, uncertain of his way along the road,
Plunges his horse into a quagmire
Thinly sheeted with frost.

(*He looks down and stamps his feet.*)

Though he pulls, the horse will not rise up,
Though he beats it the horse cannot move.

(*He makes beating motions behind himself with his fan.*)

It sinks into the mire
Till he cannot see its head.
"What shall I do now? I am finished!
All is hopeless!"—in despair
He decides to end his life on the spot.
He puts his hand upon his sword.
But still, he thinks of Kanehira—where is he?
He looks behind him, far in the distance . . .

(*He looks toward the bridgeway.*)

KANEHIRA   *But just then . . . from where can it have come?*
CHORUS   *Suddenly a lethal shaft,*
A single arrow winging from a bow,
Drives into his helmet—
A mortal wound, unbearable the pain.
Down from his mount he topples, dead,
And mingles with the earth of this faraway land.

(*He strikes his knee and kneels.*)

KANEHIRA   *This is the spot.*

(*He stands and turns to the priest.*)

First, in my place,
Pray for my lord's repose.

CHORUS (*for the Priest*).
Truly a painful story.
Then, tell me, how did Kanehira die?

KANEHIRA   *Kanehira knows nothing of what has happened.*
            One thought alone possesses his mind
            Even at moments when he is not fighting—
            To attend his lord's last moments.

            (From here on, Kanehira mimes the actions described.)

CHORUS   *Quite suddenly,*
            From the enemy ranks a voice rings out:

KANEHIRA   *"Lord Kiso has been slain!"*

CHORUS   *When Kanehira hears this voice*

KANEHIRA   *He thinks, "What is there left to hope for?"*

CHORUS   *Kanehira, his mind resolved,*

KANEHIRA   *Prepares to issue his final roar of defiance.*

CHORUS   *Setting his feet in the stirrups,*

KANEHIRA   *He cries out in a great voice:*
            "I am Imai no Shiro Kanehira,
            Vassal by birth to the house of Lord Kiso!"

            (He draws his sword and strikes a defiant posture.)

CHORUS   *Thus shouting out his name,*
            He hews his way through the horde
            Displaying the secret art
            Of one man against the strength of a thousand.
            He drives them down to the beach of Awazu;
            There, in the endless pounding of the surf
            He slashes, amuck, with rolling stroke and crosswise cut.
            Driving in, he hacks in all directions.
            He shouts:
            "Now I will show you how a man should take his life!"
            Thrusting his great blade between his teeth,
            Headlong he falls to the ground.

            (He drops his sword and gives a final stamp of the foot to indicate he has disappeared.)

            Running himself through
            He perishes.

A spectacle to stop speech,
A sight astounding to the eyes
Was Kanehira's death.

FURTHER READINGS

Arthur Waley, *The No Plays of Japan* (London: Allen & Unwin, 1921), besides containing translations of twenty famous No plays, presents an informative introduction to the No theater. Nippon Gakujutsu Shinkokai, *The Noh Drama* (Tokyo: Charles E. Tuttle, 1955) includes ten No plays and a general introduction to No theater. Other significant evaluations of No drama are James Araki, *The Ballad-Drama of Medieval Japan* (Berkeley: University of California Press, 1964), Ernest Fenellos and Ezra Pound, *The Classic Noh Theatre of Japan* (New York: New Directions, 1959) and P. G. O'Neill, *Early No Drama* (London: Lund Humphries, 1958). An introduction to the samurai is found in Paul Varley, *The Samurai* (London: Weidenfield & Nicolson, 1970).

SONGS OF KABIR

The violence that often erupted between the Muslim and Hindu inhabitants of India in the course of the nineteenth and twentieth centuries gave their British colonial administrators the general impression that the two religions were simply incompatible, and that hostile relations between them were inevitable. Certainly this was true in recent times. At the point of achieving their dream of an independent India, the Muslim and Hindu leaders of the national movement each found that they simply did not trust each other enough to face the prospect of possibly being governed by members of the other sect. The result was the partitioning of India in 1947 into a Hindu India and a Muslim Pakistan, and the mass migration of millions of people from one nation to the other, a migration that was marked by scenes of incredible hatred and savagery between groups of Muslim and Hindu refugees. Such had not always been the case, however; at times in the past, Muslims and Hindus had lived together in relative peace.

In 1192, Hindu armies were decisively defeated by Muslim invaders at the battle of Taraori in North India. The Muslims went on to conquer Delhi, from

From *Songs of Kabir*, trans. Rabindranath Tagore (New York: Macmillan, 1915), pp. 45–46, 56–57, 70–71, 75–76, 80–81, 112, 142–43.

which they ruled much of India for the next three centuries (1206–1526). In this period, North India became known to Muslims as Dar al-Islam (Abode of Islam), rather than by its former name of Dar al-Harb (Abode of War).

These Indian Muslims were far removed from Islam's Arabic origins, however. The rulers of the Delhi Sultanate were of Turkish descent, and were heavily influenced by a rich and sophisticated Persian culture that antedated Islam by a thousand years and more. They formed a tiny minority in densely populated India, so that Islamic law could not be enforced rigidly, and the sultans began compromising early. The Muslim rulers generally tried to avoid alienating the Hindu majority, although some religious zealots took delight in destroying ancient temples and sculptures and in attempting to force the Hindus to convert to Islam. Hindus successfully resisted these efforts and preserved their traditional beliefs for many of the same reasons as the Chinese of the same period were successfully resisting the foreign influence of their alien Mongol rulers.

The individual Indian would have found it difficult to convert to Islam even if he were truly won over to Muslim spiritual ideals. Hindu converts lost their standing in family, caste, and village, and so, when conversion to Islam did take place, it was as a collective phenomenon. Such conversions tended to concentrate along the periphery of Muslim territories—Baluchistan, Sind, Kashmir, and western Punjab, areas that later became Pakistan, and, above all, all of Bengal, now the Muslim nation of Bangladesh. On the other hand, some Muslims began adopting Hindu religious customs, incorporating music and dance, local shrines, and local legends into their worship. On the social level, some groups of Muslims began acting like castes—making great distinctions between *Ashraf* (immigrants) or Muslims by birth and *Ajlaf* (converts to the faith).

The period of the Delhi Sultanate saw the resurgence of devotional Hinduism. It must be remembered that this was the same era in which Jayadeva wrote the *Gitagovinda*, one of the great expressions of popular devotion to Krishna and adoration of Vishnu, whose symbol he was. The ascetic and mystical Islamic movement known as Sufism also believed in a god of love and in the personal ecstasy to be found in loving that god in return. With such basic convictions in common, it is not surprising that some sought to integrate these Hindu and Muslim beliefs into an adoration of the one true god of all. Muslim poet-saints began to express their devotion in songs written in native Indian languages, particularly Tamil in the South and Hindi in the North.

Kabir (c. 1440–1518) is one of the most famous of these poet-saints. Little is known of his life, but he probably lived near Benares. He appears to have been a member of a low-status caste of weavers who had recently converted to Islam. Both Muslims and Hindus revere the intense and elevated devotion of his poetry, and his reputation has grown in the modern, secular era for his rejection of caste and religious prejudice. It was not unusual for such poet-saints to condemn social conventions, however, and the extent to which Kabir was personally committed to social betterment remains a matter of question. Political and economic reforms are not usually essential concerns of a poet lost in the love of God.

These translations are by India's most renowned modern poet, Nobel Laureate Rabindranath Tagore, and are more polished than the vernacular preferred by Kabir.

Questions

1. What specifically Hindu and Muslim elements can you identify in these poems?
2. Would Kabir's criticism of Brahmins, caste, and other Hindu institutions be more likely to have weakened or strengthened Hinduism in this period?
3. When Kabir addresses God as "Ram," how might this differ from the use of the name in popular Hindu usage?

SONGS OF KABIR

If God be within the mosque, then to whom does this world
     belong?
If Ram be within the image which you find upon your
     pilgrimage, then who is there to know what happens
     without?
Hari is in the East: Allah is in the West. Look within your
     heart, for there you will find both Karim and Ram;
All men and women of the world are His living forms.
Kabir is the child of Allah and of Ram: He is my Guru,
     He is my Pir.

✦

The Lord is in me, the Lord is in you, as life is in every
     seed. O servant! put false pride away, and seek for
     Him within you.
A million suns are ablaze with light,
The sea of blue spreads in the sky,
The fever of life is stilled, and all stains are washed away;
     when I sit in the midst of that world.

Hark to the unstruck bells and drums! Take your delight in
love!
Rains pour down without water, and the rivers are streams
of light.
One Love it is that pervades the whole world, few there are
who know it fully:
They are blind who hope to see it by the light of reason,
that reason which is the cause of separation—
The House of Reason is very far away!

How blessed is Kabir, that amidst this great joy he sings
within his own vessel.
It is the music of the meeting of soul with soul;
It is the music of the forgetting of sorrows;
It is the music that transcends all coming in and all
going forth.

◆

It is the mercy of my true Guru that has made me to know
the unknown;
I have learned from Him how to walk without feet, to see
without eyes, to hear without ears, to drink without
mouth, to fly without wings;
I have brought my love and my meditation into the land
where there is no sun and moon, nor day and night.
Without eating, I have tasted of the sweetness of nectar;
and without water, I have quenched my thirst.
Where there is the response of delight, there is the fullness
of joy. Before whom can that joy be uttered?
Kabir says: "The Guru is great beyond words, and great is
the good fortune of the disciple."

◆

Dance, my heart! dance to-day with joy.
The strains of love fill the days and the nights with music,
and the world is listening to its melodies:
Mad with joy, life and death dance to the rhythm of this
music. The hills and the sea and the earth dance.
The world of man dances in laughter and tears.

Why put on the robe of the monk, and live aloof from the
    world in lonely pride?
Behold! my heart dances in the delight of a hundred arts;
    and the Creator is well pleased.

✦

O Lord Increate, who will serve Thee?
Every votary offers his worship to the God of his own
    creation: each day he receives service—
None seek Him, the Perfect: Brahma, the Indivisible Lord.
They believe in ten Avatars; but no Avatar can be the
    Infinite Spirit, for he suffers the results of his deeds:
The Supreme One must be other than this.
The Yogi, the Sanyasi, the Ascetics, are disputing one with
    another:
Kabir says, "O brother! he who has seen that radiance of
    love, he is saved."

✦

Lamps burn in every house, O blind one! and you cannot
    see them.
One day your eyes shall suddenly be opened, and you shall
    see: and the fetters of death will fall from you.
There is nothing to say or to hear, there is nothing to do: it
    is he who is living, yet dead, who shall never die
    again.

Because he lives in solitude, therefore the Yogi says that his
    home is far away.
Your Lord is near: yet you are climbing the palm-tree to
    seek Him.
The Brahman priest goes from house to house and initiates
    people into faith:
Alas! the true fountain of life is beside you, and you have
    set up a stone to worship.
Kabir says: "I may never express how sweet my Lord is. Yoga
    and the telling of beads, virtue and vice—these are
    naught to Him."

✦

O servant, where dost thou seek Me?
Lo! I am beside thee.
I am neither in temple nor in mosque: I am neither in
    Kaaba nor in Kailash:
Neither am I in rites and ceremonies, nor in Yoga and
    renunciation.
If thou are a true seeker, thou shalt at once see me: thou
    shalt meet Me in a moment of time.
Kabir says, "O Sadhu! God is the breath of all breath."

◆

It is needless to ask of a saint the caste to which he belongs;
For the priest, the warrior, the tradesman, and all the
    thirty-six castes, alike are seeking for God.
It is but folly to ask what the caste of a saint may be;
The barber has sought God, the washerwoman, and the
    carpenter—
Even Raidas was a seeker after God.
The Rishi Swapacha was a tanner by caste.
Hindus and Moslems alike have achieved that End, where
    remains no mark of distinction.

FURTHER READINGS

For more about Kabir, see G. H. Wescott, *Kabir and the Kabir Panth* (Cawnpore: Christ Church Mission Press, 1907; reprinted Calcutta: S. Gupta, 1953), and Charlotte Vaudeville, *Kabir* (New York: Oxford University Press, 1974). Daniel Gold, *The Lord as Guru: Hindu Saints in the Northern Indian Tradition* (New York: Oxford University Press, 1987) is an important study of the way devotional poets like Kabir have become themselves objects of worship. John Stratton Hawley and Mark Juergensmeyer, *Songs of the Saints of India* (New York: Oxford University Press, 1988), translates the works of other devotional poets. For early Hindi literature in general, see R. S. McGregor, *Hindi Literature from Its Beginnings to the Nineteenth Century* (Wiesbaden: Otto Harrassowitz, 1984).

INQUIRY ON THE GREAT LEARNING

Wang Yang-ming

In the years after 1350, the Mongol rulers of the Yuan dynasty (1279–1368) faced a rising tide of revolt, and the dynasty began to disintegrate. Out of the welter of competing forces, one paramount leader emerged: Chu Yuan-chang (1328–1398), a commoner of modest birth who had risen through the ranks. In 1368, he entered the imperial capital of Peking and founded the Ming dynasty (1368–1644). For the next 260 years, the Chinese people enjoyed an unparalleled period of peace and prosperity. The new emperor was motivated by a veneration of the culture and learning of the age that had preceded the alien rule of the hated Mongols. The result of imperial favor was a great outpouring of scholarship and literature, although all conforming to traditional models. Under the Ming emperors, Chinese culture became so fixed within this mould that it continued with little change through the succeeding dynasty, the Ch'ing (1644–1912), until the Western powers forcibly intruded new cultural forms upon the Chinese consciousness. During this long period, the Chinese were so convinced of the superiority of their culture that they could conceive of no real alternative. They turned their attention inward, rejecting the rest of the world and the foreign "barbarians" who inhabited it. China evolved, although slowly, and always within the pattern that had been set by Confucian thought and traditional art and literature.

The Ming emperors also displayed a ruling passion for order. Their cities were distinguished by symmetrical street plans, their military and civil administrations characterized by a balanced and harmonious hierarchy. The entire empire was organized into appropriate units, and taxes and labor services assigned to these units in accordance with regular and fixed principles. The imperial government interfered very little with the daily life of the peasant masses of the land, and when it did so, it acted in as unobtrusive a manner as possible. Village life in China proceeded from generation to generation in an orderly and almost changeless manner, and this suited the Ming emperors quite well.

Nowhere were the Ming principles of traditionalism and order more evident than in the imperial examination system for entrance into the civil service. It had been customary since Han times (206 B.C.–A.D. 220) to draw imperial administrators from the ranks of those men who were familiar with the Five Classics and the tenets of Confucian thought, but the system was extended and regularized under the Ming to an unprecedented degree. Not only were the

From Wang Yang-ming, "Inquiry on the Great Learning," in Wing-tsit Chan, ed. and trans., A Source Book in Chinese Philosophy (Princeton, NJ: Princeton University Press, 1963), pp. 659–67.

examination subjects restricted to the Five Classics (*The Book of Rites*, *The Book of Songs*, *The Spring and Autumn Annals*, *The Book of History*, and *The Book of Changes*) and the Four Books (*The Analects*, *The Book of Mencius*, *The Doctrine of the Mean*, and *The Great Learning*), but the only interpretation of these works acceptable to the examiners was the Neo-Confucianism of Chu Hsi (1130–1200).

Chu Hsi, building upon the foundations of Chou Tun-i, had envisioned the universe as operating in accordance with the principles of a cosmic pattern of order (*li*). Li was present in all things, and thus all things were a part of that cosmic pattern of order. To understand the pattern of the universe, one had to study physical things, determine their nature, and learn what role they played in the greater order of things. By emphasizing the study of external objects and events, Chu Hsi created a dichotomy between the human mind and the external world. His answer to this problem was that the basic nature of the human mind was good, and that this good should be cultivated.

It is probably a principle of history that any unquestioned system of thought will decline with time. When Chu Hsi's philosophy gained a monopoly in the Ming world it no longer had any competition and began to decay as lesser minds interpreted it according to their own lights. Cultivation of the mind and practice of proper conduct is more difficult than speculating about the nature of things, and many of the educated elite of the empire turned to idle speculation, paying relatively little attention to the moral questions of virtue, obligation, and proper conduct.

This tendency coincided with a period of imperial decline (c. 1450–1550) occasioned by the expansionist policies and ambitious building projects of the later Ming emperors, coupled with growing corruption and extravagance within the government. Many feared that the dynasty was in decline and that its collapse might open the gates to alien conquerors and thus bring down the empire with it, and suspected that the decline of public morality might be a contributing factor to this state of affairs. It was against this background that Wang Yangming (1472–1529) rose to prominence. Born to a noble family of Chekiang province, he entered the imperial civil service at the age of twenty-seven and embarked on a brilliant career, although one often troubled by enemies in court.

In opposition to officially accepted philosophy of Chu Hsi, Wang proclaimed that the study of external reality actually diverted the individual from his proper task of examining his own mind and will. The *li* of the universe exists only in the mind, said Wang, and only there do the principles of proper conduct lie. When one's father dies, one's respect for him does not disappear, even though his external being no longer exists. Moreover, those who spend their time investigating natural phenomena ignore their responsibility to cultivate proper conduct by conducting themselves properly. Immersed in fruitless studies, they neglect their responsibility to act selflessly in the interests of their fellow human beings. Wang suggested that one should cultivate the mind through meditation, but warned that meditation and self-realization are not ends in themselves; the proper goal of knowledge is to be able to act in accordance with the best qualities of human nature. In *The Inquiry on the Great Learning*, he set forth these principles in an orderly fashion in the form of a dialogue.

After his death, he was condemned by official decree and stripped of his honors for having contradicted Chu Hsi. A generation later, however, the empire began to recover its powers, and his contribution to its moral revitalization was recognized. He was rehabilitated, and sacrifices were offered on his behalf in the Temple of Confucius, the highest honor a Confucian scholar can attain. His moral principle that "knowledge is the beginning of conduct; conduct is the completion of knowledge" is his enduring contribution to moral philosophy and has become a basic tenet of Chinese and Japanese thought.

Questions

1. What is human nature for Wang?
2. What is the relationship between the mind and the external world?
3. How does one cultivate one's humanity? Why is there a need to do so?
4. What does Wang mean by "innate knowledge"?

INQUIRY ON THE GREAT LEARNING

Question: The *Great Learning* was considered by a former scholar [Chu Hsi] as the learning of the great man. I venture to ask why the learning of the great man should consist in "manifesting the clear character"?

Master Wang said: The great man regards Heaven and Earth and the myriad things as one body. He regards the world as one family and the country as one person. As to those who make a cleavage between objects and distinguish between the self and others, they are small men. That the great man can regard Heaven, Earth, and the myriad things as one body is not because he deliberately wants to do so, but because it is natural to the humane nature of his mind that he do so. Forming one body with Heaven, Earth, and the myriad things is not only true of the great man. Even the mind of the small man is no different. Only he himself makes it small. Therefore when he sees a child about to fall into a well, he cannot help a feeling of alarm and commiseration. This shows that his humanity (*jen*) forms one body with the child. It may be objected that the child belongs to the same species. Again, when he observes the pitiful cries and frightened appearance of birds and animals about to be slaughtered, he cannot help feeling an "inability to bear" their suffering. This shows that his humanity forms one body with birds and animals. It may be objected that birds and animals are sentient beings as he is. But when he sees plants broken and destroyed, he cannot help a feeling of pity. This shows that his humanity forms one body with plants. It may be said that plants are living things as he is. Yet even when he sees tiles and stones shattered and crushed, he cannot help a feeling of regret. This shows that his humanity forms one body with tiles and stones. This means that even the mind of the small man necessarily has the humanity that forms one body with all. Such a mind is rooted in his Heaven-endowed nature, and is naturally intelligent, clear, and not beclouded. For this reason it is called the "clear character." Although the mind of the small man is divided and narrow, yet his humanity that forms one body can remain free from darkness to this degree. This is due to the fact that his mind has not yet been aroused by desires and obscured by selfishness. When it is aroused by desires and obscured by selfishness, compelled by greed for gain and fear of harm, and stirred by anger, he will destroy things, kill members of his own species, and will do everything. In extreme cases he will even slaughter his own brothers, and the humanity that forms one body will disappear completely. Hence, if it is not obscured by selfish desires, even the mind of the small man has the humanity that forms one body with all as does the mind of the great man. As soon as it is obscured by selfish desires, even the mind of the great man will be divided and narrow like that of the small man. Thus the learning of the great man consists entirely in getting rid of the obscuration of selfish desires in order by his own efforts to make manifest his clear character, so as to restore the condition of forming one body with Heaven, Earth, and the myriad things, a condition that is originally so, that is all. It is not that outside of the original substance something can be added.

Question: Why, then, does the learning of the great man consist in loving the people?

Answer: To manifest the clear character is to bring about the substance of the state of forming one body with Heaven, Earth, and the myriad things, whereas loving the people is to put into universal operation the function of the state of forming one body. Hence manifesting the clear character consists in loving the people, and loving the people is the way to manifest the clear character. Therefore, only when I love my father, the fathers of others, and the fathers of all men can my humanity really form one body with my father, the fathers of others, and the fathers of all men. When it truly forms one body with them, then the clear character of filial piety will be manifested. Only when I love my brother, the brothers of others, and the brothers of all men can my humanity really form one body with my brother, the brothers of others, and the brothers of all men. When it truly forms one body with them, then the clear character of brotherly respect will be manifested. Everything from ruler, minister, husband, wife, and friends to mountains, rivers, spiritual beings, birds, animals, and plants should be truly loved in order to realize my humanity that forms one body with them, and then my clear character will be completely manifested, and I will really form one body with Heaven, Earth, and the myriad things. This is what is meant by "manifesting the clear character throughout the empire." This is what is meant by "regulation of the family," "ordering the state," and "bringing peace to the world." This is what is meant by "full development of one's nature."

Question: Then why does the learning of the great man consist in "abiding in the highest good"?

Answer: The highest good is the ultimate principle of manifesting character and loving people. The nature endowed in us by Heaven is pure and perfect. The fact that it is intelligent, clear, and not beclouded is evidence of the emanation and revelation of the highest good. It is the original substance of the clear character which is called innate knowledge of the good. As the highest good emanates and reveals itself, we will consider right as right and wrong as wrong. Things of greater or less importance and situations of grave or light character will be responded to as they act upon us. In all our changes and movements, we will stick to no particular point, but possess in ourselves the Mean that is perfectly natural. This is the ultimate of the normal nature of man and the principle of things. There can be no consideration of adding to or subtracting from it. If there is any, it means selfish ideas and shallow cunning, and cannot be said to be the highest good. Naturally, how can anyone who does not watch over himself carefully when alone, and who has no refinement and singleness of mind, attain to such a state of perfection? Later generations fail to realize that the highest good is inherent in their own minds, but exercise their selfish ideas and cunning and grope for it outside their minds, believing that every event and every object has its own peculiar definite principle. For this reason the law of right and wrong is obscured; the mind becomes concerned with fragmentary and isolated details and broken pieces; the selfish desires of man become rampant and the Principle of Nature is at an end. And thus the learning of manifesting character and loving people is everywhere thrown into confusion. In the past there have, of course, been people who wanted to manifest their clear character. But simply because they did not know how to abide in the highest good, but instead drove their own minds toward something too lofty, they thereby lost them in illusions, emptiness, and quietness, having nothing to do with the work of the family, the state, and the world. Such are the followers of Buddhism and Taoism. There have, of course, been those who wanted to love their people. Yet simply because they did not know how to abide in the highest good, but instead sank their own minds in base and trifling things, they thereby lost them in scheming strategy and cunning techniques, having neither the sincerity of humanity nor that of commiseration. Such are the followers of the Five Despots and the pursuers of success and profit. All of these defects are due to a failure to know how to abide in the highest good. Therefore abiding in the highest good is to manifesting character and loving people as the carpenter's square and compass are to the square and the circle, or rule and measure to length, or balances and scales to weight. If the square and the circle do not abide by the compass and the carpenter's square, their standard will be wrong; if length does not abide by the rule and measure, its adjustment will be lost; if weight does not abide by the balances, its exactness will be gone; and if manifesting clear character and loving people do not abide by the highest good, their foundation will disappear. Therefore, abiding in the highest good so as to love people and manifest the clear character is what is meant by the learning of the great man.

Question: "Only after knowing what to abide in can one be calm. Only after having been calm can one be tranquil. Only after having achieved tranquillity can one have peaceful repose. Only after having peaceful repose can one begin to deliberate. Only after deliberation can the end be attained." How do you explain this?

Answer: People fail to realize that the highest good is in their minds and seek it outside. As they believe that everything or every event has its own definite principle, they search for the highest good in individual things. Consequently, the mind becomes fragmentary, isolated, broken into pieces; mixed and confused, it has no definite direction. Once it is realized that the highest good is in the mind and does not depend on any search outside, then the mind will have definite direction and there will be no danger of its becoming fragmentary, isolated, broken into pieces, mixed, or confused. When there is no such danger, the mind will not be erroneously perturbed but will be tranquil. Not being erroneously perturbed but being tranquil, it will be leisurely and at ease in its daily functioning and will attain peaceful repose. Being in peaceful repose, whenever a thought arises or an event acts upon it, the mind with its innate knowledge will thoroughly sift and carefully examine whether or not the thought or event is in accord with the highest good, and thus the mind can deliberate. With deliberation, every decision will be excellent and every act will be proper, and in this way the highest good will be attained.

Question: "Things have their roots and their branches." A former scholar [Chu Hsi] considered manifesting the clear character as the root (or fundamental) and renovating the people as the branch (or secondary), and that they are two things opposing each other as internal and external. "Affairs have their beginnings and their ends." The former scholar considered knowing what to abide in as the beginning and the attainment of the highest good as the end, both being one thing in harmonious continuity. According to you, "renovating the people" (*hsin-min*) should be read as "loving the people" (*ch'in-min*). If so, isn't the theory of root and branches in some respect incorrect?

Answer: The theory of beginnings and ends is in general right. Even if we read "renovating the people" as "loving the people" and say that manifesting the character is the root and loving the people is the branches, it is not incorrect. The main thing is that root and branches should not be distinguished as two different things. The trunk of the tree is called the root (or essential part), and the twigs are called the branches. It is precisely because the tree is one that its parts can be called roots and branches. If they are said to be two different things, then since they are two distinct objects, how can we speak of them as root and branches of the same thing? Since the idea of renovating the people is different from that of loving the people, obviously the task of manifesting the character and that of loving the people are two different things. If it is realized that manifesting the clear character is to love the people and loving the people is to manifest the clear character, how can they be split in two? What the former scholar said is due to his failure to realize that manifesting the character and loving the people are basically one thing. Instead, he believed them to be two different things and consequently, although he knew that root and branches should be one, yet he could not help splitting them in two.

Question: The passage from the phrase, "The ancients who wished to manifest their clear character throughout the world" to the clause, "first [order their state . . . regulate their families . . .] cultivate their personal lives," can be understood by your theory of manifesting the character and loving the people. May I ask what task, what procedure, and what effort are involved in the passage from "Those who wished to cultivate their personal lives would first rectify their minds . . . make their will sincere . . . extend their knowledge" to the clause, "the extension of knowledge consists in the investigation of things"?

Answer: This passage fully explains the task of manifesting the character, loving the people, and abiding in the highest good. The person, the mind, the will, knowledge, and things constitute the order followed in the task. While each of them has its own place, they are really one thing. Investigating, extending, being sincere, rectifying, and cultivating are the task performed in the procedure. Although each has its own name, they are really one affair. What is it that is called the person? It is the physical functioning of the mind. What is it that is called the mind? It is the clear and intelligent master of the person. What is meant by cultivating the personal life? It means to do good and get rid of evil. Can the body by itself do good and get rid of evil? The clear and intelligent master must desire to do good and get rid of evil before the body that functions physically can do so. Therefore he who wishes to cultivate his personal life must first rectify his mind.

Comment. The Great Learning clearly says that there is an order from "the investigation of things" to "bringing peace to the world," but Wang says they are but one affair. To the extent that he, like other Neo-Confucianists, depended on ancient Classics for authority and used ancient Confucian terminology, he was a conservative. But he used the Great Learning in his own way.

Now the original substance of the mind is man's nature. Human nature being universally good, the original substance of the mind is correct. How is it that any effort is required to rectify the mind? The reason is that, while the original substance of the mind is originally correct, incorrectness enters when one's thoughts and will are in operation. Therefore he who wishes to rectify his mind must rectify it in connection with the operation of his thoughts and will. If, when a good thought arises, he really loves it as he loves beautiful colors, and whenever an evil thought arises, he really hates it as he hates bad odors, then his will will always be sincere and his mind can be rectified.

However, what arises from the will may be good or evil, and unless there is a way to make clear the distinction between good and evil, there will be a confusion of truth and untruth. In that case, even if one wants to make his will sincere, he cannot do so. Therefore he who wishes to make his will sincere must extend his knowledge. By extension is meant to reach the limit. The word "extension" is the same as that used in the saying, "Mourning is to be carried to the utmost degree of grief." In the Book of Changes it is said: "Knowing the utmost, one should reach it." "Knowing the utmost" means knowledge and "reaching it" means extension. The extension of knowledge is not what later scholars understand as enriching and widening knowledge. It is simply extending one's innate knowledge of the good to the utmost. This innate knowledge of the good is what Mencius meant when he said, "The sense of right and wrong is common to all men." The sense of right and wrong requires no deliberation to know, nor does it depend on learning to function. This is why it is called innate knowledge. It is my nature endowed by Heaven, the original substance of my mind, naturally intelligent, shining, clear, and understanding.

Whenever a thought or a wish arises, my mind's faculty of innate knowledge itself is always conscious of it. Whether it is good or evil, my mind's innate knowing faculty itself also knows it. It has nothing to do with others. Therefore, although an inferior man may have done all manner of evil, when he sees a superior man he will surely try to disguise this fact, concealing what is evil and displaying what is good in himself. This shows that innate knowledge of the good does not permit any selfdeception. Now the only way to distinguish good and evil in order to make the will sincere is to extend to the utmost the knowledge of the innate faculty. Why is this? When [a good] thought or wish arises, the innate faculty of my mind already knows it to be good. Suppose I do not sincerely love it but instead turn away from it. I would then be regarding good as evil and obscuring my innate faculty which knows the good. When [an evil] thought or wish arises, the innate faculty of my mind already knows it to be evil. If I did not sincerely hate it but instead carried it out, I would be regarding evil as good and obscuring my innate faculty which knows evil. In such cases what is supposed to be knowledge is really ignorance. How then can the will be made sincere? If what the innate faculty knows to be good or evil is sincerely loved or hated, one's innate knowing faculty is not deceived and the will can be made sincere.

Now, when one sets out to extend his innate knowledge to the utmost, does this mean something illusory, hazy, in a vacuum, and unreal? No, it means something real. Therefore, the extension of knowledge must consist in the investigation of things. A thing is an event. For every emanation of the will there must be an event corresponding to it. The event to which the will is directed is a thing. To investigate is to rectify. It is to rectify that which is incorrect so it can return to its original correctness. To rectify that which is not correct is to get rid of evil, and to return to correctness is to do good. This is what is meant by investigation. The *Book of History* says, "He (Emperor Yao) investigated (*ko*) heaven above and earth below"; "[Emperor Shun] investigated (*ko*) in the temple of illustrious ancestors"; and "[The ruler] rectifies (*ko*) the evil of his heart." The word "investigation" (*ko*) in the phrase "the investigation of things" combines the two meanings.

If one sincerely loves the good known by the innate faculty but does not in reality do the good as we come into contact with the thing to which the will is directed, it means that the thing has not been investigated and that the will to love the good is not yet sincere. If one sincerely hates the evil known by the innate faculty but does not in reality get rid of the evil as he comes into contact with the thing to which the will is directed, it means that the thing has not been investigated and that the will to hate evil is not sincere. If as we come into contact with the thing to which the will is directed, we really do the good and get rid of the evil to the utmost which is known by the innate faculty, then everything will be investigated and what is known by our innate faculty will not be deficient or obscured but will be extended to the utmost. Then the mind will be joyous in itself, happy and without regret, the functioning of the will will carry with it no self-deception, and sincerity may be said to have been attained. Therefore it is said, "When things are investigated, knowledge is extended; when knowledge is extended, the will becomes sincere; when the will is sincere, the mind is rectified; and when the mind is rectified, the personal life is cultivated." While the order of the tasks involves a sequence of first and last, in substance they are one and cannot be so separated. At the same time, while the order and the tasks cannot be separated into first and last, their function must be so refined as not to be wanting in the slightest degree. This is why the doctrine of investigation, extension, being sincere, and rectification is a correct exposition of the true heritage of the Sage-Emperors Yao and Shun and why it coincides with Confucius' own ideas. (*Wang Wen-ch'eng Kung ch'uan-shu*, or Complete Works of Wang Yang-ming, SPTK, 26:1b–5a)

> Comment. This is the most important of Wang's works, for it contains all of his fundamental doctrines—that the man of humanity forms one body with all things and extends his love to all, that the mind is principle, that the highest good is inherent in the mind, that to investigate things is to rectify the mind, and that the extension of innate knowledge is the way to discover the highest good and to perfect the moral life. The theory of the unity of knowledge and action is not mentioned, but since he refuses to separate the internal and the external or substance and function, the theory is clearly implied. In fact, he explicitly says that manifesting the clear character, which may be equated with knowledge, and loving the people, which is action, are identical.

FURTHER READINGS

The history and achievements of the Ming dynasty are covered in a series of excellent scholarly studies: Charles O. Hucker, *The Ming Dynasty: Its Origins and Evolving Institutions* (Ann Arbor, MI: Center for Chinese Studies, University of Michigan, 1978), Edward L. Dreyer, *Early Ming China: A Political History, 1355–1435* (Stanford, CA: Stanford University Press, 1982), and Albert Chan, *The Glory and Fall of the Ming Dynasty* (Norman, OK: University of Oklahoma Press, 1982). A journal entitled *Ming Studies* has been published from Minneapolis since 1975, and articles on major figures of the Ming period have been collected in Carrington Goodrich, ed., *Dictionary of Ming Biography, 1368–1644* (New York: Columbia University Press, 1976).

Two studies of Wang Yang-ming's life and career are provided by Tu Wei-ming, *Neo-Confucian Thought in Action: Wang Yang-ming's Youth (1472–1508)* (Berkeley: University of California Press, 1976), and Chang Yu-chuan, *Wang Shou-jen as Statesman* (Arlington, VA: University Publications of America, 1975). Two of his major works, *Inquiry on the Great Learning* and *Instructions for Practical Living* are available in Wing-tsit Chan, trans., *Instructions for Practical Living and Other Neo-Confucian Works by Wang Yang-ming* (New York: Columbia University Press, 1963). The reader interested in following Wang's philosophy further will find Carsun Chang, *The Development of Neo-Confucian Thought* (New Haven, CT: College and University Press, 1963), a useful introduction to Neo-Confucian thought in general and may wish to consult the relevant portions of Theodore de Bary and Irene Bloom, eds., *Principle and Practicality: Essays in Neo-Confucianism and Practical Learning* (New York: Columbia University Press, 1978). Julia Ching, *To Acquire Wisdom: The Way of Wang Yang-ming* (New York: Columbia University Press, 1976), provides a general study of Wang's philosophy, while Antonio S. Cua, *The Unity of Knowledge and Action: A Study in Wang Yang-ming's Moral Philosophy* (Honolulu: University Press of Hawaii, 1982), concerns himself with a fundamental principle of Wang's approach.

SACRED WRITINGS OF THE SIKHS

Guru Nanak (1469–1539), the founder of the Sikh religion, was reared as a Hindu in a small village in the Punjab, where Hindu and Muslim attitudes and ways of life had mixed over the years. Nanak was a contemporary of Babar (1483–1530), the founder of the Mughal Empire, and his life thus spanned the end of the Delhi Sultanate and the years during which the Mughals were extending their power across North India. At the same time, the West had reached the shores of India (1498), and Portuguese trading stations along the coast were soon bringing Western trading goods and Christian ideology to the land. Persian Sufic mysticism was growing stronger in the region, and the popularity of the Hindu adoration of Vishnu as a loving and earth-dwelling god continued to spread northward. In many ways, a number of disparate beliefs were beginning to coalesce in North India. Hinduism, Sufism, and Christianity were all preaching faiths in which an all-powerful god yet bound himself to humanity in love, and in which the return of that love could bring the worshipper ecstatic joy. All envisioned an ethical god, who took pleasure in the good deeds of his worshippers and who was himself the greatest good. Finally, all believed that their god, or rather his personification, dwelled at times among human beings to aid, teach, and share the sorrows of being merely human. Many saw these similarities and pondered whether all of these formulations were simply different expressions of the same ultimate reality. Nanak was one of these.

For some time after 1500, he was employed by the governor of Punjab, but experienced revelations that called him to the preaching of his beliefs. He traveled widely in this pursuit and, according to legend, visited Mecca, Tibet, and

From *Sacred Writings of the Sikhs*, trans. Jodh Singh, Kapur Singh, Bawa Harkishen Singh, Khushwant Singh; UNESCO Collection of Representative Works, Indian Series (London: Unwin Hyman; 1960).

Sri Lanka as well as much of India. For the last fifteen years of his life (1524–1539), he lived in a small village above Lahore.

Nanak's teachings resembled those of Kabir (c. 1440–1518) in many ways, being inspired by the same sources. There are enough similarities between the works of the two that Nanak is sometimes considered a disciple of Kabir. Both combined the devotionalism of the worshippers of Vishnu with the religious and social iconoclasm of the holy men of the time. They both rejected conventional forms of worship, condemned the caste system, and used the vernacular of the common people (Punjabi in the case of Nanak) rather than the classical Sanskrit or Persian of scholars and court officials. There are distinct differences, however, such as the greater consistency of Nanak's teachings and his emphasis on a brotherhood of believers that would transcend divisions of race, religion, caste, lineage, and sex.

Nanak's followers took the name *Sikh*, or disciple. According to Sikh doctrine, the divine spirit that inspired Nanak, and revealed divine wisdom and ethical principles through him, continued to dwell on earth in the persons of ten successive *gurus*, or "preceptors." These gurus were not only the religious leaders of the faith, but also governed the community of believers. The third guru began collecting the authentic versions of Nanak's hymns that had survived, and added these—974 in all—to some hymns and aphorisms by Kabir. Still others were added by the fifth guru, Arjan (1581–1606), and the whole collection, known as the *Adi Granth*, from which the poems included here are taken, began to assume the function of sacred scriptures among the Sikhs.

By the early seventeenth century Sikhism was losing some of its original eclectic inspiration and missionary fervor and was beginning to assume some of the characteristics of a closed sect. This was partially due to the conservative Muslim reaction that had followed the death of the tolerant and heterodox emperor Akbar in 1605. Rights were wrested from the Hindus, temples were closed, and many of the eclectic faiths were persecuted. The Sikhs were among these. Guru Arjan was called to the Mughal capital and died there under the most suspicious circumstances. His son, the sixth guru Hargobind (1606–1644), led the Sikhs in resisting their oppression by the Mughal administration. This further closed Sikh society to outside influences. By the end of the seventeenth century the Sikhs had evolved into a militant community, suspicious of outsiders, and with a distinctive appearance and communal cohesion in the region of the Punjab.

Conflict with the Mughals increased under the tenth guru, Gobind Singh (1675–1708), who, in 1699, initiated a militant brotherhood called the Khalsa within the Sikh community. Sikhism, originally conceived by Nanak as a brotherhood that would transcend caste distinctions by the power of their common beliefs, was dividing and developing a caste within itself. Sikhs who joined the Khalsa were baptized, not unlike the twice-born Brahman caste of the orthodox Hindus. They then adopted a distinctive appearance—uncut hair, turban, short trousers, iron bracelet, and dagger. All men baptized into the Khalsa took the name Singh as a sign of their kinship. According to tradition, Gobind Singh, all of whose sons died fighting the Mughals, declared shortly before his own death that the line of personal gurus would come to an end with him. From that time on, the authority of the guru among the Sikhs has been vested in their sacred writings (the *Adi Granth*, thereafter known as the *Guru Granth Sahib*) and in the community as a whole.

The decline of the Mughal Empire and threats by Afghan and Persian invaders in the eighteenth century accentuated the political independence, militancy, and anti-Muslim sentiment of the Sikhs. Sikhism also took on more Hindu characteristics, but reform movements in the course of the nineteenth century finally returned the religion closer to its early teachings. Nevertheless, the Sikhs have retained their militancy and fiercely independent character. Even now, Sikh separatists are engaged in a violent struggle for secession from India and the establishment of an independent Sikh nation.

Questions

1. What are the similarities and differences between Kabir and Guru Nanak?
2. What does Guru Nanak seem to think is the role of women?
3. Are there any indications that these ideas would become the basis of a religious sect? of a militant community?

SACRED WRITINGS OF THE SIKHS

There is one God,
Eternal Truth is His Name;
Maker of all things,
Fearing nothing and at enmity with nothing,
Timeless is His Image;
Not begotten, being of His own Being:
By the grace of the Guru, made known to men.

Jap: The Meditation

AS HE WAS IN THE BEGINNING: THE TRUTH,
SO THROUGHOUT THE AGES,
HE EVER HAS BEEN: THE TRUTH,
SO EVEN NOW HE IS TRUTH IMMANENT,
SO FOR EVER AND EVER HE SHALL BE TRUTH ETERNAL.

◆

There is no counting of men's prayers,
There is no counting their ways of adoration.
Thy lovers, O Lord, are numberless;
Numberless those who read aloud from the Vedas;
Numberless those Yogis who are detached from the world;

Numberless are Thy Saints contemplating,
Thy virtues and Thy wisdom;
Numberless are the benevolent, the lovers of their kind.
Numberless Thy heroes and martyrs
Facing the steel of their enemies;
Numberless those who in silence
Fix their deepest thoughts upon Thee;

How can an insignificant creature like myself
Express the vastness and wonder of Thy creation?
I am too petty to have anything to offer Thee;
I cannot, even once, be a sacrifice unto Thee.
To abide by Thy Will, O Lord, is man's best offering;
Thou who art Eternal, abiding in Thy Peace.

There is no counting fools, the morally blind;
No counting thieves and the crooked,
No counting the shedders of the innocent blood;
No counting the sinners who go on sinning;

No counting the liars who take pleasure in lies;
No counting the dirty wretches who live on filth;
No counting the calumniators
Who carry about on their heads their loads of sin.

Thus saith Nanak, lowliest of the lowly:
I am too petty to have anything to offer Thee;

I cannot, even once, be a sacrifice unto Thee.
To abide by Thy Will, O Lord, is man's best offering;
Thou who art Eternal, abiding in Thy Peace.

✦

Countless are Thy Names, countless Thine abodes;
Completely beyond the grasp of the imagination
Are Thy myriad realms;
Even to call them myriad is foolish.

Yet through words and through letters
Is Thy Name uttered and Thy praise expressed;
In words we praise Thee,
In words we sing of Thy virtues.

It is in the words that we write and speak about Thee,
In words on man's forehead
Is written man's destiny,
But God who writes that destiny
Is free from the bondage of words

As God ordaineth, so man receiveth.
All creation is His Word made manifest;
Except in the Light of His Word
There is no way.

How can an insignificant creature like myself
Express the vastness and wonder of Thy creation?
I am too petty to have anything to offer Thee;
I cannot, even once, be a sacrifice unto Thee.
To abide by Thy Will, O Lord, is man's best offering;
Thou who art Eternal, abiding in Thy Peace.

✦

Let compassion be thy mosque,
Let faith be thy prayer mat,
Let honest living be thy Koran,
Let modesty be the rules of observance,
Let piety be the fasts thou keepest;
In such wise strive to become a Moslem:

Right conduct the Ka'ba; Truth the Prophet,
Good deeds thy prayer;
Submission to the Lord's Will thy rosary;
Nanak, if this thou do, the Lord will be thy Protector.

◆

Of a woman are we conceived,
Of a woman we are born,
To a woman are we betrothed and married,
It is a woman who is friend and partner of life,
It is woman who keeps the race going,
Another companion is sought when the life-partner dies,
Through woman are established social ties,
Why should we consider woman cursed and condemned
When from woman are born leaders and rulers.
From woman alone is born a woman,
Without woman there can be no human birth.
Without woman, O Nanak, only the True One exists.
Be it men or be it women,
Only those who sing His glory
Are blessed and radiant with His Beauty,
In His Presence and with His grace
They appear with a radiant face.

◆

A true Ksatriya, of the warrior caste, is one whose valour
Shows itself in every detail of his life.
The aim of life is loving kindness,
Which he gives to the deserving,
And so becomes acceptable to God.
Any man who moved by greed, preaches falsehood,
In the end must pay the penalty for his deeds.

When the hands, feet and other parts
Of the body are besmeared with filth,
They are cleansed with water;
When a garment is defiled
It is rinsed with soapsuds;
So when the mind is polluted with sin,
We must scrub it in love of the Name.

We do not become sinners or saints,
By merely saying we are;
It is actions that are recorded;
According to the seed we sow, is the fruit we reap.
By God's Will, O Nanak,
Man must either be saved or endure new births.

✦

On hearing of the Lord,
All men speak of His greatness;
Only he that hath seen Him
Can know how great is He.
Who can conceive of His worth
Or who can describe Him?
Those who seek to describe Thee
Are lost in Thy depths.

O Great Lord, of depth unfathomable,
Ocean of virtues!
Who knoweth the bounds of Thy shores?
All the contemplatives
Have met and sought to contemplate Thee;
All the weighers of worth
Have met and sought to weigh Thy worth;
All the theologians and the mystics,
All the preachers and their teachers
Have not been able to grasp
One jot of Thy greatness.

All truths, all fervent austerities, every excellent act,
Every sublime achievement of the adepts,
Are Thy gifts, O Lord: without Thee
No man could attain perfection;
But where Thou hast granted Thy grace to a man,
Nothing can stand in his way.

How vain are the words of those that seek to praise Thee,
Thy treasuries are already filled with Thy praises;
He to whom Thou givest freely,
What should he do but praise Thee?

Saith Nanak: The True One is He
From whom all perfection springs.

FURTHER READINGS

Khushwant Singh, A *History of the Sikhs*, 2 vols. (Princeton, NJ: Princeton University Press, 1966), is a popular history of the community. Sikh scriptures have been translated and edited by W. H. McLeod, the modern Western expert on Sikhism and the Sikhs, in *Textual Sources for the Study of Sikhism* (Totowa, NJ: Barnes & Noble, 1984), while a selection of the hymns of Guru Nanak has been translated by Khushwant Singh in *Hymns of Guru Nanak* (New Delhi: Sangam, 1978).

There are numerous works on modern Sikhism, including Joseph T. O'Connell, et al., eds., *Sikh History and Religion in the Twentieth Century* (Toronto: University of Toronto Press, 1988); Richard G. Fox, *Lions of the Punjab* (Berkeley: University of California Press, 1985); and Ethne K. Marenco, *The Transformation of Sikh Society* (Portland, OR: HaPi Press, 1974).

The early history of the Sikh religion is the subject of two excellent works: W. H. McLeod, *The Evolution of the Sikh Tradition* (Delhi: Oxford University Press, 1975), is a scholarly study of the sources of early Sikh history. To this should be added the perceptive analysis of the attitudes of the early Sikhs to Hinduism presented by William O. Cole, *Sikhism and Its Indian Context, 1469–1708: The Attitude of Guru Nanak and early Sikhism to Indian Religious Beliefs and Practices* (London: Darton, Longman & Todd, 1984). Sikh history and tradition generally is discussed by a member of the faith, Harbans Singh, in *The Heritage of the Sikhs* (New Delhi: Manohar, 1983).

The Sikh gurus and their teachings lay at the heart of the Sikh religion and its evolution, and the role of the guru is considered by William O. Cole, *The Guru in Sikhism* (London: Darton, Longman & Todd, 1982). A series of biographies of some of the early gurus may be found in W. H. McLeod, *Guru Nanak and the Sikh Religion* (Oxford: Oxford University Press, 1968), the definitive work on the founder; Fauja Singh, *Guru Das (1479–1574): Life and Teachings* (New Delhi: Sterling, c. 1979); Harbans Singh, *Guru Gobind Singh (1666–1708)* (New Delhi: Sterling, c. 1979); and Balwant Anand Singh, *Guru Tegh Bahadur (1621–1675): A Biography* (New Delhi: Sterling, c. 1979).

AKBAR NAMA
Abu-l Fazl

The Mughal Empire (1526–1858) was the sixth Muslim dynasty to rule in India. During the last century of its reign, however, it was in fact sustained by the British, who utilized the Mughal emperors as figureheads for their own increasing authority in the land. Nevertheless, the Muslim Mughals left a heritage of art, architecture, literature, and law that continues to influence India today.

This continuing Mughal influence is, curiously enough, the legacy of two centuries of British rule. The British in India faced the difficult task of ruling over a hundred million subjects with only a few thousand administrators and were not eager to impose new and unfamiliar governmental forms on their tradition-loving subjects. They therefore modeled their administration after that of the Mughals, even to the point of continuing Court Persian as the language of record-keeping. For the first hundred years they ruled India, the British claimed to be no more than subjects of the Mughal emperors governing in their name. This legal fiction preserved much of the pomp and prestige of the Mughal Empire until the eve of Indian independence and created a distinctive amalgamation of Persian, Indian Muslim, Hindu, and British influences that formed the cultural and governmental traditions on which the new nation began to build in 1948.

The greatest ruler of this empire was indisputably Akbar (r. 1556–1605), grandson of the empire's founder, whose conquests and administrative reforms did much to establish Mughal power on solid ground and gain for it a century of ascendancy in North India. The greater part of Akbar's reign was spent planning and executing military campaigns. He was a heroic commander who personally led the attacks on his strongest enemies, although he preferred to negotiate a surrender than fight. He married Rajput princesses in order to win over their Hindu kinsmen and overcame the reluctance of Hindus to intermarry with Muslims by treating his new kinsmen as imperial nobility.

Although proclaiming himself a true Muslim, Akbar displayed other signs of an individualistic approach to a religion that others followed with a conservative fervor. In 1579 Akbar requested that the Portuguese send three learned men to his court, and three Jesuits led by Rudolpho Aquaviva arrived in answer to this invitation. The emperor treated them with unaccustomed deference and appointed one of them as tutor to his son Murad. This raised their hopes that he would convert to Christianity, but when it became clear that he had no intentions of doing so, they returned to Goa. What his actual intentions were is

From Abu-l Fazl, *Akbar Nama*, trans. H. Beveridge (Reprinted Delhi: Ess Ess Publications, 1977).

unclear, but his deference towards his Christian visitors aroused the suspicions of many of his co-religionists. These suspicions grew even deeper shortly thereafter when Akbar issued a decree declaring himself a *mujtahid* (infallible authority) in religious affairs, an act of presumption that outraged orthodox Muslims and led to a short-lived rebellion. He then attempted to establish a new, eclectic "Divine Faith," designed to join all in a single worship but gained little support for such a radical innovation.

Akbar's religious policies have attracted a good deal of attention over the years. He has been described alternately as a liberal Muslim who was very tolerant of other religions, or as a man who combined Indian ideas of divine kingship with Muslim Sufic mysticism. Some Pakistani scholars have argued that he was a heretic who tried to suppress Islamic orthodoxy.

These attempts to place Akbar into a preconceived sectarian category miss the point that his religious policy was one of the great strengths of his administration. His flirtation with Christianity encouraged Christian traders to favor him in the secret hope that he could be won over to their faith. His tolerance of Hinduism and his admission of Hindus to the ranks of his administration gained the empire valuable support, secured it a peaceful and relatively friendly subject population, and gained Akbar allies against ultra-orthodox Muslims who might have attempted to drive him into a holy war against the idolatrous Hindus, which would have destroyed the prosperity of the land and thus weakened the empire he was attempting to build. This is not to say that Akbar was simply playing political games; his philosophy held that the emperor was the sovereign of all his people and should act in the interests of all. He implemented reforms that were of benefit to his Hindu subjects, such as the abolition of the Muslim-imposed pilgrim tax, and he encouraged interaction among religious groups in the hope of gaining greater mutual understanding among his heterogenous people.

It was this enlightened approach to religious matters that gained him permanent fame in the verses of the *Akbar Nama*. The author, Shaikh Abu-l Fazl 'Allami (1551–1602), had come to the Mughal court, where his elder brother Faizi was court poet, in 1568. The brothers were the leaders of radical religious thought at the court, and were condemned as heretics by conservative Muslims there. Finding in Akbar a kindred spirit, Abu-l Fazl was soon converted from Akbar's servant and sycophant into his true friend and admirer. For this reason, the *Akbar Nama* is more than the simple glorification of a ruler—it is a song of sincere appreciation. Abu-l Fazl and his brother saw in Akbar both a friend and emperor, and supported and encouraged him in the tolerance and religious radicalism he seemed to be pursuing. In the end, however, neither the emperor Akbar nor the poet Abu-l Fazl could contain the forces of distrust and intolerance among the Indian people. Like Mohandas Gandhi centuries later, Akbar's dream of a united India was thwarted by the twin forces of prejudice and fanaticism. Exasperated by his heterodoxy, conservative Muslim elements joined in opposition to him, and rebellion broke out. Prince Salim, son of Akbar and a rebel leader, captured the poet Abu-l Fazl in 1602, and had him put to death. With Akbar's death in 1605, Prince Salim assumed the title Emperor Jahangir (1605–1627). An imperial policy of increasing intolerance of non-Muslims emerged over the years, and the Mughal Empire steadily lost the support of the mass of the population of India. The substitution of racist British masters for bigoted Mughal overlords was viewed as an improvement by many. The vision of Akbar and Abu-l Fazl of a land of unity and tolerance had clearly come before its time.

Questions

1. What qualities does Abu-l Fazl praise in Akbar?
2. What faults does Akbar find in the Islamic theologians?
3. Does Akbar reject Islam?

AKBAR NAMA

Although God-given wisdom and the science of Divine knowledge (theology) adorn his holy personality and illumine his actions, yet, owing to the utter marvelousness of his nature, he every now and then draws a special veil over his countenance, and exercises world-sway and speaks and acts in accordance with the requirements of the time. At the present day, when the morning-breeze of fortune is blowing, and the star of success is continually acquiring fresh radiance, he, by his practical knowledge and farsightedness, makes external ability the veil of spirituality and appraises the value of the mortifiers of the passions, and the calibre of scientists. It has been mentioned that he, in his ample search after truth, had laid the foundation of a noble seat for intellectual meetings. His sole and sublime idea was that, as in the external administration of the dominion, which is conjoined with eternity, the merits of the knowers of the things of this world had by profundity of vision, and observance of justice, been made conspicuous, and there had ceased to be a brisk market for pretence and favouritism, so might the masters of science and ethics, and the devotees of piety and contemplation, be tested, the principles of faiths and creeds be examined, religions be investigated, the proofs and evidences for each be considered, and the pure gold and the alloy be separated from evil commixture. In a short space of time a beautiful, detached building was erected, and the fraudulent vendors of impostures put to sleep in the privy chamber of contempt. A noble palace was provided for the spiritual world, and the pillars of Divine knowledge rose high.

At this time, when the centre of the Caliphate (Fathpur Sikri) was glorified by H. M.'s advent, the former institutions were renewed, and the temple of Divine knowledge was on Thursday nights illuminated by the light of the holy mind. On 20 Mihr, Divine month, 3 October 1578, and in that house of worship, the lamp of the privy chamber of detachment was kindled in the banqueting-hall of social life. The coin of the hivers of wisdom in colleges and cells was brought to the test. The clear wine was separated from the lees, and good coin from the adulterated. The wide capacity and the toleration of the Shadow of God were unveiled. Sufi, philosopher, orator, jurist, Sunni, Shia, Brahman, Jati, Siura Carbak, Nazarene, Jew, Sabi (Sabian), Zoroastrian, and others enjoyed exquisite pleasure by beholding the calmness of the assembly, the sitting of the world-lord in the lofty pulpit (mimbar), and the adornment of the pleasant abode of impartiality. The treasures of secrets were opened out without fear of hostile seekers after battle. The just and truth-perceiving ones of each sect emerged from haughtiness and conceit, and began their search anew. They displayed profundity and meditation, and gathered eternal bliss on the divan of greatness. The conceited and quarrelsome from evilness of disposition and shortness of thought descended into the mire of presumption and sought their profit in loss. Being guided by ignorant companions, and from the predominance of a somnolent fortune, they went into disgrace. The conferences were excellently arranged by the acuteness and keen quest of truth of the world's Khedive. Every time, eye and heart gained fresh lustre, and the lamp of vigils acquired new glory. The candle of investigation was lighted for those who loved darkness and sequacity. The families of the colleges and monasteries were tested. The handle of wealth and the material of sufficiency came into the grasp of the needy occupants of the summit of expectation. The fame of this faith-adorning method of world-bestowing made home bitter to inquirers and caused them to love exile. The Shahinshah's court became the home of the inquirers of the seven climes, and the assemblage of the wise of every religion and sect. The veneer and the counterfeitness of all those who by feline tricks and stratagems had come forth in the garb of wisdom were revealed. A few irreverent and crafty spirits continued their old tactics after the appearance of Truth and its concomitant convictions, and indulged in brawling. Their idea was that as in the great assemblies of former rulers the purpose of science and the designs of wisdom had been but little explored owing to the crowd of men, the inattention of the governor of the feast, the briskness of the market of praters, etc., so perhaps in this august assemblage they might succeed by the length of their tongues, and a veil might be hung over the occiput (*fararu*) of truth. The Khedive of wisdom by the glory of his mind carried out the work to a conclusion deliberately and impartially, and in this praiseworthy fashion, which is seldom found in the saints of asceticism—how then is it to be found in world rulers?—tested the various coins of mortals. Many men became stained with shame and chose loss of fame, while some acquired wisdom and emerged from the hollow of obscurity to eminence. Reason was exalted, and the star of fortune shone for the acquirers of knowledge. The bigoted 'Ulama and the routine-lawyers, who reckoned themselves among the chiefs of philosophies and leaders of enlightenment, found their position difficult. The veil was removed from the face of many of them. The house of evil-thinking coiners became the abode of a thousand suspicions and slanders. Though the wicked and crooked-minded and disaffected were always speaking foolishly about the pious Khedive, yet at this time they had a new foundation for their calumnies, and descended into the pit of eternal ruin. Inasmuch as the warmth of the Shahinshah's graciousness increases daily, and he was aware of the ignorance of those turbulent ones, he did not proceed against them with physical and spiritual vigour and with external and internal majesty. Rather, he restrained his heart and tongue from uttering his disgust, and did not allow the dust of chagrin to settle on the skirt of his soul. In a short space of time many of these fortunately fell into fatal evils and suffered losses and died, while some who were of a good sort became ashamed, and took up the work (of study) anew. From a long time it was the custom that the dull and superficial regarded the heartfelt words of holy souls as foolishness. They recognized wisdom nowhere but in the schools, and did not know that acquired knowledge is for the most part stained with doubts and suspicions. Insight is that which without schooling illuminates the pure temple of the heart. The inner soul receives rays from holy heaven. From eternity, the ocean of Divine bounties has been in motion, and the cup of those who are worthy of the world of creation is filled to the brim therefrom. Always have the magnates of Use and Wont in spite of their great knowledge sought the explanation of wisdom and ethics ('*ilm u 'amal*) from this company of the pure in heart, and have waited in the antechamber of the simple and beautiful of soul, and have gathered bliss therefrom. Accordingly histories tell of this, and its transpires in biographies (?). God be praised for that at this day the Lord of Lords of inspired (*laduni*) wisdom is represented by the Holy Personality of the Shahinshah. The difficulties of sect upon sect of mankind are made easy by the flashings of his sacred soul. The attainment of enlightenment is not the first robe of honour which the eternal needle sews. He who knows the secrets of the past, and the reader of ancient stories, is well aware of this. Still more is it known to the awakened, the truth-choosing and the acute! May the Almighty God ever keep verdant and watered this tree which is rich in spiritual and material fruit!

One night, the assembly in the 'Ibadatkhana was increasing the light of truth. Padre Radif,[1] one of the Nazarene sages, who was singular for his understanding and ability, was making points in that feast of intelligence. Some of the untruthful bigots came forward in a blundering way to answer him. Owing to the calmness of the august assembly, and the increasing light of justice, it became clear that each of these was weaving a circle of old acquisitions, and was not following the highway of proof, and that the explanation of the riddle of truth was not present to their thoughts. The veil was nearly being stripped, once for all, from their procedure. They were ashamed, and abandoned such discourse, and applied themselves to perverting the words of the Gospels. But they could not silence their antagonist by such arguments. The Padre quietly and with an air of conviction said, "Alas, that such things should be thought to be true! In fact, if this faction have such an opinion of our Book, and regard the *Furqan* (the Qoran) as the pure word of God, it is proper that a heaped fire be lighted. We shall take the Gospels in our hands, and the 'Ulama of that faith shall take their book, and then let us enter that testing-place of truth. The escape of any one will be a sign of his truthfulness." The liverless and black-hearted fellows wavered, and in reply to the challenge had recourse to bigotry and wrangling. This cowardice and effrontery displeased his (Akbar's) equitable soul, and the banquet of enlightenment was made resplendent by acute observations. Continually, in those day-like nights, glorious subtleties and profound words dropped from his pearl-filled mouth. Among them was this: "Most persons, from intimacy with those who adorn their outside, but are inwardly bad, think that outward semblance, and the letter of Muhammadanism, profit without internal conviction. Hence we by fear and force compelled many believers in the Brahman (i.e., Hindu) religion to adopt the faith of our ancestors. Now that the light of truth has taken possession of our soul, it has become clear that in this distressful place of contrarities (the world), where darkness of comprehension and conceit are heaped up, fold upon fold, a single step cannot be taken without the torch of proof, and that that creed is profitable which is adopted with the approval of wisdom. To repeat the creed, to remove a piece of skin (i.e., to become circumcised) and to place the end of one's bones on the ground (i.e., the head in adoration) from dread of the Sultan, is not seeking after God."

Verse.

Obedience is not the placing of your forehead in the dust.
Produce truth, for sincerity is not situated in the forehead.

The first step in this perilous desert is with a high courage, and an exalted determination to rise up and do battle with the protean and presumptuous car-

---

[1]Rodolfo Acquaviva, a Portuguese Jesuit.

nal soul, and by rigorous self examination to make Anger and Lust the subjects of Sultan Reason, and to erase from the heart the marks of censurable sentiments. Mayhap the Sun of Proof will emerge from behind the veil of Error and make one a truth-worshipper, and afterward he may by secret attraction draw to himself one of the inquirers after the Path. Such load-stones are produced from the mine of asceticism (*riyazat*). Or it may be that by virtue of talisman and the might of fascination he may bring him into his circle. Should the latter go astray and fall into the pit of not doing God's will, yet shall he not be stained with the dust of blame. He also said, "We blame ourselves for what we did in accordance with old rules and before the truth about faith had shed its rays on our heart."

The fortunate and auspicious, on hearing these enlightening words, hastened to the abode of the light of search and set themselves to amend their ways, while the somnolent and perverse were full of disturbance. Inasmuch as the fierce winds of indiscrimination had laid hold of the four corners of the world, he mentioned the rules of various religions, and described their various excellencies. The acute sovereign gave no weight to common talk, and praised whatever was good in any religion. He often adorned the tablet of his tongue by saying "He is a man who makes Justice the guide of the path of inquiry, and takes from every sect what is consonant to reason. Perhaps in this way the lock, whose key has been lost, may be opened." In this connexion, he praised the truth-seeking of the natives of India, and eloquently described the companionship of the men of that country in the day of disaster, and how they played away for the sake of Fidelity (lit. in the shadow of), Property, Life, Reputation, and Religion, which are reckoned as comprising the four goods of the world's market. He also dwelt upon the wonderful way in which the women of that country become ashes whenever the day of calamity arrives.

This bliss-collecting class has several divisions. Some protagonists of the path of righteousness yield up their lives merely on hearing of the inevitable lot of their husbands. Many sensualists of old times were, from ignorance and irreflection, unable to read such exquisite creatures by the lines of the forehead, or the record of their behavior, and entered with loss the ravine of experiment, and cast away recklessly the priceless jewel! Some deliberately and with open brow enter the flames along with their husband's corpse, or with some token of him who hath gone to the land of annihilation.

Some whom sacrifice of life and fellowship do not make happy, yet, from fear of men's reproach, observe the letter of love, and descend into the mouth of the fire.

He said to the learned Christians, "Since you reckon the reverencing of women as part of your religion, and allow not more than one wife to a man, it would not be wonderful if such fidelity and life-sacrifice were found among your women. The extraordinary thing is that it occurs among those of the Brahman (i.e., the Hindu) religion. There are numerous concubines, and many of them are neglected and unappreciated and spend their days unfructuously in the privy chamber of chastity, yet in spite of such bitterness of life they are flaming torches of love and fellowship." On hearing such noble recitals those present remained silent in the hall of reply, and their tongues reddened with surprise. The Divine message filled with joy all the seekers after wisdom in the august assemblage.

FURTHER READINGS

The career of Abu-l Fazl and his influence on Akbar's religious policy is detailed in Saiyid Athar Abbas Rizvi, *Religious and Intellectual History of the Muslims in Akbar's Reign, with Special Reference to Abu-l Fazl, 1556–1605* (New Delhi: Munshiram Manoharlal Publishers, 1975). Rumer Godden, *Gulbadan: Portrait of a Rose Princess at the Mughal Court* (New York: Viking Press, 1981) is the fascinating story of Akbar's aunt, who preceased Akbar by only two years, when she died in 1603 at the age of eighty. Tara Chand, *The Influence of Islam on Indian Culture* (Allahabad: Indian Press, 1954) is an important assessment of the subject. For accounts of Europeans in Akbar's India, see William Foster, *Early Travels in India, 1583–1619* (London: Oxford University Press, 1921). Akbar S. Ahmed, *Discovering Islam: Making Sense of Muslim History and Society* (New York: Routledge and Kegan Paul, 1988) is a recent work by a leading Pakistani anthropologist.

JOURNEY TO THE WEST
Wu Ch'eng-en

Buddhism, like Christianity and Islam, is composed of various sects. The two major divisions within Buddhism are the Theravada, or Hinayana, and the Mahayana schools. The Theravada sect codified its versions of the teachings of Buddha in what was called the Pali Canon. This was transmitted orally until it was finally written down in about 400 B.C. in Sri Lanka. Theravada Buddhism is generally felt to be the less hopeful philosophy, holding that the individual can achieve salvation only through the slow process of accumulating merit in life after life. Nevertheless, it is still the form of Buddhism that is dominant in Sri Lanka, Burma, and Thailand. Mahayana Buddhism derived from those early teachers who engaged in metaphysical debates with Hindus and, in the process,

From *Monkey: Folk Novel of China by Wu Ch'eng-en*, trans. Arthur Waley (New York: Grove, 1958), pp. 119, 126–27, 279, 282–84.

developed a complex and subtle set of religious doctrines. Mahayana Buddhism teaches that there have been numerous Buddhas and Buddha-figures, some of whom are devoted to aiding the devout in the attainment of salvation. The Pure Land sect, whose teachings in *The Pure Land* appear in Part II, is derived from Mahayana belief. It was Mahayana Buddhism that eventually took root in China.

The spread of Buddhism in China was a slow process, made difficult by the lack of reliable books of Buddhist teachings available to Chinese scholars. Chinese and Sanskrit are vastly different languages, and accurate translation between the two is a demanding business at best. The early process of translation was complex and prone to error. A given text was translated orally from Sanskrit into spoken Chinese, and then Chinese scholars translated the spoken version into acceptable literary Chinese. In the process much of the meaning was distorted, particularly when the Chinese attempted to understand these Sanskrit texts in terms of Chinese culture and institutions.

From about A.D. 200 to 600, China was in a state of turmoil, and communication with India was broken by Chinese withdrawal from Central Asia. Buddhism flourished in China during the period, but scholars were quite aware that the texts they were using were unreliable. One of the great intellectual adventures of this period was the effort by Chinese Buddhist scholars to produce authoritative translations of Buddhist texts. A key figure in this process was the captive monk Kumarajiva (350–409). Of mixed Indian and Central Asian descent, Kumarajiva became a monk at the age of seven and eventually became a famous translator. In about 380, a Chinese military expedition captured him and spirited him off to China where he spent the last thirty years of his life translating texts into a beautiful literary Chinese that is still studied and admired. Despite the difficulties of his task, he managed to convey the subtleties of the original Sanskrit, although it is recorded that he was never satisfied with his translations.

Chinese scholars were still not content with the texts they had, and, over the years, about a hundred Chinese pilgrims made the arduous and dangerous trek to India to collect better ones. The most famous of these pilgrims was the monk Hsuan Tsang (c. 596–664), who had mastered the doctrines taught in the various Chinese schools of Buddhism and decided that only in India could he further his understanding of the faith. Setting out in the autumn of 629, he reached India and traveled widely throughout the country, staying for a time with the great king Harsha (r. 606–647). His account of his trip, *Journey to the West (Hsi-yu Chi)*, is not only an adventurous tale, but an important source for the history and geography of India during this period. He finally returned to China in 645 and for the remainder of his life headed a translation bureau that rendered over seventy Sanskrit works into classical Chinese.

His exploits and accomplishments made Hsuan Tsang a celebrity in his own time and a legendary hero in centuries to come. Over time, fabulous legends became attached to his journey and were better known than the facts themselves. These stories were passed down as folk tales until the scholar Wu Ch'eng-en (c. 1500–1582) wrote a long novel with the same title as Hsuan Tsang's original work. He wrote the novel in popular rather than literary Chinese, and it has remained a favorite of the Chinese ever since. In the novel, Hsuan Tsang is called Tripitaka, literally "three baskets," the Sanskrit term for the canon of Buddhist scripture. Tripitaka is accompanied on his long journey by a monkey, who becomes the center of many humorous episodes, and they are joined later by a pig, a dragon transformed into a horse, and a monster named Sandy.

In addition to being a set of rollicking tales, *The Journey to the West* is also a satire on the religion and bureaucracy of the later Ming dynasty. Scholars also have read allegorical meaning into the adventures of the pilgrims, but these need not detain the reader. The selection begins as Tripitaka sets off on his journey.

Questions

1. The historical Hsuan Tsang was actually denied permission to leave China and was technically a fugitive on his pilgrimage. Why would later legends represent the journey as an embassy sent by the emperor?

2. How does India appear to the pilgrims?

3. What criticisms of China does the author have the Buddha make?

JOURNEY TO THE WEST

CHAPTER XIII

It was three days before the full moon, in the ninth month of the thirteenth year of Cheng Kuan, when Tripitaka, seen off by the Emperor and all his ministers, left the gates of Ch'ang-an. After a day or two of hard riding, he reached the Temple of the Law Cloud. The abbot and some five hundred priests, drawn up in two files, ushered him into the temple. After supper, sitting by lamplight, they discussed questions of religion and the purpose of Tripitaka's quest. Some spoke of how wide the rivers were that he must cross and how high the mountains that he must climb. Some spoke of the roads being infested by panthers and tigers, some of precipices hard to circumvent and demons impossible to overcome. Tripitaka said nothing, but only pointed again and again at his own heart. The priests did not understand what he meant, and when at last they asked him to explain, he said, 'It is the heart alone that can destroy them. I made a solemn vow, standing before the Buddha's image, to carry through this task, come what may. Now that I have started I cannot go back till I have reached India, seen Buddha, got the Scriptures, and turned the wheel of the Law, that our holy sovereign's great dynasty may forever be secure.'

✦

CHAPTER XIV

After going downhill for some way they came to the stone box, in which there was really a monkey. Only his head was visible, and one paw, which he waved violently through the opening, saying, 'Welcome, Master! Welcome! Get me out of here, and I will protect you on your journey to the West.' The hunter stepped boldly up, and removing the grasses from Monkey's hair and brushing away the grit from under his chin, 'What have you got to say for yourself?' he asked. 'To you, nothing,' said Monkey. 'But I have something to ask of that priest. Tell him to come here.' 'What do you want to ask me?' said Tripitaka. 'Were you sent by the Emperor of T'ang to look for Scriptures in India?' asked Monkey. 'I was,' said Tripitaka. 'And what of that?' 'I am the Great Sage Equal of Heaven,' said Monkey. 'Five hundred years ago I made trouble in the Halls of Heaven, and Buddha clamped me down in this place. Not long ago the Bodhisattva Kuan-yin, whom Buddha had ordered to look around for someone to fetch Scriptures from India, came here and promised me that if I would amend my ways and faithfully protect the pilgrim on his way, I was to be released, and afterwards would find salvation. Ever since then I have been waiting impatiently night and day for you to come and let me out. I will protect you while you are going to get Scriptures and follow you as your disciple.'

✦

CHAPTER XXVIII

They travelled westward for many months, and at last began to be aware that the country through which they were now passing was different from any that they had seen. Everywhere they came across gem-like flowers and magical grasses, with many ancient cypresses and hoary pines. In the villages through which they passed every family seemed to devote itself to the entertainment of priests and other pious works. On every hill were hermits practising austerities, in every wood pilgrims chanting holy writ. Finding hospitality each night and starting again at dawn, they journeyed for many days, till they came at last within a sudden sight of a cluster of high eaves and towers. 'Monkey, that's a fine place,' said Tripitaka, pointing to it with his whip. 'Considering,' said Monkey, 'how often you have insisted upon prostrating yourself at the sight of false magicians' palaces and arch impostors' lairs, it is strange that when at last you see before you Buddha's true citadel, you should not even dismount from your horse.' At this Tripitaka in great excitement sprang from his saddle, and walking beside the horse was soon at the gates of the high building. A young Taoist came out to meet them. 'Aren't you the people who have come from the east to fetch scriptures?' he asked. Tripitaka hastily tidied his clothes and looking up saw that the boy was clad in gorgeous brocades and carried a bowl of jade dust in his hand. Monkey knew him at once. 'This,' he said to Tripitaka, 'is the Golden Crested Great Immortal of the Jade Truth Temple at the foot of the Holy Mountain.' Tripitaka at once advanced bowing. 'Well, here you are at last!' said the Immortal. 'The Bodhisattva misinformed me. Ten years ago she was told by Buddha to go to China and find someone who would fetch scriptures from India. She told me she had found someone who would arrive here in two or three years. Year after year I waited, but never a sign! This meeting is indeed a surprise.' 'I cannot thank you enough, Great Immortal, for your patience,' said Tripitaka.

◆

Near the top of the hill they came upon a party of Upasakas filing through the green pinewoods, and under a clump of emerald cedars they saw bands of the Blessed. Tripitaka hastened to bow down to them. Worshippers male and female, monks and nuns pressed together the palms of their hands, crying, 'Holy priest, it is not to us that your homage should be addressed. Wait till you have seen Sakyamuni, and afterwards come and greet us each according to his rank.' 'He's always in too much of a hurry,' laughed Monkey. 'Come along at once and let us pay our respects to the people at the top.' Twitching with excitement Tripitaka followed Monkey to the gates of the Temple. Here they were met by the Vajrapani of the Four Elements. 'So your Reverence has at last arrived!' he exclaimed. 'Your disciple Hsuan Tsang has indeed arrived,' said Tripitaka, bowing. 'I must trouble you to wait here a moment, till your arrival has been announced,' said the Vajrapani. He then gave instructions to the porter at the outer gate to tell the porter at the second gate that the Vajrapani wished to report that the priest from China had arrived. The porter at the second gate sent word to the porter at the third gate. At this gate were holy priests with direct access to the Powers Above. They hurried to the Great Hall and informed the

Tathagata, the Most Honoured One, even Sakyamuni Buddha himself that the priest from the Court of China had arrived at the Mountain to fetch scriptures.

Father Buddha was delighted. He ordered the Bodhisattva, Vajrapanis, Arhats, Protectors, Planets and Temple Guardians to form up in two lines. Then he gave orders that the priest of T'ang was to be shown in. Again the word was passed along from gate to gate: 'The priest of T'ang is to be shown in.' Tripitaka, Monkey, Pigsy and Sandy, carefully following the rules of etiquette prescribed to them, all went forward, horse and baggage following. When they reached the Great Hall they first prostrated themselves before the Tathagata and then bowed to right and left. This they repeated three times, and then knelt before the Buddha and presented their passports. He looked through them one by one and handed them back to Tripitaka, who bent his head in acknowledgment, saying, 'The disciple Hsuan Tsang has come by order of the Emperor of the great land of T'ang, all the way to this Holy Mountain, to fetch the true scriptures which are to be the salvation of all mankind. May the Lord Buddha accord this favour and grant me a quick return to my native land.'

Hereupon the Tathagata opened the mouth of compassion and gave vent to the mercy of his heart: 'In all the vast and populous bounds of your Eastern Land, greed, slaughter, lust and lying have long prevailed. There is no respect for Buddha's teaching, no striving towards good works. So full and abundant is the measure of the people's sins that they go down forever into the darkness of Hell, where some are pounded in mortars, some take on animal form, furry and horned. In which guise they are done by as they did on earth, their flesh becoming men's food. Confucius stood by their side teaching them all the virtues, king after king in vain corrected them with fresh penalties and pains. No law could curb their reckless debauches, no ray of wisdom penetrate their blindness.

'But I have three Baskets of Scripture that can save mankind from its torments and afflictions. One contains the Law, which tells of Heaven, one contains the Discourses, which speak of Earth, one contains the Scriptures, which save the dead. They are divided into thirty-five sections and are written upon fifteen thousand one hundred and forty-four scrolls. They are the path to Perfection, the gate that leads to True Good. In them may be learnt all the motions of the stars and divisions of earth, all that appertains to man, bird, beast, flower, tree and implement of use; in short, all that concerns mankind is found therein. In consideration of the fact that you have come so far, I would give you them all to take back. But the people of China are foolish and boisterous; they would mock at my mysteries and would not understand the hidden meaning of our Order . . . Ananda, Kasyapa,' he cried, 'take these four to the room under the tower, and when they have refreshed themselves, open the doors of the Treasury, and select from each of the thirty-five sections a few scrolls for these priests to take back to the East, to be a boon there forever.'

FURTHER READINGS

Arthur Waley's *Monkey: Folk Novel of China by Wu Ch'eng-en* includes translations of only thirty of the one hundred chapters of the novel. There is a full translation in Wu Ch'eng-en, *The Journey to the West*, trans. Anthony C. Yu, 4 vols. (Chicago: University of Chicago Press, 1977). Hsuan Tsang's account of his journey is translated in Samual Beal, trans., *Si Yu Ki: Buddhist Records of the Western World*, 2 vols. (London: Trubner, 1883). His Chinese biography is translated in Thomas Watters, *On Yuan Chwang* (London: Royal Asiatic Society, 1905). Arthur Waley also authored a biography in *The Real Tripitaka and Other Pieces* (London: Allen & Unwin, 1952). Arthur F. Wright, *Buddhism in Chinese History* (Stanford, CA: Stanford University Press, 1959) is an excellent brief introduction to the subject.

HAGAKURE

Tsunetomo Yamamoto

From the mid-twelfth century to the restoration of imperial rule in 1867, samurai warriors played a dominant role in Japanese society. Although they initially served a primarily military function, by the seventeenth century the samurai had assumed important administrative powers and had become key figures in the government bureaucracy. The origin of this class can be traced to the decline of authority of the central government in the ninth century A.D., when local lords organized private armies of mounted warriors known as *bushi* or samurai. By the beginning of the Kamakura period (1185–1333), the samurai formed a distinct social class, governed by a strict code of conduct known as *Bushido* (the way of the warrior), a code handed down orally and through the writings of famous warriors and scholars.

Besides being proficient in martial skills, the samurai were expected to display virtues similar to those of the knights of the European Middle Ages. Qualities such as courage, honor, self-control, absolute loyalty, manly pride, and the readiness to face any hardship or make any sacrifice for lord or family were only part of the requirements of Bushido. In addition to principles drawn from Shintoism, Zen Buddhism, and Confucian moral teachings, followers of Bushido were expected to display a complete disdain for death. The bushi was,

From Yukio Mishima, *The Way of the Samurai*, trans. Kathryn Sparling (New York: Basic Books, 1977), pp. 109–14, 116–17, 119–22, 125–26, 134, 155, 164–65.

above all else, to avoid dishonor, even to the point of committing ritual suicide by disembowelment (*seppuka*).

The samurai ruled Japan essentially by the sword. The Onin War (1467–1477) and the subsequent century of civil strife reshaped Japanese society in a manner that led to profound changes in the life of the samurai. A long period of near-anarchy was ended only with reunification in 1568 and the return of peace and political stability under the rule of the Tokugawa Shoguns (1603–1867). Under the Shogunate, individual clans remained relatively independent but owed allegiance to the central government. The lord and his samurai followers comprised the leading class within each clan, but the new enforced peace required that fighting men such as the samurai find new pursuits. By the end of the seventeenth century, the great majority of samurai had left their rural homes and had relocated in the larger urban centers, where they tended to join the growing bureaucracy. Many became more involved with administration and their own self-interest and less committed to military prowess and the principles of *Bushido*.

Some samurai spoke out against the moral decay of their class and the decline of martial skills. One of these critics was Tsunetomo Yamamoto (1659–1719), a member of the powerful Nabeshima clan and, for thirty years, a devoted follower of its lord, Mitsushige Nabeshima. With the death of Nabeshima in 1700, Yamamoto renounced the world and retired to a hermitage in the mountains. Here he meditated on the principles that should guide the life of a samurai and transmitted his thoughts to his pupil, Tsuramoto Tashiro, who edited and compiled them under the title *Hagakure* (*In the Shadow of Leaves*).

Yamamoto forbade Tashiro from publishing these teachings, perhaps feeling they were too radical for the times. The manuscript was preserved for the moral and practical instruction of the House of Nabeshima and was kept by the clan as secret teachings available only to a chosen few. The *Hagakure* was kept hidden for generations, until it was finally made available to the general public in 1906. The work became quite influential, particularly among army leaders, who reinterpreted its teachings on loyalty in terms of devotion to the Japanese emperor and nation. Throughout the period of inflamed patriotism of the 1930s and World War II, the *Hagakure* was published in many editions and sold in tremendous numbers. Its opening line, "I have discovered that the way of the samurai is death," was recited by Japanese suicide pilots before departing to seek the enemy. Following the war, there was a reaction against the *Hagakure*, which came to be regarded as dangerous and subversive, and many copies were destroyed. Its popularity has subsequently revived.

The *Hagakure* is based on the acceptance of the eventuality of death. Should the samurai attempt to flee death, at that moment he ceases to be a samurai, for a readiness to die is the prerequisite for all proper action. Only if the samurai is prepared to die, is he instinctively able to act correctly. Thus, for the *Hagakure*, acceptance of death is the basis of a philosophy of action, passion, and, ultimately, freedom. It is a book about how to live, with instruction on moral and practical matters even so minor as how to behave at drinking parties and how to stifle a yawn in public. In a new and industrialized world, the teachings of the *Hagakure* have been influential in the evolution of a Bushido for modern times, and its principles are studied thoughtfully by leaders in Japanese business and industry. The *Hagakure* provides a valuable insight into Japanese attitudes and values, both past and present.

Questions

1. Yamamoto was well schooled in both Zen Buddhism and Confucian teachings. What Buddhist and Confucian influences do you find in the *Hagakure*?
2. According to the *Hagakure*, what is the most extreme manifestation of free will?
3. *Bushido* has had a profound effect on Japanese society since the twelfth century. Do you see any relationship between Bushido and aspects of modern Japanese society?

HAGAKURE

AUTHOR'S INTRODUCTION

Having surveyed the situation, I determined to repay my own debt of gratitude to the Nabeshima House[1] by being of some use in these degenerate times. If my efforts are warmly received, then all the more will I abandon selfish interest and devote my life to my domain, and even though I may be made a ronin[2] or ordered to commit ritual suicide, I shall obey calmly, thinking that it is simply part of my samurai service. Even from retirement deep in the mountains, even from the grave, though I die and am reborn again and again, the determination to serve the Nabeshima House is the first resolution of a Nabeshima samurai and my reason for living. It is, I suppose, an unseemly attitude for one who has shaved his head and retired from the secular world, but I had never desired to attain buddhahood. Even if I were to die and be reborn again seven times, I

---

[1] Powerful clan to which Yamamoto belonged.
[2] Masterless samurai.

neither expected nor wanted anything more than to be a Nabeshima samurai and to devote myself entirely to the *han*. In a word, all that is necessary for a Nabeshima samurai is that he have the strength of will to bear on his shoulders total responsibility for the ruling house of his *han*. We are all human beings. Why should one man be inferior to another? Skill and training are of no use unless one has great confidence in oneself. And if one does not use it for the peace and prosperity of the ruling house, training amounts to nothing. However, such resolution, like water boiling in a kettle, cools as easily as it was heated. Of course, there is a way to keep it from cooling. My method consists of the four vows that follow: 1) Never fall behind in the Way of the Warrior. 2) Serve your lieged lord well. 3) Be filially pious. 4) Be deeply compassionate and help all human beings.

If every morning one prays to the gods and buddhas for help in carrying out these four vows, one's strength will double and there will be no back-sliding. Just like an inchworm, one will advance slowly. Even the gods and the buddhas make such vows.

HAGAKURE: BOOK ONE

I DISCOVERED THAT THE WAY OF THE SAMURAI IS DEATH

I discovered that the Way of the Samurai is death. In a fifty-fifty life or death crisis, simply settle it by choosing immediate death. There is nothing complicated about it. Just brace yourself and proceed. Some say that to die without accomplishing one's mission is to die in vain, but this is the calculating, imitation samurai ethic of arrogant Osaka[3] merchants. To make the correct choice in a fifty-fifty situation is nearly impossible. We would all prefer to live. And so it is quite natural in such a situation that one should find some excuse for living on. But one who chooses to go on living having failed in one's mission will be despised as a coward and a bungler. This is the precarious part. If one dies after having failed, it is a fanatic's death, death in vain. It is not, however, dishonorable. Such a death is in fact the Way of the Samurai. In order to be a perfect samurai, it is necessary to prepare oneself for death morning and evening day in and day out. When a samurai is constantly prepared for death, he has mastered the Way of the Samurai, and he may unerringly devote his life to the service of his lord.

[3]A prosperous commercial and shipping center located in southern Japan.

INSIGHT AND DECISION

Some people are born with the ability to call forth instantaneous wisdom whenever the occasion demands. Others, however, must lie awake at night long afterwards, pounding their pillows in anguished concentration until they finally come up with a solution to the problem. But while such inborn differences in ability are inevitable to a certain extent, by adopting the Four Vows, anyone may develop hitherto undreamed-of wisdom. It might seem that no matter how limited one's abilities, no matter how difficult the problem, one ought to be able to find a solution if one thinks hard enough long enough, but as long as one bases one's reasoning on the "self," one will simply be wily and not wise. Human beings are foolish, and it is difficult for them to lose the "self." Even so, when faced with a difficult situation, if one sets aside the specific problem for a moment, concentrates on the Four Vows and leaves the "self," and then searches for a solution, one will not often miss.

KNOW THE LIMITS OF YOUR ABILITIES

Although we possess very little wisdom indeed, we tend to try to solve all our difficulties on the basis of it, with the unfortunate result that we become preoccupied with the self and turn our backs on the Way of Heaven, and in the end our actions become evil. Indeed to an onlooker we must seem shabby, weak, narrow-minded, and totally ineffectual. When true wisdom seems unattainable on one's own strength, it is advisable to consult with those who are wiser. Someone who is not personally involved will be able to make a clear judgment uncomplicated by personal interest and will make the proper choice. Looking at a man who makes his decisions in such an admirable way, we know that he is sturdy, reliable, firmly rooted in reality. His wisdom, gathered through consultation with others, is like the roots of a great tree, numerous and thick. There are limits to the wisdom of one man, a lone sapling blown by the wind.

THE PROPER WAY TO CRITICIZE OTHERS

Reprimanding people and correcting their faults is important; it is actually an act of charity—the first requirement of samurai service. One must take pains to do it in the proper way. It is an easy matter to find strong points and shortcomings in another man's conduct; it is equally easy to criticize them. Most people seem to believe it a kindness to tell people things they do not want to hear, and if their criticisms are not taken to heart, well, then nothing more can be done. Such an approach is totally without merit. It produces results no better than if one had set out willfully to insult and embarrass the man. It is simply a way of getting something off one's chest. Criticism must begin *after* one has discerned whether or not the person will accept it, *after* one has become his friend, shared his interests, and behaved in such a way as to earn his complete trust so that he will put faith in whatever one says. And then there is the matter of tact: One must devise the proper way to say it, and the proper moment—perhaps in a letter, perhaps on the way home from a pleasant gathering. One might start by describing one's own failures, and make him see what one is getting at without a word more than is necessary. First one praises his strengths, taking pains to encourage him and put him in the right mood, making him as receptive to one's words as a thirsty man to water. Then correct his faults. To criticize well is extremely difficult.

I know from personal experience that bad habits acquired over many years are not so easily broken. It seems to me that the properly charitable attitude is for all samurai in the service of the daimyo to be always in familiarity and friendship and to correct each other's faults the better to serve the daimyo together. By willfully embarrassing someone, one accomplishes nothing—how could such tactics be effective?

APPROACH A TASK WITH COURAGE

When I asked Yasaburo for a sample of his calligraphy, he remarked, "One should write boldly enough to cover the entire paper with a single character, with vigor enough to destroy the paper. Skill in calligraphy depends entirely on the energy and spirit with which it is executed. A samurai must proceed unflagging, never tiring or becoming dispirited, until the task is completed. That is all," and he wrote the calligraphy.

PRESENT-DAY "SALARYMEN" SET THEIR SIGHTS TOO LOW

Looking at young samurai in service these days, it seems to me they set their sights pitifully low. They have the furtive glance of pickpockets. Most of them are out for their own interests, or to display their cleverness, and even those who seem calm of heart are simply putting up a good front. That attitude will never do. Unless a samurai sets his sights on no less than offering up his life for his ruler, dying swiftly and becoming a spirit, unless he is constantly anxious about the welfare of his daimyo[4] and reports to him immediately whenever he has disposed of a problem, his concern being always to strengthen the foundations of the realm, then he cannot be called a true samurai in the service of his lord.

---

[4]Feudal lord.

In that sense, daimyo and retainer must be of the same determination. Therefore it is absolutely necessary to stand firm with a resolution so strong that not
even the gods and buddhas may cause one to swerve from one's purpose.

"THE ADVANTAGE IS TO THE ONLOOKER"

To hate evil and live one's life in righteousness is exceedingly difficult. Surprisingly enough, many errors arise from believing that it is essential to be
strictly logical and to value righteousness above all else. There is a way more
lofty than righteousness, but discovering it is no easy matter and requires wisdom of the highest order. Compared to this Way, logical principals are insignificant indeed. What one has not experienced firsthand one cannot know. And
yet, there is a means of learning the truth even though one has not been able to
discern it for oneself. The way lies in talking with other people. It is often true
that even a person who has not yet perfected himself may be able to give directions to others. The principle involved is similar to what in go[5] is called "The
advantage is to the onlooker." One speaks of "learning one's faults through contemplation," but this too is best done by talking with others. The reason is that
when one learns by listening to what others have to say and by reading books,
one transcends the limitations of one's own powers of discernment and follows
the teachings of the ancients.

THERE IS ALWAYS ROOM FOR IMPROVEMENT

I have heard that a certain master swordsman, having reached old age, made the
following statement:
   "A samurai's training lasts a lifetime, and there is a proper order to it. At
the lowest level of training, even though you practice, you do not seem to
improve, you know you are unskillful, and you believe the same of others. At
this point, needless to say, you are of no use in the service of the daimyo. At the
middle level you are still of no real use, but you are aware of your deficiencies,
and you begin to recognize the shortcomings of others. When a samurai attains
the highest level, he is able to dispose of any situation on the basis of his own
wisdom so that he no longer need follow the teachings of others; he gains confidence in his abilities, rejoices in being praised, and laments the failings of
others. Such a samurai, may we well say, is useful in the service of the daimyo.
Even above this level, there are those whose facial expressions never reveal what
they are thinking, nor do they make an exhibition of their skill—in fact, they

---

[5]Popular Japanese board game.

feign ignorance and incompetence. What is more, they respect the skill of others. In most cases I suppose this is the best that can be aspired to.

But on a still higher level there is an extreme realm that transcends the skill of ordinary mortals. One who penetrates deep into the Way of this realm realizes that there is no end to his training, and that the time will never come when he may be satisfied with his labors. Therefore, a samurai must know his shortcomings well and spend his life in training without ever feeling he has done enough. Of course he must never be overconfident, but neither should he feel inferior to others."

Yagyu, a teacher of *kendo* to the Tokugawa shoguns, is quoted as having said, "I do not know how to excel others. All I know is how to excel myself." Saying to himself, "Today I am better than I was yesterday, tomorrow I will be still better," a true samurai lives out his days in constant effort to improve. That is what training is, a process without end.

ONE SHOULD TAKE IMPORTANT CONSIDERATIONS LIGHTLY

Among the public proclamations of Lord Naoshige is the following: "One should take important considerations lightly." A commentary by Ittei Ishida (Confucian scholar of Saga Han, and Jocho Yamamoto's teacher) explains, "Small matters should be taken seriously." Truly important problems are few; they occur probably no more than twice or thrice in a lifetime. Everyday reflection will tell you this. Therefore, it is necessary to plan ahead what to do in case of a crisis, and then when the time comes, to remember the plan and dispose of the problem accordingly. Without daily preparation, when faced with a difficult situation one may be unable to reach a quick decision, with disastrous results. Therefore, may we not say that daily resolutions upon a certain course of action is the principle behind the statement, "One should take important considerations lightly"?

WHEN ONE CANNOT DECIDE WHETHER TO LIVE OR DIE, IT IS BETTER TO DIE

The famous samurai retainer Kiranosuke Shida has said, "If your name means nothing to the world whether you live or die, it is better to live." Shida is a formidable samurai, and young people have misinterpreted these words of his said in jest and have mistakenly thought he was advocating dishonorable conduct. In a postscript, he adds: "When in doubt whether to eat or not eat, it is better to refrain. When one cannot decide whether to live or die, it is better to die."

DAILY RESOLUTION

Until fifty or sixty years ago, samurai performed their ablutions every morning, shaved their heads, and perfumed their topknots. Then they cut their fingernails and toenails, filed them with pumice, and finally buffed them with *kogane* herb. They were never lazy about such matters but took great care to be well groomed. Then a samurai took a look at his long and short swords to make sure they were not rusting, wiped off the dust, and polished them. Taking such pains over one's appearance may seem foppish, but the custom did not arise from a taste for elegance or romance. One may be run through at any moment in vigorous battle; to die having neglected one's personal grooming is to reveal a general sloppiness of habit, and to be despised and mocked by the enemy. So in youth as in old age samurai took pains to look their best. Such fastidiousness may seem time-consuming and more trouble than it is worth, but it is what the Way of the Samurai is all about. Actually, it takes little trouble or time. If, always prepared to die, a samurai begins to think of himself as already dead, if he is diligent in serving his lord and perfects himself in the military arts, surely he will never come to shame; but if a samurai spends his days selfishly doing exactly as he pleases, in a crisis he will bring dishonor upon himself. Having done so, he will not even be aware of his shame, and imagining that as long as he is secure and happy nothing else matters, he will disport himself unspeakably—a thoroughly lamentable development.

A samurai who is not prepared to die at any moment will inevitably die an unbecoming death. But a samurai who lives his life in constant preparation for death—how can he conduct himself in a despicable manner? One should reflect well on this point and behave accordingly. Times have changed in the last thirty years. Now when young samurai get together they talk of money, of profit and loss, how to run a household efficiently, how to judge the value of clothing, and they exchange stories about sex. If any other topic is mentioned, the atmosphere is spoiled and everyone present feels vaguely uncomfortable. What a distressing pass things have come to! It used to be that until the age of twenty or thirty a young man never thought a mean or worldly thought, and so of course he never spoke of such things. And if in their presence older men by accident should let such a remark escape their lips, young men felt as afflicted by it as if they had been physically wounded. Apparently, the new trend has arisen because the modern age has come to value luxury and ostentation. Money alone has come to assume great importance. Certainly if young men did not have luxurious tastes inappropriate to their stations, this mistaken attitude would disappear.

On the other hand, to praise as resourceful young people who are economical and frugal is quite despicable. Frugality inevitably amounts to lacking a sense of *giri*, or personal and social obligations. Need I add that a samurai who forgets his obligations to others is mean, base, and ignoble?

DO EVERYTHING AS THOUGH TO THE DEATH

Lord Naoshige said, "The Way of the Samurai is a mania for death. Sometimes ten men cannot topple a man with such conviction." One cannot accomplish feats of greatness in a normal frame of mind. One must turn fanatic and develop a mania for dying. By the time one develops powers of discernment, it is already too late to put them into effect. In the Way of the Samurai loyalty and filial piety are superfluous; all one needs is a mania for death. Within that attitude loyalty and filial piety will come to reside.

HARDSHIP IS CAUSE FOR REJOICING

It is not enough simply to avoid feeling discouraged in the face of hardship. When disaster befalls a samurai, he must rejoice and leap at the chance to proceed with energy and courage. Well might one say that such an attitude transcends mere resignation. "When the water is high the boat rises."

A BLADE THAT REMAINS IN THE SCABBARD RUSTS

Someone once said, "There are two kinds of pride, inner and outer. A samurai who does not have both inward and outward pride is of no use." Pride may be compared to the blade of a sword, which must be sharpened and then replaced in its scabbard. From time to time it is drawn and raised to the level of one's eyebrows, wiped clean, and then replaced in its scabbard. If a samurai's sword is always drawn and he is constantly brandishing the naked blade, people will find him unapproachable, and he will have no friends. If, on the other hand, the sword is never drawn, it will rust, the blade will become dull, and people will make light of him.

SILENCE IS BEST

The best conduct with regard to speaking is to remain silent. At least if you think you can manage without speaking, do not speak. What must be said should be said as succinctly, logically, and clearly as possible. A surprising number of people make fools of themselves by talking without thinking, and are looked down upon.

START THE DAY BY DYING

Absolute loyalty to the death must be worked at every day. One begins each day in quiet meditation, imagining one's final hour and various ways of dying—by bow and arrow, gun, spear, cut down by the sword, swallowed up by the sea, jumping into a fire, being struck by lightning, crushed in an earthquake, falling off a cliff, death from illness, sudden death—and begins the day by dying. As an old man put it, "When you leave your own eaves, you enter the realm of the dead; leaving your gate, you meet the enemy." This is advocating not prudence but resolution to die.

A PREREQUISITE FOR TRUE SUCCESS

When one rises quickly in the world and one's salary is high, many people become enemies, and one's early success becomes meaningless in the long run. When, on the other hand, one is slow in making a name for oneself, many people are on one's side and one may count on still more fortune for the future. In the last analysis, it matters little whether success comes early or late; one need not worry as long as the method is acceptable to everyone. Good fortune attained with the encouragement of all is indeed genuine good fortune.

FURTHER READINGS

John Whitney Hall, *Government and Local Power in Japan: 500 to 1700* (Princeton, NJ: Princeton University Press, 1966), discusses the origins of feudalism in Japan and the nature of provincial government during the Kamakura period. The court life of the era is described in Jeffrey P. Mass, ed., *Court and Bakufu in Japan: Essays in Kamakura History* (New Haven, CT: Yale University Press, 1982). Other useful works dealing with the Kamakura period include Jeffrey P. Mass, *The Development of Kamakura Rule: 1180–1250* (Stanford, CA: Stanford University Press, 1979) and *Warrior Government in Early Medieval Japan* (New Haven, CT: Yale University Press, 1974).

John W. Hall and Jeffrey P. Mass, eds., *Medieval Japan: Essays in Institutional History* (New Haven, CT: Yale University Press, 1974) provides a collection of essays focusing on the political and institutional history of the period 794 to 1600. The Kemmu restoration and the fourteenth-century dynastic schism is covered in H. Paul Varley, *Imperial Restoration in Medieval Japan* (New York: Columbia University Press, 1971). John W. Hall and Toyoda Takeshi, eds., *Japan in the Muromachi Age* (Berkeley: University of California Press, 1977), contains a series of essays dealing with a somewhat neglected era of Japanese history in the fourteenth and fifteenth centuries. An examination of both the development of military government until the mid-fifteenth century and the effect of the Onin War is provided in H. Paul Varley, *The Onin War* (New York: Columbia University Press, 1967).

The Tokugawa period, during which the *Hagakure* was written, is the subject of a number of useful studies. Kenneth P. Kirkwood, *Renaissance in Japan*

(Rutland, VT: Tuttle, 1970), provides a cultural survey of the seventeenth century. John W. Hall and Marius B. Jansen, eds., *Studies in the Institutional History of Early Modern Japan* (Princeton, NJ: Princeton University Press, 1968), is a valuable series of essays on the Tokugawa period. The educational system of the era is discussed in Ronald P. Dore, *Education in Tokugawa Japan* (Berkeley: University of California Press, 1965). Tetsuo Najita, *Visions of Virtue in Tokugawa Japan* (Chicago: University of Chicago Press, 1987), examines the intellectual history of the period.

H. Paul Varley, *The Samurai* (London: Weidenfeld & Nicolson, 1970), briefly discusses the origins of the samurai and the evolution of the class through Tokugawa times. There are numerous translations of the *Hagakure*. Notable are Tsunetomo Yamamoto, *Bushido: Way of the Samurai*, trans. Minoru Tanaka and ed. Justin F. Stone (Albuquerque, NM: Sun Publishing, 1975) and Tsunetomo Yamamoto, *Hagakure: The Book of the Samurai*, trans. William Scott Wilson (Tokyo: Kodansha International, 1979). A fascinating personal interpretation of the *Hagakure*, written by the renowned Japanese author Yukio Mishima three years before his own suicide, is available in Yukio Mishima, *The Way of the Samurai* (New York: Basic Books, 1977). Another work, contemporary with the *Hagakure*, is Miyamoto Musashi's famous treatise, *Book of Five Rings*, trans. Victor Harris (Woodstock, NY: The Overland Press, 1982). Musashi was a wandering samurai (*ronin*) of notable martial skill who retired to a life of seclusion and meditation in 1643. He composed his *Book of Five Rings* a few weeks before his death in 1645. It is unique among books on the martial arts in that it deals with the strategy of warfare and the methods of single combat in accordance with exactly the same principles.

THE DREAM OF THE RED CHAMBER
Tsao Hsueh-ch'in

Shortly after Wu Ching-tzu finished writing his novel *The Scholars*, his fellow-southerner Tsao Hsueh-ch'in (1715–1763?) was in the northern capital of Peking, composing a masterpiece of vernacular fiction that was to become the most highly acclaimed piece of writing in all of Chinese literature. Like the author of *The Scholars*, Tsao felt the need of greater realism in literature as well as an increased reliance on personal experience. Although relatively little is

From Tsao Hsueh-ch'in, *The Dream of the Red Chamber*, trans. Chi-chen Wang (Boston: Twayne, 1958), pp. 27–47.

known about Tsao, it is clear that he had personal knowledge of the stresses and problems of a once-affluent family now losing status. His family had for generations held the highly lucrative post of commissioner of the imperial textile mills, first in Soochow and then in Nanking. His grandfather had been a patron of letters and a notable poet in his own right. His father was removed from his post for political reasons, however, and his property was confiscated. The family then moved to Peking, where it lived in reduced circumstances. By 1744, when he began writing his novel, Tsao had moved to the suburbs, where he lived for a time in dire poverty. He died in 1763, shortly after having lost his young son.

First published in 1792, the *Dream of the Red Chamber* (*Hung-lou meng*) was soon recognized as China's greatest and most beloved novel. A complex work, it provides a valuable and realistic portrayal of the aristocratic house of Chia, a formerly powerful clan in great favor with imperial authorities but now in rapid decline. It focuses on two Peking households housing five generations of the Chia family together with their numerous servants, retainers, relatives, and other hangers-on. The central figure is a young boy, Pao-yu, the hope of the house of Chia to restore their fortunes. He is outrageously spoiled by his female relatives, detests conventional learning, and prefers the company of his female cousins and the family maidservants.

He falls in love with his cousin Black Jade, a girl of delicate beauty, and the portrayal of their young affection possesses an enduring charm. As the story progresses, however, their love turns into tragedy. The desires of two members of the family have little importance when compared to the needs and aspirations of the family as a whole, and so are ignored when the time comes to arrange a marriage for Pao-yu. Phoenix, who rules the affairs of the family with a merciless efficiency and callous disregard for matters of the heart, arranges that Pao-yu should marry Precious Clasp. Stricken with grief, Black Jade dies on her lover's wedding night.

The marriage affords little happiness for Precious Clasp. Pao-yu never recovers from his bereavement. He goes off and successfully completes the examination for the imperial civil service, the achievement for which the entire family had hoped. Instead of returning home to help raise the fortunes of the house of Chia, however, he renounces the world and becomes a Buddhist monk. All that is left to Precious Clasp is the child she is expecting.

The excerpt presented here is from the novel's famous dream sequence. While visiting the neighboring family compound, Pao-yu, barely a teenager, insists on taking a nap in the bedroom of Ch'in K'o-ch'ing, the young wife of his nephew. He dreams of a celestial beauty, also named Ch'in K'o-ch'ing. Pao-yu is struck by the fact that she seems to him to combine all the charms and graces of both Black Jade and Precious Clasp. He soon enters the Great Void of Illusions Land, presided over by the Goddess of Disillusionment. At the request of his ancestors, the Goddess reprimands him for being the most lustful of men because of his potential commitment to the excessive love that afflicts the unconventional heroes of romance. She then introduces the young man to her sister for sexual initiation. Following a blissful union, Pao-yu is chased by demons and wild beasts to the brink of an impassable river. At this point, he awakens.

The dream sequence symbolizes Pao-yu's passage from childhood to adolescence, a passage in which the mysteries of love and sexuality are revealed to him, and in which the difference between love and lust are made clear. The lesson seems to have been imperfectly learned, however; that same evening Pao-yu seduces a young girl, Pervading Fragrance. The memory of pleasure has completely overcome his fear of the demons and wild beasts. The author seems to suggest that man is incorrigible once he has been exposed to the delights of sex, and that any sort of human attachment is only a source of illusion.

While the *Dream of the Red Chamber* is essentially a love story, its characters transcend time and culture. Pao-yu is not simply a spoiled and self-indulgent young man, he is a sensitive human being who does his best to conduct his life in terms of what little he knows of reality and unreality. His struggle to do so is played out in the midst of a bustling clan of dozens of people, each with his or her own individual hopes, desires, and aspirations. The author manages to people his stage in such a way as to present a profound and realistic view of the life of a noble family in eighteenth-century China, and yet to maintain such sympathy and respect for the individual suffering of the young lovers that his work remains one of the great examples of the romantic tradition in world literature.

Questions

1. Why do you think that Pao-yu was able to enjoy the trust and friendship of all the young women of the family compound?

2. What are the characters' attitudes towards religion and morality?

3. Do you think that the author is criticizing Chinese society? If so, what are his particular concerns?

4. There is a recurring contrast between love and lust in the novel. What difference does the author see between these two passions?

THE DREAM OF THE RED CHAMBER

IN WHICH BLACK JADE IS LOVINGLY WELCOMED BY HER GRANDMOTHER AND
PAO-YU IS UNWITTINGLY UPSET BY HIS COUSIN

In the meantime, Black Jade was met by more servants from the Yungkuofu. She had heard a great deal of the wealth and luxury of her grandmother's family and was much impressed by the costumes of the maidservants who had been sent to escort her to the Capital, though they were ordinary servants of the second or third rank. Being a proud and sensitive child, she told herself that she must watch every step and weigh every word so as not to make any mistakes and be laughed at.

From the windows of her sedan chair, she took in the incomparable wealth and splendor of the Imperial City, which, needless to say, far surpassed that of Yangchow. Suddenly she saw on the north side of the street an imposing entrance, consisting of a great gate and a small one on either side. Two huge stone lions flanked the approach, and over the main gate there was a panel bearing the characters "ning kuo fu."[1] The center gate was closed, but one of the side doors was open, and under it there were more than a score of manservants lounging about on long benches. A little further to the west, there was another entrance of similar proportions, with the inscription "yung kuo fu"[2] over the main gate. Black Jade's sedan was carried through the side door to the west. After proceeding a distance of an arrow's flight, the bearers stopped and withdrew, as four well-dressed boys of about seventeen came up and took their places. The maidservants alighted from their carriages and followed the sedan on foot until they reached another gate, covered with overhanging flowers. Here the bearers stopped again and withdrew. The maids raised the curtain of the sedan for Black Jade to descend.

Inside the flower-covered gate two verandas led to a passage hall with a large marble screen in the center. Beyond, there was a large court dominated by the main hall with carved beams and painted pillars. From the rafters of the side chambers hung cages of parrots, thrushes, and other pet birds. The maids sitting on the moon terrace of the main hall rose at the approach of Black Jade. "Lao Tai-tai[3] was just asking about Ku-niang,"[4] they said. Then raising the door curtain, they announced, "Lin Ku-niang is here."

---

[1] Ning kuo fu means "peace to the country mansion."
[2] Yung kuo fu means "may the country mansion long endure."
[3] Honorific designation for the mother of the master of the house.
[4] Designation for unmarried young ladies.

As Black Jade entered the door, a silver-haired lady rose to meet her. Concluding that it must be her grandmother, Black Jade was about to kneel before her, but her grandmother took her in her arms and began to weep, calling her many pet names. The attendants all wept at the touching sight. When the Matriarch finally stopped crying, Black Jade kowtowed and was then introduced to her aunts, Madame Hsing and Madame Wang, and to Li Huan, the wife of the late Chia Chu. Turning to the attendants, the Matriarch said, "Ask your young mistresses to come, and tell them they need not go to school today as there is a guest from far away." Presently the three young ladies entered, escorted by their own nurses and maids. Welcome Spring was inclined to plumpness and looked affable. Quest Spring was slender, strong-willed, and independent. Compassion Spring was yet a child.

After the introductions, tea was served. Black Jade answered the endless questions asked by her grandmother and aunts. When did her mother become ill? Who were the doctors called in to attend her? What sort of medicine did they prescribe? When did the funeral take place and who was there? The Matriarch was again in tears as Black Jade told of her mother's illness and death. She said, "Of all my children, I loved your mother best. Now she has preceded me to the grave. And I did not even have a chance to take a last look at her." Again she took Black Jade in her arms and wept.

Though her delicate features were lovely, it was evident that Black Jade was not strong. The Matriarch asked her what medicine she was taking and whether a careful diagnosis had been made.

"I have been like this ever since I can remember," she answered with a wan smile. "Some of the best-known physicians examined me and prescribed all kinds of medicine and pills, but I did not get any better. I remember that when I was about three years old, a mangy old Buddhist monk came to see my parents and asked them to give me away as a sacrifice to Buddha, saying that I would always be sick unless they let him take me away. The only other remedy, he said, was to keep me from weeping and crying and that I must never be allowed to see any of my maternal relatives. No one paid any attention, of course, to such ridiculous and farfetched talk. For the present, I am taking some ginseng pills."

"We are having some pills made," the Matriarch said, "and I will order some of yours for you."

Suddenly Black Jade heard the sound of laughter in the rear courtyard and the rather loud voice of a young woman saying, "I am late in greeting the guest from the south." Who could this be, Black Jade wondered. Everyone else was quiet and demure. This loud laughter was unsuitable to the general atmosphere of dignity and reserve. As Black Jade was thinking thus to herself, a pretty young woman came in. She was tall and slender and carried herself with grace and self-assurance. She was dressed in brighter colors than the granddaughters of the Matriarch and wore an astonishing amount of jewelry; somehow it seemed to suit her well, but there was a certain hardness about her that did not escape the careful observer.

"You wouldn't know who she is, of course," the Matriarch said to Black Jade, as the latter rose to greet the new arrival, "but she has the sharpest and cleverest tongue in this family. She is what they call a 'hot pepper' in Nanking, so you can just call her that."

One of the cousins came to Black Jade's rescue and introduced "Hot Pepper" as Phoenix, the wife of Chia Lien. Phoenix took Black Jade's hands and looked at her admiringly for a long time before returning her to the Matriarch. "What a beautiful girl!" she said. "Positively the most beautiful thing I've ever seen. No wonder Lao Tai-tai is always talking about her. But how cruel of Heaven to deprive such a lovely thing of her mother." She took out a handkerchief and began to wipe her eyes.

"Are you trying to make me cry all over again?" the Matriarch said. "Moreover, your Mei-mei[5] has just come from a long journey and she is not well. We've just succeeded in quieting her. So don't you upset her again."

"Forgive me," Phoenix said, quickly assuming a smile. "I was so overwhelmed with joy and sorrow at meeting Mei-mei that I quite forgot that Lao Tai-tai mustn't grieve too much." Again she took Black Jade's hands and asked her how old she was, whether she had had a tutor, and what medicine she was taking. She enjoined her not to be homesick, to feel perfectly at home, and not hesitate to ask for anything she wanted, and to report to her if any of the maids should be negligent or disrespectful. "You must remember, Mei-mei, that you are not in a stranger's house," she concluded.

Presently Madame Hsing took Black Jade to pay her respects to Chia Sheh. At the flower-covered gate they entered a carriage, which bore them out through the western side gate, east past the main entrance, and then entered a black-lacquered gate. It appeared to Black Jade that this compound must formerly have been a part of the garden of the Yungkuofu. It was built on a less pretentious scale than the Yungkuofu proper but it had its verandas, side chambers, flower plots, artificial rocks, and everything else that goes with a well-planned mansion. A number of maids came out to meet Black Jade and Madame Hsing as they entered the inner court. After they were seated in Madame Hsing's room, a maid was sent to inform Chia Sheh of Black Jade's presence. She said when she returned, "Lao-yeh says he is not feeling well and that, since the meeting will only renew their sorrow, he will not see the guest today. He wants Lin Ku-niang to feel at home and to regard her grandmother's house as her own."

Black Jade rose and listened deferentially while the maid delivered the message from her first uncle. Madame Hsing asked her to stay for dinner, but she declined, as etiquette required her to call on her second uncle without delay.

5Younger sister.

Madame Wang excused Black Jade from her call on Chia Cheng. "He is busy today," she said. "You will see him some other time. But there is something that I must warn you about. You will have no trouble with your sisters. You will all study and embroider together, and I am sure you will be considerate of one another and have no quarrels. But I have my misgivings about that scourge of mine. He is not home now but he will be back later, and you can see for yourself. You must not pay any attention to him. None of his sisters dare to encourage him in the least."

Black Jade had often heard her mother speak of this cousin of hers, how he was born with a piece of jade in his mouth,[6] how his grandmother doted on him and would not suffer his father to discipline him. Madame Wang must be referring to him now. "I have heard Mother speak of this elder brother," the girl said. "But what is there to fear? Naturally I shall be with my sisters, and he will be with the brothers."

"But he has not been brought up like other children," Madame Wang explained. "He lives with Lao Tai-tai and is a good deal with the girls and maids. He behaves tolerably well if left alone but, if any of the girls encourages him in the least, he becomes quite impossible and may say all sorts of wild things. That's why you must not pay any attention to him or take seriously anything he says."

On their way to dinner at the Matriarch's, they passed by Phoenix's compound. Madame Wang pointed it out to Black Jade and said, "You know now where to go if you want anything." When they arrived in the Matriarch's room, the maids were ready to serve the dinner. There were two chairs on either side of the Matriarch, and Black Jade was ushered by Phoenix to one on the left side nearest to the Matriarch, Black Jade refused the honor, but her grandmother said, "Your aunts and sister-in-law do not dine here. Besides, you are a guest today. So take the seat." Black Jade murmured an apology and obeyed. Madame Wang sat near the table, while Phoenix and Li Huan stood by and waited upon the Matriarch. The three Springs took their places according to age: Welcome Spring sat on the right, nearest the Matriarch; Quest Spring, second on the left; Compassion Spring, second on the right. Out in the courtyard many maids stood by to carry dishes back and forth from the kitchen. After dinner, the Matriarch dismissed Madame Wang, Li Huan, and Phoenix so that she could talk more freely with her granddaughters.

Suddenly there was a sound of footsteps in the courtyard and a maid announced, "Pao-yu has returned." Instead of the slovenly and awkward boy she expected to see, Black Jade looked upon a youth of great beauty and charm. His face was as bright as the harvest moon, his complexion as fresh as flowers of a spring dawn, his hair as neat as if sculptured with a chisel, his eyebrows as black as if painted with ink. He was gracious even in anger and amiable even when he

---

[6]That is, he was wealthy.

frowned. He wore a purple hat studded with precious stones and a red coat embroidered with butterflies and flowers. His jade was suspended from his neck by a multicolored silk cord.

Black Jade was startled: so familiar were his features that she felt she must have seen him somewhere before. Pao-yu, on his part, was deeply impressed by her delicate and striking features. Her beautifully curved eyebrows seemed, and yet did not seem, knitted; her eyes seemed, and yet did not seem, pleased. Their sparkle suggested tears, and her soft quick breathing indicated how delicately constituted she was. In repose she was like a fragile flower mirrored in the water; in movement she was like a graceful willow swaying in the wind. Her heart had one more aperture than Pi Kan;[7] she was noticeably more fragile than Hsi Shih.

"It seems that I have seen this Mei-mei before," Pao-yu said, with open admiration.

"Nonsense," the Matriarch said. "How could you have seen her?"

"I may not really have seen her," Pao-yu admitted. "Nevertheless, I feel as if I were meeting a friend whom I have not heard from for years."

"I'm glad to hear that," the Matriarch said, "for that ought to mean that you will be good friends."

Pao-yu sat by his cousin and asked her all sorts of questions about the south. "Have you any jade?" he asked finally.

"No, I do not have any," Black Jade answered. "It is rare, and not everybody has it as you do."

Pao-yu suddenly flared up with passion. "Rare indeed!" he cried. "I think it is a most stupid thing. I shall have none of it." He took the jade from his neck and dashed it to the floor. The maids rushed forward to pick it up and as the Matriarch took Pao-yu in her arms and scolded him for venting his anger on the precious object upon which his very life depended. Pao-yu said, weeping, "None of my sisters has anything like it. I am the only one who has it. Now this Mei-mei, who is as beautiful as a fairy, doesn't have any either. What do I want this stupid thing for?"

"Your Mei-mei did have a piece of jade," the Matriarch fabricated. "But your aunt was so reluctant to part with your Mei-mei that she took the jade from her as a memento. Your Mei-mei said she had none only because she did not want to appear boastful. As a matter of fact, her jade was even better than yours. Now put it back on before your mother hears of this." Pao-yu appeared to be satisfied with the explanation and made no protest when the Matriarch replaced the jade on his neck.

Black Jade was assigned rooms adjoining Pao-yu's in the Matriarch's apartment. As she had brought with her only her nurse and a very young maid named

[7]This is another way of saying that Black Jade is supersensitive.

Snow Duck, the Matriarch gave her Purple Cuckoo, one of her own favorite maids. Besides these, Black Jade was given four matrons and four or five maids-of-all-work, the same as the other granddaughters of the Matriarch.

Pao-yu's nurse was called Li Ma; his handmaid was Pervading Fragrance, who had also been a favorite maid of the Matriarch's. She was a good and conscientious girl and faithful to any person to whom she was assigned. Thus when she was in the Matriarch's service, she took thought for no one else. Now that she was Pao-yu's handmaid, she was entirely devoted to him. Originally she was called Pearl, but Pao-yu, because her family name was Hua (flower), gave her a new name, derived from the line, "By the pervading fragrance of the flowers, one knows that the day is warm." She was given to chiding him for his perverse behavior and was often distressed because he would not listen to her advise.

That evening after Pao-yu and Li Ma had gone to bed, Pervading Fragrance, noticing that Black Jade and Purple Cuckoo were still up, quietly went over for a visit. "Please sit down, Chieh-chieh,"[8] Black Jade said to her, and Pervading Fragrance sat down on the edge of the bed.

"Lin Ku-niang was crying just a while ago because she had unwittingly caused Pao-yu to fly into one of his mad tantrums," Purple Cuckoo said.

"Ku-niang mustn't mind him," Pervading Fragrance said to Black Jade. "You have not seen anything yet of his unpredictable ways. If you let yourself be upset by a little thing like what happened today, you will never get a moment's peace."

The next morning, after presenting herself before the Matriarch, Black Jade went to call on Madame Wang and found her talking with Phoenix and two maidservants from the house of Madame Wang's brother. Not wishing to disturb them, Black Jade joined the three Springs, who were also there for the morning presentation. From Quest Spring she learned that they were discussing what to do to help Hsueh Pan, the son of Madame Wang's sister, against whom a charge of homicide was pending in the yamen[9] of the prefect of Yingtienfu.

It should be remembered that Chia Yu-tsun had been recently appointed prefect of Yingtienfu through the good offices of Chia Cheng. Needless to say, he spared no pains in order to exonerate Hsueh Pan. It should be pointed out also that the case involved Lotus, the lost daughter of Chen Shih-yin, who was sold by her kidnapper first to a certain Feng Yuan and then to Hsueh Pan. It was in a fight over the possession of the ill-fated girl that Feng Yuan was so severely beaten by Hsueh Pan's servants that he died shortly afterward.

---

[8]Elder sister. Note the courtesy with which some of the more favored bondmaids are treated. The fact that Pervading Fragrance had been the Matriarch's maid adds to her status.
[9]Headquarters of a public official or department.

Now Hsueh Pan was an only son. His father had died when he was still a child, and as a consequence he was very much spoiled by his mother. He was all but illiterate, though he came from a family about which "there lingers the fragrance of books." He was arrogant and quick-tempered by nature and extravagant and dissolute in his ways. Though ostensibly a merchant and purchasing agent for the Imperial Household, he knew nothing of business and depended entirely upon his managers and trusted servants. His mother was the sister of General Wang Tzu-teng, commander of the metropolitan garrison, and of Madame Wang, the wife of Chia Cheng. She was therefore closely related to the Yungkuofu and was known among the Chias as Hsueh Yi-ma.[10] She was about forty years old and had, besides Hsueh Pan, a daughter named Precious Virtue, who was a few years younger than Hsueh Pan. She was both beautiful and well mannered. Her father had loved her dearly. He gave her a chance to study under a private tutor, and as a scholar she turned out to be ten times better than her brother. But after her father's death, she gave little thought to books; she realized how irresponsible her brother was and decided that she must share her mother's burdens and cares.

There were three reasons why the Hsuehs were going to the Capital. First, Hsueh Yi-ma wanted to present her daughter as a candidate for the honor of lady in waiting in the Imperial Household. Secondly, it was many years since she had seen her sister and brother. Then, Hsueh Pan wanted, ostensibly, to audit the accounts of the various family-owned stores and shops there, though his real reason was the distractions offered by the metropolis.

Shortly before the Hsuehs reached the Capital, they heard that General Wang has been appointed military inspector of nine provinces and was about to leave for his post. The news pleased Hsueh Pan, for if his mother had been able to stay with her brother as planned, he would not have been as free to do as he chose. So he suggested to his mother that they open up one of their houses in the Capital. His mother guessed his reason. "We can go to your aunt's house," she said. "I am sure she will feel offended if we do not. Besides, I have not seen her for many years and would like to be with her. If you are afraid you will not be as free as you would like, you can live by yourself, but I and your sister will stay with your aunt."

As Hsueh Yi-ma had expected, Madame Wang urged them to stay in the Yungkuofu. They were installed in Pear Fragrance Court, at the northwestern corner of the mansion. It had its own entrance from the street and was connected to Madame Wang's compound by a passageway, so that Hsueh Yi-ma and her daughter were able to visit the inner apartments of the Yungkuofu without having to go outside the gate. This they did almost every day, sometimes after lunch, sometimes in the evening. The mother would visit with the Matriarch

[10]Maternal aunt.

and her own sister, while Precious Virtue visited with the three Springs or Black Jade. Nor did Hsueh Pan have any reason for regret; he soon found among the young men of the Chia clan many boon companions with whom he could carouse, gamble, or visit the courtesans' quarters. In fact, he found that he had a great deal to learn from his new friends. For though Chia Cheng was a strict disciplinarian, he could not possibly know everything that went on in his clan. Moreover, Chia Gen, the nominal head of the clan, was far from being above reproach himself. Thus, Hsueh Pan found himself quite free to follow his own devices and gave up all thought of refurbishing one of his own houses.

IN WHICH THE DIVINE STONE PAGE DOES NOT RECOGNIZE HIS FORMER HAUNT AND THE GODDESS OF DISILLUSIONMENT FAILS TO AWAKEN HER ERSTWHILE ATTENDANT

Ever since Black Jade had arrived in the Yungkuofu, the Matriarch had lavished on her the love and tender solicitude hitherto reserved for Pao-yu. The young girl occupied an even warmer place in the Matriarch's heart than the three Springs, her real granddaughters.[11] She and Pao-yu had also been drawn close together, not only because they shared the same apartment, but also because of a natural affinity which manifested itself at their first meeting. Now there suddenly appeared on the scene Precious Virtue. Though only a trifle older than Black Jade, she showed a tact and understanding far beyond her years. She was completely unspoiled, always ready to please and enter into the spirit of the occasion and always kind to the servants and bondmaids. In contrast, Black Jade was inclined to haughtiness and held herself aloof. Thus in a short time, Precious Virtue won the hearts of all, and Black Jade could not help feeling a little jealous. Precious Virtue seemed wholly unaware of the situation her presence created.

As for Pao-yu, he was so simple in nature and so completely guileless that his behavior often struck people as odd, if not mad. He treated everyone alike and never stopped to consider the nearness of kinship of one as compared with that of another. Often he would unwittingly offend Black Jade, sometimes in his very efforts to please her. On such occasions, it was always Pao-yu who made the conciliatory gesture.

One day when the plums in the garden of the Ningkuofu were in full bloom, Yu-shih, the wife of Chia Gen, took the occasion to invite the Matriarch, Madame Wang, Madame Hsing, and other members of the Yungkuofu to a plum-flower feast. Nothing of particular note occurred; it was simply one of those many seasonal family gatherings. After dinner, Pao-yu said he felt tired and wished to take a nap.

---

[11] A daughter's child, having a different surname, is an "outside" or pseudo grandchild.

"We have a room ready for Uncle Pao," Chin-shih said to the Matriarch. "I'll take him there and see that he has a nice rest."

Now Chin-shih was Chia Jung's wife and the Matriarch's favorite great-granddaughter-in-law. She was a very beautiful young woman, possessed of a slender figure and a most gentle and amiable disposition. The Matriarch felt safe to leave Pao-yu in her hands.

The room to which Chin-shih took Pao-yu was one of the main apartments in the Ningkuofu and was luxuriously furnished, but Pao-yu took objection to the center scroll on the wall, a painting depicting the famous Han scholar Liu Hsing receiving divine enlightenment. He took an even more violent objection to the scrolls on either side of the painting on which was inscribed the couplet:

> To know through and through the ways of the world is Real
>   Knowledge;
> To conform in every detail to the customs of society is True
>   Accomplishment.

"I cannot possibly sleep in this room," he declared.

"If you do not like this room, I am afraid nothing will suit you," Chin-shih said and then added, "unless perhaps you want to use mine."

Pao-yu smiled assent, but his nurse Li Ma objected, saying, "It is hardly proper for an uncle to sleep in the bedroom of his nephew's wife."

"Don't be ridiculous," Chin-shih said, laughing. "Uncle Pao is just a boy, if he doesn't mind my saying so. Didn't you see my younger brother when he came to visit last month? He is just Uncle Pao's age but he is the taller of the two."

"Where is your brother?" Pao-yu asked, for he wanted to see what the brother of the beautiful Chin-shih was like. "Bring him and let me meet him."

"He is home, many miles from here," she answered. "You will meet him some other time."

Pao-yu detected a subtle and yet intoxicating fragrance as he entered Chin-shih's room. On the wall there was a painting by T'ang Yin, entitled "Lady Taking Nap under Begonia" and a couplet by a Sung poet:

> A gentle chill pervades her dreams because it is spring;
> The fragrance intoxicates one like that of wine.

In the center of the table was a mirror once used by Empress Wu Tse T'ien. At one side there was a golden plate on which the nimble Chao Fei-yen had danced, and on the plate there was a quince that An Lu-shan had playfully thrown at the beautiful Yang Kuei-fei. The carved bed once held the Princess Shou Yang, and the pearl curtains were made for the Princess T'ung Chang.[12]

---

[12] All famous lovers in Chinese history and legend.

"I like your room!" Pao-yu exclaimed with delight.

"It is fit for the immortals, if I may say so," Chin-shih said with a smile. She spread out the silk coverlet that was once washed by Hsi Shih and put in place the embroidered cushion that was once embraced by the Red Maid. Pao-yu's nurse withdrew after helping him to bed. Only his four handmaids—Pervading Fragrance, Bright Design, Autumn Sky, and Musk Moon—remained, and they were encouraged by Chin-shih to go outside and watch the kittens play under the eaves.

Pao-yu fell asleep almost as soon as he closed his eyes. In a dream he seemed to follow Chin-shih to some wondrous place where the halls and chambers were of jade and gold and the gardens were filled with exotic blooms. Pao-yu was filled with delight. He thought to himself that he would gladly spend the rest of his life here. Suddenly he heard someone singing on the far side of the hill.

> Spring dreams vanish like ever-changing clouds,
> Fallen flowers drift downstream never to return.
> And so lovers everywhere, heed my words,
> 'Tis folly to court sorrow and regret.

The song still lingered in Pao-yu's ears when there appeared before him a fairy goddess whose beauty and grace were unlike anything in the mortal world. Pao-yu greeted her and said, "Sister Immortal, where have you come from and where are you going? I have lost my way. Please help me."

She replied, "I am the Goddess of Disillusionment. I inhabit the Realm of Parting Sorrow in the Ocean of Regrets. I am in charge of the plaints of unhappy maidens and sad lovers, their debts of love, and their unfulfilled desires. It is not by accident that I have encountered you. My home is not far from here. I have not much to offer you, but I have some tender tea leaves, which I gathered myself, and a few jars of my own wine. I have several singers trained in exotic dances and have just completed a series of twelve songs which I call 'Dream of the Red Chamber.' Why don't you come with me?"

Chin-shih having now disappeared, Pao-yu followed the Goddess and reached a place dominated by a huge stone arch, across which was written the inscription: "Great Void Illusion Land." On either side this couplet was inscribed:

> When the unreal is taken for the real, then the real
> becomes unreal;
> Where non-existence is taken for existence, then existence
> becomes non-existence.

Passing through the arch, Pao-yu found himself standing in front of the gate of a palace, above which was the inscription: "Sea of Passion and Heaven of Love." The couplet read:

> Enduring as heaven and earth—no love however ancient
>   can ever die;
> Timeless as light and shadow—no debt of breeze and
>   moonlight can ever be repaid.

Pao-yu was still too young to understand the meaning of the couplet. He had a vague notion about love but no idea at all of what breeze and moonlight might be. He was naturally curious and said to himself that he must be sure to find out before he left the place. By this innocent thought, Pao-yu became inexplicably involved with the demons of passion.

Entering the second gate, Pao-yu saw long rows of chapels with inscriptions such as "Division of Perverse Sentiments," "Division of Rival Jealousies," "Division of Morning Weeping," "Division of Evening Lament," "Division of Spring Affections," and "Division of Autumn Sorrows."

"Would it be possible for you to take me through these chapels?" Pao-yu asked.

"No," the Goddess answered. "They contain the past, present, and future of the maidens of the entire world. Mortal eyes may not look upon them." As they walked on, Pao-yu continued to importune the Goddess until she finally yielded, saying, "You may see this one." Pao-yu looked up and saw that the chapel was inscribed "Division of the Ill-Fated." There was also this couplet:

> Sorrows of spring and sadness of autumn are all one's own
>   doing;
> A face like a flower and features like the moon are all in
>   vain in the end.

Inside, Pao-yu saw more than ten large cabinets all sealed and labeled with the names of the different provinces. Wishing to find out about his own, he went to the cabinet marked "The Twelve Maidens of the Chinling, File No. 1."

"I have heard that Chinling is a large city. Why is it that there are only twelve maidens? Just in our own family there are several hundred of them."

"We keep records of only the more important ones," the Goddess smiled indulgently.

Pao-yu looked at the next two cabinets and noted that they were marked "The Twelve Maidens of Chinling, File No. 2" and "The Twelve Maidens of Chinling, File No. 3," respectively. He opened the last cabinet and took out a large album. The first page was completely obscured by heavy mist and dark clouds. There was no foreground whatever. Inscribed on the page were the following lines:

> Clear days are rarely encountered,
> Bright clouds easily scattered.
> Her heart was proud as the sky,

> But her position was lowly on earth.
> Her beauty and accomplishments only invited jealousy,
> Her death was hastened by baseless slander
> And in vain her faithful Prince mourns. [13]

Pao-yu could make nothing of all this. On the next page there was a painting of a bunch of flowers and a broken mat, together with a poem.

> Gentle and gracious well she may be,
> Like cassia and orchid indeed she is.
> But what are these things to the young Prince
> When it is the mummer that destiny has favored? [14]

This meant even less to Pao-yu. He replaced the album and took the one in Cabinet 2. The first page was also a picture—this time a sprig of cassia at the top and below it a withered lotus flower on a dried-up pond. The accompanying poem read:

> O symbol of purity and innocence,
> Your cruel fate is least deserved.
> For in two fields one tree will grow
> And send your gentle soul to its ancient home.

Again Pao-yu failed to see the significance of the picture or poem. He tried the album in Cabinet 1 and found the pictures and poems equally baffling. He was about to try again when the Goddess, fearing that he might succeed in penetrating the secrets of Heaven if allowed to go on, took the album from him and put it back in the cabinet, saying, "Come and see the rest of the place. What is the use of puzzling over these?"

Pao-yu was led into the inner palace, which was even more splendid than what he had already seen. Several fairies came out at the call of the Goddess, but they seemed to be disappointed when they saw Pao-yu. One of them said rudely, "We thought you were going to bring Sister Crimson. Why this common creature from the mortal world?"

While Pao-yu stood in awkward silence, the Goddess explained to her fairies that she had brought him in order to enlighten him and she begged them to help her in the task. The tea, the wine, and the food were all delicious beyond anything Pao-yu had ever tasted. After the feast, the Goddess bade her fairies sing "Dream of the Red Chamber." She gave Pao-yu the manuscript so that he might follow it while it was sung. "For you may not understand this, as

---

[13] Picture and poem forecast the fate of Bright Design, one of Pao-yu's handmaids, who languished and died in disgrace.

[14] The picture represents Pervading Fragrance, whose family name means "flower." She eventually married an actor friend of Pao-yu.

you are accustomed only to mortal music," she explained. The singing was exquisite, but Pao-yu could not understand the references and allusions in the lyrics. The Goddess sighed compassionately when she saw that Pao-yu remained unenlightened.

After a while, Pao-yu began to feel sleepy and begged to be excused. The Goddess then took him to a chamber where to his astonishment he found a girl who reminded him of Precious Virtue in graciousness of manner and of Black Jade in beauty of features. He was wondering what was going to happen next when he heard the voice of the Goddess speaking to him. "In the Red Dust,"[15] she said, "the embroidered chambers are often desecrated by licentious men and loose women. What is even more deplorable are the attempts to distinguish between love of beauty and licentiousness, forgetting that one always leads to the other. The meetings at Witches' Hill and the transports of cloud and rain invariably climax what is supposedly a pure and chaste love of beauty. I am now, of course, speaking of the generality of men and women. There are rare exceptions, of which you are one. Indeed, I admire you because you are the most licentious of men."

"How could you make such an accusation!" Pao-yu protested. "I have been taken to task for not applying myself to my studies and have been severely reprimanded for it by my parents, but no one has accused me of licentiousness. Besides, I am still young. I hardly know the meaning of the word."

"Do not be alarmed," the Goddess said. "Licentiousness simply means excess, and there are all kinds of excesses. The most common kind is an insatiable greed of the flesh. We are all familiar with those coarse creatures who cannot think of beautiful women except as means for gratifying their animal desires. They are a constant danger and threat to womankind. Your licentiousness, however, is of a more subtle kind, one that can only be apprehended but not described. Nevertheless, it is just as excessive and insatiable as the kind the world is familiar with, but whereas the latter constitutes a constant danger to womankind, your licentiousness makes you a most welcome companion in the maidens' chambers. But what makes you desirable in the maidens' chambers also makes you appear strange and unnatural in the eyes of the world. It is necessary for you to experience what most men experience, so that you may know its nature and limitations. I have, therefore, arranged that you should marry my sister Chien-mei.[16] This is the night for you to consummate your union. After you have seen for yourself that the pleasures of fairyland are but thus and so, you may perhaps realize their vanity and turn your mind to the teachings of Confucius and Mencius and devote your efforts to the welfare of mankind."

[15]The world of mortals.
[16]Meaning "combining the best features of both," that is, of Precious Virtue and Black Jade.

She whispered in Pao-yu's ears the secrets of cloud and rain and pushed him toward her sister Chien-mei. Then she left them, closing the door after her. Pao-yu followed the instructions of the Goddess and disported himself with his bride in ways that may well be imagined but may not be detailed here. The next day Pao-yu went for a walk with his bride. Suddenly he found himself in a field overgrown with thorn and bramble and overrun with tigers and wolves. In front of him an expanse of water blocked the way of escape. As he tried desperately to think of what to do, the Goddess' voice spoke to him from behind, "Stop and turn back before it is too late!" As she spoke, a deafening roar issued from the water, and a horde of monsters rushed toward Pao-yu. Frantically he cried out, "Help me, Chien-mei! Help! Help!"

Thereupon he awoke, bathed in a cold sweat, as Pervading Fragrance and the other maids rushed to his bedside, saying, "Don't be afraid Pao-yu. We are all here with you."

Chin-shih, who had heard Pao-yu calling Chien-mei, wondered, "How did he happen to know my child's name?"

As Pervading Fragrance helped Pao-yu to adjust his clothes, her hand came in contact with something cold and clammy. Quickly withdrawing her hand, she asked Pao-yu what it was. Pao-yu did not answer but only blushed and gave her hand a gentle squeeze. Being a clever maid and a year or two older than Pao-yu, she too blushed and said no more. Later that evening, when she was alone with him in the apartment, she brought Pao-yu a change of clothing.

"Please don't tell anyone," Pao-yu said embarrassedly. Then he confided to her his dream. When he came to what happened in the bridal chamber, the maid blushed and laughed and covered her face with her hands. Now Pao-yu had always been very fond of the maid, so he proposed to demonstrate what the Goddess had taught him. At first Pervading Fragrance refused but in the end she acquiesced, since she knew that she would eventually be Pao-yu's concubine. Thenceforward, Pao-yu treated her with more tenderness than ever, and the maid on her part ministered to the comforts of her young master even more faithfully than before.

FURTHER READINGS

Maurice Freeman, *Family and Kinship in Chinese Society* (Stanford, CA: Stanford University Press, 1970), presents an interesting look at Chinese family life. Chung-li Chang, *The Chinese Gentry: Studies on Their Role in Nineteenth-Century Chinese Society* (Seattle: University of Washington Press, 1967), provides insight into China's gentry-official system. A fascinating portrayal of life in rural Ch'ing China is afforded by Jonathan Spence, *Death of Woman Wang* (New York: Penguin, 1979).

Klaus-Peter Koepping and Lam Lai Sing, *New Interpretation of the Dream of the Red Chamber* (Singapore: Public Press, 1973), examine the historical background of the novel, its major themes, and the importance of its analysis of social problems. Jean Knoerle, *The Dream of the Red Chamber* (Bloomington: Indiana University Press, 1972), concentrates on elements of structure and technique. An excellent discussion of the many textual problems surrounding the novel's authorship is found in Wu Shih-ch'ang, *On the Red Chamber Dream* (Oxford: Clarendon, 1961). Robert E. Hegel, *The Novel in Seventeenth-Century China* (New York: Columbia University Press, 1981) stresses the importance of seventeenth-century novels in shaping later Ch'ing fiction, including *The Dream of the Red Chamber*. C. T. Hsia, *The Classic Chinese Novel* (New York: Columbia University Press, 1968), contains a helpful study of *The Dream of the Red Chamber*.

THE TREASURY OF LOYAL RETAINERS

Takeda Izumo, Namiki Senryu,
and Miyoshi Shoraku

Written in 1748, *The Treasury of Loyal Retainers* (*Chushingura*) is perhaps the most famous and highly praised drama of popular Japanese theater. Originally written as a puppet play and later adapted for the *kabuki* theater, it quickly became the most popular drama in the entire Japanese theatrical repertoire. It has continued to captivate Japanese audiences to the present day, and its story has become part of the traditional heritage of the Japanese people. Although in many ways peculiarly Japanese, the play's popularity extends to foreign audiences, and it was probably the first work of Japanese literature to be translated into English. Its popularity stems both from its remarkable representation of Japanese life, portrayed in its elaborate and detailed character development, and from the intriguing historical events from which the story was drawn.

The play is a dramatization of an actual event known as the Ako vendetta that occurred in the early eighteenth century. Lord Asano of Ako, enraged by the conduct of a high official of the shogun (military dictator of Japan), struck the official with his sword. Because of this grave offense, Asano was ordered by the shogun to commit suicide by *seppuku* (ritual disembowelment). Asano's estates were confiscated after his death, resulting in the extinction of his noble

From Takeda Izumo, Namiki Senryu, and Miyoshi Shoraku, *Chushingura: A Puppet Play*, trans. Donald Keene (New York: Columbia University Press, 1971), pp. 104–24.

house. His armed retainers became *ronin*, or masterless samurai. Their position was extremely difficult. Their honor required that they avenge their lord's death, but he had died by the shogun's order, and vengeance in such a case was illegal. In addition, the official who had brought about Asano's downfall was both powerful and suspicious, and had them closely watched for any sign that they might be planning revenge. Nevertheless, this leaderless band, some forty-seven in number, pledged themselves to avenge their master upon the official who had been responsible for his fall. First, however, they had to lull his suspicions by convincing him that they had lost their honor, forgotten their duty, and presented no danger to him. After two years of hardship and suffering, playing the drunk and the fool, the ronin accomplished their aim and were ready to strike. On January 30, 1703, they burst into the Tokyo residence of Lord Kira Yoshinaka and killed him. They promptly carried his severed head to the temple where Lord Asano was buried and placed it on his grave. The vendetta was completed and their honor restored.

News of these events spread rapidly. The boldness of the deed and the selfless resolution of the ronin captured the imagination of people of all classes, and the forty-seven ronin were immediately acclaimed as heroes. Their action expressed the highest standards of samurai courage and loyalty, but it was also illegal. The authorities considered the case for some time, but eventually handed down the death sentence for the entire group. Partly due to public opinion, they were allowed to die honorably, by following their lord in committing seppuku. They died together on March 20, 1703, and they were interred alongside Lord Asano. Their graves continue to be a popular pilgrimage site.

Over a hundred plays have been written on the theme, but the most popular was that written by Takeda Izumo in collaboration with Namiki Senryu and Miyoshi Shoraku. It was first produced at the Takemoto Doll Theater in Osaka in 1748. The play is lengthy, consisting of eleven acts. Single acts are popular fixtures on kabuki programs, and the seventh act, "Yuranosuke at His Revels," from which this selection is taken, is a particular favorite. The act opens with Yuranosuke, the chief retainer and hero of the play, debauching himself at the stylish Ichiriki teahouse in Kyoto, apparently forgetful of both honor and revenge. Two samurai arrive with the intention of discussing revenge with him. Yuranosuke puts them off, and Heiemon, a low-ranking samurai, describes his efforts to join the vendetta. Again, Yuranosuke refuses to discuss the matter, and the samurai leave, dismayed and disgusted. Rikiya, Yuranosuke's son, then arrives and awakes his father, who is apparently in a drunken stupor. Yuranosuke is immediately awake and completely sober. He receives a letter containing information as to when the attack on Lord Kiri should be made and then sends his son away.

The villainous Kudayu appears, and Yuranosuke resumes his feigned drunkenness. After testing to see if Yuranosuke has truly forgotten revenge,

Kudayu leaves apparently satisfied, and Yuranosuke reads the letter. He discovers that Okaru, Heiemon's sister, who has sold herself into servitude to save the family, has been looking over his shoulder. He continues to feign drunkenness, promises Okaru to buy her freedom, and then leaves. Heiemon arrives, and Okaru tells him what has happened. He realizes that Yuranosuke believes that Okaru has read his letter and knows the secret of the plot, and intends to buy her freedom only to be able to silence her permanently. She decides to commit suicide, but Yuranosuke returns in time to prevent her. After hearing their story, Yuranosuke praises both brother and sister and allows Heiemon to join in the plot. The act ends with Yuranosuke discovering Kudayu hiding outside, stabbing him, and instructing Heiemon to eliminate Kudayu in a discreet fashion.

Yuranosuke is perhaps the greatest role in all of Japanese theater. Although his presence is felt throughout the play, it is only in this seventh act that he emerges as the chief character. His actions clearly illustrate the personal hardships and humiliation he and his comrades are suffering in order to further their cause, and his conduct discloses the fierce sense of honor that sustains them. For a Japanese audience, *The Treasury of Loyal Retainers* is an exaltation of the samurai code, but the play transcends this cultural limitation. It is a profound study of the meaning of honor and responsibility.

Questions

1. *The Treasury of Loyal Retainers* fascinated both nobles and commoners in Japan. Why do you think it appealed to two such different classes?

2. Would you consider this play a glorification of warlike attitudes?

3. What are some of the comic elements in "Yuranosuke at His Revels?" What function do they play?

THE TREASURY OF LOYAL RETAINERS

YURANOSUKE AT HIS REVELS

NARRATOR   If you would dally among flowers you will find in Gion a full range of colors. East, south, north, and west, with a glitter as bright as if Amida's Pure Land has been gilded anew, Gion sparkles with courtesans and geishas, so lovely as to steal away the senses of even the most jaded man, and leave him a raving fool.

KUDAYU   Is anybody here? Where's the master? Master!

MASTER   Rush, rush, rush! Who's there? Whom have I the pleasure of serving? Why, it's Master Ono Kudayu! How formal of you to ask to be shown in!

KUDAYU   I've brought a gentleman with me who's here for the first time. You seem awfully busy, but have you a room you can show this gentleman?

MASTER   Indeed I have, sir. Tonight that big spender Yuranosuke had the bright idea of gathering together all the best-known women of the Quarter. The downstairs rooms are full, but the detached wing is free.

KUDAYU   Full of cobwebs, no doubt.

MASTER   More of your usual sarcasm, sir?

KUDAYU   No, I'm just being careful not to get entangled at my age in a whore's cobweb.

MASTER   I'd never have guessed it. I can't accommodate you downstairs, then. I'll prepare an upstairs room.—Servants! Light the lamps and bring sake and tobacco.

NARRATOR   He calls out in a loud voice. Drums and samisens[1] resound from the back rooms.

KUDAYU   What do you think, Bannai? Do you hear how Yuranosuke is carrying on?

BANNAI   He seems completely out of his head. Of course, we've had a series of private reports from you, Kudayu, but not even my master Moronao suspected how far gone Yuranosuke was. Moronao told me to come up to the capital and look over the situation. He said I should report anything suspicious. I'd never have believed it if I hadn't seen it with my own eyes. It's worse than I imagined. And what has become of his son, Rikiya?

KUDAYU   He comes here once in a while and the two of them have a wild time together. It's incredible that they don't feel any embarrassment in each other's presence. But tonight I've come with a plan for worming out the innermost secrets of Yuranosuke's heart. I'll tell you about it when we're alone. Let's go upstairs.

BANNAI   After you.

KUDAYU   Well, then, I'll lead the way.

NARRATOR (*sings*)
> *Though in truth your heart*
> *Has no thought for me,*
> *Your lips pretend you are in love,*
> *With great bewitchery—*

[1] Banjo-like three-stringed instruments.

JUTARO Yagoro and Kitahachi—this is the teahouse where Yuranosuke amuses himself. It's called Ichiriki. Oh, Heiemon, we'll call you when the time comes. Go wait in the kitchen.

HEIEMON At your service, sir. Please do what you can for me.

JUTARO Is anyone there? I want to talk to somebody.

MAID Yes, sir. Who is it, please?

JUTARO We've come on business with Yuranosuke. Go in and tell him that Yazama Jutaro, Senzaki Yagoro, and Takemori Kitahachi are here. Several times we've sent a man to fetch him, but he never seems to leave this place. So the three of us have come to him. There's something we must discuss with him. We ask that he meet us. Be sure and tell him that.

MAID I'm sorry to tell you sir, but Yuranosuke has been drinking steadily for the past three days. You won't get much sense out of him, even if you see him. He's not himself.

JUTARO That may be, but please tell him what I said.

MAID Yes, sir.

JUTARO Yaguro, did you hear her?

YAGORO I did, and I'm amazed. At first I thought it was some trick of his to throw the enemy off the track. But he has abandoned himself to his pleasures more than convincingly. I simply don't understand it.

KITAHACHI It's just as I said. He's not the same man in spirit. Our best plan would be to break in on him—

JUTARO No, first we'll have a heart-to-heart talk.

YAGORO Very well, we'll wait for him here.

PROSTITUTE (*sings*) Come where my hands clap, hands clap, hands clap. (*Yuranosuke enters. He is blindfolded.*)

YURANOSUKE I'll catch you! I'll catch you!

PROSTITUTE Come on, Yura the blind man! We're waiting!

YURANOSUKE I'll catch you and make you drink.—Here!—Now I've got you! We'll have some sake! Bring on the sake! (*He grabs Jutaro, taking him for his partner in blind-man's bluff.*)

JUTARO Come to yourself, Yuranosuke. I'm Yazama Jutaro. What in the world are you doing?

YURANOSUKE Good heavens! What an awful mistake!

PROSTITUTE   Oh, the kill-joys! Look at them, Sakae. Have you ever seen such sour-looking samurai? Are they all in the same party, do you think?

SAKAE   It certainly looks that way. They all have the same fierce look.

JUTARO   Girls, we've come on business with Mr. Oboshi. We'd appreciate it if you left the room for a while.

PROSTITUTES   We guessed as much. Yura, we'll be going to the back room. Come join us soon. This way, everybody.

JUTARO   Yuranosuke, you remember me. I'm Yazama Jutaro.

KITAHACHI   I'm Takemori Kitahachi.

YATARO   And I am Senzaki Yataro. We've come here hoping to have a talk with you. I trust you're awake now?

YURANOSUKE   Thank you all for having come to see me. What have you in mind?

JUTARO   When do we leave for Kamakura?

YURANOSUKE   That's a very important question you've asked me. There's a song in *Yosaku from Tamba*[2] that goes, "When you leave for Edo, oh so far away. . . ." Ha, ha. Forgive me, gentlemen, I'm drunk.

THREE MEN   A man's character stays the same even when he's drunk, they say. If you're not in your right mind, the three of us will sober you up.

HEIEMON   Don't do anything rash, please. I hope you'll forgive me, gentlemen, but I'd like a word with him. Please hold off for a while before you start anything. Master Yuranosuke—I am Teraoka Heiemon. I am very glad to see you're in such good spirits.

YURANOSUKE   Teraoka Heiemon? Who might *you* be? Are you that fleet-footed foot soldier who was sent as a courier to the north?

HEIEMON   The same, sir. It was while I was in the north that I learned our master had committed *seppuku*, and I was dumfounded. I started off for home, running so fast I all but flew through the air. On the way I was told that his lordship's mansion had been confiscated and his retainers dispersed. You can imagine what a shock that was. I served his lordship only as a foot soldier, but I am as much indebted to him as anyone. I went to Kamakura, intending to kill Moronao, our master's enemy. For three months I watched for my chance, disguising myself as a beggar, but our enemy is guarded so strongly I couldn't even get close to him. I felt I had no choice but to disembowel

---

[2] A famous play.

myself, but I thought then of my parents in the country, and I went back home, despondent though I was. But then—surely it was a heaven-sent revelation—I learned about the league you gentlemen have formed. How happy and thankful that made me! I didn't even bother to take my things with me, but went to call on these gentlemen at their lodgings. I begged with all my heart for them to intercede in my behalf. They praised me and called me a brave fellow, and promised to plead for me with the chief. So I've come along with them here, encouraged by their assurances. Moronao's mansion—

YURANOSUKE   What's all this? You're not so much light of foot as exceedingly light of tongue. It's quite true that I felt a certain amount of indignation— about as big as a flea's head split by a hatchet—and tried forming a league of forty or fifty men, but what a crazy notion that was! I realized when I thought about it calmly that if we failed in our mission our heads would roll, and if we succeeded we'd have to commit *seppuku* afterwards. Either way, it was certain death. It was like taking expensive medicine, then hanging yourself afterwards because you couldn't pay for the cure. You're a foot soldier with a stipend of three *ryo*[3] and an allowance of three men's rations. Now don't get angry—for you to throw away your life attacking the enemy, in return for a pittance suitable for a beggar priest, would be like putting on a performance of grand *kagura* to express your gratitude for some green *nori*.[4] My stipend was 1,500 *koku*.[5] Compared to you, I might take enemy heads by the bushel and still not do my share. And that's why I gave up the idea. Do you follow me? At any rate, this uncertain world (*sings*) is just that sort of place. *Tsuten Tsutsuten Tsutsuten*.[6] Oh, when I hear the samisens playing like that I can't resist.

HEIEMON   I can't believe that is you speaking, Yuranosuke. Each man has only one life in this world, whether he's a wretch like myself with a bare income of three rations, or a rich man like you with 1,500 *koku*, and there is no high or low in the debt of gratitude we owe our master. But there's no disputing family lineage. I know it's presumptuous and rude for a miserable creature like myself to beg to join distinguished gentlemen who could have stood as deputies for our master. It's like a monkey imitating a man. But I want to go with you, even if it is only to carry your shoes or shoulder your baggage. Please take me with you. Sir, please listen to me, sir—Oh, he seems to have fallen asleep.

KITAHACHI   Come, Heiemon. There's no point in wasting any more breath on him. Yuranosuke is as good as dead. Well, Yazama and Sensaki, have you seen his true character? Shall we act as we agreed?

---

[3] A coin; three *ryo* was a small sum compared to that received by a lord's more prominent followers.
[4] That is, to offer an elaborate ritual of thanks (*kagura*) for only a simple gift of edible seaweed (*nori*).
[5] Samurai were accorded stipends of rice, measured in *koku* (about five bushels).
[6] Sounds intended to suggest the music of the samisen.

YAGORO By all means, as a warning to the others in our league. Are you ready?

NARRATOR They close in on Yuranosuke, but a cry from Heiemon stops them. With calming gestures he comes up beside them.

HEIEMON It seems to me, as I turn things over in my mind, Yuranosuke has undergone many hardships in his efforts to avenge our master, ever since they were parted by death. He has had to worry, like a hunted man, over every noise and footfall, and stifle his resentment at people's abuse. He couldn't have survived this long if he hadn't taken so heavily to drink. Wait till he's sober before you deal with him.

NARRATOR Forcibly restraining them, he leads them into the next room. Their shadows on the other side of the sliding door, cast by a light that illuminates the distinction between good and evil, are blotted out as the moon sinks behind the mountains.

Rikiya, Yuranosuke's son, having run the whole *ri*[7] and a half from Yamashina, arrives breathless. He peeps inside and sees his father lying asleep. Afraid that people may hear, he goes up to his father's pillow and rattles his sword in its scabbard, instead of a horse's bit.[8] At the clink of the hilt Yuranosuke suddenly rises.

YURANOSUKE Is that you, Rikiya? Has something urgent come up? Is that why you rattled the scabbard? Keep your voice low.

RIKIYA An express courier just brought a secret letter from Lady Kaoyo.

YURANOSUKE Was there no verbal message besides?

RIKIYA Our enemy Ko no Moronao's petition to return to his province has been granted and he will shortly start for home. Her ladyship said the details would be found in her letter.

YURANOSUKE Very good. You return home and send a palanquin for me tonight. Be off now.

NARRATOR Without a flicker of hesitation Rikiya sets off for Yamashina. Yuranosuke, worried about the contents of the letter, is about to cut the seal when a voice calls.

KUDAYU Master Oboshi! Master Yuranosuke! It's me, Ono Kudayo. I'd like a word with you.

YURANOSUKE Well! I haven't seen you in a long time. How wrinkled you've become in the year since we last met. Have you come to this house to unfurrow those wrinkles? What an old lecher you are!

---

[7] A *ri* is about 2½ miles.
[8] Samurai dozing on horseback were said to awaken to the sound of the horse's bit.

KUDAYU   Yura—they say little faults are overlooked in a great achievement. The fast life you've led here in the gay quarters, in defiance of people's criticism, will pave the foundation for your achievements. I consider you a hero, a man of great promise.

YURANOSUKE   Ha, ha. What a hard line you take! You've set up a perfect battery of catapults against me. But let's talk about something else.

KUDAYU   There's no point in pretending, Yuranosuke. Your dissipation is, in fact—

YURANOSUKE   You think it's a trick to enable me to attack the enemy?

KUDAYU   Of course I do.

YURANOSUKE   How you flatter me! I thought you'd laugh at me as a fool, a madman—over forty and still a slave to physical pleasure. But you tell me it's all a scheme to attack the enemy! Thank you, good Kudayu. You've made me happy.

KUDAYU   Then you have no intention of avenging our master Enya?

YURANOSUKE   Not in the least. I know that when we were about to turn over the house and the domain I said I would die fighting in the castle, but that was only to please her ladyship. I remember how you stalked out of the room at the time, saying that resistance would make us enemies of the shogun. But we continued our debate in deadly earnest. What idiots we were! In any case, our discussion got nowhere. We said we'd commit *seppuku* before his lordship's tomb, but one after another we stole out the back gate. I have you to thank for being able to enjoy these pleasures here, and I haven't forgotten our old friendship. Don't act so stiff! Relax with me.

KUDAYU   Yes, I see now, when I think back on the old days, that I used to be quite a fraud myself. Shall I show you my true nature and have a drink with you? How about it, Yuranosuke? The first cup we've shared in a long time.

YURANOSUKE   Are you going to ask for the cup back, as at a formal banquet?

KUDAYU   Pour the liquor and I'll drink.

YURANOSUKE   Drink up and I'll pour.

KUDAYU   Have a full cup. Here, I'll give you something to eat with it.

NARRATOR   He picks up in his chopsticks a piece of octopus that happens to be near him and holds it out to Yuranosuke.

YURANOSUKE   Putting out my hand, I accept an octopus foot. Thank you!

KUDAYU   Yuranosuke—tomorrow is the anniversary of the death of our master, Enya Hangan. The night before the anniversary is supposed to be especially important. Are you going to eat that octopus and think nothing of it?[9]

YURANOSUKE   Of course I'll eat it. Or have you had word that Lord Enya has turned into an octopus? What foolish ideas you get into your head! You and I are *ronin* now, thanks to Lord Hangan's recklessness. That's why I hold a grudge against him. I haven't the faintest intention of becoming a vegetarian for his sake, and I'm delighted to sample the fish you've so kindly provided.

NARRATOR   With the greatest aplomb he gulps down the fish in a single mouthful, a sight that stuns even the crafty Kudayu into silence.

YURANOSUKE   This fish is no good for drinking. We'll get them to wring a chicken's neck and give us chicken in the pot. Let's go to the back room. Come along, girls, and sing for us.

KUDAYU *(sings)*
> On uncertain legs he staggers off
> To the lively beat of the samisens
> Tere tsuku teretsuku tsutsuten tsutsuten . . .

YURANOSUKE *(to jesters)*   Hey, you small fry! Do you expect to be let off without getting soused?

NARRATOR   Amid all the bustle he goes within. Sagisaka Bannai, who has been observing everything from beginning to end, comes down from the second floor.

BANNAI   I've kept close watch on him, Kudayu, and I can't believe a man so rotten at the core he'd even eat animal food on the anniversary of his master's death will ever attack his enemy. I intend to report this to my master Moronao, and to recommend that he relax his precautions and open his gates.

KUDAYU   You're right, Lord Moronao need not take such precautions any more.

BANNAI   Look here—he's forgotten his sword!

KUDAYU   Yes, that really proves what a nitwit he's become. Let's examine this symbol of his samurai spirit. Why, it's rusty as a red sardine!

BANNAI   Ha, ha, ha!

KUDAYU   This certainly shows us his true nature. Your master can set his mind at rest. *(Calls.)* Where are my servants? I'm leaving. Bring my palanquin!

NARRATOR   With a shout they bring it forth.

---

[9]The offer of octopus is significant as a test of Yuranosuke's attitude because those in mourning must abstain from animal food.

KUDAYU   Now, Bannai, please get in.

BANNAI   No, sir, you're older than I. After you, please.

KUDAYU   In that case, by your leave.

NARRATOR   He gets in.

BANNAI   By the way, Kudayu, I hear that Kampei's wife is working in this place. Have you run into her here?

NARRATOR   Surprised not to receive reply, he lifts the bamboo blinds of the palanquin and sees inside a fair-sized stone.

BANNAI   Good heavens! Kudayu has turned into a stone, like Lady Sayo of Matsuura![10]

NARRATOR   He looks around him. A voice calls from under the veranda.

KUDAYU   Here I am, Bannai. I've played a trick and slipped out of the palanquin. I'm worried about the letter Rikiya brought a while ago. I'll watch what happens and let you know later on. Follow along beside the palanquin. Act as if we were leaving together.

BANNAI   I will.

NARRATOR   He nods in agreement and slowly walks beside the palanquin, pretending someone is inside.

Meanwhile, Kampei's wife Okaru is recovering in her upstairs room from intoxication; familiar now with the Quarter, she lets the blowing breezes dispel her sadness.

YURANOSUKE *(to women in the back room)*   I'll be back in a moment. Yuranosuke's supposed to be a samurai, but he's forgotten his precious sword. I'll go and fetch it. In the meantime, straighten the kakemono[11] and put some charcoal on the stove.—Oh, I must be careful not to step on that samisen and break it. Well, that's a surprise! It looks as if Kudayu's gone. *(Sings.)*

> He hears a tearful voice that cries,
> "Father! Mother!" and to his surprise,
> The words came from a parrot's beak:
> His wife had taught the bird to speak!

NARRATOR   Yuranosuke looks around the room; then, standing under the light of a lantern hanging from the eaves, he reads the long letter from Lady

[10] The Lady Sayo waved her scarf so long at the ship bearing her husband away that she finally turned to stone.

[11] Wall-hanging.

Kaoyo describing in detail the enemy's situation. The letter is in woman's language, full of polite phrases, and not easy to follow. Okaru, envious of other people happily in love, tries to read the letter from upstairs, but it is dark and the letter far away and the writing indistinct. It occurs to her that by holding out her mirror to reflect the writing she can read the message. Under the veranda, by the light of the moon, Kudayu reads the letter as it unrolls and hangs, but Yuranosuke, being no god, is unaware of this. Okaru's hair ornament suddenly comes loose and falls. Yuranosuke looks up at the sound the hides the letter behind him. Kudayu, under the veranda, is still in smiles; Okaru in the upstairs room hides her mirror.

OKARU Is that you, Yura?

YURANOSUKE Oh, it's you, Okaru. What are you doing there?

OKARU You got me completely drunk. It was so painful I've been cooling myself in the breeze, trying to sober up.

YURANOSUKE You're lucky to have such a good breeze. But Okaru, there's a little matter I'd like to discuss with you. I can't talk from here, across the rooftops, like the two stars across the Milky Way—won't you come down here for a moment?

OKARU Is this matter you'd like to discuss some favor you want to ask me?

YURANOSUKE Yes, something like that.

OKARU I'll go around and come down.

YURANOSUKE No, if you go by the staircase some maid is sure to catch you and make you drink.

OKARU What shall I do, then?

YURANOSUKE Look—luckily there's a nine-runged ladder lying here. You can use it to come down.

NARRATOR He leans the ladder against the eaves of the lower floor.

OKARU What a funny ladder! Oh, I'm afraid! It feels dangerous somehow.

YURANOSUKE Don't worry. You're way past the age for feeling afraid or in danger. You could come down three rungs at a time and still not open any new wounds.

OKARU Don't be silly. I'm afraid. It feels like I'm on a boat.

YURANOSUKE Of course it does. I can see your little boat god from here.

OKARU Ohh—you mustn't peep!

YURANOSUKE I'm admiring the autumn moon over Lake T'ung-t'ing.

OKARU I won't come down if you're going to act that way.

YURANOSUKE   If you won't come down, I'll knock you up.

OKARU   There you go again with your awful language.

YURANOSUKE   You make such a fuss anybody would think you were a virgin. I'll take you from behind.

NARRATOR   He catches her in his arms from behind and sets her on the ground.

YURANOSUKE   Tell me, did you see anything?

OKARU   No, no, I didn't.

YURANOSUKE   I'm sure you did.

OKARU   It looked like a letter from a girl friend.

YURANOSUKE   Did you read the whole thing from up there?

OKARU   Why are you grilling me so?

YURANOSUKE   It's a matter of life and death.

OKARU   What in the world are you talking about?

YURANOSUKE   I mean—I know it's an old story, Okaru, but I've fallen for you. Will you be my wife?

OKARU   Now stop it! You're lying to me.

YURANOSUKE   The truth may have started as a lie, but if I didn't really mean it, I couldn't go through with it. Say yes, please.

OKARU   No, I won't.

YURANOSUKE   But why?

OKARU   Because what you say is not truth that started as a lie, but a lie that started as truth.

YURANOSUKE   Okaru, I'll redeem your contract.

OKARU   Will you?

YURANOSUKE   I'll prove to you I'm not lying. I'll buy out your contract tonight.

OKARU   No, I have a—

YURANOSUKE   If you have a lover, you can live with him.

OKARU   Do you really mean it?

YURANOSUKE   I swear, by the providence that made me a samurai. As long as I can keep you for three days, you are at liberty to do what you please afterwards.

OKARU   I'm sure you just want me to say how happy I am before you laugh at me.

YURANOSUKE Absolutely not. I'll give the master the money at once and settle things here and now. You wait here and don't worry about anything.

OKARU Then I'll wait for you. I promise.

YURANOSUKE Don't move from the spot until I get back from paying the money. You're my wife now.

OKARU And just for three days.

YURANOSUKE Yes, I've agreed.

OKARU I'm most grateful.

NARRATOR (*sings*)

> *If ever woman was born*
> *Unlucky, I'm the one.*
> *How many pangs I've suffered*
> *For the man I love, alas.*
> *I cry alone with muffled notes*
> *Like a plover of the night.*

Okaru, hearing this song from the back room, is sunk in thought as she feels how closely its words fit herself. At that moment Heiemon suddenly appears.

HEIEMON Okaru—is that you?

OKARU Heiemon! How shaming to meet you here!

NARRATOR She hides her face.

HEIEMON There's nothing to feel ashamed about. I stopped to see Mother on my way back from the East and she told me everything. It was noble of you to have sold yourself for your husband and our master. I'm proud of you.

OKARU I am happy if you can think so kindly of me. But I have good news for you. Tonight, most unexpectedly, my contract is to be redeemed.

HEIEMON No news could please me more. Whom have we to thank for this?

OKARU Someone you know, Oboshi Yuranosuke.

HEIEMON What did you say? Your contract is to be redeemed by Oboshi Yuranosuke? Have you been intimate with him for a long time?

OKARU How could I have been? I've occasionally, perhaps two or three times, drunk with him. He said that if I had a husband I could stay with him, and if I wanted to be free he would let me go. It's almost too good to be true.

HEIEMON You mean, he doesn't know you're married to Hayano Kampei?

OKARU No, he doesn't. How could I tell him, when my being here is a disgrace to my parents and my husband?

HEIEMON   It would seem, then, he's a libertine at heart. Obviously he has no intention of avenging our master.

OKARU   No, that's not so. He has, I know it. I can't say it aloud, but I'll whisper it. *(Whispers.)*

HEIEMON   Then you definitely saw what the letter said?

OKARU   I read every word. Then we happened to look each other in the face and he began to flirt with me. Finally he talked about redeeming me.

HEIEMON   This was after you read the whole letter?

OKARU   Yes.

HEIEMON   I understand everything, then. My sister, you're doomed. You can't escape. Let me take your life.

NARRATOR   He draws his sword and slashes at her, but she jumps nimbly aside.

OKARU   What is it, Heiemon? What have I done wrong? You're not free to kill me as you please. I have my husband Kampei and both my parents too. I've been looking forward so much to seeing my parents and my husband as soon as my contract is redeemed. Whatever my offense may be, I apologize. Please forgive me, pardon me.

NARRATOR   She clasps her hands in supplication. Heiemon flings down his naked sword and gives way to bitter tears.

HEIEMON   My poor dear sister. I see you know nothing of what happened. Our father, Yoichibei, was stabbed to death by a stranger on the night of the twenty-ninth of the sixth month.

OKARU   It's not possible!

HEIEMON   You haven't heard the worst. You say you want to join Kampei as soon as you're redeemed. But he committed *seppuku* and is dead.

OKARU   Oh, no! Is it true! Tell me!

NARRATOR   She clutches him and, with a cry, collapses in tears.

HEIEMON   I understand. No wonder you cry. But it would make too long a story to tell you everything. I feel sorriest for Mother. Every time she mentions what happened she weeps, every time she remembers she weeps again. She begged me not to tell you, saying you'd cry yourself to death if you knew. I made up my mind not to tell you, but you can't escape death now. Yuranosuke is singlemindedly, fanatically motivated by loyalty. He'd have had no reason to ransom you if he didn't know you were Kampei's wife. Certainly it wasn't because he's infatuated with you. The letter you saw was of the greatest importance. He will redeem your contract only to kill you. I'm sure that's what he has in mind. Even if you tell no one about the letter, the walls have ears, and any word of the plan leaking from somebody else is sure to be blamed on you. You were wrong to have peeped into a secret letter, and you must be killed for it. Rather than let you die at a stranger's hands, I will kill you with my own hands. I can't allow any woman with knowledge of the great secret to escape, even if she's my own sister. On the strength of having killed a person dangerous to our plot I shall ask to join the league and go with the others. The sad thing about being of the lower ranks is that unless you prove to the other samurai your spirit is better than theirs, they won't let you join them. Show you understand by giving me your life. Die for my sake, sister.

NARRATOR   Okaru sobs again and again as she listens to her brother's carefully reasoned words.

OKARU   I kept thinking all the while that the reason why he didn't write me was that he'd used the money I raised as the price of my body and started on his journey. I was resentful because he hadn't even come to say good-by. It's a dreadful thing for me to say, but though Father met a horrible death he was, after all, an old man. But how sad and humiliating it must have been for Kampei to die when he was hardly thirty! I'm sure he must have wanted to see me. Why didn't anyone take me to him? What a terrible fate never even to have abstained from animal food in mourning for my husband and father. What reason have I to go on living? But if I died at your hands I'm sure Mother would hate you for it. I'll kill myself. After I'm dead, if my head or body can bring you credit, please use it for that purpose. Now I must say farewell to you, my brother.

NARRATOR   She takes up the sword.

YURANOSUKE   Stop! Wait a moment!

NARRATOR   Yuranosuke restrains her. Heiemon jumps in astonishment. Okaru cries out.

OKARU   Let me go! Let me die!

NARRATOR   Yuranosuke holds her back and she struggles, impatient for death.

YURANOSUKE   You are an admirable brother and sister. All my doubts have been resolved. Heiemon, you may join us on our eastward journey. You, Okaru, must live on so you can offer prayers for the future repose of his soul.

OKARU   I'll pray for him by going with him to the afterworld.

NARRATOR   Yuranosuke holds firmly the sword he has twisted from her grasp.

YURANOSUKE   We admitted your husband Kampei to our league, but he was never able to kill a single enemy. What excuse will he be able to offer our master when he meets him in the afterworld? This may serve as his apology!

NARRATOR   He drives the sword hard between the mats. Underneath the floor Kudayu, his shoulder run through, writhes in agony.

YURANOSUKE   Drag him out!

NARRATOR   Even before the command leaves Yuranosuke's mouth, Heiemon leaps from the veranda and resolutely drags out Kudayu, dripping with blood.

HEIEMON   Kudayu! It serves you right!

NARRATOR   He hauls him up and throws him before Yuranosuke, who grabs Kudayu by the topknot, not letting him rise, and pulls him over.

YURANOSUKE   The worm that feeds on the lion's body—that's you! You received a large stipend from your master and benefited by innumerable other kindnesses, and yet you became a spy for his enemy Moronao and secretly informed him of everything, true and false alike. The forty and more of us have left our parents and separated from our children, and have even forced our wives, who should have been our lifelong companions, to work as prostitutes, all out of the desire to avenge our late master. As soon as we wake up in the morning, then all through the day, we think about how he committed *seppuku*, and the remembrances arouse tears of impotent rage. We have racked ourselves with pain, mind and body. Tonight especially, the night before our master's anniversary, I spoke vile words of every sort, but in my heart I was practicing the most profound abstention. How dared you thrust fish before my face? What anguish I felt in my heart, not being able to accept or refuse. And how do you think I felt on the night before the anniversary of a master whose family my family has served for three generations, when the fish passed my throat? My whole body seemed to crumble to pieces all at once, and my bones felt as though they were breaking. Ahh—you fiend, you diabolical monster!

NARRATOR   He rubs and twists Kudayu's body into the ground, then breaks into tears of despair.

YURANOSUKE   Heiemon, I forgot my rusty sword a while ago. It was a sign I was meant to torture him to death with it. Make him suffer, but don't kill him.

HEIEMON   Yes, sir.

NARRATOR   He unsheathes his sword and at once leaps and pounces on Kudayu, slashing him again and again, though the wounds are superficial. He scores Kudayu's body until no part is left unscathed.

KUDAYU   Heiemon, Okaru, please intercede for me!

NARRATOR　He joins his hands in entreaty. What a repulsive sight—Kudayu, who always despised Teraoka as a lowly foot soldier, and refused to favor him with so much as a glance, now prostrates himself humbly.

YURANOSUKE　If we kill him here we'll have trouble explaining it. Pretend he's drunk and take him home.

NARRATOR　He throws a cloak over Kudayu to hide the wounds. Yazama, Senzaki, and Takemori, who have been listening in secret, fling open the sliding doors.

THREE MEN　Yuranosuke, we humbly apologize.

YURANOSUKE　Heiemon—this customer has had too much to drink. Give him some watery gruel for his stomach in the Kamo River.

HEIEMON　Yes, sir.

YURANOSUKE　Go!

FURTHER READINGS

E. Matsushima, *Chushingura* (Tokyo: Iwanami Shoten, 1964), provides a helpful treatment of both the historical background and composition of the play. James R. Brandon, ed., *Chushingura: Studies in Kabuki and Puppet Theater* (Honolulu: University of Hawaii Press, 1982), includes four articles focusing on the play and concludes with a text of the *Forty-Seven Ronin*. Sakae Shioya, *Chushingura: An Exposition* (Tokyo: Hokuseido Press, 1940), is a retelling of the historical events followed by a summary of the action of the play. Yasuji Toita, *Chushingura* (Tokyo: Sogensha, 1957), is a useful discussion of the different traditions in the performance of the play.

Three worthwhile surveys of kabuki theater are A. C. Scott, *The Kabuki Theater of Japan* (New York: Macmillan, 1966); Earl Ernst, *The Kabuki Theater* (New York: Oxford University Press, 1956); and Yasuji Toita, *Kabuki: The Popular Theater*, trans. D. Kenny (New York: Walker/Weatherhill, 1970). Donald Keene, *Bunraku: The Puppet Theater of Japan* (Tokyo: Kodansha International, 1965), presents an interesting discussion of Japanese puppet theater.

Peter Arnett, *The Theatres of Japan* (New York: Macmillan, 1969), traces the development of classical Japanese theatrical forms and their influence on modern productions. English translations of some kabuki plays are available in Samuel L. Leiter, *The Art of Kabuki* (Berkeley: University of California Press, 1979), and in James R. Brandon, trans., *Kabuki: Five Classic Plays* (Cambridge, MA: Harvard University Press, 1975). William Malm, *Nagauta: The Heart of Kabuki Music* (Tokyo: Tuttle, 1963), is an informative study of the music of the kabuki theater.

THE SCHOLARS

Wu Ching-tzu

The Scholars (Ju-lin wai-shih), completed around 1750 and first published about two or three decades later, is considered one of the greatest novels of the Chinese tradition. A loosely connected series of satirical stories revolving about various members of the scholar class, it is the first Chinese novel of significant scope that does not borrow its characters from history and legend. Its author drew heavily upon his own experiences; many of the characters of *The Scholars* were modeled on his friends and acquaintances, and his descriptions of people and places are recollections of his own observations.

A member of a scholarly family that had distinguished itself in government service during late Ming and early Ch'ing times, Wu Ching-tzu (1701–1754) appears to have been poorly prepared for a competitive official life. Although he succeeded in gaining the preliminary academic degree, he failed in subsequent civil service examinations. Having squandered his fortune, he moved his family from his native town to the city of Nanking in 1734. Here he lived the life of an idle scholar until composing his great novel.

Wu's continual failures to pass the civil service examinations embittered him toward this highly competitive system that lay at the heart of imperial government. Designed to attract the most talented individuals into government service and to weed out those less fit for service, the examination system allowed the ambitious and able scholar entry to a well-defined ladder of advancement that led to prestige, power, and wealth. *The Scholars* is primarily an attack on the absurdities of this system and the shortcomings of those involved in it. It is notable not only for its satiric portrayal of scholars and pseudo-scholars, however, but also for its descriptions of ordinary men and women functioning within their normal surroundings.

The autobiographical hero of the place is Tu Shao-ch'ing, an aristocrat who refuses to take advantage of others. Tu foolishly squanders his family fortunes through his extravagant generosity to a number of individuals who have no scruples in compromising their own honor in order to take advantage of the noble hero. Tu rejects the opportunity to enter government service and, with all his proud nonconformity, moves to the metropolis of Nanking to live among more congenial friends. Here he spends the remaining years of his life enjoying the scenic spots and engaging in intellectual conversation.

The excerpt provided here presents Tu as an appealing person, a proud and honest scholar, but prone to reckless generosity. He is not blind to the lack

From Wu Ching-tzu, *The Scholars*, trans. Yang Hsien-yi and Gladys Yang (Beijing: Foreign Language Press, 1972), pp. 387–413.

of character of the petitioners who besiege him. He is certainly aware that his steward Wang is corrupt and that many of his guests are dishonest flatterers. He is moved to tears when the dying Mr. Lou advises him to end his indiscriminate generosity and to pattern his conduct on that of his virtuous father. He cannot control himself, however, and is eventually impoverished.

The Scholars was the first Chinese work of satiric realism to detach itself from the common religious beliefs of its day. Popular Buddhism generally dictated that the virtuous always be rewarded and the wicked punished. Wu shunned this facile didacticism. In the world of *The Scholars*, as in the real world, a virtuous individual is not necessarily rewarded, and the wicked often prosper precisely because they are morally unscrupulous.

Questions

1. The Western reader often prefers a hero dedicated to a life of action. Describe Tu Shao-ch'ing's character. Do you find him admirable and virtuous? Why or why not?
2. Does the author consider ignorance or immorality the more blameworthy?
3. What relationship exists between learning and the attainment of worldly success?
4. The cornerstone of *The Scholars* is the attainment of true virtue. What constitutes true virtue for the author?

THE SCHOLARS

LIST OF PRINCIPAL CHARACTERS

Tu-shao-ching, *brilliant scholar who squanders his fortune*
Tu Shen-ching, *his cousin*
Pao Ting-hsi, *adopted son of Pao Wen-ching, son of Ni Shuang-feng*
Wei Ssu-hsuan (Fourth Mr. Wei), *Tu Shao-ching's friend*
Whiskers Wang, *Tu Shao-ching's steward*
Chang Chun-min (Iron-armed Chang), *swordsman and charlatan*
Tsang Liao-chai, *licentiate*
Hsiang Ting, *magistrate of Antung, later intendant of Ting-chang Circuit*
Mr. Lou, *an old retainer of Tu Shao-ching's family*

VISITORS CALL ON A GALLANT IN TIENCHANG COUNTY.
GOOD FRIENDS DRINK WINE IN TU SHAO-CHING'S LIBRARY

Pao Ting-hsi was amazed at the amount of money Tu Shen-ching had spent on the contest.

"Why don't I take advantage of his generosity to borrow a few hundred taels?"[1] he thought. "Then I can start another opera company, and make enough to live on."

Having reached this decision, he made himself so useful every day in the house by the river that Tu began to feel under an obligation to him. And late one night, when none of the servants were in the room, they had a frank talk.

"What do you live on, Mr. Pao?" inquired Tu. "You ought to go into some kind of business, you know."

At this question, Ting-hsi plumped down on both knees. Quite taken aback, Tu helped him up.

"What is the meaning of this?" he asked.

"You are as kind as heaven and as generous as the earth to put that question to your humble servant, sir!" cried Ting-hsi. "But I used to manage an opera company, and that is the only trade I know. If you want to befriend me, sir, will you be good enough to lend me a few hundred taels, so that I can start another company? As soon as I have money, I will repay you."

"That should be easy," said Tu. "Sit down, and let's talk it over. A few hundred taels isn't enough to start an opera company—you'll need at least a thousand. Between ourselves, I don't mind telling you that although I have a few thousand taels of ready money, I don't want to spend it at the moment. Why not? In the next year or two I expect to pass the palace examination, and after that, of course, I'll need a lot of money; so for the time being I must hold on to what I have. Regarding this company of yours, I can tell you somebody who can help. It will be the same as if I helped you myself. But you mustn't let him know I put you up to this."

"Who else but you will help me, sir?" demanded Ting-hsi.

"Steady on. Listen to me. There are seven main branches to my family. The Minister of Ceremony belonged to the fifth branch. Two generations ago, the head of the seventh branch passed first in the palace examination, and his son was prefect of Kanchow in Kiangsi. He was my uncle, and his son is my twenty-fifth cousin, Shao-ching. He's two years younger than I am, and has passed the district examination too. My uncle was an honest officer, who didn't add anything to the family estate and left no more than ten thousand taels at his death. But, like a fool, Shao-ching acts as if he had hundreds of thousands. He doesn't know the difference between good silver and bad, yet he loves to act the patron. Anyone with a bad luck story can be sure of substantial help from him.

[1] A unit of value, based on a weight of silver equal to about 1/12 pound.

Why don't you stay and help me out till autumn, when it's cooler? Then I'll give you your fare to Tienchang. I guarantee you'll get your thousand taels."

"I hope you will write me a letter of introduction for me, sir, when the time comes."

"No, no. That would never do. He likes to be the one and only patron helping anybody—he doesn't like others to join in. If I were to write, he would think I already helped you, and wouldn't trouble to do anything for you. You must apply to someone else first."

"To whom?"

"My cousin used to have an old steward called Shao, whom you ought to know."

"He came one year when my father was alive," said Ting-hsi after thinking hard. "He arranged for us to give a performance for the old mistress's birthday! I saw the Prefect of Kanchow too."

"Excellent! Old Shao is dead now, and the present steward is a thorough-going scoundrel called Whiskers Wang, whom his master trusts implicitly. My cousin's weakness is this: anybody who claims to have known his father—even a dog—wins his respect. You must call on Whiskers Wang first. The rascal likes drinking and, if you treat him to wine and persuade him to tell his master that you were a favourite with the old prefect, then Shao-ching will shower you with silver. He doesn't like to be addressed as the master, so call him 'the young master.' Another of his peculiarities is that he can't stand talk about officials or rich men. Don't tell him, for instance, how good Prefect Hsiang was to you. Keep on harping on the fact that he is the only true patron in the world. And if he asks you whether you know me, tell him you don't."

This conversation left Pao Ting-hsi overjoyed. He made himself useful in Tu's household for another two months, until the end of the seventh month when the weather began to grow cooler. Then he borrowed a few taels from Tu Shen-ching, packed his luggage, and crossed the river to travel to Tien-chang.

The day that he crossed the Yangtse, he put up for the night at Liuho. The next morning he rose early and travelled a dozen miles or more to a place called Fourth Mount, where he went into an inn and sat down. He was just going to ask for water to wash when a sedan-chair stopped at the gate. From it alighted an old man in a square cap, white gauze gown and red silk slippers who had the red nose of a heavy drinker, and a long, silky, silvery beard. As this old man came in, the inn-keeper hastened to take his luggage.

"So it is the fourth Mr. Wei," he cried. "Please take a seat inside, sir!"

As Mr. Wei entered the main room, Ting-hsi stood up and bowed. Mr. Wei returned his greeting. Ting-hsi urged him to take the seat of honour, and sat down himself in a lower place.

"I believe your name is Wei, sir," he said. "May I venture to ask your honourable district?"

"My name is Wei, and I come from Wuyi in Chuchow. What are your name and district, sir? And where are you bound for?"

"My name is Pao, and I am a native of Nanking. I am on my way to Tienchang, to visit the Mr. Tu whose grandfather was a Number One Scholar."

"Which Mr. Tu? Shen-ching or Shao-ching?"

"Shao-ching."

"There are sixty or seventy young men in the Tu family, but those are the only two who keep open house. The rest stay behind closed doors at home to prepare for the examination and look after their estates. That's why I asked straight away which of the two you meant. They are both well known all down the Yangtse Valley. Shen-ching is a most cultivated individual, but a little too effeminate for my taste. Shao-ching is a true gentleman of the old school. I'm on my way to see him too. We can travel together after we've eaten."

"Are you related to the Tu family, sir?"

"I was a classmate and sworn brother of Prefect Tu's. We were very close friends."

Upon hearing this, Ting-hsi's manner became even more respectful.

After their meal, Mr. Wei mounted his chair again. Ting-hsi hired a donkey, and trotted along beside the chair. When they reached Tienchang city gate, Mr. Wei dismounted.

"Let us walk to the house together, Mr. Pao," he said.

"Pray go on ahead in your chair, sir," replied Ting-hsi. "I want to see his steward first, before paying my respects to Mr. Tu."

"Very well," said Mr. Wei, and mounted his chair again.

When he reached Tu's house, his arrival was announced by the gatekeeper. Tu Shao-ching hastened out to meet him, and invited him into the hall, where they exchanged greetings.

"We have not seen each other for half a year, uncle," said Shao-ching. "I ought to have called to inquire after your health and that of your wife. Have you been well?"

"Quite well, thank you. There is nothing to do at home at the beginning of autumn, and I remembered your garden and reckoned the cassia must be in full blossom now. So I came to pay you a visit and drink with you."

"When tea has been served, I will invite you to have a rest in the library."

When a boy brought in tea, Tu Shao-ching gave him the order:

"Bring in Mr. Wei's baggage, and put it in the library. Then pay the chairbearers and send them away."

Presently he led Mr. Wei by a passage from the back along a winding path to the garden. As you went in you saw three rooms with an eastern exposure. A two-storeyed building on the left was the library built by the Number One Scholar, overlooking a large courtyard with one bed of *moutan* peonies and another of tree peonies. There were two huge cassia trees as well, in full bloom.

On the other side were three summer houses, with a three-roomed library behind them overlooking a great lotus pool. A bridge across this pool led you to three secluded chambers where Tu Shao-ching used to retire to study.

He invited Mr. Wei into the library with the southern exposure. The two cassia trees were just outside the window.

"Is old Lou still here?" asked Mr. Wei as he sat down.

"Mr. Lou's health has been very poor recently," replied Shao-ching, "so I have made him move into the inner library. He has just gone to sleep after taking his medicine. I'm afraid he won't be able to come out to greet you, uncle."

"If he is ill, why don't you send him home?"

"I have brought his sons and grandsons here to prepare his medicine. In this way I can inquire after his health morning and evening."

"After being with your family for thirty-odd years, hasn't the old man put by a substantial sum of money? Hasn't he bought any property?"

"After my father was appointed Prefect of Kanchow, he gave the books for the entire property to Mr. Lou. Mr. Lou was in complete charge of all financial transactions, and my father never questioned him. Apart from his salary of forty taels of silver a year, Mr. Lou didn't touch a cent. When the time came for collecting rent, he would go down to the country to visit the tenants himself; and if they prepared two dishes for him, he would send one away and eat one only. Whenever his sons or grandsons came to see him, he would pack them off after two days, and would never allow them to take a cent beyond their travelling money. In fact, he used to search them as they were leaving, to make sure none of the stewards had given them any silver. But in collecting rents or interest, if he discovered any of our friends or relatives were in difficulties, he would do his best to help them. My father knew this, but didn't query it. Sometimes when my father's debtors were unable to pay, Mr. Lou would burn their notes of hand. Though he is an old man now with two sons and four grandsons, he is still no richer than before. I feel very bad about it!"

"A true gentleman of the old school!" exclaimed Mr. Wei admiringly. "Is Shen-ching at home and well?"

"My cousin has gone to Nanking."

Just then Whiskers Wang took up his stand outside the window with a red card in his hand, but did not presume to enter.

"What is it, Wang?" asked Shao-ching, catching sight of him. "What's that in your hand?"

The steward came in and handed the card to his master.

"A man called Pao is here from Nanking," he announced "He's a theatre manager, who has been away from home for the last few years and has only just come back. Now he's crossed the river to pay his respects to you, sir."

"If he's in the theatre, tell him I have guests and can't see him. Keep his card, and ask him to leave."

"He says he was very kindly treated by our late master, sir. He wants very much to see you to thank you."

"Did my father help him out?"

"Yes, sir. One year Mr. Shao fetched his company across the river, and the prefect took a great fancy to this Pao Ting-hsi. He promised to look after him."

"In that case, show him in."

"I met this fellow Pao from Nanking on the road," said Mr. Wei.

Whiskers Wang went out to fetch Pao Ting-hsi, who advanced reverently. He looked round the spacious garden, and could see no end to it. Upon reaching the library door, he saw Tu Shao-ching sitting there with a guest. Tu was wearing a square cap, jade-coloured lined gauze gown, and pearl-decked shoes. He had a rather sallow complexion and eyebrows which rose obliquely, like a portrait of the God of War.

"That is our young master," said Whiskers Wang. "You can go in."

Pao Ting-hsi went in, knelt down and kowtowed.

"We are old friends," said Tu, helping him up. "Don't stand on ceremony."

Ting-hsi rose to his feet and exchanged greetings, first with Tu, then with Mr. Wei. Tu Shao-ching invited him to be seated on a lower seat.

"I owe your father such a debt of gratitude that even if my bones are ground to powder it will be hard to repay him," said Ting-hsi. "Because things have not gone well with me these last few years and I have been busy touring with my players, I did not come to pay my respects to the young master. Only today have I come to inquire after the young master's health. I hope you will forgive me, sir, for being so remiss."

"Just now," said Tu, "my steward Wang told me that my father took a great fancy to you, and meant to look after you. Since you are here, you must stay, and I will see what I can do for you."

"Dinner is ready, sir," announced Whiskers Wang. "Where would you like it served?"

"Why not here?" suggested Mr. Wei.

"We need a fourth," said Tu, and after a moment's hesitation called the library boy, Chia Chueh.

"Go out through the back gate and invite Dr. Chang over," he ordered.

Chia Chueh assented and left.

Presently the boy returned accompanied by a man with large eyes and a brownish moustache, who was wearing a tile-shaped cap and a wide cloth gown. Swaying as he walked in imitation of a scholar's gait, he came in, greeted them, sat down, and asked Mr. Wei's name.

"And what is your honourable name, sir?" inquired Mr. Wei, after giving his own.

"I am Chang Chun-min," was the reply, "and have served the Tu family for many years. I have a smattering of medical knowledge, and the young master does me the honour of calling me in every day to attend to Mr. Lou. How has the old gentleman been since he took his medicine today?"

Tu Shao-ching ordered Chia Chueh to go and find out.

"Mr. Lou had a nap after his medicine," reported the boy on his return. "He is awake now, and feels rather better."

"Who is *this* gentleman?" asked Chang, indicated Ting-hsi.

"This is my friend Pao from Nanking," replied Tu.

While they were speaking the table was spread, and they sat down: Mr. Wei in the seat of honour, Chang Chun-min opposite him, Tu Shao-ching in the place of host, and Pao Ting-hsi in the lowest seat. Their cups were filled, and they began to drink. The dishes to go with the wine had all been prepared at home, and were delicious. There was ham that had been hung for three years, and crabs weighing half a catty[2] each, removed from their shells before cooking.

"I have no doubt you have attained great skill in your calling," said Mr. Wei to Chang Chun-min while they were eating.

"A thorough knowledge of Wang Shu-ho[3] is not as good as experience of many diseases," quoted the doctor. "I won't deceive you, sir. I have knocked about a good deal outside without reading many books, but seeing plenty of patients. Only recently, thanks to the young master's advice, have I learned the need for book knowledge. So I am not teaching my son medicine, but have engaged a tutor for him; and he is writing compositions which he brings to show Mr. Tu. The young master always comments on them for him, and I also study these comments carefully at home, in this way learning something about literary composition. In another year or two I'll send my son in for the district examination, and he will get his share of dumplings as a candidate. Then, when he sets up in practice, he can call himself a scholarly physician!"

Mr. Wei laughed long and loud at this speech.

Then Whiskers Wang brought in another visiting card.

"Mr. Wang, the salt merchant at the North Gate, is celebrating his birthday tomorrow," he announced. "He has asked the magistrate as guest of honour, and invites you too, sir. He begs you to be sure to go."

"Tell him I have guests and cannot go," replied Tu. "How ridiculous the fellow is! If he wants a good party, why doesn't he invite those newly-rich scholars who have passed the provincial and metropolitan examinations? What time do I have to keep officials company for him?"

Whiskers Wang assented and left.

"You are a great drinker, uncle," said Tu to Mr. Wei. "You used to sit up half the night drinking with my father. We must have a good drinking session today too."

---

[2] Unit of weight equalling sixteen taels, or about 1⅓ pounds.

[3] A physician of the T'sin Dynasty, whose books are medical classics.

"Yes," replied Mr. Wei. "I hope you don't mind my saying this, friend; but though your food is first-rate, this wine bought in the market is too new. You have one jar of wine in your house which must be eight or nine years old by now. Assuming, that is, you still have it."

"I didn't know that," said Tu.

"You wouldn't know," rejoined Mr. Wei. "The year that your father went to take up his post in Kiangsi, I saw him to the boat, and he told me: 'I've buried a jar of wine in my house. When my term of office is up and I come home, we'll do some serious drinking together.' That's why I remember. Why don't you ask your household?"

"The young master couldn't have known this." Chang Chun-min smiled.

Tu Shao-ching went to the inner chambers.

"Though Mr. Tu is young, he is one of the most gallant gentlemen in these parts," declared Mr. Wei.

"The young master is so good to everyone too!" put in the doctor. "If anything, he's too open-handed. No matter who makes a request of him, he gives the fellow taels and taels of silver."

"I've never seen such a generous, noble gentleman in all my life!" chimed in Ting-hsi.

Tu Shao-ching went to the inner chambers to ask his wife if she knew anything about this wine, but she did not. He asked all the servants and maids, but none of them knew. Last of all he questioned his wet-nurse, Shao.

"There *was* such a jar," she recalled. "The year that our late master became prefect he brewed a jar of wine and buried it in a small room at the back of the seventh court-yard. He said it was to be kept for Mr. Wei. The wine was made of two pecks of glutinous rice and twenty catties of fermented rice. Twenty catties of alcohol went into it too, but not a drop of water. It was buried nine years and seven months ago, so it must be strong enough now to blow your head off. When it's dug up, don't drink it, sir!"

"Very good," said Tu.

He ordered the wet-nurse to unlock the door of the room where the wine was stored, and went in with two servants. They dug up the wine jar, and carried it to the library.

"I've found your wine, uncle!" he cried.

Mr. Wei and the two guests stood up to look at it.

"That's it!" cried Mr. Wei.

The jar was opened, and they ladled out a cupful. It stood as thick as gruel in the cup, and had a rich bouquet.

"This is capital!" exclaimed Mr. Wei. "I'll tell you how we must drink this, friend. Send out for another ten catties of wine to mix with it. We can't drink it today, so just leave it there for the present. We'll drink all day tomorrow. These two gentlemen must join us."

"We will certainly keep you company," said Chang.

"Who am I," asked Ting-hsi, "to drink this fine wine the prefect has left? Tomorrow will be the happiest day of my life!"

Presently Chia Chueh was told to fetch a lantern and escort the doctor home. Ting-hsi slept in the library with Mr. Wei, and Tu Shao-ching waited till the latter had gone to bed before retiring himself.

The next morning Pao Ting-hsi rose early and went to Whiskers Wang's room. Chia Chueh was sitting there with another servant.

"Is Mr. Wei up yet?" asked Whiskers Wang.

"He's up and washing his face," said Chia Chueh.

"Is the young master up?" the steward asked the other servant.

"He's been up a long time. He's in Mr. Lou's room, watching them prepare the medicine."

"Our master is an extraordinary man," declared Whiskers Wang. "Mr. Lou is only one of the prefect's employees! When he fell ill, our master should have given him a few taels of silver and sent him home—why keep him here and treat him as one of the family, waiting on him hand and foot?"

"How can you say that, Mr. Wang!" protested the servant. "When we prepare gruel or dishes for Mr. Lou, it's not enough for his sons and grandsons to inspect them—our master has to see them too before they can be given to Mr. Lou! The ginseng pot is kept in the mistress's room, and of course she prepares the ginseng and other medicines herself. Every morning and evening, if our master can't take in the ginseng himself, it's the mistress who takes it in to the patient. If the master hears you talking like that, he'll give you a good dressing down!"

Just then the gate-keeper came in.

"Go in, Uncle Wang, and announce that the third Mr. Tsang is here," he said. "He's sitting in the hall, waiting to see the young master."

"Go and fetch the master from Mr. Lou's room," said Whiskers Wang to the servant. "I'm not going there to ask after Lou's health!"

"This just shows how good your master is," declared Ting-hsi.

Presently Tu Shao-ching came out to see Mr. Tsang, and after exchanging greetings they sat down.

"I haven't seen you for some days, Third Brother," remarked Tu. "What have you been doing in your literary groups?"

"Your gateman told me you had a guest from some distance," said Tsang. "Shen-ching seems to be enjoying himself so much in Nanking that he doesn't want to come back."

"Uncle Wei from Wuyi is here," said Tu. "I'm preparing a feast for him today, and you must stay to it too. Let's both go to the library now."

"Wait a little," said Tsang. "I have something to say to you. Magistrate Wang here is my patron, and he's told me many times how much he admires your talent. When are you coming with me to see him?"

"I must leave it to you, Third Brother, to call on magistrates and pay your respects as a student," replied Tu. "Why, in my father's time—to say nothing of my grandfather's and great-grandfather's—heaven knows how many magistrates came here! If he really respects me, why doesn't he call on me first? Why should I call on him? I'm sorry I passed the district examination, since it means I have to address the local magistrate as my patron! As for this Magistrate Wang, who crawled out of some dust-heap to pass the metropolitan examination—I wouldn't even want him as my student! Why should I meet him? So when the salt merchant who lives at the North Gate invited me to a feast today to meet the magistrate, I refused to go."

"That's why I'm here," said Tsang. "Magistrate Wang wouldn't have accepted the invitation if the salt merchant hadn't told him you would be there too; but he wants to meet you. If you don't go, he will be very disappointed. Besides, your guest is staying here, so you can keep him company tomorrow if you go out today. Or, if you like, I'll keep your friend company today while you go to the salt merchant's."

"Please don't insist, Third Brother," said Tu. "Your patron is no lover of worth or talent; he likes to accept students simply in order to collect presents from them. He wants me as his student, does he? He must be dreaming! In any case, I have guests today; and we've cooked a seven-catty duck, and unearthed some nine-year-old wine. The salt merchant will have nothing so good to offer me! I won't hear another word about going! Come with me now to the library."

He started marching Tsang off.

"Stop a minute!" cried Tsang. "What's the hurry? I've never met Mr. Wei. I must write a card."

"All right."

Tu ordered a servant to bring an inkstone and card, and Mr. Tsang wrote: "Your kinsman and fellow candidate, Tsang Tu."

He bade the servant take this to the library, then went in with Tu Shao-ching. Mr. Wei came to the door to greet them, and they took seats. Chang Chun-min and Pao Ting-hsi, who were also there, sat down too.

"May I inquire your second name?" Mr. Wei asked Tsang.

"Mr. Tsang's second name is Liao-chai," said Tu. "He was one of the best students of my year, and is a good friend of Shen-ching's as well."

"I am delighted to make your acquaintance," said Mr. Wei.

"I have long wanted to meet you, sir," rejoined Tsang.

Tsang knew the doctor, but looking at Pao Ting-hsi he asked:

"Who is *this* gentleman?"

"My name is Pao," replied Ting-hsi. "I have just arrived from Nanking."

"If you come from Nanking, do you know Mr. Tu Shen-ching?"

"I have met the seventeenth master."

When they had breakfasted, Mr. Wei brought the wine and added ten catties of new wine to it, then ordered the servants to light plenty of charcoal and pile it when it was red by the cassia trees, setting the jar of wine on top. After the time it takes for a meal, the wine was hot. Chang Chun-min helped the servant take down the six window frames and move the table to under the eaves. They then took seats, and fresh dishes were served. Tu Shao-ching called for one gold and four jade cups, which he filled by dipping them into the wine. Mr. Wei had the gold cup, and after each drink exclaimed: "Marvellous!" They had feasted for some time when Whiskers Wang led in four servants carrying a chest. Tu asked what it was.

"This is a chestful of new autumn clothes for you, sir, and for the mistress and young gentleman. They have just been made, and I've brought them for you to check. I've already paid the tailor."

"Leave them there," said Tu. "I'll look at them when we've finished drinking."

No sooner had the chest been set down than the tailor came in.

"Tailor Yang is here," announced Whiskers Wang.

"What does he want?" asked Tu.

He stood up and saw the tailor walk into the courtyard, kneel down and kowtow, then burst out sobbing.

"What is the matter, Mr. Yang?" demanded Tu, much surprised.

"I've been working all this time in your house, sir," said the tailor. "This morning when I received my pay, I didn't know that my mother would suddenly be taken ill and die. I didn't foresee this when I went home, so I used all the money to pay my fuel and rice bills. And now I haven't got a coffin for my mother, or mourning. There's nothing I can do but come back and beg you to lend me a few taels of silver. I'll work off the debt gradually."

"How much do you want?"

"I'm a poor man. I dare not ask for a lot. Six taels, if that's not too much, sir. Otherwise four taels. I must be able to pay it back by tailoring."

"I don't want you to repay it," said Tu, much moved. "You may be in a small way of business, but you can't treat your mother's funeral casually, or you will regret it all your life. What good are a few taels? You must buy a sixteen-tael coffin at the very least; and with clothes and miscellaneous expenses you will need twenty taels altogether. I haven't got a cent in the house at the moment— wait though! This chest of clothes can be pawned for twenty taels. Wang, you take this chest for Mr. Yang, and give him all the money you can raise on it. . . . I don't want this to prey on your mind, Mr. Yang. Just forget it. You aren't drinking or gambling with my silver, but seeing to the most important event of your mother's funeral. We all have mothers, don't we? It's only right for me to help you."

The tailor carried out the chest with Whiskers Wang's help, crying as he did so. Tu Shao-ching came back to the table and sat down.

"That was a fine deed, friend!" said Mr. Wei.

Ting-hsi shot out his tongue.

"Amida Buddha!" he exclaimed. "I didn't know such a good man existed!"

They feasted all day. Since Tsang was not a heavy drinker, by the afternoon he was sick and had to be helped home. Mr. Wei and the others drank till the third watch, and broke up only when the jar of wine was empty.

But to know what followed, you must read the next chapter.

IN WHICH ARE DESCRIBED THE GALLANT DEEDS OF TU SHAO-CHING, AND THE LAST WORDS OF MR. LOU

After the party broke up, Mr. Wei slept till late the next morning, then told Tu Shao-ching that he must be leaving.

"I mean to call on your uncle and cousin," he said. "I enjoyed myself enormously at the feast you so kindly prepared yesterday! I don't suppose I shall have such a good time anywhere else. Well, I must be going. I haven't even returned your friend Tsang's call, but please give him my best regards."

Shao-ching kept him for another day. The day after that he hired chair-bearers, then took a jade cup and two costumes which had belonged to the prefect of Kanchow to Mr. Wei's room.

"You are the only sworn brother my father had, uncle," he said. "I hope you will often come to see me, and I shall visit you more often to inquire after your health. I want you to take this jade cup to drink from. And please accept these two costumes which belonged to my father, for when you wear them I shall feel I am seeing him again."

Mr. Wei accepted these gifts with pleasure. Pao Ting-hsi joined them over another pot of wine, after which rice was served. Then Tu and Ting-hsi saw Mr. Wei out of the city and bowed before his sedan-chair as he left. Upon their return, Tu went to Mr. Lou's room to see how he was. The old man affirmed that he was better, and that he would send his grandson home, keeping his son only to tend him.

Tu Shao-ching agreed with this. Then, remembering that he had no money, he sent for Whiskers Wang.

"I want you to sell my land within the dyke to that man," he told him.

"That fellow wants to get it cheap," objected Whiskers Wang. "You asked for one thousand five hundred taels, sir, but he's offered one thousand three hundred only. So I don't dare make a deal with him."

"One thousand three hundred will do."

"I just wanted to be clear on that before leaving, sir. Otherwise you might abuse me for selling it too cheaply."

"Who's going to abuse you? Hurry up and sell it. I need money right away."

"There's another thing I wanted to say, sir. When you've got the silver, I hope you'll put it to good use. It's a pity to sell your property, if you're only going to give hundreds and thousands of taels away for no reason."

"Have you seen me give silver away for no reason? You want to get something out of it, I know; but you can stow all that hypocritical talk. Be off with you now!"

"I was only making a suggestion," said Whiskers Wang.

Upon leaving the room, the steward whispered to Ting-hsi:

"Good! There's hope for you. I'm going to the dyke now to sell some land, and when I come back I'll think up a plan for you."

Whiskers Wang returned several days later having sold the land for one thousand and several hundred taels, which he brought home in a small bag.

"This is only ninety-five percent pure silver, sir," he reported to his master. "It was weighed by the market balance, which gives thirteen and a half cents less to the tael than the official balance. And he deducted twenty-three taels forty cents for the middleman there, while the witnesses to the contract took another twenty to thirty taels. We had to foot both those bills. Here is the silver, sir. Let me fetch the scales so that you can weigh it."

"Who's got the patience to listen to your fiddling accounts! Since the silver's here, why weigh it? Take it aside and have done with it!"

"I simply wanted to make it clear," said the steward.

Now that Tu Shao-ching had this silver, he called Mr. Lou's grandson to the library.

"Are you leaving tomorrow?" he asked.

"Yes, sir. Grandfather told me to go."

"I have a hundred taels of silver here for you, but you mustn't let your grandfather know about it. You have a widowed mother to keep; so take this silver home and set up in some small business which can support you both. If your grandfather recovers and your second uncle is able to leave, I shall give him a hundred taels too."

Delighted, Mr. Lou's grandson took the silver and concealed it on his person, then thanked the young master. The next day, when he took his leave, Mr. Lou would not let him be given more than thirty cents of silver for the road. When Tu Shao-ching returned from seeing him off, he found a countryman standing in the hall who knelt down and kowtowed as soon as he saw the young master.

"Aren't you Huang Ta, who looks after our ancestral temple?" asked Tu. "What are you doing here?"

"I used to live in a cottage by the ancestral temple which your father bought me," replied Huang Ta. "After all these years the place needed repairing, and I made bold to take some dead trees from your graveyard to replace the beams and pillars. But some gentlemen of your family found out, and said I'd stolen the trees. They thrashed me within an inch of my life, and sent a dozen stewards to my cottage to take back the trees, who pulled down even those parts which were all right before. Now I've nowhere to live; so I've come to beg you to speak to your clan, sir, and ask them to give me a little money for repairs from the communal fund, so that I can go on living there."

"My clan!" exclaimed Tu. "It's no use speaking to them. If my father bought you the cottage, it's obviously up to me to repair it. Since it's in ruins, how much will you need to build a new one?"

"A new one would cost a hundred taels. If I make do by repairing it, forty to fifty taels should be enough."

"Very well," said Tu. "I'm short of money at the moment, so just take fifty taels. When that's spent you can come back."

He fetched fifty taels for Huang Ta, who took the silver and left.

Then the gate-keeper came in with two cards.

"The third Mr. Tsang invites you to a feast tomorrow, sir," he announced. "This other card is to ask Mr. Pao to go along too."

"Tell the messenger to give my compliments to the third master," said Tu. "I will certainly go."

The next day he went with Pao Ting-hsi to Tsang's house. Tsang Liao-chai had prepared a good meal, and he invited Tu very respectfully to be seated and poured him wine, after which they chatted at random. Towards the end of the meal Tsang filled a cup with wine, raised it high in both hands and walked round the table to bow and present the cup to Tu. Then he knelt down.

"Brother!" he said. "I have a favour to ask."

With a start, Tu hastily set the wine on the table and knelt down to take Tsang's arm.

"Are you out of your mind, Third Brother?" he demanded. "What do you mean by this?"

"I won't get up till you've drunk that cup and promised to help me."

"I don't know what you're talking about. Get up and tell me."

Ting-hsi also tried to raise Tsang to his feet.

"Will you promise?" asked Tsang.

"Of course!" replied Tu.

"Then drink this cup of wine."

"I will drink it in a minute."

"I'm waiting for you to drain it."

Only then did Tsang stand up and resume his seat.

"Go ahead with whatever you have to say," prompted Tu.

"The examiner is at Luchow now, and it will be our turn next. The other day I tried to buy a licentiate's degree for someone, and paid the examiner's agent three hundred taels of silver. But later he told me: 'Our superiors are very strict, and I dare not sell this degree. Let me sell you a salaried scholar's rank instead, since you have already passed the preliminary test.' So I gave him my own name, and that is how I became a salaried scholar this year. But now the man who wanted to buy the licentiate's degree is demanding his money back; and if I don't return him three hundred taels, the whole business will be made public. This is a matter of life and death! You must help me, brother! If you will lend me three hundred taels of the money you got for your land to settle this business, I'll pay you back gradually. You promised just now to help."

"Pah!" exclaimed Tu. "I thought you were in real trouble when it was nothing but this all the time! You didn't have to put on such an act—kowtowing and pleading—for such a trifle! I'll give you the silver tomorrow."

"Well said!" cried Ting-hsi, clapping his hands. "Let's have large cups to drink to this!"

At once large cups were brought, and they drank until Tu was tipsy.

"Tell me, Third Brother," he said, "what made you so set on this salaried scholar's rank?"

"You wouldn't understand!" retorted Tsang. "A salaried scholar has a better chance of passing the next examination, and once you pass that you become an official. Even if you don't pass, after a dozen years you become a senior licentiate, and when you've taken the palace examination you'll be appointed a magistrate or a judge. Then I shall wear boots with knotted soles, hold court, pass sentence and have people beaten. And if gentlemen like you come to raise the wind, I'll have you locked up and fed on beancurd for a month, till you choke to death!"

"You ruffian!" cried Tu with a laugh. "You are utterly contemptible!"

"What a joke!" chuckled Ting-hsi. "You two gentlemen should each drain a cup after that."

Later that evening they parted.

The next morning Tu told Whiskers Wang to take a casket of silver over, and the steward received another six taels as his tip. On his way back he stopped at the fish shop for a bowl of noodles, and found Chang Chun-min there.

"Come over here, Mr. Whiskers, and sit with me!" called the doctor.

Whiskers Wang went over to his table, and when the noodles were brought started eating.

"I want you to do something for me," said Chang.

"What is it? Do you want a present because you've cured old Lou?"

"No, old Lou's disease is incurable."

"How much longer has he got?"

"Not more than a hundred days, probably. But you needn't tell him that. I want you to do something for me."

"Go on."

"The examiner will soon be here, and my son wants to take the examination; but I'm afraid the college authorities will say I'm an outsider. I'd like your young master to speak to them."

"That's no use." Whiskers Wang made a sign of dissent. "Our young master has never had anything to do with that lot. And he doesn't like to hear of people sitting for the examinations. If you ask him that, he'll advise you not to enter the boy!"

"What's to be done then?"

"There *is* a way. I'll tell Mr. Tu your son isn't allowed to sit; but the examination school in Fengyang was built by our young master's father, and if Mr. Tu wants to send in a candidate, who's to stop him? That'll goad him into doing something for you—he'll be willing even to spend money!"

"Handle it as you think best, Whiskers. If you pull it off, I'll not fail to thank you."

"As if I wanted thanks from you! Your son is my nephew. I'll be quite satisfied if he kowtows a few times to his old uncle when he's entered the college and is wearing a brand-new square cap and blue gown!"

This said, Chang Chun-min paid for the noodles and they left.

Whiskers Wang went home and asked the servants: "Where is the young master?"

"In the library," was the answer.

He went straight to the library, where he found Tu Shao-ching.

"I delivered the silver to the third Mr. Tsang," announced the steward. "He is very grateful to you, sir. He says you've saved him from serious trouble, and made it possible for him to become an official. Nobody else would be willing to do such a thing."

"A mere trifle," said Tu. "Why come here and gabble about it?"

"I've something else to report, sir," said the steward. "You've paid for Mr. Tsang's degree, and built a cottage for the caretaker of the ancestral temple. Very soon now the examinations are going to be held, and they'll be asking you to repair the examination school. Your father spent thousands of taels building that school, but other people have had all the advantages of it. If you were to send in a candidate, who would dare oppose him?"

"Candidates can enter themselves. Why should I send one?"

"If I had a son and you sent him in, would they dare say anything?"

"Of course not. Those college scholars are no better than slaves themselves."

"The son of Dr. Chang at the back gate has been studying. Why don't you tell him to sit for the examination?"

"Does he want to?"

"His father is an outsider—he dares not enter."

"Tell him to enter. If any scholar says anything, tell the fellow I sent him."

"Very good, sir."

With this, Whiskers Wang left.

Mr. Lou's illness was taking a turn for the worse, and Tu Shao-ching, who had invited a second physician to attend him, stayed at home in low spirits.

One day Tsang called.

"Have you heard the news?" he asked, without waiting to sit down. "Magistrate Wang is in trouble. Yesterday evening they took away his seal, and his successor is pressing him to move out of the yamen.[4] But because everyone says he is a corrupt official, no one will put him up. He's at his wit's end!"

"What is he doing?"

"He just stayed in the yamen last night. But if he doesn't move out tomorrow, he'll be in for a big loss of face! Who's going to lend him rooms, though? He'll have to move into the Old Men's Home!"

"Really?"

Tu ordered the servant to fetch Whiskers Wang.

"I want you to go at once to the yamen," he said, "and ask the attendants to inform Magistrate Wang that if he has nowhere to say, he is welcome to come here. He needs rooms badly—hurry up!"

The steward hastened off.

"You refused to meet him before," said Tsang. "What makes you offer him accommodation today? Just think, you may find yourself involved in his trouble; and if there's a riot the mob may destroy your garden!"

"Everybody knows the good my father did for this district," replied Tu. "Even if I hid bandits here, no one would break into my house. Don't worry about that, brother. As for this Mr. Wang, it's lucky for him he knew enough to respect me. To have called on him the other day would have been making up to the local magistrate; but now that he's been removed from office and has nowhere to live, it's my duty to help him. When he receives my message, he's sure to come. Wait till he arrives, and you can talk to him."

Just then the gate-keeper came in to announce: "Dr. Chang is here."

Chang Chun-min walked in, knelt down and kowtowed.

"What is it this time?" asked Tu.

"It's about this business of my son taking the examination, sir. I'm extremely grateful to you."

"I have already promised to help."

"When the scholars knew it was your wish, sir, they had no objections, but they insisted that I raise a hundred and twenty taels to help repair the

[4]Headquarters of a public official or department.

college; and where can I get so much money? That's why I've come to beg your help, sir."

"Will a hundred and twenty be enough? You won't need more later?"

"I won't need any more."

"That's easy. I'll pay it for you. All you have to do is write an application to enter the college, promising to contribute towards the repairs, and bring it here. You take it to the college for him, Third Brother. You can get the silver here."

"I am busy today," said Tsang to the doctor. "I'll go with you tomorrow."

Having expressed his thanks, Chang Chun-min left. The next moment Whiskers Wang came flying in.

"Magistrate Wang has come to call!" he announced. "He's at the gate and has left his chair."

Tu and Tsang went out to meet him. The magistrate was wearing a gauze cap and the clothes of a private citizen. He came in and bowed.

"I have long wished to make your acquaintance, sir, but lacked the opportunity," he said. "It is exceedingly good of you to put me up in your distinguished residence during my present difficulties, and I feel ashamed to trespass on your hospitality; I have therefore come to express my thanks before profiting more fully by your instructions. It is lucky my friend Tsang is here too!"

"A trifle like this is beneath Your Honour's notice," replied Tu. "Since my poor house is empty, I hope you will move in at your earliest convenience."

"I came here to ask my friend to call with me on my patron," said Tsang. "I little thought my patron would honour us first with a visit."

"Don't mention it!" said the magistrate.

He bowed his way to his chair, then left.

Tu Shao-ching kept Tsang, and gave him a hundred and twenty taels to settle Dr. Chang's business the following day; and Tsang took the silver home with him. The next day Magistrate Wang moved in. And the day after that Chang Chun-min gave a feast in Tu's house, to which Tsang and Ting-hsi were also invited.

"It's time for you to speak up," said Whiskers Wang to Ting-hsi in private. "According to my calculations, he'll soon reach the end of that silver; and if anyone else comes to ask for money, there'll be none left for you. You must speak this evening."

By this time all the guests had arrived, and the feast was laid in the library by the hall. The four of them went to the table; but before taking his seat Chang Chun-min offered a cup of wine to Tu Shao-ching to express his gratitude, then filled another cup and bowed his thanks to Tsang. During the meal they chatted at random. Then Ting-hsi addressed Tu.

"I have been here for half a year, sir, and seen you spend money like water," he said. "Even the tailor carried handfuls of silver away. But in my seven or eight months here I've had nothing but a little meat and wine—not a copper have I seen. Why should I carry on with this thankless job, getting nothing for my pains? I'd better wipe my eyes and go somewhere else to weep. I will take my leave of you tomorrow."

"Why didn't you mention this earlier, Mr. Pao?" asked Tu. "How could I know you had this on your mind? You should have spoken out."

Ting-hsi hastily filled a cup and passed it to him.

"My father and I both made a living by managing an opera company," he said. "Unhappily my father died, and instead of proving a credit to the old man I lost my capital. I have an old mother, yet I can't support her. I am the most miserable of men, unless the young master will give me some capital to take home so that I can provide for my mother."

"How admirable that an actor should show such filial piety!" exclaimed Tu. "Of course I will help you!"

Ting-hsi stood up.

"Thank you, sir, for your goodness!" he said.

"Sit down," replied Tu. "How much money do you need?"

Ting-hsi glanced at Whiskers Wang, who was standing at the foot of the table, and the steward stepped forward.

"You'll need a good deal of silver, Mr. Pao," he said. "It'll cost you five to six hundred taels I should think to get together a company and buy costumes. The young master doesn't have so much here. All he can do is give you a few dozen taels to take back across the river, and you can make a start with that."

"A few dozen taels is not enough," said Tu. "I'll give you a hundred taels to start training a company. When that's finished, you can come back again."

Ting-hsi knelt down and thanked him.

"I would have done more for you before letting you go," said Tu, stopping him, but Mr. Lou is seriously ill, and I have to be ready for any emergency."

Tsang and Chang praised Tu's generosity, and soon the party broke up.

Mr. Lou's illness was becoming daily more serious.

"My friend," he said one day, when Tu was sitting at his bedside, "I hoped I might recover, but now it doesn't look as if I shall, and I want you to send me home."

"I have not been able to do all I should for you, uncle," said Tu. "How can you speak of going home?"

"Don't be foolish! I have sons and grandsons; and though I've spent my life away from home, it's natural now to want to go home to die. No one's going to accuse you of turning me out."

"In that case I won't keep you," said Tu with tears in his eyes. "I've prepared your coffin, uncle; but now you won't be needing it, and it's not easy to take. So I'll give you a few dozen taels instead with which to buy another. The clothes and bedding are all ready, and you can take them with you."

"I will take the coffin and clothes, but don't give any more silver to my sons and grandsons. I want to leave within the next three days, and since I can't sit up I'll have to be carried in a litter. Tomorrow go to your father's shrine and inform his spirit that Mr. Lou wishes to take his leave and go home. I have been with your family for thirty years, as one of your worthy father's closest friends; and since his death your treatment of me has left nothing to be desired. Your conduct and learning are unparalleled; and your son in particular is a boy of extraordinary promise—you must bring him up to be an honest man. You are not a good manager, however, and don't make the right friends; so you will soon come to the end of your property! I like to see you acting in a just and generous manner, but you must consider with whom you are dealing. The way you are going on, all your money is being trickled out of you by people who will never repay your kindness; and while we say charity expects no reward, you should distinguish between those who deserve help and those who don't. The third Mr. Tsang and Chang Chun-min, of whom you see so much, are unscrupulous characters. And recently this Pao Ting-hsi has joined them. There are no good men among players, yet you want to be his patron. As for your steward, Whiskers Wang, he's even worse! Money is of small account, and after I'm dead you and your son must imitate your noble father in everything. If you have virtue, it doesn't matter even if you go hungry. Your closest friend is your cousin Shen-ching; but though Shen-ching is brilliant you can't trust him too far. Imitate your worthy father, and you won't go wrong. Since you set no store by officials or by your own family, this is no place for you. Nanking is a great metropolis, and there you may find friends to appreciate your talent and be able to achieve something. What's left of your property won't last long! If you take my advice, I shall die happy!"

"I shall remember all your excellent advice, uncle," replied Tu with tears in his eyes.

He went out immediately and ordered his men to hire four bearers to carry Mr. Lou to Taohung by way of Nanking, then gave Mr. Lou's son over a hundred taels to take home for his father's funeral. On the third day, he saw Mr. Lou off on his journey.

FURTHER READINGS

Ichisada Miyazaki, *China's Examination Hell*, trans. Conrad Schirokauer (New York: John Weatherhill, 1976), and Chung-li Chang, *The Chinese Gentry: Studies on Their Role in Nineteenth-Century Chinese Society* (Seattle: University of Washington Press, 1967), are useful studies of the Chinese civil service examination system and the gentry-official system it created. Tung-tsu Ch'u, *Local Government in China under the Ch'ing* (Stanford, CA: Stanford University Press, 1969), covers the duties of the various local officials of Ch'ing China. A strikingly different perspective on Ch'ing China is provided by Jonathan Spence, *The Death of Woman Wang* (New York: Penguin, 1979).

Timothy C. Wong, *Wu Ching-tzu* (Boston: Twayne, 1978), provides a useful analysis of *The Scholars* as a satire, focusing on cultural and literary factors. Robert S. Hegel, *The Novel in Seventeenth-Century China* (New York: Columbia University Press, 1981), examines the influence of seventeenth-century novels in shaping later Ch'ing fiction, *The Scholars,* and *The Dream of the Red Chamber* in particular. Also helpful in understanding the development of the Chinese novel is William Theodore de Bary, Wing-tsit Chan, and Burton Watson, *Sources of Chinese Tradition* (New York: Columbia University Press, 1960). C. T. Hsia, *The Classic Chinese Novel* (New York: Columbia University Press, 1968), is a study of six major Chinese novels, including *The Scholars.*

PART III

Discussion Questions

1. Good manners are sometimes called the cement that binds society together. In *The Dream of the Red Chamber*, how does the elaborate code of conduct act to reduce family frictions? What effect do strong-willed and direct individuals have on family harmony? What are some modern forms of good manners and proper conduct, and how do they act to reduce friction and promote harmony? Should a greater emphasis be placed on good manners in today's society? Why or why not?

2. In *The Dream of the Red Chamber,* Pao-yu is presented as a spoiled and ill-mannered youth. From what attitude of his did his lack of manners spring? We might consider his attitudes admirable, but does that excuse his lack of proper conduct? In the same work, Hsueh Pan is also presented as a spoiled and ill-mannered youth. How do his bad manners differ from those of Pao-yu, and why? Are good manners simply a social convention, or are they the necessary first step of self-discipline leading towards responsible social conduct?

3. In *The Treasury of Loyal Retainers*, how does Yuranosuke play on the difference between "proper manners" and "proper conduct?" Is the play saying that proper manners and proper conduct are two different things, and that only individuals of great principle can appreciate this distinction? What do you think? What is the difference between manners and conduct?

4. The distinction between love and physical desire is difficult to make. In *The Dream of the Red Chamber*, the Goddess of Disillusionment attempts to teach that distinction to Pao-yu. What is the difference according to the

Goddess? Can there be such a thing as love between a man and woman, or is the Goddess saying that the only real love is a concern for the welfare of humankind?

5. In *The Treasury of Loyal Retainers*, Yuranosuke tries to convince Heiemon that duty is the responsibility of those who are richer and more powerful. Heiemon argues that duty weighs equally upon all. Is Heiemon's position valid and, if so, how important an idea is this? Replace the word "duty" with "civic responsibility." Should civic responsibility bear equally upon all, or should the greater obligation of defending and preserving society be borne by those who have benefitted the most from society?

6. When speaking of justice, Aristotle says that different degrees of merit must be rewarded proportionately, not equally. In this sense, how is the behavior of Pao-yu, in *The Dream of the Red Chamber*, and Tu Shao-ch'ing, in *The Scholars*, unjust? If their behavior is unjust, is it not also antisocial?

7. Both *Hagakure* and *The Treasury of Loyal Retainers* deal extensively with the ideas of loyalty and duty. What are their views of the origins and importance of duty? Why does it make any difference to Yuranosuke and his fellow conspirators that they kill the man who was the cause of their leader's death? Does their vengeance do society any real good? If not, why do the Japanese so revere the memory of the forty-seven ronin? *Kanehira* had done his duty and avenged his lord's death before he himself was killed, and cannot understand why his spirit has not found peace but is still wandering the world. Can you tell him why he is in such a plight?

8. Wang Yang-ming, in *Inquiring on the Great Learning*, holds that "Knowledge is the beginning of action, action is the completion of knowledge." What does he mean by this? How would he assess the conduct of Tu Ch'ao-ching in *The Scholars*? How would K'ung Fu-tzu, in *The Analects* (Part I), evaluate the conduct of Tu? In terms of "proper conduct," who is the better Confucian "gentleman," Tu Ch'ao-ching or Mr. Lou, his librarian?

9. There are certain traits of character often called "the martial virtues," such as loyalty and courage, that are particularly valued in a warlike society. Consider those selections that set standards of warrior excellence, such as the *Bhagavad Gita* (Part I), *Kanehira*, *Hagakure*, and *The Treasury of Loyal Retainers*. Are there any similarities among the virtues they present? Attempt to list the virtues of the warrior in various cultures over the ages. Are there significant differences, or are the variations merely incidental? How do we regard these virtues today? Do our film and television heroes differ markedly from the heroes of the past? Why or why not?

10. There would appear to be a tendency within a pluralistic society to combine and harmonize disparate cultural elements, but this often seems to be the

result of the conscious efforts of political or intellectual leaders. Akbar, in *Akbar Nama*, attempted to create a single religion common for all; the poet Kabir, in the *Songs of Kabir*, blended various religious elements; and *The Sacred Songs of the Sikhs* are hymns of a syncretic religion. What was the value of these efforts, and how successful were they? Why do such initiatives so often seem to fail? If traditions are actually the creation of human beings, why do human beings find them so hard to change? Does tradition have a life of its own, apart from the people who belong to it?

11. Women are not emphasized in most of the selections of this part, except for *The Dream of the Red Chamber*. *The Dream* presents women at three different levels: a realistic view of women within the family compound of a numerous kindred, women as the source of sexual desire, and women as a transcendent source of disillusionment that leads men to a mature and responsible view of society and one's obligations to it. To what extent are these different views of women merely symbols of childhood, puberty, and maturity? To what extent is Okaru, in *The Treasury of Loyal Retainers*, presented as an individual and to what extent is she really a variation of the themes of degradation, loyalty, and readiness to die that characterize the forty-seven ronin? How can one tell when an author is attempting to describe real women, and when he is using the idea of women as a symbol or portraying a woman merely as a means of pointing up the character of the protagonist? Was the latter the case in Dandin's *The Perfect Bride*, in Part II? How accurately do modern authors portray women? Are their shortcomings the result of ignorance or simply because they don't really care about the true character of women?

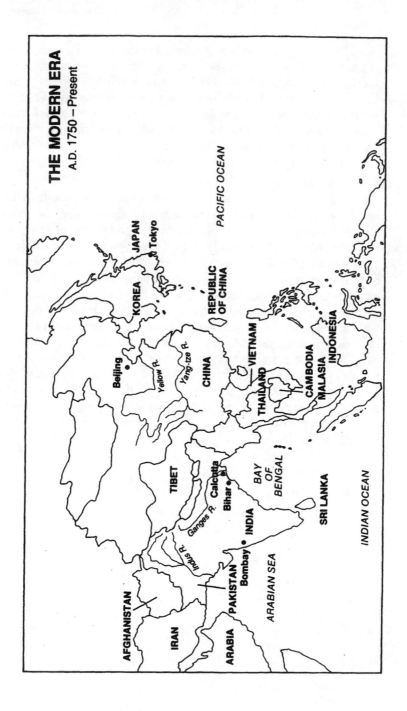

THE MODERN ERA
A.D. 1750 – Present

PACIFIC OCEAN

JAPAN
Tokyo

KOREA

REPUBLIC
OF CHINA

Beijing

Yellow R.

Yang-tze R.

CHINA

VIETNAM

THAILAND

CAMBODIA

MALASIA

INDONESIA

TIBET

Calcutta

Bihar

Ganges R.

BAY
OF
BENGAL

INDIA

Bombay

SRI LANKA

Indus R.

PAKISTAN

AFGHANISTAN

IRAN

ARABIA

ARABIAN SEA

INDIAN OCEAN

PART IV

Modernization and Tradition

Harmony in a New Era: 1750 to the Present

The last of the great European struggles for leadership in empire building was fought out in the Seven Years' War (1756–1765). Hostilities were carried to every part of the world in what eventually became the first global conflict. The main participants were England and France, and the prize was domination of the world's sea-lanes. Great Britain emerged victorious, and it was British trade and diplomacy that led Western influences in Asia for the next two centuries.

India was the first to feel the effect of Britain's hard-won supremacy. The East India Company, founded in 1600 to pursue Asian commerce, drove the French from their trading stations and seized control of the kingdom of Bihar. Now a land power in India for the first time, the Company began using its private army to control the balance of power among the various Indian states. It also initiated a policy of recruiting and training mercenary soldiers, local administrators, and managerial assistants from among the Indian population. This policy led to the creation of a class of progressive and articulate Indians. Ram Mohan Roy was such an anglicized Indian, and his *On the Burning of Widows* demonstrates the willingness of this Westernized group to question the validity of outmoded Indian values and customs. In the course of time, such British-educated Indians would play a significant role in the modernization of their country, but Ram Roy and his generation had little real influence over the course of political and military events. By 1825, the Company controlled much of India directly, and still more through client princes dependent upon the British for protection. The Company seized Sri Lanka and Malasia, and Britain controlled the passage to East Asia as surely as had Portugal three centuries earlier. In India itself, any possibility of a strong Muslim or Indian state had vanished, and the Company undertook the administration of the country.

Commerce was still Britain's first order of business, however, and great profits were realized from Chinese exports. Chinese exports exceeded British and Indian imports, however, and British merchants were forced to make up the difference in silver, a situation that created a general shortage of hard money for them. The British traders and their Indian partners developed an ingenious scheme to compensate for this disadvantage. They began to cultivate poppies in

India and ship opium to China, where its production was forbidden and where it consequently could be sold at high prices for hard cash. The British and Indian merchants were, of course, interested in expanding this lucrative market even though this entailed increasing the number of Chinese addicts. The Chinese authorities naturally attempted to halt this criminal trade, and Lien Tse-hsu, in *A Letter of Admonition to Queen Victoria*, presented a dignified plea to the British to conduct themselves in a humane manner and abandon their barbarous business. The British merchants, however, called for military and naval support to protect their markets and profits. In the Opium Wars of 1840–1842, the British destroyed Chinese navies, routed Chinese armies, and seized strategic positions all along the coast. An absolute European superiority in military technology had been forcibly demonstrated, and from this point on, the Chinese were on the defensive in their relations with the West.

While the Asian nations had turned inward, an Industrial Revolution had begun in Europe. Steam power and improved steel metallurgy had made possible ships with rapid-firing cannon that could sail Asian waters at will and ascend rivers into the interior with impunity. Steam-driven machinery and the factory system had increased Europe's productive capacity many-fold, outstripping its supply of raw materials and flooding its internal markets. In an earlier age, European merchants had sought Asian products in exchange for whatever they could sell; now they wanted to buy cheap raw materials and sell expensive manufactured goods. Western needs, if they could not be controlled, were such as to lead to the elimination of the middle classes of Asia, the creation of an ever-larger pool of cheap unskilled workers, and the draining of Asia's wealth. Furthermore, a flood of Western goods and Western management of Asia's natural resources would inevitably spell the end of the Asian nations' independence and cultural identities.

China seemed unable to meet this new threat. Many of its administrators and intellectuals seemed to be dwelling in the past. Shen Fu, in *The Sorrows of Misfortune*, shows how little Chinese life and customs had changed from Ming times, and how little room there seemed to be in Chinese society for the encouragement of individual initiative. At about the same time, the Vietnamese poet-administrator Nguyen Du chose a theme from a Ming novel for his national epic, *The Tale of Kieu*, which concludes that, in the end, even the exceptional individual is restricted by traditional conventions. In many ways this regard for the past and neglect of the present was a reflection of the attitude of the imperial government as a whole. A self-seeking and negligent administration had allowed the economic infrastructure of the country to decay even while a rapidly increasing population placed greater demands and reliance on those facilities. Canals became clogged, the dikes of the Yellow River were not maintained, and roads and bridges went unrepaired. Absentee landlordism and a corrupt administration added to the suffering of the peasant masses. Famines and floods soon devastated the country. After 1850, a series of peasant rebellions in protest of these intolerable conditions swept China, and the Manchu dynasty was able to survive only when the class of scholar-administrators rallied to its support. The Europeans took advantage of an imperial government scarcely able to manage its own affairs. Western missionaries of all sects established themselves throughout the land, the Chinese were forced to sign disadvantageous treaties, and the British took over several significant imperial administrative functions. Other Western nations soon moved in "to open up the East." Among them was France, who, in 1858, began its occupation of Vietnam.

The United States also played a role in this process. An American fleet of steam-assisted warships visited Tokyo harbor in 1853 and 1854. The Japanese government understood the significance of the power being displayed to them and agreed to open the nation for trade. Many were violently opposed to exposing Japanese society to foreigners once again, and civil war broke out. The rule of the shogun was ended, and the emperor was restored to power after almost seven hundred years of military rule. The emperor Meiji (1868–1912) took over direct rule of the country and embarked on a rapid and thorough program of Westernization aimed at preserving Japanese independence and interests. Industrialization soon allowed Japan to build up a military force on the Western model, and students were sent all over the world to study Western institutions, science, commerce, and industry. The selections from Natsume Soseki's superb Western-style novel, *Kokoro* (1914), show how quickly this policy allowed the Japanese to match Western standards even in such well-established Western cultural forms as the novel. Native traditions were ignored or even ridiculed during this hectic period, but the basic elements of Japanese culture never lost their force and constantly acted to harmonize these new influences with Japanese traditional values.

As the Company extended its telegraph lines and railways deep into the interior, India found it much harder than Japan to accept Westernization. When British power began to extend down to the village level of Indian life, both Hindus and Muslims began to fear not only the loss of political power but even the loss of their own sense of identity. In 1857, this apprehension reached a critical stage among the native troops (*sepoys*) of the Company's army, who became convinced that the British intended to force them to become Christians. A general mutiny followed, and the British were hard-pressed to control the situation. When order had been restored, the East India Company was dissolved, and the British government took over direct administration of its territories and concessions. Numerous reforms were instituted, and native

Indians were brought into the governmental and judicial systems. In this fashion, the class of anglicized Indians, both Muslim and Hindu, continued to grow and increased its admiration and support of British rule. In 1877, Victoria of England was proclaimed empress of India. While some Indians resented their loss of independence and the expanding role of English customs in Indian life, many others looked forward to the advantages they hoped to gain through membership in the world's greatest community of nations.

The Chinese government, at the same time, was faced with its own difficult choice. Were it to pursue Westernization in the Japanese fashion, its people might very well lose respect for tradition as many of the Japanese had. On the other hand, without Western technology, it would be swept under by foreign powers anxious to divide the country among themselves. The imperial administration adopted a middle road by attempting to modernize the military alone and began constructing a small but promising modern navy. In 1894, however, this navy met the new Japanese fleet and was destroyed. China's ignominious defeat in the Sino-Japanese war of 1894–1895 led to a new wave of Western encroachments. Russia, France, Germany, and Japan all forced concessions of large tracts of Chinese territory from a paralyzed imperial administration. A sense of desperation swept the country, and the emperor turned to a policy of full Westernization with the assistance of a group of reformers led by K'ang Yu-Wei, whose justification of his seeming desertion of the Confucian tradition appears in the selection *Confucius as a Social Reformer*. A period of radical reform in 1898 brought about a fierce reaction. The emperor was imprisoned, and the government taken over by the conservative and traditionalist Empress Dowager. An anti-foreign movement known as the Boxers (Society of Harmonious Fists) received official approval and carried out a deadly persecution of Westerners. As a consequence, Western troops entered China, defeated the Chinese armies who opposed them, and took control of the capital of Peking. The imperial government was further weakened, having been humiliated in the eyes of its own people as well as those of the world at large.

From the mid-nineteenth century on, nationalist movements sprang up virtually all over the world, partly in response to the fact that the economic dominance of the great powers was so easily converted into a cultural imperialism that threatened the basic institutions and very sense of identity of less highly industrialized peoples. It is not surprising, therefore, to see nationalist movements arising in the Asian nations, since nationalism appeared to many to be an important attribute of those people, such as the Japanese, who were succeeding in maintaining their political and economic independence. The first of these Asian movements to meet with any success was the revolutionary program organized by Sun Yat-sen. When rebellion broke out in China in 1911, Sun was able to step forward and proclaim the Chinese republic. Within this new republic, energetic steps were taken towards reform and modernization. Traditional Chinese values and institutions were questioned, with one of the more sweeping attacks appearing in Lu Hsun's short story, *Diary of a Madman*, in which he condemns China's entire history as having been a nightmare of the victimization of the individual.

In 1914, after a century of relative peace and steady growth, a world war broke out among the European powers. The entire affair severely shook the confidence of Europeans in their own institutions and values. Once having gotten them engaged in conflict, their leaders seemed unable to extricate them, and, over a period of four years, thirty million men and women were killed in what appeared to many to have been a meaningless and avoidable struggle. The empires of Germany, Russia, and Austria-Hungary fell, and the economies of even the victorious nations were so severely strained that they found it difficult to resume their old trading patterns. A general malaise affected Europe and was expressed in the shallow values and frenetic activity of the "jazz age" as well as in the rise of new and radical political systems such as communism and fascism. The Europeans found it difficult to resume their former confident and forceful attitude towards the rest of the world.

At the same time, the rest of the world had seen that Western values were not flawless. Each of the major Asian nations now had new reasons to struggle for sovereignty and independence. Japan had entered the war on the side of England and had swept the Germans from the Pacific Ocean, seizing their island possessions and Chinese concessions and adding them to Korea (annexed in 1910) as territories of a Japanese empire. Japan was strong and growing stronger and used that strength to expand its empire yet further. Exhilarated by Japanese victories, some young nationalists began considering institutional reforms that would further increase national strength and will, thus better preparing the country for what many had begun to consider its historic mission of dominating all of East Asia. Kita Ikki's *Outline for the Reconstruction of Japan* suggests the construction of a socialist nation; what Japan soon developed, however, was a militarized and semi-fascist one. China fell into a period of civil war (1920–1926), but had in the Kuomintang party and its modern army the tools of nationalism and found that the European powers were prepared to give way before these forces. The Chinese were able to resume their process of modernization— a process that included the continued questioning of possibly outmoded institutions. An example of this process is provided by selections from Pa Chin's novel *Family* (1931), which address the injustices and repression of the extended family system that had for so long formed a basic institution of Chinese life. Meanwhile, Indians had found that, although they were to enjoy the obligations of

British imperial subjects, British racism would not allow them to enjoy equal rights within the empire. In the midst of general disappointment, particularly among the humiliated anglicized class, India found a nationalist leader in Mohandas Gandhi (1869–1948), who not only understood the political realities of the times but had an uncanny grasp of the strengths and weaknesses of Indian society. In *Hind Swaraj*, Gandhi had proposed a national movement of passive resistance to British rule, aimed at achieving the goals of political independence, economic self-sufficiency, and cultural integrity. The British found it increasingly more difficult to rule a noncooperative India and, as Gandhi had correctly gauged, lacked the will to apply the massive force necessary to reestablish their dominance there. One perspective on the movement for national independence, and Gandhi's role in it, is provided by R. K. Narayan in his novel *Waiting for the Mahatma*.

World War II (1939–1945) further sapped the ability of the European powers to maintain their empires, and, throughout the 1950s and 1960s, those empires were relinquished. Britain did so relatively gracefully; in August 1947, the British flag was lowered, and that of India raised. The united India desired by Gandhi was not possible, however, because of traditional antipathies among the Indians themselves, and the Muslim portions of the land became the separate nation of Pakistan. What had been lost in political power, however, had been compensated for by the increased cultural homogeneity of the two states. The first twelve years of India's experience with independence is reviewed by Jawaharlal Nehru, the nation's first leader, in the selection *What is India?* He reflects here on his nation's effort to establish an identity that would conform to the necessities of the modern world while still preserving the essential qualities of national heritage.

France was less graceful in retiring from its empire and, in Vietnam, attempted to crush the independence movement led by Ho Chi Minh but failed (1945–1954). In his *Declaration of Independence*, Ho Chi Minh deliberately appealed to American values in an attempt to enlist the moral aid of the United States, but to no avail. America attempted to prevent the unification of North and South Vietnam but after a long and bloody conflict marked by the determination and readiness to sacrifice of the Vietnamese people, was forced to withdraw, leaving a nationalist Communist regime behind.

Communism also triumphed in China after a long and bitter struggle between the Chinese and their Japanese invaders (1937–1945) and a subsequent civil war (1945–1949) between the Communist forces of Mao Tse-tung and the Nationalist armies of Ch'iang Kai-shek. The peasants of the land, burdened by a century of strife and unrest, and oppressed by an antiquated and unjust landholding system, rallied to the cause of the Communists, who promised a more equitable order of things. Many had questions about what the Communists actually intended to do once in power—questions that Mao answered in his speech *On the People's Democratic Dictatorship.*

Japan was defeated in World War II and, for the first time in a thousand years of its history, suffered foreign occupation. The shock of these events contributed to a reorganization and redirection of Japanese life as thorough and rapid as the Meiji reforms a century before. The Japanese rejected territorial and military aspirations and threw their energies into economic development. They soon became one of the world's great economic powers, achieving far more through internal development than they could ever had gained through imperial expansion.

The breakup of the Japanese empire liberated Korea. After a devastating civil war between the Communist North and the Westernized South (1950–1954), the country remained divided, with the South avidly pursuing Westernization. The touching short story by O Yongsu, *Bird of Passage,* reflects upon the ravages of war and the indomitable spirit of young South Korea. South Korea did quite well in its modernization; within a single generation the country joined Japan as a major industrial nation.

Much of the history of East Asia during the period after World War II has revolved around the struggle of the Asian nations to industrialize and yet preserve their own cultural identity. By and large, they have succeeded extremely well. The technological and industrial inferiority of Asia is largely a thing of the past. In the process, the Asian nations have developed cultural identities better suited to a new age. Akira Kurosawa's film *Ikiru* (1952) shows this blending of old and new. In a thoroughly modern story, and in a thoroughly modern medium, Kurosawa effectively restates the philosophy of the Ming Confucian scholar, Wang Yang-ming, that "Knowledge is the beginning of conduct, conduct is the completion of knowledge." Old governmental and social institutions may have been discarded, but the best of the past has been preserved. The great cultural achievements of Asian traditions in literature, art, architecture, and the histories of their civilizations continue to be respected and lovingly preserved. One of the great contributions of the Asian nations to the modern world is their demonstration that various approaches to life are possible in an industrial and post-industrial world. It is not necessary that impersonal economic forces and the requirements of technological progress create a uniform and faceless world society. In the complex and diverse world of the future, it will be necessary for every people to understand and appreciate what the others have to offer. Asian history has shown that a people who are too assured of the absolute superiority of their own way of life and who refuse to learn from others will inevitably pay a price for their vanity.

THE SORROWS OF MISFORTUNE
Shen Fu

The examinations for the imperial civil service play an important role in Chinese literature, as is illustrated by *The Scholars* and *The Dream of the Red Chamber*. This is not surprising, for they played an important role in Chinese life. Every three years, young men would attend the local examinations held throughout the land. Here they would be tested on their scholarly knowledge of the traditional classics of literature and on their ability to write gracefully and correctly. Those who received the very highest marks were allowed to proceed to the examinations held in the capital at Peking, where they competed for the two highest degrees. Success at this level qualified the young man for an appointment in the imperial civil service and practically guaranteed the respect and comfort that attended high position. The prize was great, and the examinations were accordingly very competitive. It has been estimated that less than one out of five thousand men ever achieved the highest degrees.

This meant, of course, that there were many more failures than successes. The failures had received an expensive literary education and were, by and large, unfitted for trade. The lucky ones managed to obtain a position as a clerk in the office of one of the district offices. These jobs were poorly paid, were viewed with little respect, and offered scant security. Nevertheless, they were highly prized, because there were many competitors who found it difficult to earn a living in any other way.

Shen Fu was one of these failures. He was born in 1763 in the city of Soochow. His father was an irascible and sometimes tyrannical figure, a clerk who hoped his son would succeed where he had failed. This was not to be. Shen Fu took district examinations in 1778, apparently with little success. He took a job as a government clerk in 1781, but soon quit for some unknown reason. He tried going into business, working with his father, and selling his paintings. It was a hard life. He was often in debt, and more than once he was expelled from his family by his irate father. He finally found a patron and moved to Peking. In 1809, at the age of forty-six, he was writing his autobiography, *Six Records of a Floating Life*. Nothing is known of his life after this date.

The organization of the work is unusual. Rather than simply presenting a chronological account, Shen Fu discussed his life from six topical points of view. Only the first four have survived: "The Joys of the Wedding Chamber," "The Pleasures of Leisure," "The Sorrows of Misfortune," and "The Delights of Roam-

From Shen Fu, *Six Records of a Floating Life*, trans. Leonard Pratt and Chiang Su-Hui (New York: Penguin, 1983), pp. 86–92.

ing Afar." Shen Fu intended to write an autobiography, but he also produced a love story of remarkable tenderness. When he was thirteen, a marriage was arranged between him and a neighbor girl, Chen Yun. The marriage was consummated four years later, in 1780. They shared their life as intellectual partners, playmates, and companions in distress until Yun's death in 1803. When Shen Fu tries to write about his life, he constantly returns to his wife. Discussing miniature gardens, he remembers one he and Yun built together and how they would dream over it. When alluding to a classic author, he repeats a comment his wife made on the work. In short, she was so much a part of his life that he cannot write his autobiography without dwelling on her.

He was not a good husband in many ways. He fell into a drunken stupor and slept through their wedding night. He never provided her with much material comfort. When she was dying and needed medicines, they lacked money to buy them. All he could think of to do was to try to sell paintings; the thought of getting any kind of work possible seems never to have crossed his mind. He made little from his art sales and was unable to provide her with all the medicines she needed. And yet, he remembers all of the times they laughed together, even when times were hard, and how witty, sensitive, and caring she was. Rarely has married love been so tenderly and candidly portrayed.

The selection is taken from *The Sorrows of Misfortune* and narrates Yun's death and its aftermath. Shen Fu is utterly bereft after the loss of his best companion of twenty-three years. On the day that the Chinese believe the spirits of the dead return, Shen Fu seeks out the room where she died, hoping to catch one last glimpse of her, but is disappointed. He continues to try to earn a living, but spends much time at her grave remembering the good times, when they were together.

It is unknown whether Shen Fu was writing for publication or simply to comfort his own spirit, but there is no evidence that *Six Records of a Floating Life* was published during his lifetime. A partial manuscript of the work was discovered in the 1870s, and it has been published many times since then. It is a great favorite with the Chinese public and, with its tragic but tender tale of love, it is deserving of an even wider audience.

Questions

1. Why does Yun believe she is dying?
2. How do you account for the belief of Shen Fu and Yun that too much affection between husband and wife makes for a short marriage?
3. What are Yun's concerns before her death?
4. How did Shen Fu's family support him in his grief?

THE SORROWS OF MISFORTUNE

I returned to find Yun moaning and weeping, looking as if something awful had happened. As soon as she saw me she burst out, 'Did you know that yesterday noon Ah Shuang stole all our things and ran away? I have asked people to search everywhere, but they still have not found him. Losing our things is a small matter, but what of our relationship with our friends? As we were leaving, his mother told me over and over again to take good care of him. I'm terribly worried he's running back home and will have to cross the Great River. And what will we do if his parents have hidden him to blackmail us? How can I face my sworn sister again?'

'Please calm down,' I said. 'You've been worrying about it too much. You can only blackmail someone who has money; with you and me, it's all our four shoulders can do to support our two mouths. Besides, in the half year the boy has been with us, we have given him clothing and shared our food with him. Our neighbours all know we have never once beaten him or scolded him. What's really happened is that the wretched child has ignored his conscience and taken advantage of our problems to run away with our belongings. Your sworn sister at the Huas' gave us a thief. How can you say you cannot face her? It is she who should not be able to face you. What we should do now is report this case to the magistrate, so as to avoid any questions being raised about it in the future.'

After Yun heard me speak, her mind seemed somewhat eased, but from then on she began frequently to talk in her sleep, calling out, 'Ah Shuang has run away!' or 'How could Han-yuan turn her back on me?' Her illness worsened daily.

Finally I was about to call a doctor to treat her, but she stopped me. 'My illness began because of my terribly deep grief over my brother's running away and my mother's death,' said Yun. 'It continued because of my affections, and now it has returned because of my indignation. I have always worried too much about things, and while I have tried my best to be a good daughter-in-law, I have failed.

'These are the reasons why I have come down with dizziness and palpitations of the heart. The disease has already entered my vitals, and there is nothing a doctor can do about it. Please do not spend money on something that cannot help.

'I have been happy as your wife these twenty-three years. You have loved me and sympathized with me in everything, and never rejected me despite my faults. Having had for my husband an intimate friend like you, I have no regrets over this life. I have had warm cotton clothes, enough to eat, and a pleasant home. I have strolled among streams and rocks, at places like the Pavilion of the Waves and the Villa of Serenity. In the midst of life, I have been just like an Immortal. But a true Immortal must go through many incarnations before reaching enlightenment. Who could dare hope to become an Immortal in only one lifetime? In our eagerness for immortality, we have only incurred the wrath of the Creator, and brought on our troubles with our passion. Because you have loved me too much, I have had a short life!'

Later she sobbed and spoke again. 'Even someone who lives a hundred years must still die one day. I am only sorry at having to leave you so suddenly and for so long, halfway through our journey. I will not be able to serve you for all your life, or to see Fengsen's wedding with my own eyes.' When she finished, she wept great tears.

I forced myself to be strong and comforted her saying, 'You have been ill for eight years, and it has seemed critical many times. Why do you suddenly say such heartbreaking things now?'

'I have been dreaming every night that my parents have sent a boat to fetch me,' said Yun. 'When I shut my eyes it feels as if I'm floating, as if I were walking in the midst. Is my spirit leaving me, while only my body remains?'

'That is only because you are upset,' I said, 'If you will relax, drink some medicine, and take care of yourself, you will get better.'

Yun only sobbed again and said, 'If I thought I had the slightest thread of life left in me I would never dare alarm you by talking to you like this. But the road to the next world is near, and if I do not speak to you now there will never be a day when I can.

'It is all because of me that you have lost the affection of your parents and drifted apart from them. Do not worry, for after I die you will be able to regain their hearts. Your parents' springs and autumns are many, and when I die you should return to them quickly. If you cannot take my bones home, it does not matter if you leave my coffin here for a while until you can come for it. I also want you to find someone who is attractive and capable, to serve our parents and bring up my children. If you will do this for me, I can die in peace.

When she had said this a great sad moan forced itself from her, as if she was in an agony of heartbreak.

'If you part from me half way I would never want to take another wife,' I said. 'You know the saying, "One who has seen the ocean cannot desire a stream, and compared with Wu Mountain there are no clouds anywhere."'

Yun then took my hand and it seemed there was something else she wanted to say, but she could only brokenly repeat the two words 'next life.' Suddenly she fell silent and began to pant, her eyes staring into the distance. I called her name a thousand times, but she could not speak. Two streams of agonized tears flowed from her eyes in torrents, until finally her panting grew shallow and her tears dried up. Her spirit vanished in the mist and she began her long journey. This was on the 30th day of the third month in the 7th year of the reign of the Emperor Chia Ching.[1] When it happened there was a solitary lamp burning in the room. I looked up but saw nothing, there was nothing for my two hands to hold, and my heart felt as if it would shatter. How can there be anything greater than my everlasting grief?

My friend Hu Ken-tang loaned me ten golds, and by selling every single thing remaining in the house I put together enough money to give my beloved a proper burial.

Alas! Yun came to this world a woman, but she had the feelings and abilities of a man. After she entered the gate of my home in marriage, I had to rush about daily to earn our clothing and food, there was never enough, but she never once complained. When I was living at home, all we had for entertainment was talk about literature. What a pity that she should have died in poverty and after long illness. And whose fault was it that she did? It was my fault, what else can I say? I would advise all the husbands and wives in the world not to hate one another, certainly, but also not to love too deeply. As it is said, 'An affectionate couple cannot grow old together.' My example should serve as a warning to others.

The Time the Spirits Return is, according to custom, the day on which the ghosts of the recently deceased return for a visit to this world. Everything in the house must be arranged the way it was while they were alive, and, particularly, the old clothes they wore must be put on the bed and their old shoes must be put under it, so the ghost can return and see them. Around Soochow, people call this 'the closing of the eyes.' Some would engage a Taoist priest to perform a ceremony in which the spirit would first be called to the bed and then sent away, and this was called 'welcoming the ghost.' The custom in Hanchiang, however, was to set out wine and food in the room of the deceased, after which everyone would leave the house; this was called 'avoiding the ghost.' Some people had even had things stolen while they were out of the house avoiding the ghost.

My landlord was living with me when the time came for Yun's spirit to return, and he left so as to avoid it. Neighbours told me I should set out food and then go away too, but because I was hoping to catch a glimpse of her spirit when it returned, I gave them only vague answers. Chang Yu-men, who was from my home country, warned me about this: 'People have been possessed after toying with the supernatural. You should accept the existence of spirits and not try this.'

'I am staying in the house precisely because I do believe in them,' I said.

[1]Spring, 1803.

'It is dangerous to risk offending a ghost when it returns. Even if your wife's spirit does come home, there will still be a gulf between the dead and the living, so her spirit may not take shape to accept your welcome in any case. All things considered, you should avoid the ghost rather than risk running foul of it.'

I was, however, beside myself with longing for Yun, and paid him no attention. 'It is fate that determines life and death,' I said firmly. 'If you are that concerned about me, why not keep me company?'

'I will stand guard outside the door,' Chang said. 'If you see anything strange, I can come in as soon as you shout.'

I took a lantern and went into the house. I saw to it that everything was arranged the same way as before, but with the sight and sound of Yun gone I could at first not keep myself from weeping sadly. Yet I was afraid that tears would blur my vision and keep me from seeing what I wished to see, so I forced them back, opened my eyes, and sat down on the bed to wait. I touched Yun's old clothes and smelled the fragrance of her that still lingered in them. It was more than I could hear, and I felt my heart was breaking; stupefied, I began to faint away. But then I thought, how could I suddenly fall asleep while waiting for her spirit?

I opened my eyes, looked all around, and noticed that the glimmering blue flames of the pair of candles on the mat had shrunk to the size of beans. I was frightened, and seized with a cold trembling. Rubbing my hands and forehead, I gazed steadily at the candles; as I watched, both their flames gradually lengthened and grew more than a foot tall, until they scorched the paper pasted over the framework on the ceiling. Just as I was taking advantage of this light to look around, the flames suddenly shrank to their previous size.

By now, my heart was pounding and my knees were trembling, and I wanted to call in my guardian. But then I thought of Yun's gentle and impressionable spirit, and feared she might be repelled by having another man in the room. Instead I just called her name softly and prayed to her, but the room remained silent and there was nothing to be seen. The candle flames then grew bright again but did not rise up as before. I went out to tell Yu-men what had happened; he thought me very brave, not realizing that in fact I was merely transported with love the whole time.

After I lost Yun, remembering how the poet Lin Ho-ching wrote that 'the plum tree is my wife and the crane my son,' I called myself 'he who has lost the plum tree.' For the time being I buried Yun at Chinkuei Hill outside the West Gate at Yangchou, at a place usually called the Precious Pagoda of the Ho Family. I bought a plot for one coffin and left her there temporarily, in accordance with her wishes. Then I took her tablet[2] home, where my mother also grieved

[2]A memorial plaque placed in the home.

for her. Ching-chun and Feng-sen returned home, wept bitterly, and went into mourning with me.

While I was home Chi-tang approached me and said, 'Father is still angry with you, so I think you should go back to Yangchou. After father returns I will explain things and then write and let you know you may come home.'

So I took leave of my mother and said goodbye to my son and daughter, bitterly weeping the while. I returned to Yangchou, where I began to sell paintings for a living. There I often wept at Yun's grave, utterly alone and in deepest mourning. If I happened to pass by our old house, I found the sight so painful I could hardly bear it. By the time of the Double Ninth Festival, the grass on all the neighbouring graves had turned yellow, while that on Yun's grave alone remained green. The grave-keeper told me hers was a good place for a grave, because the earth spirits there were powerful.

FURTHER READINGS

The organization of Ch'ing China is thoroughly discussed in Albert Feurwerker, *State and Society in Eighteenth-Century China: The Ch'ing Empire in its Glory* (Ann Arbor: University of Michigan Press, 1976). T'ung-tou Ch'u, *Local Government under the Ch'ing* (Cambridge, MA: Harvard University Press, 1962), describes the office of the district magistrate and the work of the lesser government clerks. Ichisada Miyazaki, *China's Examination Hell*, trans. Conrad Schirokauer (New York: John Weatherhill, 1976), describes the civil service examination system. Chung-li Chang, *The Chinese Gentry: Studies on Their Role in Nineteenth-Century Chinese Society* (Seattle: University of Washington Press, 1967), discusses the scholar gentry class created by the examination system and its influence on Chinese society.

Shou-yi Ch'en *Chinese Literature: A Historical Introduction* (New York: Ronald Press, 1961), and Herbert A. Giles, *History of Chinese Literature* (New York: F. Ungar, 1967), provide general introductions to Chinese literature.

Robert Hans van Gulik, *Sexual Life in Ancient China: A Preliminary Survey of Chinese Sex and Society from c. 1500 B.C. to A.D. 1644* (Atlantic Highlands, NJ: Humanities Press, 1974), provides much useful background on the role of women in Chinese society, while Jonathan Spence, *The Death of Woman Wang* (New York: Penguin, 1979), provides a chilling account of the place of women at a still lower level of Chinese society than that of Shen Fu. *The Face of China as Seen by Photographers and Travellers*, with historical commentary by Nigel Cameron (Millerton, NY: Aperture, 1978), offers some early photographs of traditional Chinese life that record conditions probably very close to those in which Shen Fu and Chen Yun lived.

ON THE BURNING OF WIDOWS
Ram Mohan Roy

The British presence in the Indian subcontinent was longstanding. The Company of Merchants of London Trading into the East Indies, generally known as the East India Company, was chartered by Queen Elizabeth in 1600. These English merchants, along with French and Dutch traders, broke the monopoly of the Indian trade enjoyed by the Portuguese since 1500. The Company established trading stations along the coast, among them Bombay, Madras, and Calcutta, and shared the Indian trade with the Dutch and French for some time. During the Seven Years' War (1757–1763), however, Company forces defeated their competitors and established British commercial supremacy in the region. During the next century, this commercial corporation acted almost as an independent government in India, administering all British affairs there, annexing territory, forming its own army and navy, and establishing protectorates over native princes.

Company administration was limited primarily to the maintenance of law and order, revenue collection, and bureaucratic efficiency. In the first half of the nineteenth century, however, it was forced reluctantly to expand its role in other areas. Parliament coerced the Company to admit missionaries after 1813, and required it to develop a policy for the education of Indians in European-style schools. Some of the British in India had developed a high regard for the native tradition and heritage. It was Company officials who founded the Royal Asiatic Society in 1784 and promoted scholarly research into the history and civilization of India, and it was a Company employee who first recognized the relationship between Sanskrit and the Western European languages. Still others advocated providing Indians with a thoroughly British education, for both philosophical and practical reasons, the latter including gaining the Company a cheap and steady supply of well-trained, subordinate employees. A few missionaries urged that Western-style education be provided in the native spoken languages or "vernaculars" of India. The debate was settled by a resolution in 1835: the Company would train an elite group of Indians in Western subjects, and the instruction would be in English. By this time, a small stratum of English-educated Indians had come into being, and Ram Mohan Roy was outstanding among these.

From Jogendra Chunder Ghose, ed., *The English Works of Raja Ram Mohan Roy*, vol. I (1901, Delhi: Ess Ess Publications, 1977), pp. 123–28, 130–32, 134–38, 317–20.

Bengal and especially Calcutta had the most intensive contact with the British, and both areas had become cosmopolitan and bustling commercial centers. Generous land-revenue settlements put large amounts of money in the hands of Bengali zamindars, many of whom sublet their estates to others and moved into Calcutta to swell the Indian elite concentrated there. Other members of the Bengali intelligentsia learned to live by their wits in this nontraditional society, and became lawyers, tutors, translators, or journalists. This generation prospered from their contacts with British institutions and absorbed Western ideas. They studied both Sanskrit and Bengali literature and founded a school, Hindu College, specifically for the purpose of bringing the benefits of Western civilization, purged of its Christian content, to India.

Ram Mohan Roy (1774–1833) stands out from the others of this period for his personal synthesis of Western and Indian ideas. He was a social and educational reformer whose works made a deep impact on Indian intellectual life. He was an English-educated Brahmin from Bengal, a writer and orator who established newspapers, founded schools, and campaigned against social abuses such as infanticide, the ritual act of immolating a widow on her husband's funeral pyre (sati, "widow-burning"), and polygamy, all of which he believed were the results of the degeneration of India's ancient traditions. Although he eventually converted to Unitarianism, Roy continued to criticize Christian missionaries for their hostility to Indian culture and its religious ideals.

Widow-burning was practiced by members of certain higher castes, who believed it brought them great merit. As the British extended their territorial control, they attempted to suppress the practice on humane grounds. In fact, they appear to have succeeded in increasing the practice, perhaps because their opposition served to publicize and popularize the incidents that occurred. Western opposition seemed to highlight for many the Indian character of the custom. In a pamphlet published in Bengali and in English in 1818, Roy challenged that point of view by opposing the burning of widows on purely Hindu Indian grounds, drawing his arguments from Sanskrit law books. Despite his persuasive exposition, widow burning was not outlawed in Bengal until 1829, but thereafter became rare in India. Nevertheless, it has never been completely eliminated, and cases still occur.

Questions

1. What does Roy emphasize in his autobiographical sketch? What does he omit?

2. What are the strongest arguments the Advocate makes for the practice of widow-burning? How does Roy refute these?

3. What does widow-burning imply about the status of women in Hindu India?

ON THE BURNING OF WIDOWS

AUTOBIOGRAPHICAL SKETCH

MY DEAR FRIEND,

In conformity with the wish, you have frequently expressed, that I should give you an outline of my life, I have now the pleasure to give you the following very brief sketch.

My ancestors were Brahmins of a high order, and, from time immemorial, were devoted to the religious duties of their race, down to my fifth progenitor, who about one hundred and forty years ago gave up spiritual exercises for worldly pursuits and aggrandisement. His descendants ever since have followed his example, and, according to the usual fate of courtiers, with various success, sometimes rising to honour and sometimes falling; sometimes rich and sometimes poor; sometimes excelling in success, sometimes miserable through disappointment. But my maternal ancestors, being of the sacerdotal order by profession as well as by birth, and of a family than which none holds a higher rank in that profession, have up to the present day uniformly adhered to a life of religious observances and devotion, preferring peace and tranquility of mind to the excitements of ambition, and all the allurements of worldly grandeur.

In conformity with the usage of my paternal race, and the wish of my father, I studied the Persian and Arabic languages,—these being indispensable to those who attached themselves to the courts of the Mahommedan princes; and agreeably to the usage of my maternal relations, I devoted myself to the study of the Sanscrit and the theological works written in it, which contain the body of Hindoo literature, law and religion.

When about the age of sixteen, I composed a manuscript calling in question the validity of the idolatrous system of the Hindoos. This, together with my known sentiments on that subject, having produced a coolness between me and my immediate kindred, I proceeded on my travels, and passed through different countries, chiefly within, but some beyond, the bonds of Hindoostan, with a feeling of great aversion to the establishment of the British power in India. When I had reached the age of twenty, my father recalled me, and restored me to his favour; after which I first saw and began to associate with Europeans, and soon after made myself tolerably acquainted with their laws and form of government. Finding them generally more intelligent, more steady and moderate in their conduct, I gave up my prejudice against them, and became inclined in their favour, feeling persuaded that their rule, though a foreign yoke, would lead more speedily and surely to the amelioration of the native inhabitants; and I enjoyed the confidence of several of them even in their public capacity. My continued controversies with the Brahmins on the subject of their idolatry and superstition, and my interference with their custom of burning widows, and other pernicious practices, revived and increased their animosity against me; and through their influence with my family, my father was again obliged to withdraw his countenance openly, though his limited pecuniary support was still continued to me.

After my father's death I opposed the advocates of idolatry with still greater boldness. Availing myself of the art of printing, now established in India, I published various works and pamphlets against their errors, in the native and foreign languages. This raised such a feeling against me, that I was at last deserted by every person except two or three Scotch friends, to whom, and the nation to which they belong, I always feel grateful.

The ground which I took in all my controversies was, not that of opposition to *Brahminism,* but to a *perversion* of it; and I endeavoured to show that the idolatry of the Brahmins was contrary to the practice of their ancestors, and the principles of the ancient books and authorities which they profess to revere and obey. Notwithstanding the violence of the opposition and resistance to my opinions, several highly respectable persons, both among my own relation and others, began to adopt the same sentiments.

I now felt a strong wish to visit Europe, and obtain by personal observation, a more thorough insight into its manners, customs, religion, and political institution. I refrained, however, from carrying this intention into effect until the friends who coincided in my sentiments should be increased in number and strength. My expectations having been at length realised, in November, 1830, I embarked for England, as the discussion of the East India Company's charter was expected to come on, by which the treatment of the natives of India, and its future government, would be determined for many years to come, and an appeal to the King in Council, against the abolition of the practice of burning widows, was to be heard before the Privy Council; and his Majesty the Emperor of Delhi had likewise commissioned me to bring before the authorities in England certain encroachments on his rights by the East India Company. I accordingly arrived in England in April, 1831.

I hope you will excuse the brevity of this sketch, as I have no leisure at present to enter into particulars, and

I remain, &c.,

Rammohun Roy

ON THE BURNING OF WIDOWS

CONFERENCE BETWEEN AN ADVOCATE FOR, AND AN OPPONENT OF THE PRACTICE OF BURNING WIDOWS ALIVE

Advocate. I am surprised that you endeavour to oppose the practice of Concremation and Postcremation of widows, as long observed in this country.

Opponent. Those who have no reliance on the Shastru, and those who take delight in the self-destruction of women, may well wonder that we should oppose that suicide which is forbidden by all the Shastrus, and by every race of men.

Advocate. You have made an improper assertion in alleging that Concremation and Postcremation are forbidden by the Shastrus.[1] Hear what Ungira and other saints have said on this subject:

"That woman who, on the death of her husband, ascends the burning pile with him, is exalted to heaven, as equal to Uroondhooti. (1)

"She who follows her husband to another world, shall dwell in a region of joy for so many years as there are hairs in the human body, or thirty-five millions. (2)

"As a serpent-catcher forcibly draws a snake from his hole, thus raising her husband by her power, she enjoys delight along with him. (3)

"The woman who follows her husband expiates the sins of three races; her father's line, her mother's line, and the family of him to whom she was given a virgin. (4)

"There possessing her husband as her chiefest good, herself the best of women, enjoying the highest delights, she partakes of bliss with her husband as long as fourteen Indrus reign. (5)

"Even though the man had slain a Brahmun, or returned evil for good, or killed an intimate friend, the woman expiates those crimes. (6)

"There is no other way known for a virtuous woman except ascending the pile of her husband. It should be understood that there is no other duty whatever after the death of her husband." (7)

Hear also what Vyas has written in the parable of the pigeon:

"A pigeon, devoted to her husband, after his death entered the flames, and ascending to heaven, she there found her husband." (8)

---

[1] The text contains an impressive array of citations, transliterated in an antiquated form. They include the *Vedas* (Ved); *sastra* (Shastru), meaning "treatises"; *purana* (Pooran), compendia of traditional texts; *smitri*, "tradition"; Itihasa, "epic"; *Bhagavad Gita* (Bhugvet Geeta); *Katha Upanishad* (Kutopunishad); and *Mudaka Upanishad* (Moonduk Opunishad). The authorities also include the sages Anquiras (Ungira), Arundhati (Uroondhooti), Brihaspati (Vrihusputi), Gautama (Gotum), Manu (Munoo), Vajnavalkya (Yagnyuvulkyu), and Vyasa (Vyas).

And hear Hareet's words:

"As long as a woman shall not burn herself after her husband's death, she shall be subject to transmigration in a female form."   (9)

Hear too what Vishnoo the saint says:

"After the death of her husband a wife must live as an ascetic, or ascend his pile."   (10)

Now hear the words of the Bruhmu Pooran on the subject of Postcremation:

"If her lord die in another country, let the faithful wife place his sandals on her breast, and pure enter the fire."   (11)

The faithful widow is declared no suicide by this text of the Rig Ved: "When three days of impurity are gone she obtained obsequies."   (12)

Gotum says:

"To a Brahmunee after the death of her husband, Postcremation is not permitted. But to women of the other classes it is esteemed a chief duty."   (13)

"Living let her benefit her husband; dying she commits suicide."   (14)

"The woman of the Brahmun tribe that follows her dead husband cannot, on account of her self-destruction, convey either herself or her husband to heaven."   (15)

Concremation and Postcremation being thus established by the words of many sacred lawgivers, how can you say they are forbidden by the Shastrus, and desire to prevent their practice?

Opponent. All those passages you have quoted are indeed sacred law; and it is clear from those authorities, that if women perform Concremation or Postcremation, they will enjoy heaven for a considerable time. But attend to what Munoo and others say respecting the duty of widows: "Let her emaciate her body, by living voluntarily on pure flowers, roots, and fruits, but let her not, when her lord is deceased, even pronounce the name of another man. Let her continue till death forgiving all injuries, performing harsh duties, avoiding every sensual pleasure, and cheerfully practising the incomparable rules of virtue which have been followed by such women as were devoted to one only husband."   (16)

Here Munoo directs, that after the death of her husband, the widow should pass her whole life as an ascetic. Therefore, the laws given by Ungira and others whom you have quoted, being contrary to the law of Munoo, cannot be accepted; because the Ved declares, "Whatever Munoo has said is Wholesome;"   (17) and Vrihusputi, "Whatever law is contrary to the law of Munoo is not commendable."   (18) The Ved especially declares, "By living in the practice of regular and occasional duties the mind may be purified. Thereafter by hearing, reflecting, and constantly meditating on the Supreme Being, absorption in Bruhmu may be attained. Therefore from a desire during life of future fruition, life ought not to be destroyed."   (19) Munoo, Yagnyuvulkyu, and others, have then, in their respective codes of laws, prescribed to widows the duties of ascetics only. By this passage of the Ved, therefore, and the authority of Munoo and others, the words you have quoted from Ungira and the rest are set aside; for by the express declaration of the former, widows after the death of their husbands may, by living as ascetics, obtain absorption.

Advocate. What you have quoted from Munoo and Yagnyavulkyu and the text of the Ved is admitted. But how can you set aside the following text of the Rig Ved on the subject of Concremation? "O fire! let these women, with bodies anointed with clarified butter, eyes coloured with collyrium, and void of tears, enter thee, the parent of water, that they may not be separated from their husbands, but may be, in unison with excellent husbands, themselves sinless and jewels amongst women." (20)

Opponent. This text of the Ved, and the former passages from Hareet and the rest whom you have quoted, all praise the practice of Concremation as leading the fruition, and are addressed to those who are occupied by sensual desires; and you cannot but admit that to follow these practices is only optional. In repeating the Sunkulpyu of Concremation, the desire of future fruition is declared as the object. The text therefore of the Ved which we have quoted, offering no gratifications, supersedes, in every respect, that which you have adduced, as well as all the words of Ungira and the rest. In proof we quote the text of the Kuthopunishud: "Faith in God which leads to absorption is one thing; and rites which have future fruition for their object, another. Each of these, producing different consequences, hold out to man inducements to follow it. The man, who of these two chooses faith, is blessed: and he, who for the sake of reward practices rites, is dashed away from the enjoyment of eternal beatitude." (21) Also the Moonduk Opunishud: "Rites, of which there are eighteen members, are all perishable: he who considers them as the source of blessing shall undergo repeated transmigrations; and all those fools who, immersed in the foolish practice of rites, consider themselves to be wise and learned, are repeatedly subjected to birth, disease, death, and other pains. When one blind man is guided by another, both subject themselves on their way to all kinds of distress." (22)

It is asserted in the Bhugvut Geeta, the essence of all the Smritis, Poorans, and Itahases, that, "all those ignorant persons who attach themselves to the words of the Veds that convey promises of fruition, consider those falsely alluring passages as leading to real happiness, and say, that besides them there is no other reality. Agitated in their minds by these desires, they believe the abodes of the celestial gods to be the chief object; and they devote themselves to those texts which treat of ceremonies and their fruits, and entice by promises of employment. Such people can have no real confidence in the Supreme Being." (23) Thus also do the Moonduk Opunishud and the Geeta state that, "the science by which a knowledge of God is attained is superior to all other knowledge."   (24) Therefore it is clear, from those passages of the Ved and of the Geeta, that the words of the Ved which promise fruition, are set aside by the texts of a contrary import. Moreover, the ancient saints and holy teachers, and their commentators; and yourselves, as well as we and all others, agree that Munoo is better acquainted than any other lawgiver with the spirit of the Ved. And he, understanding the meaning of those different texts, admitting the inferiority of that which promised fruition, and following that which conveyed no promise of gratifications, has directed widows to spend their lives as ascetics. He has also defined in his 12th chapter, what acts are observed merely for the sake of gratifications, and what are not. "Whatever act is performed for the sake of gratifications in this world or the next is called Pruburttuk, and those which are performed according to the knowledge respecting God, are called Niburtuk. All those who perform acts to procure gratifications, may enjoy heaven like the gods; and he who performs acts free from desires, procures release from the five elements of this body, that is, obtains absorption."

Advocate. Though what you have advanced from the Ved and sacred codes against the practice of Concremation and Postcremation, is not to be set aside, yet we have had the practice prescribed by Hareet and others handed down to us.

Opponent. Such an argument is highly inconsistent with justice. It is every way improper to persuade to self-destruction by citing passages of inadmissible authority. In the second place, it is evident from your own authorities, and the Sunkulpu recited in conformity with them, that the widow should voluntarily quit life, ascending the flaming pile of her husband. But, on the contrary, you first bind down the widow along with the corpse of her husband, and then heap over her such a quantity of wood that she cannot rise. At the time too of setting fire to the pile, you press her down with large bamboos. In what passage of Hareet or the rest do you find authority for thus binding the woman according to your practice? This then is, in fact, deliberate female murder.

Advocate. Though Hareet and the rest do not indeed authorize this practice of binding, &c., yet were a woman after having recited the Sunkulpu not to perform Concremation, it would be sinful, and considered disgraceful by others. It is on this account that we have adopted the custom.

Opponent. Respecting the sinfulness of such an act, that is mere talk: for in the same codes it is laid down, that the performance of a penance will obliterate the sin of quitting the pile.   (30) Or in case of inability to undergo the regular penance, absolution may be obtained by bestowing the value of a cow, or three kahuns of cowries. Therefore the sin is no cause of alarm. The disgrace in the opinion of others is also nothing: for good men regard not the blame or reproach of persons who can reprobate those who abstain from the sinful murder of women. And do you not consider how great is the sin to kill a woman; therein forsaking the fear of God, the fear of conscience, and the fear of the Shastrus, merely from a dread of the reproach of those who delight in female murder?

Advocate. Though tying down in this manner be not authorized by the Shastrus, yet we practise it as being a custom that has been observed throughout Hindoosthan.

Opponent. It never was the case that the practice of fastening down widows on the pile was prevalent throughout Hindoosthan; for it is but of late years that this mode has been followed, and that only in Bengal, which is but a small part of Hindoosthan. No one besides who has the fear of God and man before him, will assert that male or female murder, theft, &c., from having been long practised, cease to be vices. If, according to your argument, custom ought to set aside the precepts of the Shastrus, the inhabitants of the forests and mountains who have been in the habits of plunder, must be considered as guiltless of sin, and it would be improper to endeavour to restrain their habits. The Shastrus, and the reasonings connected with them, enable us to discriminate right and wrong. In those Shastrus such female murder is altogether forbidden. And reason also declares, that to bind down a woman for her destruction, holding out to her the inducement of heavenly rewards, is a most sinful act.

Advocate. This practice may be sinful or any thing else, but we will not refrain from observing it. Should it cease, people would generally apprehend that if women did not perform Concremation on the death of their husbands, they might go astray; but if they burn themselves this fear is done away. Their families and relations are freed from apprehension. And if the husband could be assured during his life that his wife would follow him on the pile, his mind would be at ease from apprehensions of her misconduct.

Opponent. What can be done, if, merely to avoid the possible danger of disgrace, you are unmercifully resolved to commit the sin of female murder. But is there not also a danger of a woman's going astray during the lifetime of her husband, particularly when he resides for a long time in a distant country? What remedy then have you got against this cause of alarm?

Advocate. There is a great difference betwixt the case of the husband's being alive, and of his death; for while a husband is alive, whether he resides near or at a distance, a wife is under his control; she must stand in awe of him. But after his death that authority ceases, and she of course is divested of fear.

Opponent. The Shastrus which command that a wife should live under the control of her husband during his life, direct that on his death she shall live under the authority of her husband's family, or else under that of her parental relations; and the Shastrus have authorized the ruler of the country to maintain the observance of this law. Therefore, the possibility of a woman's going astray cannot be more guarded against during the husband's life than it is after his death. For you daily see, that even while the husband is alive, he gives up his authority, and the life separates from him. Control alone cannot restrain from evil thoughts, words, and actions; but the suggestions of wisdom and the fear of God may cause both man and woman to obtain from sin. Both the Shastrus and experience show this.

Advocate. You have repeatedly asserted, that from want of feeling we promote female destruction. This is incorrect, for it is declared in our Ved and codes of law, that mercy is the root of virtue, and from our practice of hospitality, &c. our compassionate dispositions are well known.

Opponent. That in other cases you shew charitable dispositions is acknowledged. But by witnessing from your youth the voluntary burning of women amongst your elder relatives, your neighbours and the inhabitants of the surrounding villages, and by observing the indifference manifested at the time when the women are writhing under the torture of the flames, habits of insensibility are produced. For the same reason, when men or women are suffering the ꞌpains of death, you feel for them no sense of compassion, like the worshippers of the female deities who, witnessing from their infancy the slaughter of kids and buffaloes, feel no compassion for them in the time of their suffering death, while followers of Vishnoo are touched with strong feelings of pity.

Advocate. What you have said I shall carefully consider.

Opponent. It is to me a source of great satisfaction, that you are now ready to take this matter into your consideration. By forsaking prejudice and reflecting on the Shastru, what is really conformable to its precepts may be perceived, and the evils and disgrace brought on this country by the crime of female murder will cease.

FURTHER READINGS

Thomas G. F. Spear, *The Oxford History of Modern India* (Delhi: Oxford University Press, 1978), is a standard survey of the subject. Arvind Sharma, ed., *Sati: Historical and Phenomenological Essays* (New Delhi: Motilal Banarsidass, 1988) is a collection of essays, with some discussion of Roy, on sati. For British policy towards widow-burning and other social abuses see Philip Woodruff, *The Men Who Ruled India: Volume One, The Founders* (London: Jonathan Cape, 1953). B. M. Sankhdher, *Rammohan Roy: The Apostle of Indian Awakening—Some Contemporary Estimates* (New Delhi: Navrang, 1989) is a collection of writings by his friends and associates after his death, many but not all laudatory in tone. C. S. Forster, *A Passage to India* (many editions) is a novel that studies how strained relations between individual British and Indians could become, and suggests some of the factors that turned many Indian intellectuals against the British.

THE TALE OF KIEU

Nguyen Du

The country of Vietnam was ruled by China for some nine hundred years, gaining its independence in 939. During this period, Chinese influence in the region was sufficient to draw Vietnam permanently into the tradition of classical Chinese civilization. Much as British and Americans find their aesthetic models and intellectual roots in the classical world of Greco-Roman civilization, so the Vietnamese regard the traditions of Han China as their cultural heritage. Even after gaining independence, the proximity of its powerful northern neighbor ensured that Chinese institutions and attitudes would continue to exert a great influence on Vietnamese development. The Le dynasty gained control in 1427 and, from their base of power in the North, maintained their rule until 1788. The Le rulers quickly became tributaries of the Chinese emperors and were guaranteed protection by them from both external and internal threats. It is not surprising, therefore, to observe that the political administration of eighteenth-century Vietnam was in many ways an imitation of that of the Ch'ing dynasty of China (1644–1911). The administration of the country was entrusted to men who had proven their worth by mastering Confucian philosophy and the Chinese literary classics. Vietnam did not possess sufficient resources to support as complete a system as Ch'ing China, but its administrators rivalled those of China in their adherence to the scholarly tradition and loyalty to the ruling dynasty.

Nguyen Du (1765–1820) was born to a Northern family that had produced generations of scholar-administrators, and he was trained to follow that career. It was his misfortune, however, to be born during the waning years of the Le dynasty. In 1771, the popular uprising known as the Tay-son revolution broke out in the southern part of the country. Under the leadership of the charismatic Nguyen Hue and espousing ideals of social justice, the movement swept over Vietnam. The Chinese sent a large army in 1788 to defend the interests of the Le ruler, but were decisively defeated, and the Le dynasty was overthrown. No sooner had Nguyen Du and his fellow scholar-officials adapted to the necessity of transferring their loyalty to a new monarch than the Tay-son movement was defeated. The victorious Nguyen emperor Gia-long (1802–1820) established a new capital, Hue, in central Vietnam, and the scholar-officials faced the task of

From Nguyen Du, *The Tale of Kieu*, trans. Huynh Sanh Thong (bilingual edition: New Haven, CT: Yale University Press, 1987), pp. 141, 143, 145, 147, 149, 151, 153, 155, 157, 159, 161, 163, 165, and 167.

transferring their loyalty once again. The task was made harder because the new dynasty was from the South and was for this reason held in some contempt by the Northerners.

Nguyen Da served the Nguyen emperor for the rest of his life in a series of minor posts and poorly-endowed sinecures. He continued to cultivate the Chinese classics and wrote a verse novel entitled *The Tale of Kieu* (*Kim Van Kieu Tan Truyen*). The novel was circulated among his friends and published only shortly after his death. It was immediately recognized as the greatest work of Vietnamese literature ever produced and has continued to be so regarded.

As is only to be expected from a scholar steeped in the Chinese classics, the work is based on a Chinese model, a novel of the Ming dynasty (1368–1644), and is rich with literary allusions. It is not a pedantic work, however, but a very human tale that raises basic moral issues of universal significance. The tangled plot revolves around a beautiful, talented, and virtuous girl named Thuy Kieu. Kieu and Kim Trong, a young scholar, fall in love at first sight, but he is called away by the death of his father. Kieu finds her family arrested on some vague charge, and sells herself into prostitution to get money to save them. She is rescued from the brothel by a young man who marries her. He has another wife, however, a member of a powerful family, who has Kieu kidnapped and made a slave in her household. Kieu flees her constant humiliation and is taken up by the warrior Tu Hai. After fives years as his wife, Kieu is again forced to flee when Tu Hai is treacherously murdered. Kieu seeks refuse in a Buddhist convent. In the excerpt presented here, the action shifts to Kieu's first love, Kim. He returns to her home to find her gone and is persuaded to marry her sister, but cannot forget Kieu. He achieves the highest grade in the imperial civil service examinations and enters the imperial service. As time passes, he hears of Kieu's continuing misfortunes and degradations. Finally, by accident, he and Kieu's family discover Kieu in her convent. Kim marries her, thus restoring her honor, but Kieu cannot make love to him. Because of her past, she says, she would feel only shame. He replies that true lovers need not share a bed. As friends and companions, they contrive to make a full and prosperous life based on mutual respect and the deepest friendship.

The key concepts in the story are personal degradation and undeserved punishment. Kieu has done nothing to deserve what happens to her, and her only sin is to submit to what she cannot avoid. Those about her use her body, but she retains control of her inner self. She will not give Kim her body, because this has been sullied, but she does share with him her untarnished spirit. This distinction between the inner and outer self is a critical one, and explains much about the character of the Vietnamese people. It is not surprising that *The Tale of Kieu* is a treasured part of their national heritage.

Questions

1. How does Kieu's family convince her to abandon the life of a Buddhist nun?
2. What objections does Kieu raise to marrying Kim? How does Kim reply to them?
3. Why does Kieu refuse to share Kim's bed?
4. What does their eventual agreement to live with separate beds disclose about their love?

THE TALE OF KIEU

As Kieu shook off the filth of all past woes, how could
  her erstwhile love know she lived here?

If Kieu had shouldered her full load of griefs, young
  Kim himself had suffered much the while.
For mourning rites he'd made that far-flung trip and from
      Liao-yang came back in half a year.
      He hurried toward his dear Kingfisher's nest and took
      one startled look—the scene had changed.
The garden was a patch of weeds and reeds.
Hushed, moon-lit windows, weather-beaten walls.
Not one lone soul—peach blossoms of last year
were smiling, flirting yet with their east wind.[1]
Swallows were rustling through the vacant house.
Grass clad the ground, moss hid all marks of shoes.
At the wall's end, a clump of thorns and briers: this
      pathway both had walked a year ago.
A silent chill was brooding over all—who could relieve the
      anguish of his heart?
      A neighbor happened by—approaching him,
Kim asked some questions he discreetly phrased.

---

[1] The east wind blows in the spring and therefore favors love.

Old Vuong? He'd somehow tangled with the law.
And Kieu? She'd sold herself to ransom him.
The family? All had moved a long way off.
And what about young Vuong and young Thuy Van?
The two had fallen on hard days of need:
he scribed, she sewed—both lived from hand to mouth.
    It was a firebolt striking from mid-sky:
Kim heard the news, was staggered by it all.
He asked and learned where all those folks had moved—he
    slowly found his way to their new home.
A tattered hut, a roof of thatch, mud walls; reed blinds in
    rags, bamboo screens punched with holes; a rain-
    soaked yard where nothing grew but weeds: the sight
    distressed and shocked him all the more.
    Still, making bold, he called outside the wall.
Young Vuong, on hearing him, rushed out at once—he
    took him by the hand, led him inside.
From their back room the parents soon appeared.
    They wept and wailed as they retold their woes:
"Young man, you know what happened to us all?
Our daughter Kieu is cursed by evil fate: she failed her word
    to you, her solemn troth.
Disaster struck our family, forcing her to sell herself and
    save her father's life.
How torn and wrenched she was when she left home!
Grief-bowed, she told us time and time again: since she had
    sworn to you a sacred oath, she begged her sister Van
    to take her place and in some way redeem her pledge
    to you.
But her own sorrow will forever last.
In this existence she broke faith with you—she'll make it
    up to you when she's reborn.
These were the words she said and said again: we graved
    them in our souls before she left.
O daughter Kieu, why does fate hurt you so?
Your Kim is back with us, but where are you?"
    The more they spoke of Kieu, the more they
    grieved—the more Kim heard them speak, the more
    he ached.
He writhed in agony, he sorely wept, his face tear-drowned
    and sorrow-crazed his mind.

It hurt him so he fainted many times and, coming to, he
    shed more bitter tears.
    When he saw Kim so desolate, old Vuong curbed his
    own grief and sought to comfort him:
"The plank's now nailed and fastened to the boat.[2]
Ill-starred and doomed, she can't requite your love.
Although you care so much for her you've lost, must you
    throw off a life as good as gold?"
    To soothe his pain, they tried a hundred ways—grief,
    smothered, flared and burned more fiercely yet.
They showed him those gold bracelets from the past and
    other keepsakes: incense, that old lute.
The sight of them rekindled his despair—it roused his
    sorrow, rent his heart again.
"Because I had to go away," he cried,
"I let the fern, the flower float downstream.
We two did take and swear our vows of troth, vows firm as
    bronze or stone, not idle words.
Though we have shared no bed, we're man and wife: how
    could I ever cast her from my heart?
Whatever it may cost in gold, in time,
I shall not quit until I see her face."
    He suffered more than all the words could say—
    stifling his sobs, he bade goodbye and left.
He hurried home, arranged a garden lodge, then he went
    back to fetch Kieu's parents there.
He saw to their well-being day and night like their own
    son, in their lost daughter's stead.
    With ink and tears he wrote away for news—agents
    he sent and missives he dispatched.
Who knows how much he spent on things, on men, and
    several times he trekked to far Lin-ch'ing.
He would search here while she was staying there.
Where should he look between the sky and sea?
He yearned and pined—he seemed to have his soul inside a
    kiln, his heart beneath a plow.
The silkworm, spinning, wasted day by day; the gaunt
    cicada, bit by frost, shrank more.

---

[2]This proverb expresses resigned acceptance of an irreversible situation.

He languished, half alive, half dead—he'd weep real tears of
    blood, but lose his soul to dreams.
        His parents took alarm because they feared what,
        gone too far, his grief might lead him to.
In haste they readied things and chose a date: an early
    marriage tied young Kim and Van.
A graceful girl, a brilliant scholar wed, uniting charms and
    gifts in their full flush.
Though he found joy in matrimonial life, how could this
    happiness outweigh that grief?
They lived together—as he came to care for his new union,
    surged his love of old.
Whenever he remembered Kieu's ordeal, he wept and felt a
    tightened knot inside.
        At times, in his hushed study, he would light the
        incense burner, play the lute of yore.
Silk strings would sigh sweet moans while scentwood smoke
    spread fragrant wisps and breezes stirred the blinds.
Then, from the steps beneath the roof, he'd hear a girl's
    faint voice—he'd glimpse what seemed a skirt.
Because he'd etched his love in stone and bronze, he'd
    dream of her and think she had come back.

        His days and nights were steeped in dismal gloom
        while spring and autumn wheeled and wheeled about.
For learned men a contest now took place: young Vuong
    and Kim attained the honor roll.[3]
Heaven's broad gate swung open—flowers hailed them in
    His Majesty's park, fame reached their heaths.
        Young Vuong still kept in mind those days long past:
        he called on Chung to settle his great debt.
He paid it off in full, then took to wife Chung's daughter,
    thus allying their two clans.
        As Kim stepped briskly on amidst blue clouds,[4] he
        thought of Kieu and sorrowed all the more.
With whom had he exchanged those vows of troth?
With whom was he now sharing jade and gold?

[3]Examinations for the *chin-shih* or highest degree, the equivalent of a doctorate.
[4]An official career for *chin-shih* graduates.

Poor fern afloat down in the troughs of waves—with honors
 blessed, he mourned her wandering life.
Then he was sent to serve in far Lin-tzu: with loved
 ones he trekked over hill and dale.
Now, in his yamen,[5] he lived leisured days amidst the lute's
 sweet sounds, the crane's soft cries.[6]
On a spring night, in her peach-curtained room,
 asleep Van dreamed and saw her sister Kieu.
When she awoke, she told her spouse at once.
He wondered, torn between mistrust and hope:
"Lin-ch'ing, Lin-tzu—they differ by one word:[7] they may
 have been mistaken each for each.
Two sisters, kindred souls, met in a dream—perchance, we
 shall receive good tidings here."
Now, working in his office, he inquired.
Old Do, one of his clerks, gave this report:
"It all began more than ten years ago—
I knew them all quite well, each name, each face.
Dame Tu and Scholar Ma went to Peking—they purchased
 Kieu and brought her back with them.
In looks and gifts she stood without a peer.
She played the lute and wrote both prose and verse.
She wished to save her virtue, fiercely fought, and tried to
 kill herself, so they used tricks.
She had to live in mud till she turned numb, then marriage
 ties attached her to young Thuc.
But his first wife laid cruel hands on her and held her in
 Wu-hsi to nip the flower.
When she betook herself from there and fled, bad luck
 would have her fall among the Bacs.
No sooner caught than she was sold once more: a cloud, a
 fern, she drifted here and there.
She happened on a man: he beat the world in wit and grit,
 shook heaven by sheer might.

[5]Official residence.
[6]Under the Sung dynasty, Chao Pien (Trieu Bien) was an honest official with a simple way of life.
When he was sent as governor to Shu (modern Szechwan) he took nothing with him but a lute and
a crane.
[7]Kim had heard reports that Kieu was in Lin-ch'ing. He now begins to suspect that the reports were
confused and that Kieu is in Lin-tzu, where Kim is now stationed.

Leading a hundred thousand seasoned troops, he came and
    stationed them throughout Lin-tzu.
Here Kieu cleared off all scores from her sad past: she
    rendered good for good or ill for ill. She proved her
    loyal heart, her kindly soul—she paid all debts, won
    praise from near and far.
I did not get to know the hero's name—for this detail please
    query Scholar Thuc."
        After he heard old Do's clear-drawn account,
Kim sent his card and bade Thuc visit him.
He asked his guest to settle dubious points:
"Where is Kieu's husband now? And what's his name?"
        Thuc answered: "Caught in those wild times of strife,
I probed and asked some questions while at camp.
The chieftain's name was Hai, his surname Tu—he won all
    battles, overwhelmed all foes.
He chanced to meet her while he was in T'ai—genius and
    beauty wed, a natural course.
For many years he stormed about this world: his thunder
    made earth quake and heaven quail!
He garrisoned his army in the East—since then, all signs
    and clues of him are lost."
        Kim heard and knew the story root and branch—
    anguish and dread played havoc with his heart:
"Alas for my poor leaf, a toy of winds!
When could she ever shake the world's foul dust?
As flows the stream, the flower's swept along—
I grieve her wave-tossed life, detached from mine.
From all our broken pledges I still keep a bit of incense
    there, and here this lute.
Its soul has fled the strings—will incense there give us its
    fire and fragrance in this life?
While she's now wandering, rootless, far from home, how
    can I wallow in soft ease and wealth?"
His seal of office he'd as soon resign—then he could cross
    all streams and scale all heights, then he would
    venture onto fields of war and risk his life to look for
    his lost love.
But heaven showed no track, the sea no trail—where could
    he seek the bird or find the fish?

While he was pausing, waiting for some news, who
    knows how often cycled sun and rain?
Now from the throne, on rainbow-tinted sheets, arrived
    decrees that clearly ordered thus:
Kim should assume new office in Nan-ping,
Vuong was transferred to functions at Fu-yang.
In haste they purchased horse and carriage, then both
    families left together for their posts.
The news broke out: The rebels had been crushed—waves
    stilled, fires quenched in Fukien and Chekiang.
Informed, Kim thereupon requested Vuong to help him
    look for Kieu along the way.
When they both reached Hang-chow, they could obtain
    precise and proven facts about her fate.
This they were told: "One day, the fight was joined.
Tu, ambushed, fell a martyr on the field.
Kieu's signal service earned her no reward: by force they
    made her wed a tribal chief.
She drowned that body fine as jade, as pearl: the Ch'ien-
    t'ang river has become her grave."
    Ah, torn asunder not to meet again!
They all were thriving—she had died foul death.
    To rest her soul, they set her tablet up, installed an
    altar on the riverbank.
The tide cast wave on silver-crested wave: gazing, all
    pictured how the bird had dropped.[8]
Deep love, a sea of griefs—so strange a fate!
Where had it strayed, the bird's disconsolate soul?[9]
    How queerly fortune's wheel will turn and spin!
Giac Duyen now somehow happened by the spot.
She saw the tablet, read the written name.
She cried, astonished: "Who are you, my friends?
Are you perchance some kith or kin of hers?
But she's alive! Why all these mourning rites?"
    They heard the news and nearly fell with shock.
All mobbed her, talked away, asked this and that:

---

[8]The fall of a wild goose is used as a metaphor for a quick, often heroic, death.
[9]According to Chinese mythology, after the daughter of Emperor Yen drowned at sea, her unhappy
soul turned into a little bird that has tried ever since to fill up the deep with twigs and pebbles.

"Her husband here, her parents over there, and there her
 sister, brother, and his wife.
From truthful sources we heard of her death, but now you
 tell us this amazing news!"
  "Karma drew us together," said the nun, "first at Lin-
  tzu, and next by the Ch'ien-t'ang.
When she would drown her beauteous body there,
I stood at hand and brought her safe to shore.
She's made her home within the Bodhi gate—our grass-
 roofed cloister's not too far from here.
At Buddha's feet calm days go round and round, but her
 mind's eye still fastens on her home."
  At what was heard all faces glowed and beamed: could
  any bliss on earth exceed this joy?
The leaf had left its grove—since that dark day, they'd
 vainly searched all streams and scanned all clouds.
The rose had fallen, its sweet scent had failed: they might
 see her in afterworlds, not here.
She's gone the way of night, they dwelt with day—now,
  back from those Nine Springs,[10] she walked on earth!
  All knelt and bowed their thanks to old Giac Duyen,
  then in a group they followed on her heels.
They cut and cleared their way through reed and rush, their
 loving hearts half doubting yet her word.
By twists and turns they edged along the shore, pushed past
 that jungle, reached the Buddha's shrine.
In a loud voice, the nun Giac Duyen called Kieu, and from
 an inner room she hurried out.
  She glanced and saw her folks—they all were here:
  Father looked still quite strong, and Mother spry;
  both sister Van and brother Quan grown up;
and over there was Kim, her love of yore.
Could she believe this moment, what it seemed?
Was she now dreaming open-eyed, awake?
Tear-pearls dropped one by one and damped her smock—
  she felt such joy and grief, such grief and joy.
  She cast herself upon her mother's knees and,
  weeping, told of all she had endured:

---

[10]The nether world or the world of the dead.

"Since I set out to wander through strange lands,
a wave-tossed fern, some fifteen years have passed.
I sought to end it in the river's mud—who could have
      hoped to see you all on earth?"
            The parents held her hands, admired her face: that
            face had not much changed since she left home.
The moon, the flower, lashed by wind and rain for all that
      time, had lost some of its glow.
What scale could ever weigh their happiness?
Present and past, so much they talked about!
The two young ones kept asking this or that while Kim
      looked on, his sorrow turned to joy.
Before the Buddha's altar all knelt down and for Kieu's
      resurrection offered thanks.
            At once they ordered sedans decked with flowers—
            old Vuong bade Kieu be carried home with them.
"I'm nothing but a fallen flower," she said.
"I drank of gall and wormwood half my life.
I thought to die on waves beneath the clouds—how could
      my heart nurse hopes to see this day?
Yet I've survived and met you all again, and slaked the
      thirst that long has parched my soul.
This cloister's now my refuge in the wilds—to live with
      grass and trees befits my age.
I'm used to salt and greens in Dhyana fare;
I've grown to love the drab of Dhyana garb.
Within my heart the fire of lust is quenched—why should I
      roll again in worldly dust?
What good is that, a purpose half achieved?
To nunhood vowed, I'll stay here till the end.
I owe to her who saved me sea-deep debts—how can I cut
      my bonds with her and leave?"
            Old Vuong exclaimed: "Other times, other tides![11]
Even a saint must bow to circumstance.
You worship gods and Buddhas—who'll discharge a
      daughter's duties, keep a lover's vows?
High Heaven saved your life—we'll build a shrine and have
      our Reverend come, live there near us."

---

[11]Now is now, and then was then.

Heeding her father's word, Kieu had to yield: she took her
    leave of cloister and old nun.
    The group returned to Kim's own yamen where, for
    their reunion, they all held a feast.
After mum wine instilled a mellow mood,
Van rose and begged to air a thought or two;
"It's Heaven's own design that lovers meet, so Kim and Kieu
    did meet and swear their troth.
Then, over peaceful earth wild billows swept, and in my
    sister's place I wedded him.
Amber and mustard seed, lodestone and pin![12]
Besides, 'when blood is spilt, the gut turns soft.'[13]
Day after day, we hoped and prayed for Kieu with so much
    love and grief these fifteen years.
But now the mirror cracked is whole again.
Wise Heaven's put her back where she belongs.
She still loves him and, luckily, still has him—still shines
    the same old moon both once swore by.
The tree still bears some three or seven plums,[14] the peach
    stays fresh[15]—it's time to tie the knot!"
    Kieu brushed her sister's speech aside and said:
"Why now retell a tale of long ago?
We once did pledge our troth, but since those days, my life
    has been exposed to wind and rain.
I'd die of shame discussing what's now past—let those
    things flow downstream and out to sea!"
    "A curious way to put it!" Kim cut in.
"Whatever you may feel, your oath remains.
A vow of troth is witnessed by the world, by earth below
    and heaven far above.
Though things may change and stars may shift their course,
    sworn pledges must be kept in life or death.
Does fate, which brought you back, oppose our love?

[12]Predestined, people are drawn together in love and marriage just as a mustard seed is attracted by amber and an iron pin or needle by lodestone.

[13]A proverb about family solidarity: When a relative gets hurt, the other members of the family cannot remain unconcerned about his or her troubles.

[14]Van implies that Kieu is not yet too old for marriage by alluding to a courtship song.

[15]The young, fresh peach tree is the image of a beautiful bride according to a wedding song.

We two are one—why split us in two halves?"
    "A home where love and concord reign," Kieu said,
    "whose heart won't yearn for it? But I believe that to
    her man a bride should bring the scent of a close bud,
    the shape of a full moon.
It's priceless, chastity—by nuptial torch, am I to blush for
    what I'll offer you?
Misfortune struck me—since that day the flower fell prey to
    bees and butterflies, ate shame.
For so long lashed by rain and swept by wind, a flower's
    bound to fade, a moon to wane.
My cheeks were once two roses—what's now left?
My life is done—how can it be remade?
How dare I, boldfaced, soil with worldly filth the homespun
    costume of a virtuous wife?[16]
You bear a constant love for me, I know—but where to
    hide my shame by bridal light?
From this day on I'll shut my chamber door: though I will
    take no vows, I'll live a nun.
If you still care for what we both once felt, let's turn it into
    friendship—let's be friends.
Why speak of marriage with its red silk thread?[17]
It pains my heart and further stains my life."
    "How skilled you are in spinning words!" Kim said.
"You have your reasons—others have their own.
Among those duties falling to her lot, a woman's chastity
    means many things.
For there are times of ease and times of stress: in crisis, must
    one rigid rule apply?
True daughter, you upheld a woman's role: what dust or dirt
    could ever sully you?
Heaven grants us this hour: now from our gate all mists
    have cleared; on high, clouds roll away.
The faded flower's blooming forth afresh, the waning moon
    shines more than at its full.

---

[16]The phrase "a skirt of coarse cloth and a thorn for a hairpin" stands for virtuous wifehood according to Confucian ethics.

[17]A crimson or red silk thread spun by the Marriage God bound a man and a woman together in wedlock.

What is there left to doubt? Why treat me like another
    Hsiao, a passerby ignored?"[18]
    He argued, pleaded, begged—she heard him through.
Her parents also settled on his plans.
Outtalked, she could no longer disagree: she hung her head
    and yielded, stifling sighs.
    They held a wedding-feast—bright candles lit all
    flowers, set aglow the red silk rug.
Before their elders groom and bride bowed low—all rites
    observed, they now were man and wife.
    In their own room they traded toasts, still shy of their
    new bond, yet moved by their old love.
Since he, a lotus sprout,[19] first met with her, a fresh peach
    bud, fifteen full years had fled.
To fall in love, to part, to reunite—both felt mixed grief
    and joy as rose the moon.
    The hour was late—the curtain dropped its fringe:
    under the light gleamed her peach-blossom cheeks.
Two lovers met again—out of the past, a bee, a flower
    constant in their love.
    "I've made my peace with my own fate," she said.
"What can this cast-off body be good for?
I thought of your devotion to our past—to please you, I
    went through those wedding rites.
But how ashamed I felt in my own heart, lending a brazen
    front to all that show!
Don't go beyond the outward marks of love—perhaps, I
    might then look you in the face.
But if you want to get what they all want, glean scent from
    dirt, or pluck a wilting flower, then we'll flaunt filth,
    put on a foul display, and only hate, not love, will
    then remain.
When you make love and I feel only shame, then rank
    betrayal's better than such love.
If you must give your clan a rightful heir, you have my
    sister—there's no need for me.

[18]Under the T'ang dynasty, young Hsiao had a beautiful wife named Lu-chu. She was abducted and offered as a concubine to the powerful general Kuo Tzu-i. After that time, she no longer recognized her former husband and looked away when she saw him in the street.
[19]The lotus is long associated with love.

What little chastity I may have saved, am I to fling it under
    trampling feet?
More tender feelings pour from both our hearts—why toy
    and crumple up a faded flower?"
    "An oath bound us together," he replied.
"We split, like fish to sea and bird to sky.
Through your long exile how I grieved for you!
Breaking your troth, you must have suffered so.
We loved each other, risked our lives, braved death—now
    we two meet again, still deep in love.
The willow in mid-spring still has green leaves—I thought
    you still attached to human love.
But no more dust stains your clear mirror now: your vow
    can't but increase my high regard.
If I long searched the sea for my lost pin,[20] it was true love,
    not lust, that urged me on.
We're back together now, beneath one roof: to live in
    concord, need two share one bed?"
    Kieu pinned her hair and straightened up her gown,
    then knelt to touch her head in gratitude:
"If ever my soiled body's cleansed of stains,
I'll thank a gentleman, a noble soul.
The words you spoke came from a kindred heart: no truer
    empathy between two souls.
A home, a refuge—what won't you give me?
My honor lives again as of tonight."
    Their hands unclasped, then clasped and clasped
    again—now he esteemed her, loved her all the more.
They lit another candle up, refilled the incense urn, then
    drank to their new joy.
His old desire for her came flooding back—he softly asked
    about her luting skill.
"Those strings of silk entangled me," she said, "in sundry
    woes which haven't ceased till now.
Alas, what's done regrets cannot undo—but I'll obey your
    wish just one more time."
    Her elfin fingers danced and swept the strings—sweet
    strains made waves with curls of scentwood smoke.

---

[20]"To grope for a pin on the bottom of the sea" is the Vietnamese equivalent of "to look for a needle
in a haystack."

Who sang this hymn to life and peace on earth?
Was it a butterfly or Master Chuang?[21]
And who poured forth this rhapsody of love?
The king of Shu or just a cuckoo-bird?[22]
Clear notes like pearls dropped in a moon-lit bay.
Warm notes like crystals of new Lan-t'ien jade.[23]
        His ears drank in all five tones of the scale—all
        sounds which stirred his heart and thrilled his soul.
"Whose hand is playing that old tune?" he asked.
"What sounded once so sad now sounds so gay!
It's from within that joy or sorrow comes—have bitter days
        now set and sweet ones dawned?"
"This pleasant little pastime," answered she, "once earned
        me grief and woe for many years.
For you my lute just sang its one last song—henceforth, I'll
        roll its strings and play no more."
        The secrets of their hearts were flowing still when
        cocks crowed up the morning in the east.
Kim spoke, told all about their private pact.
All marveled at her wish and lauded her—a woman of high
        mind, not some coquette who'd with her favors skip
        from man to man.
        Of love and friendship they fulfilled both claims—
        they shared no bed but joys of lute and verse.
Now they sipped wine, now played a game of chess,
        admiring flowers, waiting for the moon.
Their wishes all came true since fate so willed, and of two
        lovers marriage made two friends.
        As pledged, they built a temple on the hill, then sent
        a trusted man to fetch the nun.
When he got there, he found the doors shut and barred—
        he saw a weed-grown rooftop, moss-filled cracks.

---

[21] A well-known passage in the *Chuang-tzu*, a Taoist classic, reads: "Chuang Chou once dreamed that he was a butterfly, fluttering to and fro and enjoying itself. Suddenly he woke up and was Chuang Chou again. But he did not know whether he was Chuang Chou who had dreamed that he was a butterfly, or whether he was a butterfly dreaming that it was Chuang Chou."

[22] Emperor Wang ruled Shu (in modern Szechwan) as an exemplary sovereign until he fell in love with his minister's wife and had an affair with her. Discovered, he yielded the throne to the offended husband and fled into shamed seclusion in the mountains. He died there and turned into the cuckoo (or nightjar), whose mournful cry bemoans the double loss of his realm and his love.

[23] A mountain in Shensi renowned for its jade.

She'd gone to gather simples,[24] he was told:
the cloud had flown, the crane had fled—but where?
For old times' sake, Kieu kept the temple lit, its incense
    candles burning night and day.
    The twice-blessed home enjoyed both weal and
    wealth.
Kim climbed the office ladder year by year.
Van gave him many heirs: a stooping tree,[25] a yardful of
    sophoras and cassia shrubs.[26]
In rank or riches who could rival them?
Their garden throve, won glory for all times.
    This we have learned: with Heaven rest all things.
Heaven appoints each human to a place.
If doomed to roll in dust, we'll roll in dust; we'll sit on high
    when destined for high seats.
Does Heaven ever favor anyone, bestowing both rare talent
    and good luck?
In talent take no overweening pride, for talent and disaster
    form a pair.
Our karma we must carry as our lot—let's stop decrying
    Heaven's whims and quirks.
Inside ourselves there lies the root of good: the heart
    outweighs all talents on this earth.

FURTHER READINGS

Studies in English of Vietnam before the Vietnam Conflict are relatively sparse. Joseph Buttinger, *A Dragon Defiant: A Short History of Vietnam* (New York: Frederick Praeger, 1972), is a short survey concentrating on the twentieth

---

[24] Medicinal plants.

[25] A tree with down-curving branches around which cling many vines. Originally, it must have referred to a lord, who shelters and supports many dependents and retainers. In Vietnamese literary tradition, it has mainly stood for a first-rank wife as the protector of her husband's concubines. In this line, while the "stooping tree" clearly designates Van as Kim's chief spouse, it can also be broadly interpreted to mean a mother who takes good care of her numerous brood of children, a tree that casts its shadow over "a yardful of sophoras and cassia shrubs."

[26] Under the Sung dynasty, Tou Yu-chun was blessed with five brilliant sons: they all took the highest honors at literary examinations. The poet Feng Tao celebrated them in a poem as the Five Cassias. Again, under the Sung Dynasty, Wang Hu who had three sons, planted in his front yard three sophora trees in symbolic hope that they all would grow up to become ministers of state. Therefore, a yardful of sophoras means one's children, especially one's sons, for whom one entertains great expectations.

century. The foundation of an independent Vietnam is the subject of Keith W. Taylor, *The Birth of Vietnam* (Berkeley: University of California Press, 1983). Chinese influences on Vietnamese institutional development are considered in Alexander B. Woodside, *Vietnam and the Chinese Model* (Cambridge, MA: Harvard University Press, 1971), and *Historical Interaction of China and Vietnam: Institutional and Cultural Themes*, compiled by Edgar Wickberg (Lawrence, KS: Center for East Asian Studies, University of Kansas, 1969). Nguyen Khac Vien, ed., *Traditional Vietnam: Some Historical Stages* (Hanoi: Xunhasaba, 1965), is an interesting survey of Vietnamese history, with good coverage of the end of the Le dynasty and the Tay-son movement, written from a Marxist and patriotic point of view.

Maurice Durand and Nguyen Tran Huan, *A History of Vietnamese Literature*, trans. D. M. Hawke (New York: Columbia University Press, 1985), is an excellent French study newly translated into English. Some excellent examples of Vietnamese poetry are found in *The Heritage of Vietnamese Poetry*, ed. and trans. Huynh Sanh Thong (New Haven, CT: Yale University Press, 1979). The same scholar has prepared *The Tale of Kieu. A Bilingual Edition of Truyen Kieu* (New Haven, CT: Yale University Press, 1983).

LETTER OF MORAL ADMONITION TO QUEEN VICTORIA

Lin Tse-hsu

British merchants had long been established at the southern Chinese port of Canton, where several companies managed a profitable business in importing British and Indian goods with the permission of the Chinese government. Beginning in the late seventeenth century, they began to ship in Indian-produced opium and to encourage a growing Chinese market of addicts. By the 1830s, opium was commanding very high prices, and both British and other foreign trading companies had become dependent on the immense profits to be gained from drug trafficking. The foreign merchants paid little thought to the human misery they were spreading among the Chinese.

The Chinese government was not unaware of this problem; some lamented the social disintegration accompanying the spread of the opium habit,

From Ssu-yu Teng and John K. Fairbank, *China's Response to the West: A Documentary Survey, 1839–1923* (Cambridge, MA: Harvard University Press, 1954), pp. 24–27.

while others decried the currency loss that the trade was causing the empire. Yet, the imperial administration was undecided about how to proceed in the matter. Most imperial councilors felt that steps should be taken to suppress the foreign trade in the "foreign mud," as they called it, or at least to control it in order to gain the administration its share of the profits to be had. A growing minority of concerned administrators, however, advised that the government should attack the addiction itself, with the severest measures necessary. Among these was the brilliant and incorruptible Lin Tse-hsu (1785–1850), whom the emperor chose to deal with the situation at Canton.

As soon as Lin arrived in Canton, he struck at the entire network of drug supply in the area, sharply reducing the local incidence of active addiction. He also ordered translations of Western law books dealing with trade between nations. Once sure of his grounds, he wrote the appeal to Queen Victoria contained in this reading. His local efforts had their effect: the demand for opium diminished, and its price declined. The response of the foreign merchants was simply to increase their efforts to expand the local market and to find new buyers farther afield. It was now clear that the Chinese had to strike at the source of supply and force the foreigners to curtail their illicit trade. Led by the British, the merchants resisted Lin's attempts at coercion and appealed to the British government for protection against Chinese attempts to subject them to criminal prosecution. Relations between the merchants and High Commissioner Lin deteriorated, and the British moved their operations to the virtually uninhabited island of Hong Kong, where, protected by the sea, they awaited the British naval vessels whose imminent arrival they confidently expected.

Lin Tse-hsu attempted to assemble a fleet, but, in November 1839, two lightly armed Western trading vessels virtually destroyed it. It was clear that the traditional Chinese war junk, boasting spears and bowmen, was no match for Western vessels with modern cannon. This became painfully clear when a British naval expedition arrived in the summer of 1840. The Opium War had begun, and the Chinese were powerless to halt a military expedition that sailed its coasts with impunity, sacking cities, collecting ransoms, and occupying strategic locations. China had long been able to hold the foreigners at bay, confining Western traders to small enclaves, and, by and large, managing to control the degree to which Western influences were allowed to penetrate the interior. This situation had now ended; the Westerners had the upper hand and, for the immediate future, would dictate the terms of China's relations with the outside world. Commissioner Lin Tse-hsu had failed in his task and had brought this calamity on China. He was recalled to Peking in disgrace and spent the next few years in lonely exile, practicing calligraphy.

Nevertheless, Lin Tse-hsu has gone down in history, in both China and England, as a heroic figure, although perhaps a tragic one. His incorruptible character and his hopeless struggle against forces whose power he could not begin to imagine contribute to that picture, and his undelivered letter to Queen Victoria supports that view. A traditional Confucian scholar-administrator, considering England a barbarian and tributary nation, his essential nobility shines through his ignorance of the actual power relationships of the world. He proclaims that the laws of Heaven do not allow one to profit oneself by harming others and counsels the queen that the Confucian ideal of humane conduct is applicable to all. Through the stilted language, two principles are clear: do not do to others what you would not wish done to yourself, and do not return evil for good. These are sentiments with which it is hard to argue.

Questions

1. How does Lin Tse-hsu regard foreigners?
2. How does he regard the status of England and its queen?
3. What policy will China follow with regard to opium, and what policy does Lin suggest that England follow?
4. With what threat does Lin back up his requests?

LETTER OF MORAL ADMONITION TO QUEEN VICTORIA

LIN TSE-HSU'S MORAL ADVICE TO QUEEN VICTORIA, 1839

A communication: magnificently our great Emperor soothes and pacifies China and the foreign countries, regarding all with the same kindness. If there is profit, then he shares it with the peoples of the world; if there is harm, then he removes it on behalf of the world. This is because he takes the mind of heaven and earth as his mind.

The kings of your honorable country by a tradition handed down from generation to generation have always been noted for their politeness and submissiveness. We have read your successive tributary memorials saying, "In general our countrymen who go to trade in China have always received His Majesty the Emperor's gracious treatment and equal justice," and so on. Privately we are delighted with the way in which the honorable rulers of your country deeply understand the grand principles and are grateful for the Celestial grace. For this reason the Celestial Court in soothing those from afar has redoubled its polite and kind treatment. The profit from trade has been enjoyed by them continuously for two hundred years. This is the source from which your country has become known for its wealth.

But after a long period of commercial intercourse, there appear among the crowd of barbarians both good persons and bad, unevenly. Consequently there are those who smuggle opium to seduce the Chinese people and so cause the spread of the poison to all provinces. Such persons who only care to profit themselves, and disregard their harm to others, are not tolerated by the laws of heaven and are unanimously hated by human beings. His Majesty the Emperor, upon hearing of this, is in a towering rage. He has especially sent me, his commissioner, to come to Kwangtung, and together with the governor-general and governor jointly to investigate and settle this matter.

All those people in China who sell opium or smoke opium should receive the death penalty. If we trace the crime of those barbarians who through the years have been selling opium, then the deep harm they have wrought and the great profit they have usurped should fundamentally justify their execution according to law. We take into consideration, however, the fact that the various barbarians have still known how to repent their crimes and return to their allegiance to us by taking the 20,183 chests of opium from their storeships and petitioning us, through their consular officer [superintendent of trade], Elliot, to receive it. It has been entirely destroyed and this has been faithfully reported to the Throne in several memorials by this commissioner and his colleagues.

Fortunately we have received a specially extended favor from His Majesty the Emperor, who considers that for those who voluntarily surrender there are still some circumstances to palliate their crime, and so for the time being he has magnanimously excused them from punishment. But as for those who again violate the opium prohibition, it is difficult for the law to pardon them repeatedly. Having established new regulations, we presume that the ruler of your honorable country, who takes delight in our culture and whose disposition is inclined towards us, must be able to instruct the various barbarians to observe the law with care. It is only necessary to explain to them the advantages and disadvantages and then they will know that the legal code of the Celestial Court must be absolutely obeyed with awe.

We find that your country is sixty or seventy thousand *li* [three *li* make one mile, ordinarily] from China. Yet there are barbarian ships that strive to come here for trade for the purpose of making a great profit. The wealth of China is used to profit the barbarians. That is to say, the great profit made by barbarians is all taken from the rightful share of China. By what right do they then in return use the poisonous drug to injure the Chinese people? Even though the barbarians may not necessarily intend to do us harm, yet in coveting profit to an extreme, they have no regard for injuring others. Let us ask, where is your conscience? I have heard that the smoking of opium is very strictly forbidden by your country; that is because the harm caused by opium is clearly understood. Since it is not permitted to do harm to your own country, then even less should you let it be passed on to the harm of other countries—how much less to China!

Of all that China exports to foreign countries, there is not a single thing which is not beneficial to people: they are of benefit when eaten, or of benefit when used, or of benefit when resold: all are beneficial. Is there a single article from China which has done any harm to foreign countries? Take tea and rhubarb, for example; the foreign countries cannot get along for a single day without them. If China cuts off these benefits with no sympathy for those who are to suffer, then what can the barbarians rely upon to keep themselves alive? Moreover the woolens, camlets, and longells [i.e., textiles] of foreign countries cannot be woven unless they obtain Chinese silk. If China, again, cuts off this beneficial export, what profit can the barbarians expect to make? As for other foodstuffs, beginning with candy, ginger, cinnamon, and so forth, and articles for use, beginning with silk, satin, chinaware, and so on, all the things that must be had by foreign countries are innumerable. On the other hand, articles coming from the outside to China can only be used as toys. We can take them or get along without them. Since they are not needed by China, what difficulty would there be if we closed the frontier and stopped the trade? Nevertheless our Celestial Court lets tea, silk, and other goods be shipped without limit and circulated everywhere without begrudging it in the slightest. This is for no other reason but to share the benefit with the people of the whole world.

The goods from China carried away by your country not only supply your own consumption and use, but also can be divided up and sold to other countries, producing a triple profit. Even if you do not sell opium, you still have this threefold profit. How can you bear to go further, selling products injurious to others in order to fulfill your insatiable desire?

Suppose there were people from another country who carried opium for sale to England and seduced your people into buying and smoking it; certainly your honorable ruler would deeply hate it and be bitterly aroused. We have heard heretofore that your honorable ruler is kind and benevolent. Naturally you would not wish to give unto others what you yourself do not want. We have also heard that the ships coming to Canton have all had regulations promulgated and given to them in which it is stated that it is not permitted to carry contraband goods. This indicates that the administrative orders of your honorable rule have been originally strict and clear. Only because the trading ships are numerous, heretofore perhaps they have not been examined with care. Now after this communication has been dispatched and you have clearly understood the strictness of the prohibitory laws of the Celestial Court, certainly you will not let your subjects dare again to violate the law.

We have further learned that in London, the capital of your honorable rule, and in Scotland (Su-ko-lan), Ireland (Ai-lun), and other places, originally no opium has been produced. Only in several places of India under your control such as Bengal, Madras, Bombay, Patna, Benares, and Malwa has opium been planted from hill to hill, and ponds have been opened for its manufacture. For months and years work is continued in order to accumulate the poison. The obnoxious odor ascends, irritating heaven and frightening the spirits. Indeed you, O King, can eradicate the opium plant in these places, hoe over the fields entirely, and sow in its stead the five grains [i.e., millet, barley, wheat, etc.]. Anyone who dares again attempt to plant and manufacture opium should be severely punished. This will really be a great, benevolent government policy that will increase the common weal and get rid of evil. For this, Heaven must support you and the spirits must bring you good fortune, prolonging your old age and extending your descendants. All will depend on this act.

As for the barbarian merchants who come to China, their food and drink and habitation are all received by the gracious favor of our Celestial Court. Their accumulated wealth is all benefit given with pleasure by our Celestial Court. They spend rather few days in their own country but more time in Canton. To digest clearly the legal penalties as an aid to instruction has been a valid principle in all ages. Suppose a man of another country comes to England to trade, he still has to obey the English laws; how much more should he obey in China the laws of the Celestial Dynasty?

Now we have set up regulations governing the Chinese people. He who sells opium shall receive the death penalty and he who smokes it also the death penalty. Now consider this: if the barbarians do not bring opium, then how can the Chinese people resell it, and how can they smoke it? The fact is that the wicked barbarians beguile the Chinese people into a death trap. How then can we grant life only to those barbarians? He who takes the life of even one person still has to atone for it with his own life; yet is the harm done by opium limited to the taking of one life only? Therefore in the new regulations, in regard to those barbarians who bring opium to China, the penalty is fixed at decapitation or strangulation. This is what is called getting rid of a harmful thing on behalf of mankind.

Moreover we have found that in the middle of the second month of this year [April 9] Consul [Superintendent] Elliot of your nation, because the opium prohibition law was very stern and severe, petitioned for an extension of the time limit. He requested a limit of five months for India and its adjacent harbors and related territories, and ten months for England proper, after which they would act in conformity with the new regulations. Now we, the commissioner and others, have memorialized and have received the extraordinary Celestial grace of His Majesty the Emperor, who has redoubled his consideration and compassion. All those who within the period of the coming one year (from England) or six months (from India) bring opium to China by mistake, but who voluntarily confess and completely surrender their opium, shall be exempt from their punishment. After this limit of time, if there are still those who bring opium to China then they will plainly have committed a willful violation and shall at once be executed according to law, with absolutely no clemency or pardon. This may be called the height of kindness and the perfection of justice.

Our Celestial Dynasty rules over and supervises the myriad states, and surely possesses unfathomable spiritual dignity. Yet the Emperor cannot bear to execute people without having first tried to reform them by instruction. Therefore he especially promulgates these fixed regulations. The barbarian merchants of your country, if they wish to do business for a prolonged period, are required to obey our statutes respectfully and to cut off permanently the source of opium. They must by no means try to test the effectiveness of the law with their lives. May you, O King, check your wicked and sift your vicious people before they come to China, in order to guarantee the peace of your nation, to show further the sincerity of your politeness and submissiveness, and to let the two countries enjoy together the blessings of peace. How fortunate, how fortunate indeed! After receiving this dispatch will you immediately give us a prompt reply regarding the details and circumstances of your cutting off the opium traffic. Be sure not to put this off. The above is what has to be communicated. [Vermilion endorsement:] This is appropriately worded and quite comprehensive (*Te-t'i chou-tao*).

FURTHER READINGS

Gideon Chen, *Lin Tse-hsu* (Beijing, PRC: Yenching University Press, 1934; reprinted New York: Paragon, 1961) offers a full account of the imperial commissioner. Michael Greenberg, *British Trade and the Opening of China, 1800–1842* (Cambridge, UK: Cambridge University Press, 1951); Edward LeFevour, *Western Enterprise in Late Ch'ing China: A Selective Survey of Jardine, Matheson and Company, 1842–1895* (Cambridge, MA: Harvard University Press, 1968); and James Steuart, *Jardine, Matheson and Co.* (Hong Kong: n.p., 1934), all study the operations and intrigues of the major British firm engaged in the India-China trade. Peter W. Fay, *The Opium War, 1840–1842* (Chapel Hill, NC: University of North Carolina Press, 1975); Edgar Holt, *The Opium Wars in China* (London: G. P. Putnam's Sons, 1964), and Jack Beeching, *The Chinese Opium Wars* (London: Allen & Unwin, 1975), all present excellent accounts of the Opium War. Arthur Waley makes extensive use of Lin Tse-hsu's diary for the period in his brief, but eminently readable *The Opium War through Chinese Eyes* (London: Allen & Unwin, 1958), while Hsin Pao-chang also uses the diary in his extensive account, *Commissioner Lin and the Opium War* (Cambridge, MA: Harvard University Press, 1964). John K. Fairbank, *Trade and Diplomacy on the China Coast, 1842–1854*, 2 vols. (Cambridge, MA: Harvard University Press, 1953) provides an excellent and detailed account of the aftermath of the British victory in the Opium War. The establishment and growth of the British colony of Hong Kong receives a somewhat popular treatment in James Pope-Hennessey, *Half-Crown Colony: A Historical Profile of Hong Kong* (Boston: Little, Brown, 1969), while a more extensive account may be found in G. B. Endacott, *A History of Hong Kong* (London: Oxford University Press, 1958).

CONFUCIUS AS AN INSTITUTIONAL REFORMER AND THE AGE OF GREAT UNITY
K'ang Yu-wei

By the 1880s, the Chinese faced a growing dilemma. Foreign powers, such as Russia, France, Great Britian, and Japan, were exerting an increasing influence on her borders, and it was clear to many Chinese that only strenuous efforts would preserve the empire and its culture. The problem was to develop the military and economic power necessary to contend with the Western nations without being forced to adopt Western institutions and values in exchange for traditional Chinese culture. A major undertaking in this regard was the organization of a modern navy in the Yellow Sea, using Western ships with Chinese personnel. Unfortunately, corrupt imperial officials continually diverted navy funds to finance extravagant, and unproductive, projects. When attacked by the Japanese off the Yalu River in 1894, the Chinese fleet ran out of ammunition and was destroyed.

The failure of this Chinese attempt at self-defense was a signal for foreign powers to move in. Taiwan fell to the Japanese as did Korea, Russia gained a sphere of influence in Manchuria and control over Port Arthur, Britain acquired extensive new territories on the mainland opposite Hong Kong, France seized the port of Kwangchow, and it seemed to many Chinese that Westernization was now the only means by which to gain the material power necessary to preserve China's national integrity. The difficulty was how to justify such a policy in terms of Chinese values, particularly within a Confucian system that was regarded as an all-sufficient and unchanging moral structure. It was at this very time that a brilliant but erratic Confucian scholar, K'ang Yu-wei (1857–1897), proposed an ingenious solution to this perplexing problem.

From Wing-tsit Chan, trans., *A Source Book in Chinese Philosophy*. Copyright © 1963 by Princeton University Press. Excerpts, pp. 725–34, reprinted with permission of Princeton University Press.

K'ang was a member of a prominent family of administrators in the province of Kwangtung and studied for the civil service examinations from the age of twelve. He rebelled against the strictures of traditional education and spent some time as a hermit, reading Buddhist and Taoist scriptures. During a period of meditation, he achieved a Buddha-like enlightenment, and conceived himself to have become a sage with the destiny of putting "in order all under heaven." He returned to his studies in 1879 with exceptional energy and became deeply interested in the Chinese translations of Western books then appearing. He began to dream of a unified world of the future, in which the best of Western institutions and of Chinese values would be blended in a harmonious whole.

Meanwhile, his career prospered; he was successful in the Peking examinations and, in 1895, became a scholar of the prestigious Hanlin Academy. In 1897, he published a work with the radical thesis that Confucius had not edited the Five Classics, but had in fact written them as a guide to institutional reform, ascribing them to an earlier age in order to gain greater credence for his ideas. If Confucius was a social reformer, and the major Classics written to serve the cause of reform, neither the example of Confucius nor the tenets of the Five Classics were any impediment to social reform. Indeed, such reform would be thoroughly within the tradition initiated by the Great Sage. K'ang proclaimed that history evolved through three stages: Disorder, Approaching Peace and Small Tranquillity, and Great Peace and Grand Unity, and that if his proposed reforms were adopted, China would enter the era of Approaching Peace and Small Tranquillity.

In 1898, the time was ripe for such radical and visionary approaches, and the young emperor K'uang-hsu called K'ang Yu-wei to Peking to act as his major advisor. During the summer of that year, the so-called Hundred Days of reform occurred, as the emperor issued edicts reforming and revising virtually every aspect of Chinese society. Moderates and conservatives alike were appalled by the extent and intent of these measures and gathered around the Dowager Empress, the champion of traditional values and corrupt government. In September, she had the emperor seized and imprisoned; K'ang and a companion fled, but the other reform ministers, including K'ang's brother, were beheaded. Traditionalism had triumphed for the moment but had doomed the Manchu dynasty. The future belonged to the revolutionary republican movement led by Sun Yat-sen (1866–1925).

K'ang Yu-wei, unable to forsake his loyalty to the dynastic tradition, wandered from country to country in the succeeding years, attempting unsuccessfully to organize a reform party to counteract Sun Yat-sen's revolutionary movement. He returned to a republican China in 1912 and continued to work for the restoration of the imperial principle. As a consequence, he was in official disgrace when he died in 1927. Eight years later, his work *The Great Unity*, written and rewritten over the years, was finally published. The sweep of its idealistic vision of the future is startling and hardly seems to be the sober thoughts of a Confucian scholar. A careful consideration is sufficient to dispel this impression, however. The main concern of Confucian thought is how humane conduct (*jen*) may be developed, extended, and perfected. For K'ang Yu-wei, humanity itself is the all-encompassing reality of the world, and the essential characteristic of humanity is its capacity to love. With the passage of time, K'ang reasoned, love would draw all human beings together in mutual respect and affection. This would be the Age of the Great Unity. K'ang Yu-wei had simply extended the Neo-Confucian's essentially limited and peculiarly Chinese values to encompass all cultures and all peoples. Although he failed "to set in order all in the world," he left as a heritage a transcendent vision of what humans could create if allowed to follow their own best instincts.

Questions

1. How does K'ang Yu-wei relate his ideas to traditional Confucian teachings?
2. How does he show Confucius to have been a social reformer?
3. What are the causes of human suffering?
4. How does the Age of Great Unity come about?

CONFUCIUS AS A SOCIAL REFORMER AND THE AGE OF GREAT UNITY

1. THE THREE AGES

In the progress of mankind there have always been definite stages. From the clan system come tribes, which in time become nations, and from nations the Great Unification comes into existence. From the individual man the rule of tribal chieftains gradually becomes established, and from the rule of tribal chieftains the correct relationship between ruler and minister is gradually defined. From autocracy gradually comes [monarchic] constitutionalism, and from constitutionalism gradually comes republicanism. From men living as individuals gradually comes the relationship between husband and wife, and from this the relationship between father and son is gradually fixed. From the relationship between father and son gradually comes the system in which blessings are also extended to all the rest of mankind. And from this system, that of Great Unity comes into being, whereby individuals again exist as individuals [in a harmonious world without the bonds of father and son, husband and wife, and so forth].

Thus in the progress from the Age of Disorder to the Age of Rising Peace, and from the Age of Rising Peace to the Age of Great Peace, their evolution is gradual and there are reasons for their continuation or modification. Examine this process in all countries and we shall find that the pattern is the same. By observing the infant one can foretell the future adult and further the future old man, and by observing the sprout one can foretell the future tree large enough to be enclosed with both arms and further the future tree high enough to reach the sky. Similarly, by observing what the Three Systems of the Hsia (2193–1752 B.C.?), Shang (1751–1112 B.C.) and Chou (1111–249 B.C.) added to or subtracted from the previous period, one can infer the changes and modifications in a hundred generations to come.

When Confucius wrote the *Spring and Autumn Annals*, he extended it to embrace the Three Ages. During the Age of Disorder, he considered his own state (of Lu) as native and all other Chinese feudal states as foreign. In the Age of Rising Peace, he considered all Chinese feudal states as native and the outlying barbarian tribes as foreign. And in the Age of Great Peace, he considered all groups, far or near, big or small, as one. In doing this he was applying the principle of evolution.

Confucius was born in the Age of Disorder. Now that communications have extended throughout the great earth and important changes have taken place in Europe and America, the world has entered upon the Age of Rising Peace. Later, when all groups throughout the great earth, far and near, big and small, are like one, when nations will cease to exist, when racial distinctions are no longer made, and when customs are unified, all will be one and the Age of Great Peace will have come. Confucius knew all this in advance.

However, within each age there are Three Rotating Phases. In the Age of Disorder, there are the phases of Rising Peace and Great Peace, and in the Age of Great Peace are the phases of Rising Peace and Disorder. Thus there are barbarian red Indians in progressive America and primitive Miao, Yao, T'ung, and Li tribes in civilized China. Each age can further be divided into three ages. These three can further be extended (geometrically) into nine ages, then eighty-one, then thousands and tens of thousands, and then innumerable ages. After the arrival of the Age of Great Peace and Great Unity, there will still be much progress and many phases.

It will not end after only a hundred generations.

In his methods and institutions Confucius emphasized their adaptability to the times. If, in the age of primitivism and chaos, when the transforming influence of moral doctrines had not operated, one were to practice the institutions of Great Peace, it would surely result in great harm. But at the same time, if, in the Age of Rising Peace, one still clung to the institutions of the Age of Disorder, it would also result in great harm. At the present time of Rising Peace, for example, we should promote the principles of self-rule and independence and the systems of parliamentarianism and constitutionalism. If institutions are not reformed, great disorder will result. Confucius thought of these troubles and prevented them. He therefore inaugurated the doctrine of the Three Rotating Phases so that later generations may adapt and change in order to remove harm. This is Confucius' perfect humanity in establishing institutions.

2. CONFUCIUS' INSTITUTIONAL REFORMS

In high antiquity, people esteemed valor and competed in physical strength. Chaos was impending and misery prevalent. Heaven was sorry for them and decided to save them. It was not to save one generation alone but a hundred generations. Therefore Heaven produced the sagely king of spiritual intelligence. He did not become a ruler of men but a master of creation of institutions. The entire world followed him and all people, far or near, flocked to him. In the eight hundred years from the Warring States Period (403–222 B.C.) to Later Han (25–220), all scholars regarded Confucius as the king. . . . He had the actuality of people flocking to him. Therefore he had the actuality of a king. It is a matter of course that one who had the actuality of a king should have the name of a king. But the great Sage reluctantly followed the path of expediency. He humbly negated the reality of the rank and title of a king. He [promoted institutional reforms] by attributing them to ancient kings and the king of Lu, and only assumed the role of a "king behind the scene" and an "uncrowned king."

Founders of religions in all great lands have always reformed institutions and established systems. Even ancient Chinese philosophers did this. All Chinese moral institutions were founded by Confucius. His disciples received his instructions and transmitted his teachings, so that they spread over the whole empire and changed its traditional customs. Among the outstanding changes have been costumes, the three-year mourning (of one's parents' death), marriage ceremonies, the "well-field" land system, the educational system, and the civil service examination system.

Confucius was the founder of a religion. He was a sagely king with spiritual intelligence. He was a counterpart of Heaven and Earth and nourished all things. All human beings, all events, and all moral principles are encompassed in his great Way. Thus he was the Great Perfection and Ultimate Sage the human race had never had. . . .

On what basis did he become founder of a religion and a sagely king with spiritual intelligence? *Answer:* On the Six Classics. They are the works of Confucius. This was the unanimous opinion before the Han dynasty (206 B.C.–A.D. 220). Only when the student knows that the Six Classics are the works of Confucius does he understand why Confucius was a great sage, was the founder of a religion, encompassed ten thousand generations, and has been venerated as supreme. Only when a student knows that Confucius was founder of a religion and that the Six Classics are his works does he know Confucius' achievements in wiping out the Age of Disorder and bringing about the Age of Great Peace, and that everyone with blood and vital force is daily benefited by his great achievements and great virtue and should never forget it.

All the Sage wanted was to benefit the world. Therefore "his words are not necessarily [literally] truthful. . . . He simply speaks what is right." "Without evidence, they (ancient institutions) could not command credence, and not being credited, the people would not follow them." Therefore he put all institutions into operation by citing the ancient kings of the Three Dynasties as precedents and authority. If it is said that in his work a sage should not cite others as precedent and authority, then one would be equating Confucius, who possessed spiritual transforming power, with an obstinate inferior man.

4. THE AGE OF GREAT UNITY

Therefore all living creatures in the world only aim at seeking happiness and avoiding suffering. They follow no other course. There are some who take a roundabout way, take an expedient way, or zig-zag in their course, going through painful experiences without getting tired. They, too, only aim at seeking happiness. Although men differ in their nature, we can decidedly say that the way of mankind is never to seek suffering and avoid happiness. To establish institutions and inaugurate doctrines so as to enable men to have happiness but no suffering is the highest of goodness. To enable men to have much happiness and little suffering is good but not perfectly good. And to cause men to have much suffering and little happiness is no good. . . .

Having been born in an age of disorder, and seeing with my own eyes the path of suffering in the world, I wish to find a way to save it. I have thought deeply and believe the only way is to practice the way of Great Unity and Great Peace. Looking over all ways and means in the world, I believe that aside from the way of Great Unity there is no other method to save living men from their sufferings or to seek their great happiness. The way of Great Unity is perfect equality, perfect impartiality, perfect humanity, and good government in the highest decree. Although there are good ways, none can be superior.

The sufferings of mankind are so innumerable as to be unimaginable, changing from place to place and from time to time. They cannot be all listed, but let us roughly mention the major ones that are readily apparent:

(1) Seven sufferings from living: 1, rebirth, 2, premature death, 3, physical debilities, 4, being a barbarian, 5, living in frontier areas (on the fringe of civilization), 6, being a slave, and 7, being a woman.

(2) Eight sufferings from natural calamities: 1, famines resulting from floods or droughts, 2, plagues of locusts, 3, fire, 4, flood, 5, volcanic eruptions (including earthquakes and landslides), 6, collapse of buildings, 7, shipwrecks (including collisions of cars), and 8, epidemics.

(3) Five sufferings from conditions of life: 1, being a widow or widower, 2, being an orphan or childless, 3, being ill without medical care, 4, being poor, and 5, being humble in social station.

(4) Five sufferings from government: 1, punishment and imprisonment, 2, oppressive taxation, 3, military conscription, 4, the existence of the state, and 5, the existence of the family.

(5) Eight sufferings from human feelings: 1, stupidity, 2, hatred, 3, sexual love, 4, burden imposed by others, 5, toil, 6, desires, 7, oppression, and 8, class distinction.

(6) Five sufferings from being objects of honor and esteem: 1, a rich man, 2, a man of high station, 3, a man of longevity, 4, a king or emperor, and 5, a god, a sage, an immortal, or a Buddha.

All these are sufferings of human life, not to mention the conditions of sufferings of the feathered, furred, or scaly animals. But if we broadly survey the miseries of life, we shall find that all sufferings originate from nine spheres of distinction. What are these nine? The first is the distinction between states [as a cause of suffering], because it divides the world into territories and tribes. The second is class distinction, because it divides people into the honored and the humble, the pure and the impure. The third is racial distinction, which divides people into yellows, whites, browns, and blacks. The fourth is the distinction between physical forms, because it makes the divisions between male and female. The fifth is the distinction between families, because it confines the various affections between father and son, husband and wife, and brothers to those personal relations. The sixth is the distinction between occupations, because it considers the products of farmers, artisans, and merchants as their own. The seventh is the sphere of chaos, because it has systems that are unfair, unreasonable, non-uniform, and unjust. The eighth is the distinction between species, because it divides them into human beings, birds, animals, insects, and fish. And the ninth is the sphere of suffering. Suffering gives rise to suffering, and so they pass on without end and in a way that is beyond imagination. . . .

My way of saving people from these sufferings consists in abolishing these nine spheres of distinction. First, do away with the distinction between states in order to unify the whole world. Second, do away with class distinction so as to bring about equality of all people. Third, do away with racial distinction so there will be one universal race. Fourth, do away with the distinction between physical forms so as to guarantee the independence of both sexes. Fifth, do away with the distinction between families so men may become citizens of Heaven. Sixth, do away with the distinction between occupations so that all productions may belong to the public. Seventh, do away with the spheres of chaos so that universal peace may become the order of the day. Eighth, do away with the distinction between species so we may love all sentient beings. And ninth, do away with the sphere of suffering so happiness may reach its height.

In the world of Great Unity, the whole world becomes a great unity. There is no division into national states and no difference between races. There will be no war.

In the Age of Great Unity, the world government is daily engaged in mining, road building, reclamation of deserts, and navigation as the primary task.

In the Age of Great Peace, all agriculture, industry, and commerce originate with the world government. There is no competition at all.

In the Age of Great Peace, there are no emperors, kings, rulers, elders, official titles, or ranks. All people are equal, and do not consider position or rank as an honor either. Only wisdom and humanity are promoted and encouraged. Wisdom is to initiate things, accomplish undertakings, promote utility and benefits, and advance people, while humanity is to confer benefits extensively on all the people and bring salvation to them, to love people and to benefit things. There is no honor outside of wisdom and humanity.

In the Age of Great Peace, since men's nature is already good and his ability and intelligence is superior, they only rejoice in matters of wisdom and humanity. New institutions appear every day. Public benefits increase every day. The humane mind gets stronger every day. And knowledge becomes clearer every day. People in the whole world together reach the realm of humanity, longevity, perfect happiness, and infinite goodness and wisdom.

In the Age of Great Unity, since there is no more state, there is therefore no severe military discipline. As there is no ruler, there is no rebellion or instigation of disturbance. As there are no husbands or wives, there is no quarrel over women, necessity to prevent adultery, suppression of sex desires, complaint, hatred, divorce, or the calamity of murder. As there are no blood relatives of clansmen, there is no reliance on others for support, [authoritarian] admonition to do good, or litigation over inheritance. As there are no ranks or positions, there is no such thing as relying on power or strength to oppress or rob others, or resorting to intrigue or flattery to get jobs. As there is no private property, there is no litigation over land, residence, or industrial or business property. As there is no burial [but cremation], there is no litigation over grave land. As there is no tax, customs, or conscription, there is no crime of cheating or desertion. And as there is neither title nor status, there is no insulting or oppression, or such things as offense or counterattack.

In the Age of Great Peace, all people are equal. There are no servants or slaves, rulers or commanders, heads of religion or popes.

In the Age of Great Unity, all people live in public dwellings. . . . There will be automatic boats and cars. . . . New inventions appear every day. . . . There will be no difference in dress between men and women. . . . There will be no disease. . . . People think of nothing because happiness will reach its limit. They only think of immortality on earth.

FURTHER READINGS

A brief biography of K'ang Yu-wei, together with a perceptive discussion of his education and writings may be found in Richard C. Howard, "K'ang Yu-wei (1858–1927): His Intellectual Background and Early Thought," in *Confucian Personalities*, ed. Arthur Wright and Denis Twitchett (Stanford, CA: Stanford University Press, c. 1962), while a full account of his concept of the Age of Great Unity is presented in Ta T'ung-shu, *The One-World Philosophy of K'ang Yu-wei*, trans. Laurence G. Thompson (London: Allen & Unwin, 1958). K'ang's role in the abortive reform movement of 1898 is recounted in Kuke S. K. Kwong, *A Mosaic of the Hundred Days: Personalities, Politics, and Ideas of 1898*, Harvard Asian Monographs, no. 112 (Cambridge, MA: Harvard University Press, 1984). Jonathan D. Spence, *The Gate of Heavenly Peace: The Chinese and Their Revolution, 1895–1980* (New York: Viking Press, 1981), presents a history of the revolutionary era in general, concentrating on the aspirations and actions of the revolutionaries themselves, particularly K'ang Yu-wei, Lu-hsun and T'ing-ling. An even broader view is taken by John K. Fairbank, *The Great Chinese Revolution, 1800–1985* (New York: Harper & Row, 1986). A biography of K'ang's great opponent may be found in Harold Z. Schiffrin, *Sun Yat-sen: Reluctant Revolutionary* (Boston: Little, Brown, 1980). A series of collections of early photographs presents a graphic account of China as it was beginning to give way to Westernizing influences in John Thompson, *China: The Land and Its People* (Hong Kong: John Warner, 1977), covering the period 1869–1873; L. Carrington Goodrich and Nigel Cameron, *China as Seen by Photographers and Travelers, 1860–1912* (Millerton, NY: Aperture, 1978), which provides an exceptionally perceptive historical text; and Clark Worswick, *Imperial China: Photographs, 1850–1912* (New York: Pennwick-Crown, 1978).

HIND SWARAJ
Mohandas K. Gandhi

British rule in India was, by most colonial standards, remarkably efficient and, in the word the British administrators themselves preferred, benign. Yet Indians, particularly the educated class that the British were themselves fostering, felt resentment at British rule. This same class of educated Indians were so imbued with British culture as to make it difficult for them to consider using violence against their imperial masters. When an "extremist" faction of India's nationalist movement appeared in the late nineteenth century, it was suppressed, along with a short-lived terrorist outburst after 1905, on the charge of inciting revolution. The situation appeared at an impasse until an Indian leader emerged who was able to show his countrymen a way to drive out the British without violence.

Mohandas K. Gandhi (1869–1948) was born in the native state of Porbandar, in western India. His parents were Hindu, and his father and grandfather had served as prime ministers to the native prince of the region. It was decided that Gandhi should pursue law, and he was sent to London in 1888 for his legal studies. During his three years in an alien culture, he became more aware of his Indian roots and was led by his study of the *Bhagavad Gita* to a greater appreciation of the concept of selfless service. Having completed his law degree, he accepted a position in South Africa. Here he was made personally aware that, although Indians might be subjects of the same Queen as whites, they possessed few of the rights of their fellow-subjects.

Gandhi became the leader and spokesman for the Indian community and, from 1893 to 1914, he worked fearlessly and effectively to gain his countrymen rights and protection under the law. Influenced in part by the ideas of Leo Tolstoy, he developed the policy he called *satyagraha* (soul-force or truth-force), which included the use of "passive resistance." Generally speaking, satyagraha meant that one should neither obey an unjust law nor cooperate in its enforcement even at the cost of personal punishment. His application of that principle led to his imprisonment, but it also led to the British government in South Africa according the Indian population of that area a somewhat greater respect.

News of Gandhi's efforts had reached India, and when he returned home in 1915, he found himself a popular hero and much sought-after by Indian politi-

From Mohandas K. Gandhi, *Indian Home Rule by M. K. Gandhi. Being a translation of "Hind Swaraj"* (*Indian Home Rule*), *published in the Gujarati columns of Indian Opinion*, 11th and 18th December, 1909 (Phoenix, Natal: International Printing Press, 1910. [Reprinted in *The Collected Works of Mahatma Gandhi*, Vol. X. Delhi: Publications Division, Ministry of Information and Broadcasting, Government of India, 1963.]), pp. 6–7, 14–15, 19–24, 36–37, 39, 47–50, 52–53, 61, 64.

cal leaders. He undertook a year's travel about India to acquaint himself with local conditions and to begin to spread among the masses his philosophy of satyagraha. He took pains to identify himself with the Indian people in dress, speech, and way of life, and encouraged other Indian leaders to follow his lead. In this way, the Indian educated class began to be drawn away from its dependence on the British.

The Gujarati version of Gandhi's book *Hind Swaraj* was serialized in 1909 in the journal *Indian Opinion*. He reprinted the English version in India in 1921 and 1938, reaffirming his commitment to its position each time. The term Gandhi translated as "home rule" is *swaraj*, literally "self-rule." It had been in the vocabulary of extremist nationalists for years in the sense of Indian independence from British imperialism, and to most leaders of the Indian National Congress, the term implied a British view of self-government: a parliamentary model of liberal democracy. As the following excerpt shows, Gandhi used the term in more than a political sense. It has a psychological connotation, "ruling the self," which he related to traditional Indian virtues of self-control. It also implies economic self-sufficiency. Gandhi thought all the necessities of life could be met by redistribution of wealth, reducing consumption, and small-scale production. Gandhi dreamed of a united and independent India, with its economy and society centered on the traditional Indian village community, and its national spirit united by a concept of selfless service that would transcend considerations of caste, faith, race, and wealth.

Questions

1. How does Gandhi's definition of "civilization" differ from other definitions?
2. How does he explain India's subjugation to England?
3. Is Gandhi's tactic of passive resistance still viable, or was it only possible in the special conditions of the British Empire in India?

HIND SWARAJ

I have written some chapters on the subject of Indian Home Rule which I venture to place before the readers of *Indian Opinion*. I have written because I could not restrain myself. I have read much, I have pondered much, during the stay, for four months in London, of the Transvaal Indian deputation. I discussed things with as many of my countrymen as I could. I met, too, as many Englishmen as it was possible for me to meet. I consider it my duty now to place before the readers of *Indian Opinion* the conclusions, which appear to me to be final. The Gujarati subscribers of *Indian Opinion* number about 800. I am aware that, for every subscriber, there are at least ten persons who read the paper with zest. Those who cannot read Gujarati have the paper read out to them. Such persons have often questioned me about the condition of India. Similar questions were addressed to me in London. I felt, therefore, that it might not be improper for me to ventilate publicly the views expressed by me in private. . . .

The only motive is to serve my country, to find out the Truth, and to follow it. If, therefore, my views are proved to be wrong, I shall have no hesitation in rejecting them. If they are proved to be right, I would naturally wish, for the sake of the motherland, that others should adopt them.

To make it easy reading, the chapters are written in the form of a dialogue between the reader and the editor.

◆

READER: I have now learnt what the Congress has done to make India one nation, how the Partition has caused an awakening, and how discontent and unrest have spread through the land. I would now like to know your views on Swaraj. I fear that our interpretation is not the same as yours.

EDITOR: It is quite possible that we do not attach the same meaning to the term. You and I and all Indians are impatient to obtain Swaraj, but we are certainly not decided as to what it is. To drive the English out of India is a thought heard from many mouths, but it does not seem that many have properly considered why it should be so. I must ask you a question. Do you think that it is necessary to drive away the English, if we get all we want?

READER: I should ask of them only one thing, that is: "Please leave our country." If, after they have complied with this request, their withdrawal from India means that they are still in India, I should have no objection. Then we would understand that, in their language, the word "gone" is equivalent to "remained."

EDITOR: Well then, let us suppose that the English have retired. What will you do then?

READER: That question cannot be answered at this stage. The state after withdrawal will depend largely upon the manner of it. If, as you assume, they retire, it seems to me we shall still keep their constitution and shall carry on the Government. If they simply retire for the asking, we should have an army, etc., ready at hand. We should, therefore, have no difficulty in carrying on the Government.

EDITOR: You may think so; I do not. But I will not discuss the matter just now. I have to answer your question, and that I can do well by asking you several questions. Why do you want to drive away the English?

READER: Because India has become impoverished by their Government. They take away our money from year to year. The most important posts are reserved for themselves. We are kept in a state of slavery. They behave insolently towards us and disregard our feelings.

EDITOR: If they do not take our money away, become gentle, and give us responsible posts, would you still consider their presence to be harmful?

READER: That question is useless. It is similar to the question whether there is any harm in associating with a tiger if he changes his nature. Such a question is sheer waste of time. When a tiger changes his nature, Englishmen will change theirs. This is not possible, and to believe it to be possible is contrary to human experience. . . . Now will you tell me something of what you have read and thought of this civilization?

EDITOR: Let us first consider what state of things is described by the word "civilization." Its true test lies in the fact that people living in it make bodily welfare the object of life. We will take some examples. The people of Europe today live in better-built houses than they did a hundred years ago. This is considered an emblem of civilization, and this is also a matter to promote bodily happiness. Formerly, they wore skins, and used spears as their weapons. Now, they wear long trousers, and, for embellishing their bodies, they wear a variety of clothing, and, instead of spears, they carry with them revolvers containing five or more chambers. If people of a certain country, who have hitherto not been in the habit of wearing much clothing, boots, etc., adopt European clothing, they are supposed to have become civilized out of savagery. Formerly in Europe, people ploughed their lands mainly by manual labour. Now, one man can plough a vast tract by means of steam engines and can thus amass great wealth. This is called a sign of civilization. Formerly, only a few men wrote valuable books. Now, anybody writes and prints anything he likes and poisons people's minds. . . . Formerly, men worked in the open air only as much as they liked. Now thousands of workmen meet together and for the sake of maintenance work in factories or mines. Their condition is worse than that of beasts. They are obliged to work, at the risk of their lives, at most dangerous occupations, for the sake of millionaires. Formerly, men were made slaves under physical compulsion. Now they are enslaved by temptation of money and of the luxuries that money can buy. There are now diseases of which people never dreamt before, and an army of doctors is engaged in finding out their cures, and so hospitals have increased. This is a test of civilization. Formerly, special messengers were required and much expense was incurred in order to send letters; today, anyone can abuse his fellow by means of a letter for one penny. True, at the same cost, one can send one's thanks also. Formerly, people had two or three meals consisting of home-made bread and vegetables; now, they require something to eat every two hours so that they have hardly leisure for anything else.

What more need I say? All this you can ascertain from several authoritative books. These are all true tests of civilization. And if anyone speaks to the contrary, know that he is ignorant. This civilization takes note neither of morality nor of religion. Its votaries calmly state that their business is not to teach religion. Some even consider it to be a superstitious growth. Others put on the cloak of religion, and prate about morality. But, after twenty years' experience, I have come to the conclusion that immorality is often taught in the name of morality. Even a child can understand that in all I have described above there can be no inducement to morality. Civilization seeks to increase bodily comforts, and it fails miserably even in doing so.

This civilization is irreligion, and it has taken such a hold on the people in Europe that those who are in it appear to be half mad. They lack real physical strength or courage. They keep up their energy by intoxication. They can hardly be happy in solitude. Women, who should be the queens of households, wander in the streets or they slave away in factories. For the sake of a pittance, half a million women in England alone are labouring under trying circumstances in factories or similar institutions. This awful fact is one of the causes of the daily growing suffragette movement.

This civilization is such that one has only to be patient and it will be self-destroyed. According to the teaching of Mahomed this would be considered a Satanic Civilization. Hinduism calls it the Black Age. I cannot give you an adequate conception of it. It is eating into the vitals of the English nation. It must be shunned. Parliaments are really emblems of slavery. If you will sufficiently think over this, you will entertain the same opinion and cease to blame the English. They rather deserve our sympathy. They are a shrewd nation and I therefore believe that they will cast off the evil. They are enterprising and industrious, and their mode of thought is not inherently immoral. Neither are they bad at heart. I therefore respect them. Civilization is not an incurable disease, but it should never be forgotten that the English people are at present afflicted by it.

◆

The English have not taken India; we have given it to them. They are not in India because of their strength, but because we keep them. Let us now see whether these propositions can be sustained. They came to our country originally for purposes of trade. Recall the Company Bahadur. Who made it Bahadur? They had not the slightest intention at the time of establishing a kingdom. Who assisted the Company's officers? Who was tempted at the sight of their silver? Who bought their goods? History testifies that we did all this. In order to become rich all at once we welcomed the Company's officers with open arms. We assisted them. If I am in the habit of drinking *bhang* and a seller thereof sells it to me, am I to blame him or myself? By blaming the seller, shall I be able to avoid the habit? And, if a particular retailer is driven away, will not another take his place? A true servant of India will have to go to the root of the matter.

EDITOR: The causes that gave them India enable them to retain it. Some Englishmen state that they took and they hold India by the sword. Both these statements are wrong. The sword is entirely useless for holding India. We alone keep them. Napoleon is said to have described the English as a nation of shop-keepers. It is a fitting description. They hold whatever dominions they have for the sake of their commerce. Their army and their navy are intended to protect it. . . . Many problems can be solved by remembering that money is their God. Then it follows that we keep the English in India for our base self-interest. We like their commerce; they please us by their subtle methods and get what they want from us. To blame them for this is to perpetuate their power. We further strengthen their hold by quarrelling amongst ourselves. If you accept the above statements, it is proved that the English entered India for the purposes of trade. They remain in it for the same purpose and we help them to do so. Their arms and ammunition are perfectly useless.

◆

READER: I now understand why the English hold India. I should like to know your views about the condition of our country.

EDITOR: It is a sad condition. In thinking of it my eyes water and my throat gets parched. I have grave doubts whether I shall be able sufficiently to explain what is in my heart. It is my deliberate opinion that India is being ground down, not under the English heel, but under that of modern civilization. It is groaning under the monster's terrible weight. There is yet time to escape it, but every day makes it more and more difficult. Religion is dear to me and my first complaint is that India is becoming irreligious. Here I am not thinking of the Hindu or the Mahomedan or the Zoroastrian religion but of that religion which underlies all religions. We are turning away from God.

READER: How so?

EDITOR: There is a charge laid against us that we are a lazy people and that Europeans are industrious and enterprising. We have accepted the charge and we therefore wish to change our condition. Hinduism, Islam, Zoroastrianism, Christianity and all other religions teach that we should remain passive about worldly pursuits and active about godly pursuits, that we should set a limit to our worldly ambition and that our religious ambition should be illimitable. Our activity should be directed into the latter channel.

◆

READER: You have denounced railways, lawyers and doctors. I can see that you will discard all machinery. What, then, is civilization?

EDITOR: The answer to that question is not difficult. I believe that the civilization India has evolved is not to be beaten in the world. Nothing can equal the seeds sown by our ancestors. Rome went, Greece shared the same fate; the might of the Pharaohs was broken; Japan has become westernized; of China nothing can be said; but India is still, somehow or other, sound at the foundation. The people of Europe learn their lessons from the writings of the men of Greece or Rome, which exist no longer in their former glory. In trying to learn from them, the Europeans imagine that they will avoid the mistakes of Greece and Rome. Such is their pitiable condition. In the midst of all this India remains immovable and that is her glory. It is a charge against India that her people are so uncivilized, ignorant and stolid, that it is not possible to induce them to adopt any changes. It is a charge really against our merit. What we have tested and found true on the anvil of experience, we dare not change. Many thrust their advice upon India, and she remains steady. This is her beauty: it is the sheetanchor of our hope.

Civilization is that mode of conduct which points out to man the path of duty. Performance of duty and observance of morality are convertible terms. To observe morality is to attain mastery over our mind and our passions. So doing, we know ourselves. The Gujarati equivalent for civilization means "good conduct."

If this definition be correct, then India, as so many writers have shown, has nothing to learn from anybody else, and this is as it should be.

◆

READER: If Indian civilization is, as you say, the best of all, how do you account for India's slavery?

EDITOR: This civilization is unquestionably the best, but it is to be observed that all civilizations have been on their trial. That civilization which is permanent outlives it. Because the sons of India were found wanting, its civilization has been placed in jeopardy. But its strength is to be seen in its ability to survive the shock. Moreover, the whole of India is not touched. Those alone who have been affected by Western civilization have become enslaved. We measure the universe by our own miserable foot-rule. When we are slaves, we think that the whole universe is enslaved. Because we are in an abject condition, we think that the whole of India is in that condition. As a matter of fact, it is not so, yet it is as well to impute our slavery to the whole of India. But if we bear in mind the above fact, we can see that if we become free, India is free. And in this thought you have a definition of Swaraj. It is Swaraj when we learn to rule ourselves. It is, therefore, in the palm of our hands. Do not consider this Swaraj to be like a dream. There is no idea of sitting still. The Swaraj that I wish to picture is such that, after we have once realized it, we shall endeavour to the end of our life-time to persuade others to do likewise. But such Swaraj has to be experienced, by each one for himself. One drowning man will never save another. Slaves ourselves, it would be a mere pretension to think of freeing others. Now you will have seen that it is not necessary for us to have as our goal the expulsion of the English. If the English become Indianized, we can accommodate them. If they wish to remain in India along with their civilization, there is no room for them. It lies with us to bring about such a state of things.

◆

EDITOR: Passive resistance is a method of securing rights by personal suffering; it is the reverse of resistance by arms. When I refuse to do a thing that is repugnant to my conscience, I use soul-force. For instance, the Government of the day has passed a law which is applicable to me. I do not like it. If by using violence I force the Government to repeal the law, I am employing what may be termed body-force. If I do not obey the law and accept the penalty for its breach, I use soul-force. It involves sacrifice of self.

Everybody admits that sacrifice of self is infinitely superior to sacrifice of others. Moreover, if this kind of force is used in a cause that is unjust, only the person using it suffers. He does not make others suffer for his mistakes. Men have before now done many things which were subsequently found to have been wrong. No man can claim that he is absolutely in the right or that a particular thing is wrong because he thinks so, but it is wrong for him so long as that is his deliberate judgment. It is therefore meet that he should not do that which he knows to be wrong, and suffer the consequence whatever it may be. This is the key to the use of soul-force.

READER: From what you say I deduce that passive resistance is a splendid weapon of the weak, but that when they are strong they may take up arms.

EDITOR: This is gross ignorance. Passive resistance, that is, soul-force, is matchless. It is superior to the force of arms. How, then, can it be considered only a weapon of the weak? Physical-force men are strangers to the courage that is requisite in a passive resister. Do you believe that a coward can ever disobey a law that he dislikes? Extremists are considered to be advocates of brute force. Why do they, then, talk about obeying laws? I do not blame them. They can say nothing else. When they succeed in driving out the English and they themselves become governors, they will want you and me to obey their laws. And that is a fitting thing for their constitution. But a passive resister will say he will not obey a law that is against his conscience, even though he may be blown to pieces at the mouth of a cannon. . . . It is difficult to become a passive resister unless the body is trained. As a rule, the mind, residing in a body that has become weakened by pampering, is also weak, and where there is no strength of mind there can be no strength of soul. We shall have to improve our physique by getting rid of infant marriages and luxurious living. If I were to ask a man with a shattered body to face a cannon's mouth, I should make a laughing-stock of myself.

READER: From what you say, then, it would appear that it is not a small thing to become a passive resister, and, if that is so, I should like you to explain how a man may become one.

EDITOR: To become a passive resister is easy enough but it is also equally difficult. I have known a lad of fourteen years become a passive resister; I have known also sick people do likewise; and I have also known physically strong and otherwise happy people unable to take up passive resistance. After a great deal of experience it seems to me that those who want to become passive resisters for the service of the country have to observe perfect chastity, adopt poverty, follow truth, and cultivate fearlessness.

Chastity is one of the great disciplines without which the mind cannot attain requisite firmness. A man who is unchaste loses stamina, becomes emasculated and cowardly. He whose mind is given over to animal passions is not capable of any great effort. This can be proved by innumerable instances. What, then, is a married person to do is the question that arises naturally; and yet it need not. When a husband and wife gratify the passions, it is no less an animal indulgence on that account. Such an indulgence, except for perpetuating the race, is strictly prohibited. But a passive resister has to avoid even that very limited indulgence because he can have no desire for progeny. A married man, therefore, can observe perfect chastity. This subject is not capable of being treated at greater length. Several questions arise: How is one to carry one's wife with one, what are her rights, and other similar questions. Yet those who wish to take part in a great work are bound to solve these puzzles.

Just as there is necessity for chastity, so is there for poverty. Pecuniary ambition and passive resistance cannot well go together. Those who have money are not expected to throw it away, but they *are* expected to be indifferent about it. They must be prepared to lose every penny rather than give up passive resistance.

Passive resistance has been described in the course of our discussion as truth-force. Truth, therefore, has necessarily to be followed and that at any cost. In this connection, academic questions such as whether a man may not lie in order to save a life, etc., arise, but these questions occur only to those who wish to justify lying. Those who want to follow truth every time are not placed in such a quandary; and if they are, they are still saved from a false position.

Passive resistance cannot proceed a step without fearlessness. Those alone can follow the path of passive resistance who are free from fear, whether as to their possessions, false honour, their relatives, the government, bodily injuries or death.

✦

READER: What, then, would you say to the English?

EDITOR: To them I would respectfully say: "I admit you are my rulers. It is not necessary to debate the question whether you hold India by the sword or by my consent. I have no objection to your remaining in my country, but although you are the rulers, you will have to remain as servants of the people. It is not we who have to do as you wish, but it is you who have to do as we wish. You may keep the riches that you have drained away from this land, but you may not drain riches henceforth. Your function will be, if you so wish, to police India; you must abandon the idea of deriving any commercial benefit from us. We hold the civilization that you support to be the reverse of civilization. We consider our civilization to be far superior to yours. If you realize this truth, it will be to your advantage and, if you do not, according to your own proverb, you should only live in our country in the same manner as we do. You must not do anything that is contrary to our religions. It is your duty as rulers that for the sake of the Hindus you should eschew beef, and for the sake of Mahomedans you should avoid bacon and ham. We have hitherto said nothing because we have been cowed down, but you need not consider that you have not hurt our feelings by your conduct. We are not expressing our sentiments either through base selfishness or fear, but because it is our duty now to speak out boldly. We consider your schools and law courts to be useless. We want our own ancient schools and courts to be restored. The common language of India is not English but Hindi. You should, therefore, learn it. We can hold communication with you only in our national language.

✦

Let each do his duty. If I do my duty, that is, serve myself, I shall be able to serve others. Before I leave you, I will take the liberty of repeating:

1. Real home-rule is self-rule or self-control.

2. The way to it is passive resistance: that is soul-force or love-force.

3. In order to exert this force, Swadeshi in every sense is necessary.

4. What we want to do should be done, not because we object to the English or because we want to retaliate but because it is our duty to do so. Thus, supposing that the English remove the salt-tax, restore our money, give the highest posts to Indians, withdraw the English troops, we shall certainly not use their machine-made goods, nor use the English language, nor many of their

industries. It is worth noting that these things are, in their nature, harmful; hence we do not want them. I bear no enmity towards the English but I do towards their civilization.

In my opinion, we have used the term "Swaraj" without understanding its real significance. I have endeavoured to explain it as I understand it, and my conscience testifies that my life henceforth is dedicated to its attainment.

FURTHER READINGS

Numerous biographies of Gandhi have been written. Louis Fischer, *The Life of Mahatma Gandhi* (New York: Harper, 1950), is an admiring account written shortly after Gandhi's death. Gerald Gould, *Gandhi: A Pictorial Biography* (New York: Newmarket, 1983), offers a wealth of illustrations. Gandhi was himself a prolific author. *An Autobiography: The Story of My Experiments with the Truth*, trans. Mahadev Desai (Boston: Beacon, 1957), was written over a period of years up to 1925 and is unusually intimate. Martin Green, ed., *Gandhi in India in His Own Words* (Hanover, NH: University Press of New England, 1987), is an excellent collection of Gandhi's writings in India from 1920 on. Judith M. Brown, *Modern India: The Origins of an Asian Democracy* (Delhi: Oxford University Press, 1985), is a history of modern India by an expert on Gandhi's political career. Among the various works on Gandhi's thought, William Borman, *Gandhi and Non-Violence* (Albany: State University of New York Press, 1986); Martin B. Green, *The Origins of Non-Violence: Tolstoy and Gandhi in Their Historical Settings* (University Park: Pennsylvania State University Press, 1986); and Richard G. Fox, *Gandhian Utopia: Experiments with Culture* (Boston: Beacon, 1989), are recent works of particular interest.

KOKORO
Natsume Soseki

Prior to the arrival of Commodore Perry in 1853 and the restoration of imperial rule under Emperor Meiji in 1868, Japan had been isolated from the rest of the world by its own choice for over two hundred years. However, during the last thirty years of the nineteenth century this was to change dramatically. Western influence on the rest of the world became more intense, formidable, and complicated. In literature, the effect of Western contact was particularly noticeable.

From Natsume Soseki, *Kokoro*, trans. Ineko Sato (Tokyo: Hokuseido Press, 1941), pp. 250–72.

Early Meiji literature largely represented a continuation of the Tokugawa heritage, but Western literary and philosophical influences fostered the beginnings of a transition period in Japanese literature. During the Meiji period (1868–1912), Japanese literature developed distinctive qualities perhaps deriving from the interaction of Western influences with a deep sense of cultural identity on the part of Japanese authors. Meiji writers were intent on combining the best features of East and West, while remaining Japanese at the core.

The transition was completed with the maturation of such authors as Natsume Soseki (1867–1916) and Mori Ogai (1862–1922). These individuals belonged to the early Meiji generation and, unlike their predecessors, had been exposed to Western books and ideas. These were thoroughly modern writers who helped to raise Japanese literature from the stagnation of the previous two centuries. Particularly noteworthy in this period was the development of the modern Japanese novel, a literary genre in which the Japanese would distinguish themselves throughout the twentieth century. Japanese writers inherited little, Lady Muraski notwithstanding, from the native literary tradition. It was the impact of Western literary theories that stimulated the development of the modern Japanese novel. Three Western literary theories, realism, romanticism, and naturalism, were particularly influential on the Japanese novelists of the early twentieth century. Nevertheless, despite the impact of Western thought, the Japanese novel was not imitative and retained a distinctive Japanese identity and vision.

Perhaps the greatest novelist of the Meiji period was Natsume Soseki (the pen name of Natsume Kinnosuke) whose life was very indicative of the intellectual and social upheaval of the Meiji era. A marvelous storyteller, Soseki, particularly in his later novels, produced dramatic, psychologically insightful works. His main characters are generally intelligent, sensitive, and frequently lonely individuals for whom the traditions of the past have been destroyed and who are unable to adjust to the changes of the modern world.

Born in Tokyo in 1867, Soseki was the fifth son of aging parents. He experienced an unhappy and somewhat lonely childhood. He, nevertheless, made his way to Tokyo University where he distinguished himself in English studies. Following graduation, Soseki taught English in provincial secondary schools until in 1900 he was sent to England by the Japanese government for further study in English. He barely survived on a meager government stipend and had virtually no friends. He later described himself as having been "as lonely as a stray dog in a pack of wolves." His two-and-one-half-year stay in London had a tremendous impact on Soseki. It was there that he despaired of ever fully grasping the heart of a foreign literary tradition and decided to help pioneer his own country's literary future. On returning to Japan in 1903, Soseki was given the lectureship in English literature at Tokyo Imperial University. He remained in that position until 1907 when he resigned in order to devote himself full time to his writing. He was a mature man of forty at this time and had already published several notable works, including *I Am a Cat* in 1905 and *Botchan* in 1906. In 1914, he completed perhaps his greatest work, *Kokoro*, a novel examining the relationship between a young man and his mentor, called *sensei* (master or teacher).

Kokoro is a masterful study of man's isolation and incapability of love. Soseki presents a gloomy, dark picture of the human condition in a simple and dignified manner. The novel is divided into three parts and it is told in the first person. The narrator of the first two parts, "Sensei and I" and "My Parents and I," is a young student who befriends the main character, Sensei, and that of the final part, "Sensei and His Testament," is Sensei himself. Throughout the first two parts of the novel, Sensei does not appear a tragic figure. He is married, well educated, and a man of means. It is only gradually that the reader realizes that there is a dark side to him. In the final portion, which consists of Sensei's long confession just prior to his suicide, the reader finally understands Sensei's true identity and the personal tragedy that led to his fateful deed.

The young student first meets Sensei, a man some years older, on the beach at Kamakura, where they are both vacationing. The two strike up a friendship and they continue to see each other after returning to Tokyo. Throughout their relationship, Sensei remains somewhat aloof. Despite this the young man continues to seek his company and his fondness for Sensei grows. On returning to his provincial home after graduation, the young man feels alienated from his conventional parents and from the life of traditional rural society. His father, suffering from a kidney disease, takes a turn for the worst. At the moment the patient's condition reaches a crisis, the young man receives a letter from Sensei. Contained in the communication is the statement "By the time this letter reaches you I shall no longer be in this world. I shall be dead." The youth leaves his dying father and boards a train to go visit Sensei. It is on the train that he finally reads Sensei's long letter. The letter, from which the following excerpt is taken, attempts to explain his life to his young friend.

An unpleasant incident with his uncle during Sensei's youth has twisted his character and helps to prepare Sensei for the treacherous act which he will later commit. The primary themes of the novel—betrayal, guilt and loneliness—now begin to unfold. While at the university, Sensei had rented a room at the home of an army officer's widow. The woman had an attractive daughter and Sensei fell in love with her. He also had a friend at the university whom he calls "K." Sensei, in an act of generosity, invited the penniless K to move in with him. It turned out to be a terrible mistake, however, because K also fell in love with the daughter. Sensei, consumed by jealousy and aware of his friend's sensitive nature, purposely ridiculed and deeply hurt K. Having devastated his friend, Sensei then went to the widow and asked to marry her daughter. She agreed, but, before he could tell K about the engagement, the widow innocently mentioned it to him. Suffering from the pain of ridicule and betrayal, K committed suicide. The letter concludes with Sensei's account of his attempts to deal with his guilt and the loneliness that goes with it.

Questions

1. If it is true that a person's worth depends in large part on the manner in which they die, how would you describe Sensei's worth?
2. Was K's decision to commit suicide caused solely by the loss of his love? If not, what other reasons entered into his decision?
3. Do you see any evidence of the author's awareness of a conflict between old and new? Elaborate.
4. For Sensei and K, friendship and love come into conflict. Which proves stronger?
5. After reading the following excerpt from *Kokoro*, do you consider Sensei to be a noble character? Explain.
6. Why didn't Sensei confess his sin to his wife? What alternative did he take?

KOKORO

44

K's resolute character was thoroughly known to me. I knew very well too why he was irresolute about this matter only. In other words, I was triumphant, as I had added to my understanding of his usual self the knowledge of his peculiar reaction to love. But while I was chewing his word "resolution" in my mind, my sense of triumph began to fade, and finally began to flicker. I began to wonder if this might not be exceptional. I began to doubt if in his secret heart he had the final means to solve all his doubts and anguish all at once. Coming back to the word in this new light, I was surprised. Perhaps it might have been better if, at this surprise, I had searched for the real meaning of the word with an open mind. But alas! I was half blinded. I interpreted the word as his resolution only to approach the daughter. I believed with all my heart and mind that this meant the realization of his resolute character in the sphere of love.

I heard in my ears a voice whisper that I also needed the last resolution. In answer to this voice, I pulled myself together. I made up my mind that I should have to carry on the business before K, and moreover with him ignorant of it.

Silently I was waiting for the opportunity to come. But though two or three days passed, I could not catch it. I had thought I should negotiate with the *okusan* when both K and the daughter were out. But every day I found that when one was out the other was in, and could not find a single chance. I was irritated.

After a week, I could not wait any more, and pretended to be ill. The *okusan*, as well as the daughter and K, tried to get me up, but with a vague answer, I did not leave my bed till about ten. I waited for the house to become hushed, K and the daughter having gone, and finally got up. The *okusan*, seeing me, asked me what was the matter. She also advised me to stay in bed, as she would send me my breakfast. But I was too well and strong to remain in bed, and when I finished washing, I had my breakfast in the sitting-room as usual. The *okusan* served me, sitting on the other side of the long brazier. With my bowl in my hand, eating a meal which was too late for breakfast and too early for lunch, my mind was troubled by the problem of how to begin my negotiations, so I think I really looked a sufferer.

Having finished my breakfast, I began to smoke. As I did not stand up, the *okusan* could not leave her seat beside the brazier. She called the maid, and ordering her to clear the table, talked with me, as she was pouring water into the kettle and wiping the brazier. I asked her if she was particularly busy. She replied that she was not, but asked why. I said that I had something to discuss with her. She asked what it was, looking at my face. Her tone was so light that it seemed impossible for her to enter my mood, and I hesitated.

Not knowing what to do, I roamed about in idle words, and asked her if K had said anything recently. She looked as if she had never dreamed of such a thing, and asked me what it was K wanted to say. Then before I replied, she said, "Did he say something to you?"

45

I, who had not had the slightest intention of telling K's confession to the *okusan*, said, "O no." The next moment, this lie made me feel uneasy. But all that I could do was to say that it was not about K that I wanted to speak to her, as the thought came to me that he had never asked me to do anything for him. The *okusan*, saying "Yes", was waiting for my next words, and I had to begin. I said quite suddenly, "*Okusan*, please give me your daughter." She did not look so much surprised as I had expected, yet apparently was not prepared for any answer for a while, and looked at my face in silence. As I had already begun, I could not afford to be embarrassed by her scrutiny of my face, and repeated, "O please at all costs," and added, "Give her to me as my wife." The *okusan*, who was older, and far calmer than I was, and said, "Yes, but is it not too sudden?" When in an instant I replied, "Yes, I want her at once," she began to laugh, and asked me again, "Have you thought about it carefully?" And I explained to her in strong words that even though I referred to this matter suddenly I had been constantly thinking about it.

After that, we exchanged two or three questions and answers, but I forgot what they were about. The *okusan* was clear-minded and decisive like a man, and I found it much easier to deal with her in a matter like this than with an ordinary woman. "All right, you shall have her," she said. Then afterwards she said, "It seems as if you were begging me to give her, but really it is I who am to beg you to have her. As you know, she is a poor, fatherless child."

Our talk came to an end, simple and clear. I think it did not take more than a quarter of an hour from the beginning to the end. The *okusan* did not ask me anything. She said there was no need to consult their relatives, but it was all right if she told them afterwards. She clearly stated that it was not even necessary to ask the daughter. It seemed as if I, whose education was higher than hers, was more conventional and formal than she was in these matters. When I remarked that she ought to ask the daughter, if not the relatives, she said, "It is all right. How should I marry my daughter to a man whom she does not like?"

As I came back to my room, I felt queer, because things had gone on so easily. Doubts even crept into my mind from I knew not where, and I wondered if it was really all right. But the idea that my future destiny was more or less decided by this renewed everything in me.

About at lunch-time, I went to the sitting-room and asked the *okusan* when she would tell her daughter about my proposal. She said it would not matter to me when she told her, as she, who knew her daughter best, consented to this matter. I felt she was much more like a man than I was, and was going to leave her, when she stopped me and said, if I wanted her to tell the daughter as soon as possible, she would tell her this afternoon, immediately after she came back from school. I asked her to do so, and came back to my room. But when I pictured myself silently sitting at my desk and listening to the private talks of the mother and her daughter in the sitting-room, I felt it impossible to remain calm. Finally I put on my hat, and went out. At the bottom of the hill, however, I passed the daughter, who looked surprised to see me. When I took off my hat, and said, "Hullo," she asked me if I was well again, looking puzzled. I replied, "O yes, I am very well now," and quickly turned down the road toward Suidobashi.

46

I went into the street of Jinbocho from Sarugakucho and turned down the road toward Ogawamachi. It was always to poke into the second-hand bookshops that I roamed about the district, but on that day I could not bring myself to look at the worn-out books. Walking, I was incessantly thinking about the house I had just left. I thought about the *okusan*—what had passed between her and me before I came out; I imagined what she and her daughter might be doing after the latter had come back. In a word, I was, as it were, made to walk about by these imaginings. Moreover, sometimes I suddenly stood still, quite unconsciously, in the middle of the street, and wondered if at that moment the *okusan* was telling her daughter about me, and at other times, I wondered if it was all over.

I finally crossed Mansei Bridge, and went up the Myojin slope and came to Hongo Hill, then went down Kikusaka to the valley of Koishikawa. I walked about in the three wards, drawing a flat circle. Strangely the thought of K never entered my mind during this long walk. Now when I look back on those days, and ask myself why I forgot entirely about K, I cannot think of any reason. I only wonder. Was it because my mind was so concentrated on another matter that I could forget about K? But my conscience could never have allowed me to do so.

My conscience toward K revived when I opened the entrance-door and was going to enter my room, that is, at the moment when I was going to pass through his room. He was reading at his desk as usual. As usual he lifted his eyes from the book and looked at me. But he did not greet me with his usual words. He asked me, "Are you better now? Have you been to a doctor?" At that moment, I was almost tempted to knell before him and ask his pardon. This impulse was not at all a weak one. If only K and I had been standing in the middle of a heath, I am sure I should have obeyed the order of my conscience and asked his pardon on the spot. But there were other people in the house. My natural impulse was checked, and alas, did not ever again revive.

At dinner, I saw K again. K, who was completely ignorant of what had happened on that day, was only melancholy, and not the slightest sign of suspicion could be perceived in his eyes. The *okusan*, who also did not know the secret between K and me, looked happier than usual. It was only I who knew everything. I swallowed the rice which tasted like lead. The daughter did not appear at the table as usual. When the *okusan* called her, she only replied "Yes" from the next room, but did not come. As he heard this, K looked mystified, and finally asked the *okusan* what was the matter. She replied that perhaps her daughter was shy, stealing a look at me. K, wondering more, began to ask why she was shy. The *okusan*, smiling, looked at my face again.

From the moment when I sat at the table, I almost guessed what had happened by the *okusan*'s look. But I felt it would be extremely awkward if she explained everything to him at this moment. I was in great consternation, because the *okusan* was a woman who could have done such a thing. But fortunately K returned to his former silence. The *okusan*, who was in higher spirits than usual, did not proceed further. I heaved a sigh, and returned to my room. But I could not help thinking about what attitude I should take toward K in the future. I tried to invent various apologies in my mind. But there was not any worthy of being offered to K. Coward that I was, I became tired of explaining myself to him.

47

I spent two or three days in that state. During those days, the never-ceasing uneasiness because of K oppressed my mind. Even if no perceptible change had taken place in the household, I might have felt I had to do something for him. Moreover the *okusan's* tone and her daughter's attitude pricked my conscience, as they reminded me of my engagement and K. The *okusan*, who was in some ways straightforward as a man, might betray me at any moment and tell everything to K at meal-time. The daughter's attitude toward me, which became decidedly more intimate than before, might provoke K's doubts. I was put in the position that I must tell him of the new relationship established between this family and me. But it seemed a very difficult task to me, who knew my own moral weakness too well.

Not knowing what to do, I thought I should ask the *okusan* to tell him, of course in my absence. But if she told him the real story, it would make no difference except that it was indirectly told. On the other hand, if I asked her to tell a made-up story, she would certainly cross-examine me. If I were to tell her everything and ask her favour, I had to expose my weakness to my sweetheart and her mother from my own choice. As I was an honest youth, I could not help thinking that this would affect my future reputation. It seemed to be an unendurable misfortune to lose my sweetheart's trust before my marriage, however slightly it might be.

In short, I was a fool who missed his footing in trying to walk the way of honesty. Or I was a cunning man. My soul and Heaven were all that knew of this at the moment. But in order to get up again and step forward I had to announce my fall to the people around me whatever happened. I wanted to conceal my fall to the end, but at the same time, I was impelled to advance. My feet were rooted to the ground because of this dilemma and could not go any further.

Five or six days later, the *okusan* suddenly asked me if I had told K about my engagement. I replied that I had not yet done so. Then she reproved me, asking why I had not. I hardened at this question. Even now I can clearly remember the words by which the *okusan* startled me at that time.

"No wonder that he looked funny when I told him. It is very naughty of you to conceal it from such an intimate friend as he."

I asked the *okusan* if K said anything at that time. She replied that he said nothing in particular. But I could not help asking for further details. The *okusan*, who had no reason to conceal them from me, described to me K's behaviour most minutely, after a preliminary remark that there was nothing worth telling.

Considering all the *okusan* had said, K seemed to have received this final blow with calm surprise. At first he only said "Is that so?" about the new relationship formed between the daughter and me. But when the *okusan* said, "Do congratulate them on it," he looked at her face for the first time, and smiling, said, "I am so glad," and stood up. Then before he opened the sliding-door of the sitting room, he asked, turning his face towards the *okusan*, "When will they get married?" and said, "I should very much like to give them some present, but I am afraid I cannot, because I have no money." I, who sat in front of the *okusan* and listened to her talk, felt an acute pain in my breast as if it were completely choked.

48

Calculating, I found that it was more than two days since the *okusan* had told him. During those days, there was no difference in K's manner toward me, so that I had not suspected it at all. I thought that his detached air was worth admiring, even if he only managed to wear it to disguise his internal pain. When I made K and myself stand side by side in my mind and compared the two, he looked far greater than I. The thought, "I have failed as a man, even if I have triumphed in my scheme," arose like a whirlwind in my breast. I secretly blushed, thinking how much K might be despising me. But it was more painful to my self-respect to go to him now and be humiliated.

It was Saturday night when in my indecision I finally made up my mind to wait till the next day. But on that very night, K died, committing suicide. It makes me shiver even now to remember the scene. Perhaps it was not a mere accident that that night I lay with my head towards the West, though I usually lay towards the East. I happened to be awakened by the chilly draught coming over my head, then when I looked, I found that the sliding-doors between K's room and mine were open as much as the other night. But there was no black shadow of K standing there. Moved by a sudden impulse, I propped my body on my elbows and getting up, cast a sharp glance into K's room. I saw the dim lamp light, and the bed. But the quilt was piled up at the foot of the bed, as if the sleeper had found it too hot and had torn it off, and K himself lay on his stomach, with his head toward the further side of the room.

I called "Ho", but there was no answer. "What is the matter?" I called again. But K's body did not move at all. I immediately stood up and walked toward the threshold, and looked round his room by the dim lamp light.

The first impression that I received at that moment was almost like the one when K had suddenly confessed his love. As soon as my eyes glanced at the inside of the room, they lost their capacity to move, as if they had been turned into artificial ones made of glass. I stood, as if my feet had been rooted to the floor. Then when this state had passed like a squall, I again felt that I had made a terrible confusion. The dimness—the full consciousness of the irretrievable disaster—pierced my being, and in a moment cast its dismal light on my whole future. I began to tremble.

Yet I could not forget myself to the last. I soon noticed a letter on the desk. It was directed to me as I had expected. I frantically opened it. However, nothing I had expected could be found there. I had expected many sentences which would severely hurt me, and I had feared how the *okusan* and her daughter would despise me if they read the letter. When I glanced at it, I felt a great relief. (It was only from the worldly point of view that I was relieved, but it seemed exceedingly important to me.)

The content of the letter was simple, and was rather abstract. It said that he was so weak in mind and devoid of enterprising spirit that he could see no hope in his future, and therefore he would commit suicide. Then in simple phrases, his thanks for my kindness to him were added, and also another sentence asking me to take care of his affairs after his death. Then he asked me to ask the *okusan's* pardon for troubling her so much by seeking death in this way, and to let his relatives in the country know this. All necessary things were referred to in simple wording, but there was not a hint to the daughter. When I finished the letter, I realized that K had deliberately avoided the name of the daughter. What struck and pained me most was the postscript which seemed to have been added with the remnant of his Chinese ink, and which said that he should have died long before and that he could not understand why he lived on till then.

With trembling hands, I folded the letter and put it into the envelope. I deliberately put it on the desk, hoping that it would attract everybody's attention, and turning back, I saw for the first time on the sliding-door the blood that had burst forth from K's body.

49

With a sudden movement I held K's head with both my hands and lifted it a little. I wanted to have a look at his face. But as I peeped into his face which was turned toward the floor by thus lifting it, I withdrew my hands immediately. It was not only because I shuddered, but also because his head seemed to me so heavy. For a while I looked at his cold ears which I had just touched and his thick black hair which was cut short and which was not at all different from his life-time. I could not weep at all. I was only filled with fear. I not only felt the simple sensual fear caused by the scene in front of me, but was also deeply impressed by the dreadful destiny which was revealed by this friend who had suddenly changed into a cold mass.

Not knowing what to do, I went back to my room, and began to walk about the eight-mat room. My mind ordered me to do this, though I knew that there was no meaning in it. I felt I had to do something, and at the same time I thought I could not do anything. I could not help walking round and round the room, like a bear put in a pen.

Sometimes I wanted to wake up the *okusan*. But the thought that it would never do to show this scene to a woman prevented me. The strong resolution that even if I could wake her up I could never frighten the daughter oppressed me. So I resumed my pacing round and round the room.

While I was walking in this way, I lighted my lamp, and often looked at my watch. The time never passed so slowly. I don't know exactly what time I woke up, but evidently it was near the dawn. I, longing for the dawn as I walked round and round, was tortured by the dread that this darkness would go on for ever.

We used to get up before seven. This was because our lectures often began at eight. The maid, therefore, was to get up at about six. However, it was before six that I went to wake her up. Then the *okusan*, hearing me, told me that it was Sunday. She seemed to be awakened by my footsteps in the corridor. So I asked her to come to my room. She followed me, putting on her everyday *haori* over her night-dress. As soon as we entered my room, I shut the sliding-doors which had been open, and said to the *okusan* that something extraordinary had happened. She asked what it was. I pointed to the next room with my chin, and said, "Please don't be frightened." She lost colour. I said again, "Okusan, K has committed suicide." As if she were cowed, the *okusan* stood in silence, looking at my face. Then suddenly I sat down and bowed low to her, and said, "I am so sorry. It was all my fault. I am so sorry to be troubling you and your daughter." I had never thought of such a thing till the moment when I stood in front of her. But when I looked at her face, such words rushed from me unconsciously. Please interpret this in this way, that I had to beg the *okusan's* pardon, as I could not beg K's forgiveness any more. That is to say, my natural self was too strong to be controlled by my worldly self, and made me impulsively speak out the words of penitence. It was fortunate for me that the *okusan* did not take them in such a deep sense. With a pale face, but consolingly, she said, "It is a sudden unexpected accident, and no one is to be blamed." But surprise and fear gripped the muscles of her face, as if they were carved there.

50

I was sorry to show such a sight to the *okusan*, but I went and opened the sliding-doors which I had just shut. At that moment K's room was almost dark, as the oil was burnt up in the lamp. I stepped back, and with my lamp in my hands, turned to the *okusan* as I stood at the threshold. Standing behind me as if she were trying to hide herself, she peeped into the four-mat room. She would not enter the room, but asked me to open the shutters.

Her actions after that were completely to the point as was worthy of an officer's wife. I went to the doctor, and also to the police-station. I did this all because I was ordered by the *okusan*. Till such necessary proceedings were finished, she did not admit anybody to K's room.

K had died almost instantly by cutting his carotid artery with a small knife. There was no other wound to be seen. It was clear that the blood on the sliding-doors which I had seen by the dreamy dim light had gushed all at once from his neck. I looked at it again clearly by the daylight, and was surprised at the vehement power of a man's blood.

The *okusan* and I cleaned K's room, using all our brain and skill. Fortunately his blood was mostly absorbed in the quilts, and the mats on the floor were not stained very much, so it was comparatively easy to clean. We brought his body into my room, and made him lie down as if he were asleep. Then I went out to send a telegram to his home.

When I returned, incense was already being burned close to his head. As soon as I entered the room, the sacred scent greeted me, and I perceived two women sitting amidst the smoke. I saw the daughter for the first time since the event. She was weeping. The *okusan's* eyes, too, were red. I, who had forgotten to weep till then, could at last indulge in sorrow. How much was my heart relieved by this sorrow! It watered my heart which was dried up by pain and fear.

I sat in silence beside these women. The *okusan* asked to offer incense to K. I did so, and again sat without a word. The daughter did not say anything to me. Rarely she spoke to her mother a word or two, but it was all about something to be done immediately. There was yet no room in her mind to talk reminiscently about K. Still, I thought it very fortunate to have been able to spare her from the dreadful sight of the early dawn. I was afraid such a sight would destroy the beauty of a young sensitive girl. I could not forget this even when my horror was so strong that it seemed to be pervading the tips of my hair. I felt the same sort of uneasiness as I might feel if I struck a pretty innocent flower at random.

When K's father and brother came from the country, I told them my ideas about K's grave. K and I often walked in the neighbourhood of Zoshigaya, and he was very fond of the cemetery there. So I promised him, of course jokingly, that I would bury him there if he died. I wondered if it would mean anything to him now to fulfill my promise and put him in Zoshigaya. But I wanted to kneel down in front of his grave and renew my penitence every month as long as I lived. Perhaps K's father and brother felt a little obligation to me who had been helping their outcast son and brother, for they consented to my proposal.

51

On my way back from K's funeral, one of his friends asked me why K had committed suicide. Since his death, I had been tortured by this question. The *okusan* and her daughter, K's father and brother from the country, his acquaintances to whom I wrote and told of his death, and even the journalists who had nothing to do with him—all asked me the same question. Whenever I was confronted by this question, my conscience ached, as if it were pricked by a needle, and I heard a voice through the question saying, "Confess quickly that you have killed him."

I gave the same answer to everybody. I only repeated the contents of K's last letter to me, never adding a word to it. K's friend, who asked me the same question and received the same answer from me on our way back from the funeral, produced a newspaper from his breast-pocket and showed it to me. As I walked, I read the article that he pointed out to me. It stated that K's suicide was prompted by his pessimistic outlook on life due to his family trouble. Without saying anything I folded the newspaper and returned it to him. He also told me that in another newspaper they said that K had gone mad and killed himself. I had been so busy that I had had no time to read the papers, and had no idea how they treated K's death, but it had been troubling me all the same. I was very much afraid that an article might bring trouble to the *okusan* and her daughter. I especially dreaded lest the daughter's name should be referred to, however lightly. I asked him if he had come across other papers saying different things about this matter. He said these two were all he had noticed.

It was soon after this that we moved to our present house. The *okusan* and her daughter could not stand the old house. To me, too, it was a torture to be constantly reminded of the event of that night, and so we decided to move.

Two months later I safely graduated from the university, and scarcely had a half year passed since my graduation, than I was married to the daughter. Externally, everything came out as I had expected, so I should have congratulated myself on my felicity. The *okusan* and her daughter looked extremely happy. I, too, was happy. But to my happiness a dark shadow was attached, and I wondered if this happiness would finally lead me to a tragic doom.

When we were married, the daughter—no, she was already my wife, so I shall refer to her as such from now on—my wife suddenly proposed that we should visit K's grave together. Without any definite reason, I was startled, and asked her why she thought of such a thing. Then she said K would be very happy if we two went and visited his grave. I gazed intently at her innocent face, without realizing it until she asked me why I looked so strange.

To gratify her wish, I went to Zoshigaya with my wife. I washed the new grave-stone with water, and my wife put some flowers and incense in front of it. We bowed and worshipped. I am sure my wife wanted to tell K all that had happened to us, so that K could share our happiness. But all I repeated in my mind over and over again were the words that I was to blame. She rubbed K's grave-stone and said she liked it very much. It was not a very good one, but because I had gone to a stonemason myself and ordered it, she must have wished to praise it. I thought of K's bones, newly buried under this grave-stone; then I thought of my new wife, and I could not help feeling the mockery of Destiny. Then I made up my mind not to visit K's grave with my wife.

52

Such a feeling toward my dead friend lasted for a long time. This was indeed what I had feared from the beginning. Even my marriage, my long cherished hope, I went through with an uneasy mind. But because no human being can see through the future, I thought it would perhaps change my mood completely and lead me to a new life. However, when I began to live with my wife, my fragile hope was destroyed by the stern reality. As I looked at my wife, I was suddenly threatened by K. That is to say, my wife stood between K and me, and bound me to him, never releasing me from his apparition. Though everything in my wife pleased me, I wanted to shun her because of this one thing. On the other hand, this feeling of mine immediately impressed itself on her sensitive heart, and yet she could not understand the reason for it. She often cross-examined me as to what I was musing on so intently and asked me what was wrong with her. Sometimes I could laugh it off, but sometimes she became hysterical, complaining, "You must be disliking me," or "I am sure you are keeping something from me," and I was tortured.

I often thought of confessing the truth to my wife. But whenever I was on the verge of telling her, some power outside myself suddenly came upon me and restrained me. Perhaps it is not necessary to tell you why, because you understand me so well, but I feel I ought to explain this. In those days I had no intention whatever to pretend to my wife that I was a worthier man than I really was. Moreover, if I had confessed everything to my wife with a heart as honest and meek as when I faced K in my mind, she would have certainly forgiven my sin, even with tears of joy, and so I was not consulting my own interest when I hesitated. I did not confess because I could not bear to leave a black spot in her memory. Please understand that it was too painful for me to sprinkle even a drop of ink over anything so pure white.

I, who could not get rid myself of the thought of K, was always restless. I tried to bury myself in books to drive away my uneasiness, and began to work at a terrific pace. I waited for the day when I could publish the result of my studies to the world. However, this deliberate aim, too, was very painful, because it was all false and groundless, and I could no longer be absorbed in books. I folded my arms again and began to observe the world.

That my mind was relaxed because there was no need for me to work for daily bread seemed to be my wife's interpretation of my state. It was quite natural for her to think so, because she and her mother had their own property which was enough for them to live on quietly without doing anything, and I myself was in no need of a situation. Perhaps I was more or less spoilt by this. But the chief reason why I became inactive did not lie there at all. In the days when I was deceived by my uncle, I felt it to the marrow of my bones that humanity was not to be relied upon, but I still trusted myself, all the more because I condemned others. Somewhere in my mind was a belief that I was a trustworthy fellow, no matter how wicked the world was. I suddenly tottered as this belief was completely destroyed by K's death and realized that I was exactly the same kind of man as my uncle. I, who had been disgusted with other people, was now disgusted with myself, and could not move any further.

FURTHER READINGS

Any attempt at compiling a comprehensive bibliography of Soseki studies is a formidable task. What follows is simply a brief listing of both primary and secondary works from which the reader can draw upon when delving further into Natsume Soseki's life and writings. Both Beongheon Yu's *Natsume Soseki* (New York: Twayne, 1969) and *Essays on Natsume Soseki's Works*, compiled by the Japanese National Commission for UNESCO (Tokyo: Ministry of Education, 1970) provide an excellent introduction to any study of Soseki and his works. Makoto Ueda, *Modern Japanese Writers* (Stanford, CA: Stanford University Press, 1976) examines eight major modern Japanese authors including Soseki. Hisaki Yamanouchi, *The Search for Authenticity in Modern Japanese Literature* (New York: Cambridge University Press, 1978) contains seven essays on Japanese literature since 1868 including "The Agonies of Individualism" on Soseki. Edwin McClellan, "An Introduction to Soseki," *Harvard Journal of Asiatic Studies*, 20 (1959), 150–208, provides a balanced study of Soseki exclusive of his last two works. A brief biographical sketch of Soseki and an analysis of his major works is included in Edwin McClellan's *Two Japanese Novelists: Soseki and Toson* (Chicago: University of Chicago Press, 1969). Maso Miyoshi, *Accomplices of Silence: The Modern Japanese Novel* (Berkeley: University of California Press, 1974) discusses six major Japanese writers of the novel, including Soseki, and briefly examines their works.

A helpful study of Japanese intellectual life between 1868 and 1912 is available in Hilary Conroy, Sandra T. W. Davis, and Wayne Patterson, eds.,

Japan in Transition: Thought and Transition in the Meiji Era, 1868–1912 (London: Associated University Press, 1984). Yoshie Okazaki, *Japanese Literature in the Meiji Era*, trans. and adapted by V. H. Viglielmo (Tokyo: Obundsha, 1955) provides a survey of Meiji literature. Two works which are very helpful in assessing the significance of Western influence on modern Japanese culture are Inazo Nitobe, et al., *Western Influences in Modern Japan* (Chicago: University of Chicago Press, 1931) and Donald Keene, *Modern Japanese Novels and the West* (Charlottesville: University of Virginia Press, 1961).

Listed below are some of Soseki's prose writings available in English. Natsume Soseki, *I Am a Cat*, trans. Aiko Ito and Graeme Wilson (Rutland, VT: C. E. Tuttle, 1979); *Ten Nights' Dreams and Our Cat's Grave*, trans. Sankichi Hata and Dofu Shirai (Tokyo: Shito Shorin, 1934); *Within My Glass Doors*, trans. Iwao Matsuhara and E. T. Inglehart (Tokyo: Shinseido, 1928); *Botchan*, trans. Naota Ogata (Tokyo: Maruyen, 1923); *The Three-Cornered World*, trans. Alan Turney (Chicago: Henry Regnery, 1965); and *The Wayfarer*, trans. Beongcheon Yu (Detroit: Wayne State University Press, 1967).

A MADMAN'S DIARY
Lu Hsun

The twentieth century has seen China continuously shaken by internal conflict and foreign intervention. The period began with China's defeat in the war of 1894–1895 against Japan, which ushered in an era of change. A complex interaction ensued between the forces of reform, reaction, and revolution. The weakness displayed by China during the war of 1894–1895 was a beacon attracting such imperialistic powers as Britain, France, Russia, Germany, and Japan. Each of the imperialist nations sought to further their own immediate national interests at the expense of the Chinese people. As economic and political concessions were extracted from the Chinese government, resentment on the part of the Chinese grew strong. In 1900 this indignation broke out in violence. The Boxer Rebellion, encouraged by the support of the Ch'ing officials, enjoyed

From Lu Hsun, *Selected Stories of Lu Hsun*, trans. Yang Hsien-yi and Gladys Yang (Peking: Foreign Language Press, 1978), pp. 7–18. Reprinted by permission.

some initial success but ultimately was doomed to failure. China's international standing, as well as that of the Ch'ing dynasty, further declined as a result of the rebellion.

During the period from 1895 to 1911, the modern sector of the Chinese economy enjoyed a steady development due, in part, to foreign investment. This economic growth was accompanied by significant social changes, including the rise of a bourgeoisie and the emergence of an urban working class. The horrible working conditions alienated many of the working class, while, at the same time, the old family system came under increasing criticism. The new economic, political, and social demands helped to spur on a reform movement that advocated the reexamination of the "old" basic tenets of Chinese society. Many reformers contended that Western learning was needed to enable the Chinese to discard much of the old traditions, including even the teachings of Confucius. These reformers, operating chiefly through study groups and journalism, advocated the conversion of the Chinese government into a modern, constitutional government.

The Empress Dowager attempted to save the dynasty through a series of reforms, but it was too little too late, and in 1911 a revolution occurred that led to the abdication of the Manchu child-emperor on February 12, 1912. The dynastic era had ended, but the question remained as to what would replace it. The political situation in China became increasingly complicated. While a national government ruled in Peking, the real authority rested in the hands of regional leaders (warlords) who controlled their territories primarily through force of arms. The foreign presence continued throughout the period.

The destruction of the old traditions was evident particularly in the intellectual world. Revolutionary thoughts were commonplace among Chinese students residing in Tokyo and quite visible as well in magazines and schools in China. An important moment in the revolutionary movement was the founding in 1915 of the journal *Hsin Ch'ing-nien* (*New Youth*), which was to become the most influential magazine in the cultural revolution of that period. *New Youth* not only opposed the traditional teachings, but also championed the use of the vernacular in place of the old language of the classics. The campaign proved successful, and by 1930 the vernacular was employed universally in Chinese schools.

Many of the intellectuals who strongly advocated reform were on the faculty of Peking University. Their views were popular with students at this and other Chinese universities. On May 4, 1919, approximately three thousand of these students demonstrated in protest of the continued foreign interference in Chinese matters. The demonstrations became violent and were followed by more protests and strikes and by a show of support for the students by merchants and laborers. Finally, the government conceded to the protesters—those who had been detained were released, and those responsible for the arrests were forced to resign. For many, the May Fourth incident represented much of the prevailing thought initially expressed in *New Youth* and gave rise to the term "May Fourth movement" frequently employed to indicate the period from 1915 to the early 1920s. Practically every facet of traditional Chinese culture now came under criticism from intellectuals in an array of publications.

One of the leading intellectuals of the May Fourth movement was Lu Hsun, the pen name of Chou Shu-jen (1881–1936). He ranks as the single most celebrated writer in twentieth-century China and as the founder of China's new realist literature. His works enjoy immense popularity in China with an audience of approximately eight hundred million readers. Lu Hsun was born in Shao-ch'ing, Chekiang province, and received a traditional education prior to his enrollment in new-style schools in Nanking. In 1902 he was sent to Japan to study on a government scholarship. He chose medicine, but in 1906 he ended his studies in order to devote himself to literary endeavors—attuned to the problems in China, Lu Hsun felt that he could accomplish more through writing than medicine. According to Lu Hsun, in a weak and backward country, it is essential to change the spirit of the people, and he felt that literature was the best means to do this. On his return to China in 1909, his literary career stagnated until he was finally catapulted to fame in 1918 by the publication in *New Youth* of his short story *A Madman's Diary*. The work has been praised as China's first modern short story due to its use of the vernacular and its ravaging critique of traditional Chinese culture. The majority of his stories were composed between 1918 and 1925. This was the initial era of the Chinese Revolution, the time of the May Fourth movement, the establishment of the Communist Party, and the mass movement against the imperialists.

A Madman's Diary represented what could be considered a declaration of war against the long history of feudalism in China. The story portrays the author's attitude towards Chinese traditions. Despite its obvious moral seriousness, Lu Hsun's indictment that Chinese life is hypocritical and cruel is presented in an ingenious manner. Suffering from a persecution complex, the madman thinks that those around him, including his immediate family, are going to kill and eat him. To confirm his suspicions, one evening he delves into a book on Chinese history. There he discovers that, in spite of the Chinese profession of benevolence and righteousness, traditional Chinese life consists of cannibalism. It is this indictment of the "man-eating old social system," conveyed through the conflict between the oppressive social force and its deluded victim, that illuminates the reader to the truth that society not only can oppress but also can destroy. Lu Hsun's abhorrence of the old China with its "putrid morals and death-stiff language" is clearly and cleverly presented in this historic plea for reform.

Questions

1. As the madman becomes more insightful, how does he appear in the eyes of other people?

2. Does the madman's realization liberate him from the grip of the cannibalistic crowd? Does his enlightenment allow him to effect any changes in the crowd's thinking?

3. At the end of the story, the madman makes a plea that "Perhaps there are still children who have not eaten men? Save the children." What is meant by this appeal?

A MADMAN'S DIARY

Two brothers, whose names I need not mention here, were both good friends of mine in high school; but after a separation of many years we gradually lost touch. Some time ago I happened to hear that one of them was seriously ill, and since I was going back to my old home I broke my journey to call on them, I saw only one, however, who told me that the invalid was his younger brother.

"I appreciate your coming such a long way to see us," he said, "but my brother recovered some time ago and has gone elsewhere to take up an official post." Then, laughing, he produced two volumes of his brother's diary, saying that from these the nature of his past illness could be seen, and that there was no harm in showing them to an old friend. I took the diary away, read it through, and found that he had suffered from a form of persecution complex. The writing was most confused and incoherent, and he had made many wild statements; moreover he had omitted to give any dates, so that only by the colour of the ink and the differences in the writing could one tell that it was not written at one time. Certain sections, however, were not altogether disconnected, and I have copied out a part to serve as a subject for medical research. I have not altered a single illogicality in the diary and have changed only the names, even though the people referred to are all country folk, unknown to the world and of no consequence. As for the title, it was chosen by the diarist himself after his recovery, and I did not change it.

I

Tonight the moon is very bright.

I have not seen it for over thirty years, so today when I saw it I felt in unusually high spirits. I begin to realize that during the past thirty-odd years I have been in the dark; but now I must be extremely careful. Otherwise why should that dog at the Chao house have looked at me twice?

I have reason for my fear.

II

Tonight there is no moon at all, I know that this bodes ill. This morning when I went out cautiously, Mr. Chao had a strange look in his eyes, as if he were afraid of me, as if he wanted to murder me. There were seven or eight others, who discussed me in a whisper. And they were afraid of my seeing them. All the people I passed were like that. The fiercest among them grinned at me; whereupon I shivered from head to foot, knowing that their preparations were complete.

I was not afraid, however, but continued on my way. A group of children in front were also discussing me, and the look in their eyes was just like that in Mr. Chao's while their faces too were ghastly pale. I wondered what grudge these children could have against me to make them behave like this. I could not help calling out: "Tell me!" But then they ran away.

I wonder what grudge Mr. Chao can have against me, what grudge the people on the road can have against me. I can think of nothing except that twenty years ago I trod on Mr. Ku Chiu's[1] account sheets for many years past, and Mr. Ku was very displeased. Although Mr. Chao does not know him, he must have heard talk of this and decided to avenge him, so he is conspiring against me with the people on the road. But then what of the children? At that time they were not yet born, so why should they eye me so strangely today, as if they were afraid of me, as if they wanted to murder me? This really frightens me, it is so bewildering and upsetting.

I know. They must have learned this from their parents!

III

I can't sleep at night. Everything requires careful consideration if one is to understand it.

Those people, some of whom have been pilloried by the magistrate, slapped in the face by the local gentry, had their wives taken away by bailiffs, or their parents driven to suicide by creditors, never looked as frightened and as fierce then as they did yesterday.

---

[1]Ku Chiu means "ancient times." Lu Hsun had in mind the long history of feudal oppression in China.

The most extraordinary thing was that woman on the street yesterday who spanked her son and said, "Little devil! I'd like to bite several mouthfuls out of you to work off my feelings!" Yet all the time she looked at me. I gave a start, unable to control myself; then all those green-faced, long-toothed people began to laugh derisively. Old Chen hurried forward and dragged me home.

He dragged me home. The folk at home all pretended not to know me; they had the same look in their eyes as all the others. When I went into the study, they locked the door outside as if cooping up a chicken or a duck. This incident left me even more bewildered.

A few days ago a tenant of ours from Wolf Cub Village came to report the failure of the crops, and told my elder brother that a notorious character in their village had been beaten to death; then some people had taken out his heart and liver, fried them in oil and eaten them, as a means of increasing their courage. When I interrupted, the tenant and my brother both stared at me. Only today have I realized that they had exactly the same look in their eyes as those people outside.

Just to think of it sets me shivering from the crown of my head to the soles of my feet.

They eat human beings, so they may eat me.

I see that woman's "bite several mouthfuls out of you," the laughter of those green-faced, long-toothed people and the tenant's story the other day are obviously secret signs. I realize all the poison in their speech, all the daggers in their laughter. Their teeth are white and glistening: they are all man-eaters.

It seems to me, although I am not a bad man, ever since I trod on Mr. Ku's accounts it has been touch-and-go. They seem to have secrets which I cannot guess, and once they are angry they will call anyone a bad character. I remember when my elder brother taught me to write compositions, no matter how good a man was, if I produced arguments to the contrary he would mark that passage to show his approval; while if I excused evil-doers, he would say: "Good for you, that shows originality." How can I possibly guess their secret thoughts—especially when they are ready to eat people?

Everything requires careful consideration if one is to understand it. In ancient times, as I recollect, people often ate human beings, but I am rather hazy about it. I tried to look this up, but my history has no chronology, and scrawled all over each page are the words: "Virtue and Morality." Since I could not sleep anyway, I read intently half the night, until I began to see words between the lines, the whole book being filled with the two words—"Eat people."

All these words written in the book, all the words spoken by our tenant, gaze at me strangely with an enigmatic smile.

I too am a man, and they want to eat me!

IV

In the morning I sat quietly for some time. Old Chen brought lunch in: one bowl of vegetables, one bowl of steamed fish. The eyes of the fish were white and hard, and its mouth was open just like those people who want to eat human beings. After a few mouthfuls I could not tell whether the slippery morsels were fish or human flesh, so I brought it all up.

I said, "Old Chen, tell my brother that I feel quite suffocated, and want to have a stroll in the garden." Old Chen said nothing but went out, and presently he came back and opened the gate.

I did not move, but watched to see how they would treat me, feeling certain that they would not let me go. Sure enough! My elder brother came slowly out, leading an old man. There was a murderous gleam in his eyes, and fearing that I would see it he lowered his head, stealing glances at me from the side of his spectacles.

"You seem to be very well today," said my brother.

"Yes," said I.

"I have invited Mr. Ho here today," said my brother, "to examine you."

"All right," said I. Actually I knew quite well that this old man was the executioner in disguise! He simply used the pretext of feeling my pulse to see how fat I was; for by so doing he would receive a share of my flesh. Still I was not afraid. Although I do not eat men, my courage is greater than theirs. I held out my two fists, to see what he would do. The old man sat down, closed his eyes, fumbled for some time and remained still for some time; then he opened his shifty eyes and said, "Don't let your imagination run away with you. Rest quietly for a few days, and you will be all right."

Don't let your imagination run away with you! Rest quietly for a few days! When I have grown fat, naturally they will have more to eat; but what good will it do me, or how can it be "all right"? All these people wanting to eat human flesh and at the same time stealthily trying to keep up appearances, not daring to act promptly, really made me nearly die of laughter. I could not help roaring with laughter, I was so amused. I knew that in this laughter were courage and integrity. Both the old man and my brother turned pale, awed by my courage and integrity.

But just because I am brave they are the more eager to eat me, in order to acquire some of my courage. The old man went out the gate, but before he had gone far he said to my brother in a low voice, "To be eaten at once!" And my brother nodded. So you are in it too! This stupendous discovery, although it came as a shock, is yet no more than I had expected: the accomplice in eating me is my elder brother!

The eater of human flesh is my elder brother!

I am the younger brother of an eater of human flesh!

I myself will be eaten by others, but none the less I am the younger brother of an eater of human flesh!

V

These few days I have been thinking again: suppose that old man were not an executioner in disguise, but a real doctor; he would be none the less an eater of human flesh. In that book on herbs, written by his predecessor Li Shih-chen,[2] it is clearly stated that men's flesh can be boiled and eaten; so can he still say that he does not eat men?

As for my elder brother, I have also good reason to suspect him. When he was teaching me, he said with his own lips, "People exchange their sons to eat." And once in discussing a bad man, he said that not only did he deserve to be killed, he should "have his flesh eaten and his hide slept on."[3] I was still young then, and my heart beat faster for some time, he was not at all surprised by the story that our tenant from Wolf Cub Village told us the other day about eating a man's heart and liver, but kept nodding his head. He is evidently just as cruel as before. Since it is possible to "exchange sons to eat," then anything can be exchanged, anyone can be eaten. In the past I simply listened to his explanations, and let it go at that; now I know that when he explained it to me, not only was there human fat at the corner of his lips, but his whole heart was set on eating men.

VI

Pitch dark. I don't know whether it is day or night. The Chao family dog has started barking again.

The fierceness of a lion, the timidity of a rabbit, the craftiness of a fox. . . .

VII

I know their way; they are not willing to kill anyone outright, nor do they dare, for fear of the consequences. Instead they have banded together and set traps everywhere, to force me to kill myself. The behaviour of the men and women in the street a few days ago, and my elder brother's attitude these last few days, make it quite obvious. What they like best is for a man to take off his belt,

[2] A famous pharmacologist (1518–1593), author of *Ben-cao-gang-mu*, the *Materia Medica*.
[3] These are quotations from the old classic *Zuo Zhuan*.

and hang himself from a beam; for then they can enjoy their heart's desire without being blamed for murder. Naturally that sets them roaring with delighted laughter. On the other hand, if a man is frightened or worried to death, although that makes him rather thin, they still nod in approval.

They only eat dead flesh! I remember reading somewhere of a hideous beast, with an ugly look in its eye, called "hyena" which often eats dead flesh. Even the largest bones it grinds into fragments and swallows: the mere thought of this is enough to terrify one. Hyenas are related to wolves, and wolves belong to the canine species. The other day the dog in the Chao house looked at me several times; obviously it is in the plot too and has become their accomplice. The old man's eyes were cast down, but that did not deceive me!

The most deplorable is my elder brother. He is also a man, so why is he not afraid, why is he plotting with others to eat me? Is it that when one is used to it he no longer thinks it a crime? Or is it that he has hardened his heart to do something he knows is wrong?

In cursing man-eaters, I shall start with my brother, and in dissuading man-eaters, I shall start with him too.

VIII

Actually, such arguments should have convinced them long ago. . . .

Suddenly someone came in. He was only about twenty years old and I did not see his features very clearly. His face was wreathed in smiles, but when he nodded to me his smile did not seem genuine. I asked him: "Is it right to eat human beings?"

Still smiling, he replied, "When there is no famine how can one eat human beings?"

I realized at once, he was one of them; but still I summoned up courage to repeat my question:

"Is it right?"

"What makes you ask such a thing? You really are . . . fond of a joke. . . . It is very fine today."

"It is fine, and the moon is very bright. But I want to ask you: Is it right?"

He looked disconcerted, and muttered: "No. . . ."

"No? Then why do they still do it?"

"What are you talking about?"

"What am I talking about? They are eating men now in Wolf Cub Village, and you can see it written all over the books, in fresh red ink."

His expression changed, and he grew ghastly pale. "It may be so," he said, staring at me. "It has always been like that. . . ."

"Is it right because it has always been like that?"

"I refuse to discuss these things with you. Anyway, you shouldn't talk about it. Whoever talks about it is in the wrong!"

I leaped up and opened my eyes wide, but the man had vanished. I was soaked with perspiration. He was much younger than my elder brother, but even so he was in it. He must have been taught by his parents. And I am afraid he has already taught his son: that is why even the children look at me so fiercely.

IX

Wanting to eat men, at the same time afraid of being eaten themselves, they all look at each other with the deepest suspicion. . . .

How comfortable life would be for them if they could rid themselves of such obsessions and go to work, walk, eat and sleep at ease. They have only this one step to take. Yet fathers and sons, husbands and wives, brothers, friends, teachers and students, sworn enemies and even strangers, have all joined in this conspiracy, discouraging and preventing each other from taking this step.

X

Early this morning I went to look for my elder brother. He was standing outside the hall door looking at the sky, when I walked up behind him, stood between him and the door, and with exceptional poise and politeness said to him:

"Brother, I have something to say to you."

"Well, what is it?" he asked, quickly turning towards me and nodding.

"It is very little, but I find it difficult to say. Brother, probably all primitive people ate a little human flesh to begin with. Later, because their outlook changed, some of them stopped, and because they tried to be good they changed into men, changed into real men. But some are still eating—just like reptiles. Some have changed into fish, birds, monkeys and finally men; but some do not try to be good and remain reptiles still. When those who eat men compare themselves with those who do not, how ashamed they must be. Probably much more ashamed than the reptiles are before monkeys.

"In ancient times Yi Ya boiled his son for Chieh and Chou to eat; that is the old story.[4] But actually since the creation of heaven and earth by Pan Ku men have been eating each other, from the time of Yi Ya's son to the time of Hsu

[4]According to ancient records, Yi Ya cooked his son and presented him to Duke Huan of Chi who reigned from 685 to 643 B.C. Chieh and Chou were tyrants of an earlier age. The madman has made a mistake here.

Hsi-lin,[5] and from the time of Hsu Hsi-lin down to the man caught in Wolf Cub Village. Last year they executed a criminal in the city, and a consumptive soaked a piece of bread in his blood and sucked it.

"They want to eat me, and of course you can do nothing about it single-handed; but why should you join them? As man-eaters they are capable of anything. If they eat me, they can eat you as well; members of the same group can still eat each other. But if you will just change your ways immediately, then everyone will have peace. Although this has been going on since time immemorial, today we could make a special effort to be good, and say this is not to be done! I'm sure you can say so, brother. The other day when the tenant wanted the rent reduced, you said it couldn't be done."

At first he only smiled cynically, then a murderous gleam came into his eyes, and when I spoke of their secret his face turned pale. Outside the gate stood a group of people, including Mr. Chao and his dog, all craning their necks to peer in. I could not see all their faces, for they seemed to be masked in cloths; some of them looked pale and ghastly still, concealing their laughter. I knew they were one band, all eaters of human flesh. But I also knew that they did not all think alike by any means. Some of them thought that since it had always been so, men should be eaten. Some of them knew that they should not eat men, but still wanted to; and they were afraid people might discover their secret; thus when they heard me they became angry, but they still smiled their cynical, tight-lipped smile.

Suddenly my brother looked furious, and shouted in a loud voice:

"Get out of here, all of you! What is the point of looking at a madman?"

Then I realized part of their cunning. They would never be willing to change their stand, and their plans were all laid; they had stigmatized me as a madman. In future when I was eaten, not only would there be no trouble, but people would probably be grateful to them. When our tenant spoke of the villagers eating a bad character, it was exactly the same device. This is their old trick.

Old Chen came in too, in a great temper, but they could not stop my mouth, I had to speak to those people:

"You should change, change from the bottom of your hearts!" I said. "You must know that in future there will be no place for man-eaters in the world.

"If you don't change, you may all be eaten by each other. Although so many are born, they will be wiped out by the real men, just like wolves killed by hunters. Just like reptiles!"

---

[5] A revolutionary at the end of the Ching dynasty (1644–1911), Hsu Hsi-lin was executed in 1907 for assassinating a Ching official. Hsu Hsi-lin's heart and liver were eaten.

Old Chen drove everybody away. My brother had disappeared. Old Chen advised me to go back to my room. The room was pitch dark. The beams and rafters shook above my head. After shaking for some time they grew larger. They piled on top of me.

The weight was so great, I could not move. They meant that I should die. I knew that the weight was false, so I struggled out, covered in perspiration. But I had to say:

"You should change at once, change from the bottom of your hearts! You must know that in future there will be no place for man-eaters in the world. . . ."

XI

The sun does not shine, the door is not opened, every day two meals.

I took up my chopsticks, then thought of my elder brother; I know now how my little sister died: it was all through him. My sister was only five at the time. I can still remember how lovable and pathetic she looked. Mother cried and cried, but he begged her not to cry, probably because he had eaten her himself, and so her crying made him feel ashamed. If he had any sense of shame. . . .

My sister was eaten by my brother, but I don't know whether mother realized it or not.

I think mother must have known, but when she cried she did not say so outright, probably because she thought it proper too. I remember when I was four or five years old, sitting in the cool of the hall, my brother told me that if a man's parents were ill, he should cut off a piece of his flesh and boil it for them if he wanted to be considered a good son; and mother did not contradict him. If one piece could be eaten, obviously so could the whole. And yet just to think of the mourning then still makes my heart bleed; that is the extraordinary thing about it!

XII

I can't bear to think of it.

I have only just realized that I have been living all these years in a place where for four thousand years they have been eating human flesh. My brother had just taken over the charge of the house when our sister died, and he may well have used her flesh in our rice and dishes, making us eat it unwittingly.

It is possible that I ate several pieces of my sister's flesh unwittingly, and now it is my turn. . . .

How can a man like myself, after four thousand years of man-eating history—even though I knew nothing about it at first—ever hope to face real men?

XIII

Perhaps there are still children who have not eaten men?
Save the children. . . .

April 1918

FURTHER READINGS

Jonathan D. Spence, *The Gate of Heavenly Peace: The Chinese and Their Revolution, 1895–1980* (New York: Viking, 1981) examines the political development of China during the twentieth century, focusing on three people, including Lu Hsun. Mary Wright, *China in Revolution: The First Phase, 1900–1913* (New Haven, CT: Yale University Press, 1968) concentrates on the revolutionary movement in China at the beginning of the twentieth century. The revolution in China between 1915 and 1949, in particular, the relationship between China's social crisis and the revolutionary movement it bred, is analyzed in Lucien Bianco, *Origins of the Chinese Revolution*, trans. Murial Bell (Stanford, CA: Stanford University Press, 1971). The May Fourth movement is the subject of a number of works including the following: Vera Schwarcz, *The Chinese Enlightenment* (Berkeley: University of California Press, 1986) is a comprehensive examination of the movement; Yu-sheng Lin, *The Crisis of Chinese Consciousness* (Madison: University of Wisconsin Press, 1979) looks at radical anti-traditionalism in the movement; and Merle Goldman, ed., *Modern Chinese Literature in the May Fourth Era* (Cambridge, MA: Harvard University Press, 1979) studies the literature of the period.

C. T. Hsia, *A History of Modern Chinese Fiction, 1917–1957* (New Haven, CT: Yale University Press, 1971) provides an insightful look at the development of twentieth-century Chinese literature, including a chapter on Lu Hsun. The influential Chinese writers of the 1920s and 1930s are examined in Tsi-an Hsia, *The Gate of Darkness: Studies on the Leftist Literary Movement in China* (Seattle: University of Washington Press, 1968). An excellent collection of essays on Lu Hsun is available in Leo Ou-fan Lee, ed., *Lu Xun and His Legacy* (Berkeley: University of California Press, 1985). A helpful analysis of the atmosphere in which Lu Hsun wrote is provided in V. I. Semanov, *Lu Hsun and His Predecessors*, trans. Charles J. Alber (White Plains, NY: M. E. Sharpe, 1980). Leo Ou-fan Lee, *Voices from the Iron Horse: A Study of Lu Xun* (Bloomington: Indiana University Press, 1987) is a comprehensive study of the individual and his works. It includes a lengthy and useful bibliography.

Numerous anthologies containing Lu Hsun's works are available in English translation. Notable among these are Lu Hsun, *The Complete Stories of Lu*

Xun, trans. Yang Xianyi and Gladys Yang (Bloomington: Indiana University Press, 1981), Lu Hsun, *Silent China: Selected Writings of Lu Xun*, trans. and ed. Gladys Yang (New York: Oxford University Press, 1973), and Lu Hsun, *Old Tales Retold*, trans. Hsien-yi Yang and Gladys Yang (Beijing: Foreign Language Press, 1972).

AN OUTLINE FOR THE RECONSTRUCTION
OF JAPAN
Kita Ikki

After the turn of the century and especially following World War I, Japan embarked upon an era of development and change that was to culminate in the tragedy of the Pacific War. During the 1920s, a liberal civilian element controlled Japanese policy, but their position quickly eroded during the 1930s as a result of the rapid rise to power of the military. The 1930s was a turbulent, reactionary period dominated by mounting tensions encountered by Japan as it became a modern world power. Strong nationalistic sentiment fueled the demand for radical reform of domestic institutions, while, at the same time, stimulating expansionist, militaristic tendencies.

The civilian government's ties with big business and their policies of accommodation with the West and conciliation with China caused discontent among members of various patriotic organizations in Japan. The army in particular, resentful of large cuts in its budget and dissatisfied with government policies, became a hotbed of dissent. The decline of the civilian administration at the beginning of the 1930s led to a compromise government composed of professional bureaucrats, contingents of other political parties, and the armed forces. This uneasy equilibrium was broken in 1931 by Japan's invasion of Manchuria and subsequent establishment there of a puppet state. Fueled by their success in Manchuria and aided by sporadic acts of terrorism and assassination by individual terrorists at home, the military was able to reassert its power both in domestic and foreign affairs.

Many Japanese viewed the turbulent period between the two world wars as a unique opportunity to effect important changes at home and in Asia. Many Japanese intellectuals, often greatly influenced by Western ideas and policies,

From Kita Ikki, *An Outline for the Reconstruction of Japan*, in David John Lu, *Sources of Japanese History*, vol. 2, pp. 131–36. Copyright 1974 McGraw-Hill. Reprinted with permission.

attempted to guide Japan in the creation of a political system patterned after European fascism. These individuals advocated the use of the power of the state to carry out radical political and economic reforms.

Among the most vehement critics of party government was the radical nationalist Kita Ikki (1883–1937). An unusual and controversial figure, Kita became an almost legendary nationalist hero to some, while to the great majority he remained unknown or misunderstood. Kita, like other Japanese nationalists, strongly believed in Japan's national identity, the primacy of its mission, and the promise of progress through national effort. He favored immediate and drastic change in existing institutions in order to fulfill these goals. According to Kita's views, revolution was a necessary step by which a society enters the modern world, and, as a consequence, completing Japan's revolution was the duty of every Japanese patriot.

During his early years, Kita attached himself to the revolutionary activities of the Chinese nationalists. Following his disappointment at what he viewed as China's failure to produce an anti-imperialist, socialist state, Kita lived in Shanghai where he composed pamphlets advocating reforms for Japan. In 1919 he wrote his most notable treatise, *An Outline for the Reconstruction of Japan*. The work first appeared in mimeographed form in 1923 and, even though it was banned, attracted many followers including adherents among young military officers. His plan called upon the emperor to suspend the constitution and place Japan under martial law. These actions would allow the emperor complete freedom to suppress the reactionary movement by the wealthy and by the peers. The existing status quo would then be supplanted by the creation of a socialist state, which would control the national economy on behalf of the entire nation. The disproportionate development of Japanese society, in which the rich became richer and the peasants and urban workers grew poorer, would then be alleviated.

Kita's doctrine possessed great appeal to many young officers who came from poverty-stricken areas. His influence was evident in several assassination attempts and military coups staged by young military officers in the 1930s. First, in May 1932, with the intent of restoring control of the nation to the emperor and ending the parliamentary system, young military officers murdered Premier Inukai Tsuyoshi. Then on February 26, 1936, fifteen hundred troops from the army's First Division in Tokyo mutinied against the government and seized the center of the city. These rebels, inspired by Kita's doctrines, advocated similar reforms to those advocated in the 1932 coup. The insurrection failed, and Kita was subsequently implicated in the plot and executed along with other conspirators. However, his ideas of internal reform and external expansion lived on. The influence of the army increased significantly in the months that followed the February 26 incident and, ironically, the revolt is often blamed for bringing forth a "fascist" government apparently representing just what Kita is supposed to have advocated. His life and writings strongly reflect the many tensions Japan experienced in its rapid transformation into a modern urban-industrial society.

Questions

1. Kita Ikki is frequently considered to be the intellectual leader of the fascist movement in prewar Japan. What similarities do his views have with those of European fascists? What differences?
2. Kita was a strong Japanese nationalist; what in his work is specifically Japanese in tone and content?
3. How did Kita feel about the modernization of Japanese society? According to him, what was necessary in order for Japan to emerge as a modern industrial society?
4. Why did Kita feel so strongly about the need for radical reform of Japanese domestic institutions?

AN OUTLINE FOR THE RECONSTRUCTION OF JAPAN

GENERAL OUTLINE OF MEASURES FOR THE REORGANIZATION OF JAPAN, 1923

SECTION 1. THE EMPEROR OF THE PEOPLE

Suspension of the Constitution: In order to establish a firm base for national reorganization, the Emperor, with the aid of the entire Japanese nation and by invoking his imperial prerogatives, shall suspend the constitution for a period of three years, dissolve the two houses of the Diet, and place the entire country under martial law.

The true significance of the Emperor: We must make clear the fundamental principle that the Emperor is the sole representative of the people and the pillar of the state.

To clarify this doctrine, there shall be instituted a sweeping reform in the imperial court, consistent with the spirit shown by Emperor Jimmu in the founding of the nation and by Emperor Meiji in the Restoration. The incumbent Privy Councillors and other officials shall be replaced by men of ability, sought throughout the realm, capable of assisting the Emperor.

An Advisory Council shall be established to assist the Emperor. Its members, fifty in number, shall be appointed by the Emperor.

Whenever the Cabinet Council so decides or the Diet places a vote of non-confidence against him, an Advisory Council member shall submit his resignation to the Emperor. However, this procedure shall not be interpreted to mean that Council members are responsible to the Cabinet or the Diet.

Abolition of the peerage system: By abolishing the peerage system, we shall be able to remove the feudal aristocracy which constitutes a barrier between the Emperor and the people. In this way the spirit of the Meiji Restoration shall be proclaimed.

The House of Peers shall be replaced by the Deliberative Council which shall review decisions made by the House of Representatives. The Deliberative Council may reject for a single time only any decisions of the House of Representatives.

The members of the Deliberative Council shall consist of men distinguished in various fields of activities, elected by each other or appointed by the Emperor.

Popular election: All men twenty-five years of age and above shall have the right to elect and be elected to the House of Representatives, exercising their rights with full equality as citizens of Great Japan. Similar provisions shall apply to all local self-governing bodies. No women shall be permitted to participate in politics.

Restoration of people's freedom: Existing laws which restrict people's freedom and circumvent the spirit of the constitution shall be abolished. These laws include the civil service appointment ordinance, peace preservation law, press act, and publication law.

National reorganization Cabinet: A national reorganization Cabinet shall be formed during the time martial law is in effect. In addition to the existing ministries, the Cabinet shall establish such ministries of industries as described below and add a number of ministers without portfolio. Members of the reorganization Cabinet shall be selected from outstanding individuals throughout the country, avoiding those who are presently connected with military, bureaucratic, financial, or party cliques.

All present prefectural governors shall be replaced by national reorganization governors, selected in accordance with a policy similar to the one above.

National reorganization Diet: A popularly elected national reorganization Diet shall convene to discuss matters pertaining to reorganization during the time martial law is in effect. However, this Diet shall not have the power to debate those basic national reorganization policies proclaimed by the Emperor.

Granting of imperial estate: The Emperor shall set a personal example by granting to the state, the lands, forests, shares and similar properties held by the

Imperial Household. The expenses of the Imperial Household shall be limited to thirty million yen per annum appropriated from the national treasury. However, the Diet may authorize additional expenditure if the need arises.

SECTION 2: LIMITATION ON PRIVATE PROPERTY

Limitation on private property: No Japanese family shall possess property in excess of one million yen. A similar limitation shall apply to Japanese citizens holding property overseas. No one shall be permitted to make a gift of property to those related by blood or to others, or to transfer his property by other means with the intent of circumventing this limitation.

Nationalization of excess amount over limitation on private property: Any amount which exceeds the limitation on private property shall revert to the state without compensation. No one shall be permitted to resort to the protection of present laws in order to avoid remitting such excess amount. Anyone who violates these provisions shall be deemed a person thinking lightly of the example set by the Emperor and endangering the basis of national reorganization. As such, during the time martial law is in effect, he shall be charged with the crimes of endangering the person of the Emperor and engaging in internal revolt and shall be punished by death.[1]

SECTION 3: THREE PRINCIPLES FOR DISPOSITION OF LANDS

Limitation on private landholding: No Japanese family shall hold land in excess of 100,000 yen in current market value. . . .

. . . Lands held in excess of limitation on private landholding shall revert to the state. . . .

Popular ownership of lands reverted to state: The state shall divide the lands granted by the Imperial Household and the lands reverted to it from those whose holdings exceed the limitation and distribute such lands to farmers who do not possess their own lands. These farmers shall gain title to their respective lands by making annual installment payments to the state. . . .

Lands to be owned by the state: Large forests, virgin lands which require large capital investment, and lands which can best be cultivated in large lots shall be owned and operated by the state.

[1] Kita then advocates the establishment of a Council of Veterans Association as a permanent agency directly responsible to the reorganization cabinet charged with the tasks of: (1) maintaining order; (2) investigating excess property held by individuals; and (3) collecting excess amounts.

SECTION 4: CONTROL OF LARGE CAPITAL

Limitation on private property: No private industry shall exceed the limit of 10,000,000 yen in assets. A similar limitation shall apply to private industries owned by Japanese citizens overseas.

Nationalization of industries exceeding the limitation: Any industry whose assets exceed the limitation imposed on private industry shall be collectivized and operated under state control. . . .

INDUSTRIAL ORGANIZATION OF THE STATE

No. 1. Ministry of Banking: The assets of this ministry shall come from the money expropriated from large banks whose assets exceed the limitation on private industry and from individuals whose net worth exceeds the limitation on private property.

[The functions of the ministry shall include] overseas investments by utilizing its abundant assets and unified operation, making loans to other industrial ministries and to private banks, equitable adjustment of prices and currency in circulation, and guaranteeing the absolute safety of people's deposits.

No. 2. Ministry of Navigation: Ships and other assets expropriated from private lines in excess of the limitation on private property shall be utilized mainly for transoceanic voyages in order to attain supremacy of the seas. [The ministry shall also] engage in shipbuilding (naval and commercial) and other activities.

No. 3. Ministry of Mines: Large mines whose assets or market values exceed the limitation on private industry shall be expropriated and operated by this ministry. It shall also operate overseas mining industries financed by the Ministry of Banking, and engage actively in developing national mines in newly acquired colonies concurrently with the development of private mining industries.

No. 4. Ministry of Agriculture: Management of nationally-owned lands; management of Taiwan sugar industry and forestry; development of Taiwan, Hokkaido, Karafuto (Southern Sakhalin), and Chosen (Korea); development of South and North Manchuria and colonies to be acquired in the future; and management of large farms when acquired by the state.

No. 5. Ministry of Industries: Various large industries expropriated by the state shall be reorganized, unified, and expanded to form a truly large industrial combine through which all types of industries may acquire competitive advantages now possessed by comparable foreign industries. The ministry shall also operate industries urgently needed by the nation but not undertaken by private parties. Naval Steel Works and Military Ordinance Factories shall be placed under this ministry's jurisdiction and be operated by it.

No. 6. Ministry of Commerce: This ministry shall distribute all agricultural and industrial commodities produced by the state and private parties, adjust domestic commodity prices, and engage actively in overseas commerce. For this purpose, the ministry shall calculate the rates of customs duties for submission to the Cabinet.

No. 7. Ministry of Railways: This ministry shall replace the present Board of Railways and place under its unified operation the Chosen and South Manchurian Railways. It shall acquire title to railways in future colonies and engage actively in the construction of new railways.

Railways whose assets do not exceed the limitation on private industry shall be open to private operation.

Vast income of the national treasury: The vast income realized by the industrial ministries shall be sufficient for the expenditures of various service ministries and guarantee adequate living conditions for the people as described below. Therefore, with the exception of basic income taxes, all other inequitable taxes shall be abolished. Without exception, all industrial ministries shall be taxed in a manner similar to all private industries.

Monopoly of salt and tobacco shall be abolished. Based on the principle that state-owned industries and privately-owned industries can coexist, their production shall be open to private enterprise. . . . There shall be uniform taxes on both forms of production. . . .

SECTION 5: RIGHTS OF WORKERS

Functions of the Ministry of Labor: A Ministry of Labor shall be established within the Cabinet to protect the rights of all workers employed by state-owned and privately-owned industries. Industrial disputes shall be submitted to the Ministry of Labor for arbitration in accordance with a law to be enacted independently. This arbitration shall be uniformly binding on all industrial ministries, private industries, and workers.

Wages: Wages shall be in principle determined by free contract. Disputes over wages shall be resolved by the Ministry of Labor in accordance with the law described above.

Working hours: Working hours shall be uniformly set at eight hours a day. Wages shall be paid for Sundays and holidays when no work is performed. Farm workers shall receive additional wages for the overtime work performed during the busy farming seasons.

Distribution of profits to workers: One half of the net profits of private industries shall be distributed to workers employed in such industries. All workers, mental and physical, shall participate in the profit distribution proportionate to their salaries or wages. Workers shall elect their own representatives to participate in the industry's management planning and bookkeeping. Similar provisions shall apply to farm workers and landlords.

Workers employed in state-owned industries shall receive semi-annual bonuses in lieu of the profit distribution. Instead of participating in management planning and bookkeeping, such workers shall exercise their influence over the total industrial structure of the state through the House of Representatives.

Establishment of employee-shareholder system: Every private corporation shall set up a provision under which physical and mental workers in their employment shall have the right to become stockholders of the corporation.

Protection of tenant farmers: The state shall enact a separate law, based on the basic human rights, to protect tenant farmers tilling the land owned by small landlords whose holdings do not exceed the limitation on private lands.

Women's labor: Women's labor shall be free and equal to that of men. However, after the reorganization, the state shall make it a matter of national policy that the burden of labor shall not rest on the shoulders of women. In order to prepare women to replace men in providing needed labor in a national emergency, women shall receive education equal to that of men.

SECTION 6: PEOPLE'S RIGHT TO LIVE

Children's right to live: Children under fifteen years of age without both parents or father, having rights as children of the state, shall be uniformly supported and educated by the state. . . .

Support of the aged and disabled: The state shall assume the responsibility of supporting those men and women sixty years of age or over who are poor and not having their natural born or adopted sons. Similar support shall be given to those disabled and crippled persons who are poor, unable to work, and without fathers and sons.

Rights to education: National (compulsory) education shall last for a period of ten years from ages six to sixteen. Similar education shall be given to both male and female. There shall be instituted a fundamental reform in the educational system, with the aim of building a foundation for the furtherance of individual talents by imparting knowledge of worldwide scope based on the spirit of Japan and developing each individual's mind and body consistently throughout the ten-year period.

English shall be abolished and Esperanto shall become the second language[2]. . . .

---

[2]In the remaining paragraphs, Kita discusses protection of women's rights, freedom from interference by governmental officials, and rights to private property not in excess of the limitations previously imposed.

SECTION 8: RIGHTS OF THE STATE[3]

Continuation of the conscript system: The state, having rights to existence and development among the nations of the world, shall maintain the present conscript system in perpetuity. . . . Soldiers in active service shall receive stipends from the state. In the army bases and warships, there shall be no differentials in the enjoyment of provisions among the officers, soldiers, and seamen except the emblems signifying their respective ranks.

With regard to alien races residing in present and future colonies, a voluntary enlistment system may be adopted.

Positive right to start war: In addition to the right of self-defense, the state shall have the right to start a war on behalf of other nations and races unjustly oppressed by a third power. (As a matter of real concern today, the state shall have the right to start a war to aid the independence of India and preservation of China's integrity.)

As a result of its own development, the state shall also have the right to start a war against those nations who occupy large colonies illegally and ignore the heavenly way of the co-existence of all humanity. (As a matter of real concern today, the state shall have the right to start a war against those nations which occupy Australia and Far Eastern Siberia for the purpose of acquiring them.)

FURTHER READINGS

Since the 1950s, the turbulent prewar era in Japan has been the subject of numerous scholarly works. Of particular interest is George M. Wilson, *Revolutionary Nationalism in Japan: Kita Ikki, 1883–1937* (Cambridge, MA: Harvard University Press, 1969), which furnishes an insightful study of the radical Japanese nationalist. William M. Fletcher, *The Search for a New Order: Intellectuals and Fascism in Prewar Japan* (Chapel Hill: University of North Carolina Press, 1982) examines the internal dynamics that produced Japan's political and economic policies in the 1930s. The changing definitions of Japanese national objectives and policy making during the prewar era are analyzed in James B. Crowley's *Japan's Quest for Autonomy: National Security and Foreign Policy, 1930–1938* (Princeton, NJ: Princeton University Press, 1966). George M. Wilson, ed., *Crisis Politics in Prewar Japan* (Tokyo: Sophia University, 1972) provides a brief look at the internal workings of some of the major political crises that occurred in Japan during the 1930s. The most dramatic internal disturbance of

---

[3]Section 7 (omitted) outlines gradual incorporation of Chosen (Korea) in the political and administrative system of Japan proper, and application of the reorganization principles to Chosen, Taiwan, and other present and future colonies.

the period, the February 26, 1936 incident, is examined in Ben-Ami Shilloy, *Revolt in Japan: The Young Officers and the February 26, 1936 Incident* (Princeton, NJ: Princeton University Press, 1973). Richard Storry, *The Double Patriots: A Study of Japanese Nationalism* (Boston: Houghton-Mifflin, 1957) investigates the political ideas, events, and activities of Japanese nationalist groups and associations between the two world wars.

Japan's rise during the first half of the twentieth century to a position of world power is the subject of many useful texts. Notable among these is Richard Storry, *Japan and the Decline of the West in Asia, 1894–1943* (New York: Macmillan, 1979). David A. Titus, *Palace and Politics in Prewar Japan* (New York: Columbia University Press, 1974) concentrates on the structure and operation of palace politics during this period. Harry Wray and Hilary Conroy, eds., *Japan Examined: Perspectives on Modern Japanese History* (Honolulu: University of Hawaii Press, 1983) analyses important questions surrounding the development of modern Japan.

David John Lu, *Sources of Japanese History*, vol. 2 (New York: McGraw-Hill, 1974) provides a helpful collection of source material from Japan spanning the nineteenth and twentieth centuries. Another worthwhile anthology of primary works is Ivan I. Morris, *Japan 1931–1945: Militarism, Fascism, Japanism?* (Boston: Heath, 1963).

FAMILY
Pa Chin

The May Fourth era captured the imagination of the Chinese youth. They responded enthusiastically to the revolutionary ideas advocated by intellectuals in such progressive journals as *New Youth*. These magazines proposed intellectual and social reforms, emphasized the significance of Western science and technology, and strongly criticized the antiquated Chinese institutions. The May Fourth movement also had a profound effect on Chinese literature. The intellectual upheaval was accompanied by one in literature. With the fall from favor of Confucian thought among many intellectuals, literary bonds were lifted

From Pa Chin, *Family*, ed. Olga Lang (Garden City, NY: Doubleday, 1972), pp. 244–50, 252–68.

from both subject and content. Western influences, particularly European romanticism, fostered an emphasis on emotion in literature and, subsequently, stimulated revolutionary writers to view social matters as a prime concern of their writings. As time passed and economic, political, and social conditions in China failed to improve, the appeal of revolutionary doctrines increased. Authors of revolutionary conviction found much to draw upon in China's societal defects. They used their abilities to analyze and to assail traditional Chinese institutions such as the family system.

Prior to the revolution of 1911, the family had constituted the primary Chinese societal unit for millennia. The extended family, one of the oldest institutions in China, dictated that an individual was under the control of the family throughout his or her life. Oftentimes, if a person belonged to a particularly large family, three or more generations resided in a single family compound. This type of family unit represented the backbone of the traditional Chinese kinship system. The dominating principle behind this system was reflected in the Confucian kinship canons, which emphasized the relations among the various family members, including strict parental control of married sons, and the structuring of the family according to sex and age. Numerous authors attacked the evils of the old family system. These writers stressed a new role for women in the family and in society, freedom of association between male and female, marriage by free choice, more independence for the young, and a restructuring of the family unit more along the lines commonly found in the West.

Among works dealing with this subject, none was more popular than Pa Chin's (b. 1904) classic novel appropriately entitled *Family* (1931). The first volume in his *Turbulent Stream* trilogy, which deals with the decline of the Chinese family system, *Family* exposes the evils inherent in this societal organization. One of twentieth-century China's most popular and prolific writers, Pa Chin was a hero to a large number of Chinese youth during the 1930s and 1940s. An anarchist, his revolutionary humanitarianism appealed to the emotions of his readers. Pa Chin was born into a traditional upper-class family in western China and drew heavily on his own experiences for inspiration when he composed his famous trilogy.

Both his grandfather and great-grandfather had been magistrates and, shortly after Pa Chin's birth, his father assumed a similar position. His entire family, including Pa Chin's parents, uncles, aunts, brothers, sisters, cousins, nieces, nephews, and family servants lived in a traditional family compound under the direction of his grandfather. Following his father's death in 1917, Pa Chin became acutely aware of the hatred and treachery existing within his family. He reacted with disgust and anger at the many quarrels that took place between the families living together under the direction of his grandfather. He observed the cruelty and lewdness of his older male relatives and the dismal conditions of their servants. As he grew older, Pa Chin was appalled at the misery and injustice in the outside world. Heavily influenced by the new ideas of the times, he eventually became China's greatest advocate of anarchism and an inspiration to many new young writers.

Family was first published in book form in 1933 and its sequels, *Spring* and *Autumn*, were completed respectively in 1938 and 1940. The trilogy chronicles the daily life of both the young and old members of the Kao clan from 1919 to 1923 and the efforts of a few of its younger members to defy tradition and live a new life. Pa Chin describes the lives of the elders—the dinner parties, the gossiping and bickering, and the abuse of children and servants. But it is the rebellion of the younger family members that provides the stories' drama. The majority of the family's younger members are unable to liberate themselves from the cruelty of their feudal-minded elders and their lives end in despair.

In *Family*, the three Kao brothers, Chueh-hsin, Chueh-min, and Chueh-hui, struggle with the conflict between their individuality and their traditional family responsibilities. Chueh-hsin, who is modeled after the author's eldest brother, suffers the most from the oppressive system. A good-hearted individual, he allows the elders to dictate his life and vainly attempts to mend the family rifts. His brother Chueh-min, on the other hand, displays a certain degree of defiance towards his grandfather and is able to preserve his romance with his cousin Ch'in despite family interference. The third brother, Chueh-hui, who is the author's self-portrait, is the most enlightened youth in the family. Disrespectful of his elders, he often reproaches his older brothers for their cowardice in not challenging the family system. This excerpt from *Family* vividly illustrates this transitional period in revolutionary China when old and new values came into conflict and societal tensions reached a critical point.

Questions

1. According to Pa Chin, what is primarily responsible for the existence of evil? How does the individual fit into his account of evil?

2. There are many victims of the old family system. Among these, who seems to suffer the most? Explain.

3. Numerous tensions are apparent in *Family*. Discuss the primary conflicts in the novel. What does the author seem to be saying about an individual's free will to act?

FAMILY

XXVIII

It was summer holiday time. Chueh-min had much more opportunity to meet Chin. Chueh-hui[1] had much more time to spend with his young friends, to talk and work together. With renewed strength, the boys put out the new magazine, won new readers. All was going well.

That summer a big event was celebrated in the Kao family compound—the sixty-sixth birthday of the Venerable Master Kao.[2]

Preparations began early. It was to be a gala occasion. At the suggestion of Ke-ming,[3] who handled the accounts, and with the approval of the old man, a large sum of money was allotted from the family funds. As Ke-ming put it: "We collect such a huge amount of rent every year, we have more money than we know what to do with. What difference if we spend a little extra!"

Naturally, no wealthy family would let slip such a good opportunity to show off its affluence.

The festive day was fast approaching; gifts flowed in like a tide. A special office had to be set up to accept them and issue invitations. Many people were kept busy day and night. Chueh-hsin[4] took a fortnight's leave from his office to help out. The gardens were hung with lanterns and bunting; extra electric lights were added. In the main hall, a stage was built, and the best actors in the city were hired to perform three days of opera. The dramas to be presented were chosen by Ke-ting, who was an expert in such matters.

Everyone was busy except Chueh-min and Chueh-hui, who spent most of their time away from the compound. They were home only the three days of the formal celebration, when they had no choice.

Those three days were a new experience for them. Although they ordinarily disliked their family compound, at least they were familiar with it. Now, during the celebration, it changed beyond recognition. It became a theatre, a marketplace—crowded with people, noisy, full of unnatural grinning faces. Even their own room was given over to some guests whom they knew only slightly. Here a band of zither-playing blind musicians chanted birthday greetings; there another group sang lewd verses to the accompaniment of two string fiddles. Still a third group performed behind a curtain; the leering tones of the male and female voices were highly erotic; young people were not permitted to listen.

---

[1]The younger brother of Chueh-min.
[2]Head of the Kao family and the grandfather of Chueh-min.
[3]One of the three sons of Master Kao and the uncle of Chueh-min.
[4]The older brother of Chueh-min.

The operas began in the afternoon of the first day. Except for a few special birthday plays, the rest were all pieces which required skillful and subtle interpretation and were not originally included on the programme. These had been specially requested by several of the honourable guests. Whenever a portion was performed that brought blushes to the women and the young folks in the audience and smirks to the grown men, a servant with a stentorian voice would come out on the stage and read from a festively red slip of paper: "The Honourable Mr. So-and-so presents to such-and-such an actor the sum of so-much!" And the lucky actor (invariably a female impersonator) would at once profusely thank his donor, while the beneficent gentleman beamed with pompous satisfaction.

But even this did not satisfy the honourable guests. When an opera was over, the actors who had been rewarded had to drink with them at their tables, still wearing their make-up and costumes. The honourable gentlemen fondled the performers and filled them with wine; they behaved with such crass vulgarity that the younger guests were shocked and the servants whispered among themselves.

Venerable Master Kao, the shining light of all these festivities, sat up front. He gazed around briefly at what was going on, and smiled, then turned his eyes back to the stage, for the old man's favourite female impersonator had just made his entrance.

Ke-ming and the other two sons of the Venerable Master Kao circulated among the guests, looking after their wants with fawning solicitude, while Chueh-hsin trailed in their wake.

To Chueh-min and Chueh-hui it was all absolutely sickening. In this family, in these surroundings, they felt like strangers. The noisy, riotous, drunken sots seemed to them some strange species. A few faces looked vaguely familiar, yet closer examination made the boys wonder whether they had ever really seen them before. They felt completely out of place, but they were not allowed to leave because they were supposed to be acting as hosts. Like the supernumeraries in an opera, they were placed at a table with lesser guests, where they were expected to smile and drink and eat, more like machines than human beings.

Chueh-hui stuck it out the first day; that night he had bad dreams. The second day was just too much. He stayed away all afternoon between lunch and dinner. The young friends whom he visited first laughed at him, then consoled him. He finally worked up enough courage to go back and receive fresh insults (the word was Chueh-hui's). But the third day, he was unable to escape.

Mei had come with her mother, Mrs. Chien, but had gone home early because of illness. She was growing thinner by the day, and although her frailty was not yet extreme, sensitive people were touched by it, for they knew it was a sign that this lovely star would soon fall.

There were few enough sensitive people in the Kao family, but Chueh-hsin certainly was one of them. He was perhaps the most concerned about Mei. Yet there were so many invisible barriers between them—at least he thought there were—that they could only gaze at each other and converse wordlessly at a distance. They avoided all opportunities to speak together in private, thinking they could thus diminish the pain. The result was just the opposite. Chueh-hsin lost weight steadily and Mei's illness became worse; she began to cough blood.

Madam Chou[5] was very fond of Mei, but because she didn't know what was in Mei's heart, she had no way of comforting her. Actually, there was no one who could comfort Mei—not even Jui-chueh,[6] who recently had grown very close to her and knew her best.

Chin had also come to the party, and also gone home because of illness—though hers was feigned. The next day she secretly sent a note to Chueh-min, asking him to call.

Chueh-min stole away at the first opportunity, and he and Chin had a long talk. On the way home, he was very happy. Chueh-hsin met him at the entrance to the main hall and, to Chueh-min's surprise, asked:

"You've been to Chin's, haven't you?"

Chueh-min could only nod, mutely.

"I saw her servant slipping you a note; her illness wasn't real. I know all about you two." Chueh-hsin spoke in a low voice, a wry smile on his face.

Chueh-min said nothing. He too was smiling, only his was a smile of satisfaction.

Chueh-hsin saw Ke-ming approaching. He exchanged a few words with the older man. When his uncle had walked on, he again turned to Chueh-min.

"You're happy," he said softly. "You can do the things you want. I'd like to visit a sick person too, but I don't even have that much freedom. She's very ill. I know she needs me. . . ." His face twisted into an odd expression that could have been either a smile or a grimace of pain.

Moved, Chueh-min didn't know what to say. "Why don't you forget Mei?" at last he blurted awkwardly. "You're only torturing yourself. And what about Jui-chueh? You love her too, don't you?"

Chueh-hsin's face drained of colour. He stood looking at his brother in stricken silence. Suddenly, he became angry. "So you too want me to give her up? You're the same as the others! You can still talk that way at a time like this! . . ." Chueh-hsin tore himself away and walked off quickly.

Chueh-min realized that he had not given Chueh-hsin the answer he was seeking. But what other answer could he have given? Chueh-hsin said one

[5]Stepmother to Chueh-min.
[6]The wife of Chueh-hsin.

thing, but did another. Chueh-min couldn't understand the discrepancy between his Big Brother's words and his deeds. For that matter the whole family
was a puzzle to him.

His eyes wandered to the stage, where a short clown and a tall, stately
beauty were engaging in a subtle exchange of dialogue. The guests burst into
guffaws at some filthy innuendo—the honourable, the not-so-honourable, and
the completely dishonourable, guests. Chueh-min laughed scornfully.

He forgot about Chueh-hsin. Slowly, he paced back and forth, his mind
filled with his own affairs. For the first time, his prospects looked bright.

Of course it all had to do with Chin. He was very optimistic; she gave him
courage and confidence. Not only did she trust him—she had already made it
plain that she would not disappoint him. They were progressing smoothly.

At first, when they finished studying English together every day, they had
chatted about things in general. Gradually their talk had become more personal, until they understood one another completely, until they had grown so
close together that they felt unable to part. Cautiously they spoke of love—the
love affairs of their relatives and friends, of Mei and Chueh-hsin. Only much
later did their conversation get around to their own emotions. Chueh-min remembered how Chin had blushed and toyed with the pages of a book, trying to
appear calm, when she told him how much she needed him. She said she had determined to take the new road, but that there were many obstacles in her path;
she needed someone like him, someone who could understand and help her.

He and Chin already knew what was in each other's heart. All that was
lacking was an open declaration. When she sent for him today, he felt his
chance had come, and he told her what he had never dared say before, an-
nouncing heroically that he was willing to sacrifice everything for her sake.

Then she had replied. Actually, one of them had only to speak ten per
cent and the other understood the remaining ninety. They had faith in one
another, faith in their future. Their latest meeting had parted a curtain; they
had made their relationship plain. And this wonderful thing, thought Chueh-
min, had happened only today, practically just a minute ago!

His dreams for the future were very rosy and, of course, quite exaggerated.
Blinded, he could see none of the difficulties ahead. Standing on the stone
platform outside the main hall, he glanced again at the flirtatious actors on the
stage inside. Now the short clown and the stately beauty had been replaced by a
handsome hero and a pert young maid. Again the audience roared with laughter
at some vulgar sally. Chueh-min smiled contemptuously. People like this
couldn't stop him.

He gazed off into the distance, picturing an ideal life. A slap on the shoulder from a familiar hand brought him back to reality. Chueh-min turned to find
his younger brother, Chueh-hui, standing grinning behind him.

"So you've run out on them too," said Chueh-min.

"Naturally," replied Chueh-hui with a satisfied laugh. "And you . . . have another chance to sneak out!" He had guessed what Chueh-min was contemplating from the expression on his face.

Chueh-min reddened slightly. He nodded. "It's all settled between me and Chin. We've taken the first step. The problem now is the next one." His somewhat weak eyes peered happily at Chueh-hui from behind his gold-rimmed spectacles.

A fleeting smile crossed Chueh-hui's face. Even though he had told Chueh-min he thought of Chin only as a sister, even though he had loved another girl who had died for his sake, even though he had hoped that one day Chueh-min might make Chin his sister-in-law, yet when he heard that she now belonged to another, he couldn't help feeling a stab of jealousy—for he had secretly been in love with her. But at once he berated himself for harbouring such an emotion, particularly where his brother was concerned.

"Be careful. Don't take too much for granted." Though there was reason in Chueh-hui's words, they were still motivated a bit by jealousy.

"Everything's fine." Chueh-min was not in the least discouraged. "You're usually very bold. What makes you so cautious all of a sudden?"

Plainly Chueh-min had no inkling of what he was thinking. Chueh-hui immediately felt ashamed. He laughed. "You're absolutely right. I wish you luck."

[Unknown to Chueh-min, his grandfather, Master Kao, and Master Feng, head of the Feng family, privately arrange the marriage of Chueh-min to old Master Feng's grandniece.]

Chueh-min finally heard the news not only from Chueh-hui but also from his Big Brother. Chueh-hsin, acting under their grandfather's orders, had approached him to learn his reaction. Inquiring how Chueh-min felt about the matter was not the old man's idea—he issued commands and, naturally, they had to be obeyed. Chueh-hsin thought so too, although he did not approve of his grandfather's methods.

While shaken by the blow, Chueh-min was not afraid. His reply was simple. "I will decide whom I am to marry. Right now, I'm too young. I still have to finish my studies. I don't want to get married." There was a good deal more he wanted to say, but he kept it to himself.

"I can't very well tell *Yeh-yeh* that you want to make your own decisions. It's better to stress the youth aspect. But I'm afraid that won't convince him either. In our family nineteen isn't considered too young for marriage," Chueh-hsin said doubtfully. It was difficult to tell what he really advocated.

"According to you, it's hopeless, then!" said Chueh-min angrily.

"I didn't mean that," Chueh-hsin said quickly, but he had nothing to add.

Chueh-min stared at him fixedly, as if trying to read his mind. "Don't you remember what you said to me this afternoon?" the younger brother demanded. "Do you want me to re-enact your tragedy?"

"But *Yeh-yeh.* . . ." Chueh-hsin agreed with Chueh-min completely, yet he felt their grandfather's orders had to be obeyed.

"Don't talk to me about *Yeh-yeh.* I'm going to walk my own road," Chueh-min snapped. He turned and went into his room.

Chueh-min and Chueh-hui discussed the problem far into the night. Finally they agreed upon a plan of action: Resist. If that fails, run away. In any event, never give in.

Chueh-hui encouraged him, first because he sympathized with Chueh-min, and second because he wanted him to set a precedent, to blaze a new trail for other young men like him.

Fired with enthusiasm, Chueh-min immediately wrote a note to Chin, intending to send it to her the following day, secreted between the pages of a book. The note read:

> Chin:
>   No matter what you may have heard, please do not believe a word of it. People are trying to make a match for me, but I have given my heart to you and I will never go back on my pledge. Please have faith in me. You will see how courageously I can give battle, how I will fight for and win you!
>
>   Chueh-min

Chueh-min read the note over twice. This is an important memento in the annals of our love, he thought. He showed the note to Chueh-hui. "How's that?" he asked proudly.

"Splendid," replied Chueh-hui sarcastically. "Straight out of the middle ages!" And to himself he mocked: We'll soon see how courageously you "give battle"!

Now that the Venerable Master Kao's birthday celebration was over, old man Feng sent a matchmaker to formally propose the marriage of his grandniece to Chueh-min. The Venerable Master of course was entirely in favour. Madam Chou was only his daughter-in-law and Chueh-min's stepmother, not his mother; she did not think it proper to express an opinion. Chueh-hsin felt the marriage would be a serious mistake, ruining the life of another young couple. But he hadn't the courage to oppose his grandfather. He could only pray that some miracle might occur.

The matchmaking was done secretly, without Chueh-min's knowledge. Such matters were always conducted in secret; the persons involved were mere

puppets. Those who had been puppets in their youth, today were making puppets out of others. That was how it had been in the past, and that was how it
always would be—or so people like the Venerable Master Kao thought. But
they were mistaken in Chueh-min's case. He wasn't the type to submit to being
a puppet.

In contrast to the older generation, Chueh-min took active measures concerning his marriage. Without the least shyness, he made inquiries about the
proposed match. Chueh-hui became his scout. Together with Chin the two
brothers formed a committee of three. They discussed tactics—how to block the
match with old man Feng's niece, how to publicize the relationship between
Chueh-min and Chin.

As the opening stage of the battle, Chueh-min made his attitude plain to
his Big Brother. Chueh-hsin replied that it was not up to him. Chueh-min
requested his stepmother to cancel the match. Madam Chou said the decision
rested with his grandfather. But Chueh-min couldn't approach the old man
directly and he could find no one with influence to help him. In this family, the
Venerable Master Kao passed final judgement.

A few days later, Chin's mother requested him to stop calling. Mrs. Chang
was the old man's daughter. Although she sympathized with Chueh-min, as a
member of the Kao family she could not and would not help him. There was
already a rumour going around among the Kaos that Chueh-min was being
supported in his actions by his aunt Mrs. Chang because she wanted her daughter to marry him. Chin was so furious when she head this, she cried.

After the preliminary skirmish ended in total failure, Chueh-min began
the second phase of his tactics. He spread the story that unless the family respected his wishes, he would take drastic measures. Since this threat was never
permitted to reach the old man's ears, it did not produce any results either.

Then Chueh-min learned that his horoscope and that of his proposed
bride were about to be exchanged, after which a date would be set for the engagement. He heard this news only two weeks after the Venerable Master Kao's
birthday celebration.

It was then that Chueh-hsin had given the old man some indication of
Chueh-min's feelings, but to no avail.

"How dare he disagree?" the patriarch had retorted angrily. "What I say
is final!"

Chueh-min paced the garden for hours that day. His determination wavered a bit. If once he decided to run away from home, there would be no
turning back. Sustaining himself alone would be a big problem. He was very
comfortable at home; he was well provided with food and clothing. But on the
outside, how would he live? He had not made any preparations for such a move.
Yet now the problem was upon him; he had to make up his mind.

Seeking out Chueh-hsin, he came directly to the point. "Is there any hope of changing *Yeh-yeh's* mind?"

"I'm afraid not," said Chueh-hsin mournfully.

"Have you really tried to think of every possible way?" asked Chueh-min, disappointed.

"I really have!"

"What do you think I ought to do?"

"I know what's on your mind but, honestly, there's nothing I can do to help you. The best thing is to do what *Yeh-yeh* wants. In this day and age, we're fit only to be sacrificed," said Chueh-hsin sadly. He was almost weeping.

Chueh-min laughed coldly. "Still the same old policy of non-resistance! A compliant bow philosophy!" He turned on his heel and left.

XXIX

The following morning when Chueh-hsin went to pay his respects to his grandfather, the old man announced triumphantly that the marriage with the Feng family girl was all arranged. The Venerable Master said it could take place after two months and selected an auspicious day in his almanac. He told Chueh-hsin to go ahead with exchanging the horoscopes. Mumbling an assent, Chueh-hsin left, just as Chueh-hui was entering, a cryptic smile on his face.

No sooner had Chueh-hsin reached his quarters than a servant came after him with a summons from the Venerable Master Kao to return at once. Hurrying to his grandfather's study, he found the old man, seated on a sofa, berating Chueh-hui, while Mistress Chen, dressed in a light green, wide-sleeved blouse in crepe silk, her face heavily powdered and her hair smoothly done, sat perched on the arm of the patriarch's chair, and massaged his back with drumming fists. Chueh-hui stood before the old man not saying a word.

"The rebel! That such a thing could actually happen! You find Chueh-min and bring him back!" shouted the Venerable Master Kao when he saw Chueh-hsin enter. Big Brother was mystified.

The old man burst into a paroxysm of coughing and Mistress Chen increased the tempo of her drumming. "Calm yourself, Venerable Master," she pleaded. "At your age you shouldn't get yourself all worked up. They're not worth it!"

"How dare he disobey me? How dare he oppose me?" gasped the old man, red in the face. "Doesn't like the match I made for him, eh? Well, he'll have to! You bring him back here. I'm going to punish him."

Chueh-hsin murmured an assent. He was beginning to understand.

"Going to school has ruined him. I wanted you boys to take private tutoring at home, but you wouldn't listen to me. Now look what's happened! Even

Chueh-min has gone bad. He actually dares to rebel. From now on, no son of the Kao family is permitted to attend an outside school! Do you hear that?" The patriarch began to cough again.

Chueh-hsin stood flustered, his grandfather's words crashing about his head like thunder.

Chueh-hui, lined up beside his Big Brother, was quite unperturbed. Roar away, he thought, smiling inwardly. You'll soon be exposed as a paper lantern!

The old man's coughing finally ceased. Worn out, he lay back and closed his eyes. For a long time he did not speak. He looked as if he were asleep. The brothers continued standing before him respectfully, waiting. Only when Mistress Chen signalled for them to go did they tiptoe out of the room.

"Second Brother left a note for you," Chueh-hui said to Chueh-hsin when they got outside. "It's in my room. Come and read it."

"What in the world did you say to *Yeh-yeh*? Why didn't you tell me first, instead of running to him? How could you be so stupid!"

"I wanted him to know! I wanted him to realize that we're human beings, not lambs that anyone can lead to the slaughter!"

Chueh-hsin knew the barb was directed against him. It struck home, but he could only bear the pain in silence. No matter how sincerely he explained, Chueh-hui would never believe him.

In Chueh-hui's room, the boy handed him the letter. It was hard for Chueh-hsin to find the courage to read it, but at last he did:

> Big Brother,
>   I'm doing what no one in our family has ever dared to do before—I'm running out on an arranged marriage. No one cares about my fate, so I've decided to walk my own road alone. I'm determined to struggle against the old forces to the end. Unless you cancel the match, I'll never come back. I'll die first. It's still not too late to save the situation. Remember our brotherly love and do your best to help me.
>
> Chueh-min
>
> Written at 3 in the morning.

Chueh-hsin turned pale. The note dropped from his trembling fingers to the floor. "What shall I do?" he stammered. "Doesn't he understand my position?"

"It has nothing to do with your position," said Chueh-hui stiffly. "The question is what are you going to do about it?"

Chueh-hsin rose quickly, as if he had received a shock. "I'm going to bring him back," he said simply.

"You'll never find him," said Chueh-hui with a cold laugh.

"Never find him?" echoed Chueh-hsin, confused.

"No one knows where he's moved to."

"But surely you know his address. You must know. Tell me, where is he? Please tell me," Chueh-hsin begged.

"I do know. But I certainly won't tell you," said Chueh-hui firmly.

"Don't you trust me?" Chueh-hsin angrily demanded.

"It doesn't matter whether I trust you or not. Your 'policy of non-resistance,' your 'compliant bow' philosophy would be sure to bring Second Brother to grief. In a word—you're too weak!" said Chueh-hui hotly. He paced the floor with large strides.

"I must see him. Tell me his address."

"No, absolutely no!"

"You'll have to reveal it. They'll make you. *Yeh-yeh* will make you."

"I won't tell them! Even in this family, I don't think they'd resort to torture," said Chueh-hui coolly. He was aware only that he was achieving some measure of vengeance against his family. He gave no thought to what his Big Brother might be suffering.

Despondently, Chueh-hsin walked out. Before long he came back and had another talk with Chueh-hui, trying to evolve a plan. But he failed. He could offer no compromise that would satisfy both Chueh-min and his grandfather.

Later that day, a small family council was held in Madam Chou's room. Present were Madam Chou, Chueh-hsin, his wife Jui-chueh, his sister Shu-hua, and Chueh-hui. Chueh-hui stood on one side; the others arrayed themselves opposite him. They urged him to reveal Chueh-min's whereabouts; they wanted him to persuade Chueh-min to come home. They made many attractive promises—including an assurance that if Chueh-min returned a way would be found, in time, to call off the match.

But Chueh-hui was adamant.

Since no information could be obtained from Chueh-hui, and since Chueh-min's demands could not be accepted, Madam Chou and Chueh-hsin could only worriedly seek out Ke-ming and ask him to delay the exchange of the horoscopes a few days, without letting the old man know. At the same time they sent people out to try and discover where Chueh-min was hiding.

The search proved fruitless. Chueh-min was well concealed.

Ke-ming called Chueh-hui to his study and gave him a lecture—to no avail. He offered friendly guidance—to no avail. He tried argumentative exhortation—to no avail. Chueh-hui insisted he knew nothing.

Madam Chou and Chueh-hsin worked on Chueh-hui next. They pleaded with him to bring Chueh-min back. They said all Chueh-min's conditions could be met—provided he returned home first. Chueh-hui was firm. Unless he got guarantees in advance, he didn't trust anyone.

Madam Chou scolded Chueh-hui, then she wept. Although she usually left the boys to their own devices, she was genuinely interested in their welfare. The situation was serious. She didn't want anything bad to happen to them, but she was even more concerned with her reputation if this scandal should leak out. She disapproved of Chueh-hui's disrespectful attitude towards his elders, and was very dissatisfied with Chueh-min's flying in the face of the decision of the head of the family. But no matter how she tried, she couldn't think of any solution.

Confronted with a difficult problem, Chueh-hsin's only recourse was to weep. He knew that Chueh-min was right. Yet not only couldn't he help him— he had to help their grandfather oppress him. And now Chueh-hui considered him an enemy. Unless he brought back Chueh-min, he would be unable to placate the old man. But if he did make him return, he would be wounding Second Brother grievously.

No, that was something he could not do! He loved Chueh-min. His father had entrusted his two younger brothers to him on his death-bed. How could he go back on his pledge to love and cherish them? Chueh-hsin broke into sobs. He wept so bitterly that tears also came to Jui-chueh's eyes.

The Venerable Master Kao knew none of this. All that interested him was that his orders had to be obeyed, his face preserved. What others suffered as a consequence meant nothing to him. He demanded that Chueh-min be produced. He swore at Chueh-hsin. He swore at Ke-ming. At times he even swore at Madam Chou.

But all of his ranting evoked no sign of compliance from Chueh-min. His pressure was useless; Chueh-min wasn't there to be subjected to it. By now the scandal was known to everyone in the compound. Great effort was made to keep it from spreading outside.

The days passed. The Venerable Master Kao was in a perpetually bad temper. A pall of gloom hung over Chueh-hsin's household, while the other households sneered privately at his misfortune.

One day, Chueh-hui returned home after a secret meeting with Chueh-min. Leaving his desperately struggling brother was like leaving the world of light. The Kao compound depressed him dreadfully. The place was a desert; or perhaps it would be more accurate to call it a bastion of reaction, the main base of his enemy. Chueh-hui immediately sought out Chueh-hsin.

"Are you willing to help Second Brother or not?" he demanded irritably. "A whole week has already gone by."

"What can I do?" Chueh-hsin spread his hands despondently. Now you're the one who's anxious, he said to himself.

"Are you just going to let the thing drag on like this?"

"Drag on, nothing! *Yeh-yeh* says if Chueh-min doesn't return in another half month, he can stay away for ever. He'll put an announcement in the papers disowning him," said Chueh-hsin unhappily.

"Do you think *Yeh-yeh* would have the heart to do a thing like that?" Chueh-hui asked bitterly. He was still angry.

"Why wouldn't he? He's absolutely furious. He won't allow his orders to be disobeyed. Second Brother's resistance can't win."

"So you say that too. No wonder you won't help him!"

"But how can I?" Chueh-hsin considered himself the unluckiest man in the world. He had no strength whatsoever.

"When our father was dying, didn't he tell you to look after us? He'd be very disappointed in you today!" There were angry tears in Chueh-hui's eyes.

Chueh-hsin made no reply. He began to sob.

"If I were in your position, I'd never be so weak and useless, I tell you that! I'd cut the match with the Feng family with one slash of the knife, that's what I'd do!"

"But what about *Yeh-yeh*?" Big Brother asked, finally raising his head.

"*Yeh-yeh*'s era is over. Are you going to let Second Brother become a sacrifice to *Yeh-yeh*'s prejudice?"

Chueh-hsin again lapsed into silence.

"You *are* a weakling!" Chueh-hui stalked out angrily.

Alone in the room, Chueh-hsin was weighted down with misery. His "compliant bow" philosophy and his "policy of non-resistance" had failed him; he had not been able to make peace in the family. In an effort to satisfy everyone, he had given up his own happiness, but it had not brought him peace. He had willingly accepted the burden entrusted to him by his dying father; he had made every sacrifice for his younger brothers and sisters. The result was that he had driven one brother away, while the other cursed him for a weakling. What could he say to comfort himself?

After brooding thus for some time, he took up his pen and wrote an earnest letter to Chueh-min, vivisecting his own sincerity, and setting forth all his difficulties and tragic circumstances. He spoke of his love and friendship for his brothers, concluding with the plea that Chueh-min return, for the honour of the departed father, for the sake of peace in the Kao family.

Then he went to Chueh-hui and asked him to deliver the letter to Chueh-min.

Chueh-hui read the letter and wept. Shaking his head unhappily, he placed the missive back in the envelope.

Chueh-min's reply, of course, was brought by Chueh-hui. This is what it said:

> After waiting so long, I frankly was very disappointed to get a letter like this from you! All you can say is—Come back, come back! As I write this, I am sitting in a little room, like an escaped prisoner, not daring to go out for fear of being caught and brought back to my jail. The jail I mean is our home, and the jailers are the members of our family—they have banded together to destroy me without mercy.

Yes, you all want me to come home. That would solve your problems. There would be peace in the family and another victim would be sacrificed. Of course you would all be very happy, but I would be sunk in a sea of bitterness. . . . Well, you can just forget it. I won't come home unless my demands are met. Home is nothing to me but a lot of unpleasant memories.

Perhaps you wonder what makes me so bold? I wonder myself sometimes. It's my love that sustains me. I'm fighting for the happiness of two people—hers and mine.

I often think of our garden, how we played there as children together. You are my Big Brother. You must help me, for the sake of our father. For Chin too. And don't forget Cousin Mei. There's been enough heartbreak over her. Please don't let Chin become another Mei.

Tears coursed down Chueh-hsin's cheeks, but he was not aware of them. He was plunged into a dark abyss, without a ray of light, without a shred of hope. "You don't understand me," he kept mumbling. "No one understands me."

Chueh-hui stood watching him, torn between anger and pity. He not only had already read Chueh-min's letter—he had helped him write it. He had hoped the letter would move Big Brother, stir him into action, yet this was the result. He wanted to berate Chueh-hsin, but then he thought—What would be the use? Big Brother had become a man with no will of his own.

"This family is absolutely hopeless. The sooner I get out of here the better," Chueh-hui said to himself. From that moment on, he was no longer pessimistic over the chances of Chueh-min's success. This new idea intrigued him. It was a sprout that had just emerged into his consciousness, but it might grow very, very quickly.

Quite a number of people were suffering because of Chueh-min's escapade, Chueh-min himself among them. He was hiding in the home of his schoolmate, Tsun-jen, and although he was comfortable enough and Tsun-jen was very good to him, he hated being cooped up in a small room. Unable to do the things he wanted to do, unable to see the people he wanted to see, tormented by fear and longing, Chueh-min found life very difficult.

All day long he waited for news, but the only news Chueh-hui had been able to bring him so far was bad. Gradually, his hope dwindled. But it was not yet completely extinguished, and he still had the courage to go on. Chueh-hui constantly encouraged him with a promise of final victory. Chin's love, her image, gave him strength. He was sticking it out; he had no intention of surrendering.

Chin was always in his mind; he dreamed of her day and night. The more depressed he felt, the more he thought of her. And the more he thought of her, the more he longed to see her. But although she lived quite near to Tsun-jen's house, he couldn't visit her because her mother was home.

He wanted to send her a note via Chueh-hui. But when he took up his pen he found he had too much to say—he didn't know where to start. At the same time he was afraid if he didn't write her in detail, she would become worried. He decided to wait for an opportunity to talk to her face to face.

It came sooner than he expected. Chueh-hui arrived one day with the news that Mrs. Chang had gone out; he took Chueh-min to see Chin.

Leaving Chueh-min waiting outside the door, Chueh-hui went in first. "I've brought you something good, Cousin Chin," he announced cheerfully.

Chin had been lying down, reading, half-asleep, but she sat up quickly. Adjusting her hair, she asked listlessly, "What is it?" She looked pale, too tired even to smile.

"How thin you are!" Chueh-hui exclaimed in spite of himself.

"You haven't seen me in several days." Chin smiled wryly. "What about Second Brother? Why haven't I received even a single letter from him?"

"Several days? Why, I was here only the day before yesterday!"

"You don't know how time is dragging for me. Tell me quickly. What's happening with him?" Chin stared at him with large, worried eyes.

"He's given in!" Chueh-hui succumbed to an irresistible impulse to tease her.

"No! I don't believe it!"

Just at that moment, a young man stepped into her room, and Chin's eyes lit up.

"You!" she cried. Whether it was doubt, or surprise, or joy, or reproach that she felt, she didn't know herself. She rushed towards him, then checked herself abruptly and stood gazing at him, her eyes aglow.

"Yes, Chin, it's me." There was both joy and sorrow in his voice. "I meant to come much sooner, but I was afraid of running into your mother."

"I knew you'd come, I knew you'd come," she said, weeping tears of happiness. She looked reproachfully at Chueh-hui. "How could you try to fool me like that, Third Brother? I knew he'd never give in. I have faith in him." She gazed at Chueh-min lovingly, with no trace of shyness.

Chueh-hui was favourably impressed. He hadn't realized that Chin had grown so mature. Smiling, he looked at Chueh-min, who plainly was feeling very heroic at the girl's exaggerated praise. Chueh-hui acknowledged to himself that he was wrong. He had expected their meeting would be attended with tears and weeping and all the other trappings of tragedy. Such scenes were common in families like theirs.

But contrary to his expectations, they seemed to fear nothing, sustaining each other with an all-powerful mutual faith. He was delighted with them. They were a gleam of light in a dark world; they gave him hope. They didn't need his encouragement any more. Chueh-min would never bend the knee.

How easy it was for an ardent youth like Chueh-hui to believe in people!

"All right, you can quit talking like a couple of stage actors and get down to business. If you've got anything to say, say it quickly. We haven't much time." Chueh-hui grinned. "Would you like me to step out a minute?"

They both laughed but didn't answer. Ignoring Chueh-hui, they sat down on the edge of the bed, holding hands and talking affectionately. He idly picked one of Chin's books from the shelf. It was a collection of Ibsen's plays, dog-eared and underscored in places. Apparently, she had recently been reading *An Enemy of the People*.[7] She must have found encouragement in it. Chueh-hui couldn't help smiling.

He stole a glance at Chin. She and Chueh-min were engrossed in a lively conversation. Her face was radiantly beautiful. Chueh-hui felt rather envious of his brother. He turned back to *An Enemy of the People*.

After reading the first act he looked up. They were still talking. He read the second act. They still hadn't finished. He read the play through to the end. Chin and Chueh-min were chattering away, with no sign of a let-up.

"Well, how about it? What a gabby pair you two are!" Chueh-hui was growing impatient.

Chin looked up at him with a smile, and continued talking.

"Let's go, Second Brother," Chueh-hui urged, half an hour later. "You've said enough."

"Just a little longer," Chin pleaded. "It's early yet. What's your hurry?" She was holding Chueh-min's hand tightly, as if afraid he would leave.

"I must go back," said Chueh-hui, with mock stubbornness.

"Go ahead, then," Chin pouted. "My humble home isn't good enough for an aristocrat like you!" But when she saw him actually walking out, she and Chueh-min, in chorus, hastily called him to wait.

"Must you go, Third Brother? Can't you help me out a little?" Chueh-min said earnestly.

Chueh-hui laughed. "I was only fooling. But you two are much too cold to me. Chin, you haven't spoken to me, or even asked me to sit down. Now that Second Brother's here, you've forgotten me completely."

The other two also laughed.

"I've only got one mouth. I can only speak to one person at a time," Chin defended herself. "Be good now, Third Brother. Let me talk to him today. Tomorrow, you and I can talk to your heart's content." She coaxed him, as if he were a child.

---

[7] A drama by Henrik Ibsen published in *New Youth* in July–October 1918.

"Don't try to fool me. I haven't Second Brother's luck!"

Chueh-min opened his mouth to say something, but Chin cut in. "How's your luck going with Hsu Chien-ju?" she asked slyly. "Chien-ju's got it all over me. Do you like her? She's a really modern girl."

"Maybe I like her, and maybe I don't. But what's that got to do with you?" Chueh-hui retorted mischievously. He loved this kind of banter.

"They are well matched. I was thinking the same thing, myself," Chueh-min interposed.

Chueh-hui laughed and waved his hand in refusal. "No thanks. I don't want to become like you two—secret rendezvous and Shakespearean scenes!" In his heart he was thinking: What I want is you, Chin! . . . But this first thought was immediately driven away by a second: I've already sent one girl to her death. I've had enough of love. Outwardly he smiled, but it was a bitter smile.

Chueh-min's conversation with Chin at last came to an end. Now they had to part. Chueh-min hated to leave. Thinking of his lonely life in that little room, he hadn't the courage to go back. But Chueh-hui's impelling look told him that he must; there was no other way.

"I have to go," he said sadly, a note of struggle in his voice. But he didn't move. He cast about in his mind for some words to comfort Chin; all he could manage in that instant was: "Don't think about me too much," although that wasn't his meaning at all. As a matter of fact, he hoped she would think about him a great deal.

Chin stood before him, her big, luminous eyes fixed on his face, listening carefully, as if expecting him to say something out of the ordinary. He didn't. She waited, but he spoke only briefly. Disappointed, she clutched his sleeve, urging:

"Don't go yet. Stay a little longer. I still have a lot to tell you."

Chueh-min gulped down these wonderful words like the tastiest of morsels. He stared at her animated face. "All right, I won't go yet," he said with a smile—a smile so tortured that Chueh-hui, watching from the side, really thought he was going to cry.

To Chin, Chueh-min's tender gaze seemed to be gently laving her eyes, her face. "Speak," they seemed to say. "Speak. I'm listening to every word, every syllable." But she couldn't think of anything to say, and she was frantic for fear that he might leave at any moment. Still holding on to his sleeve, she blurted out the first thing that came into her mind:

"Cousin Mei has become pitifully thin lately. She coughs blood every day, though not very much. She's hiding it from her mother, and she doesn't want me to tell anyone, because she doesn't want to be given medicine. She says every day she lives is another day of misery—she'd be better off dead. Her mother is always busy entertaining and playing mahjong; she doesn't pay much attention to Mei. Yesterday I finally found the chance to tell her how sick Mei is; only now she's begun to worry. Perhaps Mei is right. But I can't stand by and watch her die. Don't say anything to Big Brother. Mei begged me not to let him know."

Suddenly Chin noticed the tears glistening behind Chueh-min's glasses. They were beginning to trickle down his cheeks. His lips trembled, but he could not speak. She understood. He was frightened that their love, too, might end in tragedy.

"I can't say any more!" she cried. She fell back a few paces, buried her face in her hands and wept.

"I really must go now, Chin," said Chueh-min unhappily. He hadn't imagined that their joyous meeting would terminate with both of them in tears. And they called themselves the new youth, the brave! . . .

"Don't go! Stay!" Chin took down her hands from her tear-stained face and stretched them towards Chueh-min.

Only Chueh-hui's restraining grasp kept Chueh-min from rushing to her. Chueh-min looked at his younger brother. Chueh-hui's eyes were dry, and they burned with a strong, steady light. Chueh-hui jerked his head in the direction of the door.

"Don't cry, Chin, I'll come again," Chueh-min said in a stricken voice. "I'm living not very far from here. I'll come as soon as there's a chance. . . . Take care of your health. I'll be sending you good news soon."

Steeling himself, he turned and walked out with Chueh-hui. Chin followed as far as the door of the main hall. There she halted and stood with her back against the frame of the doorway. Wiping her eyes, she watched them go.

The brothers reached the street with the sound of Chin's weeping still in their ears. They walked on quickly in silence, and soon arrived at Tsun-jen's house. Chueh-hui abruptly stopped in the middle of the street.

"You and Chin are bound to succeed," he said in a bright, strong voice. "We don't need any more sacrificial victims. We've had enough." Chueh-hui paused, then went on firmly, almost cruelly. "If any more sacrifices have to be made, let *them* be the victims this time!"

FURTHER READINGS

The Chinese Revolution during the twentieth century is the subject of numerous books. Among the most helpful works are Jean Chesneaux, Francoise le Barbier, and Marie Bergere, *China from the 1911 Revolution to Liberation*, trans. Paul Auster and Lydia Davis (New York: Pantheon, 1977), which provides a general survey of the early years of the Chinese Revolution (1911–1949) and Jonathan D. Spence, *The Gate of Heavenly Peace: The Chinese and Their Revolution, 1895–1980* (New York: Viking, 1981), which examines China's political development during the twentieth century. Other useful texts treating the Chinese Revolution are Edwin E. Moise, *Modern China* (London: Longman, 1986);

James Sheridan, *China in Disintegration* (New York: Free Press, 1975); Ranbir Vohra, *The Chinese Revolution, 1900–1950* (Boston: Houghton-Mifflin, 1974); and Lucien Bianco, *Origins of the Chinese Revolution, 1915–1949*, trans. Murial Bell (Stanford, CA; Stanford University Press, 1971).

Olga Lang's *Chinese Family and Society* (Hamden, CT: Archon, 1968) is a classic study of the role of the family in Chinese society. Maurice Freedman, ed., *Family and Kinship in Chinese Society* (Stanford, CA: Stanford University Press, 1970) provides a collection of essays on major aspects of Chinese family, kinship, and marriage.

Tsi-an Hsia, *The Gate of Darkness: Studies on the Leftist Movement in China* (Seattle: University of Washington Press, 1968) offers a collection of essays examining the influential Chinese writers of the 1920s and 1930s, including a section on Pa Chin. C. T. Hsia, *A History of Modern Fiction, 1917–1957* (New Haven, CT: Yale University Press, 1971) is an excellent general survey of twentieth century Chinese fiction. Ting Yi, *A Short History of Modern Chinese Literature* (Port Washington, NY: Kennikat, 1970) provides an analysis of Chinese literature from the May Fourth movement to Mao Tse-tung. Olga Lang, *Pa Chin and His Writings: Chinese Youth Between the Two Revolutions* (Cambridge, MA: Harvard University Press, 1967), is a study of Pa Chin's intellectual thought. A particularly informative text is Nathan K. Mao, *Pa Chin* (Boston: Twayne, 1978), which offers a brief biographical sketch followed by a more extensive evaluation of Pa Chin's major works. The text also includes a useful bibliography.

THE VIETNAMESE DECLARATION OF INDEPENDENCE
Ho Chi Minh

The Nguyen dynasty of Vietnam steadily lost ground, as well as influence, to the French until 1887. In that year, with the native emperors facing strife throughout the country, the French assumed complete administrative authority and reduced the Nguyen emperors to titular status. The administrators of the French protectorate reorganized the region, bringing the three sections of Vietnam—Cochinchina in the South, Annam in the central portion, and Tonkin in the North—together with Cambodia, and later Laos, to form French Indochina. Each region was administered separately, fragmenting Vietnam as never

From Ho Chi Minh, *On Revolution: Selected Writings, 1920–1966*, ed. and with an introduction by Bernard B. Fall. (New York: Praeger, 1967), pp. 143–45. Reprinted by permission.

before. The French also set out to bring French culture to the area, displacing native traditions and attempting to ally the educated Indochinese elite to the French colonial empire. Their success was greatest in the South, where they ruled directly, and weakest in Annam, where they had allowed the Nguyen emperors to maintain a native, but politically powerless, capital at Hue.

The French courted the support of the landlord class by maintaining and protecting an antiquated and inequitable system of land tenure that condemned the peasants to a life of poverty. Local elites were attracted to the support of French dominion by an excellent French school system and the promise of government jobs. The majority of the Vietnamese, however, benefited little from these arrangements except for the low-paid rubber plantation work offered them by French tire companies. Throughout the 1920s, the French forcibly suppressed nationalist sentiment and any opposition to their rule. This had the effect of driving the discontented and the nationalists underground, where they were encouraged and aided by the Soviet Union. Communist influence was thus allowed to grow stronger within the Vietnamese nationalist movement.

During the period, many Vietnamese left the country to seek other opportunities and obtain jobs, mostly menial, in Europe. One such emigrant was Ho Chi Minh (1890–1969), who left Indochina in 1911 as a messboy on an ocean liner and spent the years of World War I as a kitchen helper in London. Later, during the war years, he moved to Paris where he became a pastry cook and a member of the Communist International, although never wavering in his basic goals of Vietnamese nationalism and independence.

With the aid of funds provided by the Soviet Union, Ho returned to East Asia in 1925 and organized an Indochinese Communist party in Hong Kong. Shortly thereafter, a Nationalist party was formed in Vietnam modeled after Chiang Kai-shek's Kuomintang, which had come to power in China in 1927. A fundamental split thus formed within the nationalist movement. As the anti-colonial movement spread in Indochina in the wake of World War I, still other factions joined the movement. Among these factions were a Trotskyite party, a group of moderate reformers drawn from the traditional Confucian elite, militant Buddhist leaders, a large Indochinese Catholic minority, and the Cao Dai, who worshipped the French novelist Victor Hugo. Almost all of the nationalist groups were drawn from the Vietnamese rather than the Cambodian and Laotian populations, since the latter nurtured their traditional animosity towards the Vietnamese, rather than considering the injustices they were jointly enduring under an exploitative colonial system. Despite their common cultural heritage, however, the nationalists lacked unity and a common will.

Until the 1940s, Vietnamese nationalism continued to be fragmented and failed to unite the peasant masses. World War II changed this. Japan occupied Vietnam in 1941, discrediting French military power and using the French administration to carry out their orders. By their arrogant manner and sometimes brutal rule, the Japanese succeeded in unifying virtually all the nationalist factions in a common hatred of the Japanese and their French minions. This was the moment for which Ho Chi Minh had been waiting.

Ho Chi Minh had spent most of the 1930s in the Soviet Union, but had moved to South China, near the Vietnamese border, in 1938. Here he organized the Viet Minh as a coalition of Vietnamese nationalists under Communist leadership. After unsuccessfully trying to get aid both from the United States and Chiang Kai-shek, Ho formed an independent Viet Minh army in December 1944. In March 1945, the Japanese overturned the French regime in Vietnam, hoping to strengthen their support among conservative anti-French groups. Northern Vietnam was in the throes of a terrible famine, largely the result of Japanese mismanagement, and their bid for native support failed. Meanwhile, the war was going badly for the Japanese, and most Vietnamese sensed that the days of Japanese rule were numbered. The Viet Minh seized this occasion to cross the frontier and gain control of the provinces bordering on China. After the Japanese surrender on August 9, 1945, Viet Minh military forces occupied most of the major cities of Vietnam.

The Viet Minh proclaimed the "Democratic Republic of Vietnam" on September 2, 1945, and Ho issued a declaration of independence on the same day. The Emperor Bao Dai abdicated after twenty years and recognized the Viet Minh as the legitimate government of Vietnam. At this point the Viet Minh still had not enlisted widespread peasant support, nor had they succeeded in unifying the various disparate groups of nationalists. They were therefore very much alone when the French army arrived in 1945 to reestablish French colonial domination of Vietnam. In short order, the French had recaptured Saigon in the South, and a large anti-Communist Chinese army had occupied the North. Failing to achieve the independence proclaimed in the document provided in this selection, the Vietnamese faced enduring yet another generation of warfare.

Questions

1. At the time of this writing Ho was engaged in a civil war with France and was an avowed Communist. Why would he invoke French (as well as American) institutions?

2. French Indochina was a product of colonial rule, whereas Vietnam had been a linguistic and cultural unit for two millennia. Which of these does the *Declaration* assume to be the national unit? Why?

3. What sort of future does the declaration envisage?

THE VIETNAMESE DECLARATION OF INDEPENDENCE

All men are created equal; they are endowed by their Creator with certain unalienable Rights; among these are Life, Liberty, and the pursuit of Happiness.

This immortal statement was made in the Declaration of Independence of the United States of America in 1776. In a broader sense, this means: All the peoples on the earth are equal from birth, all the peoples have a right to live, to be happy and free.

The Declaration of the French Revolution made in 1791 on the Rights of Man and the Citizen also states: "All men are born free and with equal rights, and must always remain free and have equal rights."

Those are undeniable truths.

Nevertheless, for more than eighty years, the French imperialists, abusing the standard of Liberty, Equality, and Fraternity, have violated our Fatherland and oppressed our fellow citizens. They have acted contrary to the ideals of humanity and justice.

In the field of politics, they have deprived our people of every democratic liberty.

They have enforced inhuman laws; they have set up three distinct political regimes in the North, the Center, and the South of Viet-Nam in order to wreck our national unity and prevent our people from being united.

They have built more prisons than schools. They have mercilessly slain our patriots; they have drowned our uprisings in rivers of blood.

They have fettered public opinion; they have practiced obscurantism against our people.

To weaken our race they have forced us to use opium and alcohol.

In the field of economics, they have fleeced us to the backbone, impoverished our people and devastated our land.

They have robbed us of our rice fields, our mines, our forests, and our raw materials. They have monopolized the issuing of bank notes and the export trade.

They have invented numerous unjustifiable taxes and reduced our people, especially our peasantry, to a state of extreme poverty.

They have hampered the prospering of our national bourgeoisie; they have mercilessly exploited our workers.

In the autumn of 1940, when the Japanese fascists violated Indochina's territory to establish new bases in their fight against the Allies, the French imperialists went down on their bended knees and handed over our country to them.

Thus, from that date, our people were subjected to the double yoke of the French and the Japanese. Their sufferings and miseries increased. The result was that, from the end of last year to the beginning of this year, from Quang Tri Province to the North of Viet-Nam, more than two million of our fellow citizens died from starvation. On March 9 [1945], the French troops were disarmed by the Japanese. The French colonialists either fled or surrendered, showing that not only were they incapable of "protecting" us, but that, in the span of five years, they had twice sold our country to the Japanese.

On several occasions before March 9, the Viet Minh League urged the French to ally themselves with it against the Japanese. Instead of agreeing to this proposal, the French colonialists so intensified their terrorist activities against the Viet Minh members that before fleeing they massacred a great number of our political prisoners detained at Yen Bay and Cao Bang.

Notwithstanding all this, our fellow citizens have always manifested toward the French a tolerant and humane attitude. Even after the Japanese *Putsch* of March, 1945, the Viet Minh League helped many Frenchmen to cross the frontier, rescued some of them from Japanese jails, and protected French lives and property.

From the autumn of 1940, our country had in fact ceased to be a French colony and had become a Japanese possession.

After the Japanese had surrendered to the Allies, our whole people rose to regain our national sovereignty and to found the Democratic Republic of Viet-Nam.

The truth is that we have wrested our independence from the Japanese and not from the French.

The French have fled, the Japanese have capitulated, Emperor Bao Dai has abdicated. Our people have broken the chains which for nearly a century have fettered them and have won independence for the Fatherland. Our people at the same time have overthrown the monarchic regime that has reigned supreme for dozens of centuries. In its place has been established the present Democratic Republic.

For these reasons, we, members of the Provisional Government, representing the whole Vietnamese people, declare that from now on we break off all relations of a colonial character with France; we repeal all the international obligation that France has so far subscribed to on behalf of Viet-Nam, and we abolish all the special rights the French have unlawfully acquired in our Fatherland.

The whole Vietnamese people, animated by a common purpose, are determined to fight to the bitter end against any attempt by the French colonialists to reconquer their country.

We are convinced that the Allied nations, which at Teheran and San Francisco have acknowledged the principles of self-determination and equality of nations, will not refuse to acknowledge the independence of Viet-Nam.

A people who have courageously opposed French domination for more than eighty years, a people who have fought side by side with the Allies against the fascists during these last years, such a people must be free and independent.

For these reasons, we, members of the Provisional Government of the Democratic Republic of Viet-Nam, solemnly declare to the world that Viet-Nam has the right to be a free and independent country—and in fact it is so already. The entire Vietnamese people are determined to mobilize all their physical and mental strength, to sacrifice their lives and property in order to safeguard their independence and liberty.

FURTHER READINGS

Ho Chi Minh's writings are translated into English in the *Selected Works of Ho Chi Minh*, 4 vols. (Hanoi: Foreign Languages Publishing House, 1960–1962). John T. McAlister and Paul Mus, *The Vietnamese and Their Revolution* (New York: Harper & Row, 1970), is an excellent brief introduction. For the origins of U.S. involvement see Bernard B. Fall, *The Two Vietnams*, 2nd ed. rev. (New York: Frederick A. Praeger, 1967); and Joseph Buttinger, *The Smaller Dragon: A Political History of Vietnam* (New York: Frederick A. Praeger, 1970). David Halberstam, *Ho* (New York: Random House, 1970) is a paperback biography by the well-known journalist. David G. Marr, *Vietnamese Anti-Colonialism, 1885–1925* (Berkeley: University of California Press, 1971) is an outstanding study of the early stages of Vietnamese resistance to colonialism.

ON THE PEOPLE'S DEMOCRATIC DICTATORSHIP

Mao Tse-tung

Although China had faced increasing pressure from Western powers since the mid-eighteenth century and had contended with destructive internal uprisings, established political institutions and traditional cultural patterns were maintained with relatively little change until 1894. In that year, Japan went to war with China. China was decisively defeated and forced to yield important territories, special commercial privileges, and a crushing war indemnity to the victor. European powers quickly forced other concessions from the virtually helpless Chinese. China was thrown into turmoil, with various groups contending for

From Mao Tse-tung, *Selected Works of Mao Tse-tung*, 5 vols. (Peking: Foreign Language Press, 1969), vol. 4, 411–23. Reprinted with permission.

power to direct the course of the nation. While some groups demanded immediate Westernization, others insisted on a return to traditional Chinese values and the expulsion of foreigners and their ways. In 1900, the popular uprising against the Europeans known as the "Boxer Rebellion" occurred. The Western powers sent in an expeditionary force, capturing Peking and driving the Chinese government from its capital. It had become clear to the Chinese that they could not simply expel the foreigners, and a massive and often ill-directed program of Westernization was begun.

In 1902, a Western-style educational system was adopted, and in 1905, the system of imperial civil service examinations was abolished. This was a dramatic break with a long-established cultural and administrative system, and it signalled the widespread conclusion on the part of the Chinese that their traditional political institutions were inadequate to cope with changing conditions. Seven years later, the imperial government itself fell, and the Ch'ing dynasty (1644–1912) had come to an end. With the constant interference of the Western powers, with various contending schools of thought, and without the unifying influence that the scholar-administrator class had once provided, no force was capable of overcoming the rise to power of independent local leaders. Central government disappeared, and China entered the period known as the "era of the warlords."

In 1926, a new national force emerged, the Kuomintang, a party espousing the ideals of the democratic revolutionary Sun Yat-sen (1866–1925). Under the leadership of Ch'iang Kai-shek (1877–1975), the Kuomintang armies began eliminating the warlords and unifying the country. In the process, they found that their greatest adversary lay in the Communist party that had been established in China with Soviet encouragement in 1921. Driven from the cities, the Communists established control over extensive sections of the countryside. In 1930, Ch'iang Kai-shek undertook a series of campaigns to eradicate these areas of Communist power. By 1934, he was ready to begin the encirclement of a large zone established by Mao Tse-tung (1893–1976).

Mao was born in a small village in the province of Hunan, the son of a prosperous farmer. He graduated from the province's Western-style teacher's college in 1918, already a political radical. He took up the life of a schoolmaster, but continued his political agitation and, in 1921, was one of the founding members of the Chinese Communist party. Mao traveled extensively in the countryside and established particular rapport with the peasant class. Communist doctrine at this time taught that the revolution could come only from an industrial proletariat, and Mao's work with the rural peasants struck his colleagues as being of little worth and limited his power among the party leadership. Peasant support was essential in 1927, however, when Mao established a Communist zone in the mountains of his native province. When Ch'iang began his encirclement, Mao's zone contained over three million people. His army was no match for the massive Nationalist forces, however, and so he determined to break free and join another Communist group far to the north.

This was the famous "Long March," in which one hundred thousand men, women, and children fought their way for over six thousand miles before a small portion of them reached their final objective. Ch'iang's attempt to pursue them even here was halted in 1937 by the Japanese invasion of China. The Nationalists withdrew to the Southwest, while the Communists fought on against the Japanese in the North, gathering strength and extending their territorial control in the process. At Japan's defeat in 1945, the Red Army numbered over three million men and continued to grow during the civil war that broke out almost immediately with the Nationalists. In savage fighting, the Nationalists finally were driven to the island of Taiwan, and, in 1949, Mao declared the establishment of the People's Republic of China.

Some months before, on the twenty-eighth anniversary of the founding of the Chinese Communist party, Mao had given a speech on "The People's Democratic Dictatorship," in which he outlined the sort of government that would follow victory. This speech, provided here in full, attempts to answer questions and criticisms levelled against Mao's policies. One of the most serious criticisms was voiced by those who had believed Communist promises that victory would bring freedom and equality. Communist doctrine promises that the power of the state will be abolished, but only after a period of "consolidation" and "reeducation" known as the "dictatorship of the proletariat." Using logic strikingly similar to that of Robespierre in his famous "Speech of 17 Pluviôse," Mao explains how the Communist struggle would continue even after victory over the Nationalists.

This speech presents the Communist ideal of the "dictatorship of the proletariat." It was far less benign in practice. Tens of millions of Chinese died under Mao's leadership, many because of simple mismanagement, and many more in the name of "uniting the people and advancing steadily towards our goal." The goal of the stateless society, in which all the means of repression, exploitation, and constraint have disappeared in a universal association of free men and women, is the ideal towards which all Communist states have aspired. Needless to say, none have yet reached that goal.

Questions

1. Why had China failed to learn from the West when Japan was able to do so?
2. What have the Chinese people learned since 1900?
3. Why must there be a people's dictatorship?
4. What will the people's dictatorship accomplish?

ON THE PEOPLE'S DEMOCRATIC DICTATORSHIP

The first of July 1949 marks the fact that the Communist Party of China has already lived through twenty-eight years. Like a man, a political party has its childhood, youth, manhood and old age. The Communist Party of China is no longer a child or a lad in his teens but has become an adult. When a man reaches old age, he will die; the same is true of a party. When classes disappear, all instruments of class struggle—parties and the state machinery—will lose their function, cease to be necessary, therefore gradually wither away and end their historical mission; and human society will move to a higher stage. We are the opposite of the political parties of the bourgeoisie.[1] They are afraid to speak of the extinction of classes, state power and parties. We, on the contrary, declare openly that we are striving hard to create the very conditions which will bring about their extinction. The leadership of the Communist Party and the state power of the people's dictatorship are such conditions. Anyone who does not recognize this truth is no communist. Young comrades who have not studied Marxism-Leninism and have only recently joined the Party may not yet understand this truth. They must understand it—only then can they have a correct world outlook. They must understand that the road to the abolition of classes, to the abolition of state power and to the abolition of parties is the road all mankind must take; it is only a question of time and conditions. Communists the world over are wiser than the bourgeoisie, they understand the laws governing the existence and development of things, they understand dialectics and they can see farther. The bourgeoisie does not welcome this truth because it does not want to be overthrown. To be overthrown is painful and is unbearable to contemplate for those overthrown, for example, for the Kuomintang reactionaries whom we are now overthrowing and for Japanese imperialism which we together with other peoples overthrew some time ago. But for the working class, the labouring people and the Communist Party the question is not one of being overthrown, but of working hard to create the conditions in which classes, state power and political parties will die out very naturally and mankind will enter the realm of Great Harmony.[2] We have mentioned in passing the long-range perspective of human progress in order to explain clearly the problems we are about to discuss.

As everyone knows, our Party passed through these twenty-eight years not in peace but amid hardships, for we had to fight enemies, both foreign and domestic, both inside and outside the Party. We thank Marx, Engels, Lenin and

[1] Capitalist classes.

[2] A society based on public ownership, free from class exploitation and oppression—a lofty ideal long cherished by the Chinese people. Here the realm of Great Harmony means a communist society.

Stalin for giving us a weapon. This weapon is not a machine-gun, but Marxism-Leninism.

In his book *"Left-wing" Communism, an Infantile Disorder* written in 1920, Lenin described the quest of the Russians for revolutionary theory. Only after several decades of hardship and suffering did the Russians find Marxism. Many things in China were the same as, or similar to, those in Russia before the October Revolution. There was the same feudal oppression. There was similar economic and cultural backwardness. Both countries were backward, China even more so. In both countries alike, for the sake of national regeneration progressives braved hard and bitter struggles in their quest for revolutionary truth.

From the time of China's defeat in the Opium War of 1840,[3] Chinese progressives went through untold hardships in their quest for truth from the Western countries. Hung Hsiu-chuan,[4] Kang Yu-wei,[5] Yen Fu[6] and Sun Yat-sen were representative of those who had looked to the West for truth before the Communist Party of China was born. Chinese who then sought progress would read any book containing the new knowledge from the West. The number of students sent to Japan, Britain, the United States, France and Germany was amazing. At home, the imperial examinations were abolished and modern schools sprang up like bamboo shoots after a spring rain; every effort was made to learn from the West. In my youth, I too engaged in such studies. They represented the culture of Western bourgeois democracy, including the social theories and natural sciences of that period, and they were called "the new learning" in contrast to Chinese feudal culture, which was called "the old learning." For quite a long time, those who had acquired the new learning felt confident that it would save China, and very few of them had any doubts on this score, as the adherents of the old learning had. Only modernization could save China, only learning from foreign countries could modernize China. Among the foreign countries, only the Western capitalist countries were then progressive, as they had successfully built modern bourgeois states. The Japanese had been successful in learning from the West, and the Chinese also wished to learn from the Japanese. The Chinese in those days regarded Russia as backward, and few wanted to learn from her. That was how the Chinese tried to learn from foreign countries in the period from the 1840s to the beginning of the 20th century.

Imperialist aggression shattered the fond dreams of the Chinese about learning from the West. It was very odd—why were the teachers always commit-

---

[3]Faced with the opposition of the Chinese people to its traffic in opium, Britain sent forces in 1840–1842 to invade Kwangtung and other coastal regions of China under the pretext of protecting trade. The troops in Kwangtung, led by Lin Tse-hsu, fought a war of resistance.

[4]Leader of a peasant revolutionary war in the middle of the nineteenth century.

[5]Leader of a reform movement to establish a constitutional monarchy in the late nineteenth and early twentieth centuries.

[6]Another reformer advocating a constitutional rather than an autocratic monarchy.

ting aggression against their pupil? The Chinese learned a good deal from the West, but they could not make it work and were never able to realize their ideals. Their repeated struggles, including such a country-wide movement as the Revolution of 1911,[7] all ended in a failure. Day by day, conditions in the country got worse, and life was made impossible. Doubts arose, increased and deepened. World War I shook the whole globe. The Russians made the October Revolution and created the world's first socialist state. Under the leadership of Lenin and Stalin, the revolutionary energy of the great proletariat and labouring people of Russia, hitherto latent and unseen by foreigners, suddenly erupted like a volcano, and the Chinese and all mankind began to see the Russians in a new light. Then, and only then, did the Chinese enter an entirely new era in their thinking and their life. They found Marxism-Leninism, the universally applicable truth, and the face of China began to change.

It was through the Russians that the Chinese found Marxism. Before the October Revolution, the Chinese were not only ignorant of Lenin and Stalin, they did not even know of Marx and Engels. The salvoes of the October Revolution brought us Marxism-Leninism. The October Revolution helped progressives in China, as throughout the world, to adopt the proletarian world outlook as the instrument for studying a nation's destiny and considering anew their own problems. Follow the path of the Russians—that was their conclusion. In 1919, the May 4th Movement took place in China. In 1921, the Communist Party of China was founded. Sun Yat-sen, in the depths of despair, came across the October Revolution and the Communist Party of China. He welcomed the October Revolution, welcomed Russian help to the Chinese and welcomed cooperation of the Communist Party of China. Then Sun Yat-sen died and Chiang Kai-shek rose to power. Over a long period of twenty-two years, Chiang Kai-shek dragged China into ever more hopeless straits. In this period, during the anti-fascist Second World War in which the Soviet Union was the main force, three big imperialist powers were knocked out, while two others were weakened. In the whole world only one big imperialist power, the United States of America, remained uninjured. But the United States faced a grave domestic crisis. It wanted to enslave the whole world; it supplied arms to help Chiang Kai-shek slaughter several million Chinese. Under the leadership of the Communist Party of China, the Chinese people, after driving out Japanese imperialism, waged the People's War of Liberation for three years and have basically won victory.

Thus Western bourgeois civilization, bourgeois democracy and the plan for a bourgeois republic have all gone bankrupt in the eyes of the Chinese people. Bourgeois democracy has given way to people's democracy under the leadership of the working class and the bourgeois republic to the people's republic. This has made it possible to achieve socialism and communism through the

[7]The Revolution of 1911 overthrew the Ching dynasty.

people's republic, to abolish classes and enter a world of Great Harmony. Kang Yu-wei wrote *Ta Tung Shu*, or the *Book of Great Harmony*, but he did not and could not find the way to achieve Great Harmony. There are bourgeois republics in foreign lands, but China cannot have a bourgeois republic because she is a country suffering under imperialist oppression. The only way is through a people's republic led by the working class.

All other ways have been tried and failed. Of the people who hankered after those ways, some have fallen, some have awakened and some are changing their ideas. Events are developing so swiftly that many feel the abruptness of the change and the need to learn anew. This state of mind is understandable and we welcome this worthy desire to learn anew.

The vanguard of the Chinese proletariat learned Marxism-Leninism after the October Revolution and founded the Communist Party of China. It entered at once into political struggles and only now, after a tortuous course of twenty-eight years, has it won basic victory. From our twenty-eight years' experience we have drawn a conclusion similar to the one Sun Yat-sen drew in his testament from his "experience of forty years"; that is, we are deeply convinced that to win victory, "we must arouse the masses of the people and unite in a common struggle with those nations of the world which treat us as equals." Sun Yat-sen had a world outlook different from ours and started from a different class standpoint in studying and tackling problems; yet, in the 1920s he reached a conclusion basically the same as ours on the question of how to struggle against imperialism.

Twenty-four years have passed since Sun Yat-sen's death, and the Chinese revolution, led by the Communist Party of China, has made tremendous advances both in theory and practice and has radically changed the face of China. Up to now the principal and fundamental experience the Chinese people have gained is twofold:

1. Internally, arouse the masses of the people. That is, unite the working class, the peasantry, the urban petty bourgeoisie and the national bourgeoisie, form a domestic united front under the leadership of the working class, and advance from this to the establishment of a state which is a people's democratic dictatorship under the leadership of the working class and based on the alliance of workers and peasants.

2. Externally, unite in a common struggle with those nations of the world which treat us as equals and unite with the peoples of all countries. That is, ally ourselves with the Soviet Union, with the People's Democracies and with the proletariat and the broad masses of the people in all other countries, and form an international united front.

"You are leaning to one side." Exactly. The forty years' experience of Sun Yat-sen and the twenty-eight years' experience of the Communist Party have taught us to lean to one side, and we are firmly convinced that in order to win victory and consolidate it we must lean to one side. In the light of the experiences accumulated in these forty years and these twenty-eight years, all Chinese without exception must lean either to the side of imperialism or to the side of socialism. Sitting on the fence will not do, nor is there a third road. We oppose the Chiang Kai-shek reactionaries who lean to the side of imperialism, and we also oppose the illusions about a third road.

"You are too irritating." We are talking about how to deal with domestic and foreign reactionaries, the imperialists and their running dogs, not about how to deal with anyone else. With regard to such reactionaries, the question of irritating them or not does not arise. Irritated or not irritated, they will remain the same because they are reactionaries. Only if we draw a clear line between reactionaries and revolutionaries, expose the intrigues and plots of the reactionaries, arouse the vigilance and attention of the revolutionary ranks, heighten our will to fight and crush the enemy's arrogance can we isolate the reactionaries, vanquish them or supersede them. We must not show the slightest timidity before a wild beast. We must learn from Wu Sung[8] on the Chingyang Ridge. As Wu Sung saw it, the tiger on Chingyang Ridge was a man-eater, whether irritated or not. Either kill the tiger or be eaten by him—one or the other.

"We want to do business." Quite right, business will be done. We are against no one except the domestic and foreign reactionaries who hinder us from doing business. Everybody should know that it is none other than the imperialists and their running dogs, the Chiang Kai-shek reactionaries, who hinder us from doing business and also from establishing diplomatic relations with foreign countries. When we have beaten the internal and external reactionaries by uniting all domestic and international forces, we shall be able to do business and establish diplomatic relations with all foreign countries on the basis of equality, mutual benefit and mutual respect for territorial integrity and sovereignty.

"Victory is possible even without international help." This is a mistaken idea. In the epoch in which imperialism exists, it is impossible for a genuine people's revolution to win victory in any country without various forms of help from the international revolutionary forces, and even if victory were won, it could not be consolidated. This was the case with the victory and consolidation of the great October Revolution, as Lenin and Stalin told us long ago. This was also the case with the overthrow of the three imperialist powers in World War II and the establishment of the People's Democracies. And this is also the case

[8] A hero in the novel *Shui Hu Chuan* (*Heroes of the Marshes*) who killed a tiger with his bare hands on the Chingyang Ridge. This is one of the most popular episodes in that famous novel.

with the present and the future of People's China. Just imagine! If the Soviet Union had not existed, if there had been no victory in the anti-fascist Second World War, if Japanese imperialism had not been defeated, if the People's Democracies had not come into being, if the oppressed nations of the East were not rising in struggle and if there were no struggle of the masses of the people against their reactionary rulers in the United States, Britain, France, Germany, Italy, Japan and other capitalist countries—if not for all these in combination, the international reactionary forces bearing down upon us would certainly be many times greater than now. In such circumstances, could we have won victory? Obviously not. And even with victory, there could be no consolidation. The Chinese people have had more than enough experience of this kind. This experience was reflected long ago in Sun Yat-sen's death-bed statement on the necessity of uniting with the international revolutionary forces.

"We need help from the British and U.S. governments." This, too, is a naive idea in these times. Would the present rulers of Britain and the United States, who are imperialists, help a people's state? Why do these countries do business with us and, supposing they might be willing to lend us money on terms of mutual benefit in the future, why would they do so? Because their capitalists want to make money and their bankers want to earn interest to extricate themselves from their own crisis—it is not a matter of helping the Chinese people. The Communist Parties and progressive groups in these countries are urging their governments to establish trade and even diplomatic relations with us. This is goodwill, this is help, this cannot be mentioned in the same breath with the conduct of the bourgeoisie in the same countries. Throughout his life, Sun Yat-sen appealed countless times to the capitalist countries for help and got nothing but heartless rebuffs. Only once in his whole life did Sun Yat-sen receive foreign help, and that was Soviet help. Let readers refer to Dr. Sun Yat-sen's testament; his earnest advice was not to look for help from the imperialist countries but to "unite with those nations of the world which treat us as equals." Dr. Sun had experience; he had suffered, he had been deceived. We should remember his words and not allow ourselves to be deceived again. Internationally, we belong to the side of the anti-imperialist front headed by the Soviet Union, and so we can turn only to this side for genuine and friendly help, not to the side of the imperialist front.

"You are dictatorial." My dear sirs, you are right, that is just what we are. All the experience that Chinese people have accumulated through several decades teaches us to enforce the people's democratic dictatorship, that is, to deprive the reactionaries of the right to speak and let the people alone have that right.

Who are the people? At the present stage in China, they are the working class, the peasantry, the urban petty bourgeoisie and the national bourgeoisie. These classes, led by the working class and the Communist Party, unite to form their own state and elect their own government; they enforce their dictatorship over the running dogs of imperialism—the landlord class and bureaucrat-bourgeoisie, as well as the representatives of those classes, the Kuomintang reactionaries and their accomplices—suppress them, allow them only to behave themselves and not to be unruly in word or deed. If they speak or act in an unruly way, they will be promptly stopped and punished. Democracy is practised within the ranks of the people, who enjoy the rights of freedom of speech, assembly, association and so on. The right to vote belongs only to the people, not to the reactionaries. The combination of these two aspects, democracy for the people and dictatorship over the reactionaries, is the people's democratic dictatorship.

Why must things be done this way? The reason is quite clear to everybody. If things were not done this way, the revolution would fail, the people would suffer, the country would be conquered.

"Don't you want to abolish state power?" Yes, we do, but not right now; we cannot do it yet. Why? Because imperialism still exists, because domestic reaction still exists, because classes still exist in our country. Our present task is to strengthen the people's state apparatus—mainly the people's army, the people's police and the people's courts—in order to consolidate national defence and protect the people's interests. Given this condition, China can develop steadily, under the leadership of the working class and the Communist Party, from an agricultural into an industrial country and from a new-democratic into a socialist and communist society, can abolish classes and realize the Great Harmony. The state apparatus, including the army, the police and the courts, is the instrument by which one class oppresses another. It is an instrument for the oppression of antagonistic classes; it is violence and not "benevolence." "You are not benevolent!" Quite so. We definitely do not apply a policy of benevolence to the reactionaries and towards the reactionary activities of the reactionary classes. Our policy of benevolence is applied only within the ranks of the people, not beyond them to the reactionaries or to the reactionary activities of reactionary classes.

The people's state protects the people. Only when the people have such a state can they educate and remould themselves by democratic methods on a country-wide scale, with everyone taking part, and shake off the influence of domestic and foreign reactionaries (which is still very strong, will survive for a long time and cannot be quickly destroyed), rid themselves of the bad habits and ideas acquired in the old society, not allow themselves to be led astray by the reactionaries, and continue to advance—to advance towards a socialist and communist society.

Here, the method we employ is democratic, the method of persuasion, not of compulsion. When anyone among the people breaks the law, he too should be punished, imprisoned or even sentenced to death; but this is a matter of a few individual cases, and it differs in principle from the dictatorship exercised over the reactionaries as a class.

As for the members of the reactionary classes and individual reactionaries, so long as they do not rebel, sabotage or create trouble after their political power has been overthrown, land and work will be given to them as well in order to allow them to live and remould themselves through labour into new people. If they are not willing to work, the people's state will compel them to work. Propaganda and educational work will be done among them too and will be done, moreover, with as much care and thoroughness as among the captured army officers in the past. This, too, may be called a "policy of benevolence" if you like, but it is imposed by us on the members of the enemy classes and cannot be mentioned in the same breath with the work of self-education which we carry on within the ranks of the revolutionary people.

Such remoulding of members of the reactionary classes can be accomplished only by a state of the people's democratic dictatorship under the leadership of the Communist Party. When it is well done, China's major exploiting classes, the landlord class and the bureaucrat-bourgeoisie (the monopoly capitalist class), will be eliminated for good. There remain the national bourgeoisie; at the present stage, we can already do a good deal of suitable educational work with many of them. When the time comes to realize socialism, that is, to nationalize private enterprise, we shall carry the work of educating and remoulding them a step further. The people have a powerful state apparatus in their hands—there is no need to fear rebellion by the national bourgeoisie.

The serious problem is the education of the peasantry. The peasant economy is scattered, and the socialization of agriculture, judging by the Soviet Union's experience, will require a long time and painstaking work. Without socialism of agriculture, there can be no complete, consolidated socialism. The steps to socialize agriculture must be co-ordinated with the development of a powerful industry having state enterprise as its backbone. The state of the people's democratic dictatorship must systematically solve the problems of industrialization. Since it is not proposed to discuss economic problems in detail in this article, I shall not go into them further.

In 1924 a famous manifesto was adopted at the Kuomintang's First National Congress, which Sun Yat-sen himself led and in which Communists participated. The manifesto stated:

> The so-called democratic system in modern states is usually monopolized by the bourgeoisie and has become simply an instrument for oppressing the common people. On the other hand, the Kuomintang's Principle of Democracy means a democratic system shared by all the common people and not privately owned by the few.

Apart from the question of who leads whom, the Principle of Democracy stated above corresponds as a general political programme to what we call People's Democracy or New Democracy. A state system which is shared only by the common people and which the bourgeoisie is not allowed to own privately— add to this the leadership of the working class, and we have the state system of the people's democratic dictatorship.

Chiang Kai-shek betrayed Sun Yat-sen and used the dictatorship of the bureaucrat-bourgeoisie and the landlord class as an instrument for oppressing the common people of China. This counter-revolutionary dictatorship was enforced for twenty-two years and has only now been overthrown by the common people of China under our leadership.

The foreign reactionaries who accuse us of practising "dictatorship" or "totalitarianism" are the very persons who practise it. They practise the dictatorship or totalitarianism of one class, the bourgeoisie, over the proletariat and the rest of the people. They are the very persons Sun Yat-sen spoke of as the bourgeoisie of modern states who oppress the common people. And it is from these reactionary scoundrels that Chiang Kai-shek learned his counterrevolutionary dictatorship.

Chu Hsi, a philosopher of the Sung Dynasty, wrote many books and made many remarks which are now forgotten, but one remark is still remembered, "Deal with a man as he deals with you." This is just what we do; we deal with the imperialists and their running dogs, the Chiang Kai-shek reactionaries, as they deal with us. That is all there is to it!

Revolutionary dictatorship and counter-revolutionary dictatorship are by nature opposites, but the former was learned from the latter. Such learning is very important. If the revolutionary people do not master this method of ruling over the counter-revolutionary classes, they will not be able to maintain their state power, domestic and foreign reaction will overthrow that power and restore its own rule over China, and disaster will befall the revolutionary people.

The people's democratic dictatorship is based on the alliance of the working class, the peasantry and the urban petty bourgeoisie, and mainly on the alliance of the workers and the peasants, because these two classes comprise 80 to 90 per cent of China's population. These two classes are the main force in overthrowing imperialism and the Kuomintang reactionaries. The transition from New Democracy to socialism also depends mainly upon their alliance.

The people's democratic dictatorship needs the leadership of the working class. For it is only the working class that is most farsighted, most selfless and most thoroughly revolutionary. The entire history of revolution proves that without the leadership of the working class revolution fails and that with the leadership of the working class revolution triumphs. In the epoch of imperialism, in no country can any other class lead any genuine revolution to victory.

This is clearly proved by the fact that the many revolutions led by China's petty bourgeoisie and national bourgeoisie all failed.

The national bourgeoisie at the present stage is of great importance. Imperialism, a most ferocious enemy, is still standing alongside us. China's modern industry still forms a very small proportion of the national economy. No reliable statistics are available, but it is estimated, on the basis of certain data, that before the War of Resistance Against Japan the value of output of modern industry constituted only about 10 per cent of the total value of output of the national economy. To counter imperialist oppression and to raise her backward economy to a higher level, China must utilize all the factors of urban and rural capitalism that are beneficial and not harmful to the national economy and the people's livelihood; and we must unite with the national bourgeoisie in common struggle. Our present policy is to regulate capitalism, not to destroy it. But the national bourgeoisie cannot be the leader of the revolution, nor should it have the chief role in state power. The reason it cannot be the leader of the revolution and should not have the chief role in state power is that the social and economic position of the national bourgeoisie determines its weakness; it lacks foresight and sufficient courage and many of its members are afraid of the masses.

Sun Yat-sen advocated "arousing the masses of the people" or "giving assistance to the peasants and workers." But who is to "arouse" them or "give assistance" to them? Sun Yat-sen had the petty bourgeoisie and the national bourgeoisie in mind. As a matter of fact, they cannot do so. Why did forty years of revolution under Sun Yat-sen end in failure? Because in the epoch of imperialism the petty bourgeoisie and the national bourgeoisie cannot lead any genuine revolution to victory.

Our twenty-eight years have been quite different. We have had much valuable experience. A well-disciplined Party armed with the theory of Marxism-Leninism, using the method of self-criticism and linked with the masses of the people; an army under the leadership of such a Party; a united front of all revolutionary classes and all revolutionary groups under the leadership of such a Party—these are the three main weapons with which we have defeated the enemy. They distinguish us from our predecessors. Relying on them, we have won basic victory. We have travelled a tortuous road. We have struggled against opportunist deviations in our Party, both Right and "Left." Whenever we made serious mistakes on these three matters, the revolution suffered setbacks. Taught by mistakes and setbacks, we have become wiser and handle our affairs better. It is hard for any political party or person to avoid mistakes, but we should make as few as possible. Once a mistake is made, we should correct it, and the more quickly and thoroughly the better.

To sum up our experience and concentrate it into one point, it is: the people's democratic dictatorship under the leadership of the working class (through the Communist Party) and based upon the alliance of workers and peasants. This dictatorship must unite as one with the international revolutionary forces. This is our formula, our principal experience, our main programme.

Twenty-eight years of our Party are a long period, in which we have accomplished only one thing—we have won basic victory in the revolutionary war. This calls for celebration, because it is the people's victory, because it is a victory in a country as large as China. But we still have much work to do; to use the analogy of a journey, our past work is only the first step in the long march of ten thousand *li*.[9] Remnants of the enemy have yet to be wiped out. The serious task of economic construction lies before us. We shall soon put aside some of the things we know well and be compelled to do things we don't know well. This means difficulties. The imperialists reckon that we will not be able to manage our economy; they are standing by and looking on, awaiting our failure.

We must overcome difficulties, we must learn what we do not know. We must learn to do economic work from all who know how, no matter who they are. We must esteem them as teachers, learning from them respectfully and conscientiously. We must not pretend to know when we do not know. We must not put on bureaucratic airs. If we dig into a subject for several months, for a year or two, for three or five years, we shall eventually master it. At first some of the Soviet Communists also were not very good at handling economic matters and the imperialists awaited their failure too. But the Communist Party of the Soviet Union emerged victorious and, under the leadership of Lenin and Stalin, it learned not only how to make the revolution but also how to carry on construction. It has built a great and splendid socialist state. The Communist Party of the Soviet Union is our best teacher and we must learn from it. The situation both at home and abroad is in our favour, we can rely fully on the weapon of the people's democratic dictatorship, unite the people throughout the country, the reactionaries excepted, and advance steadily to our goal.

FURTHER READINGS

The history of China's reaction to the challenges of modernization and Western influence is perceptively discussed in John K. Fairbank, *The Great Chinese Revolution, 1800–1985* (New York: Harper & Row, 1986). Ross Terrill, *Mao: A Biography* (New York: Harper & Row, 1980), is a substantial treatment by a prolific author on modern Chinese topics. Ed Hammon, *To Embrace the Moon: An Illustrated Biography of Mao Zedong* (Berkeley: Asian Humanities Press, 1980), provides a well-illustrated but uncritical and anecdotal portrait of the subject. The most substantial recent biography is the two-volume work of Han Suyin,

---

[9] A *li* is about one-third mile.

The Morning Deluge: Mao Tse-tung and the Chinese Revolution, 1893–1954 (Boston: Little, Brown, 1972), is a detailed account of the Chinese leader's youth and career up to 1954, while *Wind in the Tower* (Boston: Little, Brown, 1976), carries the account to the time of Mao's death.

The Long March is the subject of Harrison E. Salisbury, *The Long March: The Untold Story* (New York: Harper & Row, 1985), particularly interesting because the author retraced much of the route. Edgar Snow, *Red Star Over China* (1938, many editions), not only provides a biographical sketch of Mao's career to 1937, but offers an admiring eyewitness description of the Communist base in Yenan at the beginning of the struggle with the Japanese. The history of Mao's rule in China after the Communist victory in the civil war is the subject of Maurice J. Meisner, *Mao's China: A History of the People's Republic* (New York: Free Press, 1977), while a selection of Mao's public pronouncements during that period is provided by Michael Y. M. Kau and John Long, eds., *The Writings of Mao Zedong, 1949–1976* (Armonk, NY: M. E. Sharpe, 1986).

IKIRU
Akira Kurosawa

The film has become perhaps the dominant art form of the twentieth century. It is an art form that has benefitted from wide international participation. Numerous countries have developed strong national cinemas that, while frequently drawing on other countries' film traditions, generally reflect their own cultural characteristics. Japan is one among many nations who have participated fully and prominently in the development of this modern cultural medium. The Japanese film is characterized by its individuality and by its ability to depict accurately and honestly the Japanese and the environment in which they live. It is this realistic film style that has garnered the Japanese cinema a place among the world's most distinguished film heritages. Not all Japanese films, however, have been masterpieces. Japanese film companies have frequently produced transitory entertainment comparable to grade B American westerns. Samurai movies, horror and monster films, and erotica with little artistic or social value, but

From Akira Kurosawa, *Ikiru*, trans. Donald Richie, in Howard Hibbett, ed., *Contemporary Japanese Literature* (New York: Knopf, 1983), pp. 146–88.

substantial sexual action, have been popular during the seventies and eighties. But the more ambitious and noteworthy Japanese films, with their perceptive glimpses into the Japanese mentality and, more generally, into the human condition, rank among the world's finest film accomplishments.

The Western world was late in discovering the rich film heritage of the Japanese. It was not until 1951, when Akira Kurosawa's *Rashomon* won the Grand Prix at the Venice Festival, that Western audiences were awakened to the quality of one of the finest national cinemas in existence. Movies had been popular in Japan since their first appearance in 1896. During the 1930s, Japan produced many notable silent films and in the 1950s, under the guidance of a number of masterful directors, the Japanese sound film reached its maturity. Directors such as Yasujiro Ozu, Mikio Naruse, Tadashi Imira, Kenji Mizoguchi, and Akira Kurosawa have offered the world a unique view of the Japanese people. With the death of Kenji Mizoguchi in 1956 and of Yasujiro Ozu and Mikio Naruse in the sixties, Kurosawa remains the sole living master of the Japanese film from the brilliant golden age of the 1950s.

Akira Kurosawa was born in Tokyo in 1910, the last of seven children. Initially he studied Western-style painting and made a living by painting pictures for the cooking supplements of ladies' magazines or illustrations for love stories. He turned, however, to films in 1936 after responding to a newspaper advertisement from the PCL Studios soliciting essays on the basic defects of Japanese films. He passed all the necessary examinations and started work as an assistant director. In the early 1940s he began to receive recognition for his screen writing and in 1943 directed his own script *Sugata Sanshiro*. Numerous cinema classics were to follow, including his world famous *Rashomon* in 1950, *Ikiru* in 1952, *Seven Samurai* in 1954, *Dersu Uzala* in 1975, and *Ran* in 1985. His films, while remaining Japanese in their aesthetic and historical vocabulary, are carefully crafted examinations of important universal themes, which enable his work to cross cultural boundaries.

Many of Kurosawa's films deal with the question of how we should live our lives and perhaps his finest statement on this question is found in his cinema classic *Ikiru* (*To Live*). Written in conjunction with Hashimoto Shinobu and Oguni Hideo, the film was a tremendous success and placed first on the 1952 *Kinema Jumpo* "Ten Best" list, a poll comparable in importance to the American Academy Awards. *Ikiru* is the story of a petty government bureaucrat, Kanji Watanabe, who, on discovering that he has terminal cancer, decides to undertake one meaningful act before he dies. Cutting through red tape, he manages to have a playground built for neighborhood children in what was once a disease-breeding swamp. The story is a powerful moral document on the purpose of life. Through Watanabe's struggle to find what it means to exist and to acquire some meaning for his life, he learns that he alone has responsibility for himself and for his choices. He finds his life's vindication through action. He learns that a person is simply what that person does and through this realization he discovers what it is to live.

Questions

1. Discuss Watanabe's different reactions to his impending death. When does he finally discover what it means to live?

2. Why do you think Kurosawa chose to break the film into two parts? What purpose does this serve?

3. During the wake and its successive revelations it becomes increasingly clear that Watanabe has found his vindication through action. How do those in attendance assess his actions and react to the truth?

4. Early in the film the doctor asks the intern "If you were like him, with only half a year to live, what would you do?" Taking the place of the intern, how would you answer this question? How does the film answer the question?

IKIRU

(Titles white on black; slow, rather melancholy music; then, a close-up of an X-ray negative while a voice is heard explaining.)

NARRATOR *off*   This is an X-ray picture of a stomach; it belongs to the man this story is about. Symptoms of cancer are there but he doesn't yet know anything about it.

(Cut to the City Hall, the desk of WATANABE KANJI, *Chief of the Citizens' Section. He sits behind a desk piled high with papers and is busy putting his seal to various documents. Then he stops and looks at his watch. Cut to the front of the office, the information counter; a number of women are talking with* SAKAI, *the Section Clerk. On the counter is the notice: "THIS WINDOW IS FOR YOU. IT IS YOUR LINK WITH THE CITY HALL. WE WELCOME BOTH REQUESTS AND COMPLAINTS.")*

WOMEN   And my child got a rash from that water . . . It smells bad too . . . There are millions of mosquitoes . . . Why can't you do something with the land? It would make a good playground.

(SAKAI *excuses himself and goes to* WATANABE'S *desk, telling him that some petitioners from Kuroe-cho are there.* WATANABE *tells him to send them to the Public Works Section, then looks at this watch again.*)

NARRATOR *off* This is the main character of our story, but he's not very interesting yet. He's just passing the time, wasting it, rather. It would be difficult to say that he is really alive.

(WATANABE *suddenly looks up at the sound of laughter. Cut to the office where everyone is looking at the office girl* TOYO, *who has suddenly broken into laughter.* ONO, *the Assistant Chief, speaks sharply to her, telling her to please watch her behavior during working hours. Cut back to* WATANABE, *who takes off his glasses.*)

TOYO   But it was funny.

ONO   What was?

TOYO   This joke that someone passed around.

ONO   Read it then.

(*Cut to* TOYO *standing up. She hesitates, then begins to read from a newspaper clipping.*)

TOYO *reading*   You've never had a day off, have you? No. Why? Are you indispensable? No, I just don't want them to find out they can do without me.

(*She laughs, but no one else does. Cut to* WATANABE, *who has been listening. Now he puts his glasses on again and goes back to stamping papers.*)

NARRATOR *off* This is pretty bad. He is like a corpse and actually he has been dead for the past twenty-five years. Before that he had some life in him. He even tried to work.

(WATANABE *wants to clean his seal and is looking for some paper. He opens a desk drawer full of old documents. The top one reads A PLAN TO INCREASE OFFICE EFFICIENCY. He tears off the first page, cleans his seal, throws the paper into the basket, and goes on stamping, while the* NARRATOR *continues off.*)

NARRATOR *off* But now he neither tries nor even wants to. His ambitions have been well smothered by City Hall. But, he's busy—oh, very busy. Still, he is doing little. He has to keep busy simply to stay where he is. Is this as it should be?

> (WATANABE *seems to feel uncomfortable; he takes his tablets, and drinks some water.*)

NARRATOR *off*   But before he begins to think seriously, his stomach must get worse and more useless hours must accumulate.

> (*Cut to the* WOMEN *from Kuroe-cho arriving at the office of the Public Works Section, where the* CLERK *in charge says that he is sorry, but this matter comes under the authority of the Parks Section. Wipe to the Parks Section, where the* CLERK *is telling them that the matter seems to be concerned with sanitation, hence they had better go to the Health Center. Dissolve into the Center, where they are told that the Sanitation Section will take care of them; a lively fugue is built under these scenes, based on a motif from the opening music. Wipe to the Sanitation Section, where they are told to go to the Environmental Health Section. Wipe to that Section, where they are told to go to the Anti-Epidemics Office. Wipe to that Office, where a* CLERK, *hearing it is about mosquitoes, directs them to the Pest Control Section. Wipe to that Section, where a* CLERK *swats a fly before directing them to the Sewage Section. Wipe to the Sewage Section, where a* CLERK *says that theirs was indeed formerly a sewage area but that a road ran over it, so, unless the Road Section approves . . . Wipe to the Road Section, where they are told that since the City Planning Department's policy is not yet established, they had best go there first. Wipe to the Planning Department, where they learn that the Fire Department had wanted the section reclaimed because of such poor water facilities, so they had better go there. Wipe to the Fire Department, where the* CLERK *says that it is nonsense, they do not want dirty water, it would ruin their hoses. Now if they had a swimming pool or something there, then the Fire Department might be interested. Wipe to the Children's Welfare Officer at the Educational Section, who tells them that such a big problem as this should be taken up with the City Councillor. Wipe to the Councillor's office. He is saying that he will give his personal introduction to the Deputy Mayor. Wipe to the office of that official, who is saying that he is truly happy when citizens take it upon themselves to make such suggestions, and for that reason they have established a special Citizens' Section. Wipe back to the Citizens' Section.* SAKAI *is again at the counter and does not remember them; he tells them to go to the Public Works Section. The Women become angry.*)

WOMEN   What do you think we are anyway? What does this sign here mean? Isn't it your section's responsibility? Don't worry, we won't bother you again . . .

(*They start to leave. After a moment's hesitation, he runs after them, and catches them at the door.*)

SAKAI   Just a moment, please. I'm sorry. You see, our Section Chief is out today. If you could possibly just submit a written petition.

(*All the staff stand up, to watch the women go. Quick shot of* WATANABE'S *empty desk. Dissolve to the office. Two of the staff are eating their lunch and drinking tea as they talk, back to camera.*)

SAITO   It is certainly unusual for him to be out.

ONO   Well, he hasn't been looking too well lately.

SAITO   Yes, but it wouldn't be good if he stays out too long.

ONO   Funny, though. Certainly he wouldn't take sick-leave just for a cold. Besides, I need his seal.

(*Cut to another part of the office. Two other members of the staff are eating their lunch, while they talk.*)

KIMURA   It's too bad though. Another month and he'd have had thirty years without one day off.

OHARA   Yes, but you notice that now he's away certain people seem a lot happier. Well, everyone wants to get on in the world.

(*Cut to another part of the office, where they are also having lunch.*)

SAKAI   Wonder what that medicine is he's always taking.

TOYO   Something for his stomach. And lately he hasn't been eating his noodles for lunch.

NOGUCHI   That's another record. I've never seen him eat anything else.

SAKAI   I wonder who the new Chief will be.

TOYO   What's the hurry? You have a long way to go.

(*Cut to a long shot of* ONO *and* SAITO. *They have heard* TOYO'S *remark and look up, startled.* ONO *is Assistant Chief. Cut to* WATANABE'S *empty desk. Cut to* WATANABE *walking down a hospital corridor. Dissolve to* WATANABE *at the hospital drinking-fountain, in the waiting room.* WATANABE *is trying to get a drink of water, but a man gets there before him.* WATANABE *waits, then drinks, and then looks at himself in the mirror. Cut to* WATANABE *sitting down. Another* MAN *a few chairs away comes and sits next to him.*)

MAN   Stomach trouble, eh? Me, I've got something chronic. Lately it's got so that I just don't feel right unless my stomach hurts.

(A NURSE *calls a name and the man, the same one that drank before* WATANABE *did, gets up and goes into the office.*)

MAN   Now, that fellow there. They say it's ulcers but I think it's cancer. And having cancer is the same as having a death sentence. But the doctors here always tell you it's ulcers, that an operation's unnecessary. They tell you to go on and eat anything—and when you hear that, you know you've got a year left, at the most. Your stomach always feels heavy, and it hurts; you belch a lot and you're always thirsty; either you're constipated or else you have diarrhea, and in either case your stool is always black.

(WATANABE *is feeling more and more uncomfortable. Quiet, sinister music. He changes seats but the* MAN *follows him. Shot of* WATANABE *becoming more and more uncomfortable.*)

MAN   And you won't be able to eat meat, or anything you really like, then you'll vomit up something you ate a week ago; and when that happens, you have about three months to live.

(*Cut to a long shot of* WATANABE *alone in the waiting room. The slow and melancholy music of the opening is heard. He is small in the distance, almost lost in the large waiting room. A* NURSE *suddenly calls his name; she calls it several times because he does not hear. He finally hears, and rises. The music fades. Cut to the X-ray room, two Doctors and a* NURSE *are waiting. Cut to* WATANABE *entering, then a shot of their faces as they wait for him to sit down. Quick close-up of the* DOCTOR'S *face, then* WATANABE'S.)

DOCTOR   Yes, please sit down. Well, it looks as though you have a light case of ulcers.

(*Cut to* WATANABE'S *hands. He drops the coat he is carrying. The music begins again. Cut to their faces.*)

WATANABE   Be honest with me. Tell me the truth. Tell me it's cancer.

(*The* DOCTORS' *faces; the* NURSE'S *face; the back of the young* DOCTOR'S *head—he is looking at the X-ray picture. She picks up* WATANABE'S *coat.*)

DOCTOR   Not at all. It's just a light case of ulcers, as I said.

WATANABE   Is an operation impossible?

DOCTOR   It's unnecessary. Medicine will fix you up.

WATANABE   But what shall I eat?

DOCTOR   Anything you like, so long as it's digestible.

> (*Cut to* WATANABE. *Hearing this he lowers his head so that it almost touches the deck. Wipe back to the* DOCTORS.)

YOUNGER DOCTOR   Will he last a year?

ELDER DOCTOR   No. Six months at the most. What would you do if you only had half a year to live? Miss Aihara, what would you do?

NURSE   Well, there's some poison there on the shelf.

> (*The* YOUNGER DOCTOR *turns back to look at the X-ray negative. Close-up of the negative, the sound of the buzzing of the X-ray machine is heard. Cut to the street: trucks, cars,* WATANABE *walking, but all without sound. When he tries to cross the street, a truck races past, and there is a sudden burst of sound. The traffic streams in front of* WATANABE *and he, small, on the opposite side of the street, cannot cross. Wipe to the front of* WATANABE'S *house at night. The camera slowly moves toward the front door. The sound of walking and of someone humming the song "Too Young," then the voices of* WATANABE'S *son,* MITSUO, *and his daughter-in-law,* KAZUE.)

KAZUE   There's no lights on—power gone off again, I wonder?

MITSUO   No, the neighbor's lights are on.

KAZUE   That's funny. Is your father out, I wonder? Where's the key?

MITSUO   It's in your bag.

> (*The camera has moved toward the door. Cut from an extreme close-up of part of the door to the hallway from the inside. The two of them open the door and come in.*)

KAZUE   It was open. Did that maid forget to lock up? Really, that woman forgets everything.

MITSUO   She lives so far away, that's why. It takes her so long to get home that she forgets about everything else.

KAZUE   It wouldn't cost that much more to have her live in.

MITSUO   You know Father. He'd never hear of it. Always the minor official.

(Cut to the corner of the hallway. They are moving through the dark to the bottom of the stairs.)

KAZUE It's just as cold inside as it is outside—that's what's wrong with Japanese houses.

MITSUO I always hate coming home. It would be nice to have a modern house.

(Cut to the two of them on the stairs in the dark.)

KAZUE Well, we could build one for about five hundred thousand yen, couldn't we? Though we might have to use your father's retirement pay.

MITSUO He'll get about seven hundred thousand, and a monthly pension too. And he's got about a hundred thousand saved up.

KAZUE But do you think he'll agree?

(Cut to the darkened upstairs rooms.)

MITSUO Well, he'll just have to live by himself if he doesn't. That will probably be the most effective way. After all, he can't take his money with him.

(KAZUE laughs. MITSUO finds the light and turns it on. WATANABE is at his feet; he has been sitting there in the dark. Cut to WATANABE's face, then cut to his son's.)

MITSUO Father, what's the matter?

WATANABE *in despair* Oh, nothing; nothing at all.

(He stands up, confused, then goes downstairs to his own room. Cut to MITSUO and his wife looking at each other. She begins to turn on more lights.)

KAZUE But he heard everything we said. Really, that was very rude of him. And he shouldn't have come up here, not while we were away. I call that very impolite.

MITSUO Why didn't he say what he wanted to? Why did he run away like that?

(Cut to WATANABE in his darkened room downstairs. He turns on the light. Pan with him as he goes to a small shrine in the corner of the room and opens it. Cut to MITSUO upstairs; he is lying on the bed, and KAZUE is making him move to take off the bedspread. He looks at her, and she comes and sits on the bed. She then lies down beside him.)

KAZUE   Don't look like that. Let's forget about your father and think a little more about us.

> (*They have turned on the radio and from it comes "Too Young." She turns towards him, hugs him, and tells him to hold her. Cut to* WATANABE'S *room. He is sitting before the open shrine. Cut to the small shrine and to the photograph of his dead wife inside it. Close-up of the picture. Close-up of* WATANABE *looking at it. Big close-up of the picture. Dissolve to a motor-hearse, seen through the rain-flecked windshield of a following car. The sound of windshield wipers. Cut to the back seat:* WATANABE, KIICHI, *his brother,* TATSU, *his sister-in-law (all much younger), and* MITSUO, *as a child, are going to a funeral.*)

TATSU   And she was so young, too—oh, but it must have been hard for her to leave her little boy behind.

KIICHI   Stop crying.

> (*Cut to the hearse ahead, turning a corner. Cut to the little boy,* MITSUO. *Cut to the hearse again, then back to* MITSUO; *the melancholy music of the opening is heard. [The hearse is always seen through the windshield, it's image cut by the wipers.]*)

MITSUO   We have to hurry. Mother is leaving us behind.

> (*Cut to the back seat.* WATANABE *is holding his son, tears in his eyes. Cut back to* WATANABE'S *room. From above comes the sound of the song as well as* MITSUO *and* KAZUE'S *muffled laughter. He looks up to where the sound is coming from. They seem to be making love. Cut to another room, where* WATANABE *and* KIICHI, *his brother, are talking. Both men are much younger.*)

KIICHI   You say you can't get married again because of Mitsuo, but just wait. When he grows up he's not going to be all that grateful; after he gets married himself you'll just be in the way. And that is why you ought to get married again now. My wife says that you're naturally sloppy and she says she can't stand the thought of you living all alone and getting more that way.

> (WATANABE *has been absently turning the pages of a book while his brother has been talking. Now, however, he hears his son calling him. Cut back to his room. Again he hears the voice, stands up, walks to the stairs, and starts going up them. Cut from the top of the stairs.* WATANABE *is halfway up when* MITSUO'S *voice continues off.*)

MITSUO *off* Good night. And lock up, will you?

(WATANABE *stops, then rests his head against a step, then starts back down into the darkness whispering "Mitsuo." Cut to the hallway. He slowly crosses it and locks the front door. Then from a corner he takes a baseball bat and jams it tight, as is apparently his habit, against one of the sliding doors so that it cannot be opened from the outside. Cut to a close-up of the baseball bat; at the same time, the sound of a ball being hit; the roar of the crowd; the opening music, soft under the sound of the crowd. Cut to WATANABE excitedly watching a baseball game. He turns to the MAN next to him.*)

WATANABE Mitsuo! Wasn't that a wonderful hit? See that? That batter is my—

(*Cut to the baseball game, flashpan of the young MITSUO running to home plate. Cut to WATANABE, who again shouts his son's name. Flashpan to the ball game. Something has gone wrong. Cut to WATANABE and the MAN.*)

MAN What's that guy think he's doing anyway?

(*Cut to WATANABE in his room, sitting down, the camera descending with him. Cut to WATANABE at the ball game, sitting down, the camera descending with him. Cut to WATANABE and MITSUO, the latter on a stretcher, in a hospital elevator going up, the camera ascending with them.*)

WATANABE You be brave now, Mitsuo; after all, a little appendix operation isn't anything at all.

MITSUO But, aren't you going to stay?

WATANABE I . . . I have some things to do.

(*The elevator door opens and the boy is wheeled out. WATANABE'S voice is heard repeating his son's name over and over again, as throughout the following scenes the music rises. Cut to the hallway. He is still standing there, repeating his son's name to himself. Cut to a railway station. It is wartime; the students have been mobilized and are being sent off. Hundreds of people are there: fathers, mothers, brothers, sisters, all waving flags and throwing streamers. Cut to MITSUO, now older, in his uniform. He is looking at his father, he calls his name and is very near to tears; he steps down from the train. The train starts; his father pushes him back onto it; he turns towards his father, searching for his face as the train pulls away. All of this time the voice of WATANABE can be heard calling over, "Mitsuo, Mitsuo, Mitsuo." Long dissolve from the boy's face to WATANABE in the hall. He starts to go up the stairs, but stops halfway. Dissolve to his room. He hangs up his kimono; puts his trousers under the pallet to press them, winds his pocket*) *watch and puts it on the table, reaches for the alarm clock and begins to wind, then drops it. All of this is obviously done by force of habit. Then he suddenly stops. He does not move; the seconds pass; then, without warning, he turns and crawls under the covers. He seems afraid and pulls the covers over his head. He begins to weep. A wide shot of the room. Over the huddled* WATANABE *are two framed letters on the wall. Cut to a close-up of one of them which reads: "LETTER OF COMMENDATION. MR. WATANABE KANJI IS HEREBY GIVEN RECOGNITION FOR HIS TWENTY-FIVE YEARS OF DEVOTED SERVICE." The sound of weeping continues. Cut to the hallway of the house. It is daytime.* SAKAI, *the clerk in* WATANABE'S *office, is at the door talking to the maid.)*

MAID   But he always leaves for work at the same time.

SAKAI   Huh? He hasn't been to the office for five days, hasn't even sent in an absence report. I was told to come and see what had happened.

(She goes into the house to call KAZUE. *Wipe to a telephone booth.* KAZUE *is inside talking. Cut to an office.* MITSUO *is on the telephone and we hear their conversation.)*

MITSUO   I can't believe it.

KAZUE   But it must be true, that man from his office said so.

MITSUO   But what could he be doing?

(Cut to WATANABE'S *office. The others are talking; long shot of his empty desk.)*

SAKAI   It's true, and his family was really surprised.

TOYO   But this is awful.

ONO   Well, I can make all the decisions, of course, so long as he's not here.

TOYO   But you have to go and get his seal so that I can leave.

ONO   You mean you're resigning?

(Cut to a close-up of TOYO.*)*

TOYO   Yes—this work doesn't suit me.

(Wipe to KIICHI'S *house.* MITSUO *is there. They are eating dinner.)*

MITSUO   And he's taken fifty thousand yen out of the bank, too.

KIICHI   You don't say . . . Well, maybe he's found himself a girl. Good for him if he has.

TATSU   Now, now . . .

MITSUO   But that's impossible.

KIICHI   Not at all. It's men like him who fall the hardest. Look, he's been a widower for some twenty years now. And he did it all for you, too. Now he can't stand it any longer and so he goes out and finds someone for himself.

MITSUO   That's nonsense—why, he doesn't look at all well. He's so thin, and his skin's got so dry. Have you seen him recently?

TATSU   Yes, about four days ago. One morning he came over, seemed to want to talk about something. But you know how my husband is. He just looked at him and asked if he'd come for a loan.

KIICHI   I didn't think then that he'd come wanting to talk about some woman, not looking like that.

TATSU   Now, now. My husband, you see, thinks that all men are as bad as he is. Still, Mitsuo, are you certain that something didn't happen over at your house?

MITSUO   No, not that I know of.

(*But he is evasive and will not look at his aunt and uncle. Cut to a railway crossing. It is evening, almost dark. Cut to a black dog, hunting for food in the dark. Cut to a small drinking stall. Inside a man is at the counter writing. He finishes a page and turns to the* STALL-KEEPER.)

WRITER   Would you take this over to my house? A guy from a magazine is there waiting for it. And on the way back get me some sleeping tablets.

KEEPER   But the drugstore's closed.

WRITER   Is it that late?

KEEPER   The shops close early around here.

WRITER   If I don't have those pills with my whiskey, I just don't sleep.

(*He hands the page to the* STALL-KEEPER, *crumpling the rest of the manuscript in his hand. Cut to* WATANABE *over in a dark corner; he is hardly visible. He gets up and comes over toward the* WRITER.)

WATANABE   Excuse me, but I can let you have some.

(He puts the bottle of pills on the counter in front of the WRITER, then goes back to his table. The STALL-KEEPER goes out and the black dog lopes in.)

WRITER   Thanks, may I have them at the official price?

WATANABE   Oh, I was planning to throw them away anyway.

WRITER   Then let me pay for your drinks. You're quite a drinker, aren't you? Here, let me give you a bit more.

WATANABE   No, I can't . . . I'd just throw it all up. I have gastric cancer.

WRITER *concerned*   Cancer!

WATANABE   Yes.

WRITER   Then you shouldn't drink like this.

(He puts his hand on WATANABE'S shoulder.)

WATANABE   I don't really want to talk about it . . .

WRITER   But to drink, knowing that you have cancer . . . it's like committing suicide.

(Cut to the WRITER looking at him; cut to WATANABE.)

WATANABE   No, it's not that easy. I'd thought of ending it all, but it's hard to die. And I can't die just yet. I don't know what I've been living for, all these years.

(Cut to the WRITER.)

WRITER   Do you have any children? *He receives no answer.* Well, does your stomach hurt?

(Cut to WATANABE.)

WATANABE   More than my stomach, it's . . . *He presses his chest.*

WRITER   But there must be some reason for all of this.

(A shot of both of them.)

WATANABE   No, I'm just a stupid fool, that's all. *He pours himself a cup of sake and drinks it.* I'm . . . well, I'm angry with myself. Up until a few days ago I'd never spent anything on drinking. It was only after I found that I didn't have much longer to live that I . . . *He pours himself another cup of sake.*

WRITER I understand, but you still shouldn't drink. Does it taste good?

WATANABE No, it doesn't. *He puts down his cup.* But it makes me forget. I'm drinking this expensive sake now because . . . well, because I never did before. It's like drinking poison. I mean, it seems like poison, yet it's so soothing. *He smiles.*

WRITER I know what you mean.

> *(There is some food on the table which* WATANABE *has not eaten. He sees the dog, drops the food on the floor, and the dog bolts it down. Cut back to the two men.)*

WATANABE I have about fifty thousand yen with me. I'd like to spend it having a really good time. But, and I'm ashamed to admit it, I don't know how to. If you would . . .

WRITER Are you asking me how to spend it, to show you how?

> *(A train passes very near, shaking the stall and making the bottles rattle.)*

WATANABE Yes, that is what I wanted to ask you to do.

WRITER But—

WATANABE It took me a long time to save this money, but what I mean is that now I can spend it.

> *(During the following speech, shots intercut between the two men.)*

WRITER I understand. Look, keep your money. You'll be my guest tonight. Leave it all to me. *He goes across to another table to get his bottle of whiskey; he picks it up and comes back to sit down. He looks at* WATANABE *very closely.* You know, you're very interesting. I know I'm being rude, but you're a very interesting person. I'm only a hack writer, I write trashy novels, but you've really made me think tonight. *He pours himself a glass of whiskey.* I see that adversity has its virtue—man finds truth in misfortune; having cancer has made you want to taste life. *He drinks the whiskey.* Man is such a fool. It is always just when he is going to leave it that he discovers how beautiful life can be. And even then, people who realize this are rare. Some die without ever once knowing what life is really like. You're a fine man, you're fighting against death—that's what impresses me. Up until now you've been life's slave but now you're going to be its master. And it is man's duty to enjoy life; it's against nature not to. Man must have a greed for life. We're taught that that's immoral, but it isn't. The greed to live is a virtue. *They have moved to the doorway; the sound of a train passing.* Let's go. Let's find that life you've thrown away. Tonight I'll be your Mephistopheles, but a good one, who won't ask to be paid. *He looks down at his feet.* Look, we even have a black dog!

> (*He kicks at the dog and it yelps; over this is the sound of a celeste. Cut to a close-up of a pinball machine, the ball bouncing to the sound of the celeste. Cut to the two of them in the pinball parlor.*)

WRITER See this little silver ball? That is you; that's your life. Oh, this is a marvelous machine, a marvelous machine that frees you from all of life's worries; it's an automatic vendor of dreams.

> (*Medium shot of them playing the pinball machine.* WATANABE *looks very excited. Wipe to the two of them in an enormous beer hall. They are sitting with enormous steins of beer in front of them. The writer is just about to speak when trombones, apparently part of a band, are suddenly extended over* WATANABE'S *head as he stands up. Deafening music begins. Wipe to the streets; a number of fast pans follow the* WRITER *and* WATANABE *through the crowds; shots from behind blinding neon signs and from behind the grillwork of fences; a girl races up and snatches away* WATANABE'S *hat; he turns and tries to chase her but the* WRITER *stops him.*)

WRITER No . . . girls are the most predatory of all existing mammals. To get that hat back would cost you more than its worth. But, anyway, you could buy a dozen new hats if you wanted to. Now we're going to buy you a new hat to say good-by to your old life with.

> (*Cut to them looking through an openwork screen into a small bar. Cut to them at the entrance of the bar. Medium close-up of the* WRITER *stopping to shape* WATANABE'S *new hat. Shot of them coming into the bar. From the record-player can be heard Josephine Baker's recording of "J'ai Deux Amours." The* PROPRIETRESS *and barmen stand smiling. She welcomes them, says it has been a long time, and they sit at the bar.* WATANABE *has his new hat in front of him; when she tries to take it away from him, he, instantly suspicious, grabs it and holds onto it. The* WRITER *laughs; she smiles. Camera remains on the* PROPRIETRESS *in medium close-up; the* WRITER *can be seen in the mirror behind her.*)

WRITER What's so funny? This man here has gastric cancer.

PROPRIETRESS   Then he shouldn't be drinking, should he?

WRITER   Stupid—no, take a good look at him. See, he's God and he's carrying this cross called cancer. Most people just die the minute they learn this, but not him; he's different. From that moment on he started to live.

>   (*She smiles again and the camera turns from them and pans over their glasses to the mirror behind the bar. WATANABE has put his hat back on, but his head is resting against the bar.*)

WRITER   Isn't that right?

>   (*WATANABE slowly raises his head, looks at himself in the mirror, and suddenly smiles. Wipe to a big glass-and-neon cabaret. The camera pans down the great stairwell, up which the WRITER and WATANABE are coming, forcing their way through the crowd. A couple is dancing on the landing, very close together. WATANABE cannot tear himself away from the sight; the WRITER pulls him on. Cut to the top floor. Cut to a close-up of piano hammers playing Boogie-Woogie music; a beer-drinking PIANO PLAYER, a dancing GIRL; she takes WATANABE'S hat, puts it on, dances around the room. Clsoe-ups of the piano keys; of the huge mirror which hangs above the piano; of the GIRL dancing; of WATANABE following her around the room; of the PIANO PLAYER, smiling from behind the swinging bead-curtain. WATANABE finally gets his hat back; the GIRL goes off dancing, falls against the keys of the piano, and the PIANO PLAYER turns.*)

PIANO PLAYER   You folks got any requests?

>   (*The GIRL comes over and sits on WATANABE'S lap.*)

WATANABE   "Life Is So Short."

PIANO PLAYER   I beg your pardon . . . ?

WATANABE   "Life Is So Short." *He begins to sing.* "Fall in love, dear maiden . . ."

PIANO PLAYER   Oh, that one—it's an oldie, isn't it? Okay.

>   (*He rattles off an introduction, and then pours beer down his throat; couples collect on the dance floor. Cut to the dance floor as seen through the swinging bead-curtain. As it sways back and forth, the couples one by one stop dancing, turning to look. Cut to the GIRL, she is moving slowly away from WATANABE'S chair. The camera circles, in close-up, staying on WATANABE as he sings.*)

WATANABE   *Life is so short,*
Fall in love, dear maiden,
While your lips are still red;
Before you can no longer love—
For there will be no tomorrow.

Life is so short,
Fall in love, dear maiden,
While your hair is still black;
Before your heart stops—
For there will be no tomorrow.

(Tears stream down WATANABE'S *face. There is silence. Suddenly the* WRITER *stands up, springing into the frame.)*

WRITER   That's the spirit!

(He takes WATANABE'S *arm, pulling him out of the dance hall. Cut to a strip-show, a woman dancing on a lighted platform, slow, seductive music, the camera panning around her. Cut to her feet as a garment drops. The camera moves towards the* WRITER *and* WATANABE, *both looking at the girl above them. They are both drunk.)*

WRITER   That's not art. A striptease isn't art. It's too direct. It's more direct than art. That woman's body up there. It's a big, juicy steak; it's a glass of gin; a shot of camphor; it's hormone extract, streptomycin, uranium . . . WATANABE *gulps.*

(Wipe to the streets. Both are very drunk. WATANABE *starts across the road, and is almost run over, but the car stops in time.* WATANABE *takes off his coat as though he too were doing a striptease. He stops the traffic. The* WRITER *comes and pulls him out of the road. Wipe to an enormous dance hall: a great crush of people struggling on the dance floor, cigarette smoke rising from the pack. The band is playing a mambo. Cut as each section of the band strikes up; trumpeters, trombonists, percussionists, standing against the massed dancers. Cut to* WATANABE *in the crowd, dancing with a girl who is chewing gum. She is merely discomfited by the crush; he is nearly frantic. The* WRITER *is almost asleep on his feet; his girl pinches him; he opens his eyes and yawns. Cut to a speeding car, the camera traveling alongside it, reflections sliding over the surface. Inside are* WATANABE, *the* WRITER, *and the two girls. The reflections slide over the window, past*

WATANABE'S face. He looks very ill. One of the girls is putting on lipstick; then she carefully removes her eyelashes. The other is counting a great roll of money. WATANABE looks at them, then out of the window.)

WATANABE Stop the car!

GIRL Stop the car! . . . Stop the car!

(The car stops. WATANABE opens the door and runs into the shadows. The girl looks irritated.)

WRITER *waking up* What's the matter, have we got a flat?

GIRL No, it's your friend; he's probably throwing up.

(The WRITER gets out of the car. WATANABE is slowly coming out of the shadows. In the distance over a loudspeaker comes the sound of a mambo. There is the noise of a train. WATANABE smiles—or tries to. He and the WRITER look at each other—perhaps WATANABE is remembering what he heard in the hospital, that when you begin to vomit you only have three more months to live. Both men are now completely sober. They get back into the car; the car starts.)

GIRL What are you so gloomy about? I hate gloomy people. Come on, let's sing something nice and gay.

(The girls start singing as loudly as they can; WATANABE and the WRITER stare straight ahead.)

GIRLS   *Come on'a my house, come on'a my house.*
I'm a'gonna give you everything.
I'm a'gonna give you a Christmas tree.

(Dissolve to a street near WATANABE'S house. It is day, he is on his way home, still wearing his new hat. Cut to a close-up of the hat, the camera then panning down to his face.)

TOYO *off* Mr. Watanabe!

(Cut to the street. TOYO, the office girl, is running up behind him. He turns and she catches up with him.)

TOYO Your new hat almost fooled me. *He takes off his new hat.* I was just looking for your house. Are you going to work?

WATANABE No.

TOYO Do you have your seal?

WATANABE No, it's at home.

TOYO I want to leave—and I have this new job so I'm sort of in a hurry.

WATANABE Come home with me, then.

>   *(Cut to them walking side by side.)*

WATANABE Why are you leaving?

TOYO The work is so boring. Nothing ever happens in that office. I've stood it for a year and a half now. The fact that you've been out for five days . . . *She looks at his hat* . . . and your new hat—that's all that's happened in a whole year and a half.

>   *(Cut to the upstairs room of* WATANABE'S *house.* MITSUO *is tying his tie; his wife is standing next to him.)*

MITSUO Anyway, just don't say anything to him.

KAZUE I've nothing to say to him.

MITSUO Now, don't act like that. After all, it's your fault. If you hadn't started talking about his retirement pay . . .

KAZUE Why blame everything on me? You were the one, if you remember, that started talking about money that night. He can't take his money with him, you said.

MITSUO It's funny though. Just because of that . . . he wouldn't start acting like this, just because of that. And he's always come home before. Last night was the first time he's ever stayed out all night.

KAZUE Well, let's not talk about it any more—we don't know what's wrong.

>   *(At that moment they hear something.* KAZUE *runs toward the stairs. Cut to the hall. The* MAID *takes his hat and stands looking at it. Cut to his room.* TOYO *takes his coat and puts it on a hanger. He is watching her, then turns to his desk. She walks toward him and puts her letter on his desk. As she walks around the room, she sees the framed letter of commendation on the wall.)*

TOYO Almost thirty years in that place, think of it. It gives me the willies. *She glances sideways at him.* I'm sorry.

WATANABE That's all right. You know, lately, when I look at that letter, well, I remember that joke you read out loud in the office once. It was a very true joke. I've been there almost thirty years and now I can't remember one day, can't remember one thing I did. All I know is that I was always busy and always bored.

> *(He bows his head. She looks at him, then she begins to laugh. Finally, he joins her.)*

TOYO That's the first time I've every heard you talk like that. I didn't even know you could feel like that, I really didn't.

> *(She laughs and impulsively stretches out her hands, takes his, shakes them. The door behind them opens and the MAID appears with the tea. She stops dead. Cut back to the room upstairs.)*

MITSUO Now don't be foolish. I know Uncle said the same thing, but I just can't imagine him being in love with such a young girl . . . *They sit on the bed.*

> *(Cut to WATANABE's room. He is at his desk; the girl is kneeling politely some distance away. He looks up at her over his glasses.)*

WATANABE But this is the wrong form.

> *(He looks at her; she looks away; then he takes up his seal and stamps her letter of resignation anyway. He hands it to her; she smiles.)*

WATANABE Are you going to the office today?

TOYO Oh, yes. I have to turn this in.

WATANABE If you wait a minute I'll make my absence report out. Would you take it in for me?

TOYO Why don't you go to work yourself? Everyone in the office is talking about it, they say it's "that time of life." Are you really sick? You do look pale.

WATANABE No, I . . .

TOYO Where do you go every day when you pretend to be going to work? And don't lie, either. Did you know that Mr. Sakai came here yesterday to check on you? *She suddenly laughs.* But, don't worry. After thirty years you deserve some kind of rest. I'm not going to talk about you the way Mr. Carp did.

WATANABE Mr. Carp?

TOYO   That's just my name for him—but he is just like a carp, you know. Full of airs, but he doesn't have any backbone at all, and he always acts so superior, too—even with me. Just because he makes two hundred yen a month more than I do. WATANABE *laughs and she stands up, a bit embarrassed.* Well, I'll be going now. *She takes the letters and gets her coat. He looks at her.*

(*Cut to* TOYO. *She has two large holes in her stockings.*)

WATANABE   Wait, I'll go with you.

(*Cut to the upstairs window, from the outside.* MITSUO *and his wife are looking out. Cut to the front gate,* WATANABE *and* TOYO *are coming out, both smiling. Cut to the couple in the upstairs window, watching. Cut to the couple below. She stops him, straightens his tie for him. Cut to* MITSUO *and his wife. She smirks; he looks down, worried. Cut to the staircase. The* MAID *is on her way up to share the news. Cut to the street.* WATANABE *and* TOYO *are walking and a waltz tune, played by strings and celeste, can be heard over.*)

TOYO   But you're very lucky, living in a nice house like that. Why, at my place we have three families living in two rooms. You have a son, don't you?

WATANABE   Where can I buy some women's stockings?

TOYO   You want to buy some?—they ought to be selling them somewhere around here. They're for your son's wife, aren't they? Someone told me she was very pretty.

(*Wipe to a store. They are just coming out and she is holding a pair of new stockings all wrapped up, and is smiling.*)

TOYO   I'm so excited. Why, I'd have to go without lunch for three months to buy these. But why did you get them for me?

WATANABE   You had holes in your old ones.

TOYO   But that didn't make *your* feet cold.

WATANABE   I just . . .

TOYO   I didn't mean that. *She turns and smiles.* I appreciate it a lot—very much. I only said that because I felt embarrassed.

(*Suddenly embarrassed, she walks behind him, then, laughingly, pushes him. Wipe to a tearoom. He looks at her, passes her his piece of cake. She smiles and helps herself to sugar, putting in lump after lump.*)

TOYO   Want me to tell you something? Well, I've given everyone in our office a nickname. It was something to do, so I wouldn't get so bored. Want to hear?

WATANABE   Yes.

TOYO   All right. Now, the first one is—Mr. Sea-Slug. Now, who is that? Someone that's hard to pin down, keeps squirming away. *He does not know. She giggles.* It's Mr. Ono!

(WATANABE *smiles, nods.*)

WATANABE   Of course.

TOYO   Next is Mr. Drain-Cover. Think, now. Someone who's damp all year round.

WATANABE   Mr. Ohara?

TOYO   That's right! And then there's Mr. Fly-Paper. A very sticky person. Come, you know. You don't? Mr. Noguchi. And do you want to know what I named Mr. Saito? He doesn't have anything special about him and yet he's the same all the time.

WATANABE   Saito? I don't know.

TOYO   Mr. Menu.

WATANABE   Menu?

TOYO   Yes, you know, like in cheap restaurants. The menu is always the same and it's never any good. *They both laugh.*

WATANABE   What about Kimura?

TOYO   I call him Mr. Jello because he's so weak and wobbly. I gave you a nickname too, but I won't say it. I won't because it wouldn't be nice to.

WATANABE   Please do. I wouldn't mind. Anyway, I'd like it if you made it up.

TOYO   All right. It's . . . it's Mr. Mummy. *She starts to laugh, then stops.* I'm sorry.

WATANABE   That's all right. *She begins laughing again, then he starts to laugh too.*

(*Wipe to outside the shop.*)

TOYO   Well, thanks for everything.

WATANABE   Do you have to resign today? Can't you put it off until tomorrow? Won't you stay with me today?

(*Wipe to a pinball parlor; he is teaching her how to play and she is enjoying herself. Wipe to an ice-skating rink; she is teaching him how to skate—they both fall down. Wipe to a fun-fair; they are eating noodles and laughing. Wipe to an ice-cream shop; she is eating; he smiles and gives her his portion. Wipe to a cinema; apparently a cartoon is on the screen, because she is laughing and leaning forward in her excitement; he is asleep beside her. Wipe to a Japanese-style restaurant; they are having dinner.)*

TOYO But you don't eat at all—and you really do look exhausted.

WATANABE No, I really enjoyed myself today.

TOYO But, you fell asleep in the movie. You were snoring just when the best part came.

WATANABE Well, last night . . . *He pauses and she laughs.* I can't tell this to anyone, I'm ashamed to admit it, but the reason why I've been like a mummy for the past thirty years . . . *She chokes on a glass of water* . . . Oh, don't misunderstand, I'm not angry you called me a mummy. It's true, and it couldn't be helped, it's just that . . . the reason I turned into a mummy was . . . well, it was all for my son's sake. But now he doesn't appreciate it. He . . .

TOYO Well, you can't very well blame him for that. *She smooths her new stockings.* He didn't ask you to become a mummy. Parents are all alike—my mother says just the same thing. She says: I have suffered because of you. But, if you think about it, well, I appreciate being born, I really do; but I wasn't responsible for it. *She pauses.* But why are you talking about your son like that to me?

WATANABE Well, it's just . . .

(Close-up of TOYO breaking into a smile.)

TOYO I know you love him!

(Close-up of WATANABE smiling. Wipe to the street at night. WATANABE is returning home alone. The sad music of the opening, now sounding even more desperate. Wipe to the interior of the house. WATANABE is sitting, head bowed, at one side of the table; his son is reading the newspaper on the other side; the wife is nearby, knitting.)

MITSUO It says here that the power shortage will last for a while.

WATANABE Is that so?

(Close-up of WATANABE, his head lowered, although he seems to want to say something. Close-up of the son's newspaper; close-up of the wife, busy with her knitting; close-up of WATANABE raising his head.)

MITSUO *off* It says here that this is the warmest winter in thirty years.

(WATANABE *does not hear, then realizing that something has been said, he looks up quickly.*)

WATANABE   Is that so?

(*Cut to all three of them.* WATANABE *leans forward. His hand shakes as he puts his cup down.*)

WATANABE   If you don't mind, I'd like to talk to you for a few minutes. I wanted to tell you earlier, but it isn't a very pleasant story and . . .

MITSUO   I don't want to hear it. *Suddenly puts down the paper.* I've talked the whole problem over with Uncle today, and we both think it ought to be disposed of in a businesslike way. For example, I think that our rights to your property should be made clear.

WATANABE   Mitsuo!

(KAZUE *gets up and leaves the room.* MITSUO *leans forward.*)

MITSUO   You've already spent over fifty thousand yen on her—girls nowadays!

WATANABE   Mitsuo, what are you . . . ?

MITSUO   Father! We never meddle in your affairs. We've shut our eyes to your going out every night and doing I don't know what. I just made a practical suggestion. But you must consider Kazue and her family's position in this. The idea—bringing a girl here, and holding hands too. I was terribly embarrassed when the maid told me.

(WATANABE *stands up. The camera pans with him as he hurries across the room and over to the stairs. Fade out. Then fade in to* WATANABE'S *office— his chair is vacant. Cut to various scenes of the office workers talking to each other, whispering, smiling, smirking. Someone comes up to* ONO *and whispers.* ONO, *due to be promoted now that* WATANABE *is no longer there, laughs indulgently. Over all of this the voice of the* NARRATOR *is heard.*)

NARRATOR *off*   The hero of our story has now been absent for about two weeks, and during this time, naturally, various rumors, various surmises have been repeated. All of these came to the single conclusion that Mr. Watanabe had been behaving very foolishly. Yet, to Watanabe, these same actions were the most meaningful of his entire life.

(Cut to the window of a toy factory. The machinery hums; the window rattles; the building shakes—toy rabbits are stacked in boxes along the wall. Cut to outside. TOYO and WATANABE are talking. She is wearing a turban on her head and has obviously been working—also, she is angry.)

TOYO   This isn't City Hall, you know. You can't take a whole day to do one hour's work here. Every second wasted means less money.

WATANABE   Meet me tonight—just tonight.

TOYO   I'm tired at night. I'd rather sleep. Besides, why do you want to go out with me every night? Let's just stop it. It's . . . it's unnatural.

WATANABE   Tonight—only tonight.

TOYO   No. This has to stop. Excuse me.

(She turns and runs back into the factory. He walks away. Cut to WATANABE alone among tables full of white mechanical rabbits. A door opens and she joins him.)

TOYO   All right, but tonight is absolutely the last time.

(Wipe to the second floor of a large and fancy coffee shop. WATANABE comes in and sits at TOYO'S table. In the rear, on the balcony, is a big group of boys and girls. A record-player is playing Poldini's "Waltzing Doll," and the boys and girls talk excitedly as a large birthday cake is brought up the stairs. TOYO looks at the couple next to them, then at the birthday party, then she yawns. WATANABE looks at her, leans forward.)

WATANABE   Let's take a walk.

TOYO   No, thank you. After the walk would be the noodle-shop; and after that would be the ice-cream parlor. What's the use? I know I'm being ungrateful, but I'm really bored. We don't have anything to talk about.

(Cut to WATANABE, looking at her. He lowers his head.)

TOYO   That look again . . .

(Cut back to her, in close-up.)

TOYO   You make me nervous. Why do you pay so much attention to me?

WATANABE   It's because . . .

TOYO   Because why?

WATANABE   Well, I just enjoy being with you.

TOYO   I hope it isn't love.

WATANABE   No, it's not . . .

TOYO   Why don't you speak more clearly—say what you mean!

(*Cut to* WATANABE. *He lowers his eyes.*)

TOYO *leaning forward*   Are you angry?

WATANABE   No. I don't know myself . . . *Close-up of him* . . . why I like being with you. All I know is that . . .

(*Cut to both of them at the table. The record-player begins "The March of the Wooden Soldiers."*)

WATANABE   . . . is that I'm going to die soon. I have gastric cancer.

(*Cut to a close-up of her. Cut to a close-up of him—he presses his hand against himself.*)

WATANABE   In here. You understand? I have less than a year to live. And when I found that out . . . then, somehow, I was drawn to you. Once when I was a little boy I nearly drowned. It is just that feeling. Darkness is everywhere and there is nothing for me to hold on to, no matter how I try. There is only you.

(*Close-up of her—she looks very uncomfortable.*)

TOYO   What about your son?

(*Cut to a shot of both of them;* TOYO *with her back to camera.*)

WATANABE   Don't even talk about him. I have no son; I'm all alone.

TOYO   Don't talk like that.

WATANABE   You don't understand. My son is somewhere far away, just as my parents were far away when I was drowning. I can't bear to think about it.

TOYO   But what help am I?

WATANABE   You . . . well, just to look at you makes me feel better. It . . . it warms this . . . *He looks down . . .* this mummy heart of mine. And you are kind to me. No, that's not it. It's because you are so young and healthy. No, it isn't that either. *He rises, comes to her side of the table, sits down; she is repelled, and tries to move further away.* You are so full of life and . . . and I'm envious of that. If only I could be like you for one day before I die. I won't be able to die unless I can be. Oh, I want to do something. Only you can show me. I don't know what to do. I don't know how to do it. Maybe you don't either, but, please, if you can, show me how to be like you.

TOYO   I don't know.

WATANABE   How can I be like you?

TOYO   But all I do is work and eat—that's all.

WATANABE   Really?

TOYO   Really. That and make toys like this one.

> (*She has a toy rabbit in her pocket. She takes it out, winds it up, puts it on the table in front of them; it hops toward him; she picks it up, starts it over again.*)

TOYO   That's all I do, but it's fun. I feel as if I were friends with all the children in Japan now. Mr. Watanabe, why don't you do something like that, too?

WATANABE   What can I do at the office?

TOYO   That's true. Well then, resign and find some other work.

WATANABE   It's too late.

> (*Cut to her looking at him; then cut to both of them with the mechanical rabbit between them.*)

WATANABE   No, it's not. It isn't impossible.

> (*A shot of him, with tears in his eyes. She is afraid; she moves back—"The March of the Wooden Soldiers" gets louder. He suddenly turns to her, smiling; she shrinks back.*)

WATANABE   I *can* do something if I really want to!

> (*He picks up the rabbit. Cut to the boys and girls on the balcony, they are leaning over the rail.*)

BOYS AND GIRLS   Here she comes! Happy birthday to you, happy birthday to you!

> (WATANABE *hurries past them down the stairs, the rabbit in his hand. The girl, whose birthday it is, comes up the stairs, smiling, while the others continue to sing "Happy Birthday." Cut to* TOYO, *sitting alone. The birthday party is noisy and happy but she does not turn to look, she stares straight ahead. Fade out. Then fade in to the Citizens' Section.* ONO *is coming into the office, followed by* SAITO, *the camera panning with them.)*

ONO   Oh, he'll resign soon enough—his son was here asking about his retirement pay.

SAITO   Well, then you'll be our new chief, won't you?

> (ONO *smiles, satisfied, yet trying to appear modest.)*

ONO   It's difficult to tell just yet.

> (*He is about to hang up his coat, when they both see* WATANABE'S *new hat hanging there; they look toward his desk. Cut to the desk.* WATANABE *is hunting for something, finds it and sits down.* ONO *and* SAITO *look amazed. They walk toward* WATANABE'S *desk. He looks up at them.)*

WATANABE   Here, Ono, take care of this.

> (*He hands him a document on which is written:* "PETITION FOR RECLAIMING DRAINAGE AREA—KUROE-CHO WOMEN'S ASSOCIATION." *There is a notice attached which says:* "This Petition is to be forwarded to the Public Works Section." WATANABE *tears off the notice.)*

ONO   But this petition should go—

WATANABE   No, unless we do something about it, nothing will ever be done. Everyone will have to cooperate, the Public Works Section, the Parks Section, the Sewage Section—all must cooperate. Now call me a car. I must make an inspection, and prepare a report today.

ONO   But this will be difficult.

WATANABE   No, it won't, not if you are determined.

> (*The camera pans with* WATANABE *as he hurries to put on his coat. The noon siren is heard.* ONO *hurries to follow but* WATANABE *is already out of*

the door. Cut to outside where a light rain is falling. The door swings to and ONO *follows, worried. The sound of trumpets playing the final cadence of "Happy Birthday" can be heard over.)*

NARRATOR *off* Five months later, the hero of this story died.

(A picture of WATANABE *on the funeral altar. Cut to the entire altar. It is in* WATANABE'S *room, which is now almost unrecognizable in its funeral trappings. Everything is still and there is very little movement. The entire office staff is there, as well as the* DEPUTY MAYOR, *and all* WATANABE'S *family. They are sitting on cushions laid out on either side of the altar. Cut to outside the window, looking in. They are drinking sake. The sound of a car driving up and stopping. Cut to the* DEPUTY MAYOR *listening.* MITSUO'S *wife gets up and goes to the hallway. Cut to the hallway. A group of reporters has gathered there.)*

REPORTER We'd like to see the Deputy Mayor, please, just for a few minutes.

(Cut to the room where the wake is being held. ONO *comes in and whispers to the* MAYOR.*)*

ONO Sir, those reporters . . .

(Cut to the MAYOR *politely leaving the room. Cut to the hall.)*

MAYOR Now just what's the idea—my conscience is clear.

REPORTER Are you sure? We've been finding out a few things.

2ND REPORTER And though both you and the Parks Section are claiming all the credit, wasn't it really this Watanabe who made the park?

MAYOR He was Chief of the Citizens' Section; parks fall under the Parks Section.

2ND REPORTER We know that, but what we want to know is who did all the work? The people around there all think it was this Watanabe, and they think it funny that he died there.

MAYOR What do you mean?

3RD REPORTER They think something funny is going on. For example, in your opening speech you didn't even mention Watanabe. The people there say that this wasn't right.

MAYOR If it wasn't, what would have been then?

2ND REPORTER Maybe it was a political speech.

(The MAYOR *tries to laugh. Just then a flashbulb goes off. His picture has been taken. He is disconcerted.)*

3RD REPORTER   And Watanabe was given a seat 'way in the back and was ignored. These people think that his dying like that in the park means something.

MAYOR   Do they mean that he committed suicide in the park? Deliberately sat there and froze to death?

3RD REPORTER   Yes.

MAYOR   Things like that happen in plays and novels. We happen to know what killed Watanabe. It was gastric cancer.

2ND REPORTER   Cancer?

MAYOR   Yes, an internal hemorrhage. He died quite suddenly and he didn't know that he was going to. If you doubt me, Mr. Ono here will . . . *He indicates* ONO, *who is now standing beside him . . .* Give them the name of the hospital that made the autopsy.

(Cut to the MAYOR *politely coming back into the room and sitting down. The sound of an automobile going away, dying in the distance.* ONO *returns and sits down. There is a silence; everyone feels rather uncomfortable. The* DEPUTY MAYOR *takes a cup of sake.)*

MAYOR   The way that these reporters twist the facts. *He drinks his sake, then turns to the others around him.* It's not nice to say, but they truly fail to understand the problems behind municipal projects. *They all bow, nod, smiling, agreeing.* They simply don't understand organization. Now, that park, for example. They seem to think that Mr. Watanabe built it all by himself. But that is just silly. It is probably rude of me to say this in front of his relatives, but I'm certain that Mr. Watanabe didn't have this in mind—building a park all by himself. Of course, he worked very hard toward helping and, I must admit, I was impressed by his perseverance. But it was the work of the section too. *All the section clerks nod in agreement.* And, in any event, it is complete nonsense for anyone who knows anything about the organization to say that the Chief of the Citizens' Section could go and build a park all by himself. *Everyone nods.* I'm sure that the deceased himself would be amused. *Everyone laughs.* But, then, none of us are exactly faultless, and in view of what I said at that time, perhaps we should have given more recognition to those truly responsible, since the park has now drawn so much attention. For example, the Chief of Parks . . . *That gentleman bows . . .* and his superior, the Chief of Public Works. *That gentleman also bows.*

PUBLIC WORKS CHIEF   It is good of you to say that, sir, but it is my belief that the Chief of the Parks Section and myself only pushed the plan, insofar as paper work was concerned. When I think of his honor's painstaking efforts to bring this plan to materialization, then I know that it is the Deputy Mayor himself who should be rewarded. *Everyone smiles and nods at this.*

MAYOR   No, I've been criticized—criticized even for that speech at the opening of the park. One of them called it a political speech, didn't he, Ono?

> *(He is about to say more when the* MAID *comes in and tells* MITSUO'S *wife that some women from Kuroe-cho have come to pay their respects. A group of women, many of the same who came to the Citizens' Section before, now enter the room. They do not wait to be invited, but walk directly to the altar. Many are crying. They bow before the picture; they light incense. A baby on the back of one of them starts to cry. Cut to* MITSUO, *looking at them. Cut to his wife. It is not proper for her to remain standing in the middle of the room and so she kneels. Cut to a view of the entire room. The officials are embarrassed and frowning; only one of them,* KIMURA, *is affected; he puts his hands to his eyes as though to hide tears. Then the women get up to leave the room. As the women go, they bow to the other guests and only one,* KIMURA, *bows in return. There is a long silence. Cut to* WATANABE'S *picture; cut to a closer shot; cut to one even closer—the grain of the photograph is visible. Cut to a view of the entire room. The wife, who has seen the women out, returns and sits down. The silence continues unbroken. Then the* DEPUTY MAYOR *nods to the* CHIEF OF PUBLIC WORKS *and the* CHIEF OF PARKS. *They kneel, bow to the shrine and altar, bow to the family, then politely and carefully take their leave.* ONO, *who has gone to see them out, returns.)*

ONO   It's cold, isn't it?

KIICHI   Have a drink. *He holds out a sake bottle.* Oh, I'm sorry, this sake is cold. I'll go and get some warm. How about everyone getting together, sitting a little closer together?

> *(There is a general movement, almost a scramble.* ONO *successfully gets the seat just vacated by the* MAYOR. *Others must be content with their positions. Old* OHARA *stands up too late, looks for a seat on the other side; all are taken; he sits down, grumbling. Someone asks if they had gone off to a meeting.)*

KIMURA   Yes, they couldn't bear it here any longer. Mr. Watanabe built that park, no matter what anyone says. And the Mayor knows it. That's why he . . .

ONO   Now, you're going too far. Mr. Watanabe just . . .

CLERK   It's not just because I'm in the Parks Section, but I know that our section planned and carried out the whole thing.

KIMURA   That's not what I mean.

SAITO   That's all right. We know how you feel, but why should the Chief of the Citizens' Section try to build a park anyway? It is outside his . . . his sphere of influence.

NOGUCHI   Anyway, no one built that park. It was just a coincidence. And no councillor would have done anything about it anyway, if it hadn't been that elections are coming up. KIMURA *is about to say something but* NOGUCHI *continues.* And, come to think of it, if it hadn't been for that gang that wanted to have a red-light district there, the project might not have gone so smoothly either.

OHARA   I just can't understand it. *He shakes his head, talking as though to himself.* Why should Mr. Watanabe change so? He changed so suddenly.

ONO   Yes, it was strange.

SAITO   That's it. Now that I think of it . . . Mr. Watanabe knew about his cancer. That's why.

> (*Cut to* ONO *as he turns to* MITSUO, *who has just returned with more sake.*)

ONO   We were just talking about your father—did he know he had gastric cancer?

MITSUO   If he had, he would certainly have told me. I think that Father was very fortunate in knowing nothing about it. After all, to learn something like that is just like getting a death sentence.

> (KIICHI *comes back into the room.*)

ONO   Then Saito's theory is wrong.

KIICHI   What's that?

ONO   Mr. Watanabe changed so in the last five months, and we can't understand why.

KIICHI   Oh, that. It was because of a woman. You know, often an older man tries to hold onto his youth by keeping a mistress. His complexion gets better, his eyes get brighter . . . *His wife is looking at him* . . . Anyway, I think he was keeping some woman.

ONO   Well, he did take to wearing a rather elegant hat.

(There are smiles and nods at this. SAITO *turns and looks at the picture of* WATANABE *on the altar.)*

SAITO   That hat. It really surprised me.

(Cut to the conclusion of the former scene where WATANABE *has handed the report to* ONO. *The dialogue is as before.)*

ONO   But this will be difficult.

WATANABE   No, it won't, not if you are determined.

(The camera pans with WATANABE *as he hurries to put on his coat. The noon siren is heard.)*

ONO   But—

(Cut to a vacant lot in Kuroe-cho; it is raining. WATANABE *walks around in the rain, through mud, looking at where the playground will be. One of the women runs up to him carrying an umbrella, holding it over him. Cut back to the wake.)*

SAITO   He seemed to be trying so hard. It just wasn't natural.

ONO   Well, that's true. Yet, you know, I can't believe that the influence of a woman could have . . .

KIICHI   But . . .

TATSU   Don't.

OHARA   I just can't understand it.

PARKS CHIEF   Well, there was a time when Mr. Watanabe's effort made things very difficult.

SEWAGE SECTION CLERK   You're right, but what I can't understand is why a man who had been an official for the last thirty years should—

KIMURA   That's because—

PARKS CLERK   And he really shouldn't have gone around trying to talk all the other sections into it like that. Naturally, they didn't like it—my chief in particular. He felt that the parks were all his own responsibility.

(Cut to the Parks Section. WATANABE is offering a petition. The CHIEF OF PARKS turns wearily.)

CHIEF Now, we have many park projects.

WATANABE Please. The conditions there are terrible.

CHIEF But it just isn't as easy as your plan here makes it seem.

(Cut to the same location, some time has apparently passed. WATANABE is sitting to one side; the CHIEF OF PARKS is trying to work, but cannot. He keeps glancing at WATANABE sitting there, his head bowed. Finally, the CHIEF takes the petition and, with deliberation, stamps it and puts it in the "outgoing" basket, then turns and looks at WATANABE, who does not move. Cut back to the wake.)

SAITO Mr. Watanabe just hung on until the Chief finally gave in.

PUBLIC WORKS CLERK Now that you say so, it was just the same with my boss. That Watanabe, he just wouldn't give in. Why, my chief used to turn and run when he saw him coming.

(Cut to a corridor in the City Hall. The CHIEF OF PUBLIC WORKS sees WATANABE coming, turns and hurries away, but it is too late; WATANABE has seen him and starts after him. Cut to the wake—most of the men are getting drunk.)

SANITATION CLERK But what surprised me most was the way that he, a big chief like that, acted toward clerks like me.

(Cut to the Sanitation Section. WATANABE is going up to each member of the office and bowing. Each must stand and return his bow. With each bow WATANABE murmurs, "Please," as the embarrassed clerks bow back.)

SANITATION CLERK *off* And we finally gave in too.

(Cut to the wake.)

PUBLIC WORKS CLERK We all felt sorry for him.

NOGUCHI But it was you General Affairs Section people that gave him the most trouble.

GENERAL AFFAIRS CLERK Oh, you think so?

ONO It's true. I went around with him for almost two weeks. I'll never forget it.

GENERAL AFFAIRS CLERK   I'm sorry, sir.

SAITO   But what surprised me most was that incident when . . .

SAKAI   Oh, that. That was really surprising.

> (*Cut to the stairway leading past the Citizens' Section.* WATANABE *is walking at the head of a number of women, the wives from Kuroe-cho. He goes directly up the stairs, his own clerks staring at him. In the corridor at the top he takes off his coat, gives it to one of the women to hold, and goes into a door marked "DEPUTY MAYOR'S OFFICE." Cut to the wake.*)

ONO   And that wasn't all.

SAITO   What happened in the Mayor's office?

ONO   Well, I doubt that anyone ever stood up to the Mayor like he did.

> (*Cut to the* DEPUTY MAYOR'S *office.* WATANABE *is bowing;* ONO *stands behind him.*)

MAYOR   I personally don't mind your pushing this park project like this, but some people might think that you were looking for publicity. The City Council has a lot of problems. It would be best if you'd just forget about it.

> (*This taken care of, he turns back to his friends and continues an apparently interrupted conversation.*)

MAYOR   And so I attended that party last night, but, really, the geisha nowadays are no good at all. One of them didn't open her mouth all night, and later I heard that she's a geisha only at night, it's a kind of sideline.

FRIEND   How amusing!

WATANABE   Would you . . . please reconsider. WATANABE *has gone on bowing.* ONO *is trying to make him leave. The* MAYOR *turns, incredulous; his friends look up.*

MAYOR   What did you say?

> (*Cut to* WATANABE. *He is bowing, yet looking the* MAYOR *full in the face.*)

WATANABE   About that park. Please . . . reconsider.

> (*Cut to the* MAYOR *staring at him. Cut back to* WATANABE, *staring, and* ONO *trying to pull him away. Cut back to the wake. There is silence, then laughter. Most of the men are now really drunk.*)

SAITO   Yet, judging from the results, it wasn't such a bad plan.

SAKAI   No, it was dangerous. Just think of all the . . . the spheres of influence at City Hall.

> (*Cut to* KIMURA.)

KIMURA   But the Mayor reconsidered, didn't he?

NOGUCHI   Oh, that. It was some councillor's idea. He made him do it. The whole thing was a sort of accident, you see, a kind of coincidence—you're just sentimental, that's all.

> (*There is some laughter at the word* "sentimental.")

SAKAI   Yes, that's it, sentimental.

KIMURA   I don't think so. If you can't try to understand a man like Mr. Watanabe without being thought sentimental, then the world is a dark place indeed.

NOGUCHI   And so it is—very dark.

KIMURA   I don't know what it was that was keeping Mr. Watanabe alive, but sometimes I was almost afraid for him.

> (*Cut to a corridor in the City Hall.* KIMURA *has stopped at the top of the stairs and looks at* WATANABE *in the far distance. He is leaning against the wall, with apparently no strength left. Then, very slowly, he pushes himself along the wall in the direction of the* MAYOR'S *office. Cut to a close-up of* WATANABE. *Cut back to the wake.*)

PARK SECTION CLERK   And, come to think of it, there was that day at the park site.

> (*Cut to the park site. Dust, gravel, a bulldozer. It almost runs over* WATANABE. *One of the women hurries up, pulls him back. She and several others take him to one of the houses, offer him a glass of water. He takes it and drinks some water. Cut to a close-up of* WATANABE *looking at the park site.*)

PARK SECTION CLERK *off*   When he looked at that park . . . *Cut back to the wake, the* CLERK *speaking* . . . his face just glowed. It was . . . well, it was like a man looking at his own grandchild.

KIMURA   Naturally, it was just that to him.

ONO   So, that's why . . .

KIMURA   That's why, no matter what anyone says, it was Mr. Watanabe who built that park.

NOGUCHI   But if the Mayor and the councillors hadn't done anything, there wouldn't have been any park. He just didn't take into consideration all of those . . . those spheres of influence up above.

ONO   Oh, I wouldn't say that.

NOGUCHI   No?

ONO   You remember what happened? With that gang that wanted to have a red-light district where the park is?

> (*Cut to a corridor.* WATANABE *and* ONO *are walking along it. Several men are lounging against the wall. One steps forward, taking off his dark glasses.*)

MAN   You chief of the Citizens' Section?

WATANABE   Yes, I am.

MAN   Wanted to see you. Look, mister, just don't poke your nose in any more, okay?

> (*He smiles, flicks* WATANABE'S *lapel;* WATANABE *looks at him.*)

WATANABE   Why? Who are you?

> (*The* MAN *grabs the lapels of* WATANABE'S *coat, tightens his grip.*)

MAN   Don't act stupid, I'm telling you, see? You just cut it out and don't do anything dumb any more.

> (*Cut to* WATANABE. *He is smiling. Cut to the group; the* MAN *releases him.* WATANABE *turns to go into the* MAYOR'S *office. Just then another* MAN, *obviously one of them, comes out and looks at* WATANABE.)

MAN   This is Watanabe—remember him.

> (*He stares hard at* WATANABE, *who smiles back, and then goes into the office. The gang begins to move off.* ONO *stands looking after them. The second* MAN—*the threatening killer—turns and looks at* ONO, *who turns and hurries into the office. Cut to the wake. Everyone is now drunk. Old* OHARA *is thinking, his head to one side.*)

OHARA   But it's strange. I just can't understand why he changed like that—he must have known he had cancer.

(ONO suddenly sits up, drunk, makes a gesture.)

ONO   I just remembered!

(Cut to a staircase in the City Hall. ONO is obviously lecturing WATANABE, who leans, drawn and tired, against the railing.)

ONO   Now, this is too much. You've been doing this for two weeks now. The least they could do is tell you whether they have the money or not. And the way they treat you. At least they could do it nicely—it should make you angry to be insulted this way.

WATANABE   But it doesn't. I don't have time to be angry with anyone. *He goes on down the stairs.*

(Cut to the wake. A general commotion, each person remembering something.)

ONO   And then . . .

SAITO   Now that you mention it, I remember once when . . .

(Cut to a bridge above the park site. It is sunset. WATANABE and SAITO are walking across it.)

WATANABE   Oh, how beautiful . . . *He looks up* . . . For thirty years I have never watched a sunset. Now there's no more time.

(Cut back to the wake.)

SAKAI   It's all clear now . . .

NOGUCHI   He knew he didn't have long to live.

SAITO   That clears everything up, explains everything. Now I understand why he acted that way, it wasn't strange at all, it was normal.

ONO   We'd all do the same thing ourselves.

(Cut to KIMURA.)

KIMURA   We'll all die ourselves one day.

(A general shot of the group. A pause, then OHARA moves forward.)

OHARA Look here, Ono. Now, I don't mean that . . . I mean Mr. New Chief of the Citizens' Section, that's what I mean. Look here, can't you hear me?

(Cut to ONO, drunk, pleased, and irritated, all at the same time.)

ONO I haven't been appointed yet.

OHARA All right then. Ono, what did you just say? That we'd have done the same thing ourselves? Don't make me laugh. *He drunkenly points to* ONO. You fellows couldn't do what Mr. Watanabe did. Don't make me laugh. Me, I only went to night school, and that's why I'll never be chief of any Citizens' Section. But you, Ono, someone like you! Well, just don't make me laugh.

(SAITO tries to stop OHARA; then pauses, struck with a sudden thought.)

SAITO Compared with Mr. Watanabe, all of us are just . . .

OHARA We're trash, that's what, trash. And you're trash too.

SAKAI We're all trash. Oh, there are some fine men at City Hall, but after you've worked there for a long time, it changes you.

NOGUCHI Yes, that's the place where you don't dare even think. If you do, you're dangerous. You must only act as though you're thinking and doing something.

PUBLIC WORKS CLERK That's right.

GENERAL AFFAIRS CLERK Yes, that's right.

SAITO You can't do anything. Why, to get permission for a new trash-can you have to make out enough documents to fill up that trash-can.

(SAKAI moves forward excitedly, then suddenly begins to cry.)

SAKAI And you have to put your seal on everything: stamp, stamp, stamp!

NOGUCHI The way we live is by stealing time—people complain about official corruption, but that's nothing compared with our criminal waste of time.

(ONO crawls on all fours into the middle of the room and waves his arms.)

ONO Listen, fellows! I know how you feel. I think about it too, but what can you do with such a big organization—anyway, there's no time to think.

OHARA You fool! *They all look around at him.*

SAITO   But look, Ohara. In this organization where you can't do anything, Mr. Watanabe did something, and he did it because he had cancer.

SAKAI   That's just what I wanted to say. *He begins sobbing.*

NOGUCHI   Oh, it makes me mad.

SAKAI   Me, too!

NOGUCHI   And Mr. Watanabe never got any reward at all.

(They are all crawling about on the floor.)

SAITO   Oh, but when I think of what Mr. Watanabe must have felt . . .

NOGUCHI   Whoever went and took the credit isn't even human.

OHARA   Oh, come out and say it's the Mayor.

NOGUCHI   Now, you be careful what you say.

(There is a pause. SAKAI is crying softly.)

SAKAI   But I just wonder what Mr. Watanabe felt when he was dying out there all alone in the park—just to think of it makes me feel awful.

(Most of the men begin to cry now. Among those who do not is KIMURA. Cut to WATANABE'S picture on the altar. Cut to the doorway. The MAID appears carrying WATANABE'S hat. It is now crushed and dirty.)

MAID   Excuse me, but a policeman just brought this, he found it in the park.

(Cut to a close-up of the hat in her hands. Everyone turns to look at it.)

MAID   And he said he wanted to come in and pay his respects.

(Cut. A young policemen comes in, bows, goes to the altar, prays, and then gets up to go.)

KAZUE   Thank you for coming.

KIICHI   Won't you sit down and have a drink?

(He indicates a cushion and pours the POLICEMAN a cup of sake. The POLICEMAN is ill at ease, takes the sake, puts it down. He is apparently deciding whether to speak or not.)

POLICEMAN   I . . . I saw him in the park on that night. It was about ten. No . . . *Looks at his watch . . .* it was closer to eleven, I guess. He was sitting on one of the children's swings. I thought he was probably drunk, but I didn't do anything. If I had, then maybe all of this wouldn't have happened. I am truly sorry. *The* POLICEMAN *bows.*

(*Cut to* MITSUO *looking at the hat that he now holds.*)

POLICEMAN   But he looked so, well, so happy. How can I say it? And he was singing . . . and it was in a voice that, well, moved me.

(*Cut to the park. In the distance, behind a set of climbing bars, is* WATANABE *sitting on a swing; snow is falling. He is singing. The camera pans along the bars, tracking in nearer.*)

WATANABE   *Life is so short,*
Fall in love, dear maiden,
While your lips are still red;
Before you can no longer love—
For there will be no tomorrow.

(*Dissolve to* WATANABE'S *picture over the altar. The song continues, there is a cut to the wake; shots of various faces; then of* MITSUO *standing up. Overcome, he goes into the corridor.* KAZUE, *followed by* MITSUO'S *uncle, goes out to him.*)

MITSUO   And I found a box with my name on it, on the stairs that night, and in it were his bank books and his seal, and his retirement allowance papers.

KAZUE   He must have left them . . .

MITSUO   But that was bad of him! If he knew he had cancer, why didn't he tell us? *He begins to cry; his uncle comes forward.*

KIICHI   And his mistress, why didn't she come to the funeral? Maybe there wasn't any mistress.

(*Cut to a close-up of a packing-case. In it are the framed letters of commendation, an alarm clock, a white toy rabbit. Cut back to the wake. The men are now sitting close together, very drunk, very excited. During the scene* KIMURA *leaves them and goes to kneel in front of the altar, looking up at* WATANABE'S *picture.*)

SAKAI   We must work hard.

NOGUCHI   Yes, with the spirit that Mr. Watanabe showed.

SAITO   We mustn't let his death be meaningless.

ONO   Me—I'm going to turn over a new leaf!

NOGUCHI   That's the spirit. Me, I'm going to work for the good of the public!

> *(They are all shouting, waving their arms. Only KIMURA at the altar is still and silent. Fade out. Fade in to the Citizens' Section as it was at the beginning of the film, only that ONO is now at WATANABE'S desk. SAKAI deferentially, glancing back at the information counter, comes to his side.)*

SAKAI   Excuse me, but they say that the sewage water has overflowed in Kizaki-cho.

ONO   Well, send them to the Public Works Section.

> *(Cut to KIMURA looking up sharply at these words. Cut to ONO, who stares back. Cut to KIMURA. There is the noise of a chair being pushed over as he stands up. ONO can be seen, glaring at him. Cut to KIMURA. He slowly picks up the chair and sits down. As he sits the camera descends with him. His face is obscured by the documents on his desk. It is as though he is being buried alive in them. Cut to SAKAI, apologetic at the counter.)*

SAKAI   Would you please go to the Public Works Section with this?

> *(Cut to the bridge above the park. It is sunset. KIMURA comes across the bridge on his way home. He stops to look. Cut to the park. Children are playing there and their mothers call them in for dinner. Cut to KIMURA watching them. He turns and starts off, the camera panning with him. The top of the swing comes into view. The tune "Life Is So Short," played on a solo flute, is heard over. KIMURA walks away. Fade out.)*

FURTHER READINGS

An excellent text to begin a study of Japanese cinema is Donald Richie, *Japanese Cinema* (Garden City, NY: Doubleday, 1971). Richie, an international authority on Japanese cinema, provides a chronologically arranged analysis of the major qualities of Japanese movies. Joseph L. Anderson and Donald Richie, *The Japanese Film: Art and Industry* (Princeton, NJ: Princeton University Press, 1982) is a comprehensive historical survey of the Japanese film industry. Joan Mellen, *The Waves at Genji's Door: Japan Through its Cinema* (New York: Pantheon, 1976) examines the social, political, and cultural context of Japanese movies with special attention to feminist perspectives seen through films. The great Japanese films from the 1950s and 1960s are surveyed in Keiko I. McDonald, *Cinema East* (Rutherford, UK: Farleigh Dickinson University Press; London: Associated University Press, 1983). Joan Mellen, *Voices from the Japanese Cinema* (New York: Liveright, 1975) offers a collection of interviews with major directors with emphasis on their ideologies and ambitions. A historical approach to the leading Japanese filmmakers is available in Audie Bock, *Japanese Film Directors* (Tokyo: Kodansha, 1978).

Donald Richie, *The Films of Akira Kurosawa* (Berkeley: University of California Press, 1984) provides a brief biographical sketch of the great filmmaker followed by an analysis of his films from historical, contextual, and technical viewpoints.

English translations of two of Kurosawa's greatest films, *Ikiru* and *Seven Samurai*, are available in Akira Kurosawa, *Ikiru: A Film by Akira Kurosawa*, trans. and ed. Donald Richie (New York: Simon & Schuster, 1968) and Akira Kurosawa, *Seven Samurai: A Film by Akira Kurosawa*, trans. and ed. Donald Richie (New York: Simon & Schuster, 1970). A collection of critical studies of Kurosawa's great film *Rashomon* is contained in Donald Richie, ed., *Focus on Rashomon* (Englewood Cliffs, NJ: Prentice-Hall, 1972).

THE BIRD OF PASSAGE
O Yongsu

Twentieth-century Korean literature has developed in perhaps the world's most unfavorable setting. Annexed by Japan in 1910, Korea fell under Japanese colonial rule for thirty-five years. Korea's liberation in 1945 was followed by the division of the country into "occupation zones" and then the devastation of civil war between 1950 and 1953. Subsequent revolutions in 1960 and 1961 and frequent political turmoil in the 1980s have added to the many political and spiritual crises experienced by the Korean people over the last seventy years. The literary arts in Korea not only have survived these crises but have flourished. Each period of unrest has produced a new generation of writers with new outlooks. They have responded by reshaping the literary medium in order to accommodate new values and new visions.

From O Yongsu, *The Bird of Passage*, in Peter H. Lee, ed. and trans., *Flowers of Fire: Twentieth-Century Korean Stories* (Honolulu: University of Hawaii Press, 1986), pp. 191–204.

The impact of this century of foreign influence on Korean society and literature has been immense. At the beginning of the twentieth century, Korean literature was heavily influenced by Chinese Confucianism. But the Japanese annexation in 1910 broke the dominance of Chinese Confucianism. Korea was just embarking on its transformation into the modern age, and the nature of this transformation was shaped initially by the Japanese. The long colonial rule by the Japanese and the open system after the 1945 liberation stifled the rediscovery and promotion of Korea's traditional culture. Korean intellectuals, many of whom studied abroad, formed an elite group who possessed a cosmopolitan manner of thinking. In this environment, Western influences met little opposition in Korea and secured a place above the traditional culture. Western values came to be regarded as "ideals" and traditional attitudes frequently were considered as anachronistic. The transformation from a traditional, agricultural society into a modern capitalist state produced an elemental tension between old and new.

The uneasy truce that followed the three years of devastating civil war between 1950 and 1953, in which one and a half million men, women, and children died, and two and a half million persons were wounded or injured, led to an unnatural tension in Korea. Its consequences of hate, distrust, and division still exist today. The destruction and uprooting, physical and spiritual, left indelible marks on the Korean people. The horrors of war were replaced by dire postwar economic conditions and moral confusion. Writers responded to the conditions of the times. The Korean War was the primary theme of virtually all Korean literature produced during the first decade of the postwar period. Korean writers groped for an adequate answer to explain the condition of their countrymen living in the midst of the anguish, alienation, and despair brought on by the civil war.

The disintegration of moral order is a recurring theme of postwar Korean fiction. O Yongsu's short story, *The Bird of Passage*, provides a poignant look at the injustices and absurdities of postwar society. He portrays the despair of individuals who have lost touch with the old traditions and struggle for direction in the new moral quagmire of the period. This image of the human condition is not limited to adults. It is the author's description of the young shoe-shine boy Kuch'iri that truly illuminates the reader to the horribly distorting deprivation resulting from the Korean War. In the disintegration of moral order, the young boy loses the innocence of childhood and adapts to a new kind of moral conduct.

O Yongsu was born in Onyang, South Kyongsang, on February 11, 1914 and in his early years studied in Japan from 1932 to 1939. He returned to Korea in 1939 and resided in Manchuria until the liberation in August 1945. He taught at a girls' school in Pusan until moving to Seoul in 1954 as a founding member and eventually the chief editor of the prestigious literary journal *Hyondae Munhak* (*Modern Literature*). Prior to his death in 1979, O Yongsu greatly influenced a generation of young writers. The author of more than a hundred stories, he was awarded the Asian Freedom Literature Prize in 1959, the Korean Academy of Arts Prize and the Republic of Korea's Order of Merit in 1978.

The Bird of Passage was first published in February 1958 in the *Hyondae Munhak*. Set in Seoul shortly after the Korean War it tells the story of Kuch'iri, a shoeshine boy, and his relationship with Minu, a middle-aged teacher. Minu's sedate lifestyle is abruptly disrupted by the appearance of Kuch'iri, a former acquaintance from Pusan. The shy, good-hearted, and proper teacher soon develops an emotional attachment to the shoe-shine boy, who ekes out a living on the streets of Seoul. The author, while describing their relationship with warmth and compassion, uses their story to illustrate the social, economic, and moral conditions of postwar Korean society.

Questions

1. The traditional concept of the Korean family underwent a rapid change following liberation and the ensuing civil war. Discuss the family unit as described in *The Bird of Passage*. Do you see any similarities to the Western concept of family?

2. It may be said that the devastation of the Korean War stole the innocence of childhood from many Korean children. Is Kuch'iri's lifestyle indicative of this? If so, how?

3. Describe the economic state of the postwar era. What effect do the economic conditions have on Kuch'iri?

4. Discuss the relationship between Kuch'iri and Minu. Why wouldn't Kuch'iri take Minu's money?

THE BIRD OF PASSAGE

They come with the warm weather and go away when it grows cold. Or they come with the cold and leave when it grows warm.

They always go off in search of food in flocks, and then flock together again when they return.

Such is the behavior of migratory birds. But there are some that follow a different pattern.

It happened last autumn. The leaves of the city's trees were just beginning to fall. So it must have been mid-October.

Minu was walking down Ulchiro Sixth Avenue, heading for his quarters outside the East Gate, when suddenly a shoe-shine boy was blocking his way and tugging at his sleeve. Minu was in a sour mood just then, and the sight of that grimy hand grasping the sleeve of his new suit irritated him. "No shine! Hands off!" he shouted. The boy, unabashed, kept tugging at Minu's sleeve.

"But . . . Teacher, don't you recognize me?" he asked.

Then Minu looked at the boy. Indeed it did seem that he had often seen that face before, but for a moment he could not recall where.

"In Pusan. I used to shine your shoes all the time."

Then it came back to Minu clearly. "Oh, now I remember. You're Kuch'iri, that's right. When did you come to Seoul?"

"Last spring."

"You did? You didn't do well in Pusan?"

At these words Kuch'iri released Minu's sleeve; his face fell, a tear struck the tip of his shoe, as he lowered his gaze to the pavement. Though he did not know what had happened, Minu, too, felt sad.

Kuch'iri's turtleneck pullover had tattered elbows and frayed cuffs. His trousers were glossy with dirt. He looked like any other shoeshine boy, except that the army boots he was wearing were absurdly blunt-toed and each one was big enough alone to hold both feet. They were clumsy, even comical.

Minu took out a cigaret. "Did you come alone?"

Instead of answering, Kuch'iri pulled Minu's sleeve: "Please come over here." Minu followed him into a nearby alley. Kuch'iri put down his plain wooden stool by the concrete outer wall of a house and asked Minu to sit. He wanted to shine Minu's shoes before telling his story.

Minu placed one foot on the shoeshine box. "It's been a long time since you shined my shoes. More than a year, isn't it?"

"Aren't these the same shoes you had then?"

The boy's home was in Ch'ungch'ong Province, but he could speak the Pusan dialect fluently.

"Yes, they're the same shoes. But why'd you come to Seoul? Didn't it go well at the school?"

Kuch'iri dislodged some dirt from the sole of Minu's shoe with a metal scraper and said, "Please don't ask about the school. I got into trouble."

"Trouble? What kind of trouble?"

"Just a while after you left for Seoul . . ."

"What happened?"

"Some money disappeared from the office. Seven thousand hwan."

"Really?"

"Yeah, and the Disciplinarian claimed I took it. He took me into the storeroom and gave me an awful beating."

"You mean that Mr. Ch'oe?"

"Yes. And even though I told him I didn't take it . . ."

"But whose money was it?"

"They said it was the Patriots' Club dues."

"Then what did the Disciplinarian do?"

"He said if I didn't confess by the next day he'd tell the police."

"And then?"

"Please put your other foot up."

"And?"

"The next day he stuck a pencil between my fingers and twisted it hard. I thought I'd die . . ."

"He did what?"

"So I told him I took the money; he asked how come I didn't confess earlier. And he kept asking me what I'd done with the money."

"So what did you say?"

"I told him I only confessed because of the pain, that I really didn't take the money. He said I made a fool of him and took the leg of a chair and beat me so hard that I . . ."

"Hey, enough polishing. A quick shine is all I want. So what happened next?"

"I don't know. When I opened my eyes the old janitor was splashing water on my face."

"Hmmm. And then?"

"So the janitor took me home. I was sick for days."

"Just a quick shine, I said."

"But I'll have to get that dirt off. Anyway, I was sick in bed at home, and my friend came and told me Mr. Ch'oe was asking for me. My big sister took me to him. I went limping along."

"What did he say?"

"He said they'd caught the guy who took the money. He said he was sorry, and he gave me two hundred *hwan* and told me to buy some dog soup with it."

"Who did take the money?"

"He said it was that bastard of an office boy!"

"Did you get some dog soup, then?"

"I was crying so hard. All I did was cry. My big sister was crying, too."

"Really . . . ?"

"I said I didn't want any money, and we went back home. I kept thinking of you, Teacher."

"Is that why you left for Seoul?"

"Since I was sick I couldn't make any money, so my stepmother kept telling me to get out of the house. My father got drunk and gave me a beating. So I got in with a bunch of guys who were going to Seoul and I came up here with them."

"Hm."

"Look at this, Teacher."

The boy held out his hand. The flesh of the second and third fingers was discolored, and the joints were swollen. This, he said, was due to the cruel twisting of the pencil that day. Minu gently felt the injured fingers, then released them.

"Does it still hurt?"

Kuch'iri was silent.

"How are the shoes coming?"

"They're all done."

Minu knew the boy would not let him pay so he thought he would take him for something to eat. When he up Kuch'iri stood up, too, packed up his shoeshine box, and followed along as if by agreement. When they got to the Kyerim movie theater, Kuch'iri caught Minu's sleeve again and pointed to the billboard. "Teacher, have you seen that movie?" he asked.

Minu just shook his head.

"Teacher, please go see it. I'll treat you."

For a moment Minu merely gazed dumbfounded at Kuch'iri.

"Teacher! That guy with one eye closed, holding the pistol—see? He's great!"

"Okay, I'll take you in."

"No. I've seen it. You watch it. I can get us in for free. Come on, let's go."

"Kuch'iri, the next time a good movie comes along, I'll take you to see it. I'm pretty busy today."

Kuch'iri seemed to be on the verge of tears. "Please don't go. Come see the movie. Please come with me," he said, tugging harder on Minu's sleeve.

Kuch'iri was not going to give up until Minu agreed to watch the movie. It was an awkward fix, for Minu saw that an abrupt refusal would hurt the boy's feelings. He hesitated a moment and then said, "Okay. Let's go."

Kuch'iri set down his shoeshine box at the side of the theater and left Minu standing next to it. He went to the entrance and negotiated briefly. Soon he came hurrying back, waving one arm and mincing along in his GI boots. He shouldered the shoeshine box and took the stool in one hand. With the other he led Minu along. "It's all settled," he said. "Come with me. Let's go in now."

Just as Kuch'iri had promised, he and Minu entered the theater unchallenged. When they got inside, Kuch'iri hurried up to the front, found a seat, and showed Minu to it. He whispered in his ear, "The show's continuous, you know. It'll start from the beginning again soon. You stay here and watch. I'll go shine these people's shoes over there and then I'll come back." With these words he was gone.

The film was a western. Minu's eyes were on the screen, but his own thoughts absorbed all his attention.

Minu had been teaching at W Middle School in Pusan, where he stayed until the recapture of Seoul. They called it a school, but it was a makeshift affair, just a group of tents with no fence or wall. All kinds of peddlers came there, but the shoeshine boys were the worst. Sometimes as many as seven or eight would come in one group. Over forty teachers sat back-to-back in the small office, and even a shoeshine would cause a stir. To Minu, whose responsibility it was to keep the campus in order, fell the futile task of ejecting the shoeshine boys, only to have them reappear once his back was turned. The boys swarmed to the school like flies to carrion, sometimes camping quietly beside the office and playing marbles or batting about a shuttlecock.

One day, Minu was on his way back from the washroom after having ejected that morning's crowd of shoeshine boys. One of the shoeshine boys, who had somehow managed to follow him, held out his stool and said, "Shine, sir?"

"But I just got rid of you guys!"

Minu, half smiling, half frowning, took a poke at the boy with his fist, but the boy pulled a tin out of his pocket and held it out, saying, "Teacher, this is the best American polish, you've heard of it, haven't you? I bought it yesterday. Please be my first customer." Minu had no class during the first hour, so he set his foot on the box. The boy threw himself into the job, spitting and shining the first shoe. Then, "Sir!"

"What?"

"There are too many shoeshine boys here, aren't there?"

"They're a headache!"

"I have an idea, Teacher. I'll shine all the teachers' shoes for just twenty *hwan*, and with the best polish, if you will make it so that I'm the only one allowed to shine shoes here."

"You're a greedy one!"

"Come on, let me, sir!"

It made sense. If he authorized just one boy to shine shoes, the others would not come. Moreover, the teachers welcome this new price of twenty *hwan*, instead of the usual thirty.

"I'll talk to the others about it."

"Please, sir!"

That afternoon in the general meeting Minu made the proposal. From the principal and the supervisor on down, all agreed. They decided the chosen boy should wear an armband. The next day Minu made an armband of yellow cloth with a W on it. He called the shoeshine boys together and made the announcement: "The boy wearing this armband is the only one who will be allowed to shine shoes here. There's no need for the rest of you to come anymore. You'd better go elsewhere."

However, the boys all protested, some of them pressing home their grievances: "Aren't we all refugees together here?" "That's unfair." "Choose one each day and we'll take turns." "Make it one a week . . ."

"Maybe you're right," Minu replied. "But it's been decided, so there's nothing I can do about it." Thus Minu managed to quiet the boys. Yet he could not help feeling moved when they said that they were all refugees together, for Minu himself was a refugee school teacher who had left his home in the North.

The boy who received the armband would arrive early each morning and bow smartly to each of the teachers. When the principal arrived, the boy would promptly bring his slippers, exchange them for his shoes, and begin polishing.

In a spare moment one day, Minu had his shoes shined. "How many pairs do you shine every day?"

"Including the students', it comes to about twenty pairs."

"Two times two is four . . . Can you make a profit at four hundred *hwan?*"

"It's fine."

"Is it better than before?"

"BETTER? Before it was hard to take in even two hundred a day."

"Hmmm . . . What's your name?"

"Yi Kuch'ol."

Just then the P.E. teacher came by. He said, "No, it can't be Kuch'ol— since you shine shoes you'd better change it to Kuch'iri." And so Kuch'ol came to be known as Kuch'iri.

His home was in Ch'ungch'ong Province, and his father worked down on the docks.

Lunch hour was the busiest time for Kuch'iri. Some of the teachers had their shoes shined while they ate. Working in the small teachers' office, Kuch'iri was sometimes kicked in the seat of his pants or struck on the head with a rollbook. When they were busy, the teachers would ask him to get them lunch or have him do other small tasks in place of the errandboy.

When a new principal was appointed Minu left the school and went to Seoul. He completely forgot about Kuch'iri.

Ch'oe's misunderstanding and mistreatment of the boy may have been increased by his dislike of Minu. Kuch'iri firmly refused to accept money from Minu, and this was all the more irritating. Once, when Kuch'iri said he had polished Ch'oe's shoes ten times, Ch'oe insisted that he had only done it six or seven times. At last Ch'oe derided Kuch'iri and soundly slapped his face. One day the teachers ordered lunch from the usual chophouse. Kuch'iri brought Minu's lunch first, and Ch'oe plainly showed his irritation. On one occasion Ch'oe and Minu nearly clashed openly.

When the teachers had a party, Ch'oe looked askance at Minu's gathering squid heads or leftover cooky bits and giving them to Kuch'iri; and when relief goods were distributed, Ch'oe was irritated by Minu's giving unwanted items to the boy. It was hard to know whether Ch'oe disliked Minu for taking sides with a boy he hated, or whether it was because he hated Minu that he could not stand Kuch'iri. In either case, Minu had no love for Ch'oe either.

Ch'oe could be quite cruel. For example, he would bring into the office two pupils accused of misbehaving in class. He would stand them face to face and order one to slap the other on the cheek. But eye to eye as they were, the two could only grin sheepishly. However, Ch'oe was standing there beside them, stick in hand. One pupil, seeing no escape, would lightly slap the other on the cheek. Then Ch'oe would tell the pupil who had been hit to return the blow. Helpless, the second pupil would slap back about as hard as the one he had been slapped. But the other boy, probably thinking this slap a bit harder than the first, would hit back still harder. And his comrade, thinking this slap much harder than the one he had delivered, would hit back hard indeed. But this time no threats from the teacher were necessary; the two would just go on slapping each other with all their strength until their ears and cheeks were red and swollen. Everyone would laugh at the spectacle.

As Minu sketched this portrait of Ch'oe in his mind's eye, he felt sure that Kuch'iri had been beaten all the harder on his account.

"Teacher, you see he's fallen off his horse. But it's a trick. He doesn't get killed. Watch him jump back and get away. He's really great!" Kuch'iri had come back and was sitting beside him explaining the movie.

Kuch'iri waited for Minu by the same corner every day, and each time he wanted to shine Minu's shoes. If Minu said he was busy, the boy would at least give the shoes a quick brushing. Sometimes, when Kuch'iri was busy shining someone else's shoes, Minu just went by in silence. When they met the next day, Kuch'iri would ask why Minu had not gone to work and where he had been, and he would say that he had waited for Minu until dark. One day when Minu was on his way home a little later than usual, he saw Kuch'iri, hands thrust into his pants pockets, whistling and marching along in time to the tune. It was a popular song that went ". . . though I miss my home . . ."

"What are you doing here so late?"

"I was waiting for you, Teacher," he replied, shouldering his shoeshine box and walking along after Minu.

"What for?"

"Just because . . ."

When they got to the East Gate train station, Kuch'iri simply bowed to Minu and said, "Goodbye, Teacher."

Kuch'iri lived in the second-to-last shack in the row along the bank of the stream just outside the station. One time, thinking it odd that Kuch'iri went into the station every evening, Minu had asked him where he lived. Kuch'iri took his sleeve and drew him to the ticket gate, where he pointed out the shack just opposite. He said he lived there with an old lady who raised bean sprouts and sold them in the market.

Minu would leave work as early as possible, knowing that Kuch'iri was waiting for him. Somehow Kuch'iri had found a permanent place in his heart. This was Minu's weakness: if a neighbor's dog wagged its tail at him, he would feel fond of it. Or perhaps it was partly that Minu's youngest nephew was still in the North, where there was no way to get news of him, and whenever Minu saw Kuch'iri it was just like seeing the little nephew who had always tagged after him.

"How long are you going to go on shining shoes?"

"Why?"

"That's a job for little kids, you know."

Kuch'iri was silent.

"How old are you now?"

"On New Year's I'll turn fourteen."

"Wouldn't you like to get a job as a carpenter, or iron-worker?" Such were Minu's hopes for the boy, and he had thoughts of sending him to night school.

"Well, what do you want to do?"

"I want to make some money so I can open a shoe store."

"Hm? A shoe store?"

"In Pusan, at the head of our alley."

"Why on earth there?"

"So I can show it to that kid."

"What kid?"

"My stepmother's kid."

"But still, he's your brother, isn't he?"

"Him? I can't stand that brat. Because of him I've been beaten enough. And my big sister, too. She's always getting a licking because of him. I really feel sorry for my big sister. If I open a shoe store, she can come live with me."

"It takes a lot of money to open a shoe store. Do you have any saved up?"

Kuch'iri looked at Minu with a quick grin and rubbed harder with the polishing cloth. "I've saved six thousand *hwan* since I came to Seoul. Plus nine hundred I gave to the old woman to help her with her bean sprout business."

"How did you get to know her?"

"One day she asked me to open her bean sprout bucket for her. I could tell by her dialect that she was from Ch'ungch'ong, too."

"Does she have a family?"

"She says her husband died last year, and her son was killed in the war."

It was two days before Christmas.

Kuch'iri had been shining Minu's shoes once every two or three days but had refused to accept payment. Now Kuch'iri looked so cold that Minu handed him two thousand *hwan* and said, "Here, buy yourself a shirt. How can you go around in those clothes in the winter?"

Kuch'iri stared at the money and back at Minu, and deftly thrust the bills back into Minu's pocket. "I don't want it. I don't want your money."

Minu pulled the money back out and stuck it under Kuch'iri's nose. "Come on, take it," he said.

"I don't want it!"

"Hurry up and take it."

Kuch'iri did not move.

"Look, how can I accept your favors then?"

Minu dropped the money in front of Kuch'iri and turned away. But Kuch'iri, stumbling in his oversized boots, came from behind and stood in his path. "I don't want money. I don't want it." Wiping his eyes with his fist, he held the money out to Minu. Passersby turned to watch.

"What are you crying for?" Minu said.

"I don't want it. Money . . ."

This was a predicament. "Okay, then, bring your things and come with me."

Again Kuch'iri shoved the money back into Minu's overcoat pocket. He shouldered his stool and box and followed along. The two went into a restaurant and ordered two bowls of dumpling soup.

"Why do you wait for me every day?"

Kuch'iri lowered his gaze.

"Speak up!"

"Because I like you!"

"What do you mean, you like me?"

"I just do."

"Just do? What . . . ? Really!"

The waiter brought the soup.

"But look, Kuch'iri." Again Minu got out his money. "Look, you shine my shoes and then I'll buy you a shirt, okay? That's what people do at Christmas. So buy a shirt with this and start wearing it tomorrow, won't you?"

"But I don't want you to give me any money!"

"You're a stubborn little . . . Look, if you don't do what I tell you, I won't come by here and I won't let you shine my shoes anymore. How would you like that?"

Kuch'iri sniffed.

"Your nose is running into your soup."

Kuch'iri snuffled, and with a look of reproach for Minu he took the money.

They had left the restaurant and were walking side by side. Minu asked, "Do you want to see a movie? I'll treat you."

"No, thank you. I've got to go home now."

"What for?"

"The old woman can't see too well at night anymore."

"So what do you do?"

I carry water and sort bean sprouts for her."

They did not meet the next day, for it was Sunday.

When Kuch'iri saw Minu on Christmas morning, he was beaming as he held out his arms to show off the jacket he had gotten in a second-hand clothes shop. He also showed him a can of shoe polish he had bought with the change. Minu was pleased and said, "That's good. But you could use a haircut, too."

They say the peak season for shoeshine boys begins when the forsythia bloom, as people emerge into the fine weather wanting to look their best after a long winter indoors. For Kuch'iri work was plentiful, and he said that he could earn in one day now what during the winter had taken two days to earn.

While he was polishing Minu's shoes one day, Kuch'iri said, "Teacher, your shoes are all worn out."

"Yes, it's time to buy a new pair."

"Don't buy any. I'll get you some high-quality American ones from a guy I know." He measured Minu's foot with a cord.

A few days later Kuch'iri told him, "Teacher, I asked him to get the shoes. He says he'll get the best. It's okay if they're secondhand, isn't it?"

"What's the price?"

"Let's see . . . They'll sell them cheap to us, say about four or five thousand *hwan*."

"That low?"

"Yeah. On the black market a good pair of American shoes'll go for at least ten thousand *hwan* even if they're used."

After that, Kuch'iri worried about his offer each time he shined Minu's shoes. "I saw the guy yesterday and he says he'll get them soon," he would say, and then mutter something to himself.

One Saturday in early May, Minu left work somewhat earlier than usual. Kuch'iri was nowhere to be seen, though his box and stool lay abandoned on the ground. Thinking that Kuch'iri must have gone to the washroom, Minu sat down on the stool and took out a cigaret.

A glamour like that of quarrelling urchins came from a nearby alleyway. Minu smoked his cigaret and waited, but still Kuch'iri did not return. Thinking Kuch'iri might be watching the fight, Minu stepped into the alley. There from behind he saw a young man, apparently smartly dressed, surrounded by four or five shoeshine boys. The young man was striking somebody. He wore rubber slippers on his feet and held a pair of leather shoes in his hand. Minu moved closer, thinking that the boy being struck resembled Kuch'iri.

"Teacher, go away. Don't come in here. It's nothing." It was Kuch'iri. Blood dribbled from his nose and smeared his face.

"Kuch'iri! What's going on here?"

Kuch'iri, spitting blood and wiping the side of his mouth, yelled almost desperately, "Teacher, go away. It's nothing. Please go away!"

With that the young man turned and looked angrily at Minu. "Who are you?" he asked.

Minu had no ready answer, but hesitated a moment and then said, "It doesn't matter who I am, but what on earth . . ."

Kuch'iri took his chance to escape. He ran down the alley with all his might and was rounding the corner before the surprised young man uttered a curse and ran after him.

Minu thought to himself, "Whatever it's all about, I just hope Kuch'iri doesn't get caught." He asked the shoeshine boys standing there what had happened to Kuch'iri. But as if by agreement they did not say a word and slipped away. At that point, a boy came to pick up Kuch'iri's stool and box. The boy said that he was a friend of Kuch'iri, and that he would take care of Kuch'iri's things. Minu consented and had the boy shine his shoes, hoping to find out more. "Hey, what was that all about," he asked.

The boy glanced up at him and answered, "He was caught stealing shoes at the restaurant over there."

"Kuch'iri was?"

"Him and another kid, but the other one got away and Kuch'iri got caught."

Minu's head began to swim and his eyesight blurred. He shut his eyes for a moment to calm himself. "It was all because of that promise of his," he muttered. He was angered by this breach of faith, but he felt sorry for Kuch'iri. "If I see him, I'll really teach him a lesson, the little thief." Yet even as he said this, Minu really felt as if he would burst into tears if he met Kuch'iri now.

"Ha, if I'd only caught that bastard I've have bashed his skull in like a chestnut?" It was the young man with the shoes, coming back out of breath.

"What happened?"

"He got away."

Minu was relieved.

"Look at this. It hasn't been a week since I bought these shoes." He took off the rubber slippers, put on the shoes, and headed off across the trolley line.

From that day on Kuch'iri was nowhere to be found.
On the fourth day Minu went to the shack outside the train station where the old lady who sold bean sprouts lived. The old lady did live there, he was told, but the door was latched; she must have been at the market.

Every day on his way to and from work, Minu stopped at Kuch'iri's old shoeshine spot. About ten days or so later, another boy took over the spot. Setting his foot on the box Minu asked, "Do you know Kuch'iri, who used to shine shoes here?"
"Yeah, I know him. He's gone to an American army base up near the DMZ."[1]
"Alone?"
"No, he joined a group of guys who were going up there." The boy said that every summer groups of shoeshine boys went to the American army bases to make money. It would be autumn before they returned, the boy said in reply to Minu's query.

A wearisome August passed, and then September drew to a close.
Autumn came late that year.

One day, as leaves were beginning to fall along the streets, Minu glanced up at the sky. A flock of geese flew by in a neat V, on their way from somewhere to somewhere else. Minu was deeply moved: "Kuch'iri, too, will be coming back soon," he thought.

FURTHER READINGS

Ki-baik Lee, *A New History of Korea*, trans. Edward W. Wagner (Cambridge, MA: Harvard University Press, 1984) is a good general interpretative history of Korea. Shannon McCune, *Korea: Land of Broken Calm* (Princeton, NJ: Van Nostrand, 1967) focuses on Korea during the twentieth century. A useful examination of Korean political culture and development in the twentieth century is available in Gregory Henderson, *Korea: The Politics of the Vortex* (Cambridge, MA: Harvard University Press, 1968). The *Korean Cultural Series* provides a wealth of information pertaining to Korean social and cultural conditions. Of particular interest is the sixth volume in this series, *Korean Society*, ed. Chun

[1] Demilitarized zone.

Shin-yong (Seoul, Korea: International Cultural Foundation, 1976), which treats Korean family and social systems, social strata, and traditionalism. Paul Crane, *Korean Patterns* (Seoul, Korea: Hollym, 1967) provides a useful account of traditional Korean values, attitudes, and customs. A brief assessment of the changes in family life, site, and composition resulting from the Korean War, industrialization, and American influence is available in Hyo-Chai Lee, "The Changing Family in Korea," *Bulletin of Korea Research Center*, 29 (December, 1968), pp. 87–99.

James Irving Matray, *The Reluctant Crusade* (Honolulu: University of Hawaii Press, 1985) discusses American foreign policy in Korea between 1941 and 1950. Without Parallel, Frank Baldwin, ed., *The American-Korean Relationship since 1945* (New York: Pantheon, 1974) is a collection of articles focusing on American involvement in Korea from 1945 to 1972. The liberation of Korea and the allied occupation from 1945 to 1948 is the subject of Bruce Cumings, *The Origins of the Korean War* (Princeton, NJ: Princeton University Press, 1981). Notable among the many works dealing with the Korean War are John M. Carew, *Korea: The Commonwealth at War* (London: Cassell, 1967); Bevin Alexander, *Korea: The First War We Lost* (New York: Hippocrene, 1986); and Donald Knox, *The Korean War: Pusan to Chosin* (San Diego: Harcourt Brace Jovanovich, 1985). Burton I. Kaufman, *The Korean War* (Philadelphia: Temple University Press, 1986) offers an insightful study of foreign policy issues, which places the war in broad domestic and international perspective.

Korean fiction has undergone an exciting development during the twentieth century. Examples from this bountiful harvest of new fiction are available in *Korea Journal*, a monthly publication of the Korean National Commission for UNESCO, Seoul, Korea. The most comprehensive collection of twentieth-century Korean short stories is Peter H. Lee, ed., *Flowers of Fire* (Honolulu: University of Hawaii Press, 1974), which contains twenty-one stories by seventeen writers. The representation of works from the post-liberation years is especially good. Chong-un Kim, "Images of Man in Postwar Korean Fiction," *Korean Studies* (Honolulu: University Press of Hawaii for the Center for Korean Studies, 1978), vol. II, pp. 1–28, briefly discusses the works of fiction produced during the postwar decades in Korea. Marshall R. Pihl, "Engineers of the Human Soul: North Korean Literature Today," *Korean Studies* (Honolulu: University Press of Hawaii for the Center for Korean Studies, 1977), vol. I, pp. 63–110, is a helpful introduction to the contemporary North Korean short story and the North Korean literary policy. While the short story form continues to represent modern Korea's best known works, the novel has also flourished. The twentieth century has produced a number of Koreans who compose in Western languages. Li Mirok, *The Yalu Flows: A Korean Childhood* (East Lansing: Michigan State University Press, 1956); Younghill Kang, *The Grass Roof* (Chicago: Follett, 1966);

and Richard Kim, *The Martyred* (New York: George Braziller, 1964) and *Lost Names: Scenes from a Korean Boyhood* (New York: Frederick A. Praeger, 1970) all deal with the disintegration of traditional systems and values. Examples of twentieth-century Korean poetry are contained in Won Ko, trans., *Contemporary Korean Poetry* (Iowa City: University of Iowa Press, 1970) and Peter H. Lee, trans., *Poems from Korea: A Historical Anthology* (Honolulu: University Press of Hawaii, 1974).

WHAT IS INDIA?
Jawaharlal Nehru

The last British viceroy, Lord Louis Mountbatten, had decided to grant India independence within the British Commonwealth of Nations on August 15, 1947, but adopted the demand of the Muslim minority, concentrated in the West and East, that the land be partitioned into two nations, India and Pakistan. Boundaries were to be settled by arbitration on the basis of population, at least in theory. Hundreds of Indian princes, some governing territories larger than many nation-states, could not be dealt with in such summary fashion, but they were forced to choose within which of the new states they wished their lands to be included. It was difficult for the governments of newly independent and separate states of Pakistan and India to adjust to a situation that many dedicated Indian leaders, including Gandhi, had prayed would never occur.

A constituent assembly, elected in 1946 to draft a constitution for an undivided India, had formulated the document under which India lives today. It was progressive and modern, embodying all of the liberal democratic aspirations of the Indian National Congress and reflecting in particular Nehru's viewpoint. Gandhi had envisioned a decentralized state based on the fundamental social, political, and economic unit of the traditional Indian village, and warned that, within a centralized state, the mutual distrust of Muslims and Hindus would surely lead to conflict. Both his idealism and political realism were ignored as many Indian leaders began to dream of the power that they thought could only come with centralization and nationalism. Many of those dedicated people who still followed Gandhi's leadership and relied on his judgment left the government.

Some Indian National Congress leaders, who feared the capitalism that had led Britain to dominate and exploit India for so long, proposed a more

From Jawaharlal Nehru, *India Today and Tomorrow*, in Sarvepalli Gopal, ed., *Jawaharlal Nehru, An Anthology* (Oxford, UK: Oxford University Press, 1983), pp. 225–30.

socialist constitution with strong measures against official corruption. Although some of these proposals were eventually adopted by Prime Minister Indira Gandhi, Nehru tried at the time to maintain a delicate balance between socialists and communists on the left and Hindu revivalists on the right. The latter won few concessions in the constitution except for minor policies such as protection of cows, regarded as sacred by the Hindus. Nevertheless, Hindus have remained politically active and have gained power as time has passed. Currently a large segment of the Indian population believes that India should promote and protect the religion and culture of the majority. Needless to say, that majority is Hindu.

India had, then, three distinct, and conflicting, visions of its economic future at the time of independence. Besides Nehru's democratic socialist concept and Gandhi's ideas of rural self-sufficiency that were carried on by his followers after his death, there was a liberal capitalist vision. The spokesman for this point of view within the Congress party was Sardar Vallabhbhai Patel. Indians debated the many issues involved with these conflicting economic philosophies: the roles of Gandhian village and cottage industries, which were not important to Nehru but were central to everything Gandhi had done; the instruments through which the government would guide and control the economy; the possible nationalization of private enterprises; the role of state enterprises; the future of foreign capital; and many others.

Like Nehru, Patel wanted to build a strong, centralized industrial state to defend the nation and to raise the standard of living of the Indian people. Nehru, however, distrusted capitalists, thought capitalism was outmoded, and was not convinced that capitalism would lead to social justice or improve the lot of most of the Indian population. Feeling that such progress could be accomplished only under governmental direction, he wanted not only centralized planning but governmental ownership of industry. In those cases where business was privately owned, such as where foreign capital investment was involved, Nehru felt that tight governmental control and regulation were necessary.

Patel, on the other hand, distrusted the government and wanted to strengthen the private sector. Nehru compromised on the general issue, partly to reassure foreign investors, who had been a large part of the British colonial economy and constituted a legacy to the new nation. The first two five-year plans established by the Indian government were based on mixed private and government ownership of industry, and this approach has remained the basic developmental strategy for the government of India ever since. Indian private enterprise was protected from foreign competition and cottage industries were protected from industrial competition.

In 1959, against a background of Muslim-Hindu slaughters and cruel mass migrations of people from one new nation to the other, the wrenching assassination of Gandhi in 1949, and the bitter controversies through which the Indian leaders finally hammered out a national policy, Prime Minister Jawaharlal Nehru looked at the India he was helping to build and attempted to place the birth-pangs of the new nation within the context of the long history of Indian civilization. Reflecting on his administration's emphasis on economic, industrial, and technological growth, he realized that India could drift into a materialism that would be a betrayal of the inspiration of Gandhi and constitute a break with a long and rich Indian tradition. Harmonizing that heritage with the driving economic and technological forces of the modern world was India's challenge for the future.

Questions

1. In light of what you have read about India, how accurate is Nehru's review of Indian history?

2. How does Nehru's attitude towards Marxism and socialism differ from typical American attitudes?

3. Does Nehru seem realistic or unrealistic in his hope for the reconciliation of Indian tradition on one hand and science and technology on the other?

4. Does India seem to have realized Nehru's hopes in the past three decades?

WHAT IS INDIA?

To endeavor to understand and describe the India of today would be the task of a brave man. To describe tomorrow's India would verge on rashness.

What is India? That is a question which has come back again and again to my mind. The early beginnings of our history filled me with wonder. It was the past of a virile and vigorous race with a questing spirit and an urge for free inquiry and, even in its earliest known period, giving evidence of a mature and tolerant civilization. Accepting life and its joys and burdens, it was ever searching for the ultimate and the universal. It built up a magnificent language, Sanskrit, and through this language, its arts and architecture, it sent its vibrant message to far countries. It produced the Upanishads, the Gita and the Buddha.

Hardly any language in the world has probably played that vital part in the history of a race which Sanskrit has. It was not only the vehicle of the highest thought and some of the finest literature, but it became the uniting bond for India, in spite of its political division. The *Ramayana* and the *Mahabharata* were woven into the texture of millions of lives in every generation for thousands of years. I have often wondered, if our race forgot the Buddha, the Upanishads and the great epics, what then will it be like! It would be uprooted and would lose the basic characteristics which have clung to it and given it distinction throughout these long ages. India would cease to be India.

Gradually deterioration set in. Thought lost its freshness and became stale, and the vitality and exuberance of youth gave place to crabbed age. Instead of the spirit of adventure there came lifeless routine, and the broad and exciting vision of the world was cabined and confined and lost in caste divisions, narrow social customs and ceremonials. Even so, India was vital enough to absorb the streams of people that flowed into her mighty ocean of humanity and she never quite forgot the thoughts that had stirred her in the days of her youthful vigor.

Subsequently, India was powerfully influenced by the coming of Islam and Muslim invasions. Western colonial powers followed, bringing a new type of domination and a new colonialism and, at the same time, the impact of fresh ideas and of the industrial civilization that was growing up in Europe. This period culminated, after a long struggle, in independence and now we face the future with all this burden of the past upon us and the confused dreams and stirrings of the future that we seek to build.

We have all these ages represented in us and in our country today. We have the growth of nuclear science and atomic energy in India, and we also have the cowdung age.

In the tumult and confusion of our time, we stand facing both ways, forward to the future and backwards to the past, being pulled in both directions. How can we resolve this conflict and evolve a structure for living which fulfils our material needs and, at the same time, sustains our mind and spirit? What new ideals or old ideals varied and adapted to the new world can we place before our people, and how can we galvanize the people into wakefulness and action?

For the present, in India we are rightly absorbed in the Five-Year Plans and in a tremendous effort to raise our people's living standards. Economic progress is essential and a prerequisite for any other type of advance. But a doubt creeps into our minds. Is this by itself enough or is something else to be added on to it? The Welfare State is a worthwhile ideal, but it may well be rather drab. The examples of states which have achieved that objective bring out new problems and difficulties, which are not solved by material advance alone or by a mechanical civilization. Whether religion is necessary or not, a certain faith in a worthwhile ideal is essential to give substance to our lives and to hold us together.

Change is essential but continuity is also necessary. The future has to be built on the foundations laid in the past and in the present. To deny the past and break with it completely is to uproot ourselves and, sapless, dry up. It was the virtue of Gandhiji to keep his feet firmly planted in the rich traditions of our race and our soil and, at the same time, to function on the revolutionary plane. Above all, he laid stress on truth and peaceful means. Thus he built on old foundations, and at the same time, oriented the structure towards the future.

When Islam came to India in the form of political conquest it brought conflict. It had a twofold effect. On the one hand, it encouraged the tendency of Hindu society to shrink still further within its shell; on the other, it brought a breath of fresh air and fresh ideals, and thus had a certain rejuvenating influence. Hindu society had become a closed system. The Muslims who came from outside brought their own closed system with them. Hence the great problem that faced India during the medieval period was how these two closed systems, each with its strong roots, could develop a healthy relationship. Wise rulers like Akbar and others realized that the only hope for the future lay in some kind of harmony being established.

The philosophy and the world outlook of the old Hindus was amazingly tolerant; and yet they had divided themselves up into numerous separate caste groups and hierarchies. The Muslims had to face a new problem, namely how to live with others as equals. In other countries where they had gone, their success was so great that this problem did not really arise. They came into conflict with Christendom and through hundreds of years the problem was never solved. In India, slowly a synthesis was developed. But before this could be completed, other influences came into play.

The new liberal thought of the West and industrial processes began to affect the mind and life of India. A new nationalism developed, which was inevitably against colonialism and sought independence, and yet which was being progressively affected by the new industrial civilization as well as the language, literature and ways of the West.

Rammohun Roy came, seeking some kind of a synthesis between old India and modern trends. Vivekananda brought back something of the vigour of old Indian thought and dressed it in a modern garb. Political and cultural movements grew up and culminated in Gandhiji and Rabindranath Tagore.

In Europe there had been a fierce conflict between science and traditional religion, and the cosmology of Christianity did not fit in at all with scientific theories. Science did not produce that sense of conflict in India and Indian philosophy could easily accept it without doing any vital injury to its basic conceptions.

In India, as elsewhere, two forces developed—the growth of nationalism and the urge for social justice. Socialism and Marxism became the symbol of this urge for social justice and, apart from their scientific content, had a tremendous emotional appeal for the masses.

Living is a continual adjustment to changing conditions. The rapidity of technological change in the last half century has made the necessity of social change greater than ever, and there is a continual maladjustment. The advance of science and technology makes it definitely possible to solve most of the economic problems of the world and, in particular, to provide the primary necessities of life to everyone all over the world. The methods adopted will have to depend upon the background and cultural development of a country or a community.

Internationally, the major question today is that of world peace. The only course open is for us to accept the world as it is and develop toleration for each other. It should be open to each country to develop in its own way, learning from others, and not being imposed on by them. Essentially, this calls for a new mental approach. The Panch-sheel, or the Five Principles, offer that approach.

There are conflicts within a nation. In a democratic apparatus with adult suffrage, those conflicts can be solved by normal constitutional methods.

In India we have had most distressing spectacles of conflict based on provincialism or linguism. In the main, it is conflict of class interests that poses problems today, and in such cases vested interests are not easy to displace. Yet we have seen in India powerful vested interests like those of the old princes and of the big jagirdars, talukdars and zamindars being removed by peaceful methods, even though that meant a break-up of a well-established system which favoured a privileged few. While, therefore, we must recognize that there is class conflict, there is no reason why we should not deal with it through these peaceful methods. They will only succeed, however, if we have a proper objective in view clearly understood by the people.

We have deliberately laid down as our objective a socialist pattern of society. Personally I think that the acquisitive society, which is the base of capitalism, is no longer suited to the present age. We have to evolve a higher order more in keeping with modern trends and conditions and involving not so much competition but much greater cooperation. We have accepted socialism as our goal not only because it sees to us right and beneficial but because there is no other way for the solution of our economic problems. It is sometimes said that rapid progress cannot take place by peaceful and democratic methods. I do not accept this proposition. Indeed, in India today any attempt to discard democratic methods would lead to disruption and would thus put an end to any immediate prospect of progress.

The mighty task that we have undertaken demands the fullest cooperation from the masses of our people. The change we seek necessitates burdens on our people, even on those who can least bear them; unless they realize that they are partners in the building of a society which will bring them benefits, they will not accept these burdens or give their full cooperation.

Whether in land or industry, or in the governmental apparatus, institutional changes become necessary from time to time as functions change. A new set of values will replace those that have governed the old acquisitive society based on the profit motive. The problem before us is ultimately to change the thinking and activities of hundreds of millions of people, and to do this democratically by their consent.

India today presents a very mixed picture of hope and anguish, of remarkable advances and at the same time of inertia, of a new spirit and also the dead hand of the past and of privilege, of an overall and growing unity and many disruptive tendencies. Withal there is a great vitality and a ferment in people's minds and activities.

It is a remarkable thing that a country and a people rooted in the remote past, who have shown so much resistance to change in the past, should now be marching forward rapidly and with resolute steps.

What will emerge from the labour and the tumults of the present generation? I cannot say what will tomorrow's India be like. I can only express my hopes and wishes. I want India to advance on the material plane—to fulfil her Five-Year Plans to raise the standards of living of her vast population; I want the narrow conflicts of today in the name of religion or caste, language or province, to cease, and a classless and casteless society to be built up where every individual has full opportunity to grow according to his worth and ability. In particular, I hope that the curse of caste will be ended, for there cannot be either democracy or socialism on the basis of caste.

Four great religions have influenced India—two emerging from her own thought, Hinduism and Buddhism, and two coming from abroad but establishing themselves firmly in India, Christianity and Islam. Science today challenges the old concepts of religion. But if religion deals not with dogmas and ceremonials, but rather with the higher things of life, there should be no conflict with science or *inter se* between religions. It might be the high privilege of India to help in bringing about this synthesis. That would be in India's ancient tradition inscribed on Asoka's edicts.

Tomorrow's India will be what we make it by today's labours. We have started on this pilgrimage with strong purpose and good heart, and we shall reach the end of the journey, however long that might be.

What I am concerned with is not merely our material progress, but the quality and depth of our people. Gaining power through industrial processes, will they lose themselves in the quest of individual wealth and soft living? That would be a tragedy, for that would be a negation of what India has stood for in the past and, I hope, in the present time also as exemplified by Gandhiji.

Can we combine the progress of science and technology with this progress of the mind and spirit also? We cannot be untrue to science, because that represents the basic fact of life today. Still less can we be untrue to those essential principles for which India has stood in the past throughout the ages.

FURTHER READINGS

Jawaharlal Nehru's writings are literary accomplishments as well as political documents. Foremost among them are *The Discovery of India* (New York: John Day, 1947). The standard biography is Michael Brecher, *Nehru: A Political Biography* (London: Oxford University Press, 1959). Some of the questions raised by Nehru are discussed in Ainslie T. Embree, *India's Search for National Identity* (New York: Knopf, 1972). Craig Baxter, et al., *Government and Politics in South Asia* (Boulder: Westview Press, 1987) covers the political history of all the South Asian states since independence. Lloyd I. Rudolph and Susanne Hoeber Rudolph, *In Pursuit of Lakshmi: The Political Economy of the Indian State* (Chicago: University of Chicago Press, 1987) examines the interactions between the economy and politics in the Republic of India since 1947.

WAITING FOR THE MAHATMA
R. K. NARAYAN

Mohandas Gandhi's reputation in India has never waned even though the nation's political course has taken directions he would have opposed, and scholars have interpreted and reinterpreted his contribution to Indian nationalism and the winning of independence. He is seen alternately as a saint, master political strategist, and utopian dreamer, but, in whatever guise, remains a figure of compelling interest in the Indian memory and imagination. A charismatic leader of such proportions is difficult to evaluate or analyze, and it is unlikely that historians and political scientists ever will succeed in mapping the true dimensions of his influence on India. It remains for the artists and creative writers to attempt to make an assessment. It is not unlikely that Gandhi will be transformed into a legend in the process, and the reader of this selection will be left to judge whether or not that transformation may not already be underway.

Several important novels have taken up the theme of Gandhi and his effect on India, including Raja Rao's *Kanthapura* (London: Allen & Unwin, 1938), and Mulk Raj Anand's *Untouchable* (Bombay: Jaico, 1956), but most attempt to portray Gandhi within a political context and thus lose something of the power of Gandhi's individual personality.

From R. K. Narayan, *Waiting for the Mahatma* (Chicago: University of Chicago Press, 1981), pp. 62, 64–67, 69–72, 78–80, 84–85.

R. K. Narayan's *Waiting for the Mahatma* avoids this problem by largely ignoring the major political events of the time. The novel concentrates on depicting Gandhi as a real person among ordinary people, rather than as the saintly strategist of the independence movement. Narayan also avoids confronting Gandhi directly and thus being forced to describe and explain him. Gandhi appears frequently throughout the book, but he is described primarily in his relations to a young boy named Sriram and a young girl, Bharati, whom Sriram has fallen in love with. Sriram's caustic grandmother, other campaigners in the Indian independence movement, and various people who attempt to exploit Gandhi for their own ends are also included in the cast of characters. In this fashion the figure of Gandhi becomes a multifaceted reflection of a few people with whom he has come in contact. Moreover, this approach allows Narayan to present a realistic view of the lives and concerns of a few common people living in uncommon times. The novel thus offers us a different view of the last years of British rule in India.

Narayan is a major Indian novelist, and many of his stories are set in Malgudi, a fictional town resembling Mysore in South India. *Waiting for the Mahatma* (1955) initially had a mixed reception, partly due to the unconventional characterization of Gandhi, and partly because it appeared between his two most popular works, *The Financial Expert* (1953) and *The Guide* (1958). It is now considered one of his finest efforts.

Waiting for the Mahatma is the story of an introverted young man who is transformed by his ardent attachment to a disciple of Gandhi. The novel opens with the introduction of Sriram in about 1938, an orphan whose father had died in the service of the British in World War I and whose mother had died giving birth to him. Sriram has been raised by his Granny, who had saved his father's monthly pension payments and turned the bank account over to him on his twentieth birthday. With no need to work for a living, he leads an indolent and passionless life until meeting Bharati, a young girl whose devotion to the Mahatma leaves her no time for romantic involvement. In order to be near her, Sriram joins the nationalist movement and finally wins her when Gandhi approves their union on the day of his death in 1948. Despite this tragic conclusion, the novel is a richly humorous portrayal of middle-class Indian life in the last decade before independence.

In the following passage, Narayan portrays Sriram's conversion to Gandhi's movement, but leaves room for the reader to wonder what the young man's motivations truly are; perhaps he is not even sure of that himself. As the passage opens, the smitten Sriram has followed Bharati to a camp Gandhi has set up among the hovels of the untouchable city sweepers while on a visit to Malgudi. He offers to join the movement, and Bharati tells him to return at 3:00 A.M. When he does so, he unexpectedly finds himself face to face with Gandhi.

Questions

1. Does Sriram join with Gandhi exclusively because of his attraction to Bharati, or could he have other motives?
2. What does Sriram like and dislike about the life of Gandhi's volunteers?
3. How does Granny respond to Gandhi's campaign and to Sriram's intentions to take part in it?

WAITING FOR THE MAHATMA

Granny had slept fitfully. She had gone up to Kanni's shop five times during the evening to enquire if anyone had seen Sriram, and sent a boy who had come to make a purchase there to look for Sriram everywhere. At last the schoolmaster who lived up the street told her as he passed her house,

'Your pet is in Mahatma's camp. I saw him.'

'Ah! What was he doing there?' asked Granny alarmed. For her the Mahatma was one who preached dangerously, who tried to bring untouchables into the temples, and who involved people in difficulties with the police. She didn't like the idea. She wailed, 'Oh, master, why did you allow him to stay on there? You should have brought him away. It is so late and he has not come home. As his old teacher you should have weaned him away.'

'Don't worry, madam, he is perfectly safe. How many of us could have the privilege of being so near the Mahatma? You must be happy that he is doing so well! Our country needs more young men like him.'

Granny replied, 'It is teachers like you who have ruined our boys and this country,' and turned in, slamming the door.

◆

He stood at the entrance to Mahatmaji's hut, holding his breath. It was very difficult to decide what he should do now. She had asked him to be present at the portals of the Great Presence, but perhaps she had been fooling him.

◆

The door of Mahatmaji's hut was half open. Light streamed out through the gap. Sriram went towards it like a charmed moth. If he had paused to reflect he would not have believed himself to be capable of repeating a foolhardy act a second time. But through lack of sleep, and tension of nerves, a general reck-lessness had come over him, the same innocent charge that had taken him tumbling into the hut the previous evening took him there again now. He peeped in like a clown. The door was half open; he had over-estimated its width from a distance, for he could not peep in without thrusting his head through.

'Oh, there he is!' cried Bharati, with laughter in her voice. 'You may open the door if you wish to come in,' she said. Sriram felt again that the girl was making fun of him. Even in the great presence, she didn't seem to care. Here at least Sriram had hoped she would speak without the undertone of mischief. He felt so irritated at the thought that he replied with all the pungency he could muster in his tone: 'You have—I waited for you there—'

'Come in, come in,' said the Mahatma. 'Why should you be standing there? You could have come straight in.'

'But she asked me to wait outside,' said Sriram, stepping in gingerly. From the door to where the Mahatma sat the distance was less than ten feet, but he felt he was taking hours to cover it. His legs felt weak and seemed to intertwine, he seemed to be walking like a drunkard, a particularly dangerous impression to create in the Mahatma, who was out to persuade even the scavengers to give up drinking. In a flash it occurred to him that he ought to have a sensible answer ready if the Mahatma should suddenly turn round and ask, 'Have you been drinking toddy or whisky?'

But his trial came to an end, when Gandhi said, 'Bharati has just been mentioning you.' He spoke while his hands were busy turning a spinning wheel, drawing out a fine thread. A man sitting in a corner, with a pad resting on his knee, was writing. Mahatmaji himself as always was doing several things at the same time. While his hands were spinning, his eyes perused a letter held before him by another, and he found it possible too to put in a word of welcome to Sriram. Through the back door of the hut many others were coming in and passing out. For each one of them Mahatmaji had something to say.

He looked up at Sriram and said: 'Sit down, young man. Come and sit as near me as you like.' There was so much unaffected graciousness in his tone that Sriram lost all fear and hesitation. He moved briskly up. He sat on the floor near Mahatmaji and watched with fascination the smooth turning of the spinning wheel. Bharati went to an inner part of the hut, threw a swift look at Sriram, which he understood to mean, 'Remember not to make a fool of yourself.'

The Mahatma said, 'Nowadays I generally get up an hour earlier in order to be able to do this: spinning a certain length is my most important work: even my prayer comes only after that. I'd very much like you to take a vow to wear only cloth made out of your own hands each day.'

'Yes, I will do so,' promised Sriram.

When the gong in the Taluk Office struck four, the Mahatma invited Sriram to go out with him for a walk.

✦

During the last fifteen minutes of this walk the Mahatma said nothing; he walked in silence, looking at the ground before him. When the Mahatma was silent the others were even more so, the only movement they performed was putting one foot before another on the sand, keeping pace with him: some were panting hard and trying hard to suppress the sound. The Mahatma's silence was heavy and pervasive, and Sriram was afraid even to gulp or cough, although he very much wanted to clear his throat, cough, sneeze, swing his arms about. The only sound at the moment was the flowing of the river and the twitter of birds. Somewhere a cow was mooing. Even Bharati, the embodiment of frivolity, seemed to have become sombre. The Mahatma pulled out his watch, looked at it briefly and said, 'We will go back, that is all the walk I can afford today.' Sriram wanted to ask, 'Why!' But he held his tongue. The Mahatma turned to him as they were walking back, 'You have a grandmother, I hear, but no parents.'

'Yes. My grandmother is very old.'

'Yes, she must be, otherwise how can you call her a grandmother?' People laughed, Sriram too joined in this laughter out of politeness.

'Does she not miss you very much when you are away for so long?'

'Yes, very much. She gets very angry with me. I don't know what to do about it,' said Sriram courageously rushing ahead. He felt pleased at having said something of his own accord, but his only fear was that Bharati might step in and say something nasty and embarrassing, but he was happy to note that Bharati kept her peace.

Mahatmaji said: 'You must look after your granny too, she must have devoted herself to bringing you up.'

'Yes, but when I am away like this she is very much upset.'

'Is it necessary for you to be away from her so much?'

'Yes, Bapu, otherwise how can I do anything in this world?'

'What exactly do you want to do?'

It was now that Sriram became incoherent. He was seized with a rush of ideas and with all the confusion that too many ideas create. He said something, and the Mahatma watched him patiently, the others too held their breath and watched, and after a few moments of struggle for self-expression, Sriram was able to form a cogent sentence. It was the unrelenting pressure of his subconscious desires that jerked the sentence out of his lips, and he said, 'I like to be where Bharati is.' The Mahatma said, 'Oh, is that so!' He patted Bharati's back and said, 'What a fine friend you have! You must be pleased to have such a devoted friend. How long have you known him?'

Bharati said like a shot, 'Since yesterday. I saw him for the first time sitting in your hut and I asked him who he was.'

Sriram interposed and added, 'But I knew her before, although I spoke to her only yesterday.'

The Mahatma passed into his hut, and went on to attend to other things. Many people were waiting for him. Bharati disappeared into the Mahatma's hut the moment they arrived. Sriram fell back and got mixed up with a crowd waiting outside. He felt jealous of Bharati's position. She sought him out later and said, 'You are probably unused to it, but in Bapu's presence we speak only the absolute truth and nothing less than that, and nothing more than that either.'

He took her to task: 'What will he think of me now when he knows that I have not known you long enough and yet—'

'Well, what?' she twitted him.

'And yet I wish to be with you and so on.'

'Why don't you go in and tell him you have been speaking nonsense and that you were blurting out things without forethought or self-control? Why couldn't you have told him that you want to serve the country, that you are a patriot, that you want to shed your blood in order to see that the British leave the country? That is what most people say when they come near the Mahatma. I have seen hundreds of people come to him, and say the same thing.'

'And he believes all that?' asked Sriram.

'Perhaps not, but he thinks it is not right to disbelieve anyone.'

'But you say we must only speak the truth in his presence.'

'If you can, of course, but if you can't, the best thing to do is maintain silence.'

'Why are you so angry with me, is it not a part of your duty not to be angry with others?' asked Sriram pathetically.

'I don't care,' said Bharati, 'this is enough to irritate even the Mahatma. Now what will he think of me if he realizes I am encouraging a fellow like you to hang about the place, a fellow whom I have not known even for a full day yet!'

Sriram became reckless, and said breezily, 'What does it matter how long I have known you? Did you think I was going to lie to him if you had not spoken before I spoke?'

These bickerings were brought to an end by someone calling 'Bharati' from another hut. Bharati abandoned him and disappeared from the spot.

Bharati's words gave him an idea. He realized his own omission, and proposed to remedy it next time he walked with the Mahatma. Sriram's anxiety lest he fall asleep when the Mahatma was up kept him awake the whole night. He shared the space on the floor with one of the men in the camp. It was a strange feeling to lie down in a hut, and he felt he was becoming a citizen of an entirely new world. He missed the cosy room of his house in Kabir Lane, he missed the two pillows and the soft mattress and the carpet under it; even the street noises of Kabir Street added much to the domestic quality of life, and he missed it badly now. He had to adopt an entirely new mode of life. He had to live, of his own choice, in a narrow hut, with thatch above, with a dingy, sooty smell hanging about everything. The floor had been swept with cow dung and covered with a thin layer of sand. He had to snuggle his head on the crook of his arm for a pillow.

◆

[Sriram spends a day in the camp and learns of the volunteers' commitment to poverty, nonviolence, self-suffering, and Indian independence, after which he felt ready to speak to Gandhi again.]

Sriram was told that he could accompany Mahatmaji in his tour of the villages on condition that he went home, and secured Granny's approval. Sriram tried to slur the matter over, he said it would not be necessary, he hinted he was an independent man used to such outings from home. The Mahatma's memory was better than that. He said with a smile, 'I remember you said that she didn't like to see you mixing with us.'

Sriram thought it over and said, 'Yes, master, but how can I for ever remain tied to her? It is not possible.'

'Are you quite sure that you want to change your style of life?' asked the Mahatma.

'I can think of nothing else,' Sriram said. 'How can I live as I have lived all these years?' He threw a quick glance at Bharati as she came in with some letters for the Mahatma. Her look prevented him from completing the sentence, which would have run, 'And I always wish to be with Bharati and not with my grandmother.'

The Mahatma said, 'I shall be happy to have you with us as long as you like, but you must first go home and tell your grandmother and receive her blessing. You must tell her frankly what you wish to do, but you must cause her no pain.'

Sriram hesitated. The prospect of facing Granny was unnerving. The thought of her was like the thought of an unreal troublesome world, one which he hoped he had left behind for ever: the real world for him now was the one of Bharati, Gorpad, unslaughtered naturally dying animals, the Mahatma, spinning wheels. He wanted to be here all the time; it seemed impossible for him to go back to Kabir Street, that *pyol*, and that shop, and those people there who treated him as if he were only eight years old. He stood before the Mahatma as if to appeal to him not to press him to go and face his grandmother, but the master was unrelenting. 'Go and speak to her. I don't think she is so unreasonable as to deny you your ambitions. Tell her that I would like to have you with me. If you tour with me the next two weeks, you will observe and learn much that may be useful to you later in life. Tell her she will feel glad that she let you go. Assure her that I will look after you safely.' Every word filled him with dread when he remembered the terms in which Granny referred to the Mahatma. He dared not even give the slightest indication as to how she would react. He felt a great pity for the Mahatma, so innocent that he could not dream of anyone talking ill of him. He felt angry at the thought of Granny, such an ill-informed, ignorant and bigoted personality! What business had she to complicate his existence in this way? If he could have had his will he would have ignored his grandmother, but he had to obey the Mahatma now.

He said, 'All right, sir. I will go and get my granny's blessing. I'll be back early tomorrow.'

◆

[He summons up his courage and returns home. Apparently made anxious by his absence, Granny feeds him delicacies and ridicules the lifestyle of the volunteers.]

◆

Sriram was horrified. 'What do you take the Mahatma for! Do you know, he won't even wear sandals made of the hide of slaughtered animals!'

Granny was seized by a fit of laughter. Tears rolled down her cheeks. 'Won't wear sandals!' she cried in uncontrollable laughter. 'Never heard of such a thing before! How do they manage it? By peeling off the skin of animals before they are slaughtered, is that it?'

'Shut up, Granny!' cried Sriram in a great rage. 'What an irresponsible gossip you are! I never thought you could be so bad!'

Granny for the first time noticed a fiery earnestness in her grandson, and gathered herself up. She said: 'Oh! He is your God, is he?'

'Yes, he is, and I won't hear anyone speak lightly of him.'

'What else can I know, a poor ignorant hag like me! Do I read the newspapers? Do I listen to lectures? Am I told what is what by anyone? How should I know anything about that man Gandhi!'

'He is not a man; he is a Mahatma!' cried Sriram.

'What do you know about a Mahatma, anyway?' asked Granny.

Sriram fidgeted and rocked himself in his chair in great anger. He had not come prepared to face a situation of this kind. He had been only prepared to face a granny who might show sullenness at his absence, create difficulties for him when he wanted to go away and exhibit more sorrow and rage than levity. But here she was absolutely reckless, frivolous, and without the slightest sense of responsibility or respect. This was a situation which he had not anticipated, and he had no technique to meet it. It was no use, he realized, showing righteous indignation: that would only tickle the old lady more and more, and when the time came for him to take her permission and go, she might become too intractable.

Granny came back to her original mood after all these unexpected transitions. She said: 'You must eat your dinner, my boy,' very earnestly. She bustled about again as if for a distinguished visitor. She pulled a dining leaf out of a bundle in the kitchen rack, spread it on the floor, sprinkled a little water on it, and drew the bronze rice pot nearer, and sat down in order to be able to serve him without getting up again. The little lamp wavered in its holder. He ate in silence, took a drink of water out of the good old brass tumbler that was by his side; he cast a glance at the old bronze vessel out of which rice had been served to him for years. He suddenly felt depressed at the sight of it all. He was oppressed with the thought that he was leaving these old associations, that this was really a farewell party. He was going into an unknown life right from here. God knew what was in store for him. He felt very gloomy at the thought of it all. He knew it would be no good ever talking to his granny about his plans, or the Mahatma or Bharati. All that was completely beyond her comprehension. She would understand only edibles and dinner and fasting at night in order to impress a neighbour with her austerity. No use talking to her about anything. Best to leave in the morning without any fuss. He had obeyed Mahatmaji's mandate to the extent of seeing her and speaking to her. The Mahatma should be satisfied and not expect him to be able to bring about a conversion in the old lady's outlook, enough to earn her blessing.

Granny was very old, probably eighty, ninety, or a hundred. He had never tried to ascertain her age correctly. And she would not understand new things. At dead of night, after assuring himself that Granny was fast asleep, he got up, scribbled a note to her by the night lamp, and placed it under the brass pot containing water on the window sill, which she was bound to lift first thing in the morning. She could carry it to a neighbour and have it read to her if she had any difficulty in finding her glasses. Perhaps she might not like to have it read by the neighbours. She would always cry: 'Sriram, my glasses, where are the wretched glasses gone?' whenever anything came to her hand for reading, and it would be his duty to go to the cupboard, and fetch them. Now he performed the same duty in anticipation. He tip-toed to the almirah, took the glasses out of their case silently, and returned to the hall, leaving the spectacle case open, because it had a tendency to close with a loud clap. He placed the glasses beside his letter of farewell, silently opened the door, and stepped into the night.

FURTHER READINGS

There are several literary critiques of Narayan's work, including William Walsh, *R. K. Narayan: A Critical Appreciation* (London: Heinemann, 1982), and M. K. Naik, *The Ironic Vision: A Study of the Fiction of R. K. Narayan* (New Delhi: Sterling, 1983). R. K. Narayan, *My Days* (New York: Viking, 1974) is a collection of autobiographical sketches. Of particular interest to students is his second novel, *The Bachelor of Arts* (1937, Chicago: The University of Chicago Press, 1980), which describes a young man's last year of college and first year after graduation. His experiences on a lecture tour of universities in the United States are humorously recounted in R. K. Narayan, *Reluctant Guru* (Delhi: Hind, 1974).

PART IV

Discussion Questions

1. K'ang Yu-wei, in *Confucius as a Social Reformer*, makes K'ung Fu-tzu into a successful social activist. Why did K'ang feel it important to portray K'ung in this way, and how did this view correspond to recent Confucian thought, particularly that of Wang Yang-ming, in *An Inquiry on the Great Learning* (Part III)? In *The Great Unity*, K'ang envisions a future unified world. Is his vision that of a world in which *all* traditional cultures have been eliminated? Or is it fundamentally a Confucian world? How would you feel about living in such a world?

2. Natsume Soseki's novel, *Kokoro*, revolves around the concepts of personal honor and sense of responsibility. How does Sensei's suicide in any way compensate for his dishonorable actions? How does his sense of responsibility for the death of his friend affect the responsibility he should have felt for the well-being of his wife? Is Sensei's suicide a selfish action? Where does the sense of personal honor come from? Is it based on real moral principles, or is it mostly a matter of social custom or even simple self-indulgence? How did Kieu, in *The Tale of Kieu*, endure disgrace and still maintain her sense of honor?

3. What arguments does Ram Mohan Roy make against traditional practices in *On the Burning of Widows?* Consider his argument that abandonment of the practice would be in better accord with tradition than its continuance. Is this a serious point, or is it merely a rhetorical appeal to conservative opinion? Do you see a tradition among Indian leaders such as Gandhi, in *Hind Swaraj*, and Nehru, in *What is India?*, of consciously seeking to preserve what is best in Indian tradition and of harmonizing needed changes with that tradition? Why did Mao Tse-tung, in *The People's Democratic Dictatorship*, Lu Hsun, in *A Madman's Diary*, and Kita Ikki, in *Outline for the Reconstruction of Japan*, not follow a similar policy?

4. How is the distinction between the inner self and the outer self fundamental to understanding *The Tale of Kieu?* How does the character of Kuch'iri, in *Bird of Passage*, show how important this distinction is? To what extent can Kieu and Kuch'iri be taken as symbols for Vietnam and Korea respectively? What would you think of the proposition that, on the national scale, the inner self corresponds to traditional culture and the outer self to the government and economy? Do Americans make the same distinction between inner and outer self on the personal level, or are we driven primarily by the opinion others have of us?

5. The family was probably the fundamental institution of traditional China, as can be seen from *The Classic of Filial Piety* (Part I) and *The Dream of the Red Chamber* (Part III). It provided the individual with his or her basic identity, but could also be destructive of individual initiative and self-respect. How did his family affect the life of Shen Fu in *The Sorrows of Misfortune?* What light does Pa Chin's *Family* cast on the weaknesses of the institution? Were these families regulated in accordance with the principles set forth by Chu Hsi in *Reflection of Things at Hand?* If not, would these families have been different under proper Confucian governance? What elements were necessary to make the traditional Chinese family system work? Are the same elements necessary in the average American family?

6. Many people in India regard Mohandas Gandhi as having been divine and refer to him as the Mahatma (Great Soul). Why did Sriram, in *Waiting for the Mahatma*, regard him as godlike? What do you see in the thought and expression of *Hind Swaraj* that would have led so many people to have had such affection and respect for Gandhi? Was he in fact a Krishna figure fitted for modern times? Gandhi was deeply affected by the message of the *Bhagavad Gita* (Part I). What reflections of the *Bhagavad Gita* do you see in *Hind Swaraj?* How would Wang Yang-ming, in the *Inquiry on the Great Learning* (Part III), have felt about Gandhi? Would Gandhi have made a good Confucian? Why or why not?

7. To what extent is Kurosawa's *Ikiru* a restatement of Wang's philosophy, in *Inquiry on the Great Learning* (Part III), on the relationship between action and knowledge? Is this relationship an important one? How would you explain it in terms of modern American life?

8. K'ang Yu-wei, in *Confucius as a Social Reformer*, and Lu Hsun, in *A Madman's Diary*, both advocated a radical reform of China's traditional institutions. In what ways do their approaches differ? Does the fact that K'ang was a traditional Confucian scholar and Lu trained in medicine have anything to do with their differences? There are also similarities in their basic concerns. What are these, and what do they owe to the Confucian ideals of proper proportion and humane conduct?

9. Ho Chi Minh, in *The Vietnamese Declaration of Independence*, and Gandhi, in *Hind Swaraj*, discuss the justifications for their peoples' desire for independence from France and Great Britain respectively. What reasons are adequate justification for a people to end a government rather than seek a change in that government's policies? Which of the reasons advanced by these leaders would have seemed valid to Abraham Lincoln in 1861? Does the fact that India and Vietnam are different racially and culturally from Great Britain and France have anything to do with the issue? If so, how can the United States have any objection to the independence of Puerto Rico?

10. One of the traditional roles of the Confucian scholar-administrator was to instruct the ruler in the ways of humane conduct and of maintaining a correct sense of proportion. Read *The Analects* (Part I), and then read Lin Tse-hsu's *Letter of Admonition to Queen Victoria*. How effectively is Lin performing his traditional task for Queen Victoria? Political leaders often become so concerned about their political fortunes or impressed by their own authority that they forget that their duty is to rule well. Do you think that an institution such as the Confucian scholar-advisor would be of value in American government? How would such a system work?

11. The disintegration of traditional Asian family life is a frequent theme, either explicit or implicit, in modern Asian literature. How is this factor reflected in *Kokoro*, *Bird of Passage*, *Waiting for the Mahatma*, and *Ikiru*? Is the large family group, with its complex pattern of obligations, conventions, and authority, simply unsuited to the demands of modern life? What factors have contributed to the loss of familial relations in the selections cited above? By comparison, how has the structure of the traditional American family fared under industrialization, and what particular factors have affected it most significantly? Is it possible that the family as we know it will not exist in the world of the future? What do you think the effects would be on the individual and on society?

144   THE PURE LAND   From *Buddhist Texts through the Ages,* ed. and trans. Edward Conze, et al. Copyright © 1954 Philosophical Library. Reprinted by permission.

149   COLD MOUNTAIN POEMS   Reprinted by permission of Grove Press, a division of Wheatland Corporation. Copyright © 1965 by Grove Press, Inc.

160   THE POETRY OF LI PO AND TU FU   "Thought While Studying," "Written in Behalf," and "Drinking Alone," by Li Po, translated by Joseph J. Lee and Irving Yuching Lo, and "Meandering River," "Random Pleasures," "Farewell Of," and "Frontier Songs" by Tu Fu, translated by Irving Yuching Lo and Ronald C. Miao. From *Sunflower Splendor: Three Thousand Years of Chinese Poetry,* edited by Wu-Chi Liu and Irving Yuching Lo. Copyright © 1975 by Wu-Chi Liu and Irving Yuching Lo. Reprinted by permission of Doubleday, a division of Bantam, Doubleday, Dell Publishing Group, Inc.

174   MAN'YOSHU: A COLLECTION OF TEN THOUSAND LEAVES   Reprinted from *An Introduction to Japanese Court Poetry,* with translations by the author and Robert Brower, by Earl Miner with permission of the publishers, Stanford University Press, © 1968 by the Board of Trustees of the Leland Stanford Junior University.

189   APPRAISAL OF WOMEN ON A RAINY NIGHT   From *The Tale of Genji* by Lady Murasaki, translated by Arthur Waley. Published by George Allen & Unwin, Ltd. and Houghton Mifflin Co.

207   REFLECTIONS OF THINGS AT HAND   Chu Hoi, *Reflections of Things at Hand,* trans. Wing-tsit Chan and Lu Tsu-chien. Copyright © 1967 Columbia University Press. Used by permission.

224   GITAGOVINDA   Barbara Stollen Miller, ed. and trans., *Love Song of the Dark Lord: Jayadeva's Gitagovinda.* Copyright © 1977, Columbia University Press. Used by permisson.

256   CONFESSIONS OF LADY NIJO   Excerpts from *The Confessions of Lady Nijo* by Lady Nijo, translation by Karen Brazel, translation copyright © 1973 by Karen Brazel. Used by permission of Doubleday, a division of Bantam, Doubleday, Dell Publishing Group, Inc.

280   KANEHIRA   From Zeami, *Kanehira,* trans. Stanleigh H. Jones, Jr., in *Twenty Plays of the No Theatre,* ed. Donald Keene. Copyright © 1970, Columbia University Press. Used by permission.

299   INQUIRY ON THE GREAT LEARNING   Chan, W., ed., *A Source Book in Chinese Philosophy.* Copyright © 1963 Princeton University Press. Excerpt, pp. 659–67, reprinted with permission of Princeton University Press.

309   SACRED WRITINGS OF THE SIKHS   Extract taken from *Sacred Writings of the Sikhs* by Bhai Jodh Singh, Kapur Singh, Bawa Harkishen Singh, and Khush-